Mobil ✧✧ Travel Guide

Texas

2006

ExxonMobil
Travel Publications

Acknowledgements

We gratefully acknowledge the help of our representatives for their efficient and perceptive inspections of the lodging and dining establishments listed; the establishments' proprietors for their cooperation in showing their facilities and providing information about them; and the many users of previous editions who have taken the time to share their experiences. Mobil Travel Guide is also grateful to all the talented writers who contributed entries to this book.

www.mobiltravelguide.com

Front cover photo: Riverwalk, San Antonio, Texas

ISBN: 0-7627-3936-3

ISSN: 1550-1094

Manufactured in the United States of America.

10 9 8 7 6 5 4 3 2 1

Contents

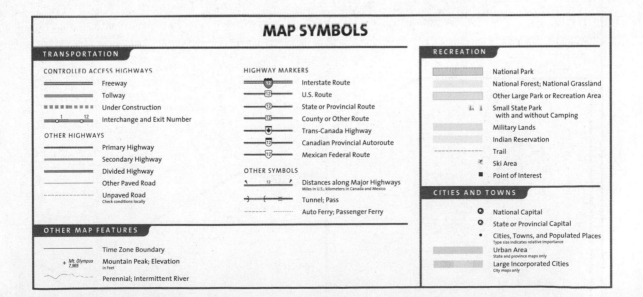

MAP SYMBOLS

TRANSPORTATION

CONTROLLED ACCESS HIGHWAYS
Freeway
Tollway
Under Construction
Interchange and Exit Number

OTHER HIGHWAYS
Primary Highway
Secondary Highway
Divided Highway
Other Paved Road
Unpaved Road
Check conditions locally

HIGHWAY MARKERS
Interstate Route
U.S. Route
State or Provincial Route
County or Other Route
Trans-Canada Highway
Canadian Provincial Autoroute
Mexican Federal Route

OTHER SYMBOLS
Distances along Major Highways
Miles in U.S.; kilometers in Canada and Mexico
Tunnel; Pass
Auto Ferry; Passenger Ferry

OTHER MAP FEATURES
Time Zone Boundary
Mt. Olympus   Mountain Peak; Elevation
7,965   in Feet
Perennial; Intermittent River

RECREATION
National Park
National Forest; National Grassland
Other Large Park or Recreation Area
Small State Park
  with and without Camping
Military Lands
Indian Reservation
Trail
Ski Area
Point of Interest

CITIES AND TOWNS
National Capital
State or Provincial Capital
Cities, Towns, and Populated Places
Type size indicates relative importance
Urban Area
State and province maps only
Large Incorporated Cities
City maps only

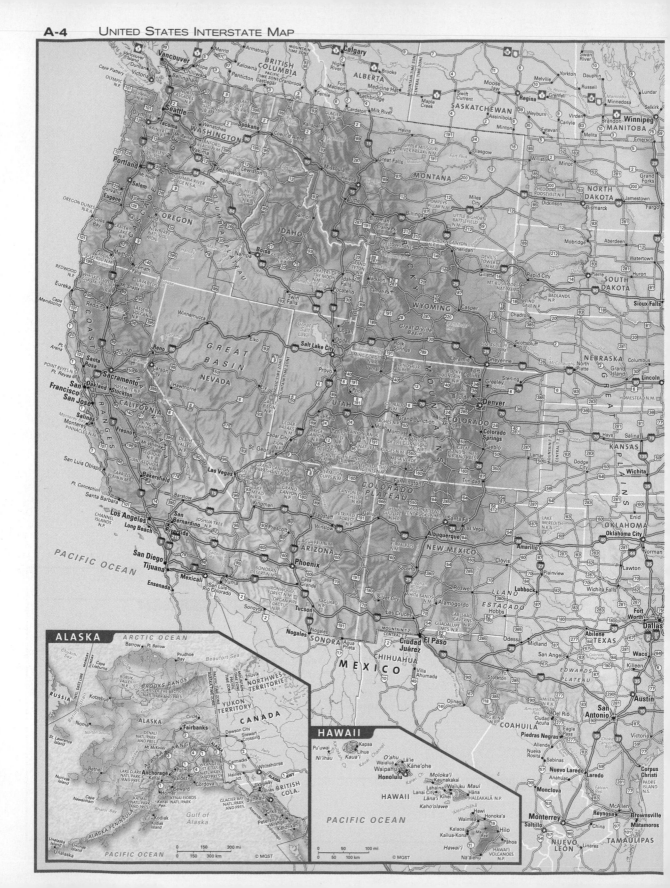

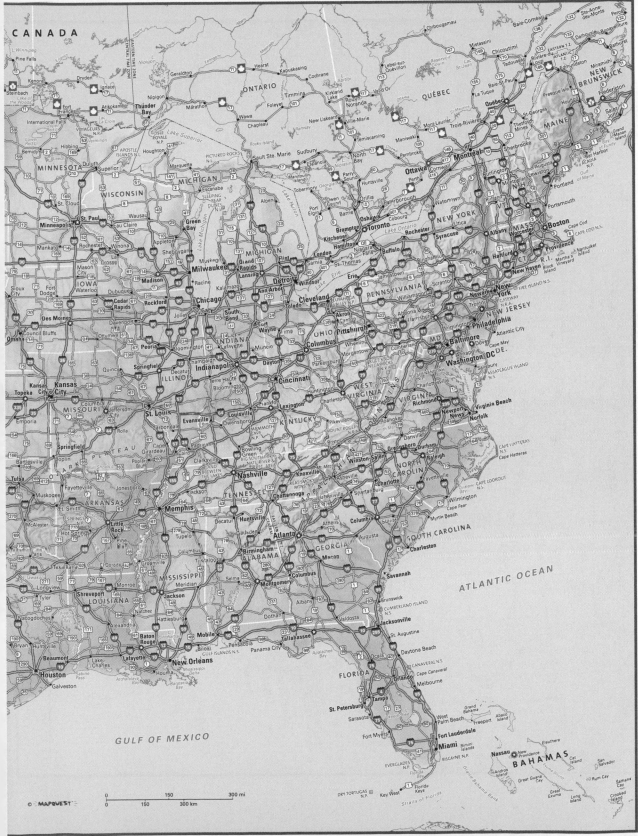

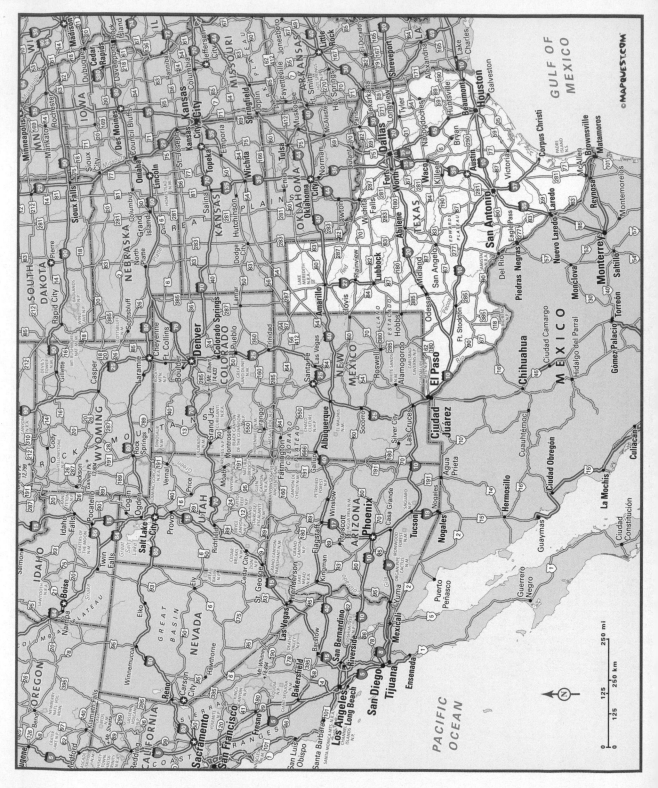

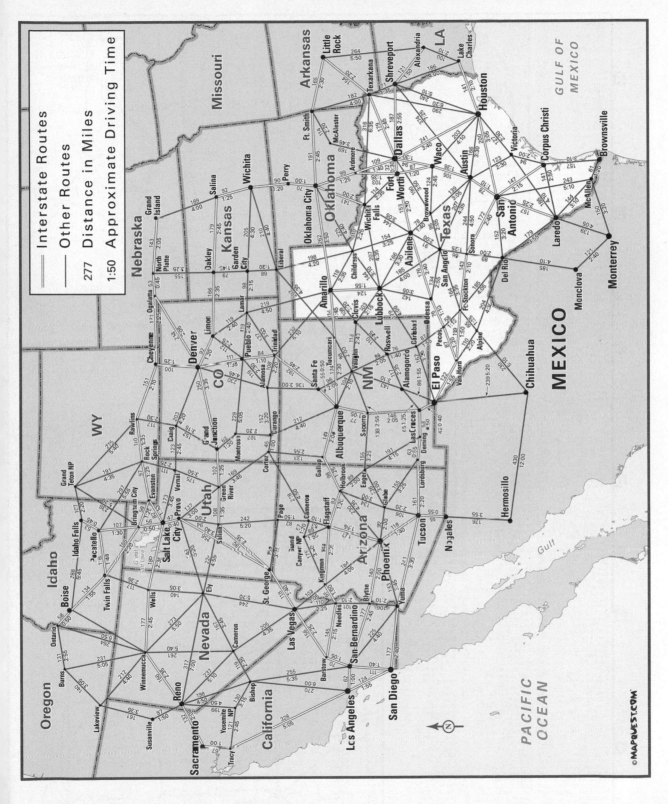

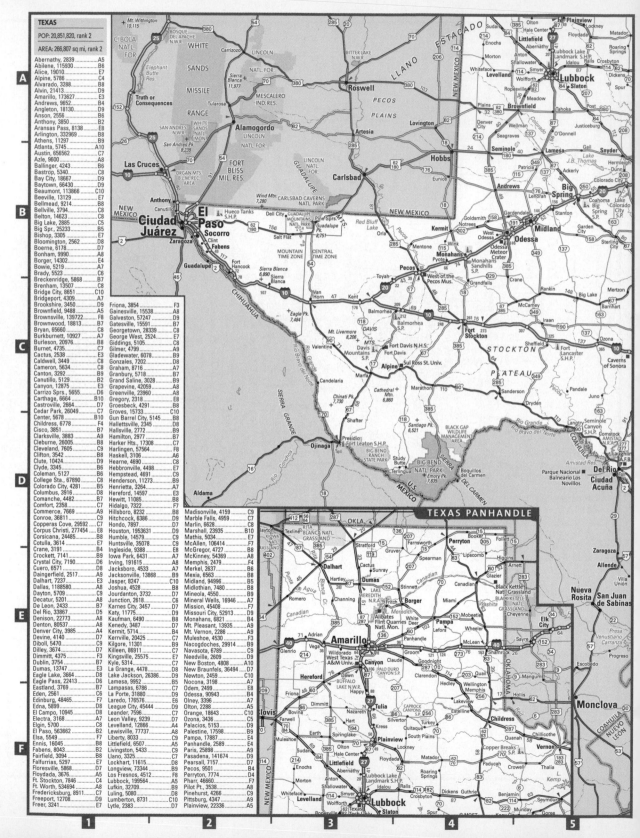

TEXAS

POP: 20,851,820, rank 2

AREA: 266,807 sq mi, rank 2

Abernathy, 2839 .... A5
Abilene, 115930 .... B6
Alice, 19010 .... E7
Alpine, 5786 .... C4
Alvarado, 3288 .... B8
Alvin, 21413 .... D9
Amarillo, 173627 .... E3
Andrews, 9652 .... B4
Angleton, 18130 .... D9
Anson, 2556 .... B6
Anthony, 3850 .... B2
Aransas Pass, 8138 .... E8
Arlington, 332969 .... B8
Athens, 11297 .... B9
Atlanta, 5745 .... A10
Austin, 656562 .... C7
Azle, 9600 .... A8
Ballinger, 4243 .... B6
Bastrop, 5340 .... C8
Bay City, 18667 .... D9
Baytown, 66430 .... D9
Beaumont, 113866 .... C10
Beeville, 13129 .... E7
Bellmead, 9214 .... B8
Bellville, 3794 .... C8
Belton, 14623 .... C8
Big Lake, 2885 .... C5
Big Spr., 25233 .... B5
Bishop, 3305 .... E7
Bloomington, 2562 .... D8
Boerne, 6178 .... D7
Bonham, 9990 .... A8
Borger, 14302 .... E4
Bowie, 5219 .... A7
Brady, 5523 .... C6
Breckenridge, 5868 .... B7
Brenham, 13507 .... C8
Bridge City, 8651 .... C10
Bridgeport, 4309 .... A7
Brookshire, 3450 .... D9
Brownfield, 9488 .... A5
Brownsville, 139722 .... F8
Brownwood, 18813 .... B7
Bryan, 65660 .... C8
Burkburnett, 10927 .... A7
Burleson, 20976 .... B8
Burnet, 4735 .... C7
Cactus, 2538 .... E3
Caldwell, 3449 .... C8
Cameron, 5634 .... C8
Canton, 3292 .... B9
Canutillo, 5129 .... B2
Canyon, 12875 .... E3
Carrizo Sprs., 5655 .... D6
Carthage, 6664 .... B10
Castroville, 2664 .... D7
Cedar Park, 26049 .... C7
Center, 5678 .... B10
Childress, 6778 .... F4
Cisco, 3851 .... B7
Clarksville, 3883 .... A9
Cleburne, 26005 .... B8
Cleveland, 7605 .... C9
Clifton, 3542 .... B8
Clute, 10424 .... D9
Clyde, 3345 .... B6
Coleman, 5127 .... B6
College Sta., 67890 .... C8
Colorado City, 4281 .... B5
Columbus, 3916 .... D8
Comanche, 4482 .... B7
Comfort, 2358 .... C7
Commerce, 7669 .... A9
Conroe, 36811 .... C9
Copperas Cove, 29592 ...... C7
Corpus Christi, 277454 .... E8
Corsicana, 24485 .... B8
Cotulla, 3614 .... E7
Crane, 3191 .... B4
Crockett, 7141 .... B9
Crystal City, 7190 .... D6
Cuero, 6571 .... D8
Daingerfield, 2517 .... A9
Dalhart, 7237 .... E3
Dallas, 1188580 .... A8
Dayton, 5709 .... C9
Decatur, 5201 .... A8
De Leon, 2433 .... B7
Del Rio, 33867 .... D5
Denison, 22773 .... A8
Denton, 80537 .... A8
Denver City, 3985 .... A4
Devine, 4140 .... D7
Diboll, 5470 .... C9
Dilley, 3674 .... D7
Dimmitt, 4375 .... F3
Dublin, 3790 .... B7
Dumas, 13747 .... E3
Eagle Lake, 3664 .... D8
Eagle Pass, 22413 .... D6
Eastland, 3769 .... B7
Eden, 2561 .... C6
Edinburg, 48465 .... F7
Edna, 5899 .... D8
El Campo, 10945 .... D8
Electra, 3168 .... A7
Elgin, 5700 .... C8
El Paso, 563662 .... B1
Elsa, 5549 .... F7
Ennis, 16045 .... B8
Fabens, 8043 .... B2
Fairfield, 3094 .... B8
Falfurrias, 5297 .... E7
Floresville, 5868 .... D7
Floydada, 3676 .... A5
Ft. Stockton, 7846 .... C4
Ft. Worth, 534694 .... A8
Fredericksburg, 8911 ...... C7
Freeport, 12708 .... D9
Freer, 3241 .... E7

Friona, 3854 .... F3
Gainesville, 15538 .... A8
Galveston, 57247 .... D9
Gatesville, 15591 .... B7
Georgetown, 28339 .... C8
George West, 2524 .... E7
Giddings, 5105 .... C8
Gilmer, 4799 .... A9
Gladewater, 6078 .... B9
Gonzales, 7202 .... D8
Graham, 8716 .... A7
Granbury, 5718 .... B7
Grand Saline, 3000 .... B9
Grapevine, 42059 .... A8
Greenville, 23960 .... A8
Gregory, 2318 .... E8
Groesbeck, 4291 .... B8
Groves, 15733 .... C10
Gun Barrel City, 5145 ..... B8
Hallettsville, 2345 .... D8
Hallsville, 2772 .... B9
Hamilton, 2977 .... B7
Harker Hts., 17308 .... C7
Harlingen, 57564 .... F8
Haskell, 3106 .... A6
Hearne, 4690 .... C8
Hebbronville, 4498 .... E7
Hempstead, 4691 .... C9
Henderson, 11273 .... B9
Henrietta, 3264 .... A7
Hereford, 14597 .... E3
Hewitt, 11085 .... B8
Hidalgo, 7322 .... F7
Hillsboro, 8232 .... B8
Hitchcock, 6386 .... D9
Hondo, 7897 .... D7
Houston, 1953631 .... C9
Humble, 14579 .... C9
Huntsville, 35078 .... C9
Ingleside, 9388 .... E8
Iowa Park, 6431 .... A7
Irving, 191615 .... A8
Jacksboro, 4533 .... A7
Jacksonville, 13868 .... B9
Jasper, 8247 .... C10
Joshua, 4528 .... B8
Jourdanton, 3732 .... D7
Junction, 2618 .... C6
Karnes City, 3457 .... D7
Katy, 11775 .... C9
Kaufman, 6490 .... B8
Kenedy, 3487 .... D7
Kermit, 5714 .... B4
Kerrville, 20425 .... C7
Kilgore, 11301 .... B9
Killeen, 86911 .... C7
Kingsville, 25575 .... E7
Kyle, 5314 .... C7
La Grange, 4478 .... D8
Lake Jackson, 26386 .... D9
Lamesa, 9952 .... B5
Lampasas, 6786 .... C7
Laredo, 176576 .... E6
La Porte, 31880 .... C9
League City, 45444 .... D9
Leander, 7596 .... C7
Leon Valley, 9239 .... D7
Levelland, 12866 .... A4
Lewisville, 77737 .... A8
Liberty, 8033 .... C9
Littlefield, 6507 .... A5
Livingston, 5433 .... C9
Llano, 3325 .... C7
Lockhart, 11615 .... D8
Longview, 73344 .... B9
Los Fresnos, 4512 .... F8
Lubbock, 199564 .... A5
Lufkin, 32709 .... B9
Luling, 5080 .... D8
Lumberton, 8731 .... C10
Lytle, 2383 .... D7

Madisonville, 4159 .... C9
Marble Falls, 4959 .... C7
Marlin, 6628 .... C8
Marshall, 23935 .... B10
Mathis, 5034 .... E7
McAllen, 106414 .... F7
McGregor, 4727 .... B8
McKinney, 54369 .... A8
Memphis, 2479 .... F4
Merkel, 2637 .... B6
Mexia, 6563 .... B8
Midland, 94996 .... B5
Midlothian, 7480 .... B8
Mineola, 4550 .... B9
Mineral Wells, 16946 ...... A7
Mission, 45408 .... F7
Missouri City, 52913 ...... D9
Monahans, 6821 .... B4
Mt. Pleasant, 13935 .... A9
Mt. Vernon, 2286 .... A9
Muleshoe, 4530 .... F2
Nacogdoches, 29914 .... B9
Navasota, 6789 .... C9
Needville, 2609 .... D9
New Boston, 4808 .... A10
New Braunfels, 36494 ...... D7
Newton, 2459 .... C10
Nocona, 3198 .... A7
Odem, 2499 .... E8
Odessa, 90943 .... B4
Olney, 3396 .... A7
Olton, 2288 .... A5
Orange, 18643 .... C10
Ozona, 3436 .... C5
Palacios, 5153 .... D9
Palestine, 17598 .... B9
Pampa, 17887 .... E4
Panhandle, 2589 .... E4
Paris, 25898 .... A9
Pasadena, 141674 .... C9
Pearsall, 7157 .... D7
Pecos, 9501 .... B4
Perryton, 7774 .... D4
Pharr, 46060 .... F7
Pilot Pt., 3538 .... A8
Pinehurst, 4266 .... C9
Pittsburg, 4347 .... A9
Plainview, 22336 .... A5

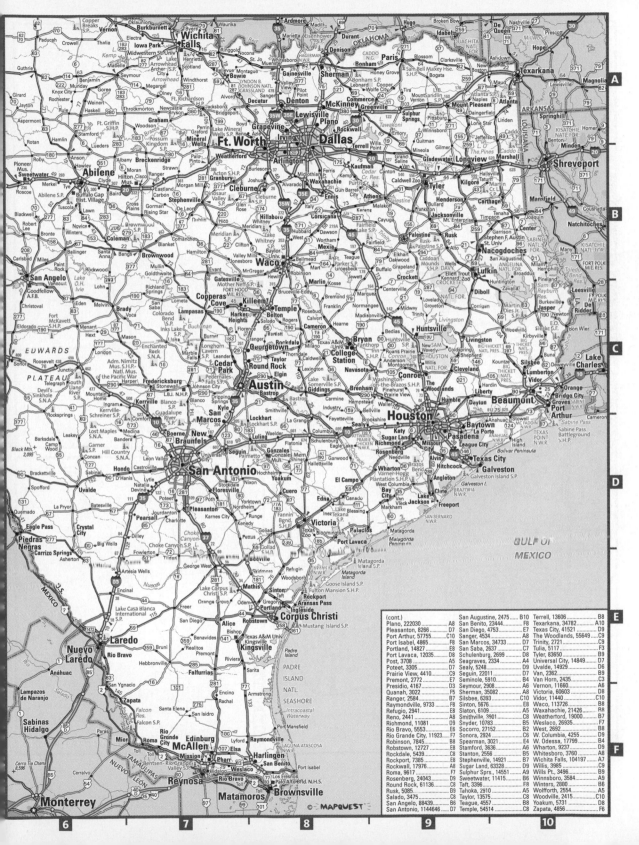

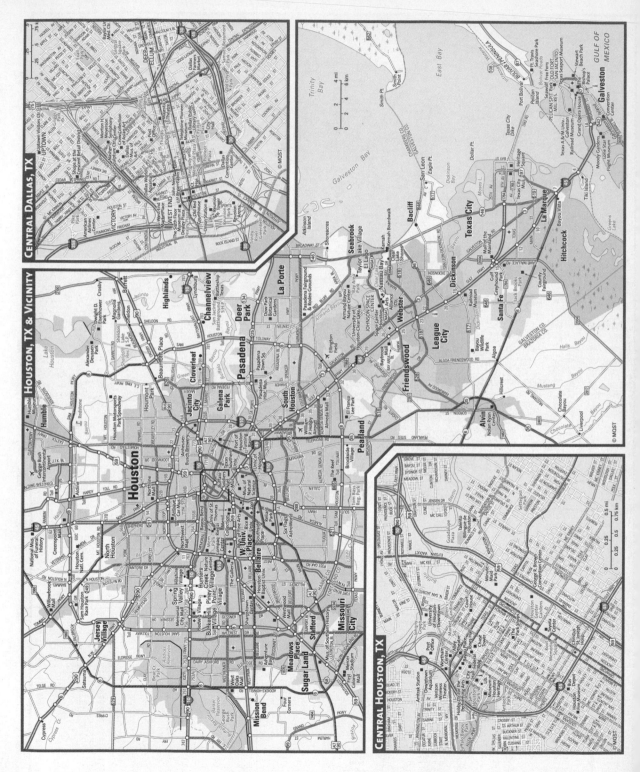

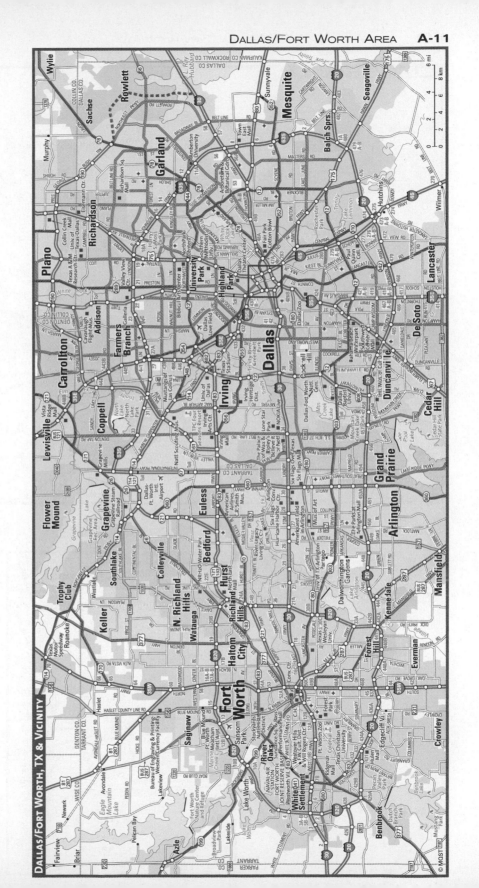

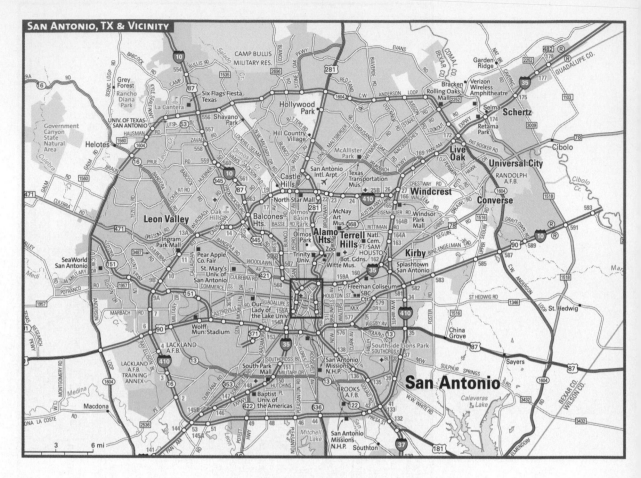

SAN ANTONIO, TX & VICINITY

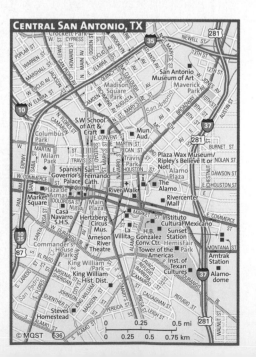

CENTRAL SAN ANTONIO, TX

© MQST

Mileage Chart

Row / column cities (top to bottom along the right edge, and left to right along the bottom):

WICHITA, KS · WASHINGTON, DC · VANCOUVER, BC · TORONTO, ON · TAMPA, FL · SEATTLE, WA · SAN FRANCISCO, CA · SAN DIEGO, CA · SAN ANTONIO, TX · SALT LAKE CITY, UT · ST. LOUIS, MO · RICHMOND, VA · RENO, NV · RAPID CITY, SD · PORTLAND, OR · PORTLAND, ME · PITTSBURGH, PA · PHOENIX, AZ · PHILADELPHIA, PA · ORLANDO, FL · OMAHA, NE · OKLAHOMA CITY, OK · NEW YORK, NY · NEW ORLEANS, LA · NASHVILLE, TN · MONTRÉAL, QC · MINNEAPOLIS, MN · MILWAUKEE, WI · MIAMI, FL · MEMPHIS, TN · LOUISVILLE, KY · LOS ANGELES, CA · LITTLE ROCK, AR · LAS VEGAS, NV · KANSAS CITY, MO · JACKSON, MS · INDIANAPOLIS, IN · HOUSTON, TX · EL PASO, TX · DETROIT, MI · DES MOINES, IA · DENVER, CO · DALLAS, TX · CLEVELAND, OH · CINCINNATI, OH · CHICAGO, IL · CHEYENNE, WY · CHARLOTTE, NC · CHARLESTON, WV · CHARLESTON, SC · BURLINGTON, VT · BUFFALO, NY · BOSTON, MA · BOISE, ID · BISMARCK, ND · BIRMINGHAM, AL · BILLINGS, MT · BALTIMORE, MD · ATLANTA, GA · ALBUQUERQUE, NM

Legend (bottom left):

Distances in chart are in miles.
To convert miles to kilometers,
multiply the distance in miles
by 1.609

Example:
New York, NY to Boston, MA
= 215 miles or 346 kilometers
(215 x 1.609)

© MapQuest.com, Inc.

Welcome

Dear Traveler,

Since its inception in 1958, Mobil Travel Guide has served as a trusted advisor to auto travelers in search of value in lodging, dining, and destinations. Now in its 48th year, the Mobil Travel Guide is the hallmark of our ExxonMobil family of travel publications, and we're proud to offer an array of products and services from our Mobil, Exxon, and Esso brands in North America to facilitate life on the road.

Whether you're looking for business or pleasure venues, our nationwide network of independent, professional evaluators offers their expertise on thousands of travel options, allowing you to plan a quick family getaway, a full-service business meeting, or an unforgettable Mobil Five-Star celebration.

Your feedback is important to us as we strive to improve our product offerings and better meet today's travel needs. Whether you travel once a week or once a year, please take the time to contact us at www.mobiltravelguide.com. We hope to hear from you soon.

Best wishes for safe and enjoyable travels.

Lee R. Raymond
Chairman and CEO
Exxon Mobil Corporation

A Word to Our Readers

Travelers are on the roads in great numbers these days. They're exploring the country on day trips, weekend getaways, business trips, and extended family vacations, visiting major cities and small towns along the way. Because time is precious and the travel industry is ever-changing, having accurate, reliable travel information at your fingertips is critical. Mobil Travel Guide has been providing invaluable insight to travelers for more than 45 years, and we are committed to continuing this service well into the future.

The Mobil Corporation (known as Exxon Mobil Corporation since a 1999 merger) began producing the Mobil Travel Guide books in 1958, following the introduction of the US interstate highway system in 1956. The first edition covered only five Southwestern states. Since then, our books have become the premier travel guides in North America, covering all 50 states and Canada.

Since its founding, Mobil Travel Guide has served as an advocate for travelers seeking knowledge about hotels, restaurants, and places to visit. Based on an objective process, we make recommendations to our customers that we believe will enhance the quality and value of their travel experiences. Our trusted Mobil One- to Five-Star rating system is the oldest and most respected lodging and restaurant inspection and rating program in North America. Most hoteliers, restaurateurs, and industry observers favorably regard the rigor of our inspection program and understand the prestige and benefits that come with receiving a Mobil Star rating.

The Mobil Travel Guide process of rating each establishment includes:

- Unannounced facility inspections

- Incognito service evaluations for Mobil Four-Star and Mobil Five-Star properties

- A review of unsolicited comments from the general public

- Senior management oversight

For each property, more than 450 attributes, including cleanliness, physical facilities, and employee attitude and courtesy, are measured and evaluated to produce a mathematically derived score, which is then blended with the other elements to form an overall score. These quantifiable scores allow comparative analysis among properties and form the basis that we use to assign our Mobil One- to Five-Star ratings.

This process focuses largely on guest expectations, guest experience, and consistency of service, not just physical facilities and amenities. It is fundamentally a relative rating system that rewards those properties that continually strive for and achieve excellence each year. Indeed, the very best properties are consistently raising the bar for those that wish to compete with them. These properties proactively respond to consumers' needs even in today's uncertain times.

Only facilities that meet Mobil Travel Guide's standards earn the privilege of being listed in the guide. Deteriorating, poorly managed establishments are deleted. A Mobil Travel Guide listing constitutes a positive quality recommendation; every listing is an accolade, a recognition of achievement. Our Mobil One- to Five-Star rating system highlights its level of service. Extensive in-house research is constantly underway to determine new additions to our lists.

- The Mobil Five-Star Award indicates that a property is one of the very best in the country and consistently provides gracious and courteous service, superlative quality in its facility, and a unique ambience. The lodgings and restaurants at the Mobil Five-Star level consistently and proactively respond to consumers' needs and continue their commitment to excellence, doing so with grace and perseverance.

- Also highly regarded is the Mobil Four-Star Award, which honors properties for outstanding achievement in overall facility and for providing very strong service levels in all areas. These award winners provide a distinctive experience for the ever-demanding and sophisticated consumer.

◎ The Mobil Three-Star Award recognizes an excellent property that provides full services and amenities. This category ranges from exceptional hotels with limited services to elegant restaurants with a less-formal atmosphere.

◎ A Mobil Two-Star property is a clean and comfortable establishment that has expanded amenities or a distinctive environment. A Mobil Two-Star property is an excellent place to stay or dine.

◎ A Mobil One-Star property is limited in its amenities and services but focuses on providing a value experience while meeting travelers' expectations. The property can be expected to be clean, comfortable, and convenient.

Allow us to emphasize that we do not charge establishments for inclusion in our guides. We have no relationship with any of the businesses and attractions we list and act only as a consumer advocate. In essence, we do the investigative legwork so that you won't have to.

Keep in mind, too, that the hospitality business is ever-changing. Restaurants and lodgings—particularly small chains and stand-alone establishments—change management or even go out of business with surprising quickness. Although we make every effort to double-check information during our annual updates, we nevertheless recommend that you call ahead to make sure the place you've selected is still open and offers all the amenities you're looking for. We've provided phone numbers; when available, we also list fax numbers and Web site addresses.

We hope that your travels are enjoyable and relaxing and that our books help you get the most out of every trip you take. If any aspect of your accommodation, dining, or sightseeing experience motivates you to comment, please drop us a line. We depend a great deal on our readers' remarks, so you can be assured that we will read your comments and assimilate them into our research. General comments about our books are also welcome. You can write to us at Mobil Travel Guide, 7373 N Cicero Ave, Lincolnwood, IL 60712, or send an e-mail to info@mobiltravelguide.com.

Take your Mobil Travel Guide books along on every trip you take. We're confident that you'll be pleased with their convenience, ease of use, and breadth of dependable coverage.

Happy travels!

How to Use This Book

The Mobil Travel Guide Regional Travel Planners are designed for ease of use. This book begins with a general introduction that provides a geographical and historical orientation to the state and gives basic statewide tourist information, from climate to calendar highlights to seatbelt laws. The remainder of the book is devoted to travel destinations within the state—mainly cities and towns, but also national parks and tourist areas—which are arranged in alphabetical order.

The following sections explain the wealth of information you'll find about those travel destinations: information about the area, things to see and do there, and where to stay and eat.

Maps and Map Coordinates

At the front of this book in the full-color section, we have provided state maps as well as maps of selected larger cities to help you find your way around once you leave the highway. You'll find a key to the map symbols on the Contents page at the beginning of the map section.

Next to most cities and towns throughout the book, you'll find a set of map coordinates, such as C-2. These coordinates reference the maps at the front of this book and help you find the location you're looking for quickly and easily.

Destination Information

Because many travel destinations are close to other cities and towns where travelers might find additional attractions, accommodations, and restaurants, we've included cross-references to those cities and towns when it makes sense to do so. We also list addresses, phone numbers, and Web sites for travel information resources—usually the local chamber of commerce or office of tourism—as well as pertinent statistics and, in many cases, a brief introduction to the area.

Information about airports, ground transportation, and suburbs is included for large cities.

Driving Tours and Walking Tours

The driving tours that we include for many states are usually day trips that make for interesting side excursions, although they can be longer. They offer you a way to get off the beaten path and visit an area that travelers often overlook. These trips frequently cover areas of natural beauty or historical significance.

Each walking tour focuses on a particularly interesting area of a city or town. Again, these tours can provide a break from everyday tourist attractions. The tours often include places to stop for meals or snacks.

What to See and Do

Mobil Travel Guide offers information about nearly 20,000 museums, art galleries, amusement parks, historic sites, national and state parks, ski areas, and many other types of attractions. A white star on a black background ★ signals that the attraction is a must-see—one of the best in the area. Because municipal parks, public tennis courts, swimming pools, and small educational institutions are common to most towns, they generally are not mentioned.

Following an attraction's description, you'll find the months, days, and, in some cases, hours of operation; the address/directions, telephone number, and Web site (if there is one); and the admission price category. The following are the ranges we use for admission fees, based on one adult:

✪ **FREE**

✪ **$** = Up to $5

✪ **$$** = $5.01-$10

✪ **$$$** = $10.01-$15

✪ **$$$$** = Over $15

Special Events

Special events are either annual events that last only a short time, such as festivals and fairs, or longer, seasonal events such as horse racing, theater, and summer concerts. Our Special Events listings also include infrequently occurring occasions that mark certain dates or events, such as a centennial or other commemorative celebration.

Listings

Lodgings, spas, and restaurants are usually listed under the city or town in which they're located. Make sure to check the related cities and towns that appear right beneath a city's heading for additional options, especially if you're traveling to a major metropolitan area that includes many suburbs. If a property is located in a town that doesn't have its own heading, the listing appears under the town nearest it, with the address and town given immediately after the establishment's name. In large cities, lodgings located within 5 miles of major commercial airports may be listed under a separate "Airport Area" heading that follows the city section.

LODGINGS

Travelers have different wants and needs when it comes to accommodations. To help you pinpoint properties that meet your particular needs, Mobil Travel Guide classifies each lodging by type according to the following characteristics.

Mobil Rated Lodgings

☼ **Limited-Service Hotel.** A limited-service hotel is traditionally a Mobil One-Star or Mobil Two-Star property. At a Mobil One-Star hotel, guests can expect to find a clean, comfortable property that commonly serves a complimentary continental breakfast. A Mobil Two-Star hotel is also clean and comfortable but has expanded amenities, such as a full-service restaurant, business center, and fitness center. These services may have limited staffing and/or restricted hours of use.

☼ **Full-Service Hotel.** A full-service hotel traditionally enjoys a Mobil Three-Star, Mobil Four-Star, or Mobil Five-Star rating. Guests can expect these hotels to offer at least one full-service restaurant in addition to amenities such as valet parking, luggage assistance, 24-hour room service, concierge service, laundry and/or dry-cleaning services, and turndown service.

☼ **Full-Service Resort.** A resort is traditionally a full-service hotel that is geared toward recreation and represents a vacation and holiday destination. A resort's guest rooms are typically furnished to accommodate longer stays. The property may offer a full-service spa, golf, tennis, and fitness facilities or other leisure activities. Resorts are expected to offer a full-service restaurant and expanded amenities, such as luggage assistance, room service, meal plans, concierge service, and turndown service.

☼ **Full-Service Inn.** An inn is traditionally a Mobil Three-Star, Mobil Four-Star, or Mobil Five-Star property. Inns are similar to bed-and-breakfasts (see below) but offer a wider range of services, most significantly a full-service restaurant that serves at least breakfast and dinner.

Specialty Lodgings

Mobil Travel Guide recognizes the unique and individualized nature of many different types of lodging establishments, including bed-and-breakfasts, limited-service inns, and guest ranches. For that reason, we have chosen to place our stamp of approval on the properties that fall into these two categories in lieu of applying our traditional Mobil Star ratings.

☼ **B&B/Limited-Service Inn.** A bed-and-breakfast (B&B) or limited-service inn is traditionally an owner-occupied home or residence found in a residential area or vacation destination. It may be a structure of historic significance. Rooms are often individually decorated, but telephones, televisions, and private bathrooms may not be available in every room. A B&B typically serves only breakfast to its overnight guests, which is included in the room rate. Cocktails and refreshments may be served in the late afternoon or evening.

☼ **Guest Ranch.** A guest ranch is traditionally a rustic, Western-themed property that specializes in stays of three or more days. Horseback riding is often a feature, with stables and trails found on the property. Facilities can range from clean, comfortable establishments to more luxurious facilities.

Mobil Star Rating Definitions for Lodgings

✪ ★ ★ ★ ★ ★ : A Mobil Five-Star lodging provides consistently superlative service in an exceptionally distinctive luxury environment, with expanded services. Attention to detail is evident throughout the hotel, resort, or inn, from bed linens to staff uniforms.

✪ ★ ★ ★ ★ : A Mobil Four-Star lodging provides a luxury experience with expanded amenities in a distinctive environment. Services may include, but are not limited to, automatic turndown service, 24-hour room service, and valet parking.

✪ ★ ★ ★ : A Mobil Three-Star lodging is well appointed, with a full-service restaurant and expanded amenities, such as a fitness center, golf course, tennis courts, 24-hour room service, and optional turndown service.

✪ ★ ★ : A Mobil Two-Star lodging is considered a clean, comfortable, and reliable establishment that has expanded amenities, such as a full-service restaurant on the premises.

✪ ★ : A Mobil One-Star lodging is a limited-service hotel, motel, or inn that is considered a clean, comfortable, and reliable establishment.

Information Found in the Lodging Listings

Each lodging listing gives the name, address/location (when no street address is available), neighborhood and/or directions from downtown (in major cities), phone number(s), fax number, total number of guest rooms, and seasons open (if not year-round). Also included are details on business, luxury, recreational, and dining facilities at the property or nearby. A key to the symbols at the end of each listing can be found on the page following the "A Word to Our Readers" section.

For every property, we also provide pricing information. Because lodging rates change frequently, we list a pricing category rather than specific prices. The pricing categories break down as follows:

✪ **$** = Up to $150

✪ **$$** = $151-$250

✪ **$$$** = $251-$350

✪ **$$$$** = $351 and up

All prices quoted are in effect at the time of publication; however, prices cannot be guaranteed. In some locations, short-term price variations may exist because of special events, holidays, or seasonality. Certain resorts have complicated rate structures that vary with the time of year; always confirm rates when making your plans.

Because most lodgings offer the following features and services, information about them does not appear in the listings:

✪ Year-round operation

✪ Bathroom with tub and/or shower in each room

✪ Cable television in each room

✪ In-room telephones

✪ Cots and cribs available

✪ Daily maid service

✪ Elevators

✪ Major credit cards accepted

🔍 Although we recommend every lodging we list in this book, a few stand out—they offer noteworthy amenities or stand above the others in their category in terms of quality, value, or historical significance. To draw your attention to these special spots, we've included the magnifying glass icon to the left of the listing, as you see here.

SPAS

Mobil Travel Guide is pleased to announce its newest category: hotel and resort spas. Until now, hotel and resort spas have not been formally rated or inspected by any organization. Every spa selected for inclusion in this book underwent a rigorous inspection process similar to the one Mobil Travel Guide has been applying to lodgings and restaurants for more than four decades. After spending a year and a half researching more than 300 spas and performing exhaustive incognito inspections of more than 200 properties, we narrowed our list to the 48 best spas in the United States and Canada.

Mobil Travel Guide's spa ratings are based on objective evaluations of more than 450 attributes. Approximately half of these criteria assess basic expectations, such as staff courtesy, the technical proficiency and skill of the employees, and whether the facility is maintained properly and hygienically. Several standards address issues that impact a guest's physical comfort and convenience, as well as the staff's ability to impart a sense of personalized service and anticipate clients' needs. Additional criteria measure the spa's ability to create a completely calming ambience.

The Mobil Star ratings focus on much more than the facilities available at a spa and the treatments it offers. Each Mobil Star rating is a cumulative score achieved from multiple inspections that reflects the spa management's attention to detail and commitment to consumers' needs.

Mobil Star Rating Definitions for Spas

✪ ★ ★ ★ ★ ★ : A Mobil Five-Star spa provides consistently superlative service in an exceptionally distinctive luxury environment with extensive amenities. The staff at a Mobil Five-Star Spa provides extraordinary service above and beyond the traditional spa experience, allowing guests to achieve the highest level of relaxation and pampering. A Mobil Five-Star spa offers an extensive array of treatments, often incorporating international themes and products. Attention to detail is evident throughout the spa, from arrival to departure.

✪ ★ ★ ★ ★ : A Mobil Four-Star spa provides a luxurious experience with expanded amenities in an elegant and serene environment. Throughout the spa facility, guests experience personalized service. Amenities might include, but are not limited to, single-sex relaxation rooms where guests wait for their treatments, plunge pools and whirlpools in both men's and women's locker rooms, and an array of treatments, including at a minimum a selection of massages, body therapies, facials, and a variety of salon services.

✪ ★ ★ ★ : A Mobil Three-Star spa is physically well appointed and has a full complement of staff to ensure that guests' needs are met. It has some expanded amenities, such as, but not limited to, a well-equipped fitness center, separate men's and women's locker rooms, a sauna or steam room, and a designated relaxation area. It also offers a menu of services that at a minimum includes massages, facial treatments, and at least one other type of body treatment, such as scrubs or wraps.

RESTAURANTS

All Mobil Star rated dining establishments listed in this book have a full kitchen and offer seating at tables; most offer table service.

Mobil Star Rating Definitions for Restaurants

✪ ★ ★ ★ ★ ★ : A Mobil Five-Star restaurant offers one of few flawless dining experiences in the country. These establishments consistently provide their guests with exceptional food, superlative service, elegant décor, and exquisite presentations of each detail surrounding a meal.

✪ ★ ★ ★ ★ : A Mobil Four-Star restaurant provides professional service, distinctive presentations, and wonderful food.

✪ ★ ★ ★ : A Mobil Three-Star restaurant has good food, warm and skillful service, and enjoyable décor.

✪ ★ ★ : A Mobil Two-Star restaurant serves fresh food in a clean setting with efficient service. Value is considered in this category, as is family friendliness.

✪ ★ : A Mobil One-Star restaurant provides a distinctive experience through culinary specialty, local flair, or individual atmosphere.

Information Found in the Restaurant Listings

Each restaurant listing gives the cuisine type, street address (or directions if no address is available), phone and fax numbers, Web site (if available), meals served, days of operation (if not open daily year-round), and pricing category. Information about appropriate attire is provided, although it's always a good idea to call ahead and ask if you're unsure; the meaning of "casual" or "business casual" varies widely in different parts of the country. We also indicate whether the restaurant has a bar, whether a children's menu is offered, and whether outdoor seating is available. If reservations are recommended, we note that fact in the listing. When valet parking is available, it is noted in the description. In many cases, self-parking is available at the restaurant or nearby.

Because menu prices can fluctuate, we list a pricing category rather than specific prices. The pricing categories are defined as follows, per diner, and assume that you order an appetizer or dessert, an entrée, and one drink:

- ✪ **$** = $15 and under
- ✪ **$$** = $16-$35
- ✪ **$$$** = $36-$85
- ✪ **$$$$** = $86 and up

Again, all prices quoted are in effect at the time of publication, but prices cannot be guaranteed.

Although we recommend every restaurant we list in this book, a few stand out—they offer noteworthy local specialties or stand above the others in their category in terms of quality, value, or experience.

To draw your attention to these special spots, we've included the magnifying glass icon to the left of the listing, as you see here.

SPECIAL INFORMATION FOR TRAVELERS WITH DISABILITIES

The Mobil Travel Guide symbol indicates that an establishment is not at least partially accessible to people with mobility problems. When the symbol follows a listing, the establishment is not equipped with facilities to accommodate people using wheelchairs or crutches or otherwise needing easy access to doorways and rest rooms. Travelers with severe mobility problems or with hearing or visual impairments may or may not find the facilities they need. Always phone ahead to make sure that an establishment can meet your needs.

Understanding the Symbols

What to See and Do

★ = One of the top attractions in the area

$ = Up to $5

$$ = $5.01 to $10

$$$ = $10.01 to $15

$$$$ = Over $15

Lodgings

$ = Up to $150

$$ = $151 to $250

$$$ = $251 to $350

$$$$ = Over $350

Restaurants

$ = Up to $15

$$ = $16 to $35

$$$ = $36 to $85

$$$$ = Over $85

Lodging Star Definitions

★★★★★ A Mobil Five-Star lodging establishment provides consistently superlative service in an exceptionally distinctive luxury environment with expanded services. Attention to detail is evident throughout the hotel/resort/inn from the bed linens to the staff uniforms.

★★★★ A Mobil Four-Star lodging establishment is a hotel/resort/inn that provides a luxury experience with expanded amenities in a distinctive environment. Services may include, but are not limited to, automatic turndown service, 24-hour room service, and valet parking.

★★★ A Mobil Three-Star lodging establishment is a hotel/resort/inn that is well appointed, with a full-service restaurant and expanded amenities, such as, but not limited to, a fitness center, golf course, tennis courts, 24-hour room service, and optional turndown service.

★★ A Mobil Two-Star lodging establishment is a hotel/resort/inn that is considered a clean, comfortable, and reliable establishment, but also has expanded amenities, such as a full-service restaurant on the premises.

★ A Mobil One-Star lodging establishment is a limited-service hotel or inn that is considered a clean, comfortable, and reliable establishment.

Restaurant Star Definitions

★★★★★ A Mobil Five-Star restaurant is one of few flawless dining experiences in the country. These restaurants consistently provide their guests with exceptional food, superlative service, elegant décor, and exquisite presentations of each detail surrounding the meal.

★★★★ A Mobil Four-Star restaurant provides professional service, distinctive presentations, and wonderful food.

★★★ A Mobil Three-Star restaurant has good food, warm and skillful service, and enjoyable décor.

★★ A Mobil Two-Star restaurant serves fresh food in a clean setting with efficient service. Value is considered in this category, as is family friendliness.

★ A Mobil One-Star restaurant provides a distinctive experience through culinary specialty, local flair, or individual atmosphere.

Symbols at End of Listings

🄳 Facilities for people with disabilities not available

🐾 Pets allowed

⛷ Ski in/ski out access

⛳ Golf on premises

🎾 Tennis court(s) on premises

🏊 Indoor or outdoor pool

🏋 Fitness room

✈ Major commercial airport within 5 miles

🏃 Business center

Making the Most of Your Trip

A few hardy souls might look back with fondness on a trip during which the car broke down, leaving them stranded for three days, or a vacation that cost twice what it was supposed to. For most travelers, though, the best trips are those that are safe, smooth, and within budget. To help you make your trip the best it can be, we've assembled a few tips and resources.

Saving Money

ON LODGING

Many hotels and motels offer discounts—for senior citizens, business travelers, families, you name it. It never hurts to ask—politely, that is. Sometimes, especially in the late afternoon, desk clerks are instructed to fill beds, and you might be offered a lower rate or a nicer room to entice you to stay. Simply ask the reservation agent for the best rate available. Also, make sure to try both the toll-free number and the local number. You may be able to get a lower rate from one than from the other.

Timing your trip right can cut your lodging costs as well. Look for bargains on stays over multiple nights, in the off-season, and on weekdays or weekends, depending on the location. Many hotels in major metropolitan areas, for example, have special weekend packages that offer leisure travelers considerable savings on rooms; they may include breakfast, cocktails, and/or dinner discounts.

Another way to save money is to choose accommodations that give you more than just a standard room. Rooms with kitchen facilities enable you to cook some meals yourself, reducing your restaurant costs. A suite might save money for two couples traveling together. Even hotel luxury levels can provide good value, as many include breakfast or cocktails in the price of a room.

State and city taxes, as well as special room taxes, can increase your room rate by as much as 25 percent per day. We are unable to include information about taxes in our listings, but we strongly urge you to ask about taxes when making reservations so that you understand the total cost of your lodgings before you book them.

Watch out for telephone-usage charges that hotels frequently impose on long-distance, credit-card, and other calls. Before phoning from your room, read the information given to you at check-in, and then be sure to review your bill carefully when checking out. You won't be expected to pay for charges that the hotel didn't spell out. Consider using your cell phone if you have one; or, if public telephones are available in the hotel lobby, your cost savings may outweigh the inconvenience of using them.

Here are some additional ways to save on lodgings:

- Stay in B&B accommodations. They're generally less expensive than standard hotel rooms, and the complimentary breakfast cuts down on food costs.

- If you're traveling with children, find lodgings at which kids stay free.

- When visiting a major city, stay just outside the city limits; these rooms are usually less expensive than those in downtown locations.

- Consider visiting national parks during the low season, when prices of lodgings near the parks drop by 25 percent or more.

- When calling a hotel, ask whether it is running any special promotions or if any discounts are available; many times reservationists are told not to volunteer these deals unless they're specifically asked about them.

- Check for hotel packages; some offer nightly rates that include a rental car or discounts on major attractions.

ON DINING

There are several ways to get a less expensive meal at an expensive restaurant. Early-bird dinners are popular in many parts of the country and offer considerable savings. If you're interested in visiting a Mobil Four- or Five-Star establishment, consider going at lunchtime. Although the prices are probably still relatively high at midday, they may be half of those at dinner, and you'll experience the same ambience, service, and cuisine.

ON ENTERTAINMENT

Although many national parks, monuments, seashores, historic sites, and recreation areas may be used free of charge, others charge an entrance fee and/or a usage fee for special services and facilities. If you plan to make several visits to national recreation areas, consider one of the following money-saving programs offered by the National Park Service:

✪ **National Parks Pass.** This annual pass is good for entrance to any national park that charges an entrance fee. If the park charges a per-vehicle fee, the pass holder and any accompanying passengers in a private noncommercial vehicle may enter. If the park charges a per-person fee, the pass applies to the holder's spouse, children, and parents as well as the holder. It is valid for entrance fees only; it does not cover parking, camping, or other fees. You can purchase a National Parks Pass in person at any national park where an entrance fee is charged; by mail from the National Park Foundation, PO Box 34108, Washington, DC 20043-4108; by calling toll-free 888/467-2757; or at www.nationalparks.org. The cost is $50.

✪ **Golden Eagle Sticker.** When affixed to a National Parks Pass, this hologram sticker, available to people who are between 17 and 61 years of age, extends coverage to sites managed by the US Fish and Wildlife Service, the US Forest Service, and the Bureau of Land Management. It is good until the National Parks Pass to which it is affixed expires and does not cover usage fees. You can purchase one at the National Park Service, the Fish and Wildlife Service, or the Bureau of Land Management fee stations. The cost is $15.

✪ **Golden Age Passport.** Available to citizens and permanent US residents 62 and older, this passport is a lifetime entrance permit to fee-charging national recreation areas. The fee exemption extends to those accompanying the permit holder in a private noncommercial vehicle or, in the case of walk-in facilities, to the holder's spouse and children. The passport also entitles the holder to a 50 percent discount on federal usage fees charged in park areas, but not on concessions. Golden Age Passports must be obtained in person and are available at most National Park Service units that charge an entrance fee. The applicant must show proof of age, such as a driver's license or birth certificate (Medicare cards are not acceptable proof). The cost is $10.

✪ **Golden Access Passport.** Issued to citizens and permanent US residents who are physically disabled or visually impaired, this passport is a free lifetime entrance permit to fee-charging national recreation areas. The fee exemption extends to those accompanying the permit holder in a private noncommercial vehicle or, in the case of walk-in facilities, to the holder's spouse and children. The passport also entitles the holder to a 50 percent discount on usage fees charged in park areas, but not on concessions. Golden Access Passports must be obtained in person and are available at most National Park Service units that charge an entrance fee. Proof of eligibility to receive federal benefits (under programs such as Disability Retirement, Compensation for Military Service-Connected Disability, and the Coal Mine Safety and Health Act) is required, or an affidavit must be signed attesting to eligibility.

A money-saving move in several large cities is to purchase a **CityPass.** If you plan to visit several museums and other major attractions, CityPass is a terrific option because it gets you into several sites for one substantially reduced price. Currently, CityPass is available in Boston, Chicago, Hollywood, New York, Philadelphia, San Francisco, Seattle, southern California (which includes Disneyland, SeaWorld, and the San Diego Zoo), and Toronto. For more information or to buy one, call toll-free 888/330-5008 or visit www.citypass.net. You can also buy a CityPass from any participating CityPass attraction.

Here are some additional ways to save on entertainment and shopping:

✪ Check with your hotel's concierge for various coupons and special offers; they often have two-for-one tickets for area attractions and coupons for discounts at area stores and restaurants.

✪ Purchase same-day concert or theater tickets for half-price through the local cheap-tickets outlet, such as TKTS in New York or Hot Tix in Chicago.

☼ Visit museums on their free or "by donation" days, when you can pay what you wish rather than a specific admission fee.

ON TRANSPORTATION

Transportation is a big part of any vacation budget. Here are some ways to reduce your costs:

☼ If you're renting a car, shop early over the Internet; you can book a car during the low season for less, even if you'll be using it in the high season.

☼ Rental car discounts are often available if you rent for one week or longer and reserve in advance.

☼ Get the best gas mileage out of your vehicle by making sure that it's properly tuned up and keeping your tires properly inflated.

☼ Travel at moderate speeds on the open road; higher speeds require more gasoline.

☼ Fill the tank before you return your rental car; rental companies charge to refill the tank and do so at prices of up to 50 percent more than at local gas stations.

☼ Make a checklist of travel essentials and purchase them before you leave; don't get stuck buying expensive sunscreen at your hotel or overpriced film at the airport.

FOR SENIOR CITIZENS

Always call ahead to ask if a discount is being offered, and be sure to carry proof of age. Additional information for mature travelers is available from the American Association of Retired Persons (AARP), 601 E St NW, Washington, DC 20049; phone 202/434-2277; www.aarp.org.

Tipping

Tips are expressions of appreciation for good service. However, you are never obligated to tip if you receive poor service.

IN HOTELS

☼ Door attendants usually get $1 for hailing a cab.

☼ Bell staff expect $2 per bag.

☼ Concierges are tipped according to the service they perform. Tipping is not mandatory when you've asked for suggestions on sightseeing or restaurants or for help in making dining reservations. However, a tip of $5 is appropriate when a concierge books you a table at a restaurant known to be difficult to get into. For obtaining theater or sporting event tickets, $5 to $10 is expected.

☼ Maids should be tipped $1 to $2 per day. Hand your tip directly to the maid, or leave it with a note saying that the money has been left expressly for the maid.

IN RESTAURANTS

Before tipping, carefully review your check for any gratuity or service charge that is already included in your bill. If you're in doubt, ask your server.

☼ Coffee shop and counter service waitstaff usually receive 15 percent of the bill, before sales tax.

☼ In full-service restaurants, tip 18 percent of the bill, before sales tax.

☼ In fine restaurants, where gratuities are shared among a larger staff, 18 to 20 percent is appropriate.

☼ In most cases, the maitre d' is tipped only if the service has been extraordinary, and only on the way out. At upscale properties in major metropolitan areas, $20 is the minimum.

☼ If there is a wine steward, tip $20 for exemplary service and beyond, or more if the wine was decanted or the bottle was very expensive.

☼ Tip $1 to $2 per coat at the coat check.

AT AIRPORTS

Curbside luggage handlers expect $1 per bag. Car-rental shuttle drivers who help with your luggage appreciate a $1 or $2 tip.

Staying Safe

The best way to deal with emergencies is to avoid them in the first place. However, unforeseen situations do happen, so you should be prepared for them.

IN YOUR CAR

Before you head out on a road trip, make sure that your car has been serviced and is in good working order. Change the oil, check the battery and belts, make sure that your windshield washer fluid is full and your tires are properly inflated (which can also improve your gas mileage). Other inspections recommended by the vehicle's manufacturer should also be made.

Next, be sure you have the tools and equipment needed to deal with a routine breakdown:

- Jack
- Spare tire
- Lug wrench
- Repair kit
- Emergency tools
- Jumper cables
- Spare fan belt
- Fuses
- Flares and/or reflectors
- Flashlight
- First-aid kit
- In winter, a windshield scraper and snow shovel

Many emergency supplies are sold in special packages that include the essentials you need to stay safe in the event of a breakdown.

Also bring all appropriate and up-to-date documentation—licenses, registration, and insurance cards—and know what your insurance covers. Bring an extra set of keys, too, just in case.

En route, always buckle up! In most states, wearing a seatbelt is required by law.

If your car does break down, do the following:

- Get out of traffic as soon as possible—pull well off the road.
- Raise the hood and turn on your emergency flashers or tie a white cloth to the roadside door handle or antenna.
- Stay in your car.
- Use flares or reflectors to keep your vehicle from being hit.

IN YOUR HOTEL

Chances are slim that you will encounter a hotel or motel fire, but you can protect yourself by doing the following:

- Once you've checked in, make sure that the smoke detector in your room is working properly.
- Find the property's fire safety instructions, usually posted on the inside of the room door.
- Locate the fire extinguishers and at least two fire exits.
- Never use an elevator in a fire.

For personal security, use the peephole in your room door and make sure that anyone claiming to be a hotel employee can show proper identification. Call the front desk if you feel threatened at any time.

PROTECTING AGAINST THEFT

To guard against theft wherever you go:

- Don't bring anything of more value than you need.
- If you do bring valuables, leave them at your hotel rather than in your car.
- If you bring something very expensive, lock it in a safe. Many hotels put one in each room; others will store your valuables in the hotel's safe.
- Don't carry more money than you need. Use traveler's checks and credit cards or visit cash machines to withdraw more cash when you run out.

For Travelers with Disabilities

To get the kind of service you need and have a right to expect, don't hesitate when making a reservation to question the management about the availability of accessible rooms, parking, entrances, restaurants, lounges, or any other facilities that are important to you, and confirm what is meant by "accessible."

The Mobil Travel Guide ⊡ symbol indicates establishments that are not at least partially accessible to people with special mobility needs (people using wheelchairs or crutches or otherwise needing easy access to buildings and rooms). Further information about these criteria can be found in the earlier section "How to Use This Book."

A thorough listing of published material for travelers with disabilities is available from the Disability Bookshop, Twin Peaks Press, Box 129, Vancouver, WA 98666; phone 360/694-2462; disabilitybookshop.virtualave.net. Another reliable organization is the Society for Accessible Travel & Hospitality (SATH), 347 Fifth Ave, Suite 610, New York, NY 10016; phone 212/447-7284; www.sath.org.

Border-Crossing Regulations

In addition to a driver's license or military ID, proof of citizenship—a passport or certified birth certificate—is required for travel into Mexico for US citizens ages 18 and over. Children under age 18 traveling with their birth certificates are not required to have photo IDs, but it is highly recommended. A child under age 18 traveling to Mexico without both legal guardians must have a notarized letter of consent from the nontraveling parent(s) granting permission for the child to travel. The notarized letter of consent is not waived even when the minor has his or her own passport.

Canadian citizens crossing into Mexico must have a valid Canadian passport or government-issued birth certificate along with a government-issued photo ID, such as current driver's license or military ID. Mexican citizens residing in the US must have a Mexican passport, or Matricula Consular; a Certificate of Nationality issued by the Mexican Consulate with photo ID; a birth certificate with recent photo ID; or Mexican voter registration papers with photo ID. A US Resident Alien Registration Card is no longer an acceptable travel document for entry into Mexico.

Resident aliens of the US must carry a valid national passport; a Mexican visa may be required. A US Alien Registration Card is no longer an acceptable travel document for entry into Mexico.

If you plan to travel beyond the border cities or stay in Mexico for longer than 72 hours, you must purchase a Mexican tourist card, available from Mexican consulates, Mexican border crossing points, Mexican tourism offices, airports within the border zone, and most airlines serving Mexico. If you're driving your car beyond the border area, you are required to purchase an automobile permit, which costs about $20. Get a copy of the current border regulations from the nearest Mexican consulate or tourism office before crossing, and make sure that you understand them. A helpful booklet, Know Before You Go, can be obtained free of charge from the nearest office of the US Customs Service or online at www.customs.treas.gov.

Your automobile insurance is not valid in Mexico; for a short visit, get a one-day policy before crossing. You may find it more convenient to unload all baggage before crossing than to go through a thorough customs inspection upon your return. At customs, you must declare your purchases. Each traveler may bring up to $800 worth of goods purchased in Mexico back into the United States duty free. In addition, federal regulations permit each US citizen 21 years of age or older to bring back 1 quart of alcoholic beverage duty free in a 30-day period. Travelers are not permitted to bring in plants, fruits, or vegetables. State regulations vary, so check locally before entering Mexico. New regulations may be issued at any time.

US currency is accepted in all border cities.

For more information about traveling to Mexico, including safety information, look for the US State Department's Consular Information Sheet at travel.state.gov/mexico.html, or request it by fax by calling 202/647-3000.

Important Toll-Free Numbers and Online Information

Hotels

Adams Mark 800/444-2326
www.adamsmark.com
AmericInn 800/634-3444
www.americinn.com
AmeriHost Inn 800/434-5800
www.amerihostinn.com
Amerisuites 800/833-1516
www.amerisuites.com
Baymont Inns 877/229-6667
www.baymontinns.com
Best Inns & Suites 800/237-8466
www.bestinn.com
Best Value Inn 888/315-2378
www.bestvalueinn.com
Best Western 800/780-7234
www.bestwestern.com
Budget Host Inn 800/283-4678
www.budgethost.com
Candlewood Suites 888/226-3539
www.candlewoodsuites.com
Clarion Hotels 800/252-7466
www.choicehotels.com
Comfort Inns and Suites 800/252-7466
www.comfortinn.com
Country Hearth Inns 800/848-5767
www.countryhearth.com
Country Inns & Suites 800/456-4000
www.countryinns.com
Courtyard by Marriott 800/321-2211
www.courtyard.com
Cross Country Inns (KY and OH) 800/621-1429
www.crosscountryinns.com
Crowne Plaza Hotels and Resorts 800/227-6963
www.crowneplaza.com
Days Inn 800/544-8313
www.daysinn.com
Delta Hotels 800/268-1133
www.deltahotels.com
Destination Hotels & Resorts 800/434-7347
www.destinationhotels.com
Doubletree Hotels 800/222-8733
www.doubletree.com
Drury Inn 800/378-7946
www.druryinn.com
Econolodge 800/553-2666
www.econolodge.com

Embassy Suites 800/362-2779
www.embassysuites.com
ExelInns of America 800/367-3935
www.exelinns.com
Extended StayAmerica 800/398-7829
www.extendedstayhotels.com
Fairfield Inn by Marriott 800/228-2800
www.fairfieldinn.com
Fairmont Hotels 800/441-1414
www.fairmont.com
Four Points by Sheraton 888/625-5144
www.fourpoints.com
Four Seasons 800/819-5053
www.fourseasons.com
Hampton Inn 800/426-7866
www.hamptoninn.com
Hard Rock Hotels, Resorts, and Casinos 800/473-7625
www.hardrock.com
Harrah's Entertainment 800/427-7247
www.harrahs.com
Hawthorn Suites 800/527-1133
www.hawthorn.com
Hilton Hotels and Resorts (US) 800/774-1500
www.hilton.com
Holiday Inn Express 800/465-4329
www.hiexpress.com
Holiday Inn Hotels and Resorts 800/465-4329
www.holiday-inn.com
Homestead Studio Suites 888/782-9473
www.homesteadhotels.com
Homewood Suites 800/225-5466
www.homewoodsuites.com
Howard Johnson 800/406-1411
www.hojo.com
Hyatt 800/633-7313
www.hyatt.com
Inns of America 800/826-0778
www.innsofamerica.com
InterContinental 888/567-8725
www.intercontinental.com
Joie de Vivre 800/738-7477
www.jdvhospitality.com
Kimpton Hotels 888/546-7866
www.kimptongroup.com
Knights Inn 800/843-5644
www.knightsinn.com
La Quinta 800/531-5900
www.laquinta.com

Le Meridien 800/543-4300
www.lemeridien.com

Leading Hotels of the World 800/223-6800
www.lhw.com

Loews Hotels 800/235-6397
www.loewshotels.com

MainStay Suites 800/660-6246
www.mainstaysuites.com

Mandarin Oriental 800/526-6566
www.mandarin-oriental.com

Marriott Hotels, Resorts, and Suites 800/228-9290
www.marriott.com

Microtel Inns & Suites 800/771-7171
www.microtelinn.com

Millennium & Copthorne Hotels 866/866-8086
www.millenniumhotels.com

Motel 6 . . . . 800/466-8356
www.motel6.com

Omni Hotels 800/843-6664
www.omnihotels.com

Pan Pacific Hotels and Resorts 800/327-8585
www.panpac.com

Park Inn & Park Plaza 888/201-1801
www.parkinn.com

The Peninsula Group . . . . Contact individual hotel
www.peninsula.com

Preferred Hotels & Resorts Worldwide 800/323-7500
www.preferredhotels.com

Quality Inn 800/228-5151
www.qualityinn.com

Radisson Hotels 800/333-3333
www.radisson.com

Raffles International Hotels and Resorts . . . 800/637-9477
www.raffles.com

Ramada Plazas, Limiteds, and Inns 800/272-6232
www.ramada.com

Red Lion Inns 800/733-5466
www.redlion.com

Red Roof Inns 800/733-7663
www.redroof.com

Regent International 800/545-4000
www.regenthotels.com

Relais & Chateaux 800/735-2478
www.relaischateaux.com

Renaissance Hotels 888/236-2427
www.renaissancehotels.com

Residence Inn 800/331-3131
www.residenceinn.com

Ritz-Carlton 800/241-3333
www.ritzcarlton.com

RockResorts 888/367-7625
www.rockresorts.com

Rodeway Inn 800/228-2000
www.rodeway.com

Rosewood Hotels & Resorts 888/767-3966
www.rosewoodhotels.com

Select Inn 800/641-1000
www.selectinn.com

Sheraton 888/625-5144
www.sheraton.com

Shilo Inns 800/222-2244
www.shiloinns.com

Shoney's Inn 800/552-4667
www.shoneysinn.com

Signature/Jameson Inns 800/822-5252
www.jamesoninns.com

Sleep Inn 877/424-6423
www.sleepinn.com

Small Luxury Hotels of the World 800/525-4800
www.slh.com

Sofitel 800/763-4835
www.sofitel.com

SpringHill Suites 888/236-2427
www.springhillsuites.com

St. Regis Luxury Collection 888/625-5144
www.stregis.com

Staybridge Suites 800/238-8000
www.staybridge.com

Summerfield Suites by Wyndham 800/833-4353
www.summerfieldsuites.com

Summit International 800/457-4000
www.summithotels.com

Super 8 Motels 800/800-8000
www.super8.com

The Sutton Place Hotels 866/378-8866
www.suttonplace.com

Swissôtel 800/637-9477
www.swissotel.com

TownePlace Suites 888/236-2427
www.towneplace.com

Travelodge 800/578-7878
www.travelodge.com

Vagabond Inns 800/522-1555
www.vagabondinns.com

W Hotels 888/625-5144
www.whotels.com

Wellesley Inn and Suites 800/444-8888
www.wellesleyinnandsuites.com

WestCoast Hotels 800/325-4000
www.westcoasthotels.com

Westin Hotels & Resorts 800/937-8461
www.westin.com

Wingate Inns............................800/228-1000
www.wingateinns.com
Woodfin Suite Hotels...................800/966-3346
www.woodfinsuitehotels.com
WorldHotels..........................800/223-5652
www.worldhotels.com
Wyndham Hotels & Resorts..............800/996-3426
www.wyndham.com

Airlines

Air Canada...........................888/247-2262
www.aircanada.ca
AirTran...............................800/247-8726
www.airtran.com
Alaska Airlines........................800/252-7522
www.alaskaair.com
American Airlines......................800/433-7300
www.aa.com
America West.........................800/235-9292
www.americawest.com
ATA..................................800/435-9282
www.ata.com
Continental Airlines...................800/523-3273
www.continental.com
Delta Air Lines........................800/221-1212
www.delta.com
Frontier Airlines......................800/432-1359
www.frontierairlines.com
Hawaiian Airways......................800/367-5320
www.hawaiianair.com
Jet Blue Airlines.......................800/538-2583
www.jetblue.com
Midwest Express......................800/452-2022
www.midwestexpress.com

Northwest Airlines.....................800/225-2525
www.nwa.com
Southwest Airlines.....................800/435-9792
www.southwest.com
Spirit Airlines.........................800/772-7117
www.spiritair.com
United Airlines........................800/241-6522
www.united.com
US Airways...........................800/428-4322
www.usairways.com

Car Rentals

Advantage............................800/777-5500
www.arac.com
Alamo...............................800/327-9633
www.goalamo.com
Avis.................................800/831-2847
www.avis.com
Budget..............................800/527-0700
www.budget.com
Dollar...............................800/800-4000
www.dollarcar.com
Enterprise...........................800/325-8007
www.enterprise.com
Hertz...............................800/654-3131
www.hertz.com
National.............................800/227-7368
www.nationalcar.com
Payless.............................800/729-5377
www.paylesscarrental.com
Rent-A-Wreck.com.....................800/535-1391
www.rent-a-wreck.com
Thrifty...............................800/847-4389
www.thrifty.com

Meet The Stars

Mobil Travel Guide 2006 *Five-Star* Award Winners

CALIFORNIA
Lodgings
The Beverly Hills Hotel, *Beverly Hills*
Chateau du Sureau, *Oakhurst*
Four Seasons Hotel San Francisco,
  San Francisco
Hotel Bel-Air, *Los Angeles*
The Peninsula Beverly Hills, *Beverly Hills*
Raffles L'Ermitage Beverly Hills, *Beverly Hills*
The Ritz-Carlton, San Francisco, *San Francisco*

Restaurants
Bastide, *Los Angeles*
The Dining Room, *San Francisco*
The French Laundry, *Yountville*
Gary Danko, *San Francisco*

COLORADO
Lodgings
The Broadmoor, *Colorado Springs*
The Little Nell, *Aspen*

CONNECTICUT
Lodging
The Mayflower Inn, *Washington*

DISTRICT OF COLUMBIA
Lodging
Four Seasons Hotel Washington, DC,
  Washington

FLORIDA
Lodgings
Four Seasons Resort Palm Beach, *Palm Beach*
The Ritz-Carlton Naples, *Naples*
The Ritz-Carlton, Palm Beach, *Manalapan*

GEORGIA
Lodgings
Four Seasons Hotel Atlanta, *Atlanta*
The Lodge at Sea Island Golf Club,
  St. Simons Island

Restaurants
The Dining Room, *Atlanta*
Seeger's, *Atlanta*

HAWAII
Lodging
Four Seasons Resort Maui at Wailea, *Wailea,
  Maui*

ILLINOIS
Lodgings
Four Seasons Hotel Chicago, *Chicago*
The Peninsula Chicago, *Chicago*
The Ritz-Carlton, A Four Seasons Hotel, *Chicago*

Restaurant
Charlie Trotter's, *Chicago*

MAINE
Restaurant
The White Barn Inn, *Kennebunkport*

MASSACHUSETTS
Lodgings
Blantyre, *Lenox*
Four Seasons Hotel Boston, *Boston*

NEW YORK
Lodgings
Four Seasons, Hotel New York, *New York*
The Point, *Saranac Lake*
The Ritz-Carlton New York, Central Park,
  New York
The St. Regis, *New York*

Restaurants
Alain Ducasse, *New York*
Jean Georges, *New York*
Masa, *New York*
per se, *New York*

NORTH CAROLINA
Lodging
The Fearrington House Country Inn, *Pittsboro*

PENNSYLVANIA
Restaurant
Le Bec-Fin, *Philadelphia*

SOUTH CAROLINA
Lodging
Woodlands Resort & Inn, *Summerville*

Restaurant
Dining Room at the Woodlands, *Summerville*

TEXAS
Lodging
The Mansion on Turtle Creek, *Dallas*

VERMONT
Lodging
Twin Farms, *Barnard*

VIRGINIA
Lodgings
The Inn at Little Washington, *Washington*
The Jefferson Hotel, *Richmond*

Restaurant
The Inn at Little Washington, *Washington*

Mobil Travel Guide has been rating establishments with its Mobil One- to Five-Star system since 1958. Each establishment awarded the Mobil Five-Star rating is one of the best in the country. Detailed information on each award winner can be found in the corresponding regional edition listed on the back cover of this book.

Four- and Five-Star Establishments in Texas

Texas

★ ★ ★ ★ ★ Lodging
The Mansion on Turtle Creek, *Dallas*

★ ★ ★ ★ Lodgings
Four Seasons Hotel Austin, *Austin*
Four Seasons Hotel Houston, *Houston*
Four Seasons Resort and Club Dallas at Las Colinas,
    Dallas/Fort Worth Airport Area
The St. Regis Houston, *Houston*
Watermark Hotel & Spa, *San Antonio*

★ ★ ★ ★ Spas
Trellis, The Spa at the Houstonian, *Houston*
Watermark Spa at the Watermark Hotel & Spa,
    San Antonio, TX

★ ★ ★ ★ Restaurants
Abacus, *Dallas*
Café at the Four Seasons, *Austin*
The French Room, *Dallas*
Le Reve, *San Antonio*
Nana, *Dallas*
Quattro, *Houston*
Restaurant at the Mansion on Turtle Creek, *Dallas*

Texas

The long, turbulent history of Texas as we know it, goes back to 27 years after Columbus arrived in America. In 1519, Alonzo Alvarez de Piñeda explored and charted the Texas coast. Alvar Núñez Cabeza de Vaca, shipwrecked near Galveston, wandered across Texas beginning in 1528. Inspired by the tales of de Vaca, Coronado entered the state from New Mexico, bringing with him Fray Juan de Padilla, the first missionary, who was later killed by the Native Americans he tried to convert.

In 1821, Mexico won its independence from Spain, and Texas became a part of the new Mexican republic. At about this time, Moses Austin and his son, Stephen F. Austin, received permission to settle 300 American families on the Brazos. This was the beginning of Anglo-American Texas. Dissatisfaction with Mexican rule led to the Texas Revolution and the taking of San Antonio, later temporarily lost when the Alamo fell. The Revolution came to an end on the plain of San Jacinto when General Sam Houston's outnumbered troops successfully charged the Mexican Army on April 21, 1836, and Texas became an independent republic. It remained so until December 29, 1845, when Texas became the 28th state of the Union.

The character of Texas changes markedly from region to region. While the face of western Texas is largely that of the open range, eastern Texas is home to plantations where rice, sugar cane, and cotton are grown. Northern Texas is the land of the *Llanos Estacado* (staked plains), but to the southwest stand mountain ranges with 59 peaks at an altitude of more than 6,000 feet. South Texas is dotted with citrus groves that thrive in its semitropical climate, as do the beach lovers that populate hundreds of miles of sand along the Gulf Coast and on the barrier islands. Central areas have an abundance of man-made lakes, making fishing and boating popular pastimes.

Population: 20,851,820
Area: 268,601 square miles
Elevation: 0-8,749 feet
Peak: Guadalupe Peak (Culberson County)
Entered Union: December 29, 1845 (28th state)
Capital: Austin
Motto: Friendship
Nickname: Lone Star State
Flower: Bluebonnet
Bird: Mockingbird
Tree: Pecan
Fair: September-October in Dallas
Time Zone: Central ar.d Mountain
Web Site: www.traveltex.com
Fun Facts:
- More species of bats live in Texas than in any other part of the United States.
- More wool comes from the state of Texas than from any other state in the United States.

Industry exceeds agriculture in the Houston-Beaumont area, including a space industry that contributes millions of dollars to the state's economy. Much of the nation's oil is produced in Texas, and it also ranks at the top of the cotton and livestock industries.

When to Go/Climate

Most of Texas is relatively warm and dry. Exceptions are the Panhandle, which can get cold in winter, and east Texas and the Gulf Coast, which are often humid and wet. Tornado season runs from March through May in the north Texas plains; hurricanes are most common in August and September along the Gulf Coast.

Calendar Highlights

JANUARY

Cotton Bowl Classic *(Dallas). Phone 214/634-7525 (parade); 214/638-2695 (tickets).*

FEBRUARY

Houston Livestock Show & Rodeo *(Houston). Astrodome. Phone 713/791-9000. Largest event of its kind in the world.*

APRIL

Fiesta San Antonio *(San Antonio). Phone 210/227-5191. Celebrating Texas heroes since 1891 with three major parades (one on the San Antonio River), sports, and food. More than 150 events held throughout city.*

MAY

Byron Nelson Golf Classic *(Dallas). Four Seasons Resort and Club. Phone 972/717-2500.*

Cinco de Mayo Celebration *(Del Rio). Phone 830/775-3551. Festival of food, music, and dance to celebrate the Mexican victory over Spain.*

JUNE

Juneteenth Festival *(Houston). Phone toll-free 800/365-7575. Music festival celebrating the abolition of slavery in June 1865.*

AUGUST

Texas Folklife Festival *(San Antonio). Institute of Texan Cultures, HemisFair Park. Phone 210/458-2249. Crafts, folk music, dancing, entertainment, and food representing more than 30 ethnic groups in Texas.*

SEPTEMBER

Pioneer Days *(Fort Worth). Fort Worth Stockyards. Phone 817/626-7921. Commemorates pioneer settlement along the Trinity River and early days of the cattle industry.*

State Fair of Texas *(Dallas). State Fair Park. Phone 214/565-9931. America's largest state fair.*

Tri-State Fair *(Amarillo). Phone 806/376-7767. Second largest after State Fair. Week-long festival, rodeo, and carnival with New Mexicans and Oklahomans.*

OCTOBER

WWII Flying Air Show *(Midland). Midland International Airport. Contact Chamber of Commerce, phone 915/563-1000.*

DECEMBER

Harbor Lights Celebration *(Corpus Christi). Contact Convention & Visitors Bureau, phone 361/881-1888 or toll-free 800/678-6232. Lighting of boats in marina. Christmas trees at Art Museum of South Texas.*

Las Posadas *(San Antonio). River Walk. Phone 210/224-6163. Song and candlelight procession has been a tradition for more than 250 years. Held in conjunction with Fiesta de las Luminarias, the fiesta of lights, when the River Walk is lined with candles. Reenactment of the Holy Family's search for an inn. Evening ends with piñata party in Plaza Juarez in La Villita.*

Wonderland of Lights *(Marshall). Contact Chamber of Commerce, phone 903/935-7868. Christmas festival. Courthouse, entire neighborhoods decorated by 7 1/2 million lights.*

AVERAGE HIGH/LOW TEMPERATURES (° F)

Dallas/Fort Worth

Jan 54/33	May 83/63	Sept 88/67
Feb 59/37	June 92/70	Oct 79/56
Mar 68/46	July 97/74	Nov 67/45
Apr 76/55	Aug 96/74	Dec 58/36

Houston

Jan 61/40	May 85/64	Sept 88/68
Feb 65/43	June 90/71	Oct 82/58
Mar 71/50	July 93/72	Nov 72/50
Apr 78/58	Aug 93/72	Dec 65/42

Parks and Recreation

There are approximately 1,000 roadside parks

WEST TEXAS: GHOST TOWNS, GHOST LIGHTS, AND DUDE RANCHES

From El Paso, drive east on Interstate-10 and south on Highway 90 to Marfa, site of the filming of *Giant* and home of the mysterious Marfa Ghost Lights and a mile-high golf course. Follow Highway 67 south through the Chinati Mountains to the ghost mining town of Shafter and to Presidio, then east on Ranch Road 170 (also called The River Road), one of the nation's most scenic drives. Follow the Rio Grande over steep hills and into dry gulleys, past the Big Bend Ranch State Park to the town of Lajitas, with lodgings, a saloon, dining, and a horseback trip outfitter. Head west again along Ranch Road 170 to Terlingua, a quicksilver (mercury) mining ghost town and host of the giant Chili Cook-off in November. This is the western entry point to Big Bend National Park, a rugged and forbidding expanse of 801,163 acres and Chisos Mountains scenery where hiking, camping, backcountry, and rafting trips can last from one day to three weeks. From this point, either follow Highway 118 north from Terlingua through the Del Norte Mountains to Alpine, with its excellent natural history museum, railroad hotel, galleries, and dining; or take Highway 385 north from Big Bend to Marathon, a much smaller town with an excellent historic hotel, a few art galleries, and Glass Mountains glory. Then travel north on Highway 118 to Fort Davis, home to sensational hiking at Davis Mountains State Park, dude ranch stays, frontier fort and buffalo soldier history exploration at Fort Davis National Historic Site, and an unforgettable galaxy study at McDonald Observatory. Allow at least four days. **(Approximately 500 miles)**

maintained by the Texas Department of Transportation. Tables, benches, grills, and rubbish incinerators are provided. Some have water.

Water-related activities, hiking, horseback riding, various other sports, picnicking and camping, as well as visitor centers are available in many of Texas's state parks. The daily per-vehicle entrance fee at most parks ranges from $2-$5; annual Texas Conservation Passport, $50. Camping: primitive $4-$9/night; water only $6-$12/night; water and electricity $9-$16/night; water, electricity, and sewer $10-$16/night; screened shelter $15-$32/night. Cabins $35-$75/night, depending on size. Pets on leash only; pets not allowed in buildings, cabins, or screened shelters. Most parks accept reservations up to 11 months in advance when you call the Central Reservation Center at 512/389-8900. Reservations require payment for each facility reserved in an amount equal to one day's user fee. Contact Texas Parks & Wildlife, Reservations, 4200 Smith School Rd, Austin 78744; phone 512/389-8950 or toll-free 800/792-1112.

FISHING AND HUNTING
Nonresident fishing license: 5-day $20-$30; annual $30. Freshwater trout or saltwater stamp, $7. Annual nonresident hunting license: $100 for small game; $250 for big game. Nonresident 5-day small game license, $35. Nonresident spring turkey license, $100. Banded bird area license $10. Stamps required for white-winged dove, $7; turkey, $5; and migratory waterfowl, $7 (state) and $15 (federal). All annual licenses expire August 31. Fees are subject to change. For complete information, send for "Texas Parks & Wildlife Outdoor Annual" from the Parks & Wildlife Department, 4200 Smith School Rd, Austin 78744. Phone 512/389-8950 or toll-free 800/792-1112 in Texas.

Driving Information

Safety belts are mandatory for all persons in the front seat of a vehicle. Children under 5 years must be in approved passenger restraints anywhere in the vehicle: ages 2-4 may use a regulation safety belts or approved safety seats; children under age 2 must use approved safety seats. For further information, phone toll-free 800/452-9292.

INTERSTATE HIGHWAY SYSTEM
The following alphabetical listing of Texas towns in this book shows that these cities are within 10 miles of the indicated interstate highways. Check a highway map for the nearest exit.

Highway Number	Cities/Towns within 10 Miles
Interstate 10	Baytown, Beaumont, El Paso,

Fort Stockton, Gonzales, Houston, Kerrville, Orange, Ozona, San Antonio, Seguin, Sonora, Van Horn.

Interstate 20	Abilene, Arlington-Grand Prairie, Big Spring, Dallas, Dallas/Fort Worth Airport Area, Eastland, Fort Worth, Kilgore, Longview, Marshall, Midland, Monahans, Odessa, Pecos, Sweetwater, Tyler, Weatherford.
Interstate 27	Amarillo, Canyon, Lubbock, Plainview.
Interstate 30	Arlington-Grand Prairie, Dallas, Dallas/Fort Worth Airport Area, Greenville, Mount Pleasant, Sulphur Springs, Texarkana.
Interstate 35	Arlington-Grand Prairie, Austin, Cleburne, Dallas, Dallas/ Fort Worth Airport Area, Denton, Fort Worth, Gainesville, Georgetown, Hillsboro, Laredo, New Braunfels, San Antonio, San Marcos, Temple, Waco.
Interstate 37	Corpus Christi, San Antonio.
Interstate 40	Amarillo, Shamrock.
Interstate 45	Corsicana, Dallas, Ennis, Fairfield, Galveston, Houston, Huntsville, Texas City.

Additional Visitor Information

The *Texas Almanac,* an excellent compendium published every two years by the *Dallas Morning News,* may be obtained from the Gulf Publishing Company, PO Box 2608, Houston 77252.

The Texas Department of Transportation operates 12 travel information centers on main highways entering the state, and also the Judge Roy Bean Visitor Center in Langtry and an information center in the state capitol complex. They also distribute free maps and travel literature by mail, including the *"Texas State Travel Guide."* Write to Texas Department of Transportation, PO Box 5064, Austin 78763. Phone toll-free 800/452-9292 (daily 8 am-6 pm) or 800/888-8839 (24-hour travel kit hotline).

Abilene (B-6)

See also Eastland, Sweetwater

Founded 1881
Population 115,930
Elevation 1,738 ft
Area Code 915
Information Convention & Visitors Bureau, 1101 N 1st St, 79601; phone 915/676-2556 or toll-free 800/727-7704
Web Site www.abilene.com/visitors

Abilene is a major retail, educational, medical, and employment center for a 22-county area. Its economy is based primarily on the petroleum industry, agri-business, and a major military installation.

What to See and Do

Abilene State Park. *150 Park Rd 32, Tuscola (79562). 16 miles SW on FM 89 to Park Rd 32.* Phone 915/572-3204. Approximately 600 acres with Texas Longhorn herd. Swimming pool (Memorial Day-Labor Day; fee), bathhouse; picnicking, improved campsites (dump station). Nearby Lake Abilene has fishing. (Daily) **$$**

Abilene Zoological Gardens. *Nelson Park, 2070 Zoo Ln, Abilene. Near junction of Loop 322 and Hwy 36.* Phone 915/676-6085. www.abilenetx.com/zoo/zoo_home.htm. Approximately 13 acres; includes indoor plant and animal habitat facility with live specimens in museum setting. (Sun-Sat 9 am-5 pm; closed Jan 1, Thanksgiving, Dec 25) **$$**

Buffalo Gap Historic Village. *133 Williams St, Buffalo Gap. 8 miles S on Hwy 89.* Phone 915/572-3365. More than 15 restored original buildings, including the first Taylor County Courthouse and jail; Museum of the Old West. Tour includes a film on history of Texas. (Mid-Mar-mid-Nov, daily; rest of year, Fri-Sun; closed Thanksgiving, Dec 25) **$$**

Dyess Air Force Base. *226 Commissary Rd Bldg, Abilene (79607). W on Business 20, then S on Spur 312. Stop at gate for temporary pass.* Phone 915/696-5609. An Air Combat Command base, first home of the B-1B bomber. Also has C-130s, T-38s. Linear Air Park includes 30 vintage display aircraft (daily). **FREE**

Fort Phantom Hill and Lake. *14 miles N on FM 600.* Phone 915/677-1309. Ruins of 1850s frontier fort, built to protect gold miners traveling to California. Lake has water sports (some fees). (Daily) **FREE**

Grace Museums. *102 Cypress St, Abilene. Phone 915/673-4587.* The former Grace Hotel (1909), now restored and renovated, serves as the home of the Museums of Abilene. Inside is the Art Museum featuring permanent and special exhibits. The Historical Museum traces Abilene's history from 1900 to 1945 through photos and memorabilia. The Children's Museum offers many hands-on activities. (Mon-Sat; closed holidays) Free admission Thurs evenings. **$$**

Oscar Rose Park. *7th and Mockingbird sts, Abilene. Phone 915/676-6217.* Picnicking, playground, pool, gym, tennis center; community and children's theater, amphitheater; senior citizen center. There are 25 other city parks. **FREE**

Special Events

Celebrate Abilene. *Downtown, 1101 N 1st St, Abilene. Phone 915/676-2556.* Art festival, railroad festival, children's activities, stew cook-off. Mid-Apr.

West Texas Fair & Rodeo. *1801 E South 11th St, Abilene. Phone 915/677-4376.* Fri after Labor Day.

Limited-Service Hotels

★★AMBASSADOR SUITES. *4250 Ridgemont Dr, Abilene (79606). Phone 325/698-1234; fax 325/698-2771. www.ambassadorabilene.com.* This hotel is located directly across the street from the Mall of Abilene, with shops, theaters, and other convenient services within walking distance. 176 rooms, 3 story, all suites. Pets accepted; fee. Complimentary full breakfast. Check-out noon. Restaurant, bar. Indoor pool, whirlpool. Airport transportation available. **$**

★BEST WESTERN MALL SOUTH. *3950 Ridgemont Dr, Abilene (79606). Phone 325/695-1262; toll-free 800/346-1574; fax 325/695-2593. www.bestwestern.com.* 61 rooms, 2 story. Pets accepted, some restrictions; fee. Complimentary continental breakfast. Check-out noon. Outdoor pool. Airport transportation available. **$**

★LA QUINTA INN. *3501 W Lake Rd, Abilene (79601). Phone 325/676-1676; fax 325/672-8323. www.lq.com.* 106 rooms, 2 story. Pets accepted, some restrictions. Complimentary continental breakfast. Check-out noon. Outdoor pool. **$**

Addison (A-8)

Web Site www.addisontexas.net

Restaurants

★★ ADDISON CAFE. *5290 Belt Line Rd, Addison (75254). Phone 972/991-8824; fax 972/991-8839.* Easily one of the most refined dining experiences in Addison, this café provides a lavish French menu and sophisticated service to match. Salmon Napoleon, duck confit with mushrooms, and a salad of pepper-crusted seared goat cheese over baby greens with a walnut-tarragon vinaigrette add up to a wonderfully memorable dinner. American, French menu. Lunch, dinner. Closed holidays. Bar. **$$**

★★ ANDIAMO. *4151 Belt Line Rd, Addison (75001). Phone 972/233-1515; fax 972/233-2477.* A pretty retreat in Addison's Belt Line restaurant row, this café delivers on the promise of fine fare from central Italy. Calamari puttanesca is dressed in a lemony white wine sauce with olives and capers, and the house sole special features sautéed fish in champagne sauce with shrimp and angel hair pasta. A suggested villa garden setting makes even a Tuesday dinner feel special. Italian menu. Lunch, dinner. Closed Sun; holidays. **$$**

★★ CHAMBERLAIN'S. *5330 Belt Line Rd, Addison (75254). Phone 972/934-2467; fax 972/661-5350. www.chamberlainsrestaurant.com.* One of Dallas's palaces of prime beef, this sleek, contemporary dining room woos even noncarnivores with lovely works in shrimp remoulade, beefsteak tomatoes in blue cheese vinaigrette, and seared, peppered tuna steak. Beef lovers swoon over peppercorn steak in cognac sauce and cool-centered filet mignon with garlic mashed potatoes. Steak menu. Dinner. Closed holidays. Bar. Children's menu. Valet parking. **$$$**

★★ FOGO DE CHÃO. *4300 Belt Line Rd, Addison (75001). Phone 972/503-7300; fax 972/503-7303. www.fogodechao.com.* If you're in a carnivorous mood, this upscale, aromatic Brazilian churrascaria is the place to indulge. Fifteen all-you-can-eat grilled and roasted meats waft through the room on spits, borne by efficient "gauchos" who descend upon you at your whim. The massive salad bar and side dishes represent the other food groups—but at this price, save room for plenty of meat. Brazilian steakhouse. Lunch, dinner. Closed Thanksgiving, Dec 25. Bar. Children's menu. Valet parking. **$$$**

★★KAMPAI SUSHI & GRILL. *4995 Addison Cir, Addison (75001). Phone 972/490-8888.* Tucked into Addison's high-end shopping and residential center, the hip and super-contemporary Kampai suits the young neighborhood. Beautiful sushi renditions augment a menu laden with sashimi salad in a sesame dressing, spicy crawfish rice, crab Rangoon, and tempura-fried ice cream. Japanese menu. Lunch, dinner. Outdoor seating. **$$$**

★★LOMBARDI MARE. *5100 Belt Line Rd #410, Addison (75254). Phone 972/503-1233; fax 972/503-6279.* The aquatic décor, prompt, efficient service, palate-teasing fresh Italian seafood, and busy bar scene combine to make this upscale North Dallas eatery a must for those who like to people-watch while enjoying some of the best seafood in the city. Italian, seafood menu. Lunch, dinner, brunch. **$$$**

★★SAMBUCA. *15207 Addison Rd, Addison (75001). Phone 972/385-8455; fax 972/239-3790. www.sambucajazzcafe.com.* American menu. Dinner. Closed holidays. Casual attire. **$$$**

Alice (E-7)

See also Corpus Christi, Kingsville

Population 19,010
Elevation 205 ft
Area Code 361
Zip 78332
Information Chamber of Commerce, 612 E Main, PO Box 1609; phone 361/664-3454
Web Site www.alicetx.org

This is a farming, livestock, natural gas, and oil town. It is situated on the gently sloping subtropical Gulf Plain, where mesquite, hackberry, and live oak flourish. Alice is also a center of uranium production in southern Texas.

What to See and Do

Lake Corpus Christi State Park. *Park Rd 25, Mathis. 25 miles NE on Hwy 359, then 2 miles NW on Park Rd 25. Phone 361/547-2635.* Approximately 21,000 acres. Swimming, water-skiing, fishing, boating (ramp); picnicking (shelters), tent and trailer sites (dump station). (Daily) **$$**

Special Events

Fiesta Bandana. *Plaza Park, Cameron St, Alice (78332). Phone 361/664-3455.* Nightly entertainment; carnival, queen's court, talent show, folk dancers. Six days in early May.

Jim Wells County Fair. *JWC Fairgrounds, 3001 S Johnson, Alice (78332). Phone 361/664-3454.* Mid-Oct.

Alpine (C-4)

See also Fort Stockton, Marfa

Founded 1882
Population 5,768
Elevation 4,481 ft
Area Code 915
Zip 79830
Information Chamber of Commerce, 106 N Third St; phone 915/837-2326
Web Site www.alpinetexas.com

Alpine lies in a high valley, with the Glass Mountains to the east, the Davis Mountains to the north, and the Del Norte Mountains to the south. It is the home of Sul Ross State University, and it serves as a business center for ranching in the Big Bend area of west Texas.

Local mountain and desert plants include piñon pine, juniper, sotol, and a great variety of cacti. Pronghorn antelope, mountain lions, white-tailed deer, and javelina can be seen in the area.

What to See and Do

Driving tour. Davis Mountains and McDonald Observatory. (Approximately 100 miles) Drive 26 miles Northwest on Highway 118, a mountain road through scenic country, to

Davis Mountains State Park. *Hwy 118 NW, Fort Davis. Phone 915/426-3337.* A 2,250-acre park. Picnicking, playground, hiking trails, restaurant, lodge, tent and trailer sites (dump station). (Daily) **$$**

Fort Davis. (Population 900, altitude 5,050 feet) Highest town in Texas. Just outside town are the restored ruins of

Fort Davis National Historic Site. *N Hwy 17, Fort Davis. Phone 915/426-3224.* A famous frontier outpost garrisoned from 1854 to 1891. Museum, visitor center; restored and refurnished officers' quarters, barracks, commissary, and kitchen; sound reproduction of 1875 Retreat Parade; slide show; living history programs in summer. Self-guided trail; transportation for handicapped (free). (Daily; closed Dec 25) Golden Age Passport accepted (see MAKING THE MOST OF YOUR TRIP). Contact Superintendent, PO Box 1379, Fort Davis 79734. **$$**

McDonald Observatory. *At the base of Mount Locke. Phone 915/426-3640.* Has a 107-inch reflecting telescope; solar viewing, video presentations. Guided tours (fee); evening star parties at visitors center (Tues, Fri, and Sat evenings). (Daily; closed Jan 1, Thanksgiving, Dec 25) **$$**

Museum of the Big Bend. *Hwy 90, Alpine. Sul Ross State University, E of town via Hwy 90, entrance #2. Phone 915/837-8143.* Local Spanish, Native American, Mexican, and pioneer artifacts and historical displays. (Tues-Sun) **DONATION**

Limited-Service Hotels

★ ★ **INDIAN LODGE.** *N Hwy 118, Fort Davis (79734). Phone 432/426-3254; fax 432/426-2022. www.tpwd.state.tx.us.* Pueblo-style lodge with rustic décor is located on hillside. State-owned, operated. All park facilities available. 39 rooms, 3 story. Check-in 3 pm, check-out noon. Restaurant. Outdoor pool. **$**
🔁

★ ★ **LIMPIA HOTEL.** *Main St, Fort Davis (79734). Phone 432/426-3237; toll-free 800/662-5517; fax 432/426-3983. www.hotellimpia.com.* Built in 1912 of locally mined pink limestone. 38 rooms, 2 story. Pets accepted, some restrictions; fee. Check-in 3 pm, check-out noon. Restaurant, bar. **$**
🐾

Restaurant

★ ★ **REATA.** *203 N 5th St, Alpine (79830). Phone 432/837-9232; fax 432/837-9234. www.reata.net.* Southwestern menu. Lunch, dinner. Closed Sun-Mon; Thanksgiving, Dec 25. Bar. Children's menu. Casual attire. Reservations recommended. Outdoor seating. Private club. **$$**

Amarillo (E-3)

See also Canyon, Clarendon, Dalhart, Dumas, Fritch, Hereford, Pampa, Shamrock

Settled 1887
Population 173,627
Elevation 3,676 ft
Area Code 806
Information Convention and Visitor Council, 1000 S Polk St, 79101; phone 806/374-1497 or toll-free 800/692-1338
Web Site www.amarillo-cvb.org

This is the Panhandle, once known as the *Llano Estacado* (staked plain). It is open-range cattle country covered by tall, robust buffalo grass. It was, and in many ways still is, the raw, weather-beaten, hearty, Old West. But the hide huts of the buffalo hunters on the prairie have given way to a modern, attractive city where the economy is based on cattle, irrigated farming, tourism, diversified industry, oil, natural gas, and helium production.

The flatlands of the Panhandle were once generally regarded as worthless and uninhabitable. But buffalo hides at $3.75 and the use of buffalo bones for fertilizer made buffalo hunting a source of wealth for those who dared to cross into this area, heavily populated with Native Americans. Later, ranchers moved in to graze their cattle, and in 1877, the railroad arrived. "Ragtown," as it was first called, became Amarillo, which is Spanish for "yellow." An early promoter was so delighted with the name, which was derived from the color of a nearby creek bank, that he painted all his buildings a bright yellow. The yellow rose remains a symbol of Amarillo's colorful past.

What to See and Do

Amarillo Museum of Art. *2200 S Van Buren, Amarillo (79109). Phone 806/371-5050. www.amarilloart.org.* Features broad range of paintings, photographs, sculptures, and textiles from 20th-century American art to Southeast Asian treasures. Exhibits change every seven weeks. (Tues-Fri 10 am-5 pm, Sat-Sun from 1 pm; closed holidays) **FREE**

American Quarter Horse Heritage Center & Museum. *2601 I-40 E, Amarillo (79104). At Quarter Horse Dr. Phone 806/376-5181. www.aqha.com.* Many hands-on and interactive exhibits, video presentations, artifacts, and live demonstrations on the history and significance of "America's breed." Heritage Gallery traces chronology of development; Performance Gallery includes rodeo, ranching, and racing aspects, and features the American Quarter Horse Hall of Fame. Research library; 70-seat orientation theater. (Memorial Day weekend-Labor Day weekend: Mon-Sat 9 am-5 pm; rest of year: Mon-Sat 9 am-5 pm, Sun noon-5 pm; closed Jan 1, Thanksgiving, Dec 25) **$**

Carson County Square House Museum. *Hwy 207 and 5th St, Panhandle. 26 miles NE via Hwy 60. Phone 806/537-3524. www.squarehousemuseum.org.* Museum depicts the history and development of the Texas Panhandle region from the era of Native American hunters through ranching and railroads to the discovery of oil and the industrialization of the region. Complex includes historic house, furnished dugout dwelling, Santa Fe caboose, barn, branding diorama, pioneer bank, general store, windmill, blacksmith shop, natural history hall, and two art galleries. (Mon-Sat 9 am-5 pm, Sun from 1 pm; closed holidays) **FREE**

Don Harrington Discovery Center. *1200 Streit Dr, Amarillo (79106). 5 miles W on I-40, 1 mile N of Coulter exit. Phone 806/355-9548. www.dhdc.org.* Exhibits focus on science, health, and technology; more than 75 hands-on exhibits. Planetarium shows, 360 degree films (summer). Helium Monument is a steel memorial to the gas found in abundance in the area; also includes a time capsule. (Tues-Sat 9:30 am-4:30 pm, Sun from noon; closed holidays) **$**

Livestock auction. *E 3rd and Manhattan sts, Amarillo (79104). Phone 806/373-7464.* More than 200,000 cattle sold each year. (Mon-Sun 8 am-5 pm; closed holidays) **FREE**

Palo Duro Canyon State Park. *11450 Park Rd 5, Canyon (79015). 18 miles S on I-27, then 10 miles E on Hwy 217. Phone 806/488-2227. www.palodurocanyon.com.* (See CANYON)

Thompson Park. *509 E 7th Ave, Amarillo (79101). Phone 806/378-3036.* Pool (June-Aug, daily; fee); amusement park (mid-Mar-Sept, daily; fee). Amarillo Zoo has animals indigenous to the plains (Tues-Sun). **FREE**

Wonderland Amusement Park. *2601 Dumas Dr at Thompson St, Amarillo (79105). N on Hwy 87/287 N, River Rd exit. Phone toll-free 800/383-4712. www.wonderlandpark.com.* 25 rides and 30 attractions, including a double-loop roller coaster and water rides. (Apr-May: Sat-Sun from 1 pm; closing times vary;

June-mid-Aug: Mon-Fri 7-10:30 pm, Sat-Sun 1-10 pm; mid-Aug-early Sept: Sat-Sun 1-10 pm) **$$$$**

Special Events

Coors Ranch Rodeo. *Tri-State fairgrounds, 3301 E 10th Ave, Amarillo. Phone 806/376-7767.* Mid-June.

Tri-State Fair. *3301 E 10th Ave, Amarillo (79104). Phone 806/376-7767. www.tristatefair.com.* Second largest after State Fair. Mid-Sept. **$$**

Limited-Service Hotels

★ **DAYS INN.** *1701 I-40 E, Amarillo (79102). Phone 806/379-6255; toll-free 800/329-7466; fax 806/379-8204. www.daysinn.com.* 119 rooms, 5 story. Pets accepted; fee. Complimentary full breakfast. Check-in 3 pm, check-out 11 am. Outdoor pool. Airport transportation available. **$**
🐾 ☄

★ **HAMPTON INN.** *1700 I-40 E, Amarillo (79103). Phone 806/372-1425; toll-free 800/426-7866; fax 806/379-8807. www.hamptoninn.com.* 116 rooms, 2 story. Pets accepted, some restrictions. Complimentary continental breakfast. Check-out noon. Outdoor pool. **$**
🐾 ☄

★ ★ **HOLIDAY INN.** *1911 I-40 E, Amarillo (79102). Phone 806/372-8741; toll-free 800/465-4329; fax 806/372-2913. www.holiday-inn.com.* 248 rooms, 4 story. Pets accepted; fee. Check-in 3 pm, check-out noon. Restaurant, bar. Fitness room. Indoor pool, children's pool, whirlpool. Business center. **$**
🐾 🏋 ☄ 🚶

Restaurant

★ ★ **BIG TEXAN STEAK RANCH.** *7701 I-40 E, Amarillo (79118). Phone 806/372-6000; fax 806/371-0099. www.bigtexan.com.* Steak menu. Breakfast, lunch, dinner, brunch. Bar. Children's menu. Casual attire. **$$**

Angleton (D-9)

See also Brazosport, Galveston, Houston

Population 18,130
Elevation 31 ft
Area Code 979
Zip 77515
Information Chamber of Commerce, 445 E Mulberry,

PO Box 1356, 77516; phone 979/849-6443
Web Site www.angleton.tx.us

What to See and Do

Varner-Hogg Plantation State Historical Park. *1702 N 13th St, West Columbia (77486). 15 miles W via Hwy 35. Phone 979/345-4656.* Stately house (circa 1835) in 66-acre park. Period furnishings; family memorabilia. Tours (Wed-Sun, fee). Picnicking. **FREE**

Special Event

Brazoria County Fair. *901 S Downing, Angleton (77156). Phone 979/849-6416. www.bcfa.org* Rodeo, livestock exhibition, exhibits. Ten days in early Oct.

Aransas Pass (E-8)

See also Corpus Christi, Port Aransas, Rockport

Founded circa 1830
Population 8,138
Elevation 5 ft
Area Code 361
Zip 78336
Information Chamber of Commerce, 130 W Goodnight, 78336; phone toll-free 800/633-3028
Web Site www.aransaspass.org

Shipping from Corpus Christi passes through the waterway called Aransas Pass to the Gulf. The town is a shrimp boat and resort headquarters, with some industrial plants. Boats for deep-sea and bay fishing can be rented; duck hunting in December and January is popular. Aransas Pass is the northern gateway to Port Aransas (see) and Mustang Island.

Special Event

Shrimporee. *130 W Goodnight Ave, Aransas Pass (78336). Phone 361/758-2750.* Parade, arts and crafts, entertainment. Late Sept.

Limited-Service Hotel

★ **DAYS INN.** *410 E Goodnight Ave, Aransas Pass (78336). Phone 361/758-7375; toll-free 877/430-2444; fax 361/758-8105. www.daysinn.com.* 32 rooms. Complimentary continental breakfast. Check-in 2 pm, check-out noon. High-speed Internet access, wireless Internet access. Fitness room. Outdoor pool. **$**
🧍 🏊

Arlington-Grand Prairie (B-8)

See also Cleburne, Dallas, Dallas/Fort Worth Airport Area, Denton, Ennis, Fort Worth, Granbury, Hillsboro

Population 261,721
Elevation 616 ft
Area Code Arlington, 817; Grand Prairie, 972
Information Arlington Convention & Visitors Bureau, 1905 E Randol Mill Rd, 76011; phone 817/265-7721 or toll-free 800/433-5374. Grand Prairie Tourist Information located at I-30 and Belt Line Rd; phone 972/263-9588 or toll-free 800/288-8386
Web Site www.arlington.org

What to See and Do

Legends of the Game Baseball Museum. *1000 Ballpark Way, Suite 400 Arlington (76011). Located off I-30 between Dallas and Fort Worth. Entrance is on the S side of The Ballpark. Phone 817/273-5600.* If you're batty about the game of baseball, you'll want to swing through this 24,000-square-foot museum at The Ballpark in Arlington, home of the Texas Rangers. It showcases more than 140 baseball artifacts, the most you'll see anywhere in the country outside the Hall of Fame in Cooperstown, New York. We're talking the bats, gloves, jerseys, trophies, and more of legends such as Hank Aaron, Ty Cobb, Lou Gehrig, and Babe Ruth. Other exhibits focus on the Rangers and their history. In the Learning Center, interactive fun scores a home run with kids and fans of all ages. For example, you can feel the sting when you catch a Nolan Ryan fastball, and find the sweet spot on a bat. (Daily; closed Mon Nov-Mar, also Thanksgiving, Dec 25) **$$**

Palace of Wax. *601 E Safari Pkwy, Grand Prairie. I-30 at Belt Line Rd exit N. Phone 972/263-2391.* Onion-domed structure houses a collection of wax figures in exhibits with themes including Hollywood, history, religion, fairy tales, horrors, and the Old West. Visitors can view a figure-making studio to see actual pieces under construction. Gift shop, concession, arcade. (Daily; closed Thanksgiving, Dec 25) **$$$$**
Also here is

Ripley's Believe It or Not! *601 E Safari Pkwy, Grand Prairie (75050). Phone 972/263-2391.* Features galleries filled with antiques, oddities, curiosities, and illusions from the collection of Robert L. Ripley.

River Legacy Living Science Center. *703 NW Green Oaks Blvd, Arlington. Phone 817/860-6752.* Hands-on, interactive exhibits depicting the thriving ecosystem along the Trinity River. (Tues-Sat; closed holidays). **$**

Six Flags Over Texas. *2201 Road to Six Flags, Arlington (76010). Park is located just W of the junction of Hwy 360 and I-30. Phone 817/530-6000. www.sixflags.com.* Few fun-loving families roll into north Texas without boarding one of this park's roller coasters for a hair-raising ride up, down, and all around. When the thrill's over, the daredevils all offer the same advice: hang on tight, especially on the Texas Giant, which has been ranked the country's number-one wooden roller coaster. The Superman Tower of Power, the park's tallest ride at 325 soaring feet, provides bursts of compressed air that shoots bravehearts up to the ride's top (making them feel like the comic hero himself) and then "turbo drops" them down. Plenty of other exciting rides offer tamer thrills, such as the Silver Star Carousel, with turn-of-the-century wooden horses. In all, this 205-acre fun factory has more than 100 rides, shows, and other attractions that make kids squeal with delight. (Daily) **$$$$**

Texas Rangers (MLB). *Ameriquest Field, 1000 Ballpark Way, Arlington-Grand Prairie. Jct Hwy 360 and I-30. Phone 817/273-5222. www.texasrangers.com.* Team plays at Ameriquest Field in Arlington. (Apr-Sept) **$$**

Special Event

Horse racing. *1000 Lone Star Pkwy, Arlington-Grand Prairie. Phone 972/263-7223.* Pari-mutuel thoroughbred racing (mid-Apr-late July, Wed-Sun). Quarter Horse Fall Meeting of Champions (early Oct-late Nov, Thurs-Sun). Also simulcast thoroughbred racing (daily).

Limited-Service Hotels

★ ★ **COURTYARD BY MARRIOTT.** *1500 Nolan Ryan Expy, Arlington (76011). Phone 817/277-2774; toll-free 800/321-2211; fax 817/277-3103. www.courtyard .com.* 147 rooms, 3 story. Check-in 3 pm, check-out noon. High-speed Internet access. Fitness room. Indoor pool, outdoor pool, whirlpool. **$**
🖈 ⌖

★ **FAIRFIELD INN.** *2500 E Lamar Blvd, Arlington (76006). Phone 817/649-5800; toll-free 800/228-2800; fax 817/649-5800. www.fairfieldinn.com.* 108 rooms, 3 story. Complimentary continental breakfast. Check-in 3 pm, check-out noon. Outdoor pool. **$**
⌖

Full-Service Hotel

★ ★ ★ **HILTON ARLINGTON.** *2401 E Lamar Blvd, Arlington (76006). Phone 817/640-3322; toll-free 800/ 445-8667; fax 817/633-1430. www.arlingtontx.hilton .com.* This full-service hotel is convenient to the Dallas/ Fort Worth Airport and shopping. 308 rooms, 15 story. Check-in 3 pm, check-out noon. High-speed Internet access. Restaurant, bar. Fitness room. Outdoor pool, whirlpool. Airport transportation available. Business center. **$**
🖈 ⌖ 🖈

Restaurants

★ ★ ★ **CACHAREL.** *2221 E Lamar Blvd, Arlington (76006). Phone 817/640-9981; fax 817/633-5737. www.cacharel.net.* Located on the ninth floor of the Brookhollow Tower Two building and just 15 minutes from downtown Dallas or Fort Worth, this inviting country French restaurant features panoramic views of Arlington and serves new French cuisine with exquisite sauces. French menu. Lunch, dinner. Closed Sun; holidays. Bar. Children's menu. Business casual attire. Reservations recommended. **$$$**

★ ★ **PICCOLO MONDO.** *829 Lamar Blvd E, Arlington (76011). Phone 817/265-9174; fax 817/226-3474. www.piccolomondo.com.* Italian menu. Lunch, dinner. Closed Jan 1, Thanksgiving, Dec 25. Bar. Business casual attire. Reservations recommended. **$$**

Athens (B-9)

See also Corsicana, Palestine, Tyler

Population 11,297
Elevation 492 ft
Area Code 903
Zip 75751
Information Chamber of Commerce, 1206 S Palestine, PO Box 2600; phone 903/675-5181 or toll-free 800/755-7878
Web Site www.athenscc.org

Special Event

Texas Fiddlers' Contest and Reunion. *Phone 903/675-1859.* Last Fri in May.

The University of Texas, the Capitol, and Downtown

People can't seem to agree whether the University or the Capitol represents the heart of Austin. The two grew up together and sit side-by-side, so it's important to see both. Begin on Guadalupe Street at about 24th Street, which is universally known as The Drag. Along this stretch are bookstores, music stores, clothing stores, and exceptional people-watching. To the immediate east is the main campus of the University of Texas; turn left (east) onto 22nd Street and walk about three blocks to the University of Texas tower, the South's largest bell carillon. This 1930s Beaux Arts tower was the horrifying site of a gunman's murderous rampage in 1966. Walk north along Speedway to 24th Street and turn right (east) on 24th; continue to Trinity. There awaits the Texas Memorial Museum, a 1936 beauty housing natural history exhibits. Hike another block east to Red River, where the Lyndon Baines Johnson Library and Museum offers an in-depth look at the life and administration of the late president.

Now double back toward the middle of campus, following San Jacinto Boulevard south to 21st Street. Take 21st Street west to its intersection with University Avenue, and drink in the sight of the Littlefield Fountain, a glorious, unforgettable sculpture erected in 1933 to honor World War I veterans.

Walk south from the fountain along University to Martin Luther King Boulevard, turning left (east) to MLK at Congress Avenue. The Bob Bullock Texas History Museum offers state-of-the-art exhibits, collections, an IMAX theater, café, and museum store. Walk south on Congress five blocks to the State Capitol building—a beautiful, 1888 domed design in pink granite. Immediately southeast of the capitol is the visitor center, at the corner of 11th and Brazos streets. Walk west on 11th to Colorado Street to see the Governor's Mansion, a stately, Greek Revival house that's been home to every governor since 1856.

Backtrack a block to Congress and turn right (south). On the left (east) side of the street is the Austin Museum of Art's downtown location and, across Eighth Street, the Jones Center for Contemporary Art. Take a moment to examine the old Majestic Theater at Seventh and Congress, which was built in 1915 and had its name changed to Paramount Theater in 1929. Also at Seventh and Congress, note the Stephen F. Austin Hotel, a lovely 1924 creation with a comfortable, ground-floor bar. Continue south on Congress another block to Sixth Street and turn left (east) for one block to the splendid Driskill Hotel, an 1886 landmark. Roam along Sixth Street to see several blocks of late 19th-century architecture in brick and limestone and to poke around art galleries, bistros, and music venues, or continue south on Congress to the Mexic-Arte Museum at Fourth and Congress.

Limited-Service Hotels

★ **BEST WESTERN INN ON THE HILL.** *2050 Hwy 31 E, Athens (75751). Phone 903/675-9214; toll-free 800/892-3819; fax 903/675-5963. www.bestwestern.com.* 110 rooms, 2 story. Check-out noon. Bar. Outdoor pool. **$**

★ ★ **SPANISH TRACE INN.** *716 E Tyler St, Athens (75751). Phone 903/675-5173; toll-free 800/488-5173; fax 903/677-1528.* 80 rooms, 2 story. Check-out noon. Restaurant. Outdoor pool. **$**

Specialty Lodging

The following lodging establishment is approved by Mobil Travel Guide, but due to its unique and individualized nature has not been given a traditional Mobil Star rating. Included in this listing you may find bed-and-breakfasts, limited-service inns, guest ranches, and other unique hotel properties.

THE BIRDHOUSE. *103 E Kaufman St, Mabank (75147). Phone 903/887-1242; toll-free 888/474-5885; fax 903/887-7621. www.inn-guide.com/birdhouse.* 4 rooms, 3 story. Complimentary full breakfast. Check-in 4-9 pm, check-out noon. **$**

Austin (C-7)

See also Bastrop, Burnet, Georgetown, Johnson City, La Grange, San Antonio, San Marcos

Founded 1839
Population 656,562
Elevation 550 ft
Area Code 512
Information Convention & Visitors Bureau, 201 E 2nd St, 78701; phone 512/478-0098 or toll-free 800/926-2282
Web Site www.austintexas.org

In 1838, a party of buffalo hunters that included Mirabeau B. Lamar, vice president of the Republic of Texas, camped at a pleasant spot on the Colorado River. In 1839, Lamar, then president of the republic, suggested this same spot as the site of a permanent capital. On high ground and far away from the fever dangers of the coast country, the site was selected even though it was on the frontier. Named for Stephen F. Austin, son of Moses Austin, leader of the first American colony in Texas, the new capital was planned—and planned well. Situated at the foot of the Highland Lakes chain, the site was blessed with lakes—Austin and Town—which today wind their way through the heart of the city. The Capitol building, at the head of Congress Avenue, was later built on one of the hills that rises from the Colorado River Valley.

A city of handsome buildings, modern Austin boasts a unique version of New Orleans's Bourbon Street—Old Pecan Street. This seven-block strip of renovated Victorian and native limestone buildings on East 6th Street between Congress Avenue and Interstate 35 is a National Registered Historic District with more than 60 restaurants, clubs, and shops. On weekends, thousands gather to enjoy the street performers and nightlife.

As a state center of science, research, education, and government, Austin's economy is diversified between the state bureaucracy, the University of Texas, and the research and manufacturing of high-technology electronics.

What to See and Do

Arboretum at Great Hills. *10000 Research Blvd, Austin (78759). Phone 512/338-4437. www.simon.com.* This 45-store suburban shopping center attracts an upscale crowd with familiar favorites such as Barnes & Noble, Bath & Body Works, Pottery Barn, Restoration Hardware, The Sharper Image, and Tommy Bahama. The open-air, well-landscaped center lives up to its name nicely, with lots of green trees that help keep shoppers cool in the summer sunshine. Just across the street, a chic Saks Fifth Avenue (9722 Great Hills Dr; phone 512/231-3700) anchors a smaller shopping center called the Arboretum Market. (Mon-Wed, Fri-Sat 10 am-9 pm, Thurs to 8 pm, Sun noon-6 pm; closed Easter, Dec 25) **FREE**

Austin Children's Museum. *201 Colorado St, Austin (78701). Phone 512/472-2499. www.austinkids.org.* Through its interactive galleries, this 7,000-square-foot museum aims to entertain and educate children up to age 9. In its Global City exhibit, for example, tykes take on the roles of adults—they can go grocery shopping, order lunch at a diner, pretend that they're doctors or construction workers, and more. In other fun exhibits, they learn about Austin's history, explore the world of water, experience life on a Texas ranch, and take a star turn on center stage. (Tues-Sat 10 am-5 pm, Sun noon-5 pm; closed holidays) **$$**

Austin Lyric Opera. *901 Barton Springs Rd, Austin (78704). Performances are at the Bass Concert Hall inside the Performing Arts Building on the University of Texas campus, at the intersection of 23rd St and Robert Dedman Dr. Phone 512/472-5995; toll-free 800/316-7372. www.austinlyricopera.org.* Since 1986, this opera company has kept Austin's hills alive with the sound of music, winning critical acclaim for its lyrical presentations. International artists and rising young American singers often team up to stage the company's three-opera season, which runs from November through March. (Performances held Mon, Thurs-Sat)

Austin Museum of Art. *823 Congress Ave, Austin (78701). Phone 512/495-9224. www.amoa.org.* Changing exhibits of American art since 1900; performances, films, lectures, art classes. (Tues-Wed, Fri-Sat 10 am-6 pm, Thurs to 8 pm, Sun noon-5 pm; closed holidays) **$**

Austin Steam Train Association. *610 Brazos St, #210, Austin (78767). Hwy 183 at FM 1431. Phone 512/477-8468. www.austinmuseums.org.* Vintage steam train makes scenic journey from Cedar Park and Plaza Saltillo; some trips feature hors d'oeuvres, musical entertainment, and drinks. (Mon-Fri 9 am-4 pm) **$$**

Austin Zoo. *10807 Rawhide Trail, Austin (91808). Phone 512/288-1490.* Features more than 100 species of rescued animals. (Daily 10 am-6 pm; closed Thanksgiving, Dec 25) **$$**

Ballet Austin. *University of Texas at Austin Performing Arts Building, 23rd St and Robert Dedman Dr, Austin. Performances are at the Bass Concert Hall. Phone 512/476-2163. www.balletaustin.org.* The sure-footed members of this troupe just gotta dance, and appreciative audiences applaud their pointed toes and fancy footwork when the curtain's up. The troupe presents a four-series season that stretches from October to May, and the dancers typically take more than a few innovative steps in the various productions. Each year, the ballet also presents a fifth program, *The Nutcracker.* (Oct-May: Fri-Sat 8 pm, Sun 2 pm; closed holidays) **$$$$**

Barton Creek Greenbelt. *2201 Barton Springs Rd, Austin (78746). Begins at Barton Springs Pool. Phone 512/472-1267. www.texasclimbers.com/crags/greenbelt.* Hikers and bikers get quite a workout on this 7 1/2-mile urban trail, as do rock climbers. Yes, rock climbers. Sheer limestone walls up to 40 feet tall border the greenbelt, and they're perfect for scaling. If you can pull your own weight, the climbing's especially good at the Gus Fruh, Loop 360, and Spyglass access points along the trail. (Daily 5 am-10 pm)

Bob Bullock Texas State History Museum. *1800 N Congress Ave, Austin (78711). Phone 512/936-8746; toll-free 866/369-7108. www.thestoryoftexas.com.* Explore the three floors of this 34,000-square-foot Texas-size museum and you'll learn all you ever wanted to know—and probably even more—about the Lone Star State. Through more than 700 artifacts and numerous interactive displays, you'll be transformed into a walking encyclopedia of Texas history, beginning with the first meetings between Native Americans and European explorers. An IMAX theater is equipped with 2-D and 3-D capabilities, and the Texas Spirit Theater rocks with special effects. (Mon-Sat 9 am-6 pm, Sun noon-6 pm; closed holidays) **$$**

⭐ **Elisabet Ney Museum.** *304 E 44th St, Austin (78751). At Ave H. Phone 512/458-2255. www.ci.austin.tx.us/elisabetney.* Former studio of Elisabet Ney, 19th-century German-Texan portrait sculptor. Houses a collection of her works, some of which stand in the Texas and US capitols. (Wed-Sun 10 am-5 pm, Sun from noon; closed holidays) **FREE**

Forest Creek Golf Club. *99 Twin Ridge Pkwy, Round Rock (78664). Phone 512/388-2874. www.forestcreek.com. Golf Digest* magazine named this par-72, 7,147-yard gem the finest public golf course in central Texas—a good reason to drive about 30 miles north of downtown Austin to do some long-distance driving with your clubs. A tip: try to mix power with finesse because of consistent scheme variations. You also get help from your golf cart's global positioning system, which tells you the exact distance to the hole and alerts you to hazards. The rest is up to you. (Daily dawn to dusk; closed Dec 25) **$$$$**

French Legation Museum. *802 San Marcos St, Austin (78702). Phone 512/472-8180. www.frenchlegationmuseum.org.* (1841) Housed the charge d'affaires to the Republic of Texas. Creole architecture and furnishings. Restored house and gardens, reconstructed carriage house, French Creole kitchen. (Tues-Sun 1-4:30 pm; closed holidays) **$$**

Governor's Mansion. *1010 Colorado, Austin (78701). Between 10th and 11th sts, in Capitol Complex. Phone 512/463-5516 (recording). www.txfgm.org.* (1856) Greek Revival architecture, American Federal and Empire furnishings. Contains former governors' memorabilia. Tours (Mon-Thurs 10-11:40 am; closed state holidays and special occasions). No purses, bags, or backpacks permitted on mansion grounds. **FREE**

Highland Lakes. *www.highlandlakes.com.* Seven hydroelectric dams cross the Colorado River, creating a continuous series of lakes for nearly 150 miles upstream. Lake Buchanan and Lake Travis are the largest; Town Lake and Lake Austin are located within the Austin city limits. Fishing, boating; camping (except on Town Lake). Many varied accommodations on the shores of each.

Lady Bird Johnson Wildflower Research Center. *4801 La Crosse Ave, Austin (78739). Phone 512/292-4200. www.wildflower.org.* Native plant botanical garden of national renown begun with generous grant from former First Lady, who added to her legacy by launching a national roadside beautification program in the 1960s. Numerous courtyards, terraces, arbors, and meadows, as well as an observation tower, café, gift store, and nature trail. (Tues-Sun 9 am-5:30 pm; closed holidays) **$$**

McKinney Falls State Park. *5808 McKinney Falls Pkwy, Austin (78744). 13 miles SE of the state capitol in Austin off Hwy 183. Phone 512/243-1643. www.tpwd.state.tx.us/park/mckinney.* Just a short drive from downtown, escape into the great outdoors at this 744-acre park in south Austin. During the daylight hours, check out the park's namesake falls or take your pick from numerous recreational activities, including fishing, hiking, mountain biking, and swimming in Onion Creek. While enjoying all this back-to-nature fun, you'll likely spot armadillos, raccoons, white-tailed deer, and other wildlife. After dark, stargaze from your campsite under the Texas sky. (Daily 8 am-10 pm) **$**

Mexic-Arte Museum. *419 Congress Ave, Austin (78768). Phone 512/480-9373. www.mexic-artemuseum.org.* Nonprofit arts organization exhibits contemporary and historical art focusing on Latino culture. Museum store. (Mon-Thurs 10 am-6 pm, Fri-Sat 10 am-5 pm, Sun noon-5 pm; closed holidays) **$$**

Neill-Cochran House. *2310 San Gabriel, Austin (78705). Phone 512/478-2335. www.neill-cochranmuseum.org.* (Circa 1855) Greek Revival house built of native Austin limestone and Bastrop pine; furnishings from the 18th to 20th centuries. (Wed-Sun 2-5 pm; closed holidays) **$**

★ **O. Henry Home and Museum.** *409 E 5th St, Austin (78701). Phone 512/472-1903. www.ci.austin.tx.us/ parks/ohenry.htm.* Victorian cottage was the residence of writer William Sydney Porter (O. Henry); original furnishings. Special events. (Wed-Sun noon-5 pm; closed holidays) **FREE**

Sixth Street. *SE of the Capitol Complex on Sixth St between Congress Ave and I-35. Phone 512/974-2000 (City of Austin Information). www.ci.austin.tx.us/ downtown/sixthmap.htm.* Austin bills itself as the Live Music Capital of the World, and this lively street helps the city back up that mighty big boast. In this funky entertainment district, sometimes likened to New Orleans' Bourbon Street, you'll hear a rousing med-ley of music—from rock and hip-hop to soul and jazz—in the many bars and nightclubs that often get jammed with a younger, party-hearty crowd. Just wander down this loud street of quaint old build-ings and pop into any of the hotspots that catch your fancy. Should you want a good laugh instead of a good beat, opt for Esther's Follies (525 E Sixth St, phone 512/320-0198), an irreverent comedy club long known in these parts for keeping its patrons in stitches. Other diversions include pool halls, tattoo parlors, and restaurants.

South Congress Avenue Shopping. *S Congress Ave, Austin (78704). From Riverside to Oltorf St.* Forget mainstream malls with all those familiar retail chains and come to the shopping area nicknamed "SoCo." In this bohemian shopping district, quirky rules.

One-of-a-kind stores with names like Lucy in Disguise, New Bohemia, and Uncommon Objects sell everything from vintage clothes and kitschy antiques to 1950s furniture, Mexican imports, and much more. You have to make this fabulously funky scene to fully appreciate it. A few popular restaurants, such as Guero's Taco Bar, cater to hungry shoppers.

State Capitol. *1100 Congress Ave, Austin (78701). Phone 512/463-0063. www.capitol.state.tx.us.* It's no secret that the Lone Star State thinks big, so it's no surprise that its 115-year-old capitol ranks as the country's largest statehouse, with about 18 acres of floor space. That's one big building, even by Texas standards. You can explore much of it on your own, or take a guided tour for plenty of insider info about its architecture and contents. If the legislature is in session, take a seat in the Senate or House chamber and watch all the political wrangling (pun intended) as lawmakers debate the issues of the day. At the nearby Capitol Complex Visitors Center (112 E 11th St, phone 512/305-8400), learn even more about the statehouse and the state through numerous historical and interactive exhibits. For example, the 12-minute film *Beyond the Dome* takes you back inside the capi-tol to hidden places not seen on the tour. (Mon-Fri 8:30 am-4:30 pm, Sat 9:30 am-3:30 pm, Sun noon-3:30 pm; closed holidays) **FREE** On grounds are

> **Capitol Complex Visitors Center.** *112 E 11th St, Austin. Phone 512/305-8400.* Oldest government building in the state has information on tours; bro-chures, exhibits. Gift shop. (Daily; closed holidays) **FREE**

> **Texas State Library.** *Lorenzo de Zavata State Archives and Library Building, 1201 Brazos St, Austin. Phone 512/463-5514. www.tsl.state.tx.us.* Houses historical documents, including Texas Declaration of Independence; 45-foot mural offers view of Texas history. (Mon-Fri 8 am-5 pm; genealogy library Tues-Sat 8 am-5 pm; closed holidays) **FREE**

University of Texas at Austin. *2613 Wichita St, Austin (78712). Phone 512/471-3434. www.utexas.edu.* (1883) (48,000 students) Its 15 colleges and schools and 75 departments offer some 6,500 courses, providing 260 different degree programs. The general information desk in the rotunda of the main building offers sched-ules of campus events. Tours (May-Dec: Mon-Sat 2 pm; rest of year: Mon-Fri 11 am and 2 pm, Sat 2 pm) Attractions include

Harry Ransom Humanities Research Center. *21st and Guadalupe sts, Austin (78705). Phone 512/471-8944. www.hrc.utexas.edu.* Collections of rare books and manuscripts. Gutenberg Bible on display. (Tues-Wed, Fri 10 am-5 pm, Thurs to 7 pm, Sat-Sun noon-5 pm; closed holidays) **FREE**

Lyndon Baines Johnson Library & Museum. *2313 Red River, Austin (78705). On campus, one block W of I-35. Phone 512/916-5137. www.lbjlib.utexas.edu.* Exhibits on "Great Society," international affairs, oval office, first lady's gallery, head-of-state gifts; presidential history presented through memorabilia of political campaigns from Washington to Reagan. Changing exhibits on US history. Archives collection of documents available for research. (Daily 9 am-5 pm; closed Dec 25) **FREE**

Texas Memorial Museum of Science and History. *2400 Trinity St, Austin (78705). Phone 512/471-1604. www.tmm.utexas.edu.* Natural history exhibits dedicated to geology, paleontology, zoology, anthropology, and history. Special events. (Mon-Fri 9 am-5 pm, Sat from 10 am, Sun from 1 pm; closed holidays) **FREE**

Veloway. *Slaughter Creek Metropolitan Park, 4103 Slaughter Ln, Austin (78749). Phone 512/974-6700. www.ci.austin.tx.us/parks/trails.htm.* Bicyclists and in-line skaters have this winding pathway all to themselves. No walkers, no joggers, and, of course, no cars. The paved-asphalt loop stretches for 3.1 miles through more than 100 green acres of scenic parkland rife with natural foliage and wildlife, from rabbits and foxes to mice and squirrels. You'll feel far from the maddening crowd as you tone those thighs. (Daily) **FREE**

Warehouse District. *W of Congress Ave and S of Sixth St in downtown Austin. Phone 512/474-5171; toll-free 800/926-2282. www.austintexas.org.* Southwest of bustling East Sixth Street, nightclubs and restaurants make this nine-block district yet another hot hangout. But here, you'll party with mostly business professionals who prefer a more upscale scene. You'll score plenty of live music at swinging spots such as Antone's (213 W Fifth St, phone 512/320-8424), the city's best-known blues club; and Bitter End B-Side (311 Colorado St, phone 512/478-2462), where the soft jazz mixes nicely with martinis. Ahhh!

Zilker Metropolitan Park. *2100 Barton Springs Rd, Austin (78746). Phone 512/472-4914. www.ci.austin.tx.us/zilker.* Locals will tell you that this 351-acre park near downtown is the city's most be-loved, and they're mighty proud of it. The main come-on is Barton Springs Pool, a spring-fed watering hole that stretches for 1,000 feet. You'll find the swimming a chilling experience, with the water temperature averaging 68 degrees year-round. Brrrrr! Park officials sometimes close the pool for water-quality reasons, but numerous other enticements keep fun-seekers coming to Zilker when they do. A miniature train and a well-equipped playground keep kids grinning from ear to ear even when they can't jump into the water. Adults come for the hike-and-bike trails, a botanical garden, a hillside theater, a nature center, a variety of athletic fields, and more. The park has lovely picnic areas, so bring something tasty to chow down on in the Texas outdoors. (Daily 5 am-10 pm) **$** Includes

Barton Springs Pool. *2101 Barton Springs Rd, Austin (78746). Phone 512/476-9044.* Spring-fed natural swimming pool nearly as long as a football field. (Apr-Oct) **$**

Zilker Botanical Gardens. *2220 Barton Springs Rd, Austin (78746). Phone 512/477-8672. www.ci.austin.tx.us.* **FREE**

Zilker Hillside Theater. *2101 William Barton Dr, Austin (78704). Phone 512/397-1463.* (See SPECIAL EVENTS)

Special Events

Austin Fine Arts Festival. *Republic Sq Park, 5th and Guadalupe sts, Austin. Phone 512/458-6073. www.austinfineartsfestival.org.* Fine arts and crafts, children's events, music, food. Apr. **$$**

Congress Avenue Bridge Bat Colony. *Congress Avenue Bridge, Austin (78746). Bridge crosses Town Lake just S of downtown. Phone 512/416-5700.* North America's largest urban bat colony, with up to 1.5 million of these nocturnal creatures, takes up residence in Austin from mid-March to early November each year. They roost all day under the Congress Avenue Bridge, just south of downtown, out of sight, out of mind. But come dusk, the flying mammals usually make their presence known. In a noisy exit that can last up to 45 minutes, they come flocking out in droves to spend the evening feasting on tasty insects throughout the city. Their nightly appearance makes for a splendid spectacle that draws hundreds of wide-eyed onlookers to the shores of Town Lake. Many of the curious come with picnic baskets, as well as lawn chairs or blankets for their viewing comfort; others take bat cruises. On summer weekends, representatives of Bat

Conservation International offer interesting insight at the *Austin American-Statesman's* Bat Observation Area, which you'll find lakeside at the southeast corner of the bridge. Mid-Mar-early Nov. **FREE**

Highland Lakes Bluebonnet Trail. Highland Lakes communities feature arts, crafts, and activities during wildflower season. Two weekends in early Apr.

Old Pecan Street Arts Festival. *1710 S Lamar Blvd, Austin (78704). Phone 512/441-9015. www.roadstar productions.com.* First weekend in May and last weekend in Sept.

Saveur Texas Hill Country Wine. *98 San Jacinto Blvd, Austin (78701). Phone 512/542-9463. www.texas wineandfood.org.* If you appreciate good eats, bring your hearty appetite to the state's largest wine and food festival. Each year, more than 5,000 food lovers and about 100 celebrity chefs, cookbook authors, and wine experts converge on the Texas Hill Country for five savory days of wining and dining mixed with cooking classes and culinary talk. At venues throughout the city, the festival hosts more than 35 events ranging from black-tie to down-home. Early Apr. **$$$$**

Star Texas Fair and Rodeo. *7311 Decker Ln, Austin (78724). www.staroftexas.org.* Features rodeo performances. Late Mar.

Zilker Hillside Theater. *Zilker Park, 2100 Barton Springs Rd, Austin (78704). Phone 512/397-1463. www.zilker.org.* Free drama, ballet, classic films, musicals, and symphony concerts under the stars. Major musical featured each summer. Early Apr-Oct.

Limited-Service Hotels

★ ★ **COURTYARD BY MARRIOTT AUSTIN CENTRAL.** *5660 I-35 N, Austin (78751). Phone 512/458-2340; toll-free 800/321-2211; fax 512/458-8525. www.courtyard.com.* Located in the heart of Austin's business district, this modern hotel also attracts a fair number of sports enthusiasts drawn to the several area golf courses and events at nearby Concordia University and the University of Texas. Business travelers may make use of in-room high-speed Internet access and fax, printing, and copying services as well as meeting rooms and a PC. 198 rooms, 9 story. Complimentary full breakfast. Check-in 3 pm, check-out noon. High-speed Internet access, wireless Internet access. Restaurant. Fitness room. Outdoor pool, whirlpool. Business center. **$**
🧍 ➳ 🏃

★ ★ **DOUBLETREE GUEST SUITES.** *303 W 15th St, Austin (78701). Phone 512/478-7000; toll-free 800/222-8733; fax 512/478-3562. www.doubletree.com.* Located just two blocks from the state capitol, this hotel has a contemporary design. 189 rooms, 15 story, all suites. Pets accepted, some restrictions; fee. Check-in 3 pm, check-out noon. High-speed Internet access. Restaurant, bar. Fitness room. Outdoor pool, whirlpool. Business center. **$$**
🐾 🧍 ➳ 🏃

★ ★ **DOUBLETREE HOTEL.** *6505 I-35 N, Austin (78752). Phone 512/454-3737; toll-free 800/866-3126; fax 512/419-0102. www.doubletree.com.* This Doubletree welcomes guests with the warm richness of its Spanish colonial décor with Saltillo tile flooring, dark moldings, rows of archways, and lush plants. Enjoy more of the greenery, as well as waterscapes, in the multilevel indoor courtyard. The location puts you near popular food and shopping venues, and the hotel's complimentary shuttle will transport you to attractions that are a little farther afield. 350 rooms, 6 story. Pets accepted; fee. Check-in 3 pm, check-out noon. High-speed Internet access. Restaurant, bar. Fitness room. Outdoor pool, whirlpool. Business center. **$**
🐾 🧍 ➳ 🏃

★ ★ **EMBASSY SUITES DOWNTOWN/TOWN LAKE.** *300 S Congress Ave, Austin (78704). Phone 512/469-9000; toll-free 800/362-2779; fax 512/480-9164. www.embassysuites.com.* This high-rise hotel boasts a soaring atrium with lush greenery and more than one waterfall. Order your complimentary breakfast cooked as you like and meet up with fellow guests again at the manager's social hour each afternoon, during which you can enjoy an alcoholic beverage if you like, a nonalcoholic drink if you don't, and a light snack. In the evening, take an easy walk to view the famous Bat Flight over the Colorado River. Every suite has a bedroom and a sitting room, each with its own TV, and the hotel makes every accommodation for business travelers. 262 rooms, 9 story, all suites. Pets accepted; fee. Check-in 3 pm, check-out noon. High-speed Internet access, wireless Internet access. Restaurant, bar. Fitness room. Indoor pool, whirlpool. **$$**
🐾 🧍 ➳

★ **LA QUINTA INN.** *2004 I-35 N, Round Rock (78681). Phone 512/255-6666; fax 512/388-3635. www.lq.com.* 116 rooms, 3 story. Pets accepted, some restrictions; fee. Complimentary continental breakfast. Check-out noon. Fitness room. Outdoor pool, whirlpool. **$**

★ ★ **RADISSON HOTEL & SUITES.** *111 E Cesar Chavez St, Austin (78701). Phone 512/478-9611; toll-free 800/333-3333; fax 512/473-8399. www.radisson.com.* Located in the heart of downtown and overlooking Town Lake, this hotel is convenient to many attractions, including the University of Texas and Austin's famous Sixth Street. A 10-mile Hike-and-Bike Trail around the lake is a nice alternative to the hotel's fitness center. T.G.I. Friday's restaurant serves familiar fare. 413 rooms, 12 story. Pets accepted, some restrictions; fee. Check-in 3 pm, check-out noon. High-speed Internet access. Restaurant, two bars. Fitness room. Outdoor pool. Business center. **$**

Full-Service Hotels

★ ★ ★ **CROWNE PLAZA HOTEL AUSTIN.** *500 I-35 N, Austin (78701). Phone 512/480-8181; toll-free 800/227-6963; fax 512/457-7990. www.crowneplaza.com.* Centrally located in the heart of downtown, this atrium-style hotel's ornate and richly furnished interior is echoed in the flower-bedecked outdoor courtyard with a tiered fountain as the centerpiece. Some of the guest rooms overlook this calming scene; others offer a bird's-eye view of downtown. This full-service hotel caters to both leisure and business travelers with equal attentiveness. Opting for the Executive/Club Floor gives you access to the business center, daily buffet breakfast and cocktail hour, and a CD player. 254 rooms, 18 story. Pets accepted, some restrictions; fee. Check-in 3 pm, check-out noon. High-speed Internet access, wireless Internet access. Two restaurants, bar. Fitness room. Outdoor pool, whirlpool. Business center. **$$**

★ ★ ★ **THE DRISKILL.** *604 Brazos St, Austin (78701). Phone 512/474-5911; toll-free 800/252-9367; fax 512/474-2214. www.driskillhotel.com.* The Driskill has been an Austin landmark since its opening in 1886. Developed by a wealthy cattle baron, this eponymous hotel welcomes guests to a world of privilege. The gleaming marble floors and glorious stained-glass skylights of the magnificent lobby are the first signs of the gracious style of this unique hotel, defined by its inimitable Texan hospitality and international sophistication. The rooms and suites are located in the original hotel and in the adjacent 1929

tower, offering visitors the chance to experience the rich, dark ambience of the historic rooms or the fresh, light colors of the Texas Hill Country-inspired tower rooms. Well-appointed business and fitness centers are among the perks here, and the Driskill Grill remains one of Austin's most cherished dining spots. 189 rooms, 4 story. Pets accepted, some restrictions; fee. Check-in 3 pm, check-out noon. High-speed Internet access, wireless Internet access. Two restaurants, two bars. Fitness room. Business center. **$$**

★ ★ ★ ★ **FOUR SEASONS HOTEL AUSTIN.** *98 San Jacinto Blvd, Austin (78701). Phone 512/478-4500; toll-free 800/545-4000; fax 512/478-3117. www.fourseasons.com.* Texan hospitality and charm are particularly evident at the Four Seasons Hotel Austin. Close to downtown and the entertainment district, this hotel enjoys a parklike setting of rolling hills overlooking Town Lake. The traditional décor is enlivened with playful touches indicative of the region, including cow prints and wildflower arrangements. The guest rooms are luxurious without being pretentious, and the intuitive service is always on hand to exceed expectations. Guests absorb the tranquility here, whether lingering poolside or enjoying a gourmet picnic on the sprawling grounds. The peaceful setting is the focal point at this hotel; both the Café (see) and the Lobby Lounge boast expansive views. Diners are introduced to renowned Hill Country cuisine, which blends elements from American, Asian, continental, and Southwestern cuisines to create palate-pleasing sensations. 291 rooms, 9 story. Pets accepted, some restrictions. Check-in 3 pm, check-out noon. Restaurant, bar. Fitness room. Outdoor pool, whirlpool. Business center. **$$$**

★ ★ ★ **HYATT REGENCY AUSTIN.** *208 Barton Springs Rd, Austin (78704). Phone 512/477-1234; toll-free 800/633-7313; fax 512/480-2069. www.austin.hyatt.com.* This contemporary hotel is located on the shore of Town Lake in downtown Austin. Just four blocks from the convention center and one block from the auditorium, it makes a convenient base for exploring the city. This contemporary hotel's location on the shore of Town Lake at the south end of downtown opens up a world of nature's charms for guests. The indoor/outdoor lobby has a stream running through it and an outdoor lounging area perfect for admiring the Austin skyline or the grace of the bats flying over the Colorado River. You can walk or jog the lakeside trail or rent a bike and pedal the 9 miles. You can take advantage of riverboat tours, paddleboats, and canoes. On top of all this, the hotel's location makes it a convenient base for exploring the city, and it boasts up-to-date amenities for business travelers. 447 rooms, 17 story. Pets accepted; fee. Check-in 3 pm, check-out noon. High-speed Internet access. Restaurant, bar. Fitness room. Outdoor pool, whirlpool. Business center. **$**

★ ★ ★ **INTERCONTINENTAL HOTEL STEPHEN F. AUSTIN.** *701 Congress Ave, Austin (78701). Phone 512/457-8800; fax 512/457-8896. www.austin.intercontinental.com.* 189 rooms, 16 story. Check-in 3 pm, check-out noon. High-speed Internet access. Restaurant, two bars. Fitness room. Indoor pool, whirlpool. Business center. **$$**

★ ★ ★ **LAKE AUSTIN SPA RESORT.** *1705 Quinlan Park Rd, Austin (78732). Phone 512/372-7300; toll-free 800/847-5637. www.lakeaustin.com.* 40 rooms. Children over 15 years only. Check-in 3 pm, check-out noon. High-speed Internet access. Restaurant, bar. Fitness room. Indoor pool, outdoor pool, whirlpool. Business center. **$$$$**

★ ★ ★ **THE MANSION AT JUDGES' HILL.** *1900 Rio Grande, Austin (78705). Phone 512/495-1800; toll-free 800/311-1619; fax 512/691-4461. www.judgeshill.com.* 48 rooms. Check-in 3 pm, check-out noon. High-speed Internet access. Restaurant, bar. Airport transportation available. **$$$**

★ ★ ★ **MARRIOTT AUSTIN AT THE CAPITOL.** *701 E 11th St, Austin (78701). Phone 512/478-1111; toll-free 800/228-9290; fax 512/478-3700. www.marriott.com/ausdt.* This downtown hotel is just blocks from the state capitol and the University of Texas campus and steps away from the Sixth Street entertainment area—close enough to judge for yourself whether Austin's claims of being the live-music capital of the world are true. The Frank Erwin Center, host to everything from pop and country music concerts to stand-up comedians to basketball and wrestling, is practically next door. 365 rooms, 16 story. Pets accepted; fee. Check-in 3 pm, check-out noon. High-speed Internet access. Restaurant, bar. Fitness room. Indoor pool, outdoor pool, whirlpool. Business center. **$**

★ ★ ★ **MARRIOTT AUSTIN NORTH.** *2600 LaFrontera Blvd, Austin (78681). Phone 512/733-6767; toll-free 800/228-9290; fax 512/733-6868. www.marriott.com.* 295 rooms, 8 story. Check-in 3 pm, check-out noon. High-speed Internet access, wireless Internet access. Restaurant, bar. Fitness room. Indoor pool. Business center. **$**

★ ★ ★ **OMNI AUSTIN HOTEL.** *700 San Jacinto Blvd, Austin (78701). Phone 512/476-3700; toll-free 800/843-6664; fax 512/397-4888. www.omnihotels.com.* 375 rooms, 20 story. Pets accepted, some restrictions; fee. Check-in 3 pm, check-out noon. High-speed Internet access, wireless Internet access. Restaurant, bar. Fitness room. Outdoor pool, whirlpool. Business center. **$$**

★ ★ ★ **OMNI AUSTIN SOUTHPARK.** *4140 Governors Row, Austin (78744). Phone 512/448-2222; toll-free 800/843-6664; fax 512/442-8028. www.omnihotels.com.* This contemporary hotel is close to the lake, area parks, and shopping. 313 rooms, 14 story. Pets accepted, some restrictions; fee. Check-in 3 pm, check-out noon. Wireless Internet access. Restaurant, two bars. Fitness room. Indoor pool, outdoor pool, whirlpool. Airport transportation available. Business center. **$**

★ ★ ★ **RENAISSANCE HOTEL.** *9721 Arboretum Blvd, Austin (78759). Phone 512/343-2626; toll-free 800/468-3571; fax 512/346-7953. www.renaissance hotels.com.* This hotel is part of the Arboretum complex, which holds more than 50 specialty shops, cinemas, and several restaurants, as well as a small lake surrounded by nature trails. It is close to the area's high-tech companies, making it a good choice for business travelers. 478 rooms, 10 story. Pets accepted. Check-in 3 pm, check-out 1 pm. High-speed Internet access. Three restaurants, two bars. Fitness room. Indoor pool, outdoor pool, whirlpool. Business center. **$$**

Full-Service Resort

★ ★ ★ **BARTON CREEK RESORT.** *8212 Barton Club Dr, Austin (78735). Phone 512/329-4000; toll-free 800/336-6158; fax 512/329-4597. www.bartoncreek.com.* Tucked away on 4,000 acres in Texas Hill Country west of Austin, Barton Creek Resort beckons active-minded travelers seeking a country getaway. Impeccable service and stylish interiors are only the beginning at this all-encompassing resort, where the accommodations feature handsome furnishings, continental influences, and soothing earth tones. Spacious and comfortable, the guest rooms even feature a bath and a half for additional convenience. Four 18-hole golf courses are the resort's centerpiece. Designed by legendary course architects Tom Fazio, Arnold Palmer, and Ben Crenshaw, the courses are designed to challenge and inspire with their cliffside fairways and rolling greens. Guests also play tennis on 11 courts, exercise at the fitness center, and unwind at the world-class spa. After all this activity, appetites are big for Southwestern specialties, barbecue, and other American favorites at the Hill Country Dining Room, Barton Creek Lakeside, and Austin Grill. 296 rooms, 5 story. Check-in 4 pm, check-out noon. High-speed Internet access. Three restaurants, three bars. Children's activity center. Fitness room, fitness classes available, spa. Indoor pool, outdoor pool, children's pool, whirlpool. Golf, 72 holes. Tennis. Airport transportation available. Business center. **$$$**

Restaurants

★ ★ ★ ★ CAFÉ AT THE FOUR SEASONS.
98 San Jacinto Blvd, Austin (78701). Phone 512/478-4500; fax 512/477-0704. www.fourseasons.com. With panoramic views of Town Lake and the lush, surrounding park grounds, the Café at the Four Seasons is a delightful setting to enjoy the kitchen's signature "regional Hill Country cuisine." If you are not familiar with this cuisine, you're in for a treat. This daring brand of fare fuses American, Southwestern, continental, and Asian themes on a canvas of local ingredients. Chiles, citrus, smoke, herbs, and spices all play a part in the menu's success. The Café is perfect for warm-weather dining; the outdoor terrace, overlooking the wildflower gardens and shaded by large trees, offers a peaceful setting to relax and savor the cuisine and the restaurant's vast wine selection. If tabletops are too formal, opt for the picnic basket, which is prepared and delivered—along with a denim blanket—to the tree of your choice on the lawn overlooking the lake. American menu. Breakfast, lunch, dinner. Bar. Children's menu. Casual attire. Reservations recommended. Valet parking. Outdoor seating. **$$$**

★ ★ CHEZ NOUS.
510 Neches St, Austin (78701). Phone 512/473-2413; fax 512/236-8486. Tucked into a historic neighborhood near the University of Texas campus, this lovely dining spot delights gourmands and anyone else in search of a fine meal. Perfect for first dates, quiet business lunches or dinners, and birthdays, Chez Nous made its name with a prix-fixe menu that satisfies with salade Lyonnaise, smoked trout pate, veal tenderloin in a brandy demi-glace, and chocolate mousse. Bistro-style café. French menu. Lunch, dinner. Closed Mon. Casual attire. **$$**

★ ★ CHEZ ZEE.
5406 Balcones Dr, Austin (78731). Phone 512/454-2666; fax 512/454-5003. www.chez-zee.com. American menu. Lunch, dinner, late-night, brunch. Closed Thanksgiving, Dec 25. Bar. Children's menu. Casual attire. Reservations recommended. Valet parking. Outdoor seating. **$$**

★ COUNTY LINE ON THE HILL.
6500 W Bee Cave Rd, Austin (78746). Phone 512/327-1742; fax 512/328-9478. www.countyline.com. Barbecue, steak menu. Dinner. Closed Jan 1, Thanksgiving, Dec 24-26. Bar. Children's menu. Outdoor seating. **$$**

★ ★ ★ DRISKILL GRILL.
604 Brazos St, Austin (78701). Phone 512/474-5911; toll-free 800/252-9367; fax 512/474-2214. www.driskillgrill.com. Guests will find delightful dining in an elegant, romantic setting at this outstanding new American restaurant in the Driskill hotel(see). (Lyndon and Lady Bird Johnson are rumored to have had their first date here.) Fine china and exceptional service by a knowledgeable staff create an impressive setting. American menu. Dinner. Closed Sun-Mon. Bar. Business casual attire. Reservations recommended. Valet parking. **$$$**

★ ★ ★ FONDA SAN MIGUEL.
2330 W North Loop, Austin (78756). Phone 512/459-4121; fax 512/459-5792. www.fondasanmiguel.com. One of the Texas pioneers in the service of authentic foods from deep within Mexico's interior, this gorgeous hacienda has been famous for its extraordinary food since 1976. Dishes that astound with flavor and resonate with honesty are ceviche Veracruzano, enchiladas suizas, and calamares with chipotle salsa. A superior wine list and a knockout brunch make this one of Austin's more memorable spots. Mexican menu. Dinner, Sun brunch. Bar. Business casual attire. Reservations recommended. Valet parking. **$$**

★ ★ GREEN PASTURES.
811 W Live Oak, Austin (78704). Phone 512/444-4747; fax 512/444-3912. www.greenpastures.citysearch.com. This magnificent Victorian mansion, once the childhood home of the late, beloved humorist John Henry Faulk, was opened as a restaurant by sister Mary Faulk Koock in 1945. The center of lovely dining is best known for its Plantation

Sunday Brunch, at which brandy milk punch or mimosas set the tone for a spread of salads, meats from a carving station, and numerous other warm dishes, as well as elegant desserts. Brilliant peacocks roam the grounds, and music from a grand piano transports you to another time. American, French menu. Lunch, dinner, Sun brunch. Bar. Children's menu. Business casual attire. Reservations recommended. Valet parking. **$$$**

★ ★ ★ **HUDSON'S ON THE BEND.** *3509 Ranch Rd 620 S, Austin (78734). Phone 512/266-1369; fax 512/266-1399. www.hudsonsonthebend.com.* Chefs Jeff Blank and Shanny Lott call their brand of cuisine "Cooking Fearlessly," and they have the cookbook to prove it. The fruits of their boundless imaginations show up in appetizers such as baby back ribs marinated in Coca-Cola and sauced with orange-ginger barbecue glaze and rattlesnake cakes atop chipotle cream sauce, and entrées such as guajillo-rubbed salmon filet and pepita-crusted lamb chops. A true Austin experience not to be missed in a native stone house surrounded by flower and herb gardens. Southwestern menu. Dinner. Closed Thanksgiving, Dec 25. Bar. Casual attire. Reservations recommended. Outdoor seating. **$$$**

★ ★ ★ **JEFFREY'S RESTAURANT & BAR.** *1204 W Lynn St, Austin (78703). Phone 512/477-5584; fax 512/474-7279. www.jeffreysofaustin.com.* The inventive cuisine of chef David Garrido blends his penchant for Latin flavors with classic training, resulting in gems such as crispy fried oysters with yucca root chips over a honey-habañero aioli and beef tenderloin with pecorino-rosemary potatoes and a sauce filled with wild mushrooms and flavored with brandy. Jeffrey's food became so popular with a certain former Texas governor that a second location had to be opened in Washington, DC. Ask about the four-course tasting menu. American menu. Dinner. Closed Dec 25-Jan 1. Bar. Business casual attire. Reservations recommended. Valet parking. **$$$**

★ ★ **LOUIE'S 106.** *106 E 6th, Austin (78701). Phone 512/476-1997; fax 512/476-2892. www.louies106.net.* Mediterranean menu. Lunch, dinner, late-night. Closed holidays. Bar. Children's menu. Business casual attire. Reservations recommended. Valet parking. **$$**

★ ★ **MATT'S EL RANCHO.** *2613 S Lamar Blvd, Austin (78704). Phone 512/462-9333; fax 512/462-9028. www.mattselrancho.com.* Mexican, Southwestern, seafood menu. Lunch, dinner. Closed Tues; holidays. Bar. Children's menu. Outdoor seating. **$$**

★ **OASIS-LAKE TRAVIS.** *6550 Comanche Trail, Austin (78732). Phone 512/266-2442; fax 512/266-9296. www.oasis-austin.com.* Mexican, American menu. Lunch, dinner. Closed Thanksgiving, Dec 25. Bar. Children's menu. Outdoor seating. **$$**

★ **PAPPADEAUX.** *6319 I-35 N, Austin (78752). Phone 512/452-9363; fax 512/452-8541. www.pappadeaux.com.* Cajun, seafood menu. Lunch, dinner. Closed Thanksgiving, Dec 25. Bar. Children's menu. Casual attire. Outdoor seating. **$$**

★ ★ ★ **RUTH'S CHRIS STEAK HOUSE.** *107 W 6th St, Austin (78701). Phone 512/477-7884; toll-free 800/544-0808; fax 512/477-5411. www.ruthschris-austin.com.* Steak menu. Dinner. Closed holidays. Bar. Business casual attire. Reservations recommended. Valet parking. **$$$**

★ ★ **SHORELINE GRILL.** *98 San Jacinto Blvd, Austin (78701). Phone 512/477-3300; fax 512/477-6392. www.shorelinegrill.com.* American menu. Lunch, dinner. Closed Jan 1, Dec 25. Bar. Children's menu. Casual attire. Reservations recommended. Valet parking. Outdoor seating. **$$$**

★ ★ **ZOOT.** *509 Hearn St, Austin (78703). Phone 512/477-6535; fax 512/482-0512. www.zootdining.com.* American menu. Dinner. Closed holidays. Children's menu. **$$$**

Bandera (D-7)

See also Kerrville, San Antonio

Founded 1850
Population 957
Elevation 1,257 ft
Area Code 830
Zip 78003
Information Convention & Visitors Bureau, PO Box 171; phone 830/796-3045 or toll-free 800/364-3833
Web Site www.tourtexas.com/bandera

This authentic Western town, known as the "Cowboy Capital of the World," offers fishing all year and hunting for wild turkey and white-tailed deer in season. Rodeos and country-western dances are popular pastimes here.

What to See and Do

Frontier Times Museum. *506 13th St, Bandera. Phone 830/796-3864.* Early Texas and frontier items; Western art gallery; bell collection; South American items; genuine shrunken head. (Daily; closed holidays) **$**

Special Event

Cowboy Capital PRCA Rodeo. *Mansfield Park Rodeo Arena, 2454 Hwy 16 N, Bandera (78003). Phone toll-free 800/364-3833.* Parade, dances. Memorial Day weekend.

Specialty Lodgings

The following lodging establishments are approved by Mobil Travel Guide, but due to their unique and individualized nature have not been given a traditional Mobil Star rating. Included in this listing you may find bed-and-breakfasts, limited-service inns, guest ranches, and other unique hotel properties.

DIXIE DUDE RANCH. *Ranch Rd 1077, Bandera (78003). Phone 830/796-4481; toll-free 800/375-9255; fax 830/796-4481. www.dixieduderanch.com.* On a 725-acre working ranch. Family-style meals; buffets, cookouts. 21 rooms. Closed one week around Dec 25. Complimentary full breakfast. Check-in 2 pm, check-out 11 am. Restaurant. Outdoor pool, children's pool, whirlpool. **$$**

MAYAN DUDE RANCH. *350 Mayan Ranch Rd, Bandera (78003). Phone 830/796-3312; fax 830/796-8205. www.mayanranch.com.* Forty-seven miles northwest of San Antonio, this ranch is located on 340 acres of lowlands and hill country and has been family owned and operated for nearly 50 years. There are two horse rides daily. Authenticated dinosaur tracks on property. 68 rooms, 2 story. Complimentary full breakfast. Check-in 1 pm, check-out noon. Restaurant (public by reservation), bar. Children's activity center. Outdoor pool, whirlpool. Tennis. **$**

SILVER SPUR DUDE RANCH. *9266 Hwy 1077, Bandera (78003). Phone 830/796-3037; fax 830/796-7170. www.silverspur-ranch.com.* 14 rooms. Complimentary full breakfast. Check-in 3 pm, check-out 11 am. Restaurant. Outdoor pool. **$**

Bastrop (C-8)

See also Austin, La Grange, San Marcos

Population 5,340

Elevation 374 ft
Area Code 512
Zip 78602
Information Chamber of Commerce, 927 Main St; phone 512/321-2419
Web Site www.bastropchamber.com

Bastrop, named for Felipe Enrique Neri, Baron de Bastrop, is the seat of Bastrop County, one of the 23 original counties of the Republic of Texas. First settled in 1829 to protect commerce on the Old San Antonio Road, the town was subject to many Native American raids and was virtually abandoned in 1836. In 1839, it was resettled and has since flourished. The timber from the "Lost Pines of Texas," so named because the nearest similar vegetation is 100 miles away, was used in the building of the capitol at Austin.

What to See and Do

Bastrop State Park. *Hwy 21 E, Bastrop. 1 mile E via Hwy 71, Park Rd 1. Phone 512/321-2101.* These 5,000 acres include a forest of the "Lost Pines of Texas." Swimming pool (Memorial Day-Labor Day, daily; fee), fishing; hiking trail, 18-hole golf, picnicking, improved campsites, RV facilities, cabins. (Daily) **$$**

Buescher State Park. *FM 153 Rd, Smithville. 12 miles SE via Hwy 71, then NE on FM 153, Park Rd 1. Phone 512/237-2241.* Approximately 1,000 acres. Fishing, boating (no gas motors permitted); hiking trail, picnicking, playground, improved campsites (dump station), shelters. (Daily) **$$**

Lake Bastrop Park. *Hwy 21 E, Bastrop. North Shore Recreation Area, 3 miles N on Hwy 95, then E on FM 1441. Phone 512/303-7666. (Lower Colorado River Authority)* Includes a 906-acre lake. Daily entrance permit includes swimming, water-skiing, fishing, boating (launch fee); picnicking, camping (hook-ups, dump station), unfurnished cabins. (Daily) **$$**

Baytown (D-9)

See also Galveston, Houston

Settled 1824
Population 66,430
Elevation 33 ft
Area Code 281
Information Chamber of Commerce, 4721 Garth Rd, Suite C, PO Box 330, 77522; phone 281/422-8359

Web Site www.baytownchamber.com

Progressing from a small sawmill and store settlement to a Confederate shipyard to oil boomtown in 1916, Baytown today has industries related to oil refineries, petrochemicals, and synthetic rubber. Water sports, fishing, and hunting are popular pastimes.

What to See and Do

Anahuac National Wildlife Refuge. *509 Washington Ave, Anahuac. 20 miles S of I-10 on Hwys 61, 562 to FM 1985, connecting with gravel road for 3 miles. Phone 409/267-3337.* This 28,564-acre refuge, bounded by East Galveston Bay and the Intracoastal Waterway, is primarily for migrating and wintering waterfowl; more than 250 bird species include 30 varieties of geese and duck as well as pelicans, roseate spoonbills, ibis, and egrets. Natural marshlands provide food and shelter. Animals include American alligator, nutria, and river otter. Saltwater fishing for crab and flounder; freshwater fishing only in designated areas; seasonal waterfowl hunting east of Oyster Bayou. Restrooms, but no drinking water, available. **FREE**

Baytown Historical Museum. *220 W Defee, Baytown. Phone 281/427-8768.* Contains artifacts pertaining to local and pioneer history. (Tues-Sat) **FREE**

Lynchburg Ferry. *1001 S Lynchburg Rd, Baytown. Phone 281/424-3521.* Oldest operating ferry in Texas, shuttling travelers across the mouth of the San Jacinto River since 1824. Trip provides access to San Jacinto Battleground and Battleship USS *Texas* (see HOUSTON).

Limited-Service Hotel

★ **HAMPTON INN.** *7211 Garth Rd, Baytown (77521). Phone 281/421-1234; toll-free 800/426-7866; fax 281/421-9825. www.hamptoninn.com.* 69 rooms, 3 story. Complimentary continental breakfast. Check-out noon. Outdoor pool, whirlpool. **$**
🏊

Beaumont (C-10)

See also Orange, Port Arthur

Founded 1835
Population 113,866
Elevation 24 ft
Information Convention & Visitors Bureau, 801 Main, Suite 100, PO Box 3827, 77704; phone 409/880-3749 or toll-free 800/392-4401
Web Site www.beaumontcvb.com

On January 10, 1901, a group of men working under Anthony Lucas were glumly, but determinedly, drilling for oil. Suddenly, the pipe catapulted into the air, and oil spouted 200 feet high. This was the Lucas well in the Spindletop field. Promoters, toughs, petty thieves, and soldiers of fortune rushed to Beaumont, but the town soon brought things under control. Later, another oil pool deeper than the original was discovered.

Located on the Neches River deep ship channel, which connects with the Intracoastal Waterway and the Gulf of Mexico, Beaumont is an important inland port and industrial city. Chemicals, synthetic rubber, oil equipment, forest products, and ships are produced here. Rice is grown in the surrounding area and milled in Beaumont.

What to See and Do

Art Museum of Southeast Texas. *500 Main St, Beaumont. Phone 409/832-3432. www.amset.org.* A permanent collection of 19th- and 20th-century American paintings, sculpture, prints, drawings, photography, contemporary folk art, decorative arts. Hosts national and international traveling exhibitions. Gift shop. (Daily; closed holidays) **FREE**

Babe Didrikson Zaharias Memorial Museum. *1750 I-10 E, exit 854, Beaumont. Phone 409/833-4622.* Trophies, artifacts, and memorabilia of "the world's greatest woman athlete." Also houses the Beaumont Visitor Information Center. (Daily; closed Dec 25) **FREE**

Cattail Marsh. *1350 Langham Rd, Beaumont. W on I-10 to Walden Rd, S to Tyrell Park entrance. Phone 409/842-0458. www.cityofbeaumont.com/pout.htm.* A 900-acre constructed wetland includes more than 375,000 plants and attracts more than 350 bird species annually. Recreational activities include bird-watching, hiking, and biking on more than 8 miles of gravel roads. Tyrell Park is adjacent and offers picknicking, Frisbee, 18-hole golf, and children's playgrounds. (Daily) **FREE**

Edison Plaza Museum. *350 Pine St, Beaumont. Phone 409/981-3089.* Largest collection of Thomas A. Edison artifacts west of the Mississippi and the only electric industry museum in the South. Exhibits focus on Edison's inventions concerning electric light and power, the rising costs of electricity today, the future of electricity, and alternative energy sources. Includes Edison phonographs, mimeograph, dictating machine, and personal items from Edison's estate. (Mon-Fri or by appointment; closed holidays) **FREE**

Jefferson Theatre. *345 Fannin St, Beaumont. Phone 409/835-5483.* Full performance arts venue. Host to vaudeville in 1927 and various live performances today. Located in the orchestra pit is the original Robert Morton Wonder Organ, with 778 pipes. **FREE**

John Jay French Museum (Historic House). *2995 French Rd, Beaumont. Phone 409/898-3267.* (1845) Restored Greek Revival country house, re-created tannery and blacksmith shop. (Tues-Sat; closed holidays) **$$**

McFaddin-Ward House. *1906 Calder Ave, Beaumont. Phone 409/832-2134.* (1906) Historic house museum, Beaux-Arts Colonial-style with original family furnishings. Silver collection, Oriental rugs, porcelain, and glass; carriage house. (Tues-Sun; closed holidays) Reservations requested. Children over 8 years only. **$$**

Spindletop/Gladys City Boomtown Museum. *US 69 and University Dr, Lumberton. Phone 409/835-0823.* Re-creation of turn-of-the-century oil town; 15 buildings include pharmacy, surveyor's office, saloon, photography studio; all contain period furnishings, artifacts. Self-guided tour. (Tues-Sun; closed holidays) **$$** On grounds is

> **Lucas Gusher Monument.** A Texas granite shaft, 58 feet high, erected to commemorate the discovery of the first major oil field on the Gulf Coastal Plain.

Texas Energy Museum. *600 Main St, Beaumont. Phone 409/833-5100.* Extensive modern facility encompassing history, science, and technology of energy. Permanent educational exhibits include a 120-foot-long "History Wall," which traces energy from the 18th century to the present; a 135-gallon saltwater aquarium; and an exhibit on the 1901 "Spindletop" oil boom, featuring two lifelike animated robots. (Tues-Sun; closed holidays) **$**

Tyrrell Historical Library. *695 Pearl St, Beaumont. Phone 409/833-2759.* (1903) Served as the First Baptist Church until 1926. It now houses historical documents and art collections and serves as a center for genealogical research. (Tues-Sat) **FREE**

Special Events

Neches River Festival. *2643 North St, Beaumont (77702). Phone 409/835-2443; toll-free 800/392-4401.* Mid-Apr.

South Texas State Fair. *2700 Gulf St, Beaumont. Phone 409/832-9991; toll-free 800/392-4401.* Ten days in early Oct.

Limited-Service Hotels

★ **BEST WESTERN JEFFERSON INN.** *1610 I-10 S, Beaumont (77707). Phone 409/842-0037; toll-free 800/780-7234; fax 409/842-0057. www.bestwestern.com.* 120 rooms. Pets accepted. Complimentary continental breakfast. Check-out noon. Outdoor pool. **$**

★★ **HOLIDAY INN.** *3950 I-10 S, Beaumont (77705). Phone 409/842-5995; toll-free 800/465-4329; fax 409/842-7810. www.holiday-inn.com.* 253 rooms, 8 story. Pets accepted; fee. Check-out noon. Restaurant, bar. Fitness room. Indoor pool, whirlpool. Airport transportation available. Business center. **$**

Full-Service Hotel

★★★ **HILTON HOTEL.** *2355 I-10 S, Beaumont (77705). Phone 409/842-3600; toll-free 800/774-1500; fax 409/842-1355. www.hilton.com.* Directly off the interstate in the center of the Golden Triangle, this hotel has a Southwestern décor accented with tile, stone, and earth tones. 284 rooms, 9 story. Check-out noon. Restaurant, bar. Fitness room. Outdoor pool. Airport transportation available. **$**

Restaurants

★ **CHULA VISTA.** *1135 N 11th St, Beaumont (77702). Phone 409/898-8855; fax 409/898-8977.* Mexican menu. Lunch, dinner. Closed Thanksgiving, Dec 25. Bar. Children's menu. Outdoor seating. **$$**

★ **HOFFBRAU STEAKS.** *2310 N 11th St, Beaumont (77703). Phone 409/892-6911; fax 409/899-3100. www.hoffbrausteaks.com.* Steak menu. Lunch, dinner. Closed Jan 1, Dec 25. Bar. Children's menu. Outdoor seating. **$$**

Big Bend National Park

Web Site www.nps.gov/bibe

108 miles S of Alpine on Hwy 118 or 69 miles S of Marathon on Hwy 385 to Park Headquarters.

In this park the Rio Grande, southern boundary of the United States, flows through awe-inspiring canyons with sheer rock walls rising 1,500 feet above the water; south of Marathon, the river makes the extraordinary 90-degree bend for which the park is named. This rocky wilderness, once home to dinosaurs, boasts more than 1,200 species of plants, particularly cacti in the lowest areas and juniper, piñon, oak, and scattered stands of Arizona pine, Douglas fir, Arizona cypress, and aspen in the uplands. Deer, coyote, peccaries (javelina), and more than 400 bird species may be found amid scenery as stark and magnificent as anywhere in the United States. The Sierra del Carmen and other mountain ranges visible from the park are across the border in Mexico.

The visitor center at Panther Junction contains orientation exhibits for visitors (daily); at Persimmon Gap, the entrance from Marathon, there is also a visitor contact station. At Chisos Basin, about 7 miles off the connecting road within the park (watch for sign), there is a visitor center, a store, restaurant, and motel; tent and trailer campgrounds (no hook-ups; limit 24 feet). Rio Grande Village, 20 miles southeast of Panther Junction, offers a visitor center; tent and trailer campground and RV park (vehicle must accept full hook-ups); a store; shower facilities; gas; laundromat. Castolon, 35 miles southwest of Panther Junction, has a tent and trailer campground (no hook-ups) and small store. Some fees.

Floating the Rio Grande and overnight backpacking is free by permit only; inquire at visitor centers. There are several self-guided trails. Park Service naturalists frequently conduct nature walks and talks. Further information, including activity schedules, can be obtained at all visitor centers in park or by contacting the Superintendent, PO Box 129, Big Bend National Park 79834; phone 915/477-2251.

It is possible to drive within this 800,000-acre park to Santa Elena Canyon and to Boquillas Canyon. Both drives offer much scenery. The trip between Alpine, the park, and Marathon totals about 190 miles. To get the most out of Big Bend, plan to spend at least one night.

Fill gas tank, check oil, and carry water before entering the park. Most people go into the park by one route and out by the other.

Big Spring (B-5)

See also Midland, Snyder

Founded 1881
Population 25,233
Elevation 2,397 ft
Area Code 915
Zip 79720
Information Chamber of Commerce, 215 W 3rd St, PO Box 1391, 79721; phone 915/263-7641 or toll-free 800/734-7641

Big Spring was once a feeding ground for buffalo. Comanches and pioneers fought bitterly for hunting and water rights in the early years. Big Spring is now a farm and ranch center with varied industries. Nearby lakes offer fishing, boating, picnicking, and camping.

What to See and Do

Big Spring State Park. *1 Scenic Dr, Big Spring. 1 mile W on FM 700 to Park Rd 8. Phone 915/263-4931.* A 370-acre park, with picnic grounds and playground. View from top of mountain; prairie dog colony. Hiking; interpretive trail. (Day use only) (Daily) **$$**

Heritage Museum. *510 Scurry St, Big Spring. Phone 915/267-8255.* Themed exhibits, including Indian artifacts, ranching, and oil production; large longhorn collection; Western art; changing exhibits, demonstrations. (Tues-Sat; closed holidays) **$**

Lake Colorado City State Park. *4582 Farm to Market, #2836, Big Spring (79512). 36 miles E via I-20, then 6 miles S via FM 2836. Phone 915/728-3931.* A 500-acre area. Swimming, water-skiing, fishing, boating (ramp); picnicking, playground, improved camping, tent and trailer sites. (Daily) **$$**

Potton House. *200 Gregg St, Big Spring. Phone 915/263-0511.* (1901) Restored turn-of-the-century Victorian-style house; furnishings brought from

England by original owners. (Tues-Sat afternoon; closed holidays) **$**

Special Events

Gem & Mineral Show. *Dora Roberts Bldg, fairgrounds, Big Spring. Phone toll-free 800/734-7641.* First weekend in Mar.

Howard County Fair. *Phone toll-free 800/734-7641.* Third week in Aug.

Rattlesnake Roundup. Contact Chamber of Commerce. Late Mar.

Limited-Service Hotel

★ **SUPER 8.** *700 W I-20, Big Spring (79720). Phone 432/267-1601; toll-free 800/800-8000; fax 432/267-6916. www.super8.com.* 155 rooms, 2 story. Complimentary continental breakfast. Check out noon. Restaurant. Fitness room. Outdoor pool, children's pool. **$**
🏋 🖼

Bonham (A-8)

See also Denison, Greenville, Paris, Sherman

Founded 1837
Population 9,990
Elevation 605 ft
Area Code 903
Zip 75418
Information Chamber of Commerce, 110 E First St; phone 903/583-4811
Web Site www.bonhamchamber.com

Bonham was named for James Butler Bonham, a defender of the Alamo. It is located in the blackland prairie south of the Red River, near the boundary between Texas and Oklahoma.

What to See and Do

Bonham State Park. *3 1/2 miles SE via Hwy 78, FM 271. Entrance on Park Rd 24. Phone 903/583-5022.* On 261 acres. Swimming, fishing; picnicking, 10-mile mountain bike trail, improved campsites (dump station). (Daily) **$$**

Fort Inglish Village. *1/2 mile W on Hwy 82. Phone 903/640-0506.* Blockhouse is a replica of first building in Bonham (1837), built to protect settlers. Log structures, including blacksmith shop, residential cabin,

schoolhouse/church, and general store have been moved from surrounding county to form a settlement. Living history demonstrations of pioneer skills. (Apr-Aug, Tues-Sun) **FREE**

Lake Bonham Recreation Area. *6 miles N. Phone 903/583-8001.* Swimming, water-skiing, fishing, boating (launch); nine-hole and miniature golf, playground, tent and trailer sites (dump station, no hook-ups). Some fees.

Sam Rayburn House. *1 mile W on Hwy 82. Phone 903/583-5558. www.thc.state.tx.us/samrayhouse/srhdefault.html.* (1916) Guided tour of house and grounds. (Mon-Fri, hours vary; closed holidays) **FREE**

Sam Rayburn Library and Museum. *800 W Sam Rayburn Dr, Bonham. 1/2 mile W on Hwy 82. Phone 903/583-2455.* Affiliated with the University of Texas at Austin. Honors the man who was Speaker of the US House of Representatives for 17 1/2 years. In the library is an exact copy of the Speaker's Capitol office, which contains a fireplace that was in the US House of Representatives for 92 years, and a crystal chandelier, more than a century old, that has hung in both the White House and the Capitol. The library also contains Rayburn's papers; published proceedings from the first Continental Congress; books by and about leading political figures and American history. (Daily; closed holidays) **FREE**

Special Event

Fannin County Fair. *Fort Inglish Park, Hwys 121 and 82, Bonham (75418). Phone 903/583-7453.* Third weekend in Oct.

Brackettville (D-6)

See also Del Rio, Eagle Pass, Uvalde

Population 1,876
Elevation 1,110 ft
Information Kinney County Chamber of Commerce, PO Box 386; phone 830/563-2466

What to See and Do

❎ **Alamo Village.** *FM 674 N, Brackettville (78832). 7 miles N on Ranch Rd 674. Phone 830/563-2580. www.alamovillage.com.* Built for the John Wayne movie *The Alamo* (1959). Buildings include a stage depot, bank, jail, and replica of the Alamo. Entertainment (Memorial Day-Labor Day); walk-in museums, trading post, store, cantina. (Daily 9 am-5 pm; closed week of Dec 25) **$$$**

Brazosport (D-9)

See also Angleton, Houston

Population 49,541
Elevation 0-20 ft
Area Code 979
Information Visitor & Convention Council, 420 TX 332, Clute 77531; phone 979/265-2505 or toll-free 888/477-2505
Web Site www.brazosport.org

Brazosport, with the deepwater Brazos Harbor on the Gulf, is a composite of cities including Brazoria, Clute, Freeport, Jones Creek, Lake Jackson, Oyster Creek, Quintana, Richwood, and Surfside. One of the state's largest chemical plants extracts chemicals from seawater here. Fishing, both sport and commercial (shrimp), is important to the area.

What to See and Do

Brazosport Museum of Natural Science. *400 College Dr, Lake Jackson. Phone 979/265-7831.* Emphasizing local flora and fauna; archaeological finds. Shell exhibits with collections for public study; Children's Hall; paleontology, mineralogy, and ivory displays; marine life exhibits; aquarium, simulated underwater diorama. (Mon-Sat; closed holidays) **FREE**

Special Events

Festival of Lights. *91 Lake Rd, Lake Jackson. Phone 979/297-4533.* Sat before Thanksgiving.

Fishin' Fiesta. *Bridge Harbor Yacht Club, Freeport.* July.

Great Texas Mosquito Festival. *100 Parkview Dr, Clute. Phone 949/265-2508.* Last weekend in July.

Riverfest. *318 W Park St, Brazosport. Phone 979/233-3306.* Last weekend in Apr.

Shrimp Boil and Auction. *Freeport Park, Hwy 288, Freeport (77541). Phone 979/297-9922.* Late Aug.

Limited-Service Hotels

★ **LA QUINTA INN.** *1126 W Hwy 332, Clute (77531). Phone 979/265-7461; toll-free 800/531-5900;*

fax 979/265-3804. www.lq.com. 135 rooms, 2 story. Pets accepted, some restrictions. Complimentary continental breakfast. Check-in 3 pm, check-out noon. Outdoor pool. **$**

★ ★ **SWISS CHEROTEL BRAZOSPORT HOTEL AND CONFERENCE CENTER.**
925 Hwy 332 W, Lake Jackson (77566). Phone 979/297-1161; toll-free 800/544-2119; fax 979/297-1249. www.cherotel.com. 142 rooms, 2 story. Pets accepted; fee. Check-in 3 pm, check-out noon. High-speed Internet access. Restaurant, bar. Fitness room. Indoor pool, outdoor pool. Business center. **$**

Brenham (C-8)

See also Bryan/College Station

Founded 1844
Population 13,507
Elevation 350 ft
Area Code 979
Zip 77833
Information Washington County Chamber of Commerce, 314 S Austin St; phone 979/836-3695 or toll-free 888/273-6426
Web Site www.brenhamtx.org

Brenham is the county seat for Washington County, known as the "Birthplace of Texas," where the Texas Declaration of Independence was signed on March 2, 1836. Nestled in the green rolling hills of central Texas, the county offers a wide range of historical and natural attractions for all ages. Bluebonnets and other wildflowers bloom in profusion along country roads in March and April.

What to See and Do

Antique Rose Emporium. *10000 FM 50, Brenham. 12 miles NW on FM 50. Phone 979/836-5548. www.antiqueroseemporium.com.* Eight-acre garden center beautifully landscaped on early settler's homestead with old garden roses, native plants, cottage garden perennials, and wildflowers. Restored buildings include 1855 stone kitchen, 1840s log corn crib, 1850s saltbox house, and 1900s Victorian home. Tours (groups by reservation). (Mon-Sat 9 am-6 pm, Sun 11 am-5:30 pm; closed holidays) **FREE**

Baptist Historical Center. *12 miles N at intersection of FM 50 and 390. Phone 979/836-5117.* Museum with exhibits on Sam Houston, including wardrobe; history of Texas Baptists; history of city of Independence. Baptist Church (organized in 1839, present building 1872) was the site of the baptism of Sam Houston. Contains historic century-old church bell, relics. (Wed-Sat; closed Jan 1, Dec 25) Across the highway are the graves of Houston's wife and mother-in-law, who requested burial within sound of the church bell. Ruins of old Baylor College, 1/2 mile W on FM 390. **FREE**

Blue Bell Creamery. *1101 S Horton St, Brenham. FM 577, 2 miles off Hwy 290. Phone 979/830-2197; toll-free 800/327-8135.* 45-minute tours of ice cream manufacturing plant. Free samples. Country store. (Mon-Fri) **$$**

Lake Somerville. *15 miles NW on TX 36. Phone 979/535-7763.* Fishing, boating (ramps); hiking, picnicking, concession, camping, cabins, tent and trailer facilities. The state of Texas operates Birch Creek and Nails Creek state parks on the lake. The US Army Corps of Engineers operates three additional recreation areas.

Monastery of St. Clare Miniature Horse Ranch. *9 miles NE via Hwy 105. Phone 979/836-9652.* Home of Franciscan Poor Clare nuns. Pastures, barn. "Art Barn" gift shop sells handmade ceramics. Self-guided tours (free). Forty-five-minute guided tours (fee). (Limited hours; closed religious holidays).

Pleasant Hill Winery. *1441 Salem Rd, Brenham.* Winery and vineyards tours. Tasting room, gift shop. Tours (reservations required). (Weekends; closed holidays) **FREE**

Stephen F. Austin State Historical Park. *Approximately 30 miles S via Hwy 36, off I-10. Phone 979/885-3613.* Site of San Felipe, seat of Anglo-American colonies in Texas. Monuments; replica of Austin's house. Bathhouse, fishing; picnicking, playground, gift shop, camping (tent and trailer sites, shelters). Some fees. (Daily) **$$**

Washington-on-the-Brazos State Historical Park. *14 miles NE on Hwy 105, then 5 miles NE on FM 912. Phone 936/878-2214. www.birthplaceoftexas.com.* Putting the spotlight on the story of independence and Texas's beginnings, the State spent 10 years and more than $6 million developing a plethora of worthy attractions at its Washington-on-the-Brazos State Park—the site of the signing of Texas's declaration of independence from Mexico. There's no fee to enter the state park and enjoy its extensive biking trails, picnic areas, and Visitor Services Complex (including interactive historical exhibits, full-service restaurant and gift shop). Nominal fees for the three other main attractions—the Star of Republic Museum, Independence Hall, and the Barrington Living History Farm—are well worth it. The museum houses a collection of more than 20,0000 artifacts and depicts the story of the Republic of Texas through interactive exhibits, audiovisual presentations, and more. Kids will love the farm, a restored 1950s Brazos River Valley cotton plantation, where costumed volunteers demonstrate everything from cooking to butchering livestock, and soap- and candle-making. Call ahead for information on special seasonal events. (Daily 8 am-sundown) **FREE** On grounds are

> **Anson Jones Home.** Residence of last president of the Republic of Texas; period furnishings. Guided tours (Daily). **$$**

> **Independence Hall.** Replica of hall in which Texas Declaration of Independence was signed. (Daily) **$$**

> **Star of the Republic Museum.** *Washington (77880). Phone 979/878-2214. www.starmuseum.org.* Exhibits on history and culture of the Republic of Texas; audiovisual programs; research library. Tours. (Daily 10 am-5 pm; closed Thanksgiving, Dec 24-Jan 1) **$**

Special Events

Bluebonnet Trails/Wildflowers Tours. *Phone toll-free 888/273-6486.* Drive through countryside combining wildflowers with early Texas history; free maps. Late Mar-Apr.

Texas Independence Day Celebration. *Washington-on-the-Brazos State Historical Park, 401 Guadalupe St, Brenham. Phone 979/878-2214.* Reenactments, musical performances, tours of historic park. Weekend nearest Mar 2.

Washington County Fair. *1305 E Horton, Brenham (77834). Phone 979/836-4112.* Held annually since 1868. Rodeos, carnival, entertainment, food. Third Wed-Sat in Sept.

Specialty Lodging

The following lodging establishment is approved by Mobil Travel Guide, but due to its unique and individualized nature has not been given a traditional Mobil Star rating. Included in this listing you may find bed-and-breakfasts, limited-service inns, guest ranches, and other unique hotel properties.

ANT STREET INN. *107 W Commerce St, Brenham (77833). Phone 979/836-7393; toll-free 800/481-1951; fax 979/836-7595. www.antstreetinn.com.* Guests often lounge in the balcony rocking chairs overlooking a tranquil courtyard. This quaint bed-and-breakfast is located in the historic Ant Street district of downtown. Built in 1899, the restored guest rooms have turn-of-the-century décor, antiques, vaulted ceilings, wood floors and oriental rugs. 16 rooms, 2 story. Children over 12 years only. Complimentary full breakfast. Check-in 3 pm, check-out 11 am. High-speed Internet access, wireless Internet access. **$$**

Brownsville (F-8)

See also Harlingen, Port Isabel, South Padre Island

Founded 1848
Population 139,722
Elevation 33 ft
Area Code 956
Information Brownsville Chamber of Commerce, 1600 E Elizabeth St, 78520; phone 956/542-4341
Web Site www.brownsvillechamber.com

While breezes off the Gulf make Texas's southernmost city cooler than many other cities farther north, its tropical climate remains clear. Palms, royal poinciana, citrus trees, bougainvillea, papaya, and banana trees line the streets. Brownsville and nearby South Padre Island are year-round resort areas.

Brownsville is an air, rail, and highway port of entry between the United States and Mexico and an international seaport with a 17-mile ship channel to the Gulf. Red grapefruit, oranges, lemons, limes, sorghum, and winter vegetables are grown and shipped from here. Brownsville is also an important shrimp boat port and deep-sea fishing center. The Mexican city of Matamoros is just across the Rio Grande.

Fort Taylor (later Fort Brown) was established in 1846, after Texas entered the Union. Construction of the fort precipitated the Mexican War, which began at Palo Alto Battlefield. The final land battle of the Civil War was also fought nearby. Raids of the area by Mexican bandits continued well into the early 20th century.

What to See and Do

Freshwater fishing. *In many lakes and canals.* Bass, crappie, and catfish.

Gladys Porter Zoo. *500 Ringgold St, Brownsville. Phone 956/546-2177. www.gpz.org.* Outstanding 31-acre zoo with more than 1,900 animals in their natural setting; reptile collection, free-flight aviary, children's zoo, aquarium, Australian exhibit. (Mon-Fri 9 am-5 pm, Sat-Sun 9 am-5:30 pm; closed holidays.) **$$$**

Gray Line bus tours. *2600 Padre Blvd, South Padre Island. Phone toll-free 800/321-8720.* Contact PO Box 2610, South Padre Island 78597.

Matamoros, Tamaulipas, Mexico. (Population 500,000) Across the Rio Grande. This is a colorful and interesting Mexican border city, with diversified industry making it one of Mexico's wealthiest towns. Life centers around the Plaza de Hidalgo and the streets that reach out from it. The market, four blocks from the plaza on Calle (street) 9 and Calle 10, is an open mall of small stands. (No fruit may be brought back to the United States. For Border Crossing Regulations, see MAKING THE MOST OF YOUR TRIP.)

Palmitto Ranch Battlefield. *Marker is 12 miles E on Hwy 4.* Site of the final land engagement of the Civil War (May 12-13, 1865). Confederate troops prevailed but were ordered to surrender upon learning of Lee's capitulation at Appomattox more than a month before.

Palo Alto Battlefield National Historic Site. *1623 Central Blvd, Brownsville. 6 miles N of town on FM 1847, near junction FM 511. Visitor center with museum is on the second floor of IBC Bank Building. Phone 956/541-2785.* Historical marker gives details of the artillery battle that began the Mexican War here on May 8, 1846. **FREE**

Port Brownsville. *1000 Foust Rd, Brownsville. 6 miles NE on International Blvd. Phone toll-free 800/378-5395.* Harbor for shrimp boats and ships transporting various commodities. **FREE**

Resaca de la Palma. *North end of town, vicinity Paredes Line Rd and Coffee Port Rd, Brownsville.* Site of the second Mexican War battle, May 9, 1846. General Zachary Taylor defeated Mexican General Mariano Arista. Historical markers give details.

Saltwater fishing. On Laguna Madre Bay, in the ship channels, or in the Gulf by charter boats from Port Isabel or South Padre Island.

Special Event

Charro Days. *455 E Elizabeth St, Brownsville (78520). Phone 956/546-3721.* Parades, concerts, special events. Late Feb-early Mar.

Limited-Service Hotels

★ **BEST WESTERN ROSE GARDEN INN.** *845 N Expy 77/83, Brownsville (78520). Phone 956/546-5501; toll-free 800/780-7234; fax 956/546-6474. www.bestwestern.com.* 121 rooms, 2 story. Complimentary full breakfast. Check-in 2 pm, check-out noon. Outdoor pool. **$**

★ ★ **FOUR POINTS BY SHERATON.** *3777 N Expy, Brownsville (78520). Phone 956/547-1500; fax 956/547-1550. www.fourpoints.com.* 141 rooms, 2 story. Pets accepted, some restrictions; fee. Complimentary full breakfast. Check-in 3 pm, check-out noon. High-speed Internet access, wireless Internet access. Restaurant, bar. Fitness room. Outdoor pool, whirlpool. Airport transportation available. Business center. **$**

Full-Service Resort

★ ★ **RANCHO VIEJO RESORT.** *1 Rancho Viejo Dr, Rancho Viejo (78575). Phone 956/350-4000; toll-free 800/531-7400; fax 956/350-9681. www.playrancho.com.* 65 rooms, 2 story. Check-in 4 pm, check-out noon. Restaurant, bar. Fitness room. Outdoor pool, children's pool. Golf. Tennis. **$**

Restaurant

★ ★ **LOS CAMPEROS.** *1442 International Blvd, Brownsville (78520). Phone 956/546-8172; fax 956/541-7315.* Mexican menu. Lunch, dinner, late-night. Bar. Casual attire. Reservations recommended. **$$**

Brownwood (B-7)

See also Comanche

Population 18,813

Elevation 1,342 ft
Area Code 915
Information Brown County Chamber of Commerce, 521 E Baker, PO Box 880, 76804; phone 915/646-9535
Web Site www.ci.brownwood.tx.us

Almost in the exact center of Texas, Brown County is rich farm and ranch land, producing cattle, sheep, goats, poultry, pecans, and grain crops.

What to See and Do

Douglas MacArthur Academy of Freedom. *Austin and Coggin sts, Brownwood. Howard Payne University campus. Phone 915/649-8700.* Includes Hall of Christian Civilization, with one of Texas's largest murals; Mediterranean Hall, with reproduction of the Rosetta Stone; and MacArthur Exhibit Gallery, containing memorabilia of the famous general. Tours (daily; closed school holidays). **FREE**

Lake Brownwood State Park. *16 miles NW on Hwy 279, then 6 miles E on Park Rd 15. Phone 915/784-5223.* Approximately 540 acres on a 7,300-acre lake. Swimming, fishing, boating (ramps); hiking trails, picnicking, concessions (seasonal), multiuse campsites, RV facilities, cabins, shelters. (Daily) **$**

Limited-Service Hotel

★ **DAYS INN.** *515 E Commerce St, Brownwood (76801). Phone 325/646-2551; fax 325/643-6064. www.daysinn.com.* 138 rooms, 2 story. Pets accepted; fee. Complimentary continental breakfast. Check-out noon. Outdoor pool, whirlpool. **$**

Bryan/ College Station (C-8)

See also Brenham, Huntsville

Population 65,660
Elevation Bryan, 367 ft; College Station, 308 ft
Area Code 979
Information Bryan/College Station Convention & Visitors Bureau, 715 University Dr E, College Station 77840; phone 979/260-9898 or toll-free 800/777-8292
Web Site www.b-cs.com

This rich farming area is home to a number of nationalities, blended together into a thriving community. Bryan and College Station have become a space research, industrial, and wholesale-retail trade center. Hunting, fishing, and camping are popular year-round.

What to See and Do

Brazos Valley Museum of Natural History. *3232 Briarcrest Dr, Bryan. Phone 979/776-2195.* Exhibits focus on archaeology and natural history of the Brazos Valley; includes hands-on Discovery Room featuring live animals. (Mon-Sat; closed holidays) **$$$**

Messina Hof Wine Cellars. *4545 Old Reliance Rd, Bryan (77808). 5 miles NE of Bryan on Hwy 21, Old Reliance exit, then follow signs. Phone 979/778-9463; toll-free 800/736-9463. www.messinahof.com.* Winery and vineyard tours, lakeside picnic area. Tasting room, gift shop. Tours (fee). (Mon-Fri 8:30 am-5:30 pm; closed Thanksgiving, Dec 25) **FREE**

Texas A&M University. *Rudder Tower Visitors Center 1st Floor College Station, College Station (77843). Phone 979/845-5851.* (1876) (44,000 students) This school is the oldest public institution of higher education in the state. It ranks among the top ten institutions in research and development. Enrollments in engineering, agriculture, business, veterinary medicine, and architecture are among the largest in the country. On its attractive 5,200-acre campus, limited tours are available of the creamery, the oceanography-meteorology building with observation deck, the Memorial Student Center art exhibits, rare gun collection, nuclear science center, cyclotron, and branding iron exhibit. Aggieland Visitor Center has audiovisual programs (Mon-Fri; two-week advance notice requested). Also located here is

> **Museum at the George H. W. Bush Presidential Library.** *1000 George Bush Dr W, College Station (77845). Phone 979/691-4000; fax 979/691-4050. www.bushlibrary.tamu.edu.* The George Bush Presidential Library and Museum is located on the West Campus of Texas A&M University. The museum contains approximately 60,000 historical objects ranging from Head of State Gifts, gifts from the American people, and personally used items. The archives contains more than 38 million pages of personal papers and official documents from George Bush's vice presidency and presidency as well as personal records from his public career. (Daily 9:30 am-5 pm, Sun noon-5 pm; closed Jan 1, Thanksgiving, Dec 25) **$$**

Limited-Service Hotels

★ **BEST WESTERN INN AT CHIMNEY HILL.** *901 University Dr, College Station (77840). Phone 979/260-9150; toll-free 800/267-7750; fax 979/846-0467. www.bestwestern.com.* 98 rooms, 2 story. Complimentary continental breakfast. Check-in 3 pm, check-out noon. Outdoor pool, whirlpool. **$**

★ **HAMPTON INN.** *320 S Texas Ave, College Station (77840). Phone 979/846-0184; toll-free 800/426-7866; fax 979/268-5807. www.hamptoninn.com.* 133 rooms, 4 story. Complimentary full breakfast. Check-in 3 pm, check-out noon. High-speed Internet access, wireless Internet access. Outdoor pool. **$**

★ **LA QUINTA INN.** *607 Texas Ave S, College Station (77840). Phone 979/696-7777; toll-free 800/531-5900; fax 979/696-0531. www.lq.com.* 176 rooms. Pets accepted. Complimentary continental breakfast. Check-in 3 pm, check-out noon. Outdoor pool. Airport transportation available. Texas A & M University opposite. **$**

Full-Service Hotel

★ ★ ★ **HILTON COLLEGE STATION AND CONFERENCE CENTER.** *801 University Dr E, College Station (77840). Phone 979/693-7500; toll-free 800/774-1500; fax 979/846-7361. www.hiltoncs.com.* This hotel and conference center is just 2 miles from Texas A&M and often hosts university-related business and social events. 303 rooms, 11 story. Pets accepted, some restrictions. Check-in 4 pm, check-out noon. High-speed Internet access, wireless Internet access. Restaurant, bar. Fitness room. Outdoor pool, whirlpool. Airport transportation available. **$**

Restaurant

★ **JOSE'S.** *3824 Texas Ave S, Bryan (77802). Phone 979/268-0036; fax 979/846-8370.* Mexican menu. Lunch, dinner. Closed Mon; holidays. Children's menu. Casual attire. **$**

Burnet (C-7)

See also Austin, Georgetown, Johnson City, Killeen

Founded 1849
Population 4,735
Elevation 1,300 ft
Area Code 512
Zip 78611
Information Chamber of Commerce, 703 Buchanan Dr; phone 512/756-4297
Web Site www.burnetchamber.org

This resort town is in the Highland Lakes region, which is an area of geologic interest that attracts many rockhounds.

What to See and Do

Fort Croghan Museum. *703 Buchanan Dr, Burnet. 1 mile W on Hwy 29. Phone 512/756-8281.* One of eight frontier forts established in 1848-1849 to protect settlements. Two original stone buildings, blacksmith shop, one-room schoolhouse relocated buildings; visitor center; museum displays 1,400 early pioneer artifacts; displays relating to Civilian Conservation Corps. (Apr-Sept, Thurs-Sat) **DONATION**

Inks Lake State Park. *9 miles W on Hwy 29, then S on Park Rd 4. Phone 512/793-2223.* A 1,200-acre recreation area. Swimming, fishing, boating (ramps); hiking, golf, concessions, campsites (dump station). (Daily) **$$**

Lake Buchanan. *3 miles W on Hwy 29. Phone 512/793-2803.* Larger than Inks Lake; water sports.

Longhorn Cavern State Park. *6 miles S on Hwy 281, then 6 miles W on Park Rd 4. Phone 512/756-4680.* In the Highland Lakes country on the Colorado River, this 639-acre tract provides picnicking facilities in addition to a museum of the Civilian Conservation Corps (CCC) and the extremely large cavern. Guided tours. (Daily) **$$$**

Special Event

Bluebonnet Festival. *On the square, Burnet.* Second weekend in Apr.

Canyon (E-3)

See also Amarillo, Hereford

Population 12,875
Elevation 3,551 ft
Area Code 806
Zip 79015
Information Chamber of Commerce, 1518 5th Ave, PO Box 8; phone 806/655-1183

This former cattle town, now the seat of Randall County, originated as the headquarters of the once huge T-Anchor Ranch.

What to See and Do

Palo Duro Canyon State Park. *12 miles E on Hwy 217 to Park Rd 5. Phone 806/488-2227. www.tpwd.state.tx.us/park/paloduro.* Approximately 16,400 acres of colorful scenery. Hiking trail, saddle horses (fee). Picnicking, concession, improved campsites (dump station). (See SPECIAL EVENT) (Daily) **$**

Panhandle-Plains Historical Museum. *2401 4th Ave, Canyon. On campus of West Texas A&M University. Phone 806/651-2244.* Texas's largest state museum; exhibits include Western heritage, petroleum, paleontology, transportation, and fine art. (Daily; closed holidays) **$$**

Special Event

Texas. *Amphitheater, Palo Duro Canyon State Park, Canyon. Phone 806/655-2181.* Musical drama by Paul Green depicting Texas life in the 1880s. Outdoors. Pre-performance barbecue. Thurs-Tues evenings. Mid-June-late Aug.

Specialty Lodging

The following lodging establishment is approved by Mobil Travel Guide, but due to its unique and individualized nature has not been given a traditional Mobil Star rating. Included in this listing you may find bed-and-breakfasts, limited-service inns, guest ranches, and other unique hotel properties.

HUDSPETH HOUSE. *1905 4th Ave, Canyon (79015). Phone 806/655-9800; toll-free 800/655-9809; fax 806/655-7457. www.hudspethinn.com.* This restored house (1909) is on the Texas Historical Register.

8 rooms, 3 story. Complimentary full breakfast. Check-in 4 pm, check-out 11 am. **$**

Childress (F-4)

See also Quanah, Vernon

Population 6,778
Elevation 1,877 ft
Area Code 940
Zip 79201
Information Chamber of Commerce, PO Box 35; phone 940/937-2567
Web Site childresstexas.com

What to See and Do

Childress County Heritage Museum. *210 3rd St NW, Childress. Phone 940/937-2261.* Housed in a historic US Post Office building; prehistoric and Native American artifacts; cattle, cotton, and railroad industry exhibits; farming, ranching, and pioneer displays; period rooms, antique carriage room. (Mon-Fri or by appointment) **FREE**

Special Event

Childress County Old Settlers' Reunion. *Rodeo Arena, Childress. Phone 940/937-2567.* Celebrated for more than 100 years. Memorial, parade, barbecue, rodeo, dance. Three days third weekend in July.

Clarendon (E-4)

See also Amarillo

Founded 1878
Population 1,974
Elevation 2,727 ft
Area Code 806
Zip 79226

Information Chamber of Commerce, 318 S Kearney,

PO Box 730; phone 806/874-2421 or toll-free

800/579-4023

What to See and Do

Greenbelt Lake. *6640 Lake Park Dr, #104, Clarendon. 4 miles N on Hwy 70. Phone 806/874-2746.* Swimming,

water-skiing, fishing, boating (ramps, marina); 18-hole golf (fee), picnicking, camping, tent and trailer sites (hook-ups, dump station). Some fees. (Daily) **$**

Saints Roost Museum. *Hwy 70 S, Clarendon. Phone 806/874-2746.* (Thurs-Sun; closed holidays) **FREE**

Cleburne (B-8)

See also Arlington-Grand Prairie, Dallas, Fort Worth, Granbury, Hillsboro, Stephenville

Population 26,005
Information Chamber of Commerce, 1511 W Henderson St, PO Box 701; phone 817/645-2455
Web Site www.cleburnechamber.com

Cleburne is an industrial, trading, and shipping town with surrounding dairy, small grain, and livestock farms and several manufacturing plants.

What to See and Do

Cleburne State Park. *5800 Park Rd 21, Cleburne (76031). 6 miles SW on Hwy 67, then 6 miles SW on Park Rd 21. Phone 817/645-4215.* Approximately 500 acres. Swimming, fishing, boating (ramp, rentals); hiking, picnicking, concession, improved camping, tent and trailer sites (dump station). (Daily) **$**

Dinosaur Valley State Park. *Farm Rd 205 and Park Rd 59, Cleburne (76043). 24 miles SW on Hwy 67 to Park Rd 59, near Glen Rose. Phone 254/897-4588. www.tpwd.state.tx.us.* Approximately 1,500 acres. The highlight is the well-preserved dinosaur tracks in the riverbed, along with two fiberglass dinosaur models—one, a towering 70 feet tall. Swimming, fishing; hiking, mountain biking, picnicking, playground, camping, tent and trailer sites (hook-ups, dump station). (Daily 8 am-10 pm) **$**

Layland Museum. *201 N Caddo St, Cleburne. Phone 817/645-0940.* Southwest Native American collection, early pottery, fossils; Civil War exhibit, local history, Santa Fe Railroad caboose, and artifacts; research library. (Mon-Fri; closed holidays) **FREE**

Special Events

Christmas Candle Walk. *Phone 817/641-7433.* Tour of houses. Early Dec.

Sheriff's Posse PRCA Rodeo. *Phone 817/373-2382.* Weekend mid-June.

Comanche (B-7)

See also Brownwood, Stephenville

Population 4,482
Elevation 1,358 ft
Information Chamber of Commerce, 100 Indian Creek Dr, PO Box 65; phone 915/356-3233

In its early days, Comanche was a supply point for ranchers who dared to push their herds into Native American country. Gangs of outlaws, including John Wesley Hardin, raided the town periodically. Comanche's commerce is based on agriculture, cattle, dairy products, and light manufacturing.

What to See and Do

Bicentennial Park. *On town square.* Features Fleming Oak (more than 200 years old), historical markers, and stone columns from 1890 courthouse.

Comanche County Museum. *Moorman Rd, Comanche. 1 mile W via Hwy 36.* Area history; 13 rooms of memorabilia. (Sat-Sun, limited hours; also by appointment) **DONATION**

Old Cora. *SW corner of town square.* (1856) Oldest original existing courthouse in the state.

Proctor Lake. *Rtes 1 and 71A, Comanche (76442). 10 miles NE on Hwys 67/377. Phone 254/879-2424.* Swimming, water-skiing, fishing, boating (ramps); picnicking (fee), camping, tent and trailer sites (most with electricity; fee). (Daily) **$**

Corpus Christi (E-8)

See also Alice, Aransas Pass, Kingsville, Port Aransas, Rockport

Founded 1839
Population 277,454
Elevation 35 ft
Area Code 361
Information Convention & Visitors Bureau, 1201 N Shoreline, 78401; phone 361/881-1888 or toll-free 800/678-6232
Web Site www.corpuschristi-tx-cvb.org

Corpus Christi was established as a trading post by Colonel Henry L. Kinney in 1839. When the US Army moved in for the Mexican War in 1846, it was described as a "small village of smugglers and lawless men with but few women and no ladies." In its early days, Corpus Christi grew and prospered as ranching prospered. Natural gas and oil were discovered in the early 1900s, but the city has remained a livestock and industrial center.

Corpus Christi Bay provides a landlocked harbor with a ship channel to the Gulf through Aransas Pass and Port Aransas. The bay also makes this a resort area, with fishing, swimming, and water sports.

What to See and Do

Art Museum of South Texas. *1902 N Shoreline, Corpus Christi (78401). Phone 361/825-3500. www.stia.org.* Built by internationally renowned architect Philip Johnson to make the most of Corpus Christi's generous sunlight and gorgeous bayside view, the starkly white Art Museum of South Texas is as much a work of art as the paintings it houses. While the permanent collection spans a wide variety of styles and mediums, the museum's most comprehensive groupings are works by Texas artists and contemporary works on paper. Large-scale abstract paintings by Texas modernist Dorothy Hood are displayed in the Singer Gallery, and photographs by Houston-based artist Michele Wambaugh are featured in the Historical Gallery. If you come with family on a weekend, kids will appreciate the museum's interactive playroom, which offers drawing and painting programs, art activities and games, a reading room, and plenty of space to roam. Traveling exhibits change every three or four months. (Tues-Sun; closed holidays) **$**

Asian Cultures Museum & Educational Center. *1809 N Chaparral, Corpus Christi (78401). Phone 361/882-2641. www.geocities.com/asiancm.* Best known for its collection of more than 2,800 Hakata dolls, Corpus Christi's Asian Cultural Museum is one of five such museums in the United States and the only one in Texas. Founded in 1974, the museum's core artifacts were collected or commissioned by Mrs. Billie Trimble Chandler during a 17-year teaching stint in Japan and include Noh theater masks, opera costumes, Chinese porcelain, and lacquerware. A 5-foot bronze Amida Budda and rickshaw are two of the most popular attractions. Traveling exhibits change several times a year. In 2003, the museum launched an Indian art exhibit with a corresponding festival featuring the food, dance, and music of India. Educational Center classes range from origami and calligraphy to flower arranging. Call ahead to see if your visit will correspond with one of these unique culturally enriching sessions. (Tues-Sat 9 am-5 pm; closed holidays) **$**

Corpus Christi Greyhound Racetrack. *5302 Leopard St, Corpus Christi (78408). Off I-37 at Navigation Blvd. Phone 361/289-9333. www.corpuschristidogs.com.* A night at Texas's first racetrack is a popular way for Corpus Christi citizens to cap their sun-soaked days. Thirteen live greyhound races are presented Wednesday through Sunday evenings at 7:30 pm. Matinees are featured on Wednesday, Friday, Saturday, and Sunday at 1:30 pm. (Extra matinees are added on Memorial Day, Independence Day, and Labor Day weekends.) Full card simulcasts of greyhound and thoroughbred races begin daily at 11 am. Concession stands and cocktails are available in both the grandstand and clubhouse areas, and the track's full-service dining room is open on Friday and Saturday. (Closed Easter, Thanksgiving, Dec 24) **$**

Corpus Christi Museum of Science & History. *1900 N Chaparral St, Corpus Christi (78401). Phone 361/883-2862. www.cctexas.com.* Linen sails billow in the Gulf Coast breeze, and wooden ship hulls creak and bob. There's nothing stuffy about this exhibit! Built in Spain to commemorate the 500th anniversary of Christopher Columbus's voyages to the New World, stunningly accurate reproductions of the *Pinta* and *Santa Maria* sailing vessels (now moored outside the museum in Corpus's ship channel) have been prized possessions of the museum since 1993. Guided tours of the ships, which were built using the same materials that 15th-century shipbuilders would have used, are offered every hour on the half hour. Equally compelling are the collections inside the museum proper, which happens to be Texas's marine archaeology repository—including artifacts from many famous shipwrecks, such as the one involving three Spanish treasure ships that ran aground on Padre Island in 1554. There's also a history collection with 28,000 items representing the history and culture of the people of South Texas, a Children's Wharf interactive kids' section, and exhibits featuring reptiles and shells of the area. (Tues-Sat 10 am-5 pm, Sun from noon; closed holidays) **$$**

Fishing. Fishing boats leave downtown Corpus Christi marina for bay fishing trips and at other piers, including Deep Sea Headquarters and Fisherman's Wharf in Port Aransas for Gulf trips. Skiffs for redfish trout fishing in Laguna Madre may be rented at John F. Kennedy Causeway.

Flagship Cruises. *Corpus Christi Marina, Peoples St Slip 49, Corpus Christi. Phone 361/884-1693.* (Wed-Mon 3 pm; closed Tues, Thanksgiving, Dec 25) **$$$**

Fun Time Coach USA bus tours. *5857 Agnes, Corpus Christi (78406). Phone 361/289-7965. www.coachusa.com.* Casino tours to Louisiana.

Great Texas Coastal Birding Trail. *Phone 512/389-4936. www.tpwd.state.tx.us/birdingtrails/coastal_trail.htm.* Spoonbills and egrets, plovers and terns—Texas is a bird-watcher's paradise, with more species (600-plus) than any other state. Seventy-five percent of these species can be viewed along the Texas Gulf Coast, which explains the location of this spectacular series of trails winding through 43 Texas coastal counties. Divided into three parts—upper, lower, and central—each section of the trail includes 12 to 16 color-coded loops. The Texas Parks & Wildlife Department has drawn up incredibly detailed maps (available at travel centers and chambers of commerce) with information about birds you're likely to see at each location, the best seasons to visit, and food and lodging available in each vicinity. Visitors to the Corpus Christi area can't miss the Mustang Island loop of the trail, which starts with a free ferry ride across the bay to Port Aransas (watch for bottle-nosed dolphins and brown pelicans on the way over) and proceeds south down the island. **FREE**

Heritage Park. *1581 N Chaparral, Corpus Christi (78401). Phone 361/883-0639.* Nine turn-of-the-century houses in this district give visitors a glimpse of high Victorian architecture in Corpus Christi. (Mon-Sat 9 am-5 pm; closed Sun, Thanksgiving, Dec 25) **$$**

Padre Staples Mall. *5488 S Padre Island Dr, Corpus Christi (78401). Phone 361/991-5718.* One of the region's two largest malls, with 1.1 million square feet and 140 shops and services, Padre Staples has tenants that run the gamut from anchor stores Dillard's, JCPenney, Foley's, and Bealls to national chains such as Gymboree, Abercrombie and Fitch, and the Gap. Other shops include Limited Express, Motherhood Maternity, Foot Locker, and the Disney Store. The pleasant skylit interior has a tropical feel created by plenty of live plants and Spanish tile accents. The mall's Venetian-style, double-decker carousel is a popular feature, attracting more than a million visitors a year. Also a highlight, the mall—which is independently owned and operated—hosts special and seasonal events in its center court, ranging from the Girl Scout Cookie Celebrity Stackoff to visits from the Easter Bunny and Santa. A food court offers snacks and meals. (Mon-Sat 10 am-9 pm, Sun noon-6 pm; closed Thanksgiving, Dec 25)

South Texas Institute for the Arts. *1902 N Shoreline Blvd, Corpus Christi (78401). Phone 361/825-3500. www.stia.org.* Contains the Art Museum of South Texas, Creative Arts Center, and Center for Hispanic Arts. Building designed by Philip Johnson; permanent and changing exhibits. Free admission Thurs. (Tues-Sat 10 am-5 pm, Sun from 1 pm; closed holidays) **$**

⭐ **Texas State Aquarium.** *Corpus Christi Beach, 2710 N Shore Line Blvd, Corpus Christi (78402). Phone 361/881-1200; toll-free 800/477-4853. www.texas stateaquarium.org.* Ten major indoor and outdoor exhibit areas focus on marine plant and animal life indigenous to the Gulf of Mexico; changing exhibits; approximately 350,000 gallons of saltwater and more than 250 species of sea life. Visitors enter the museum under the signature waterfall, which symbolizes immersion into the study of marine life in the Gulf of Mexico. Throughout the summer, the aquarium offers a SeaCamp for grade school children interested in marine biology. The exhibit, Dolphin Bay, strives to protect dolphins that lack the skills to survive in the wild. (Mon-Sat 9 am-5 pm, Sun 10 am-6 pm; closed Thanksgiving, Dec 25) **$$$**

USS *Lexington* Museum in the Bay. *Corpus Christi Bay, 2914 N Shoreline Blvd, Corpus Christi (78403). Just off State Hwy 181. Phone 361/888-4873; toll-free 800/523-9539. www.usslexington.com.* Popularly known as the "Blue Ghost" or "Lady Lex," the USS *Lexington* was the last World War II Essex Class aircraft carrier to remain in US Naval service. Decommissioned in 1991 and opened to the public in 1992 as a naval aviation museum, the ship, now permanently moored in Corpus Christi Bay, is an awe-inspiring 910 feet (more than three football fields) long and 16 decks high. Tours highlight Lady Lex's eventful past: the ship served the United States longer and set more records than any carrier in the history of naval aviation. Memorabilia and artifacts date from 1943 to 1991 and include 19 vintage aircraft, ranging from an F-14 Tomcat to an SBD-3 Dauntless. Exhibits also display crewready rooms, air operations, captain's and admiral's quarters, the commander's stateroom, the dental clinic, and more. For added entertainment, visit the 44-foot-wide and three-stories-tall Joe Jessel Mega Theater, the only large-format theater aboard a World War II aircraft carrier. (Memorial Day-Labor Day: daily 9 am-6 pm; rest of year: daily 9 am-5 pm; closed Thanksgiving, Dec 25) **$$$**

Special Events

Bayfest. *1517 N Chaparral St, Corpus Christi (78401). Phone 361/887-0868. www.bayfesttexas.com.* Six blocks downtown closed to private vehicles; shuttle buses and trains. International foods, arts and crafts, entertainment. Late Sept. **$$**

Bay Jammin' Concerts. *Cole Park Anderson Amphitheater, 1700 Ocean Dr, Corpus Christi (78404).* Contemporary music. Thurs evenings June-mid-Aug.

Buccaneer Days. *402 S Shoreline Blvd, Corpus Christi (78401). Phone 361/882-3242. www.bucdays.com.* Beauty pageant, parades, rodeo, BBQ challenges, sports events, carnival, music festival, art jamboree, and drama. Early Apr-May.

C-101 C-Sculptures. *501 Tupper Ln, Corpus Christi (78417). Phone 361/289-0111. www.c101.com/cs-sculpting.html.* Sand castle building and sculpting. June.

Harbor Lights Celebration. *Phone 361/985-1555.* Lighting of boats in marina. Lighting of 70-foot tree of lights. Children's parade. Gingerbread and holiday tree village. First weekend in Dec.

Summer Bayfront Concerts. *1700 Ocean Dr, Corpus Christi (78404).* Classic music and show tunes. Thurs evenings in summer.

Texas Jazz Festival. *509 Lawrence St, Corpus Christi (78401). Phone 361/883-4500. www.texasjazz-fest.org.* Concerts. Oct. **FREE**

Velocity Games. *615 N Upper Broadway, Suite 1800, Corpus Christi (78477). In South Cole Park at Oleander Point. Phone 361/888-7500; toll-free 866/946-3922. www.velocitygames.us.* Extreme water sportsters have long made Corpus Christi one of their top destinations. The shallow, warm waters and high wind speeds along this section of the Gulf are perfect for sports like windsurfing and kiteboarding. Capitalizing on this, Velocity Games, one of America's large-scale extreme sports events (an expanded version of the US Open Windsurfing Regatta and Kiteboarding Championships), makes Corpus Christi its home. Held over Memorial Day weekend, the event attracts more than 250 amateur and pro competitors and close to 10,000 spectators. Events include BMX, skateboarding, kiteboarding, and windsurfing with pro exhibitions in BMX, skateboarding, and wakeboarding, plus live music, food, and retail vendors. Memorial Day weekend. **FREE**

Limited-Service Hotels

★ **COMFORT INN.** *3925 S Padre Island Dr, Corpus Christi (78415). Phone 361/225-2500; toll-free 800/228-5150; fax 361/225-3000. www.choicehotels.com.* 68 rooms, 2 story. Complimentary continental breakfast. Check-in 2 pm, check-out noon. High-speed Internet access. Fitness room. Outdoor pool, whirlpool. Business center. **$**

★ ★ **EMBASSY SUITES.** *4337 S Padre Island Dr, Corpus Christi (78411). Phone 361/853-7899; fax 361/851-1310. www.embassysuites.com.* With spacious two-room suites, this typical atrium structure hotel is located in the business and retail district. The hotel is close to a racetrack, art museum and many other attractions. 150 rooms, 3 story, all suites. Pets accepted, some restrictions; fee. Complimentary full breakfast. Check-in 4 pm, check-out noon. High-speed Internet access, wireless Internet access. Restaurant, bar. Fitness room. Indoor pool, whirlpool. Airport transportation available. Business center. **$**

★ ★ **HOLIDAY INN.** *1102 S Shoreline Blvd, Corpus Christi (78401). Phone 361/883-5731; toll-free 800/465-4329; fax 361/883-9079. www.holidayinncorpus.com.* 368 rooms, 7 story. Pets accepted; fee. Check-in 4 pm, check-out noon. Wireless Internet access. Restaurant, two bars. Fitness room. Beach. Indoor pool, whirlpool. Airport transportation available. **$**

★ **LA QUINTA INN.** *5155 I-37 N, Corpus Christi (78408). Phone 361/888-5721; toll-free 800/531-5900; fax 361/888-5401. www.lq.com.* 121 rooms, 2 story. Pets accepted. Complimentary continental breakfast. Check-in 2 pm, check-out noon. Outdoor pool. **$**

★ ★ **RADISSON HOTEL CORPUS CHRISTI BEACH.** *3200 Surfside Blvd, Corpus Christi (78403). Phone 361/883-9700; toll-free 800/333-3333; fax 361/883-1437. www.radisson.com/corpuschristitx.* This property is conveniently located on Corpus Christi Beach next to the USS *Lexington* and Texas State Aquarium. The outdoor pool features a swim-up bar and waterfall. A kite museum is off the lobby. 139 rooms, 7 story. Check-in 4 pm, check-out 11 am.

High-speed Internet access. Two restaurants, bar. Fitness room. Beach. Outdoor pool, children's pool, whirlpool. Business center. **$**

Full-Service Hotels

★ ★ ★ **OMNI CORPUS CHRISTI HOTEL BAYFRONT TOWER.** *900 N Shoreline Blvd, Corpus Christi (78401). Phone 361/887-1600; toll-free 800/843-6664; fax 361/887-6715. www.omnihotels.com.* Visitors can gaze from their private balcony at 131 miles of sand outside this bayfront hotel. More than 24,000 square feet of meeting space attracts groups, but the sailing, swimming, and ocean fishing makes this a great leisure destination as well. 475 rooms, 20 story. Pets accepted, some restricitons; fee. Check-in 3 pm, check-out noon. High-speed Internet access, wireless Internet access. Two restaurants, bar. Fitness room. Indoor pool, outdoor pool, children's pool, whirlpool. Airport transportation available. Business center. **$$**

★ ★ ★ **OMNI CORPUS CHRISTI HOTEL MARINA TOWER.** *707 N Shoreline Blvd, Corpus Christi (78401). Phone 361/887-1600; toll-free 800/843-6664; fax 361/887-6715. www.omnihotels.com.* 346 rooms, 20 story. Pets accepted, some restrictions; fee. Check-in 3 pm, check-out noon. Restaurant, bar. Fitness room. Indoor pool, outdoor pool, whirlpool. Airport transportation available. **$**

Full-Service Resort

★ ★ **HOLIDAY INN.** *15202 Windward Dr, Corpus Christi (78418). Phone 361/949-8041; toll-free 888/949-8041; fax 361/949-9139. www.sunspreeresorts.com.* 149 rooms, 6 story. Check-in 4 pm, check-out 11 am. Restaurant, bar. Fitness room. Beach. Outdoor pool, children's pool, whirlpool. **$**

Restaurants

★ **CITY DINER AND OYSTER BAR.** *622 N Water St, Corpus Christi (78401). Phone 361/883-1643; fax 361/883-7063.* Seafood, steak menu. Lunch, dinner. Bar. Children's menu. Casual attire. **$$**

★ **WATER STREET OYSTER BAR.** *309 N Water St, Corpus Christi (78401). Phone 361/881-9448; fax 361/888-7783. www.waterstreetco.com.* High ceilings, oak furniture. Seafood menu. Lunch, dinner, brunch. Bar. Children's menu. Casual attire. Outdoor seating. **$$**

Corsicana (B-8)

See also Athens, Dallas, Ennis, Hillsboro

Population 24,485
Elevation 411 ft
Area Code 903
Zip 75110
Information Corsicana Area Chamber of Commerce, 120 N 12th St; phone 903/874-4731
Web Site www.corsicana.org

While drilling for fresh water in 1894, citizens of Corsicana were surprised to strike oil instead. With that discovery, one of the first commercial wells west of the Mississippi was dug. This site has now been preserved as Petroleum Park, located on 12th Street in town. Mobil Oil had its beginnings in Corsicana as Magnolia Oil with the construction of the first oil refinery in Texas in 1897. This refinery was also the first of its kind in the West. The rotary drill bit now in universal use was developed by a Corsicanan.

Industries include oil field machinery, textiles, clothing, and food products. Cotton and small grains are grown in the rich blackland of the area, and beef cattle are another important industry.

What to See and Do

Cook Center. *3100 W Collin St, Corsicana. Adjacent to Navarro College. Phone toll-free 800/988-5317.* Houses 60-foot domed planetarium, the largest in Texas; museum; indoor and outdoor fossil fuel exhibits. Movie and laser shows (fee). (Mon-Fri; closed holidays) **$$**

Navarro Mills Lake. *1175 Farm Rd 667, Corsicana (76679). 20 miles SW on Hwy 31. Phone 254/578-1431; toll-free 800/284-2267. www.swf-wc.usace.army.mil/navarro.* Swimming, water-skiing, fishing, boating (ramps); nature trail, picnicking, playgrounds, tent and trailer sites (hook-ups, dump station; fee), shower facilities. Camping reservations accepted nine days in advance. (Daily) **$$**

Pioneer Village. *912 W Park Ave, Corsicana. Phone 903/654-4846.* Seventeen restored buildings, including house, store, blacksmith shop, trading post, old barn, general shed, tack shed, children's playhouse, gristmill, jail cell, carriage house with antique vehicles, museums; pre-Civil War documents. (Mon-Sat 10 am-5 pm, Sun noon-5 pm; closed holidays) **$$**

Robert S. Reading Indian Artifact Collection. *Navarro College, 3206 W 7th Ave, Corsicana (75110). 3 miles W on Hwy 31. Phone 903/874-6501.* One of the largest collections of arrow points (47,000-54,000) and artifacts in the Southwest. Tours (by appointment). (Mon-Fri; closed holidays) **FREE**

Crockett (B-9)

See also Huntsville, Lufkin, Palestine

Population 7,141
Elevation 366 ft
Area Code 936
Information Houston County Chamber of Commerce, 1100 Edmiston Dr, PO Box 307; phone 936/544-2359 or toll-free 888/269-2359
Web Site www.crockett.org

Incorporated as the seat of Houston County on December 29, 1837, Crockett is one of the oldest towns in Texas. The town site was donated by A. E. Gossett, a veteran of the Battle of San Jacinto; he named the town in honor of Davy Crockett and the county in honor of Sam Houston. There are historic structures in town and a spring where Davy Crockett is said to have camped on the way to the Alamo.

The 161,478-acre Davy Crockett National Forest (see LUFKIN) lies 6 miles to the east. The ranger station for the Neches Ranger District is in Crockett.

What to See and Do

Mission Tejas State Historical Park. *Hwy 21 and Park Rd 44, Crockett (75844). 22 miles NE via Hwy 21 near Weches, enter on Park Rd 44. Located adjacent to the Davy Crockett National Forest. Phone 936/687-2394.* Named for Mission San Francisco de los Tejas, the first Spanish mission in Texas. Mission commemorative building; log house (1828-1838). Lake fishing; hiking and nature trails, picnicking, playground, tent and trailer sites (hook-ups, showers). (Daily) **$$**

Monroe-Crook House. *707 E Houston, Crockett. Phone 936/544-5820.* (1854) Greek Revival house built by the great-nephew of James Monroe. (Wed, Sat-Sun) **$**

Special Events

Crockett Heritage Festival. *Phone 936/544-2359.* Military reenactments, costumed characters. Last weekend in Oct.

Grapeland Peanut Festival. *Phone 936/544-2359.* Second weekend in Oct.

World's Champion Fiddlers' Festival. *1100 Edmiston Dr, Crockett (75835). Phone 936/544-2359.* Second weekend in June.

Dalhart (E-3)

See also Amarillo

Population 7,237
Elevation 3,985 ft
Area Code 806
Zip 79022
Information Chamber of Commerce, 102 E 7th St, PO Box 967; phone 806/249-5646
Web Site www.dalhart.org

Special Event

XIT Rodeo & Reunion. *Phone 806/249-5646.* DRCA rodeo. 5K "Empty Saddle" run, parade, free barbecue, pony express races, tractor pull, fiddlers contest, arts and crafts, dances, antique car show. Early Aug.

Limited-Service Hotel

★ **DAYS INN.** *701 Liberal St, Dalhart (79022). Phone 806/244-5246; toll-free 800/329-7466; fax 806/244-0805. www.daysinn.com.* 42 rooms, 2 story. Pets accepted. Complimentary continental breakfast. Check-in 3 pm, check-out 11 am. Fitness room. Indoor pool, whirlpool. **$**

Dallas (A-8)

See also Arlington-Grand Prairie, Cleburne, Corsicana, Dallas/Fort Worth Airport Area, Denton, Ennis, Greenville, Hillsboro, McKinney

Founded 1841
Population 1,188,580
Elevation 468 ft
Area Code 214 and 972

Information Dallas Convention & Visitors Bureau, 325 N St. Paul St, Suite 2000, 75201; phone 214/571-1000
Web Site www.dallascvb.com
Suburbs Arlington-Grand Prairie, Denton, Ennis, Fort Worth, Greenville, McKinney. (See individual alphabetical listings.)

The city of Dallas, the Southwest's largest business center, is also one of the nation's leading fashion centers. A variety of businesses and industries make their homes in Dallas, primarily those involved in oil, aerospace, and insurance. Far from the typical image of a Texas city, Dallas is a well-dressed, sophisticated city that tends toward formality. A major convention city, Dallas is accustomed to showing visitors a good time and is well equipped to do so.

The city originated with the establishment of John Neely Bryan's trading post on the Upper Trinity River in 1841. Two years later, the town was named Dallas, after one of several men by that name—no one is quite sure which. By the mid-1870s, Dallas had become a thriving business town, with a cosmopolitan air unique to the region.

The cultivation of Dallas's urbane cultural persona began in 1855 with the arrival of French, Swiss, and Belgian settlers looking to build a Utopian colony. Among them were scientists, artists, writers, naturalists, and musicians. The colony was a failure, but the nucleus of culture remained in the heart of this young community on the frontier. Today ballet, symphony, opera, and theater are still enjoyed in Dallas, as are numerous museums and exhibitions.

Additional Visitor Information

For additional accommodations, see DALLAS/FORT WORTH AIRPORT AREA, which follows DALLAS.

For further information contact the Dallas Convention & Visitors Bureau, 1201 Elm St, Suite 2000, 75270; phone 214/571-1000; the visitor information center, North Park Center; or the visitor information center at West End Market Place, 603 Munger.

Public Transportation.

Buses (Dallas Area Rapid Transit), phone 214/979-1111.

What to See and Do

African American Museum. *Fair Park, 3536 Grand Ave, Dallas (75210). Phone 214/565-9026. www.aamdallas.org.* This magnificent building of ivory-hued stone houses a library, research center, and numerous permanent and visiting exhibits. (Tues-Fri noon-5 pm, Sat from 10 am, Sun from 1 pm; closed holidays) **FREE**

Angelika Film Center and Café. *5321 E Mockingbird Ln, Dallas (75206). Phone 214/841-4700. www.angelikafilmcenter.com/dallas.* If your taste in movies leans toward the avant-garde, you'll want to be seated in one of the Angelika's eight theaters when the lights go dim. Its wall-to-wall screens showcase some of the most talked-about foreign, independent, and specialty films in current release. A café and lounge draw a hip crowd to the lobby of this stylish cinema, located in a trendy entertainment district with other restaurants and shops. (Box office opens Mon-Thurs 10 am-midnight, Fri-Sat 10 am-2 am; closed Sun) **$$**

Biblical Arts Center. *7500 Park Ln, Dallas (75225). Park Ln at Boedeker; 1 block W of Central Expy (Hwy 75). Phone 214/691-4661. www.biblicalarts.org.* The facility features early Christian-era architecture; the museum/gallery areas display biblical art. A life-size replica of the Garden Tomb of Christ is located in the Atrium Courtyard. A highlight is the light and sound presentation of the 124-by-20-foot oil painting "Miracle at Pentacost" featuring more than 200 biblical figures (fee). (Tues-Sat 10 am-5 pm, Sun 1-5 pm; June-Aug, daily; closed holidays) **FREE**

Cedar Hill State Park. *1570 FM 1382, Cedar Hill (75104). Phone 972/291-3900. www.tpwd.state.tx.us/park/cedarhil.* Just a short drive southwest of Dallas, escape the city and pursue your outdoor activity of choice at this 1,826-acre urban nature preserve on the Joe Pool Reservoir. In these cedar-covered hills, the park offers hiking, mountain biking, boating, fishing, swimming, camping, bird-watching, and more. At the Penn Farm Agricultural History Center, learn how hardworking Texas farmers cultivated the land from the mid-1800s to the mid-1900s. (Daily 8 am-10 pm) **$**

Coach USA bus tours. *710 E Davis St, Grand Prairie (75050). Phone 972/263-0294; toll-free 800/256-4723. www.coachusa.com.* Daylong sightseeing tours to area casinos. **$$$$**

Conspiracy Museum. *110 S Market St, Dallas (75202). Phone 214/741-3040.* This museum features displays, films, and old newspaper articles about the assassinations of famous politicians, including John F. Kennedy Jr. and his brother Robert. (Daily 10 am-6 pm) **$$**

Dallas Arboretum Gardens. *8525 Garland Rd, Dallas (75218). On White Rock Lake. Phone 214/515-6500. www.dallasarboretum.org.* Several themed gardens situated on 66 acres, including a trial garden for research. Featured areas include the Jonsson Color Garden, the Palmer Fern Dell, the Sunken Gardens, and the Lay Ornamental Garden. Also on-site are fountains, sculptures, and two historic mansions. Self-guided tours. (Daily 9 am-5 pm; closed holidays) **$$**

Dallas Cowboys (NFL). *Texas Stadium, 2401 E Airport Fwy, Irving (75062). Phone 972/785-5000 (tickets). www.dallascowboys.com.* Professional football team. **$$$$**

Dallas Farmers' Market. *1010 S Pearl St, Dallas (75201). Phone 214/670-5880. www.dallasfarmersmarket.org.* Who doesn't like to bite into produce fresh from the farm? That's just what you can get at the area's largest outdoor market, on 8 1/2 prime acres in the southeast corner of downtown. The spacious facility can accommodate up to 1,000 vendors who sell fruit, vegetables, meats, specialty items, and flowers grown in Texas and elsewhere. You can also find pottery, furniture, and handcrafted jewelry at the International Fair section of the market, or sign up for a cooking class with some of the best chefs in Dallas. (Daily 6 am-6 pm; closed Jan 1, Thanksgiving, Dec 25) **FREE**

Dallas Galleria. *13350 N Dallas Pkwy, Dallas (75240). Phone 972/702-7100. www.dallasgalleria.com.* This handsome multilevel mall makes shopping an event all its own, as befits this clothes-minded city. The store directory reads like a Who's Who list for retail: Cartier, Versace, Gucci, Louis Vuitton, Macy's, Nordstrom, Saks Fifth Avenue, and Tiffany & Co., to name a few. In all, nearly 200 stores will tempt you with the latest fashions and trendiest merchandise. Also, you can dine in any of 28 restaurants and food outlets, or go gliding on the ice. (Mon-Sat 10 am-9 pm, Sun noon-6 pm; closed Thanksgiving, Dec 25) **FREE**

Dallas Market Center Complex. *2100 N Stemmons Frwy, Dallas (75207). Phone 214/655-6100. www.dallasmarketcenter.com.* The world's largest wholesale merchandise mart consists of the World Trade Center, Trade Mart, Market Hall, International Apparel Mart-Dallas, and International Menswear Mart-Dallas. Tours by appointment (fee).

Dallas Mavericks (NBA). *American Airlines Center, 2500 Victory Ave, Dallas (75219). Phone 214/747-6287. www.nba.com/mavericks.* This professional basketball team is owned by the flamboyant Mark Cuban. **$$$$**

Dallas Museum of Art. *1717 N Harwood St, Dallas (75201). Phone 214/922-1200. www.dm-art.org.* Paintings by such masters as Degas, Monet, Renoir, and van Gogh are among the 22,000 pieces of artwork in this museum's permanent collection, with about 3,500 on display at any given time. Especially noteworthy are its African, Asian, and Pacific collections, particularly objects from Africa and Indonesia, such as a rare Kongo power figure and an 11th-century bronze sculpture of the Hindu god Shiva Nataraja. Other galleries feature European, American, and contemporary art. For a breath of fresh air, stroll through the museum's sculpture garden. Free admission the first Tues of the month. (Tues-Wed, Fri-Sun 11 am-5 pm; Thurs to 9 pm; closed Jan 1, Thanksgiving, Dec 25) **$$**

Dallas Stars (NHL). *2601 Avenue of the Stars, Frisco (75034). Phone 214/467-8277. www.dallasstars.com.* Team plays at Dr. Pepper StarCenters in Duncanville, Euless, FRisco, Plano, Valley Ranch, and Grapevine Mills. **$$$$**

Dallas Symphony Orchestra. *Morton H. Meyerson Symphony Center, 2301 Flora St, Dallas (75201). Phone 214/692-0203. www.dallassymphony.com.* Classical and pops programs; also pop, jazz, and country artists. (Sept-May) **$$$$**

Dallas Theater Center. *3636 Turtle Creek Blvd, Dallas (75219). Phone 214/522-8499. www.dallastheater center.com.* (1959) Professional theater, occupies two performing spaces. The building at 3636 Turtle Creek Blvd, designed by Frank Lloyd Wright, houses the Kalita Humphreys Theater (approximately 500 seats); at 2401 Flora St is the Arts District Theater, with flexible seating and staging arrangements. (Sept-May, Tues-Sun) **$$$$**

Dallas Zoo. *650 E S.R.L. Thornton Frwy, Dallas (75203). S on I-35, Marsalis exit. Phone 214/670-5656. www.dallas-zoo.org.* More than 1,400 mammals, reptiles, and birds on 85 landscaped acres. The 25-acre "Wilds of Africa" exhibit features a 1-mile monorail ride, nature trail, African Plaza, chimpanzee forest, and gorilla conservation research center; animals roam freely through six naturalistic habitats. Parking fee. (Daily 9 am-5 pm; closed Dec 25) **$$$**

Deep Ellum. *West of Hwy 75, mainly on Elm, Main, and Commerce sts. www.ondaweb.com/deep_ellum.* If you want to get a little freaky, this 170-acre bohemian district fits the bill. In this large cluster of renovated warehouses just west of downtown, popular restaurants do business right alongside funky live-music clubs, eclectic shops, and even tattoo parlors. The artsy scene heats up at night, and the later it gets, the younger the crowd and the more bizarre the people-watching: spiky hair dyed red or green and the like.

Fair Park Dallas. *1300 Robert B. Cullum Blvd, Dallas (75210). Phone 214/670-8400. www.dallasmetroplex.org.* Comprising 277 landscaped acres with Art Deco buildings and numerous entertainment and cultural facilities. Site of the annual state fair (see SPECIAL EVENTS), one of the world's largest expositions. (Daily; hours vary for different events) Here are

Age of Steam Railroad Museum. *Fair Park, 3800 Parry Ave, Dallas (75226). Phone 214/428-0101. www.dallasrailwaymuseum.com.* A collection of steam locomotives and passenger cars, including a locomotive weighing 1.2 million pounds and the electric locomotive that pulled Robert F. Kennedy's funeral train. (Wed-Sun 10 am-5 pm, weather permitting; closed holidays) **$**

Dallas Museum of Natural History. *3535 Grand Ave, Dallas (75210). Phone 214/421-3466. www.dallasdino.org.* Fifty habitat groups exhibit diverse plant and animal life of Texas. Fossil hall exhibits animals of prehistoric Texas, including a reconstructed tenontosaurus. Changing exhibits. (Mon-Sat 10 am-5 pm, Sun noon-5 pm; closed Jan 1, Thanksgiving, Dec 25) **$$**

Dallas World Aquarium. *1801 N Griffin St, Dallas (75202). Phone 214/720-2224. www.dwazoo.com.* More than 375 species of marine, freshwater, and tropical fish, amphibians, and reptiles. (Daily 10 am-5 pm; closed Thanksgiving, Dec 25) **$$$**

Hall of State. *3939 Grand Ave, Dallas. Phone 214/ 421-0281. www.hallofstate.com.* Historic landmark; fine example of American Art Deco architecture. Murals, statuary, and changing exhibits depict the history of Texas. (Tues-Sat 9 am-5 pm, Sun from 1 pm; closed Jan 1, Dec 25) Research Center located in East Texas Room; lower floor houses Dallas Historical Society offices. **FREE**

Music Hall. *909 1st Ave, Dallas. At Parry. Phone 214/565-1116.* Performances by the Dallas Opera;

Dallas Summer Musicals and concerts. (See SPECIAL EVENTS)

SBC Cotton Bowl. *Fair Park, Dallas (75210). Phone 214/634-7525. www.sbccottonbowl.com.* Scene of the college football classic each January 1 and other special events throughout the year.

The Science Place. *1318 2nd Ave, Dallas (75210). Phone 214/428-5555. www.scienceplace.org.* Hands-on exhibits on energy, chemistry, physics, medical sciences, growth, and development; "Kids Place" exhibit; IMAX Theatre. (Late May-mid-Aug: Mon-Sat 9:30 am-5:30 pm, Sun 11:30 am-5:30 pm; rest of the year: Tues-Fri 9:30 am-4:30 pm, Sat to 5:30 pm, Sun 11:30 am-5:30 pm) Planetarium shows (daily). **$$$**

Texas Discovery Gardens. *3601 Martin Luther King Jr. Blvd, Dallas (75210). Phone 214/428-7476. www.texasdiscoverygardens.org.* Gardens; tropical conservatory; Xeriscape Garden; display with Braille markers. (Daily; closed Jan 1, Thanksgiving, Dec 24-25) **$**

Grapevine Lake. *110 Fairway Dr, Dallas (76051). Via Hwy 26. Phone 817/481-4541. www.swf-wc.usace.army.mil/grapevine.* Swimming, water-skiing, fishing, boating (ramps, rentals); hiking, bicycle and bridle trails, picnicking, camping (tent and trailer sites; hook-ups, dump station). Fee for camping, some recreation areas. (Daily; hours vary; some areas close at sunset or 9 pm)

John F. Kennedy Memorial Plaza. *Houston and Market sts, Dallas.* A 50-foot monument, designed by Philip Johnson, was erected in 1969 and is situated 200 yards from the spot where the president was assassinated. (Daily, 24 hours) **FREE**

McKinney Avenue Transit Authority. *3153 Oak Grove, Dallas (75204). Phone 214/855-0006. www.mata.org.* Four restored vintage electric trolley cars operate over a 3-mile route, mainly along McKinney Ave, which connects central Dallas (beginning at Ross Ave and St. Paul St) with McKinney Ave's popular restaurants, nightclubs, and shops. Some tracks date back 100 years to Dallas's original trolley system. (Daily) **FREE**

Meadows Museum. *5900 Bishop Blvd, Dallas (75275). Phone 214/768-2516. meadowsmuseum.smu.edu.* El Greco. Goya. Picasso. Velazquez. At this 66,000-square-foot art haven on the campus of Southern Methodist University, focus on one of the largest and most comprehensive collections of Spanish

artwork beyond Spain's borders. You'll be moved by Baroque canvases, Impressionist landscapes, modernist abstractions, Renaissance altarpieces, rococo oil sketches, and more in eye-pleasing exhibits that span a thousand years of Spanish heritage. The collection includes more than 750 pieces, with about 100 usually on display. (Wed-Sun, Mon-Tues by appintment only; closed holidays) **FREE**

Meadows School of the Arts. *Southern Methodist University campus, Bishop and Binkley Blvd. Phone 214/768-2787. www.smu.edu.* Houses Greer Garson Theatre, with classic thrust stage design, Bob Hope and Margo Jones theaters, with university productions; Caruth Auditorium, a 490-seat concert hall with Fisk pipe organ. (Aug-May; some fees). Also Meadows Museum, with the most encyclopedic collection of 15th-20th-century Spanish art in the United States; sculpture garden. (Daily; closed school holidays) **$$$**

NorthPark Center. *1030 Northpark Center, Dallas (75225). Phone 214/361-6345. www.northparkcenter.com.* In this fashion-conscious city, some of the best-dressed locals do their shopping in this pleasant mall in an affluent area. High-end stores such as Brooks Brothers, Coach, Kenneth Cole New York, Lord & Taylor, Neiman-Marcus, and Tiffany & Co. cater to the mall's upscale neighbors. But you'll find a broader range of prices at other stores, including Banana Republic, Dillard's, Foley's, and the Gap. In all, the Center has 120 shops and restaurants. (Mon-Sat 10 am-9 pm, Sun noon-6 pm; closed Easter, Thanksgiving, Dec 25) **FREE**

Old City Park Museum. *1717 Gano St, Dallas (75215). Phone 214/421-5141. www.oldcitypark.org.* Lovely Victorian homes, turn-of-the-century commercial buildings, a school, and a church are among the 38 historic structures that introduce visitors to how Dallas looked and how its citizens lived between 1840 and 1910. The museum, which also includes a working farm, is spread over 13 green acres just south of downtown. Explore the grounds on your own or take the one-hour guided tour offered each afternoon at 1:30 pm (2:30 pm on Sun). (Tues-Sat 10 am-4 pm, Sun noon-4 pm; Jan-Feb, Aug, Tues-Sun noon-4 pm; closed holidays) **$$**

⭐ **The Sixth Floor Museum at Dealey Plaza.** *411 Elm St, Dallas (75202). Phone 214/747-6660 (recording). www.jfk.org.* President John F. Kennedy was tragically assassinated in Dallas more than 40 years ago, on November 22, 1963, and many people still come to town curious to learn more about that fateful day. In a moving tribute to the fallen leader, this downtown museum helps visitors recall the president's life, death, and legacy through artifacts, historic films, interpretive displays, and photographs. Collectively, it stirs the emotions, as does the site itself—the former Texas School Book Depository, where a sniper's nest and rifle were found on the sixth floor after the horrifying shots rang out. In one of the memory books, record your personal recollections of this shocking day in American history, or simply share your feelings. You won't be alone if you shed a tear or two. (Daily 9 am-6 pm; closed Dec 25) **$$**

Sur La Table. *4527 Travis St, Suite A, Dallas (75205). Phone 214/219-4404. www.surlatable.com.* In the 1970s, Seattle spawned this clearinghouse for hard-to-find kitchen gear, and it soon became known as a source for cookware, small appliances, cutlery, kitchen tools, linens, tableware, gadgets, and specialty foods. Sur La Table has since expanded to include cooking classes (**$$$$**), chef demonstrations, and cookbook author signings, as well as a catalog and online presence. Cooking connoisseurs discover such finds as cool oven mitts, zest graters, copper whisks, onion soup bowls, and inspired TV dinner trays. (Daily 10 am-6 pm; closed holidays)

Texas Rangers (MLB). *1000 Ballpark Way, Arlington (76011). Jct of Hwy 360 and I-30. Phone 817/273-5222. texas.rangers.mlb.com.* Games are played at The Ballpark at Arlington. **$$**

Tour 18 Dallas. *8718 Amen Corner, Flower Mound (75022). Phone 817/430-2000. www.tour18golf.com.* Play some of the most talked-about golf holes in America without having to cart your clubs from coast to coast. All 18 holes at this duffer's dream-come-true simulate some of the great ones throughout the country, such as No. 17 at Sawgrass and No. 1 at Cherry Hill. (Seasonal; closed Dec 25) **$$$$**

Viking Culinary Arts Center. *4531 McKinney Ave, Dallas (75205). Phone 214/526-3942. www.vikingrange.com.* Give your home-cooked meals a hearty flavor boost with cooking classes at this upscale retail store, an affiliate of the Viking Range Corp, manufacturer of high-end kitchen appliances. Learn from staff instructors and guest chefs who heat up ovens in the area's best restaurant kitchens. The daily instruction runs the gamut from soufflé workshops to ethnic weeknight dinners. Some classes are taught lecture-style with demonstrations; others are hands-on, meaning bring your apron. Shop for utensils, cookware, and cookbooks after class, or browse the appliance show-

room. (Mon-Fri 10 am-9 pm, Sat to 6 pm, Sun from noon; closed Thanksgiving, Dec 25) **$$$$**

White Rock Lake Park. *8100 Doran Cir, Dallas (75218). 5 miles NE on Garland Rd. Phone 214/670-4100. www.dallascityhall.org.* For a good workout, join the locals who keep their bodies buff by running, walking, or biking the scenic 9.33-mile trail that wraps around this in-town lake on the city's east side. Or just kick back and hang out, sunning on the lawn, hooking a fish or two, or raiding your picnic basket in one of the shady picnic areas. Playgrounds keep the kids smiling. (Daily) **FREE**

Special Events

Dallas Boat Show. *Dallas Market Hall, 2200 Stemmons Frwy, Dallas (75220). Phone 469/549-0673. www.dallasboatshow.net.* Late Jan-early Feb and mid-July. **$$**

Dallas Opera. *The Music Hall at Fair Park, 909 First Ave, Dallas (75210). Phone 214/443-1000 (tickets). www.dallasopera.org.* Internationally famed opera seasons. Call or visit the opera's Web site for schedule and tickets. Mid-Nov-late Feb. **$$$$**

Dallas Summer Musicals. *Music Hall, Fair Park, 909 First Ave, Dallas (75210). Phone 214/565-1116. www.dallassummermusicals.org.* Featuring Broadway musicals; Tues-Sun. June-early Oct.

EDS Byron Nelson Championship. *4150 N Macarthur Blvd, Irving (75038). Phone 214/742-3896. www.eds.com/byron_nelson/index.shtml.* (See Dallas/Fort Worth Airport Area) **$$$$**

SBC Cotton Bowl Classic. *Fair Park, 3750 Midway Plz, Dallas (75210). Phone 214/634-7525. www.sbccottonbowl.com.* College football's national championship game that was founded in 1937 by J. Curtis Sanford, a wealthy oilman. Usually Jan 1. **$$$$**

Scarborough Faire Renaissance. *2511 FM 66, Waxahachie (75167). 30 miles S on I-35 E, exit 399A. Phone 972/938-1888. www.scarboroughrenfest.com.* Re-creation of a 16th-century English village at market time; entertainment, jousting, crafts, games, food and drink. Eight weekends, mid-Apr-early June. **$$$**

State Fair of Texas. *Fair Park, 3921 Martin Luther King Jr. Blvd, Dallas (75210). Phone 214/565-9931. www.bigtex.com.* Features livestock shows, midway rides, carnival games, craft shows, music performances, and "Big Tex." Sept-Oct. **$$$$**

Limited-Service Hotels

★ ★ **COURTYARD BY MARRIOTT.** *2150 Market Center Blvd, Dallas (75207). Phone 214/653-1166; toll-free 800/321-3211; fax 214/653-1892. www.courtyard.com.* Just off the interstate and conveniently located in Dallas's business district, this budget-friendly hotel is great for both business and leisure travelers. The hotel features wood and marble décor in addition to all the amenities modern travelers expect. 184 rooms, 5 story. Check-in 3 pm, check-out noon. High-speed Internet access, wireless Internet access. Restaurant, bar. Fitness room. Outdoor pool, whirlpool. Airport transportation available. Business center. **$**

★ ★ **COURTYARD BY MARRIOTT.** *2383 Stemmons Trail, Dallas (75220). Phone 214/352-7676; toll-free 800/628-8108; fax 214/352-4914. www.courtyard.com.* 146 rooms, 3 story. Check-in 3 pm, check-out noon. High-speed Internet access, wireless Internet access. Restaurant, bar. Fitness room. Outdoor pool, whirlpool. Business center. **$**

★ ★ **COURTYARD BY MARRIOTT.** *6840 N Dallas Pkwy, Plano (75024). Phone 972/403-0802; fax 972/378-9245. www.courtyard.com.* Designed with the business traveler in mind, this property offers sitting areas, large desks and a convenient location near many major corporations. 153 rooms, 3 story. Check-in 3 pm, check-out noon. Restaurant, bar. Fitness room. Outdoor pool. **$**

★ ★ **DOUBLETREE HOTEL.** *4099 Valley View Ln, Dallas (75244). Phone 972/385-9000; fax 972/458-8260. www.doubletree.com.* 290 rooms. Check-in 3 pm, check-out noon. High-speed Internet access. Restaurant, bar. Fitness room. Outdoor pool. Airport transportation available. Business center. **$**

★ ★ **DOUBLETREE HOTEL.** *8250 N Central Expy, Dallas (75206). Phone 214/691-8700; fax 214/706-0187. www.dallascampbellcentre.doubletree.com.* This Hilton chain is minutes north of downtown and across the street from exclusive shopping at North Park Mall. All rooms in the gleaming tower have floor-to-ceiling windows, and some floors boast views of the city skyline. 302 rooms, 21 story. Pets accepted, some restrictions; fee. Check-in 3 pm, check-out 11 am. Restaurant, bar. Fitness room. Tennis. **$**

★ ★ **HILTON GARDEN INN ADDISON.** *4090 Belt Line Rd, Addison (75001). Phone 972/233-8000; toll-free 877/782-9444; fax 972/239-8777. www.hiltongardeninn.com.* 96 rooms, 3 story. Check-in 3 pm, check-out noon. Restaurant, bar. Children's activity center. Fitness room. Outdoor pool. Golf. Business center. **$**

★ ★ **HOLIDAY INN.** *2645 LBJ Fwy, Dallas (75234). Phone 972/243-3363; toll-free 800/465-4329; fax 972/243-6682. www.holiday-inn.com.* With a great location and affordable rates, this hotel is near area restaurants and shopping and offers complimentary shuttle service within 5 miles. With additional amenities for the business traveler, the comfortable accommodations here will suit every kind of guest. 377 rooms, 6 story. Check-in 3 pm, check-out noon. Restaurant, bar. Fitness room. Indoor pool, outdoor pool, whirlpool. **$**

★ ★ **THE MAGNOLIA HOTEL.** *1401 Commerce St, Dallas (75201). Phone 214/915-6500; toll-free 888/915-1110; fax 214/253-0053. www.magnoliahotels.com.* Although it is housed in the historic Magnolia building, topped with a striking Pegasus statue that has become an icon of the city, this hotel surprises guests with an eclectic and modern theme. Located in the heart of downtown, this hotel is near the American Airlines Center—home of the Dallas Mavericks and Stars—and the Dallas Convention Center, not to mention the city's best shopping and dining. 330 rooms, 18 story. Pets accepted; fee. Complimentary continental breakfast. Check-in 3 pm, check-out 11 am. Bar. Fitness room. Whirlpool. **$$**

★ ★ **MARRIOTT SUITES DALLAS MARKET CENTER.** *2493 N Stemmons Fwy, Dallas (75207). Phone 214/905-0050; toll-free 800/627-7468; fax 214/905-0050. www.marriott.com.* 266 rooms, 12 story, all suites. Pets accepted; fee. Check-in 3 pm, check-out noon. High-speed Internet access. Restaurant, bar. Fitness room. Outdoor pool, whirlpool. Airport transportation available. Business center. **$**

★ ★ **SHERATON SUITES MARKET CENTER.**
2101 N Stemmons Fwy, Dallas (75207). Phone 214/747-3000; toll-free 800/325-3535; fax 214/742-5713. www.starwood.com. French doors and marble baths grace each of this property's suites. The location is convenient for visitors of the nearby convention center or the Dallas Market Center, World Trade Center, and Apparel Mart, all of which are across the street. 251 rooms, 11 story, all suites. Pets accepted; fee. Check-in 3 pm, check-out noon. High-speed Internet access. Restaurant, bar. Fitness room. Indoor pool, outdoor pool, whirlpool. Business center. **$**

🐾 🏋 🛏 🚶

★ ★ **WYNDHAM DALLAS MARKET CENTER.**
2015 Market Center Blvd, Dallas (75207). Phone 214/741-7481; toll-free 800/996-3426; fax 214/747-6191. www.wyndham.com. 228 rooms, 11 story. Check-in 3 pm, check-out noon. High-speed Internet access, wireless Internet access. Restaurant, bar. Fitness room. Outdoor pool. **$**

🏋 🛏

Full-Service Hotels

★ ★ ★ **THE ADOLPHUS.** *1321 Commerce St, Dallas (75202). Phone 214/742-8200; toll-free 800/221-9083; fax 214/651-3588.* Beer baron Adolphus Busch built this luxury property in 1912, and subsequent renovations have kept the downtown jewel sparkling, making it the *grande dame* of Dallas hotels. Through the years, queens, celebrities, and other notables have checked in and enjoyed its baroque splendor, not to mention its plush rooms and suites lavishly decorated with Queen Anne and Chippendale furnishings. The elegant French Room rates as one of the city's best restaurants, with classic French cooking updated for contemporary tastes. The Bistro and Walt Garrison Rodeo Bar and Grill offer less formal dining. Wednesday through Sunday, the hotel serves high tea in the lobby living room. Its central location makes the Adolphus a good choice for business travelers, but its old-world charm sets just the right mood for a romantic getaway. 433 rooms, 21 story. Check-in 3 pm, check-out 1 pm. High-speed Internet access, wireless Internet access. Three restaurants, three bars. Fitness room. Business center. **$$**

🏋 🚶

★ ★ ★ **CROWNE PLAZA.** *14315 Midway Rd, Addison (75001). Phone 972/980-8877; toll-free 800/222-7696; fax 972/991-2740. www.crowneplaza.com.*

Located in the Addison business district outside of Dallas, this property caters to the business traveler. Complimentary shuttle service is provided to the nearby famous Galleria shopping mall. 429 rooms, 4 story. Pets accepted; fee. Restaurant. Fitness room. Outdoor pool, whirlpool. Airport transportation available. Business center. **$$**

🐾 🏋 🛏 🚶

★ ★ ★ **THE FAIRMONT DALLAS.** *1717 N Akard St, Dallas (75201). Phone 214/720-2020; toll-free 800/441-1414; fax 214/720-7405. www.fairmont.com.* Located in the Dallas arts district, this hotel is close to the financial district, cultural activities, and the West End Historic Area. 551 rooms, 25 story. Pets accepted, some restrictions; fee. Check-in 3 pm, check-out noon. High-speed Internet access. Restaurant, two bars. Fitness room. Outdoor pool. Business center. **$$**

🐾 🏋 🛏 🚶

★ ★ ★ **HILTON AT LINCOLN CENTER.** *5410 LBJ Frwy, Dallas (75240). Phone 972/934-8400; fax 972/701-5244. www.hilton.com.* 500 rooms. Check-in 3 pm, check-out noon. High-speed Internet access. Restaurant, bar. Fitness room. Indoor pool, whirlpool. Airport transportation available. Business center. **$$$**

🏋 🛏 🚶

★ ★ ★ **HILTON DALLAS PARK CITIES.** *5954 Luther Ln, Dallas (75225). Phone 214/368-0400; fax 214/369-9571. www.dallasparkcities.hilton.com.* Within walking distance of upscale shopping and easily accessible from downtown Dallas, this immaculate hotel is a solid choice for group events like weddings and business meetings. Upscale furnishings grace the guest rooms, while a rooftop pool and an extensive fitness center are convenient amenities for fitness enthusiasts and families. 224 rooms. Check-in 4 pm, check-out noon. High-speed Internet access. Restaurant, bar. Fitness room. Outdoor pool, whirlpool. **$**

🏋 🛏

🔍 ★ ★ ★ **HOTEL CRESCENT COURT.** *400 Crescent Ct, Dallas (75201). Phone 214/871-3200; fax 214/871-3272.* Located in the fashionable uptown area of Dallas, the recently renovated Hotel Crescent Court is the essence of chic European style. Designed by renowned architect Philip Johnson, the impressive exterior resembles a French chateau with a contemporary twist. Situated within a complex of luxury shops and trendy restaurants, this hotel has one of Dallas's finest addresses. Priceless antiques, artwork, and Louis XIV tapestries define the public spaces, while the guest rooms provide refined shelter. Spiral staircases add romance in the suites, and lovely French doors open out to the well-tended grounds. Little extras, like luxurious linens and warm and attentive service, make the guest experience exceptional. The fitness center and spa are committed to well-being, with state-of-the-art equipment, sensational treatments, and healthy cuisine. Patrons dine on superb New American dishes in the lovely setting of Beau Nash restaurant. This brasserie-style venue is one of the city's most popular restaurants. 220 rooms, 7 story. Pets accepted, some restrictions; fee. Check-in 3 pm, check-out noon. High-speed Internet access, wireless Internet access. Three restaurants, bar. Fitness room (fee), fitness classes available, spa. Outdoor pool, whirlpool. Business center. **$$$**

★ ★ ★ **HOTEL LAWRENCE DALLAS.** *302 S Houston St, Dallas (75202). Phone 214/761-9090; toll-free 877/396-0334; fax 214/761-0740. www.hotellawrence.com.* 118 rooms. Pets accepted, some restrictions; fee. Check-in 3 pm, check-out noon. High-speed Internet access. Restaurant, bar. Airport transportation available. Business center. **$**

★ ★ ★ **HOTEL ZAZA.** *2332 Leonard St, Dallas (75201). Phone 214/468-8399; toll-free 800/597-8399; fax 214/468-8397. www.hotelzaza.com.* This luxury boutique hotel is located in the trendy Uptown district, where many young Dallas professionals live and hang out. Given the neighborhood, the developers gave the hotel a unique look to help attract the stylish crowd. The exterior says French chateau; the interior says hip, hip, hip. Although plenty of nightlife lies within blocks of its front door, you don't have to venture outside for your evening entertainment. Sip cocktails in the Dragonfly bar, a see-and-be-seen kind of place, and then dine at Dragonfly, where celebrated chef Stephan Pyles helped create a savory Mediterranean menu with Asian influences. Come bedtime, get comfy in your spacious guest room with an oversized television, or in one of the individually decorated suites with themes ranging from Bohemian to Out of Africa. 145 rooms, 4 story. Pets accepted; fee. Check-in 3 pm, check-out noon. High-speed Internet access. Restaurant, bar. Fitness room, spa. Outdoor pool, whirlpool. **$$**

★ ★ ★ **HYATT REGENCY DALLAS.** *300 Reunion Blvd, Dallas (75207). Phone 214/651-1234; toll-free 800/633-7313; fax 214/742-8126. www.hyattregencydallas.com.* This hotel is located in the heart of downtown, within walking distance of the Dallas Convention Center. 1,122 rooms, 28 story. Check-in 3 pm, check-out noon. High-speed Internet access, wireless Internet access. Four restaurants, two bars. Fitness room. Outdoor pool, whirlpool. Business center. **$$**

★ ★ ★ **INTERCONTINENTAL HOTEL DALLAS.** *15201 Dallas Pkwy, Addison (75001). Phone 972/386-6000; fax 972/991-6937. www.intercontinental.com.* 549 rooms, 16 story. Check-in 2:30 pm, check-out noon. Restaurant, bar. Fitness room. Indoor pool, whirlpool. Tennis. Business center. **$$$**

★ ★ ★ ★ ★ **THE MANSION ON TURTLE CREEK.** *2821 Turtle Creek Blvd, Dallas (75219). Phone 214/559-2100; fax 214/528-4187.* Situated on almost 5 acres in Dallas's exclusive residential neighborhood, The Mansion on Turtle Creek is only five minutes from the businesses of downtown. Once a private home, this 1920s Italian-Renaissance mansion retains the ambience of a distinguished residence. The hotel welcomes guests to its refined accommodations, where French doors open to private balconies, suites have marble fireplaces, and original works of art adorn the walls. From the business and fitness centers to the salon and outdoor pool, guests are ensured a comfortable stay. The tradition of a gentlemen's club is alive at the bar, where hunting trophies decorate the hunter-green walls, while the Pool Terrace is perfect for light fare in the warm sunshine. No visit to Dallas is complete without reservations at the Restaurant (see), where culinary superstar Dean Fearing crafts sophisticated Southwestern cuisine in a magnificent setting. 143 rooms, 9 story. Pets accepted, some restrictions; fee. Check-in 3 pm, check-out noon. High-speed Internet access, wireless Internet access. Two restaurants, bar. Fitness room, spa. Outdoor pool, whirlpool. Airport transportation available. Business center. **$$$$**

★ ★ ★ **MARRIOTT DALLAS ADDISON QUORUM BY THE GALLERIA.** *14901 Dallas Pkwy, Dallas (75240). Phone 972/661-2800; toll-free 800/811-8664; fax 972/934-1731. www.marriott.com/dalqc.* Visitors to the many local Fortune 500 headquarters flock to this hotel located near the Galleria, which makes it an ideal spot for shoppers as well. On-site facilities and services include a coffee shop, cocktail lounge, and rental car desk, while business-friendly rooms are equipped with work desks, speaker phones, and high-speed Internet access. 548 rooms, 12 story. Check-in 3 pm, check-out 1 pm. High-speed Internet access. Restaurant, bar. Fitness room. Indoor pool, outdoor pool, whirlpool. Tennis. Business center. **$$**

★ ★ ★ **MARRIOTT SOLANA.** *5 Village Cir, Westlake (76262). Phone 817/430-5000; toll-free 800/ 228-9290; fax 817/430-4870. www.marriott.com.* 198 rooms, 7 story. Check-in 3 pm, check-out noon. High-speed Internet access. Restaurant, bar. Fitness room. Outdoor pool, whirlpool. Business center. **$$**

★ ★ ★ **THE MELROSE HOTEL DALLAS.** *3015 Oak Lawn Ave, Dallas (75219). Phone 214/ 521-5151; toll-free 800/635-7673; fax 214/521-2470. www.melrosehotel.com.* When just another chain hotel won't do, consider the inviting Melrose in the Oak Lawn/Turtle Creek area. Built in 1924, the hotel used to attract celebrities with its old-world charm, but guests now tend to be business travelers, people attending meetings, and couples on weekend getaways. No two of its oversized rooms are alike, except for their stylish décor, European marble baths, and a few other amenities, all of which help ensure a comfortable stay. Locals crowd into the cozy Library Bar to sip cocktails (especially the martinis), chat with friends, and listen to relaxing piano music. Many then take a seat in the elegant Landmark Restaurant, where the eclectic menu features fresh, market-select items from around the country. 184 rooms, 8 story. Pets accepted, some restrictions; fee. Check-in 3 pm, check-out noon. High-speed Internet access. Restaurant, bar. Fitness room. **$$**

★ ★ ★ **OMNI DALLAS HOTEL AT PARK WEST.** *1590 LBJ Fwy, Dallas (75234). Phone 972/ 869-4300; toll-free 800/788-6644; fax 972/869-3295. www.omnihotels.com.* 337 rooms, 12 story. Pets accepted, some restrictions; fee. Check-in 3 pm, check-out noon. Restaurant, bar. Fitness room. Outdoor pool, whirlpool. Airport transportation available. Business center. **$$**

★ ★ ★ **RENAISSANCE DALLAS HOTEL.** *2222 N Stemmons Fwy, Dallas (75207). Phone 214/631-2222; toll-free 800/811-8893; fax 214/905-3814. www.*

renaissancehotels.com. A sleek, elliptical-shaped tower with a pink granite façade, this hotel attracts corporate clients visiting the adjacent Dallas Market Center and Apparel Mart or the nearby Texas Stadium and Dallas Convention Center. Dining options include T-Bones Steakhouse and the casual Charisma. 518 rooms, 30 story. Pets accepted, some restrictions; fee. Check-in 3 pm, check-out noon. High-speed Internet access, wireless Internet access. Two restaurants, bar. Fitness room. Outdoor pool, whirlpool. Business center. **$$**

★ ★ ★ **RENAISSANCE RICHARDSON HOTEL.** *900 E Lookout Dr, Richardson (75082). Phone 972/367-2000; fax 972/367-3333. www.renaissance hotels.com.* 336 rooms, 12 story. Check-out noon. Restaurant, bar. Fitness room. Indoor pool, whirlpool. Business center. **$$**

★ ★ ★ **SHERATON DALLAS BROOKHOLLOW HOTEL.** *1241 W Mockingbird Ln, Dallas (75247). Phone 214/630-7000; toll-free 800/442-7547; fax 214/640-9221. www.sheraton.com.* Ideally located just 10 minutes from downtown Dallas, and 30 minutes from Six Flags and Hurricane Harbor, this hotel has something for everyone. 348 rooms, 13 story. Pets accepted, some restrictions; fee. Check-in 3 pm, check-out noon. Restaurant, bar. Fitness room. Outdoor pool. Airport transportation available. **$$**

★ ★ ★ **THE STONELEIGH HOTEL.** *2927 Maple Ave, Dallas (75201). Phone 214/871-7111; fax 214/721-1072.* The European feel of this hotel is evident from the burgundy awning and stone-lion-flanked entrance to the rose-colored walls and floral accents of the guest rooms. Operating since 1924, the property now offers fine continental cuisine in its Seville dining room. 153 rooms, 11 story. Pets accepted; fee. Check-in 3 pm, check-out noon. High-speed Internet access, wireless Internet access. Restaurant, bar. Fitness room. Airport transportation available. Business center. **$**

★ ★ ★ **THE WESTIN CITY CENTER, DALLAS.** *650 N Pearl St, Dallas (75201). Phone 214/979-9000; fax 214/953-1931.* 407 rooms, 16 story. Pets accepted, some restrictions. Check-in 3 pm, check-out noon. High-speed Internet access, wireless Internet access. Restaurant, bar. Fitness room. Business center. **$$**

★ ★ ★ **THE WESTIN GALLERIA DALLAS.**
13340 Dallas Pkwy, Dallas (75240). Phone 972/934-9494; toll-free 800/228-3000; fax 972/450-2979. www.westin.com. Located within the Galleria center, this hotel provides access to more than 200 shops, several restaurants, and entertainment. 432 rooms, 17 story. Check-in 3 pm, check-out 1 pm. High-speed Internet access. Two restaurants, three bars. Fitness room. Outdoor pool. Business center. **$$$**

★ ★ ★ **THE WESTIN PARK CENTRAL.** *12720 Merit Dr, Dallas (75251). Phone 972/385-3000; fax 972/991-4557. www.westin.com.* This atrium lobby hotel is located right at Park Central. It is convenient to downtown Dallas and the airports. 536 rooms, 20 story. Pets accepted, some restrictions. Check-in 3 pm, check-out noon. Restaurant, bar. Fitness room. Outdoor pool, whirlpool. Business center. **$$**

★ ★ ★ **WYNDHAM ANATOLE HOTEL.** *2201 Stemmons Fwy, Dallas (75207). Phone 214/748-1200; toll-free 800/996-3426; fax 214/761-7520. www.wyndham.com.* 1,610 rooms, 27 story. Check-in 3 pm, check-out noon. High-speed Internet access, wireless Internet access. Five restaurants, six bars. Children's activity center. Fitness room (fee), fitness classes available, spa. Two indoor pools, outdoor pool, whirlpool. Tennis. Business center. **$$**

Full-Service Resort

★ ★ ★ **THE WESTIN STONEBRIAR RESORT.** *1549 Legacy Dr, Fresco (75034). Phone 972/668-8000; toll-free 888/627-8441; fax 972/668-8100. www.westin.com/stonebria.* 301 rooms, 10 story. Check-in 3 pm, check-out noon. Restaurant, bar. Children's activity center. Fitness room. Outdoor pool, whirlpool. Golf. Business center. **$$$**

Full-Service Inn

★ ★ ★ **HOTEL ST. GERMAIN.** *2516 Maple Ave, Dallas (75201). Phone 214/871-2516; toll-free 800/683-2516; fax 214/871-0740. www.hotelstgermain.com.* Despite its location in the bustling Uptown district, this intimate boutique hotel offers its guests secluded getaways in grand style. All seven of its suites are richly decorated with turn-of-the-century antiques from France and New Orleans, and each has a work-ing fireplace. Can you get any more romantic? Yes, come nightfall, with a candlelight dinner in a grand dining room that overlooks a New Orleans-style garden courtyard. The hotel serves the French cuisine on antique Limoges china. Before or after dinner, make a toast or two in the Parisian-style champagne bar in the parlor. 7 rooms, 3 story. Pets accepted, some restrictions; fee. Complimentary full breakfast. Check-in 4 pm, check-out noon. Restaurant, bar. **$$$**

Specialty Lodging

The following lodging establishment is approved by Mobil Travel Guide, but due to its unique and individualized nature has not been given a traditional Mobil Star rating. Included in this listing you may find bed-and-breakfasts, limited-service inns, guest ranches, and other unique hotel properties.

COURTYARD ON THE TRAIL. *8045 Forest Trail, Dallas (75238). Phone 214/553-9700 ; fax 214/553-5542. www.courtyardonthetrail.com* 3 rooms. Check-in 3-6 pm, check-out 11 am. **$**

Spa

★ ★ ★ **THE SPA AT THE CRESCENT.** *400 Crescent Ct, Dallas (75201).Phone 214/871-3232; toll-free 800/828-4772. www.crescentcourt.com.* With its stately décor, comprehensive treatment menu, and spacious fitness center, The Spa at The Crescent has earned a loyal following among local denizens in the know. From classic European treatments to therapies hailing from exotic locales, a world of relaxation awaits. Fifteen different massages—including Swedish, deep tissue, reflexology, hot and cool stone, and Thai—and a variety of traditional European kurs entice guests. The thermal mineral kur covers you with a moor mud wrap, soaks you in a mineral-rich bath, and massages you for 30 minutes with a soothing cream. The thalasso kur harnesses the power of seaweed and algae with a wrap, a bath, and a massage, while the Crescent herbal kur begins with a chamomile scrub, followed by an aromatic bath and a massage. Choose from an extensive menu of aromatic baths, including herbal, thalasso, Hungarian kur, anti-cellulite red wine, and aromatherapy mineral.

Body treatments include paraffin dips to hydrate skin, body brushing to exfoliate and moisturize, and skintonic body contouring to reduce cellulite. Four types of body wraps, including a moor mud wrap and an essential oil wrap, eliminate toxins, tone the body, and improve circulation. The wine and honey wrap, available seasonally, employs a combination of wine yeast extract, honey, and organic essential oils, while the natural spirulina wrap uses algae harvested from the lakes of Southern California. To indulge yourself, book a Lady Primrose specialty treatment, available exclusively at The Crescent. The English garden ritual, which includes a sensual bath and a soothing massage, is all about the fragrant scent and the tranquil quality of roses. Lady Primrose's green tea ritual includes a gentle sugar scrub, a detoxifying soak, and a peaceful massage. Ancient Balinese traditions as well as Ayurvedic treatments, such as a shirodhara, are also available. Try a Bali spice ritual that uses a mixture of clove, ginger, and native spices to alleviate muscle aches.

In addition to aromatherapy, vitamin C, and oxygen facials, The Rosewood Skin Institute performs glycolic peels, lymphatic drainage facials, microdermabrasion, and Lam probe treatments, which help improve minor skin conditions.

Restaurants

★ ★ ★ **2900.** *2900 Thomas Ave, Dallas (75204). Phone 214/303-0400.* In Uptown's small but fabulous State-Thomas Historic District, this dark, quiet bistro offers elegant renditions of some ordinary dishes, such as pan-seared Hudson Valley foie gras over black-eyed peas with applewood-smoked bacon and barbecued venison short ribs in a whiskey sauce. Sweet endings include bread pudding with Granny Smith apples and caramel, as well as a menu of ports and cognacs. A thoughtfully prepared wine list adds to the appeal. American menu. Dinner. Closed Sun-Mon. Bar. Casual attire. **$$$**
🄳

★ ★ ★ ★ **ABACUS.** *4511 McKinney Ave, Dallas (75205). Phone 214/559-3111; fax 214/559-3113. www.abacus-restaurant.com.* A lively young crowd gathers at Abacus, a cool, modern space that could easily make the top restaurant designers in the country swoon. To match the stylish room—garnet-red walls, tall floral arrangements, and long, multicolored banquettes, the kitchen, led by chef/owner Ken Rathbun, offers a vibrant selection of contemporary global fare that wildly and successfully incorporates the flavors and cooking styles of the Mediterranean, the Southwest, and the Pacific Rim. The menu is divided into small plates (appetizer-sized dishes), a dazzling selection of sushi and sashimi, and big plates

(entrée-sized dishes). The signature lobster-scallion shooters—small fried lobster dumplings served in sake cups with a red chile and coconut sake sauce—are a head-turning treat. International/Fusion menu. Dinner. Closed Sun; holidays. Bar. Business casual attire. Reservations recommended. Valet parking. **$$$**

★ ★ **ABYSSINIA.** *7015 Greenville Ave, Dallas (75231). Phone 214/691-0033.* Forget the utensils. At this spacious, super-casual African outpost, guests eat with their hands, pinching bites of the rich, flavorful dishes with pieces of thin, spongy bread called injera. Doro wat, or chicken marinated in lemon and garlic and stewed in a textured sauce of onion, ginger, and hot red pepper, and missir wat, a puree of lentils, butter, and spices, are among the most popular offerings. Ethiopian menu. Lunch, dinner, late-night. Bar. Casual attire. Outdoor seating. **$**

★ ★ **ADELMO'S.** *4537 Cole Ave, Dallas (75205). Phone 214/559-0325. www.adelmos.com.* One bite into the amuse dish of pickled, spicy vegetables, and you'll know that flavor treats are in store at this intimate bistro that's perfect for dates and elegant business outings. Lobster-packed black ravioli, pork loin medallions in a caper-mustard sauce, and chocolate-walnut cake in chocolate buttercream with berries and whipped cream typify the kitchen's lavish offerings. Mediterranean menu. Lunch, dinner. Closed Sun; holidays. Bar. **$$$**

★ ★ ★ **AL BIERNAT'S.** *4217 Oak Lawn Ave, Dallas (75219). Phone 214/219-2201. www.albiernats. com.* The privileged Highland Park neighborhood provides the perfect setting for one of Dallas's loveliest steak dinners. A Kobe-style cut with a blackened crust and a ruby interior is the crowning glory, while lobster, lamb chops, à la carte sides, and chocolate bread pudding round out the menu. Patrons delight in a wine list of more than 600 selections, and fine details are found in everything from stemware to delicious breads from Empire Baking Company. Steak menu. Lunch, dinner. Closed holidays. Bar. Free valet parking. **$$$**

★ **AL-AMIR.** *7402 Greenville Ave, Dallas (75231). Phone 214/739-2647. www.alamirdallas.com.* A well-kept North Dallas secret, this dinner spot keeps late hours for night owls in search of Lebanese goodies, including hummus, baba ghanoush, stuffed grape leaves, and savory lamb over a bed of rice-vermicelli. Middle Eastern menu. Dinner, late-night. Closed Mon-Tues. Bar. Casual attire. **$**
🄳

★ ★ **ALI-BABA.** *1905 Greenville Ave, Dallas (75206). Phone 214/823-8235. www.alibabacafe.com.* Authentic to the owners' familial recipes back home in Syria, this small neighborhood hangout resonates with warmth and rich, exotic flavors. Simple dishes such as rice and vermicelli sautéed in olive oil and dashed with saffron, and possibly the best tabbouleh in Texas, are among the devoted clientele's favorites. Middle Eastern menu. Lunch, dinner. Closed Sun-Mon. **$$**

★ ★ **ANTARES.** *300 Reunion Blvd, Dallas (75207). Phone 214/712-7145.* Occupying the sphere serving as a Dallas skyline fixture for more than a quarter century, this restaurant within Reunion Tower offers an incomparable view as a side dish. Worthy of the revolving surroundings are such menu picks as roasted duck quesadillas, baked chicken stuffed with boursin cheese and artichoke hearts, and pistachio-crusted salmon with fennel slaw. American menu. Lunch, dinner, Sun brunch. Bar. Children's menu. Casual attire. **$$**

★ ★ **ARC-EN-CIEL.** *3555 W Walnut St, Dallas (75042). Phone 972/272-2188.* French for "rainbow," Arc-En-Ciel also is known as a place that brings sunshine into the mouths of its faithful following. Long a favorite in Garland, a suburb northeast of Dallas, this Chinese standout brings mobs of diners in daily for dim sum and an appealing balance of specialties, such as steamed cherrystone clams in a pot with chopped onions and fresh jalapeños. Chinese menu. Lunch, dinner. Casual attire. **$$**

★ ★ **ARCODORO/POMODORO.** *2708 Routh St, Dallas (75201). Phone 214/871-1924; fax 214/871-3141. www.arcodoro.com.* Combined sister restaurants unfold within a sprawl of villa rooms that suggest lazy evenings under a Tuscan moon. Beautiful presentations include veal medallions with rosemary and wild mushrooms, baby calamari in black squid sauce over polenta, and ravioli plumped with scallops and shrimp in a creamy pistachio treatment. Italian menu. Lunch, dinner, late-night. Closed Jan 1, Dec 25. Bar. Business casual attire. Reservations recommended. Valet parking. Outdoor seating. **$$**

☿ ★ ★ **AUGUST MOON.** *5340 Wayzata Blvd, Dallas. Phone 972/881-0071; fax 972/881-1904. www.augustmoon.com.* A favorite in the North Dallas/Plano area since the 1980s, August Moon coddles customers with five-flavor shrimp, pad Thai noodles, fish in a basil-lemongrass sauce, mussels baked in their shells, and pork tenderloin in black bean sauce. Nice finds at the buffet include salmon sushi and barbecued chicken. Chinese menu. Lunch, dinner. Children's menu. **$$**
ⓑ

★ ★ ★ **AURORA.** *4216 Oak Lawn Ave, Dallas (75219). Phone 214/528-9400. www.auroradallas.com.* Mesmerizing work by the gypsy/chef Avner Samuel, who watches from his open kitchen as though a captain on his ship, stuns even the most demanding palates in this jewel box of a restaurant just outside Highland Park. Limoges china, Christofle silver, and a vanilla glow from chandeliers declare utter refinement, as do dishes such as warm egg custard infused with white truffles, diver scallops over chestnut-potato puree, and roasted duck with duck confit and a sweet potato-roasted apple tart. French menu. Dinner. Closed Sun. Bar. Jacket required. Reservations recommended. **$$$**

★ ★ **AVANTI CAFE AT FOUNTAIN PLACE.** *1445 Ross Ave, Dallas (75202). Phone 214/965-0055; fax 214/965-0057. www.avantirestaurants.com.* Tucked into the downtown center called Fountain Place, the sibling to Avanti on McKinney Avenue offers dining with a view of a bubbling waterscape. Compelling choices include herb-crusted calamari, pan-seared sea bass in a champagne-lemon sauce, and white chocolate cheesecake. Italian menu. Lunch, dinner. Closed Sat-Sun. Bar. Casual attire. Outdoor seating. **$$**

★ ★ **AVANTI RISTORANTE.** *2720 McKinney Ave, Dallas (75204). Phone 214/871-4955. www.avantirestaurants.com.* Is it Italian or Mediterranean? Doesn't matter, because Avanti puts rewarding, lively flavors on the plate with gusto. A classic Caesar makes a beautiful opener, followed by veal scallopini with artichokes, escargots in puffed pasty, or lobster tail in a champagne-saffron sauce. Thoughtful servers anticipate everything, making every patron feel extra special. Italian menu. Lunch, dinner, late-night. Bar. Casual attire. **$$$**

★ ★ **AVILA'S MEXICAN RESTAURANT.** *4714 Maple Ave, Dallas (75219). Phone 214/520-2700.* This tiny café on the well-worn restaurant row near Oak Lawn and the Market Center is a hidden gem with a loyal following. An expert blending of Tex-Mex, Old Mexico home cooking, and family recipes results in a rustic tortilla soup, cheese enchiladas blanketed in a poblano-cream sauce, and chicken in a velvety dark mole sauce. Mexican menu. Lunch, dinner. Closed Sun. Bar. Casual attire. **$$**

★ **BARBEC'S.** *8949 Garland Rd, Dallas (75218). Phone 214/321-5597.* A mainstay in the White Rock Lake area, this landmark coffee shop serves breakfast all day, but you can find lunch and dinner here, too. The biscuits are renowned, but the burgers and chicken-fried steak are good bets, too. American menu, diner. Breakfast, lunch, dinner. Children's menu. Casual attire. No credit cards accepted. **$**

★ ★ **BEAU NASH.** *400 Crescent Ct, Dallas (75201). Phone 214/871-3200; fax 214/871-3224.* A deep sense of style makes diners forget that this Crescent Court restaurant is within a hotel. The site of countless power breakfasts and lunches, the Uptown favorite packs in visitors and locals alike with beautiful works like smoked salmon timbale with lemon crème fraiche and caviar and seared tuna with wasabi aioli and pear-jicama salad. The gorgeous marble floors and a stunning painted ceiling create a suitably serene setting for the kitchen's creations. American menu. Breakfast, lunch, Sun brunch. Bar. Children's menu. Business casual attire. Reservations recommended. Valet parking. Outdoor seating. **$$$**

★ ★ **BLUE FISH.** *3519 Greenville Ave, Dallas (75206). Phone 214/824-3474.* One of Dallas's first restaurants to offer a fine list of lovely sake choices, Blue Fish does so with style at its sake bar. Along with the chic sake sampler, consider the Tiger's Eye among many sushi choices, as well as one of the rice bowls or the lush, marinated meat skewers from the wood-fired grill. The colorful setting is hip and friendly, and service is congenial. Japanese, sushi menu. Lunch, dinner, late-night. Bar. Casual attire. **$$**

★ **BREADWINNERS.** *3301 McKinney Ave, Dallas (75204). Phone 214/754-4940; fax 214/754-0721. www.breadwinnerscafe.com.* Breakfast, lunch, dinner. Closed holidays. Children's menu. **$$**

★ ★ **BUGATTI RISTORANTE.** *3802 W NW Hwy, Dallas (75220). Phone 214/350-2470. www.bugattis.net.* Named for an elegant racing machine, this Bachman Lake-area nook offers a quiet dining experience that's never stuffy. Traditional favorites such as lasagna, veal Marsala, and chicken cacciatore please the palate, while slightly trendier works in pizza, salads, and fish keep the menu interesting. Italian menu. Lunch, dinner. Bar. Casual attire. **$$**

★ **BUTCHER SHOP.** *808 Munger Ave, Dallas (75202). Phone 214/720-1032.* Picky about how your steak is cooked? Then do it yourself at this casual, comfortable spot in downtown's West End Historic District. Pick a cut from the monster offerings, which range from a 14-ounce filet to a 28-ounce T-bone, plus prime rib and chicken, and then head over to the grill and get to work. Steak menu. Dinner. Bar. Casual attire. **$$**

★ **CAFE ISTANBUL.** *5450 W Lovers Ln, Ste 222, Dallas (75209). Phone 214/902-0919. www.cafe-istanbul.net.* Sink into the cozy yellow-and-blue surroundings and allow the thoughtful staff to pamper your soul and taste buds at this favorite near University Park. Fresh vegetable kebabs complement pureed eggplant and lamb shank in rich fashion, while chicken breasts surround a filling of pistachios, pine nuts, rice, and red pepper on an ever-evolving menu. Middle Eastern menu. Lunch, dinner. Closed Mon. Bar. Casual attire. Outdoor seating. **$$**

★ **CAFE IZMIR.** *3711 Greenville Ave, Dallas (75206). Phone 214/826-7788; fax 214/824-1224.* Brothers Beau and Ali Nazary delight a small army of nightly regulars with their fresh dishes from a menu that can change on a whim. The tapas-style offerings can range from mixed olives and dolma to kebabs and grilled asparagus, while fixed-price meals typically offer a parade of salads, grilled vegetables, and grilled meats. Nice wine picks come from Greece, Lebanon, Spain, and Chile. Mediterranean menu. Dinner. Closed Dec 25. Casual attire. **$$**

★ ★ **CAFE MADRID.** *4501 Travis St, Dallas (75205). Phone 214/528-1731.* The city's first authentic Spanish restaurant and tapas bar has matured with sophistication. A long list of small plates includes the winning potato omelet with a dollop of garlic-parsley aioli, manchego cheese slices with green apple and grapes, tuna empanadas, and a shiitake tart. A kick-back place with wooden tables, chairs, and floors, Madrid also offers great Spanish wines at good prices. Spanish, tapas menu. Lunch, dinner. Closed Sun. Bar. Casual attire. Outdoor seating. **$$**

★ ★ ★ **CAFE PACIFIC.** *24 Highland Park Village, Dallas (75205). Phone 214/526-1170; fax 214/526-0332.* The pride of the exalted Park Cities has been a Big D favorite since the 1980s, thanks to such joys as the chilled fruits de mer platter with its lump crabmeat, jumbo shrimp, lobster tail, and Blue Point oysters. Halibut with papaya salsa is among the choice grilled selections, and one that's easy to pair with a suitable wine from a list structured by price ranges. The setting is most civilized, due in no small part to a polished, professional staff outfitted in starched white

DALLAS/TEXAS   **51**

jackets. Seafood menu. Lunch, dinner. Closed Sun; holidays. Bar. Valet parking. Outdoor seating. **$$$**

★ ★ ★ **CAPITAL GRILLE.** *500 Crescent Ct, Suite 135, Dallas (75201). Phone 214/303-0500; fax 214/303-0523. www.thecapitalgrille.com.* American menu. Lunch, dinner, late-night. Closed July 4, Thanksgiving, Dec 25. Bar. Business casual attire. Reservations recommended. Valet parking. **$$$**

★ ★ ★ **CARAVELLE.** *400 N Greenville Ave, Richardson (75081). Phone 972/437-6388; fax 972/437-5418.* A beloved haunt in North Dallas, this red-and-pink dining room never fails to please with an expertly executed menu of dishes from varying Chinese regions and Vietnam. Among the customer favorites are salt-crusted prawns in the shell that are wok-fried and served on a lettuce-onion bed with pickled vegetables and a hot pot of hot-and-sour fish soup that can serve a group. Ginger-onion lo mein is a huge hit with vegetarians, and everyone loves the patient, considerate staff. Chinese, Vietnamese menu. Lunch, dinner. **$$$**

★ **CELEBRATION.** *4503 W Lovers Ln, Dallas (75209). Phone 214/351-2456; fax 214/904-1716. www.celebrationrestaurant.com.* American menu. Lunch, dinner. Closed Thanksgiving, Dec 24-25. Bar. Children's menu. **$$**

★ ★ ★ **CHEZ GERARD.** *4444 McKinney Ave, Dallas (75205). Phone 214/522-6865; fax 214/522-0127. www.chezgerardrestaurant.com.* A reigning queen on the haute cuisine scene since 1984, this legendary charmer continues to please the most discerning palates in town. Particularly cozy, with wood floors, windows with lacy curtains, and candlelight, Gerard is all about romance. There's much to love in a dish of foie gras with black currants, veal medallions with wild mushrooms and a port-laced cream sauce, and an elegant wine list that offers unusual finds. French menu. Lunch, dinner. Closed Sun; holidays. Bar. Outdoor seating. **$$**

⊡

★ **CISCO GRILL.** *6630 Snider Plz, Dallas (75205). Phone 214/363-9506.* Tucked into the vintage shopping center known as Snider Plaza, a pearl earring's throw from the campus of Southern Methodist University, this casual café was among the first to bring contemporary dining to the neighborhood. Look for menu items like black bean enchiladas and frilly salads. Southwestern menu. Lunch, dinner. Closed Sun. Casual attire. **$**

★ ★ **CITY CAFÉ.** *5757 W Lovers Ln, Dallas (75209). Phone 214/351-2233; fax 214/351-1936.* The darling of the Miracle Mile on the edge of the Park Cities, City Café soothes weary souls with its intimacy, imparted by lace-curtained windows, antiques, and lavish plates. Lemon-thyme butter dresses a roasted chicken, tomato risotto cushions osso buco in fennel, and tiny quail are packed with shallots and wrapped in bacon. Don't miss the lovely brunch. American menu. Lunch, dinner, Sun brunch. Closed holidays. Bar. Valet parking. Outdoor seating. **$$$**

★ ★ **CIUDAD.** *3888 Oak Lawn, Dallas (75219). Phone 214/219-3141; fax 214/219-3291. www.ciudaddf.com.* Seemingly plucked from a palace in Mexico City's most elegant quarter, this delight from Monica Greene exudes a lush blend of hospitality and style. An oversized martini glass holds a ceviche made with octopus, conch, and prawns with bits of sweet onion, pineapple and vanilla, while the cumin-dusted lamb chops rest atop strips of sautéed fennel next to a masa pudding plump with cheese and ancho chiles. Don't miss the unbelievable margaritas. Mexican menu. Dinner, late-night, Sun brunch. Closed Jan 1, Thanksgiving, Dec 25. Bar. Casual attire. Reservations recommended. Outdoor seating. **$$**

★ **CREMONA BISTRO.** *3136 Routh St, Dallas (75201). Phone 214/871-1115.* Old-fashioned and comforting, this Oak Lawn-area stronghold will outlast all trends in the Dallas dining scene with ease. Devotees count on solid renditions of lasagna, cannelloni, crab claws, shrimp scampi, and manicotti, and they're rewarded with live music on weekends. Italian menu. Lunch, dinner. Casual attire. **$$**

★ **DE TAPAS.** *5100 Belt Line Rd, Dallas (75254). Phone 972/233-8553.* Tapas, those small plates of appetizing Spanish nibbles to be shared with friends over drinks, make up the entire menu at North Dallas hangout. Nearly three dozen selections include tomatoes topped with garlic and parsley, potato omelet, sautéed shrimp, and cheeses and olives. Spanish, tapas menu. Lunch, dinner. Bar. Casual attire. Outdoor seating. **$**

★ ★ ★ **DEL FRISCO'S DOUBLE EAGLE STEAK HOUSE.** *5251 Spring Valley Rd, Dallas (75254). Phone 972/490-9000; fax 972/934-0867.* This majestic steakhouse is decorated with dark mahogany, marble, mirrors and chandeliers. Wait for a table at the beautiful hand-carved bar and listen to the lively, decked-out crowd. Prime beef stars at this beef palace, which knows exactly how to put on a deluxe din-

www.mobiltravelguide.com

ner. Savvy servers make the evening pure pleasure, helpfully guiding diners through sensational choices like sherry-rich mock turtle soup, towers of thick-cut onion rings, silken ribeyes, sumptuous sides of Parmesan-cream spinach, and desserts of four-layer lemon-cream cake. Finer wines and cognacs are popular too. American, steak menu. Dinner. Valet parking. **$$**

★ ★ **DELI NEWS.** *17062 Preston Rd, Ste 100, Dallas (75248). Phone 972/733-3354; fax 972/733-3355.* Way up north near Campbell Road, this Russian outpost delights with beef stroganoff, chicken Kiev, and lamb kebabs, as well as hot pastrami on rye that's baked on-site. Excellent bagels bring in fans by the carloads, and homemade soups such as borscht and matzo ball conjure up happy memories. Don't miss the Red Square omelet, with spinach, sautéed onions, and mushrooms, at breakfast. Deli menu. Breakfast, lunch, dinner. Children's menu. **$$**

★ ★ **DOVIE'S.** *14671 Midway Rd, Dallas (75001). Phone 972/233-9846.* Upscale twists on meat-and-potatoes favorites make this an Addison store to find. Occupying a 1930s rock farmhouse where film star and war hero Audie Murphy once lived, Dovie's brings smiles with rainbow trout, pot roast, and Sunday brunch. American menu. Lunch, dinner, Sun brunch. Closed Mon. Bar. Casual attire. **$$**

★ ★ ★ **DRAGONFLY.** *2332 Leonard St, Dallas (75201). Phone 214/550-9500.* One of Dallas's hippest nightspots is also a mind-boggling restaurant with exotic, urbane design elements. Dishes bearing heavy influences from Japan, Thailand, Vietnam, China, and Morocco resonate with bold flavors and creativity. Among the menu's pleasures are pot stickers stuffed with rock shrimp and laced with lobster butter over a crisp, cool salad of pear slices and watercress; black cod slicked with a miso glaze; and a tagine of fish cooked with preserved lemons and garlic over a pillow of couscous. International/Fusion menu. Breakfast, lunch, dinner, brunch. Bar. Casual attire. **$$$**

★ ★ ★ **EAST WIND.** *2800 Routh St, Dallas (75201). Phone 214/745-5554. www.eastwinddallas.com.* Making a successful transition from Deep Ellum to Uptown, this Vietnamese favorite is what made Dallas gain a deeper appreciation for southeast Asian cuisine. Elegant offerings include beef carpaccio, grilled catfish, and beautifully wrought salads topped with marinated fish and meats. Linger over a glass of wine or the potent, sweet iced coffee. Pan-Asian menu. Lunch, dinner. Bar. Casual attire. **$$$**

★ **EL PASEO MEXICAN RESTAURANT.** *100 W Main St, Azle (76020). Phone 817/444-8811.* Mexican menu. Lunch, dinner. Closed Mon. Casual attire. **$**

★ ★ **FERRARI'S ITALIAN VILLA.** *14831 Midway Rd, Addison (75001). Phone 972/980-9898.* The aromas emanating from wood-burning ovens assure you that you've come to the right place. Pizzas bear thin, crispy crusts and fresh toppings; pastas are homemade and lovingly dressed; and meat dishes get thoughtful herb and seasoning treatments. Desserts here are worth the calories, too. Italian menu. Lunch, dinner. Bar. Children's menu. Casual attire. **$$$**

★ ★ **FERRE RISTORANTE.** *3699 McKinney Ave, Ste 106, Dallas (75204). Phone 214/522-3888.* A hot spot in Uptown's West Village features a beautiful-people scene in the bar area and a dining room where foodies gather over lovely, stylized Italian cuisine. Elegant starters include roasted portobello mushroom slices laden with a lusty basil-laced mascarpone cheese blended with Dungeness crab. Winning entrées include linguine decorated with tender calamari rings, firm rock shrimp, baby clams and plump mussels. Italian menu. Lunch, dinner, Sun brunch. Bar. Casual attire. Outdoor seating. **$$$**

★ ★ ★ ★ **THE FRENCH ROOM.** *1321 Commerce St, Dallas (75202). Phone 214/742-8200; toll-free 800/223-5652; fax 214/651-3588. www.hoteladolphus.com.* Tucked into the elegant Hotel Adolphus, The French Room is a charming spot for delicious and sophisticated Francophile fare. Softly lit and decorated with marble floors, crystal chandeliers, and ceilings painted with dreamlike murals of clouds and angelic cherubs, The French Room is ideal for upscale, intimate dining. Unlike most menus, the one at The French Room does not contain prices; rather, diners are charged per number of courses consumed. Order many, because each is more delectable than the next. As a between-courses treat, you'll receive a refreshing, palate-cleansing scoop of sorbet in a precious frosted glass flower. Couple the sorbet with the fact that entrées arrive cloaked in silver domes, and you might run from The French Room for fear of death by pretension, but don't fret. Despite its attention to classic details, it isn't at all stuffy. French menu. Dinner. Closed Sun-Mon; also first two weeks of July. Bar. Jacket required. Reservations recommended. Valet parking. **$$$**

★ ★ ★ **FUSION.** *4334 Lemmon Ave, Dallas (75219). Phone 214/521-3536. www.fusion-restaurant.com.* Exactly as the name implies, here's a menu that brings together the best of Asian cuisines. Under the guidance of chef John Le, creativity shines in such dishes as black cod and the flash-fried Tex-Mex roll, which is a rotund roll filled with escolar, avocado, onion, chilies, and salsa, within a panko-crusted jacket. A pretty setting makes for a special meal. Pan-Asian menu. Lunch, dinner. Bar. Casual attire. Outdoor seating. **$$$**

★ **GENNIE'S BISHOP GRILL.** *321 N Bishop Ave, Dallas (75208). Phone 214/946-1752.* An Oak Cliff institution in the historic Bishop Arts District, this paragon of home cooking brings hungry hordes in search of fattening solace. Chicken-fried steak, giant yeast rolls, and homemade pies are all noteworthy. American menu. Lunch. Closed Sat-Sun. Children's menu. Casual attire. No credit cards accepted. **$**

○ ★ ★ **GERSHWIN'S.** *8442 Walnut Hill Ln, Dallas (75231). Phone 214/373-7171; fax 214/373-9604. www.gershwinsrestaurant.com.* Enduring in a fickle town, the classic from the 1980s gets splashes of sophistication in candlelight and starched table linens. Rabbit spring rolls with a hoisin sauce make a good starter, and sumptuous osso buco over butternut squash risotto and halibut wrapped in leek ribbons are fine entrées. Smart service and a decent wine list add to Gershwin's appeal. American menu. Lunch, dinner. Closed Sun; holidays. Bar. Children's menu. Valet parking. Outdoor seating. **$$$**

★ ★ **THE GRAPE.** *2808 Greenville Ave, Dallas (75206). Phone 214/828-1981; fax 214/826-2187.* Diners at Dallas's original cava continue to swoon over the elegantly wrought food and thoughtfully prepared wine list as they have since the bistro opened in 1973. The signature mushroom soup remains among the best tastes in town, and a changing menu of dishes includes the likes of baked oysters in a flaky chile crust and a tandoori barbecue pork chop. American menu. Lunch, dinner. **$$$**

★ ★ **THE GREEN ROOM.** *2715 Elm St, Dallas (75226). Phone 214/748-7666. www.thegreenroom.com.* The original upscale café in the music neighborhood called Deep Ellum, the Green Room offers a killer deal in its Feed Me Menu. Each of four courses is the chef's choice, with such delights as king salmon cake in lemon sauce, Caesar salad with spicy crostini, New England striped bass, and apple tart in phyllo with a caramel sauce. Sophistication plus a funky setting equals pure pleasure. Eclectic menu. Dinner.

Closed Jan 1, Thanksgiving, Dec 25. Bar. Casual attire. Reservations recommended. Valet parking. Outdoor seating. **$$$**

★ ★ **HANA JAPANESE.** *14865 Inwood Rd, Dallas (75001). Phone 972/991-8322.* An intriguing mix of Asian cuisines is evidenced in pretty sushi offerings alongside such unusual finds as the Malaysian specialty, beef rending, the Thai tofu stay, and the Chinese Hainanese chicken. Lucky bamboo, pale woods, and paper screens lend a soft, serene spirit. Japanese menu. Lunch, dinner. Closed Sun. Bar. Casual attire. **$$**

★ ★ **HEDARY'S LEBANESE OVEN & GRILL.** *7915 Belt Line Rd, Dallas (75254). Phone 972/233-1080.* A transplant from Fort Worth, this family-owned and -run dining room is typically filled with diners who appreciate flavorful, handmade Lebanese dishes. No can openers or microwaves are found in the kitchen, so you know that the falafel, kibbi, roasted chicken with lemon and onion, hummus, and tabouleh you're eating is the freshest anywhere. Middle Eastern menu. Lunch, dinner. Closed Mon. Bar. Casual attire. **$$**

★ **HENK'S EUROPEAN DELI.** *5811 Blackwell St, Dallas (75231). Phone 214/987-9090.* Henk's hearty, authentic works in Wiener schnitzel and bratwurst will satisfy even the most voracious appetite. The Black Forest cake deserves a good look, too. Good take-out deli offerings should be noted. German, European menu. Breakfast, lunch, dinner. Children's menu. Casual attire. **$$**

○ ★ ★ **HOFSTETTERS SPARGEL CAFE.** *4326 Lovers Ln, Dallas (75225). Phone 214/368-3002; fax 214/368-8766.* As fresh as crisp asparagus—hence the name spargel—this sleek dining room serves inspired cuisine of Germany, Austria, and Switzerland that dispels notions of heavy, ponderous dishes from the old world. Menu brights include cold poached salmon in a creamy dill-mustard sauce and lamb chops in a mint pesto with pan-fried polenta, alongside more traditional fare, such as veal sautéed in a mushroom sauce spiked with Riesling. German menu. Lunch, dinner, brunch. Bar. Children's menu. Casual attire. **$$**

○ ★ **HOLY SMOKES.** *8611 Hillcrest Rd, Dallas (75225). Phone 214/691-7427.* Smoke from hickory wood fires imbues the meats at this upstart with unforgettable, deep flavor. Lush chunks of pulled pork, surprisingly moist turkey breast, sliced brisket, and pork ribs are seductive, as is black bean-corn salad and tart, fried green tomatoes. Try the barbecue

Frito pie, with chopped brisket and jalapeno slices. American, barbecue menu. Lunch, dinner. Bar. Casual attire. **$$**

★ ★ **HONG KONG ROYALE.** *221 W Polk, Richardson (75081). Phone 972/238-8888.* Chinese menu. Lunch, dinner. Casual attire. **$$**

★ ★ **IL SOLE.** *4514 Travis St, Dallas (75205). Phone 214/559-3888.* Years of traveling through Italy, France, and the California wine country went into planning, designing, and crafting the space and menu at this Highland Park favorite. Gorgeous plates of calamari, escargot, and beef carpaccio get treatments varying from red chiles, cilantro, Muscat, and arugula. Seared scallops over a ragu of tender beef rib meat with polenta and broccoli rabe send taste buds soaring. The wine list wows with selections and half-glass options. Italian menu. Dinner. Bar. Casual attire. **$$$**

★ ★ **INDIA PALACE.** *12817 Preston Rd, Dallas (75230). Phone 972/392-0190.* Pretty chandeliers and table linens dress up this place— a quiet, serene den in which to linger over an extensive menu of savory, sometimes spicy Northern Indian offerings. The emphasis is on tandoor items, such as chicken, lamb, and shrimp. Don't pass up the lovely naan and other breads. Indian menu. Lunch, dinner. Children's menu. **$$**

★ ★ **IRIS.** *5405 W Lovers Ln, Dallas (75209). Phone 214/352-2727.* Tucked between home-design shops at Inwood and Lovers, this cool, gray room is adorned with local artists' renderings of the delicate iris flower, and tables are graced by some of the finest food in all of Dallas. Chef Russell Hodges thrills the palate with such pearls as lemon-infused risotto topped with Parmesan shavings and drops of white truffle oil and accompanied by giant prawns and crisp asparagus. Velvety foie gras on toast points gets a dab of huckleberry-port sauce, while roasted rack of lamb shines beneath dollops of fresh mint pureed with apricot chutney and dates. American menu. Dinner. Closed Sun-Mon. Bar. Casual attire. **$$$**

★ ★ **JASMINE.** *4002 Belt Line Rd, Dallas (75001). Phone 972/991-6867.* One of the myriad offerings in Addison's restaurant row, Jasmine offers a view of the bustling retail community from its second-story perch. Favorite menu picks include pork-filled dumplings with a spicy hoisin dipping sauce, a garlic-lavish braised eggplant with fried rice, and ginger-laced stone crab. Chinese menu. Lunch, dinner. Bar. Casual attire. **$$**

★ ★ **JAVIER'S.** *4912 Cole Ave, Dallas (75205). Phone 214/521-4211. www.javiers.net.* A lovely series of elegant hacienda rooms transports well-heeled patrons to a stylish Mexico City setting. Cuisine from the interior ranges from lush black bean soup and red snapper in a sauce of tomatoes and peppers to the silken beef tenderloin stuffed with Chihuahua cheese and daubed with a dark red chile sauce. Mexican menu. Dinner. Closed holidays. Bar. Valet parking. **$$**

★ ★ ★ **JEROBOAM.** *1501 Main St, Dallas (75201). Phone 214/748-7226.* From the creators of the sublime Green Room comes Dallas's most modern French menu. Named for the three-liter wine bottle, this slick urban bistro fills the lobby of the exquisite 1913 Kirby Building in the revitalizing downtown district. Classic French works such as pate, cassoulet, and veal shank pot au feu mingle with new treatments, while newer ideas like skate tickle with creativity. The French wine list is an encyclopedic tour for the oenophile but offers a thoughtful balance of prices and values. American menu. Dinner. Closed Sun. Bar. Casual attire. **$$$**

★ ★ **KALACHANDJI'S.** *5430 Gurley Ave, Dallas (75223). Phone 214/821-1048; fax 214/823-7264. www.kalachandjis.com.* Hidden away in an East Dallas residential quarter, the home of the North Texas Hare Krishnas is a popular destination for its lacto-vegetarian cuisine and unbeatable Indian flavors. The dining courtyard within the ornate palace walls is a great setting in which to enjoy lentils, curries, pakora, jasmine and basmati rices, and myriad masala works. International menu. Lunch, dinner. Closed Mon; Dec 25-Jan1. Casual attire. Outdoor seating. **$**

★ **KEL'S.** *5337 Forest Ln, Dallas (75244). Phone 972/458-7221.* North Dallas's tried-and-true spot for home cooking serves up solid blue-plate specials, such as fried chicken, pork chops, and meatloaf, with sides of fresh veggies. Good breakfasts can be counted on as well. American menu. Breakfast, lunch, dinner. Children's menu. Casual attire. **$**

★ ★ **KIRBY'S STEAKHOUSE.** *3525 Greenville Ave, Dallas (75206). Phone 214/821-2122. www.kirbys steakhouse.com.* A specialty steakhouse since the 1950s, a revamping in the late 1990s breathed new life into this Lower Greenville landmark. Candlelight softens this macho beef arena, where best bets include prime rib and tournedos in béarnaise sauce. American menu. Dinner. Bar. Children's menu. Casual attire. Outdoor seating. **$$$**

★ **KITCHEN AT PRESTON TRAIL.** *17370 Preston Rd, Ste 415, Dallas (75252). Phone 972/818-3400.* Fried chicken, chicken enchiladas, and smoked turkey salad are among the goodies that keep the Kitchen's trendy North Dallas crowd happy. Layer cakes and lemon bars make for sweet endings. American menu. Lunch, dinner. Closed Sat-Sun. Casual attire. Outdoor seating. **$**

★ ★ **LA CALLE DOCE.** *1925 Skillman Ave, Dallas (75206). Phone 214/824-9900; fax 214/823-2983. www.lacalledoce.com.* This family-owned favorite in the Lakewood neighborhood is a lively joint with refurbished cement floors, colorful Mexican pottery, and low lighting. Outstanding efforts from the kitchen include big bowls of fresh ceviche, a seafood soup of shrimp, clam, and mussels, as well as pan-fried whole tilapia and steak Tampiqueña with cheese and avocado. Mexican menu. Lunch, dinner. Outdoor seating. **$$**

★ ★ **LA DUNI LATIN CAFE.** *4620 McKinney Ave, Dallas (75205). Phone 214/520-7300. www.laduni.com.* An enchanting room near Highland Park presents compelling samples of cuisine from Cuba, Central and South America, and Spain. Pounded green plantains make a good base for sampling a selection of mojos (sauces made from roasted peppers, fresh herbs, and marinated veggies), while dishes such as roasted chicken in champagne and oranges sing of simple, gastronomic joy. Count on phenomenal desserts, excellent wine choices, and the best mojitos in Dallas, too. Latin American menu. Lunch, dinner. Closed Mon. Bar. Casual attire. Outdoor seating. **$$**

★ ★ **LA TRATTORIA LOMBARDI.** *2916 N Hall St, Dallas (75204). Phone 214/954-0803; fax 214/954-1821. www.latrattorialombardi.com.* For more than 20 years, this mainstay in the Uptown neighborhood of art galleries and theaters has won over legions of fans with helpful, watchful service and fresh, inventive dishes. Top picks include the warm antipasti dish of crab fingers in garlic butter, osso buco, and tiramisu. Italian menu. Lunch, dinner, Sun brunch. Casual attire. **$$$**

★ ★ ★ **LANDMARK.** *3015 Oak Lawn Ave, Dallas (75219). Phone 214/522-1453; toll-free 800/635-7673; fax 214/521-0702. www.melrosehotel.com.* Within the historic Melrose Hotel in Uptown lies one of the finer culinary experiences to be had in Dallas, thanks to the cuisine genius of chef Doug Brown. Tender braised veal cheeks with truffle-infused mashed potatoes and basil-marinated grilled shrimp with cucumber-mango salad are examples of the seriously seductive dishes typically offered. A seven-course tasting menu, with or without wine pairings, is a must. Elegant, understated décor incorporates vintage marble and new oil paintings, creating a setting ideal for business meetings and romantic rendezvous. American menu. Breakfast, lunch, dinner, late-night, Sun brunch. Bar. Business casual attire. Reservations recommended. Valet parking. **$$$**

★ ★ ★ **LAVENDOU.** *19009 Preston Rd, Suite 200, Dallas (75225). Phone 972/248-1911; fax 972/248-1660. www.lavendou.com.* Cozy and sophisticated, this café done in lavender and yellow comforts with its authentic cuisine and welcoming service. Classic fare includes duck in herbes de Provence and black currants, scallops with black truffles in puff pastry, and Grand Marnier soufflé. The thoughtfully wrought wine list is a plus. French menu. Lunch, dinner. Closed Sun. Bar. Children's menu. Casual attire. Reservations recommended. Outdoor seating. **$$$**

★ ★ **LE RENDEZVOUS.** *5934 Royal Ln, Suite 120, Dallas (75230). Phone 214/739-6206; toll-free www.lerendezvous.net.* Authentic French cuisine and classic treatments have made Le Rendezvous a neighborhood favorite in Preston Hollow in a relatively short time. Onion soup gratinée Lyonnaise and ham quiche with baby spinach salad make a perfect lunch, while sautéed sweetbreads and a dessert of tarte tatin provide the pitch-perfect dinner. French menu. Lunch, dinner. Bar. Casual attire. Outdoor seating. **$$$**

★ **LEONARDO'S.** *9741 Preston Rd, Dallas (75034). Phone 972/335-1244.* A bargain-hunter's delight in Frisco, this humble café makes dishes from scratch and takes pride in its admirable Alfredo sauce. Don't miss the chicken cacciatore and garlic rolls. Italian menu. Lunch, dinner. Closed Sun. Casual attire. **$**

★ ★ ★ **LOCAL.** *2936 Elm St, Dallas (75226). Phone 214/752-7500.* Smart diners know to call well ahead to snag one of the coveted 50 seats inside this modest space in Deep Ellum. A study in understated refinement and a delicious sense of realness, Local is memorable for creativity and utter simplicity in fresh, seasonal fare. Consider starting with a plate of bibb lettuce and arugula topped with slices of pan-fried pear and chunks of Maytag blue cheese, followed by seared, citrus-rubbed salmon over pearly couscous with crunchy sugar snap peas. Don't miss the course of artisan cheeses, nor the smart wine list. American menu. Dinner. Closed Sun-Tues. Casual attire. Reservations recommended. **$$$**

★ ★ **LOLA.** *2917 Fairmount St, Dallas (75201). Phone 214/855-0700; fax 214/871-7202. www.lola4dinner.com.* An exquisite food affair is assured at every seating in this Uptown darling, which should be undertaken by only the most serious foodies. Dishes might include such wonders as Moroccan-influenced yellow corn soup, roasted lamb loin, crab claws atop lemon risotto, and sublime cheese selections. The service is informed and enthusiastic, interesting wines are found in all price categories, and the walls of this tastefully simple 1930s cottage are hung with framed oil paintings. French menu. Dinner. Closed Sun-Mon. Bar. Business casual attire. Reservations recommended. Valet parking. Outdoor seating. **$$$**
🅳

★ **LUCKY'S CAFE.** *3531 Oak Lawn Ave, Dallas (75219). Phone 214/522-3500.* The joyful noise at this sincerely casual diner comes from regulars ranging from well-heeled arts patrons to disheveled partiers, all delighted about sitting down to Mexican egg dishes, pecan French toast, wood-grilled chicken, and homemade apple pie. Diner. Breakfast, lunch, dinner. Bar. Casual attire. **$**

★ ★ **LUNA DE NOCHE.** *7602 N Jupiter Rd, Dallas (75044). Phone 972/414-3616.* Tuna tacos and vegetarian nachos provide contemporary balance to Mexican standards, such as spicy beef enchiladas, nachos, and quesadillas. If you dare, sip an Eclipse—the margarita topped off with raspberry liqueur. The original of a three-location outfit, this one's tucked deep inside a shopping center. Mexican menu. Lunch, dinner, Sat and Mon brunch. Closed Sun. Bar. Casual attire. **$$**

★ ★ **MAGUIRE'S.** *17552 N Dallas Pkwy, Dallas (75287). Phone 972/818-0068; fax 972/818-4572. www.maguiresrestaurant.com.* A sophisticated, clubby setting fits in well with the upscale steakhouse neighbors, but this dining room feels somehow more casual, thanks to comforting dishes such as Thai chicken wings and chicken tortilla soup. Meatloaf gets a special wild mushroom treatment, and chicken enchiladas are bathed in sour cream. A good wine list is a bonus at this stunning restaurant just off the tollway in North Dallas. International menu. Lunch, dinner, Sun brunch. **$$$**

★ **MAI'S.** *4812 Bryan St, Dallas (75204). Phone 214/826-9887.* A small but happy little gem in near east Dallas offers the best in Southeast Asian cuisine with fresh, flavorful presentations. Cool imperial rolls are stuffed with shrimp, chicken, lettuce, crunchy bean sprouts, cilantro, and mint leaves, and gratifying hot pots are filled with tangles of noodles with fresh vegetables, seafood and meat. Asian, Vietnamese menu. Lunch, dinner. Closed Sun. Casual attire. No credit cards accepted. **$**

★ ★ **MAINSTREAM FISH HOUSE.** *11661 Preston Rd, #153, Dallas (75230). Phone 214/739-3474.* You'll be transported to an East Coast fishing village at this Preston Hollow favorite, where families pack in for fresh catches of salmon, trout, catfish, crab, and shrimp, among others. The kitchen does a nice job with sauces, fresh herbs, and seasonings, as well as intriguing side dishes. Mainstream is sometimes noisy, but always fun. Seafood menu. Lunch, dinner. Bar. Casual attire. **$$**

★ **MARGAUX'S.** *2404 Cedar Springs Rd, Dallas (75201). Phone 214/740-1985.* A quiet spot in Uptown, this New Orleans-style café offers the charm and style of the loveliest French Quarter spots in the form of soups, sandwiches, salads, and a few entrées. Mostly a lunch place, it serves dinner on Thursday. Cajun/Creole menu. Lunch. Closed Sat-Sun. Casual attire. **$**

★ ★ **MARIE GABRIELLE.** *2728 N Harwood St, Dallas (75201). Phone 214/871-2097; fax 214/871-2502. www.marie-gabrielle.com.* Perhaps one of the best breakfast-and-lunch spots in the downtown vicinity, this pretty restaurant with a garden setting surprises with a smart mix of dishes ranging from comforting to chic. King Ranch chicken is a hit, as are Thai noodle soup and spring rolls filled with flank steak. American menu. Breakfast, lunch. Closed Sat-Sun. Casual attire. Outdoor seating. **$**

★ ★ **MARIO & ALBERTO.** *12817 Preston Valley Ctr, Suite 425, Dallas (75230). Phone 972/980-7296; fax 972/980-7297.* A brightly colored, simple setting provides the right mood for enjoying delights such as sliced beef with garlic and chilies accompanied by a cheese enchilada in ranchero sauce and a pecan-topped green salad. The shrimp flauta is a great starter, and coconut ice cream provides the perfect finish. Mexican menu. Lunch, dinner. Closed Sun; Jan 1, Thanksgiving, Dec 25. Bar. Children's menu. Casual attire. **$$**

★ **MATTITO'S CAFE MEXICANO.** *3011 Routh St, Dallas (75201). Phone 214/526-8181.* As colorful as a piñata and as lively as a fiesta, this hangout is the most popular Mexican dining spot in Uptown. Patrons, who crowd into booths and tables filling a series of rooms, sip margaritas and tuck into plates of grilled meats and fresh fish, as well as creative versions of enchiladas and tacos. Mexican menu. Lunch, dinner. Bar. Children's menu. Casual attire. **$$**

★ ★ ★ **MAY DRAGON.** *4848 Belt Line Rd, Dallas (75240). Phone 972/392-9998.* Cozy and serene, this longtime winner in North Dallas wins over customers with plum picks, such as Peking duck, kung pao beef, lettuce wraps filled with diced pork, and traditional pupu platters. Chinese menu. Lunch, dinner, late-night. Bar. Casual attire. **$$$**

★ **MECCA.** *10422 Harry Hines Blvd, Dallas (75220). Phone 214/352-0051.* In an aged industrial district, this landmark diner has kept generations of big eaters with happy bellies at breakfast and lunch. A no-nonsense setting is ideal for big plates of eggs, biscuits, and cream gravy and lunches of meatloaf and mashed potatoes. Diner, American menu. Breakfast, lunch. Closed Sun. Casual attire. **$**

★ **MERCADO JUAREZ.** *1901 W Northwest Hwy, Dallas (75220). Phone 972/556-0796.* A bright interior with colorful furnishings, along with a mariachi band, makes this one of the more festive Tex-Mex places around. Fajitas, enchiladas, and nachos are among the favorite menu choices, while the bar posts steady margarita sales. Mexican menu. Lunch, dinner. Casual attire. **$**

★ ★ ★ **THE MERCURY GRILL.** *11909 Preston Rd #1418, Dallas (75206). Phone 972/960-7774; fax 972/960-7988.* One of the most compelling reasons to visit the Preston-Forest shopping area is to taste the work of popular chef Chris Ward, who coddles his admirers with such dishes as crispy duck confit paired with roasted peaches and mousseline potatoes; a warm bread salad made with shaved fresh artichokes, oversized croutons, and herbed cream cheese; and Kobe flank steak with tamarind-infused plums and caramelized scallions. Lovely wines and skillful service make for a prized experience. International menu. Lunch, dinner. Bar. **$$$**

★ ★ **MI COCINA.** *77 Highland Park Village, Dallas (75205). Phone 214/521-6426; fax 214/559-3850.* Expect to find this Park Cities hangout packed to the rafters day and night with singles, couples on dates, and families. They come for the enchiladas in sunset sauce, the fajita salad, platters of grilled vegetables, and the bodacious Lucychanga. Beware of the mambo taxi, the blended margarita-sangria mixture is sweetly dangerous. Mexican menu. Lunch, dinner. **$$**

★ ★ **MIRABELLE.** *17610 Midway Rd, Dallas (75287). Phone 972/733-0202.* Elegance and style set a certain mood at this North Dallas beauty, where orange walls, oil paintings, and silver-plated chargers are as eye-catching as the food is palate-pleasing. Seafood from Hawaii and Central and South America are inviting, but you'll find meats such as duck breast in a molasses-bourbon sauce irresistible. The 6,000-bottle wine cellar is sure to offer a gratifying choice. American menu. Dinner. Closed Mon. Bar. Casual attire. **$$$**

★ ★ **MODO MIO.** *18352 Dallas Pkwy, Dallas (75287). Phone 972/713-9559; fax 972/713-7521.* Far-north Dallas gets its due in fine Italian fare at this well-loved café. Good everyday bets include linguine with clams and garlic and ravioli stuffed with portobello mushrooms, as well as filet mignon with sage, garlic, and tomato-infused butter sauce. A good wine list adds to the appeal. Italian menu. Lunch, dinner. Closed Sun; holidays. **$$$**

★ ★ **MOMO'S ITALIAN.** *9191 Forest, Dallas (75243). Phone 972/234-6800; fax 972/480-8213. www.momosrestaurant.com.* Eight salt and freshwater fish aquariums are featured here. Italian menu. Lunch, dinner. Children's menu. **$$**

★ ★ **MONICA'S ACA Y ALLA.** *2914 Main St, Dallas (75226). Phone 214/748-7140. www.monicas.com.* A favorite in Deep Ellum since the early 1990s, Monica's is a corner of cool—with good food to boot. Regulars adore the Mexican lasagna, packed with chicken, black beans, and corn, as well as the tamale steamed in a banana leaf. Expect loud crowds at night, particularly on Sunday salsa dance nights. Mexican menu. Lunch, dinner. Closed Mon; holidays. **$$**

★ ★ ★ **MORTON'S, THE STEAKHOUSE.** *501 Elm St, Dallas (75202). Phone 214/741-2277; fax 214/748-6360. www.mortons.com.* Situated downtown, Morton's is famous for its animated signature tableside presentation. Patrons select their own cuts of meat at the table. Steak menu. Dinner. Closed holidays. Bar. Valet parking. **$$$**

★ ★ ★ ★ **NANA.** *2201 Stemmons Frwy, Dallas (75207). Phone 214/761-7470; fax 214/761-7819. www.nanarestaurant.com.* American menu. Dinner, late-night. Bar. Business casual attire. Reservations recommended. Valet parking. **$$$**

★ ★ ★ **NANDINA.** *5631 Alta Ave, Dallas (75206). Phone 214/826-6300.* Named for the heavenly (or sacred) bamboo plant, this sleek showplace has Zen inspirations trickling from a stone water wall, slipping around corners of seductive, contemporary dining rooms and sliding along a curved marble sushi bar. The menu offers a tapas-style approach to Asian dining, with choices including sashimi salad, lettuce wraps filled with chicken and cashews, beef strip loin dabbed with citrus and red chile, and Vietnamese shrimp pancake. Pan-Asian menu. Lunch, dinner. Closed Sun. Bar. Casual attire. Outdoor seating. **$$**

★ ★ **NATALIE'S.** *5944 Royal Ln, Dallas (75230). Phone 214/739-0362.* More interesting than the usual tearoom, this Preston Hollow jewel has made a name for itself with an ambitious menu that exceeds expectations. A chicken salad revved up with chutney and sublime homemade pies are among worthy considerations. American, Italian menu. Lunch, dinner. Bar. Casual attire. **$**

★ ★ **NERO'S ITALIAN.** *2104 Greenville Ave, Dallas (75206). Phone 214/826-6376.* There's not a more charming, intimate spot for romantic dinners than this Lower Greenville favorite. Tiny pink lights decorate rooms painted red and hung with ornately framed paintings, and diners cozy up in comfy booths to enjoy the signature bread topped with sun-dried tomato spread and melted mozzarella. Don't miss the red snapper festooned with shrimp and artichoke hearts in lemon, garlic, and butter or the gnocchi in gorgonzola-walnut cream. Italian menu. Breakfast, lunch, dinner, late-night. Casual attire. **$$**

★ ★ ★ **NEWPORT'S SEAFOOD.** *703 McKinney Ave, Dallas (75202). Phone 214/954-0220; fax 214/969-0934.* Tucked into the old Dallas Brewery & Bottling Works, Newport's was one of the first places to open in the West End and to fly in fresh seafood daily. Newport's thrives by spoiling diners with creative dishes and conscientious service. Although the setting is rustic, the restaurant surprises with such productions as ahi tuna sashimi in a sake-soy sauce; sherry-spiked lobster bisque; pasta with calamari, shrimp, Greek olives, herbs, and feta; and reliable renditions of such favorites as filet mignon with broiled lobster. Seafood menu. Lunch, dinner. Closed holidays. Bar. Casual attire. **$$$**

★ ★ ★ **NICK AND SAM'S STEAK AND FISH.** *3008 Maple Ave, Dallas (75201). Phone 214/871-7444; fax 214/871-7663. www.nick-sams.com.* Steeped in a throwback spirit of elegant dinner clubs, this cavernous, sophisticated beef palace in Uptown serves exceptional prime steaks. Spectacular, bone-in ribeyes need no adornment, although the house-made steak sauce and horseradish cream are divine, and the selection

of iced, fresh mollusks is always very good. There's an award-winning wine list as well as several good wines by the glass, which diners may even taste first. American menu. Dinner, late-night. Closed holidays. Bar. Business casual attire. Reservations recommended. Valet parking. **$$$**

★ ★ **OLD SAN FRANCISCO STEAK HOUSE.** *10965 Composite Dr, Dallas (75220). Phone 214/357-0484; fax 214/357-6592. www.osfsteakhouse.com.* One of the older steak joints in town, this kitschy standby evokes images of the gold rush days in its décor. Giant blocks of cheese are served as appetizers with big, hot bread loaves—but you'll want to leave room for the giant hand-cut steaks and fresh seafood. Steak menu. Dinner. Bar. Children's menu. Casual attire. **$$**

★ ★ **OLD WARSAW.** *2610 Maple Ave, Dallas (75201). Phone 214/528-0032; fax 214/871-1965. www.theoldwarsaw.com.* Since 1949, Dallas's first home of haute French-continental cuisine has been the destination for high rollers and those who want to entertain lavishly in a setting seemingly staged by 1940s Hollywood. Strolling violinists, crystal chandeliers, baroque frames on paintings, and formal service pamper, while a menu of lobster crepes, steak tartare, sweetbreads with chestnuts, and chateaubriand fulfill yearnings for fine foods of another time. French menu. Dinner, late-night. Bar. Jacket required. Reservations recommended. Valet parking. **$$$**

★ ★ **PALOMINO.** *500 Crescent Ct #165, Dallas (75201). Phone 214/999-1222; fax 214/999-1115. www.palomino.com.* A showplace within the stylish complex known as the Crescent, this Uptown hangout features a busy bar area and a bustling dining room. Red figures prominently, as does glass, in an energetic setting. The wood-burning oven produces excellent crisp-crusted pizzas, and the open kitchen sends such delights as roasted garlic chicken, butternut risotto, sliced lamb on focaccia, and a chocolate soufflé out to appreciative tables. American menu. Lunch, dinner. Closed holidays. Bar. Children's menu. Casual attire. Reservations recommended. Valet parking. Outdoor seating. **$$**

★ ★ ★ **PAPPAS BROS. STEAKHOUSE.** *10477 Lombardy Ln, Dallas (75220). Phone 214/366-2000; fax 214/366-2222. www.pappasbros.com.* This bustling, beautifully appointed restaurant serves a limited menu of prime aged steaks, salmon, and lobster. With one of the most extensive wine lists in the city (more than 1,500 varieties), the options can be overwhelming. Luckily, the service is attentive and accommodating, and the servers are glad to help. Steak menu. Dinner. Closed Sun. **$$$**

★ ★ **PARIGI.** *3311 Oak Lawn Ave, Dallas (75219). Phone 214/521-0295.* Uptown-Oak Lawn crowds stay happy with lavish cuisine and thoughtful service in the art-filled setting near galleries and the Dallas Theater Center. Rich tapenade on baguette slices is the perfect prelude to a bowl of penne tossed with chopped fresh tomatoes, artichoke hearts, and fresh garlic or chile-dusted diver scallops in sour cream laced with tomato, cilantro, and lemon. American, French, Italian menu. Lunch, dinner, brunch. Bar. Casual attire. Outdoor seating. **$$$**

★ ★ ★ **PARIS VENDOME.** *3699 McKinney Ave Suite 200, Dallas (75204). Phone 469/533-5663.* This upbeat, chic bistro in Uptown's West Village does French with flirty panache. Chef Chris Ward wows his legions of fans by striking a balance between comfort and luxury with coq au vin with spaetzle, a monster prime beef tenderloin burger topped with foie gras, pretty mussels in a broth of white wine and shallots, and steak topped with Roquefort butter with a haystack of frites on the side. French menu. Lunch, dinner. Bar. Casual attire. Outdoor seating. **$$$**

★ ★ **PATRIZIO.** *25 Highland Park Village, Dallas (75205). Phone 214/522-7878; fax 214/443-0714.* Lively clusters of regulars keep the energy at a fever pitch in this Highland Park hangout in the chic shopping enclave called the Village. Baked ziti shares the menu with a good bruschetta, while pasta primavera with grilled vegetables and angel hair pasta with artichokes offer more modern approaches to carbohydrate classics. Italian menu. Lunch, dinner. Closed Jan 1, Thanksgiving, Dec 25. Bar. Valet parking. Outdoor seating. **$$**

★ ★ **PAUL'S PORTERHOUSE.** *10960 Composite Dr, Dallas (75220). Phone 214/357-0279. www.pauls porterhouse.com.* Western bronze sculptures loaned by regular customers are among the sights you'll enjoy while cooling your heels and waiting for a table at this beef palace. Although steak reigns, the menu also offers varied fish dishes as well as game picks, such as rabbit. Seafood, steak menu. Lunch, dinner. Casual attire. **$$**

★ ★ **PIETRO'S.** *5722 Richmond Ave, Dallas (75206). Phone 214/824-6960.* A family operation just off Lower Greenville, this homey spot has been feeding Dallasites comforting plates of filling Italian fare for decades. Start with fried artichoke hearts and calamari, but be sure to leave room for spaghetti carbonara and manicotti stuffed with crabmeat. Italian menu. Dinner. Closed Mon. Bar. Casual attire. **$$**

★ ★ **POPOLOS.** *707 Preston Royal Shopping Ctr, Dallas (75230). Phone 214/692-5497. www.popolos.com.* Intimate and stylish, this Preston Hollow sophisticate pampers diners with pretty Mediterranean works. Look for starters such as bruschetta and goat cheese-cucumber salad, and then follow up with something as inspired as wood-oven pizzas and hickory-grilled steaks. Mediterranean menu. Lunch, dinner. Bar. Casual attire. **$$$**

★ ★ **PRIMO'S.** *3309 McKinney Ave, Dallas (75204). Phone 214/220-0510.* Long an Uptown favorite for fresh, robust Tex-Mex fare, this is the spot you're most likely to see Dallas chefs dining on their time off. The botanas platter combines appetizers such as stuffed jalapeños, nachos, and quesadillas, and rewarding entrée choices include mesquite-grilled carne asada topped with white cheese and poblano chile strips. Tex-Mex menu. Lunch, dinner, late-night. Bar. Casual attire. **$**

★ **PURPLE COW DINER.** *6025 Preston Rd, Dallas (75230). Phone 214/373-0037.* A haven for kids and parents with nerves of steel, this happy, noisy space features a purple train on tracks high on the walls and a décor of cows in purple and pink. Go for the chili-cheese dog, burger topped with pepper cheese, and silky-smooth chocolate shakes. Diner, American menu. Lunch, dinner. Children's menu. Casual attire. **$**

★ ★ ★ **PYRAMID GRILL.** *1717 N Akard, Dallas (75201). Phone 214/720-5249; fax 214/720-5282. www.fairmont.com.* Long a favorite downtown destination within the Fairmont Hotel, this elegant dining room has evolved from a fussy, formal spot to a comfortable, cozy spot with soft lighting, piano music, and a pleasant staff. Lobster bisque lingers from the earlier years, while grilled fish and steak suggest an updating to meet today's tastes. Look for a high-style wine list. American menu. Breakfast, lunch, dinner, Sun brunch. Bar. Children's menu. Business casual attire. Reservations recommended. Valet parking. **$$$**

★ ★ ★ **RESTAURANT AT HOTEL ST. GERMAIN.** *2516 Maple Ave, Dallas (75201). Phone 214/871-2516; fax 214/871-0740. www.hotelstgermain.com.* No dining experience is more sumptuous than the one at this tiny hotel in Uptown. The fixed-price, seven-course affair is had by

reservation only, and it's wise to book one of the petite restaurant's tables well in advance. Diners pre-order from the menu, which changes monthly and typically offers such treasures as the appetizer flan holding wild mushrooms and Gruyere cheese. French menu. Dinner. Closed Sun-Mon; Jan 1, Thanksgiving, Dec 25. Jacket required. Reservations recommended. Valet parking. Outdoor seating. **$$$$**
🅳

★ ★ ★ **RESTAURANT AT THE MANSION ON TURTLE CREEK.** *2821 Turtle Creek Blvd, Dallas (75219). Phone 214/559-2100; toll-free 888/767-3966; fax 214/528-4187. www.mansiononturtlecreek.com.* The Mansion on Turtle Creek has long been known for its spirited Southwestern cuisine. After nearly two decades at the Mansion, chef/owner Dean Fearing's food is as exciting as ever, with up-to-the-minute dishes that brazenly (and brilliantly) combine Southern, Southwestern, and Texas influences, with the occasional nod to Asia and beyond. The restaurant was designed as a Mediterranean-inspired mansion and boasts a classic, old-world charm with its leaded glass windows, carved woodwork, and a bas-relief ceiling. The room is sedate and formal, though comfortable, especially since men are no longer required to wear jackets and ties. Mr. Fearing, a gregarious host, helps make the experience less formal and more fun by making his way around the dining room, taking time to check in with regulars and greet newcomers. Southwestern menu. Lunch, dinner, Sun brunch. Bar. Children's menu. Reservations recommended. Valet parking. **$$$**

★ ★ **ROYAL THAI.** *5500 Greenville Ave, Dallas (75206). Phone 214/691-3555.* A pioneer in Thai dining in Dallas, this Old Town landmark is a pretty spot for relaxing over a series of dishes that bring Southeast Asia to Texas. Try the chicken soup with lime leaves, lemongrass, and basil, as well as the satay, pad Thai noodle dish, and any of the fragrant, herbal-rich curry dishes. Thai menu. Lunch, dinner. Casual attire. **$$**

★ ★ **ROYAL TOKYO.** *17721 Dallas Pkwy, Suite 100, Dallas (75287). Phone 214/368-3304; fax 214/368-0585.* Dallas's original sushi spot has relocated to a northern address in a shopping center but still pleases with skillfully wrought fresh-fish hits. The toro, tuna, yellowtail, and freshwater eel are excellent, as are dishes featuring shrimp tempura, baked scallops, noodles, and the exalted Kobe beef. Traditional seating is available. Japanese menu. Lunch, dinner. Closed Thanksgiving, Dec 25. Bar. Children's menu. **$$$**

★ ★ ★ **RUTH'S CHRIS STEAK HOUSE.** *17840 Dallas Pkwy, Dallas (75235). Phone 972/250-2244; fax 927/250-1590. www.ruthschris.com.* This Dallas location offers the classic steakhouse experience with its wood paneling, traditional menu, and excellent service. Steak menu. Dinner. Closed Thanksgiving, Dec 25. Bar. Casual attire. Valet parking. **$$$**

★ ★ **S & D OYSTER COMPANY.** *2701 McKinney Ave, Dallas (75204). Phone 214/880-0111.* One of the first places to open in the rejuvenating Uptown in the 1970s, this stalwart fish house occupies a historic brick grocery building that is sure to withstand the district's overwhelming development. A New Orleans spirit occupies the place—an unexpected find in the mix of elegant eateries in Uptown—where oysters on the half-shell, barbecued shrimp, well-smoked beef brisket, pork ribs, baked potato casserole, spinach salad, peach cobbler, cold beer, and RC Cola are served with a smile. Seafood menu. Lunch, dinner. Closed Sun. Bar. Casual attire. **$$**

★ **SAL'S PIZZA.** *2525 Wycliff Ave, Dallas (75219). Phone 214/522-1828.* New York-style pizzas star at this standby in the Market Center area, but the simple café also offers a generous selection of appetizers such as shrimp scampi, and entrées, including veal chops and cannelloni. Italian menu, pizza. Lunch, dinner, late-night. Bar. Casual attire. **$**

★ ★ ★ **THE SAMBA ROOM.** *4514 Travis St, Dallas (75205). Phone 214/522-4137; fax 214/522-4442.* Turning heads with its spicy, exotic dishes and sultry atmosphere, this den of Nuevo Latino cuisine off Knox Street and near Highland Park keeps patrons happy with Key lime margaritas, mojitos, and a hefty menu of lusty dishes. Try the corn pancakes with shredded beef and melted cheeses; the paella with seafood, chicken, and sausage; and the sugar cane-skewered lamb over lentil salsa. Cuban, Latin American, Jamaican menu. Dinner, late-night, Sun brunch. Closed Dec 25. Bar. Casual attire. **$$$**

★ ★ **SAMBUCA JAZZ CAFE.** *2120 McKinney Ave, Dallas (75201). Phone 214/744-0820. www.sambuca jazzcafe.com.* The shotgun space in a vintage downtown building provides room for legions of hip diners and drinkers, many of whom come for the eats and stay for the live jazz. Gorgonzola salad with walnuts, chicken stuffed with dried fruit and mascarpone, and pasta with shellfish typify the stylish menu offerings. American menu. Lunch, dinner, late-night. Bar. Casual attire. Outdoor seating. **$$$**

★ **SAMMY'S BBQ.** *2126 Leonard St, Dallas. Phone 214/880-9064; fax 214/871-7597.* This longtime, family-run restaurant is a serious favorite among locals. An anomaly in the gentrified Uptown district, this simple barbecue joint is beloved for its chopped beef sandwiches, spinach salad, and homemade pies. Barbecue menu. Lunch. Closed Sun. Bar. Casual attire. **$**

★ ★ ★ **SEVENTEEN SEVENTEEN.** *1717 Harwood St, Dallas (75201). Phone 214/880-0158.* Artful dishes worthy of Dallas Museum of Art surroundings have made this a downtown dining destination favored by fashionable diners outfitted in silk and jewels. Start with a dish of tempura shrimp over baby greens in a Thai vinaigrette, cradled in a crispy won ton basket. For the main course, choose from many delicious options, like a quesadilla stuffed with smoked chicken and dabbed with a roasted tomatillo salsa, and a pan-seared pork chop in a soy glaze over stir-fried rice in a baked acorn squash. American menu. Lunch. Closed Sat-Mon. Bar. Casual attire. Outdoor seating. **$$**

★ ★ ★ **SEVY'S GRILL.** *8201 Preston Rd, Dallas (75225). Phone 214/265-7389; fax 214/265-8949.* Steady popularity growth at this Park Cities favorite can be credited to an ever-evolving menu that does nothing but shimmer with inspiration. Goat cheese crostini and shrimp-crab cakes offer a taste of appetizer bliss, while entrée success lies in dishes such as grilled salmon dusted in red chile powder and resting on a cool pool of tomatillo-lime sauce. Skillful service allows dates and business types to converse, although the bar-crowd noise early in the evening may distract. American menu. Lunch, dinner. Closed holidays. Bar. Valet parking. Outdoor seating. **$$**

★ ★ ★ **SMITH & WOLLENSKY.** *18438 Dallas Pkwy, Dallas (75287). Phone 972/930-9200. www.smith andwollensky.com.* American menu. Dinner, late-night. Bar. Casual attire. Outdoor seating. **$$$**

★ **SMOKEY JOHN'S DEPOT.** *1820 W Mockingbird Ln, Dallas (75235). Phone 214/352-2752.* A train theme makes this Market Center joint a family-friendly spot. A menu of pork ribs, beef brisket, baked chicken, and smoked sausage takes care of big appetites. American, barbecue menu. Lunch. Closed Sun. Children's menu. Casual attire. **$**

★ **SONNY BRYAN'S.** *2202 Inwood Rd, Dallas (75235). Phone 214/357-7120.* This is the original location of a Texas legend, which bears no less than a James Beard Award for superior regional cuisine. Tiny and ancient, the shack holds a few school desks at which to eat big ribs and brisket sandwiches. Several other locations are found around the Metroplex. American, barbecue menu. Lunch. Closed Sun. Children's menu. Casual attire. **$**

★ **SONNY BRYAN'S.** *302 N Market St, Dallas (75202). Phone 214/744-1610.* American, barbecue menu. Lunch, dinner. Children's menu. **$**

★ ★ **ST. PETE'S DANCING MARLIN.** *2730 Commerce St, Dallas (75226). Phone 214/698-1511. www.dancingmarlin.com.* Bars are plentiful in Deep Ellum, but few serve meals with the creativity found in this joint. Linguine and penne come with your choice of a dozen or so treatments, pizza gets interesting with feta and clams among the available toppings, and baklava is among the dessert options. American menu. Lunch, dinner. Bar. Casual attire. Outdoor seating. **$$**

★ ★ ★ **STEEL.** *3102 Oak Lawn Ave, Suite 100, Dallas (75219). Phone 214/219-9908; fax 214/219-9929.* Tucked into the back of the Centrum Building in Uptown, this chic, Zen-infused corner of cool attracts a fashionable crowd in search of sensational sushi, inspired Asian dishes, and excellent wines. The red clam nigiri sushi is superb, as is the Japanese ceviche creation of octopus, squid, clam, and crab in a miso vinaigrette. Warm dishes worth a long look are sea bass in miso and sake and orange-spiked Korean beef. Pan-Asian menu. Lunch, dinner. Closed Jan 1, Dec 25. Bar. Casual attire. Reservations recommended. **$$$**

★ ★ **STONELEIGH P.** *2926 Maple Ave, Dallas (75201). Phone 214/871-2346; fax 214/871-2348. www.stoneleighp.com.* Fashioned from a World War I-era pharmacy, the P remains the lovable, offbeat barroom-reading room it's been since 1973. Known for its burger with melted provolone and chipotle-laced mayo on a rustic roll, the P also does a mean quesadilla and a great steamed artichoke. Wash it all down with a Bass Ale. American menu. Lunch, dinner, late-night. Closed Jan 1, Thanksgiving, Dec 25. Bar. Casual attire. Outdoor seating. **$$**

★ **THE STRING BEAN.** *7879 Spring Valley Rd, Dallas (75254). Phone 972/385-3287.* In North Dallas, a menu of pure comfort food means generous helpings of chicken and dumplings, meatloaf, pot roast, pork chops, and oodles of vegetables alongside. Families love this restaurant. American menu. Lunch, dinner. Children's menu. Casual attire. **$$**

★ ★ **SULLIVAN'S STEAKHOUSE.** *17795 N Dallas Pkwy, Dallas (75287). Phone 972/267-9393. www.sullivansteakhouse.com.* Named for the famous pugilist of a century past, this upscale monument to prime beef is both comfortable and sophisticated. Elegant cuts of steak and pretty fish are expertly cooked, and service is polished. Side dishes, desserts, and wines are satisfying as well. Steak menu. Lunch, dinner. Bar. Casual attire. Outdoor seating. **$$$**

★ ★ **SUSHI-SAKE.** *220 W Campbell Rd, Dallas (75080). Phone 972/470-0722.* One of the best bets for Asian cuisine in Richardson, this is the spot for traditional nigiri sushi, as well as maki and sashimi. Beef tataki, soft-shell crab, and crunchy fried oysters are worth due consideration. Have a look, too, at the chilled sake offerings. Japanese, sushi menu. Lunch, dinner. Closed Sun. Casual attire. **$$**

★ ★ **SUZE.** *4345 W Northwest Hwy, Dallas (75220). Phone 214/350-6135.* The quintessential neighborhood bistro for refined palates, this small spot tucked into a modern shopping center in near North Dallas spoils its loyal clientele with inventive dishes and smooth service. Spinach salad decorated with blue cheese, applewood-smoked bacon, onion strips, and mushrooms is a good foil to the plate of tart, fried green tomatoes with a chunky red tomato sauce. Chicken stuffed with fresh sage and Spanish ham over Roquefort polenta is simply dreamy. American menu. Dinner. Closed Sun-Mon. Casual attire. **$$$**

★ ★ **TEI TEI ROBATA BAR.** *2906 N Henderson, Dallas (75206). Phone 214/828-2400; fax 214/821-5633. www.teiteirobata.com.* Seemingly more Vancouver than Dallas, this sleek, gorgeous space lets diners focus on the chefs working behind oak-burning grills. The ice-filled robata box stocks all manner of fresh finned and shelled fish for guests to pick out for dinner. Sashimi, Kobe steaks, lobster soup, and a fine variety of chilled sakes are offered too. The Patami Room (no shoes) seats 6-12 people. Japanese menu. Dinner. Closed Mon. Casual attire. **$$$**
🅓

★ ★ **TEPPO.** *2014 Greenville Ave, Dallas (75206). www.teppo.com.* Small but unceasingly chic, this hangout on Lower Greenville serves exceptional sushi, sashimi, and yakitori in an ultracontemporary space. Two blackboards are crammed with daily specials and the printed menu brims with temptations, making decisions tough. Some tempting options include squid sashimi over crushed ice; smoked salmon sushi; and aromatic, freshly grilled skewers of chicken and green onion or sirloin and fresh garlic cloves and marinated vegetables with chicken livers. Gracious service and a nice wine list make this a winner. Japanese menu. Dinner. Closed Mon. **$$$**
🅓

★ ★ **TERILLI'S.** *2815 Greenville Ave, Dallas (75206). Phone 214/827-3993. www.terillis.com.* Since the late 1980s, this mainstay in the Lower Greenville stretch of cafés and nightspots has been filled with the buzz of a vibrant clientele. Half come for the jazz and wine, while others flock in regularly for pastas, salads, and the signature rosemary skewers holding grilled shrimp, scallops, and artichoke hearts. Italian menu. Lunch, dinner, Sun brunch. Children's menu. Outdoor seating. **$$**

★ **TEXADELPHIA.** *5500 Greenville Ave, Suite 600, Dallas (75206). Phone 214/265-8044.* Begun in Austin, this sandwich shop does justice to the Texas-sized appetite. Specialties include a Philly cheesesteak-style sandwich, which you can jazz up with jalapeños. Chips and salsa bring a Tex-Mex element to the mix. American menu. Lunch, dinner. **$**

★ ★ **TEXAS DE BRAZIL.** *2727 Cedar Springs Rd, Dallas (75201). Phone 214/720-1414.* Roaming gauchos wielding giant swords of grilled meats transport diners to the Brazilian pampas, where this churrascaria style of dining reigns. For a fixed price, choose from some two dozen kinds of meats, along with numerous side dishes. Brazilian, steak menu. Dinner. Bar. Casual attire. **$$$**

★ ★ **TEXAS LAND & CATTLE COMPANY.** *3130 Lemmon Ave, Dallas (75204). Phone 214/526-4664. www.texaslandandcattle.com.* This San Antonio-based chain offers elaborate works in beef and a setting that's surprisingly homey and casual. Start with a giant wedge of iceberg coated in nubby blue cheese dressing, and then dig into a hefty, tender steak. Sports on TV and cold beer keep the bar area busy and happily noisy. Southwestern, steak menu. Lunch, dinner. Bar. Children's menu. Casual attire. **$$$**

★ ★ **THAI GARDEN.** *6090 Campbell Rd, Dallas (75248). Phone 972/248-8861.* Chinese influences infiltrate the Thai menu here, which varies its offerings from fried crab-cream cheese bundles and garlic chicken or beef with broccoli to pad Thai and, for dessert, mango with sticky rice. Thai menu. Lunch, dinner. Closed Sun. Bar. Casual attire. **$$**

★ **THOMAS AVE. BEVERAGE CO.** *2901 Thomas Ave, Dallas (75204). Phone 214/979-0452.* What every neighborhood should have—a bar that also serves excellent food. This Uptown favorite matches the fun of shooting pool with the serious flavors found in dishes like roasted chicken with herbed goat cheese and hummus with sun-dried tomatoes. American menu. Lunch, dinner. Bar. Casual attire. Outdoor seating. **$$$**

★ ★ **TONY'S WINE WAREHOUSE.** *2904 Oak Lawn Ave, Dallas (75219). Phone 214/520-9463; fax 214/559-4093.* Décor in the form of stacked cardboard wine boxes telegraphs this bistro's casual approach to dining and sipping. Customers shop for their dinner wines in the retail area and then sit down to a bountiful meal of shrimp-mushroom casserole, veal piccata, sautéed asparagus in puff pastry, and the like. American menu. Lunch, dinner. Closed Sun; holidays. **$$**

★ ★ **TRAMONTANA.** *8220 Westchester Dr, Dallas (75225). Phone 214/368-4188; fax 214/368-4194.* Named for the wind that blows over the Pyrenees, this stateside oasis in a Park Cities shopping center amazes even jaded foodies. Chef/owner James Neel wows diners with his wild mushroom soufflé, caramelized salmon with lemongrass beurre blanc, and potato-crusted calamari. The cozy dining room and imaginative wine list are plusses. American menu. Lunch, dinner. Closed Sun-Mon; holidays. **$$$**

★ ★ **TUPINAMBA.** *12270 Inwood Rd, Dallas (75244). Phone 972/991-8148.* Fountains, potted greenery, and pretty patio detailing make Tupinamba a more scenic setting than the average Tex-Mex place. A loyal Dallas following makes regular visits here for nachos loaded with chicken, beef, beans, and cheese, and for chili-topped enchiladas and sizzling beef and shrimp fajitas. Tex-Mex menu. Lunch, dinner. Bar. Casual attire. **$$**

★ **TWO ROWS RESTAURANT & BREWERY.** *5500 Greenville Ave, Dallas (75206). Phone 214/696-2739.* A tremendously popular, noisy sports bar in the Old Town area, this watering hole also boasts an ambitious kitchen. Menu picks include pizza with tropical toppings, grilled salmon, seafood pasta, and spicy chicken wings. American menu. Lunch, dinner, late-night. Bar. Casual attire. Outdoor seating. **$$**

★ ★ **UNCLE JULIO'S.** *4125 Lemmon, Dallas (75219). Phone 214/520-6620.* Mexican, Spanish menu. Lunch, dinner. Children's menu. Casual attire. **$$**

★ ★ **WAKA.** *18900 Dallas Pkwy, Dallas (75287). Phone 972/713-6451.* Fashionable but satisfying, Waka manages to match its style with substance. Elegant Japanese dishes include rice bowls topped with pan-seared tuna and squid and miso-marinated salmon over Asian pickles, while Chinese offerings include dim sum. The menu also exhibits French inspirations, as in the foie gras with bean sprouts and Japanese yams. Pan-Asian menu. Lunch, dinner. Closed Sun. Casual attire. **$$$**

★ ★ **WATEL'S.** *2207 Allen St, Dallas (75214). Phone 214/720-0323. www.watels.com.* Refined but not especially fussy, the comfortably elegant dining room in Uptown offers divine creations from Belgian-born chef/owner Rene Peeters. Roasted eggplant soup; Provençal tapenade; and large, smoked sea scallops over blank linguine in a citrus dressing are savvy starter courses. Entrees such as veal sweetbreads in a creamy chive sauce and lobster Napoleon atop spinach in Cognac-laced mushrooms between puff pastry layers show Peeters' deft touch. French menu. Lunch, dinner. Bar. Casual attire. **$$$**

★ ★ **YAMAGUCHI BAR & SUSHI.** *7713 Inwood Rd, Dallas (75209). Phone 214/350-8660.* Tetsuji Yamaguchi's laid-back, simple cubbyhole on the outskirts of the Park Cities gives equal due to sushi, sashimi, and cooked Japanese specialties. The beef tataki is winning, as are the sashimi sampler, grilled meats, and noodle bowls. Cool sake is smooth as glass, too. Plan to linger with friends over a series of courses. Japanese menu. Lunch, dinner. Bar. Casual attire. **$$**

★ ★ **YORK STREET.** *6047 Lewis St, Dallas (75206). Phone 214/826-0968.* Tables within this intimate cuisine haven in the Lakewood area of East Dallas have become among the hottest in town. Chef/owner Sharon Hage rewrites one-fourth of her menu daily, depending on the freshest goods available from her meat, fish, and produce purveyors. Standouts include such dishes as mussels with fresh horseradish and smoked ham and hanger steak with creamed potatoes. American menu. Dinner. Closed Sun, Mon; holidays. **$$**

★ **ZIZIKI'S.** *4514 Travis St, Suite 122, Dallas (75205).* Outlasting the fickle trends of the Knox Street neighborhood, this pretty tavern and café comforts with cool surroundings and soothes with a lavish menu of seafood, meats, and salads. Don't miss the artichoke dip. Mediterranean menu. Lunch, dinner. Closed holidays. Bar. Children's menu. Casual attire. Outdoor seating. **$$$**

Dallas/Fort Worth Airport Area (A-8)

See also Arlington-Grand Prairie, Dallas, Fort Worth

Web Site www.dfwairport.com

Public Transportation

Airport Information Dallas/Fort Worth International Airport Phone 972/574-8888

Lost and Found Phone toll-free 866/342-5339

Airlines Aeromexico, Air Canada, Air Tran Airways, Allegro, America West, American Airlines, American Eagle, American Trans Air, Atlantic Southeast, British Airways, Champion Air, ComAir, Continental Airlines, Delta Air Lines, Frontier Airlines, Korean Air, Lufthansa, Mesa Airlines, Midwest Airlines, Northwest Airlines, SkyWest Airlines, Sol Air, Sun Country, TACA Airlines, United Airlines, US Airways

Special Event

EDS Byron Nelson Championship. *4150 N MacArthur Blvd, Irving (75038). At the Four Seasons Resort and Club. Phone 214/742-3896. www.golfweb.com/ tournaments/r019.* This annual tournament always entices with one of the largest purses on the PGA Tour, so some of golf's brightest stars hit the links to try topping its leader board. Mid-May. **$$$$**

Limited-Service Hotels

★ ★ **HILTON GARDEN INN LAS COLINAS.** *7516 Las Colinas Blvd, Irving (75063). Phone 972/444-8434; fax 972/910-9246.* This hotel is conveniently located in the DFW/Los Colinas area and features finely decorated rooms. 174 rooms, 5 story. Complimentary continental breakfast. Check-out noon. Bar. Fitness room. Outdoor pool. Business center. **$$**

★ **HOMEWOOD SUITES LAS COLINAS.** *4300 Wingren Blvd, Irving (75039). Phone 972/556-0665; fax 972/401-3765. www.homewood-suites.com.* 136 rooms, all suites. Pets accepted, some restrictions; fee. Check-in 3 pm, check-out noon. High-speed Internet access. Fitness room. Outdoor pool, whirlpool. Business center. **$**

Full-Service Hotel

★ ★ ★ **OMNI MANDALAY HOTEL.** *221 E Las Colinas Blvd, Irving (75039). Phone 972/556-0800; toll-free 800/843-6664; fax 972/556-0729. www.omni hotels.com.* Travelers to the Dallas area are treated to the best of both worlds at the Omni Mandalay Hotel. This full-service hotel remains close to the city center, yet it is tucked away on 5 acres fronting Lake Carolyn in a peaceful suburban setting. A rich, sophisticated décor defines this hotel, where the rooms and suites spoil visitors with abundant creature comforts and advanced technology. Golf and tennis are nearby, and the hotel has its own fitness center, spa, and lakeside pool. Dining decision-making is delightfully difficult here, where guests can dial in for room service 24 hours a day, enjoy a poolside meal, savor an Italian specialty at Trevi's, grab a snack at Morsels, or imbibe a cocktail at Les Jardin or Aperitif. 421 rooms, 28 story. Pets accepted, some restrictions; fee. Check-in 3 pm, check-out noon. Wireless Internet access. Restaurant, bar. Fitness room. Outdoor pool, whirlpool. Business center. **$**

Full-Service Resort

★ ★ ★ **FOUR SEASONS RESORT AND CLUB DALLAS AT LAS COLINAS.** *4150 N MacArthur Blvd, Irving (75038). Phone 972/717-0700; toll-free 800/332-3442; fax 972/717-2550. www.four seasons.com.* The Four Seasons Resort and Club Dallas at Las Colinas is only moments from downtown Dallas, yet it feels like it's a million miles away. Set on 400 rolling acres, the resort is a sports enthusiast's paradise. Home to the PGA's Byron Nelson Championship, the two golf courses accommodate players of all levels. Those guests looking to perfect their game appreciate the Byron Nelson Golf School and plentiful practice areas. The 12-court tennis facility attracts players with its climate-controlled indoor courts and sunny outdoor courts. Three outdoor pools, one indoor pool, and a children's pool keep swimmers satisfied, and the Sports Club's spa smoothes out the kinks with its variety of massages and treatments. Guests work up hearty appetites after active days, and the resort's six restaurants and bars serve up flavorful cuisine to meet the challenge. 357 rooms, 9 story. Pets accepted, some restrictions. Check-in 3 pm, check-out noon. Six restaurants, bars. Fitness room, spa. Indoor pool, three outdoor pools, children's pool, whirlpool. Golf. Tennis. Business center. **$$$**

Restaurants

★ ★ ★ **CAFE ON THE GREEN.** *4150 N MacArthur Blvd, Irving (75038). Phone 972/717-0700; fax 972/717-2486. www.fshr.com.* Sleek, cool, and refined, this wondrous room within the Four Seasons Las Colinas Resort and Spa sets the pace for all pan-Asian dining rooms in north Texas. German-born chef Christof Syre brings years of work in Hong Kong to produce lovely touches in griddled Dungeness crab cake with a sweetish, smoky sauce; curried mango-orange soup with lump crab; and blackened tuna steak with mango-cilantro chutney. Spa menu choices help virtuous diners stick with their programs. American menu. Breakfast, lunch, dinner, Sun brunch. Bar. Valet parking. **$$$**

★ ★ **HANASHO.** *2938 N Belt Line Rd, Irving (75062). Phone 972/258-0250.* A longtime favorite in Irving, this attractive restaurant claims a devoted clientele. Sushi, sashimi, gyoza, teriyaki, noodle dishes, and tempura offerings are among the best-selling menu items. Japanese, sushi menu. Lunch, dinner. **$$$**
🅳

★ ★ **LA BISTRO.** *722 Grapevine Hwy, Hurst (76054). Phone 817/281-9333; fax 817/498-9039.* Italian menu. Lunch, dinner. Closed holidays. Bar. Children's menu. Casual attire. Reservations recommended. **$$**

★ ★ ★ **VIA REAL.** *4020 N MacArthur Blvd, Irving (75038). Phone 972/650-9001; fax 972/541-0215. www.viareal.com.* Situated adjacent to the Four Seasons Las Colinas Resort, this popular restaurant has been serving its Mexican and Southwestern cuisine for more than 11 years. The warm upscale Santa Fe décor complements the traditional Mexican dishes, as well as the seafood from Mexico's coastal regions. Southwestern, Mexican menu. Lunch, dinner, Sun brunch. Bar. **$$$**

Del Rio (D-5)

See also Brackettville, Eagle Pass, Uvalde

Founded 1868
Population 33,867
Elevation 948 ft
Information Chamber of Commerce, 1915 Avenue F; phone 830/775-3551.
Web Site www.drchamber.com

On the Rio Grande with San Felipe Springs supplying water to thousands of acres, Del Rio is a green spot in the desert. Laughlin Air Force Base, of the Air Education Training Command, is 6 miles east. Private ranches in the area offer hunting for a variety of game, including white-tailed deer, javelina, and turkey.

What to See and Do

Amistad (Friendship) National Recreation Area. *Del Rio (78840). 12 miles NW on Hwy 90. Phone 830/775-7491.* An international project. Six miles long, the dam forms a lake of more than 65,000 acres extending up the Rio Grande, Devil's, and Pecos rivers. Stone statue of Tlaloc, Aztec rain god, towers over the Mexican end of the dam; 4,000-year-old pictographs in rock shelters in the area. Two marinas with boat ramps, gas, stores, and full facilities. Water sports, swimming; primitive camping. Contact Amistad National Recreation Area, HCR 3 Box 5J, 78840. (Daily) **FREE**

Ciudad Acuña, Mexico. Across the border. Visitors often make the short trip over the river to this quaint Mexican town. Shopping, restaurants, and nightlife all serve as attractions to the tourist. (For Border Crossing Regulations, see MAKING THE MOST OF YOUR TRIP.)

Continental Ranch Tour. *300 W Nicholson, Del Rio (78840). 50 miles NW of Del Rio in Val Verde County. Phone 830/775-6957.* All-day tour of 90-year-old ranch, including ranch headquarters, domestic livestock, native plants, rock formations, and undeveloped scenic areas of the Pecos River. Tour includes snacks and picnic lunch overlooking Pecos River. Participants should be in good physical condition and be willing to ride two hours over rough terrain. By appointment only (call for reservations). **$$$$**

Firehouse. *120 E Garfield, Del Rio. Phone 830/775-0888. www.delrioarts.org.* The Del Rio Council for the Arts maintains an art gallery; classes and workshops in arts and special interest areas. (Mon-Sat; closed holidays) **FREE**

Judge Roy Bean Visitor Center. *Loop 25 Torres Ave, Langtry. 60 miles NW on Hwy 90. Phone 915/291-3340.* For years, Bean was "the law west of the Pecos." Preserved by the state of Texas, his saloon-courtroom, the "Jersey Lily," is a historic landmark. Dioramas with sound; cactus garden. Department of Transportation visitor center. (Daily; closed holidays) **FREE**

Seminole Canyon State Historical Park. *Hwy 90 W, Comstock. 41 miles NW via Hwy 90, 10 miles W of*

Comstock. *Phone 915/292-4464*. On 2,172 acres. Hiking, picnicking, camping. Prehistoric pictograph sites. Guided tours into canyon (Wed-Sun). **$$**

Val Verde Winery. *100 Qualia Dr, Del Rio. Phone 830/775-9714. www.texaswinetrails.com/val.htm.* Texas's oldest licensed winery, founded in 1883, is operated by the third generation of the Qualia family. Tours, tasting. (Mon-Sat 10 am-5 pm; closed holidays) **FREE**

Whitehead Memorial Museum. *1308 S Main St, Del Rio. Phone 830/774-7568.* Memorabilia of early Southwest; Cadena folk art; grave of Judge Roy Bean; replica of Bean's Jersey Lily Saloon, hacienda and chapel, doctor's office; cabins, store, barn. (Tues-Sun; closed holidays) **$$**

Special Events

Cinco de Mayo Celebration. *Phone 830/774-8541.* Entertainment, dance, food, crafts. May 5.

Diez y Seis de Septiembre. *Brown Plaza, 201 Ave P, Del Rio. Phone 830/774-8541.* Concerts, food booths, music. Sept 16.

Fiesta de Amistad. *1915 Ave F, Del Rio (78840). Phone 830/775-3551.* Mid-late Oct.

George Paul Memorial Bull Riding. *Val Verde County Fairgrounds, 2006 N Main, Del Rio (78840). Phone 830/775-9595.* Top riders in the world compete. Late Apr.

Limited-Service Hotel

★ **LA QUINTA INN.** *2005 Ave F, Del Rio (78840). Phone 830/775-7591; toll-free 800/531-5900; fax 830/774-0809. www.lq.com.* 101 rooms, 2 story. Pets accepted. Complimentary continental breakfast. Check-in 3 pm, check-out noon. Outdoor pool. **$**

Denison (A-8)

See also Bonham, Gainesville, Sherman

Founded 1872
Population 22,773
Elevation 767 ft
Area Code 903
Information Chamber of Commerce, 313 W Woodard St, PO Box 325, 75021; phone 903/465-1551
Web Site www.denisontx.com

President Dwight D. Eisenhower was born in Denison. It is an industrial and transportation center manufacturing clothing, fabricated metal, food products, and drilling equipment.

What to See and Do

Denison Dam. *351 Corps Rd, Denison (75020). 5 miles NW on Hwy 91. Phone 903/465-4990.* Large earth-filled dam impounds Lake Texoma. Water sports; resorts. Camping (fees in some areas). Visitor center.

Eisenhower Birthplace State Historical Park. *208 E Day St, Denison. At Lamar Ave, 4 blocks E of Hwy 69. Phone 903/465-8908.* Restored house; furnishings; some of Eisenhower's personal items. Interpretive center; picnicking. (Tues-Sun; closed Jan 1, Thanksgiving, Dec 25) **$**

Eisenhower State Park. *50 Park Rd 20, Denison (75020). 5 miles NW on Hwy 91, then 2 miles W on FM 1310 to Park Rd 20. Phone 903/465-1956. www.tpwd.state.tx.us/park/eisenhow.* Approximately 400 acres. Swimming, fishing (lighted pier), boating (ramps, marina); hiking trails, picnicking, playground; improved campsites, RV facilities (dump stations). (Daily) **$**

Grayson County Frontier Village. *Loy Lake Rd, Hwy 75 exit 67, Denison. 2 miles SW via Hwy 75, Loy Lake Rd exit. Phone 903/463-2487.* Town replica from 1800s; 15 original structures, museum. (Daily) **FREE**

Special Events

National Aerobatic Championships. *Grayson County Airport, 4700 Airport Dr, Denison (75020). Phone 903/786-2904.* Second and third weeks in Sept.

Texoma Lakefest Regatta. *132 Grandpappy Dr, Denison (75020). Phone 903/465-1551.* Regatta, dance, lake activities. Mid-Apr.

Denton (A-8)

See also Arlington-Grand Prairie, Dallas, Fort Worth, Gainesville, McKinney

Population 80,537
Elevation 662 ft
Information Convention & Visitor Bureau, 414 Parkway St, PO Drawer P, 76202; phone 940/382-9693 or toll-free 888/381-1818
Web Site www.denton-chamber.org

This pleasant town and county seat has diversified industry; it also serves as a farm supply and shipping point. Much scientific research is carried on at the University of North Texas and Texas Woman's University.

What to See and Do

Denton County Courthouse Museum. *110 W Hickory, 1st floor, Denton. Phone 940/349-2850; toll-free 800/346-3189.* Memorabilia and artifacts depicting Denton County history; large collections of rare antique dolls and guns; rare blue glass; Native American artifacts. (Tues-Sat afternoons; closed holidays) **FREE**

Lewisville Lake. *Lake Park and Mill St, Lewisville (75057). 1 mile SE via I-35 E. Phone 972/434-1666.* This 23,000-acre lake is surrounded by 11 developed park areas. Three marinas and a fishing barge provide service to boaters and anglers; swimming. Some fees. (Daily)

Ray Roberts Lake State Park. *FM 455, Pilot Point. Approximately 12 miles NE via Hwy 380 and Hwy 377. Phone 940/686-3408.* This lake was formed by the damming of the Trinity River. The Isle du Bois Unit on the south side of the lake and the Johnson Branch Unit on the north side both offer swimming, fishing piers (cleaning stations), boating (launch, docks); nature, hiking, bridle trails; picnicking, playgrounds, primitive and improved camping, and tent and trailer sites. Other areas offer limited facilities. (Daily) **$**

Texas Woman's University. *304 Administration Dr, Denton (76201). University Dr and Bell Ave, NE part of town. Phone 940/898-3456.* (1901) (9,000 students) Graduate school and Institute of Health Sciences are coeducational. This 270-acre campus includes University Gardens; art galleries in Fine Arts Building; DAR Museum with "Gowns of First Ladies of Texas" collection in Adminstrative Conference (by appointment); and the Blagg-Huey Library with "Texas Women—A Celebration of History," a self-guided tour with photos and artifacts (Daily; closed holidays) **FREE** Also on campus is

> **Little-Chapel-in-the-Woods.** Designed by O'Neil Ford. Stained-glass windows, carved wood, mosaics made by students. A National Youth Administration (NYA) project dedicated by Eleanor Roosevelt in 1939. (Daily) **FREE**

Special Event

North Texas State Fair and Rodeo. *2217 N Carroll Blvd, Denton (76202). Phone 940/387-2632.* Nine days in late Aug.

Limited-Service Hotel

★ ★ **RADISSON HOTEL DENTON AND EAGLE POINT GOLF CLUB.** *2211 I-35 E N, Denton (76205). Phone 940/565-8499; fax 940/384-2244. www.radisson.com.* 150 rooms, 8 story. Pets accepted, some restrictions; fee. Restaurant, bar. Fitness room. Outdoor pool. Golf. Business center. **$**

Restaurant

★ **TRAIL DUST STEAKHOUSE.** *Hwy 380, Aubrey (76227). Phone 940/440-3878; fax 940/365-3154. www.traildust.com.* American menu. Dinner. Closed Thanksgiving, Dec 25. Bar. Children's menu. **$$**

Dumas (E-3)

See also Amarillo

Population 13,747
Elevation 3,668 ft
Area Code 806
Zip 79029
Information Moore County Chamber of Commerce, PO Box 735; phone 806/935-2123

Oil was discovered in Dumas in 1926. Today, Dumas is noted for its large natural gas fields and for the production of between 60 and 70 percent of the nation's helium.

Special Event

Dogie Days Celebration. *McDade Park.* Food booths, carnival rides, dances, barbecue, parade. First weekend in June.

Limited-Service Hotel

★ **COMFORT INN.** *1620 S Dumas Ave, Dumas (79029). Phone 806/935-6988; toll-free 800/262-0038; fax 806/935-6924. www.comfortinn.com.* 51 rooms, 2 story. Complimentary continental breakfast. Check-in 1 pm, check-out 11 am. High-speed Internet access. Fitness room. Indoor pool, whirlpool. **$**

Eagle Lake (D-8)

See also Houston

Population 3,664
Elevation 170 ft
Area Code 409
Zip 77434
Information Chamber of Commerce, 408 E Main St, phone 409/234-2780
Web Site www.elc.net/city.of.eagle.lake

A popular area for duck and goose hunting, this region produces large rice harvests, oil, natural gas, sand, and gravel. A sanctuary for the coastal prairie chicken is nearby.

What to See and Do

Attwater Prairie Chicken National Wildlife Refuge. *3013 Farm Market Rd, Eagle Lake (77434). 7 miles NE off FM 3013. Phone 409/234-3021. www.texasbirding.net.* Approximately 8,000 acres along banks of San Bernard River. Protected area for the endangered Attwater prairie chicken; large numbers of migratory and resident species. In spring, refuge is filled with wildflowers. (Daily; office Mon-Fri) **FREE**

Prairie Edge Museum. *408 E Main, Eagle Lake. Phone 409/234-2780.* Exhibits depicting area history, life on the prairie, flora and fauna, early rice farming equipment. (Sat-Sun, and by appointment) **FREE**

Special Event

Magnolia Homes Tour. *425 Spring St, Columbus (78934). 18 miles NW. Phone 409/732-8385.* Ten early Texas and Victorian houses are opened for tours; antiques show; parade; food. Four days in mid-May.

Eagle Pass (D-6)

See also Brackettville, Del Rio, Uvalde

Founded 1849
Population 22,413
Elevation 726 ft
Area Code 830
Information Chamber of Commerce, 400 Garrison St, PO Box 1188, 78853; phone 830/773-3224
Web Site www.eaglepasstexas.com

Eagle Pass is across the Rio Grande from Piedras Negras, Coahuila, Mexico (for Border Crossing Regulations see MAKING THE MOST OF YOUR TRIP). A toll bridge connects the two cities. Eagle Pass is the port of entry to Mexican Highway 57, the Constitution Highway to Mexico City via Saltillo and San Luis Potosi.

What to See and Do

Fort Duncan Park. *480 S Adams, Eagle Pass (78852). Enter at Adams or Monroe st. Phone 830/773-4343.* Ten restored buildings of the fort (1849) that once housed 10,000 troops; museum (Mon-Fri). In the park are ballfields, picnic area, playground, and a golf course. (Daily) **FREE**

Piedras Negras, Mexico. (Population 280,000) Many pleasant restaurants and nightclubs. Contact the Chamber of Commerce.

Limited-Service Hotels

★ **BEST WESTERN EAGLE PASS.** *1923 Loop 431, Eagle Pass (78852). Phone 830/758-1234; toll-free 800/992-3245; fax 830/758-1235. www.bestwestern.com.* 40 rooms, 2 story. Pets accepted, some restrictions. Complimentary continental breakfast. Check-in 2 pm, check-out noon. Wireless Internet access. Outdoor pool. Business center. **$**
🐾 🛏️ 🏃

★ **LA QUINTA INN.** *2525 E Main St, Eagle Pass (78852). Phone 830/773-7000; toll-free 800/531-5900; fax 830/773-8852. www.lq.com.* 130 rooms, 2 story. Pets accepted. Complimentary continental breakfast. Check-in 1 pm, check-out noon. Outdoor pool. **$**
🐾 🛏️

Eastland (A-8)

See also Abilene, Fort Worth, Weatherford

Population 3,769
Elevation 1,421 ft
Area Code 254
Zip 76448
Information Chamber of Commerce, 102 S Seaman; phone 254/629-2332

Eastland is the home of the legend of "Old Rip," a Texas horned toad alleged to have survived for 31 years (1897-1928) sealed in the cornerstone of the county courthouse. A minor publicity sensation resulted for the town when the cornerstone was opened and the reptile discovered. Today, the remains of Old Rip are on view in the county courthouse.

Edinburg (F-7)

See also Harlingen, McAllen, Mission

Founded 1907
Population 48,465
Elevation 91 ft
Area Code 956
Zip 78539
Information Chamber of Commerce, 602 W University Dr, PO Box 85; phone 956/383-4974
Web Site www.edinburg.com

Edinburg, with its year-round growing conditions, is a leading agricultural and citrus market for oranges, grapefruit, and vegetables.

What to See and Do

Hidalgo County Historical Museum. *121 E McIntyre, Edinburg. Phone 956/383-6911.* Exhibits depict regional history of Rio Grande Valley, south Texas and northern Mexico; includes Native American items, Spanish exploration, Mexican War, ranch life, steamboats, bandit era. Housed partly in 1910 County Jail Building with hanging room (used once in 1913) and original gallows trapdoor. (Tues-Sun; closed holidays) **$$**

Special Event

Fiesta Hidalgo. Five days, last weekend in Feb.

El Paso (B-2)

See also Guadalupe Mountains National Park

Founded 1827
Population 563,662
Elevation 3,762-6,700 ft
Area Code 915
Information Convention & Visitors Bureau, 1 Civic Center Plaza, 79901; phone 915/534-0653 or toll-free 800/351-6024
Web Site www.elpasocvb.com

The first authenticated expedition here was by Rodriguez Chamuscado in 1581. Juan de Oñate named the place El Paso del Norte in 1598. Several missions were founded in the area beginning in 1659. They are now considered to be among the oldest continuously active parishes in the United States. Over the years several ranches were established. The first actual settlement in what is now downtown El Paso was in 1827, adjacent to the ranch of Juan Maria Ponce de Leon.

The town remained wholly Mexican throughout the Texas Revolution. In 1846, it surrendered to US forces engaged in fighting the Mexican War. In 1848, it was divided between present day Ciudad Juárez and what was to become El Paso proper. The border was placed in the middle of the Rio Grande, according to the terms of the treaty of Guadalupe Hidalgo. By provision of the Chamizal Treaty of 1963, the boundary has been changed, giving back to Mexico about 700 acres cut off by the shifting of the river. The disputed area was made into parkland on both sides of the border.

A military post was established in 1846 and a trading post in 1852. In 1854, the military post was named Fort Bliss. By this time, the Butterfield Stage Line from St. Louis to San Francisco was carrying gold seekers to California through El Paso.

Fort Bliss was captured by Texas troops of the Confederate Army in 1861 as part of a campaign to win New Mexico. The campaign failed, and the troops gradually withdrew. El Paso returned to Union hands by the end of the Civil War.

Spanish and English are mutually spoken in both El Paso and Ciudad Juárez. International spirit runs heavy between these two cities, as does the traffic. This spirit is reflected in the Civic Center complex and in the Chamizal National Memorial.

Along with more than 400 manufacturing plants ranging from oil refineries to food processing facilities, El Paso is also home to a military training center and one of the largest air defense centers in the world.

What to See and Do

Border Jumper Trolleys. *1 Civic Center Plz, El Paso (79901). Phone 915/544-0062. www.borderjumper.com.* Offers trolley rides around El Paso and into Mexico. Tours include the Juárez Tour, Mission Trail Tour (year-round, except in Dec), Christmas Lights Tour (early-mid-Dec), and the annual Ghost Tour (Oct). **$$$**

Chamizal National Memorial. *800 S San Marcial St, El Paso (79905). Enter from Paisano Dr; near Cordova Bridge. Phone 915/532-7273. www.nps.gov/cham.* The 55-acre area commemorates peaceful settlement of a boundary dispute between Mexico and the United States. Exhibits and bilingual movie tell story of the settlement; bilingual guide service. Special events include theater performances (see SPECIAL EVENTS). Visitor center (daily 8 am-5 pm). (Daily 5 am-10 pm; closed Jan 1, Thanksgiving, Dec 25) **FREE**

Ciudad Juárez, Mexico. Offers a different and fascinating experience. The markets in Ciudad Juárez have a wide variety of goods, and the stores offer better shopping than most Mexican border cities. Bullfights, fairs, and festivals abound. The best way to cross the border is to park in a lot on El Paso Street, at the bridge, and walk. Take advantage of the El Paso/Juárez trolley tour from The Border Jumper Trolley Company (see above). (For Border Crossing Regulations, see MAKING THE MOST OF YOUR TRIP.)

Concordia Cemetery. *2703 S Meridian St, El Paso (79930). NW of I-10 and Hwy 54. Phone 915/562-7062.* Established in 1856, this had become a primary burial site for El Paso by the 1880s. The Boot Hill section holds the grave of gunfighter John Wesley Hardin.

El Paso Holocaust Museum and Study Center. *401 Wallenberg Dr, El Paso (79912). Phone 915/833-5656.* Exhibits detail the tragic events that led from the rise of Nazi Germany and anti-Semitism to death camps and, eventually, liberation. Event speakers include liberators and survivors. (Tues-Thurs, Sun 1-4 pm)

El Paso Mission Trail. *Drive E 12 miles on I-10 to Zaragosa Rd, then S 2 1/2 miles to Alameda Ave; turn left and then immediate right onto S Old Pueblo Rd, which leads to*

San Elizario. *At intersection of farm roads and I-10, 15 miles SW of downtown El Paso.* The Presidio Chapel (1843) was built to replace the one first established in 1780. San Elizario was the site of the Salt War, a bitter struggle over rights to salt found in flats to the east.

Scenic drive. *Go N on Mesa St to Rim Rd and turn E, which will lead you to Scenic Dr.* The drive to the south end of Mount Franklin gives a magnificent view of El Paso and Ciudad Juárez, particularly at night.

Socorro. *Socorro Rd, El Paso.* The Mission here (circa 1680) is the oldest parish church in continual use in the United States.

Tigua Cultural Center. *305 Ya Ya Ln, El Paso (79907). Phone 915/859-5287.* The Tigua people, whose origins can be traced to 1500 BC, maintain a cultural center, two restaurants, and a gift shop. Presentations of Tigua dances and bread-baking (Sat-Sun). (Tues-Sun 8:30 am-5 pm) **FREE**

Ysleta. *301 S Schultz, El Paso (79907).* (1682) Oldest mission in Texas. When founded, Ysleta was on the Mexican side of the Rio Grande, but the river shifted, leaving it in Texas. The Mission Nuestra Señora del Carmen is on Highway 80 and south Old Pueblo Road. Preservation and upkeep is continuous. Some of the surrounding lands have been in cultivation every year since its founding. This is one of the few places in the United States where Egyptian long-staple cotton has been grown successfully.

El Paso Museum of Art. *1 Arts Festival Plz, El Paso (79901). Phone 915/532-1707. www.elpasoartmuseum. org.* Exhibits spanning six centuries of paintings and sculpture include American, Mexican Colonial, and pre-Columbian art, Kress Collection of Italian Renaissance works; changing exhibits. (Tues-Sat 9 am-5 pm, Fri to 7 pm, Sun noon-5 pm; closed holidays) **FREE**

El Paso Museum of History. *12901 Gateway W, El Paso (79927). I-10 and Americas Ave. Phone 915/858-1928.* Hispanic, Native American, United States artifacts and El Paso history dioramas; changing exhibits. (Tues-Sat 9 am-4 pm, Sun 1-4:50 pm; closed holidays) **DONATION**

Fort Bliss. *Chaffe Rd, Building #56, El Paso (79916). Enter at Robert E. Lee Gate, 1 mile E of airport. Phone 915/568-2121. www.bliss.army.mil.* Once the largest cavalry post in the US, Fort Bliss is now the home of the US Army Air Defense Center, one of the largest air defense centers in the world, where troops from all allied nations train. On base are

Old Fort Bliss. *Pershing and Pleasanton rds, El Paso (79916). Phone 915/568-4518.* Five adobe buildings replicate the original Fort Bliss army post. Period rooms contain items pertaining to the history of the fort. Includes military and civilian artifacts from 1850s to present. (Daily 9 am-4:30 pm; closed holidays) **FREE**

US Army Air Defense Museum. *Sheridan and Pleasanton rds, El Paso (79916). Building #1735 on Marshall Rd.* Phone 915/568-5412. Audiovisual exhibits on history of United States anti-aircraft gunnery and other military subjects. Changing exhibits; weapons park. (Daily 9 am-4:30 pm; closed holidays) **FREE**

Hueco Tanks State Historic Site. *6900 Hueco Tanks Rd, #1, El Paso (79938). 32 miles NE off Hwy 62, Ranch Rd 2775.* Phone 915/857-1135. *www.tpwd.state.tx.us/park/hueco.* More than 850 acres of cave and rock formations, ancient pictographs, vegetation, and wildlife. This is a semi-oasis in the desert where rainfall is trapped in natural basins or "huecos." Park facilities include picnicking, improved campsites (hook-ups, dump station). Rock climbing. (Oct-late Apr: daily 8 am-6 pm; May-late Sept: Mon-Thurs 8 am-6 pm, Fri-Sun 7 am-7 pm) **$**

Magoffin Home State Historic Site. *1120 Magoffin Ave, El Paso (79901).* Phone 915/533-5147. *www.tpwd.state.tx.us/park/magoffin/magoffin.htm.* Example of early territorial architecture (1875). Sun-dried adobe combined with Greek Revival detail created the Southwestern living style. Original family furnishings. (Daily 9 am-4 pm; closed holidays) **$**

University of Texas at El Paso. *500 University Dr, El Paso (79902). Off I-10, Schuster exit.* Phone 915/747-5000. *www.utep.edu.* (1914) (17,000 students) The Sun Bowl, seating 53,000, is on campus along with the Centennial Museum. Fine Arts Center with art exhibits, drama, and musical productions (fee).

Wilderness Park Museum. *4301 Transmountain Rd, El Paso (79924). Transmountain Rd at Gateway S.* Phone 915/755-4332. Archaeological and ethnological exhibits of the Southwest and man's adaptation to a desert environment; nature trail. Guided tours (by appointment). (Tues-Sun 9 am-4:45 pm; closed holidays) **FREE**

Special Events

Chamizal Festival. *Chamizal National Memorial, 800 S San Marcial St, El Paso (79905).* Phone 915/532-7273. *www.nps.gov/cham.* Celebration of international folklife. Musicians, dancers. Oct.

El Paso Symphony Orchestra. *Abraham Chavez Theater, 1 Civic Center Plaza, El Paso (79901).* Phone

915/532-3776. *www.epso.org.* Sixteen concerts with solo artists September-April. Also summer concerts and special events. **$$$$**

Fiesta de las Flores. *El Paso County Coliseum, 4100 E Paisano St, El Paso (79905).* Phone 915/542-3464. Carnival festivities with a Latin flavor. Labor Day weekend.

Horse racing. **Sunland Park Race Course,** *1200 Futurity Dr, Sunland Park (88603). 6 miles W, just off I-10 in New Mexico.* Phone 505/874-5200. *www.sunlandpark.com.* Thoroughbred and quarter horse racing. Pari-mutuel betting. Water-ski shows on infield lake (Sat-Sun, weather permitting). Casino (daily noon-midnight). (Nov-Apr: daily from 9 am)

Siglo de Oro. *Chamizal National Memorial, 800 S San Marcial St, El Paso (79905).* Phone 915/532-7273. Festival of Classical Spanish drama wtih performances by professional and collegiate groups from Spain, Puerto Rico, Mexico, and the United States. Late Feb-early Mar.

Southwestern International Livestock Show & PRCA Rodeo. *4100 E Paisano St, El Paso (79905).* First two weeks in Feb.

St. Anthony's Day Celebration. *Ysleta del Sur Reservation, 119 S Old Pueblo Dr, El Paso (79907).* Phone 915/859-7913. Religious patron saint of the Tiguas; special food and ceremonies. June.

Sun Carnival. *4100 Rio Bravo St, El Paso (79902).* Phone 915/533-4416. *www.sunbowl.org.* Festivities and sporting events; ending with the Sun Bowl. Thanksgiving weekend-Dec.

Viva El Paso. *McKelligon Canyon Amphitheatre, 3 McKelligon Canyon Rd, El Paso (79930).* Phone 915/565-6900; toll-free 800/915-8482. Outdoor musical that chronicles the story of the stuggles of the early Indian, Spanish, and Mexican settlers. June-Aug.

Limited-Service Hotels

★ **COMFORT INN.** *900 N Yarbrough Dr, El Paso (79915).* Phone 915/594-9111; toll-free 800/424-6423; fax 915/590-4364. *www.comfortinnelpaso.com.* 200 rooms, 3 story. Pets accepted, some restrictions; fee. Complimentary continental breakfast. Check-in 3 pm, check-out noon. Outdoor pool, whirlpool. Airport transportation available. **$**

★ ★ **EMBASSY SUITES.** *6100 Gateway Blvd E, El Paso (79905). Phone 915/779-6222; toll-free 800/362-2779; fax 915/779-8846. www.embassysuites.com.* Located in the business district, this atrium hotel is close to the airport and the Mexican border. 184 rooms, 8 story, all suites. Complimentary full breakfast. Check-in 3 pm, check-out noon. High-speed Internet access. Restaurant, bar. Fitness room. Indoor pool, whirlpool. Airport transportation available. Business center. **$**

★ ★ **HOLIDAY INN.** *900 Sunland Park Dr, El Paso (79922). Phone 915/833-2900; toll-free 800/465-4329; fax 915/833-6338. www.holiday-inn.com/elpaso-sunlnd.* On hill overlooking Sunland Park. 178 rooms, 2 story. Pets accepted; fee. Check-in 3 pm, check-out noon. Restaurant, bar. Fitness room. Outdoor pool, whirlpool. Airport transportation available. Business center. **$**

★ **LA QUINTA INN.** *6140 Gateway Blvd E, El Paso (79905). Phone 915/778-9321; toll-free 800/531-5900; fax 915/779-1505. www.lq.com.* 121 rooms, 2 story. Pets accepted. Complimentary continental breakfast. Check-in 1 pm, check-out noon. Fitness room. Outdoor pool. Airport transportation available. **$**

Full-Service Hotel

★ ★ ★ **CAMINO REAL HOTEL EL PASO.** *101 S El Paso St, El Paso (79901). Phone 915/534-3000; toll-free 800/769-4300; fax 915/534-3024. www.caminoreal.com.* Located downtown, next to the convention center and performing arts theater, this renovated historic hotel (1912) features a lobby bar covered by an original Tiffany glass dome. 359 rooms, 17 story. Pets accepted, some restrictions; fee. Check-in 3 pm, check-out noon. High-speed Internet access. Restaurant, bar. Fitness room. Outdoor pool. Airport transportation available. Business center. **$**

Restaurants

★ ★ **BELLA NAPOLI.** *6331 N Mesa St, El Paso (79912). Phone 915/584-3321.* Italian, American menu. Lunch, dinner. Closed Mon, Tues; Thanksgiving, Dec 25; week of July 4. Outdoor seating. **$$**

★ **CASA JURADO.** *4772 Doniphan Dr, El Paso (79922). Phone 915/833-1151; fax 915/833-1152.* Mexican menu. Lunch, dinner. Closed Mon; holidays. Bar. Casual attire. **$**

★ ★ **CATTLEMAN'S STEAKHOUSE AT INDIAN CLIFFS RANCH.** *3045 S Fabens-Carlsbad Rd, Fabens (79838). Phone 915/544-3200; fax 915/764-4168. www.cattlemanssteakhouse.com.* A children's zoo and playground are featured here. Seafood, steak menu. Lunch, dinner. Bar. Children's menu. Casual attire. **$$**

★ ★ **JAXON'S.** *4799 N Mesa St, El Paso (79912). Phone 915/544-1188; fax 915/544-0638. www.jaxons.com.* American menu. Lunch, dinner. Closed Thanksgiving, Dec 25. Bar. Children's menu. Casual attire. Reservations recommended. **$$**

★ ★ **SENOR JUAN'S GRIGGS.** *9007 Montana Ave, El Paso (79925). Phone 915/598-3451.* Mexican, American menu. Lunch, dinner. Closed Thanksgiving, Dec 25. Bar. **$$**

★ ★ **STATE LINE.** *1222 Sunland Park Dr, El Paso (79922). Phone 915/581-3371; fax 915/833-4843. www.countyline.com.* Barbecue menu. Lunch, dinner. Closed Jan 1, Thanksgiving, Dec 24-25. Bar. Children's menu. Casual attire. **$$**

Ennis (B-8)

See also Arlington-Grand Prairie, Corsicana, Dallas

Population 16,045
Elevation 548 ft
Area Code 972
Zip 75119
Information Chamber of Commerce, 108 Chamber of Commerce Dr, PO Box 1177, 75120; phone 972/878-2625
Web Site www.ennis-chamber.com

Ennis has preserved many historical buildings in the downtown area. The town is also noted for the Bluebonnet Trails, which are at their best in April (see SPECIAL EVENTS).

What to See and Do

Lake Bardwell. *4000 Observation Dr, Ennis (75119). 4 1/2 miles SW on Hwy 34. Phone 972/875-5711.* Beaches, water-skiing, fishing, boating (ramps, marina); nature trail, picnicking, tent and trailer sites (electric and water hook-ups, dump station). Some fees. (Daily)

Special Events

Bluebonnet Trails. Garden Club-sponsored 40 miles of fields in profusion of blooming wildflowers. Contact the Chamber of Commerce. Mid-late Apr.

National Polka Festival. *Phone 972/878-2625.* Parade, Czech costumes, arts and crafts fair. Memorial Day weekend.

Specialty Lodging

The following lodging establishment is approved by Mobil Travel Guide, but due to its unique and individualized nature has not been given a traditional Mobil Star rating. Included in this listing you may find bed-and-breakfasts, limited-service inns, guest ranches, and other unique hotel properties.

BONNYNOOK INN. *414 W Main, Waxahachie (75165). Phone 972/938-7207; toll-free 800/486-5936; fax 972/938-7700. www.bonnynook.com.* The film *Bonnie and Clyde* was done in this small town, home of this bed-and-breakfast. Old-world elegance with 20th-century comfort. 5 rooms, 2 story. Pets accepted, some restrictions. Complimentary full breakfast. Check-in 4 pm, check-out noon. **$**

Fairfield (B-8)

See also Palestine

Population 3,094
Elevation 461 ft
Area Code 903
Zip 75840
Information Chamber of Commerce, 900 W Commerce, PO Box 956; phone 903/389-5792
Web Site www.fairfieldtx.com

What to See and Do

Burlington-Rock Island Railroad Museum. *208 S 3rd Ave, Teague. 10 miles SW via Hwy 84. Phone 903/739-2408. www.therailroadmuseum.com.* Housed in the 1906 depot of the old Trinity & Brazos Valley Railroad; railroad artifacts, items of local history, genealogical records; also two-room log house. Tours by appointment. (Sat-Sun 1-5 pm; closed holidays) **$**

Fairfield Lake State Park. *123 State Park Rd 64, Fairfield (75840). NE on Hwy 84 to FM 2570, then E on FM 3285. Phone 903/389-4514.* More than 1,400 acres. Swimming, water-skiing, fishing, boating (ramps); hiking trails, picnicking, playground, improved campsites (dump station). Guided boat tours of bald eagle habitats (fee). (Daily) **$**

Freestone County Historical Museum. *302 Main St, Fairfield. Phone 903/389-3738.* Old county jail (1857), two log cabins, old church, antiques exhibit, county history items, old telephone exhibit, artifacts of seven wars, Civil War letters; quilts. Tours. (Wed, Fri-Sat, also Sun afternoons; closed holidays) **$$**

Fort Stockton (C-4)

See also Alpine, Monahans, Pecos

Founded 1859
Population 7,846
Elevation 2,954 ft
Area Code 915
Zip 79735
Information Chamber of Commerce, 1000 Railroad Ave, PO Box C; phone 915/336-2264 or toll-free 800/336-2166
Web Site www.fortstockton.org

Fort Stockton grew around a military post established in 1859 at Comanche Springs; the springs had previously been a watering place on the California Trail, the San Antonio-San Diego Stage Line, and on the Comanche War Trail, which extended from Chihuahua to Arkansas. Today, the area surrounding Fort Stockton has more than 100,000 acres of irrigated land producing pecans, vegetables, alfalfa, grain, wine grapes, and cotton; the area is also known for cattle, sheep, and goat ranches, and for its many oil and gas wells. Fort Stockton is rich in preserved landmarks.

What to See and Do

Annie Riggs Hotel Museum. *301 S Main St, Fort Stockton. Phone 915/336-2167.* (1899) Turn-of-the-century hotel, later run as a boarding house; 14 of the original 15 rooms feature displays on local history and the town's development. Self-guided tours. (Daily; closed holidays) **$**

Old Fort Stockton. *4 blocks off Hwy 290 at Rooney St, between 2nd and 5th sts and at Water and 8th sts. Phone 915/336-2400. www.tourtexas.com/fortstockton/*

ftstockriggs.html. Some of the original 24-inch adobe-walled officers' quarters, the old guardhouse, and the fort cemetery remain; rebuilt barracks kitchen. Self-guided tours (maps available at Chamber of Commerce Tourist Center). (Mon-Sat 10 am-noon and 1-5 pm, Sun 1:30-5 pm; closed holidays) **$**

Special Event

Water Carnival. *Comanche Springs Swimming Pool, 103 W Callaghan, Fort Stockton (79735). Phone toll-free 800/336-2166.* Mid-July.

Limited-Service Hotels

★ ★ BEST WESTERN SWISS CLOCK INN.
3201 W Dickinson, Fort Stockton (79735). Phone 432/336-8521; toll-free 800/780-7234; fax 432/336-6513. www.bestwestern.com. 112 rooms, 2 story. Pets accepted. Complimentary full breakfast. Check-in 2:30 pm, check-out noon. Restaurant. Outdoor pool. **$**

🐾 🏊

★ LA QUINTA INN. *1537 N Hwy 285, Fort Stockton (79735). Phone 432/336-9781; toll-free 800/531-5900; fax 432/336-3634. www.lq.com.* 97 rooms, 2 story. Pets accepted, some restrictions. Complimentary continental breakfast. Check-in 1 pm, check-out noon. Outdoor pool. **$**

🐾 🏊

Fort Worth (A-8)

See also Arlington-Grand Prairie, Cleburne, Dallas/Fort Worth Airport Area, Denton, Eastland, Granbury, Mineral Wells, Weatherford

Founded 1849
Population 534,694
Elevation 670 ft
Area Code 817
Information Convention & Visitors Bureau, 415 Throckmorton, 76102; phone 817/336-8791 or toll-free 800/433-5747
Web Site www.fortworth.com
Suburbs Arlington-Grand Prairie, Cleburne, Denton, Granbury, Weatherford. (See individual alphabetical listings.)

Somewhere between Dallas and Fort Worth is the dividing line between the East and the West. Dallas is sophisticated and fashionable; Fort Worth is proudly simple and open. The city's predominant industry, cattle (for a long time symbolized by the historic Fort Worth Stockyards), has been joined by the oil, grain, aircraft, and computer industries, creating a modern metropolis full of shops, restaurants, theaters, and nightspots that somehow continue to reflect a distinctly Western character.

In the mid-19th century, Fort Worth was a camp (never a fort) with a garrison to protect settlers. It was later named Fort Worth in honor of General William J. Worth, a Mexican War hero. After the Civil War, great herds of longhorn cattle were driven through the area en route to the Kansas railheads. Cowboys camped with their herds outside of town and "whooped it up" at night.

By 1873, the Texas & Pacific Railroad had reached a point 26 miles east when its backers, Jay Cooke & Co, failed. The population fell from 4,000 to 1,000, and a Dallas newspaper commented that Fort Worth was a place so dead that a panther was seen sleeping on the main street. In response to this insult, Fort Worth called itself "Panther City," and the long-term feud between Fort Worth and Dallas had begun.

A group of citizens headed by K. M. Van Zandt formed the Tarrant County Construction Company and continued the building of the railroad. In 1876, the T&P had a state land grant that would expire unless the road reached Fort Worth before the legislature adjourned. While efforts were made to keep the legislature in session, practically everybody in Fort Worth went to work on the grading and laying of track.

The legislature finally decided to adjourn in two days. It seemed impossible that the line could be finished. The desperate Fort Worthians improvised cribs of ties to bridge Sycamore Creek and for 2 miles laid the rails on ungraded ground. The city council is said to have moved the city limits east to meet it. The first train, its whistle tied down, wheezed into town on July 19, 1876. Fort Worth had become a shipping point.

In 1882 the free school system was begun, and the first flour mill started operations. In 1883, the Greenwall Opera House was host to many famous stars. In 1870 a local banking institution, now known as Nations Bank, opened. Oil did not come in until 1917, but in the years before and since, Fort Worth has continued to grow. The headquarters for several well-known American companies are located in Fort Worth.

Public Transportation

Buses (Transportation Authority of Fort Worth), phone 817/215-8600.

Airport For additional accommodations, see DALLAS/FORT WORTH AIRPORT AREA, which follows DALLAS.

What to See and Do

150 Years of Fort Worth Museum. *1501 Montgomery St, Fort Worth (76102). Phone 817/255-9300. www.fort worthmuseum.org/firesta.html.* Museum recounts the history of the city in a series of photographs and artifacts on view in Fire Station No. 1, the city's first fire station, built in 1907. (Daily 9 am-8 pm) **FREE**

Amon Carter Museum. *3501 Camp Bowie Blvd, Fort Worth (76107). Phone 817/738-1933. www.carter museum.org.* This major collection of American paintings, photography, and sculpture includes works by Winslow Homer, Georgia O'Keeffe, Grant Wood, Thomas Cole, Frederic Remington, and Charles Russell; changing exhibits. The building was designed by Philip Johnson. (Tues-Wed, Fri-Sat 10 am-5 pm, Thurs to 8 pm, Sun noon-5 pm; closed holidays) **FREE**

Bass Performance Hall. *525 Commerce St, Fort Worth (76102). Phone 817/212-4280. www.basshall.com.* Opened in 1998, the $65 million masterpiece has been hailed as "the last great hall built in the 20th century." Home to the Van Cliburn International Piano Competition, the Fort Worth Symphony, the Fort Worth Opera, and the Fort Worth/Dallas Ballet. National touring productions and special concerts are offered here as well. (Closed holidays) **$$$$**

Bayard H. Friedman Tennis Center. *3609 Bellaire Dr N, Fort Worth (76109). Phone 817/257-7960. www.tennis.tcu.edu.* On the campus of Texas Christian University, tall green trees frame this center, making for a pleasant setting to serve and volley or hug the baseline. Whatever your style of play, you're sure to work up a good sweat and tone those thighs as you try to ace your opponent. Go for your best shots on one of 16 outdoor courts ($) or five indoor ones ($$$$). (Mon-Fri 9 am-9 pm, Sat-Sun 9 am-7:30 pm; closed holidays)

Benbrook Lake. *7001 Lake Side Dr, Fort Worth (76113). 4 miles S of I-20 off 77. Phone 817/292-2400.* Swimming, water-skiing, fishing, boating (ramps, marinas); horseback riding, golf, picnicking, concession, camping (tent and trailer sites). Fees may be charged at some recreation areas. (Daily) **$$**

Botanic Garden. *3220 Botanic Garden Blvd, Fort Worth (76107). Phone 817/871-7686. www.fwbg.org.* More than 150,000 plants of 2,000 species include native plants and tropical plants. Conservatory ($), fragrance garden, rose gardens, perennial garden, trial garden. Extensive Japanese garden with bridges, waterfalls, teahouses. (Daily 8 am-dusk) **FREE**

Bureau of Engraving and Printing's Western Currency Facility Tour and Visitor Center. *9000 Blue Mound Rd, Fort Worth (76131). Phone 817/231-4000; toll-free 866/865-1194. www.moneyfactory.com.* See money (bills from $1 to $50) being printed as you walk along an enclosed walkway suspended over the production floor. Two floors of interactive displays showcase the history of currency and the printing process. Theater, gift shop, vending areas. Call ahead to schedule a tour. Tours (Mon-Fri 10:30 am-6 pm) **FREE**

Burger's Lake. *1200 Meandering Rd, Fort Worth (76114). Phone 817/737-3414. www.burgerslake.com.* On a steamy Texas day, cool off in this old-fashioned swimming hole, a 1-acre, spring-fed lake with a sandy bottom. Five diving boards, a 20-foot slide, and a trapeze over the water keep kids happy, and lifeguards keep them safe. Catch the sun's rays on two sandy beaches, or escape them under big shade trees spread across the 30-acre grounds. When the clan gets hungry, the park has plenty of charcoal grills and picnic tables, or you can head to the snack bar. (Mid-May-Aug, daily 9 am-7:30 pm) **$$**

Casa Mañana Theatre. *3101 W Lancaster, Fort Worth (76107). At Lancaster and University Dr. Phone 817/332-2272. www.casamanana.org.* Large geodesic dome houses professional performances ranging from Broadway shows to children's theater. (Tues-Sun evening performances, Sat-Sun matinees)

Eagle Mountain Lake. *NW via Hwy 199 and Farm Rd 1220.* A 9,200-acre impoundment on the West Fork of the Trinity River, the lake is home to Fort Worth Boat Club, which sponsors numerous sailing regattas. Water sports enthusiasts are served well by several marinas, which offer watercraft rentals, gas docks, restaurants, and cafés. Beaches, parks, boat ramps, bait shops.

Fort Worth Museum of Science & History. *1501 Montgomery St, Fort Worth (76107). Phone 817/255-9300; toll-free 888/255-9300. www.fortworthmuseum.org.* Exhibits on fossils, anthropology, geology, natural sciences, and history. Hands-on, changing, and permanent exhibits. (Daily; closed Thanksgiving, Dec 24-25) **$$$** Also here are

Noble Planetarium. *1501 Montgomery St, Fort Worth (76107). Phone 817/255 9300. www.fortworthmuseum.org/noble.html.* Shows change periodically. Public shows (daily). **$$**

Omni Theater. *1501 Montgomery St, Fort Worth. Phone 817 255 9300.* Seventy-millimeter Omnimax films are screened on an 80-foot projection dome. Films change periodically. (Daily; closed Thanksgiving, Dec 24-25) **$$$**

Fort Worth Nature Center & Refuge. *9601 Fossil Ridge Rd, Fort Worth (75135). 4 miles W of I-820, off Hwy 199. Phone 817/237-1111.* A 3,600-acre wildlife habitat. Nature trails; picnicking. Visitor center. (Tues-Sat 9 am-5 pm, Sun noon-5 pm; closed Thanksgiving, Dec 25) **FREE**

⭐ **Fort Worth Stockyards National Historic District.** *121 E Exchange Ave, Fort Worth (76106). From downtown Fort Worth, head N on N Main St to Exchange Ave, the gateway to the Stockyards. Phone 817/626-7921. www.fortworthstockyards.org.* Yee-haw! Walk these streets and see something you can't see anywhere else in America—a daily cattle drive with genuine Texas cowboys herding big, beefy steers down the way. This lively district, listed on the National Register of Historic Places, celebrates all things Western in its 15 square blocks. Down an ice-cold longneck beer in the saloon. Cheer on the bull riders at the rodeo. Get decked out in Western duds from one of the many stores, and then go for a spin on the Texas-size dance floor at Billy Bob's Texas. If you're lucky, a country star might be croonin' some hit tunes at the happenin' honky-tonk, the world's largest. Restaurants and a hotel also welcome visitors. (Daily) Also here are

Billy Bob's Texas. *2520 Rodeo Plaza, Fort Worth (76106). Phone 817/624-7117. www.billybobstexas.com.* Family fun center and country music nightclub offer live entertainment, bull riding, video and arcade games, billiards, dancing, and a restaurant. (Mon-Sat 11-2 am, Sun noon-2 am) **$$**

Old Trail Driver's Park. *28th and Decatur sts, Fort Worth. E of the stockyards.* Adjacent to the stockyards, to the west is Rodeo Park.

Stockyards Museum. *131 E Exchange Ave, Suites 111-114, Fort Worth (76106). Phone 817/625-5082.* Featuring the 1986 Texas Sesquicentennial Wagon

Train Collection, this museum also contains memorabilia and hands-on artifacts of the stockyards era, the meatpacking industry, and the railroad. (Mon-Sat 10 am-5 pm, Sun 12-5 pm; closed holidays) **DONATION**

Fort Worth Water Garden. *Between Houston and Commerce sts, Fort Worth. Just S of Fort Worth/Tarrant County Convention Center.* Enormous concrete, terraced water gardens containing a wide variety of foliage, trees, and spectacular water cascades and fountains. (Daily) **FREE**

Fort Worth Zoo. *1989 Colonial Pkwy, Fort Worth (76110). In Forest Park; I-30 to University Dr, then 1 mile S (follow signs). Phone 817/759-7555. www.fortworthzoo.com.* This is a 68-acre beastly attraction with 5,000-plus animals. One of the zoo's exhibits, Texas Wild! is an 8-acre spectacle that takes you on a zoological trek across the Lone Star State, introducing you to the flora and fauna in six regions. Its many interactive displays keep kids entertained while they learn. Sneaky. They can milk a simulated cow, climb in a beehive, and more. A train ride and carousel add to the fun. Elsewhere, take a good look at all the wild creatures you expect to eyeball, plus a few you don't. For example, it's one of only two United States zoos with all four Great Ape species in residence: bonobos, chimpanzees, gorillas, and orangutans. No wonder families like monkeying around on these grounds.(Apr-mid-Oct: Mon-Fri 10 am-5 pm, Sat-Sun to 6 pm; mid-Oct-mid-Feb: daily 10 am-4 pm; mid-Feb-Apr: daily 10 am-5 pm) **$$**

Hell's Half Acre to Sundance Square. *100 E 8th St, Fort Worth (76102). At Main. Phone 817/253-5909.* Guided walking tour of historic downtown Fort Worth. Filled with anecdotal stories of city's past and present, and tips on points of interest. Approximately 2 1/2 hours. Call ahead for reservations. **$$$**

Jubilee Theatre. *506 Main St, Fort Worth (76102). Phone 817/338-4411. www.jubileetheatre.org.* A primary venue for African American theater in Texas, productions enjoy long runs and consistently good critical response. (Call for schedule) **$$$$**

Kimbell Art Museum. *3333 Camp Bowie Blvd, Fort Worth (76107). Phone 817/332-8451. www.kimbellart.org.* With its worldwide reputation for excellence, the Kimbell draws plenty of art lovers through its doors and into its 22,000 square feet of galleries, where innovative use of natural light enhances the viewing. And you're sure to like what you see, given the quality of the museum's 331-piece permanent collection. Its holdings span from antiquity to the 20th century, with masterpieces by the likes of Cézanne, El Greco, Matisse, Monet, Picasso, Rembrandt, and Velazquez. Few other museums in the Southwest can match its Asian arts in particular, with standouts such as *Earth Spirit,* an eighth-century Chinese Tang Dynasty sculpture. The Kimbell also showcases selected pieces of pre-Columbian and African art, as well as Greek, Roman, Egyptian, and Near Eastern antiquities. Plus, the museum hosts some of the country's most talked-about traveling exhibitions (fees for special exhibitions vary). (Tues-Thurs, Sat 10 am-5 pm, Fri noon-8 pm, Sun noon-5 pm; closed holidays) **FREE**

Lake Worth. *9 miles NW on Hwy 199.* Boating, fishing; picnicking.

Log Cabin Village. *2100 Log Cabin Village Ln, Fort Worth (76109). Phone 817/926-5881. www.logcabinvillage.org.* The pioneers who claimed Texas as their own in the 1800s lived a much different life than modern-day Texans do. No electric lights. No air-conditioning. No luxury homes with backyard swimming pools. Tour the log houses in this village, which are furnished with authentic artifacts, and you'll see how rustic life was way back when. Costumed "interpreters" help take you back to those days. Spinners twist natural wool into thread, a miller grinds shelled corn into meal, and more. (Tues-Fri 9 am-4 pm, Sat-Sun 1-5 pm; closed holidays) **$**

Maverick Fine Western Wear. *100 E Exchange Ave, Fort Worth (76106). Phone 817/626-1129; toll-free 800/282-1315. www.maverickwesternwear.com.* Want to shop where country music stars score some of their dazzlin' duds—from boots and hats to shirts and skirts? Then two-step your way over to this high-end store in the Stockyards (see) for snazzy Wild West attire that's mostly uptown, not down-home. You'll find top-name brands for men, women, and children, and you'll probably pay top dollar for them. Order a beer or glass of wine at the bar to revive your spirits. (Mon-Thurs 10 am-6 pm, Fri-Sat 10 am-10 pm, Sun 11 am-6 pm; closed holidays)

Modern Art Museum of Fort Worth. *3200 Darnell St, Fort Worth (76107). Phone 817/738-9215; toll-free 866/824-5566. www.mamfw.org.* Even if you've visited Texas's oldest art museum in the past, you won't recognize it now. In December 2002, the museum packed up its belongings and moved to a stunning new 153,000-square-foot facility with 53,000 square feet of galleries, five times what it had before. You can now gaze at much more of the 2,600-piece permanent collection of post-World War II international art, which includes works by modern masters such as Francis Bacon and Andy Warhol. You'll be awed by drawings, paintings, photographs, prints, sculpture, site-specific installations, and videotapes/discs. Major traveling exhibits add still more variety to the marvelous mix (fee for special exhibition tickets). But you'll be impressed even before you step inside to begin your visual voyage. From the outside, the museum's five long, flat-roofed pavilions seemingly float in a 1 1/2-acre pond—it's quite a sight. (Tues-Thurs, Sat 10 am-5 pm, Fri 10 am-8 pm, Sun 11 am-5 pm; Tues 10 am-8 pm early Sept-mid-Nov; closed holidays) **$**

Scenic drive. Through Trinity and Forest parks on the Clear Fork of the Trinity River. These beautiful parks have bicycle trails, a duck pond, zoo, and miniature train.

Sol Y Luna. *900 Houston St, Fort Worth (76102). www.padrinocigars.com/solyluna.htm.* Slip into something fashionably casual and make the scene at this hip hangout with a split personality. On the first floor, order a martini (or other classic cocktail) and make good conversation in a laid-back, stylish setting. In the cozy cigar room, sink into an overstuffed chair and puff on a hand-rolled stogie while sipping cognac by the fireplace. For more of a club scene, descend the stairs to a dimly lighted basement, where the music and action get cranked up several decibels.

Sundance Square Entertainment District. *4th and Main sts, Fort Worth (76102). Throckmorton and Calhoun sts between 2nd and 5th sts. www.sundance square.com.* Shopping, dining, art, and entertainment district of brick streets and renovated turn-of-the-century buildings. Markers along a self-guided walking tour commemorate historic locations and events; the 300 block of Main Street is especially associated with the city's colorful history and with such characters of the Old West as Butch Cassidy; the Sundance Kid; and Luke Short, an infamous Western gambler who gunned down the town's marshal in front of the notorious White Elephant Saloon.

Thistle Hill. *1509 Pennsylvania Ave, Fort Worth (76104). At Summit Ave. Phone 817/336-1212. www.thistlehill.org.* (1903) This restored mansion was built by one of the cattle barons who made Fort Worth a major city. Guided tours (Mon-Fri 11 am-2 pm, Sun 1-3 pm; closed holidays). **$$**

Trinity River Trails. *300 N Main St, Fort Worth (76102). Pick up the trails in downtown Fort Worth at Heritage Park. Phone 817/926-0006. www.trwd.com.* To get yourself pumped up, go walking, biking, running, or inline skating along any of these scenic trails, which border the Trinity River and stretch for 32 miles in various directions from downtown. The west route will take you through an especially serene, heavily wooded area about 2 miles from the central business district. Go southwest and you'll pass through popular Trinity Park and the city's cultural district. In some sections, the trails are paved; in others, they're crushed limestone. (Daily) **FREE**

⭐ **Will Rogers Memorial Center.** *3401 W Lancaster St, Fort Worth (76107). Phone 817/871-8150.* Will Rogers statue, Memorial Coliseum, Tower, Auditorium, Amon Carter Jr. Exhibit Hall, Equestrian Center. Many community events are held here, including horse shows, boxing, circuses, rodeos.

William Edrington Scott Theater. *1300 Gendy, Fort Worth (76107). Phone 817/738-6509.* This 500-seat theater located in the Fort Worth Community Arts Center features plays and opera performances. (Year-round)

Special Events

MAIN Street Fort Worth Arts Festival. *Downtown, Main St, Fort Worth. Phone 817/336-2787. www.msfwaf.org.* Nine blocks of historic Main Street become a marketplace for arts, food, and live entertainment. One of the largest events of its kind. Mid-Apr.

Southwestern Exposition & Livestock Show. *Will Rogers Memorial Center, 3401 W Lancaster Ave, Fort Worth (76107). Phone 817/877-2400. www.fwstockshow rodeo.com.* Mid-Jan–early Feb.

Texas Motor Speedway. *3545 Lone Star Cir, Fort Worth (76177). Phone 817/215-8500. www.texasmotorspeed way.com.* NASCAR, Indy Racing League, and a variety of other racing events and classes. Call or visit Web site for racing schedule. **$$$$**

Limited-Service Hotel

★ ★ **COURTYARD BY MARRIOTT DOWNTOWN.** *601 Main St, Fort Worth (76102). Phone 817/885-8700; toll-free 800/321-2211; fax 817/885-8303. www.courtyard.com/dfwms.* Within walking distance of all of Fort Worth's restaurants, attractions, and night life, this contemporary hotel's prime loca-

tion makes it ideal for visitors to the city. Relax in the whirlpool or work out in the hotel's fitness room to unwind after a long day. 203 rooms, 20 story. Check-in 3 pm, check-out noon. High-speed Internet access. Bar. Fitness room. Outdoor pool, whirlpool. Business center. **$**
🧍 🛏 🏃

Full-Service Hotels

🔑 ★ ★ ★ **THE ASHTON HOTEL.** *610 Main St, Fort Worth (76102). Phone 817/332-0100; toll-free 866/327-4866; fax 817/332-0110. www.theashtonhotel.com.* Small, intimate, and luxurious best describe this boutique hotel, which occupies a historic downtown building built in 1915. All of its guest rooms have king-size beds that invite slumber with their Italian Frette linens, plush duvets, and down pillows. Some rooms have a claw-foot whirlpool tub nestled away in a corner, 12-foot ceilings, and good views of Main Street. Custom-designed mahogany furniture helps give the entire hotel a rich, inviting look. Sample the New American cuisine dished up in Café Ashton, or, if you're with a small group of up to 20, book the Wine Cellar for private dining. Work off the calories in the small fitness center. 39 rooms, 6 story. Pets accepted; fee. Check-in 3 pm, check-out noon. High-speed Internet access. Restaurant, bar. Fitness room. **$$$**
🐾 🏃

★ ★ ★ **DORAL TESORO HOTEL & GOLF RESORT.** *3300 Championship Pkwy, Fort Worth (76177). Phone 817/961-0800; fax 817/961-0900. www.doraltesoro.com.* 286 rooms. Check-in 3 pm, check-out noon. High-speed Internet access. Two restaurants, two bars. Fitness room. Outdoor pool, whirlpool. Golf, 18 holes. Business center. **$$**
✈ 🧍 🛏 ⛳ 🏃

★ ★ ★ **RENAISSANCE FORTH WORTH WORTHINGTON HOTEL.** *200 Main St, Fort Worth (76102). Phone 817/870-1000; toll-free 888/236-2427; fax 817/338-9176. www.renaissancehotels.com.* 504 rooms, 12 story. Pets accepted, some restrictions; fee. Check-in 3 pm, check-out noon. High-speed Internet access. Two restaurants, two bars. Fitness room. Indoor pool, whirlpool. Tennis. Business center. **$$**
🐾 🧍 🛏 🎾 🏃

★ ★ ★ **STOCKYARDS HOTEL.** *109 E Exchange Ave, Fort Worth (76106). Phone 817/625-6427; toll-free 800/423-8471; fax 817/624-2571. www.stockyardshotel*

.com. Check into this hotel and turn back time to the days of cattle drives and cattle rustlers. Located in Fort Worth's Stockyards, a national historic district, the hotel dates to the early 1900s, when it offered an elegant Old West theme to businessmen and ranchers in town for the booming livestock market. Completely restored in the 1980s, the property still has that Old West feel. The guest rooms have Western, Native American, Mountain Man, or Victorian décor. Instead of the typical lobby bar, there is Booger Red's Saloon, where saddles serve as barstools. The Western touch really heats up in H3 Ranch, a steakhouse with a hickory wood grill. 52 rooms, 3 story. Pets accepted; fee. Check-in 3 pm, check-out noon. High-speed Internet access. Restaurant, bar. **$$**

Specialty Lodging

The following lodging establishment is approved by Mobil Travel Guide, but due to its unique and individualized nature has not been given a traditional Mobil Star rating. Included in this listing you may find bed-and-breakfasts, limited-service inns, guest ranches, and other unique hotel properties.

TEXAS WHITE HOUSE. *1417 Eighth Ave, Fort Worth (76104). Phone 800/279-6491; toll-free 800/279-6491; fax 817/923-0410. www.texaswhitehouse.com.* 5 rooms. Complimentary full breakfast. Check-in 3-6 pm, check-out noon. **$**

Restaurants

★ **ANGELO'S.** *2533 White Settlement Rd, Fort Worth (76107). Phone 817/332-0357; fax 817/336-3091. www.angelosbbq.com.* Barbecue menu. Lunch, dinner. Closed Sun; holidays. Children's menu. Casual attire. **$**

★ ★ ★ **ANGELUNA.** *215 E 4th St, Fort Worth (76102). Phone 817/334-0080; fax 817/334-0903. www.angelunabasshall.com.* With a great downtown location close to Sundance Square and directly in front of the beautiful Bass Performing Hall, this restaurant features a large and attractive marble-top bar. The innovative menu offers a variety of appetizers, pizzas, pastas, and main entrees. Italian, Mediterranean menu. Lunch, dinner. Bar. Business casual attire. Reservations recommended. Valet parking. Outdoor seating. **$$$**

★ ★ **BELLA ITALIA WEST.** *5139 Camp Bowie Blvd, Fort Worth (76107). Phone 817/738-1700.* Italian

menu. Lunch, dinner. Closed holidays. Bar. Outdoor seating. **$$**

★ ★ **BISTRO LOUISE.** *2900 S Hulen St, Suite 40, Fort Worth (76109). Phone 817/922-9244; fax 817/922-8148. www.bistrolouise.com.* Mediterranean menu. Lunch, dinner, Sun brunch. Closed holidays. Bar. Children's menu. Outdoor seating. **$$**

★ ★ **BLUE MESA GRILL.** *1600 S University Dr, Fort Worth (76107). Phone 817/332-6372; fax 817/332-6398. www.bluemesagrill.com.* Southwestern menu. Lunch, dinner, Sun brunch. Closed Thanksgiving, Dec 25. Bar. Children's menu. Casual attire. Outdoor seating. **$$**

★ ★ **CLASSIC CAFE.** *504 N Oak, Roanoke (76262). Phone 817/430-8185; fax 817/491-1432. www.theclassiccafe.com.* American menu. Lunch, dinner. Closed Sun; holidays. Bar. Children's menu. Casual attire. Reservations recommended. **$$$**

★ **EDELWEISS.** *3801 Southwest Blvd #A, Fort Worth (76116). Phone 817/738-5934; fax 817/738-6946. www.edelweissrestaurant.com.* German, American menu. Dinner. Closed Sun-Mon; holidays. **$$**

★ **FIESTA MEXICAN.** *3233 Hemphill St, Fort Worth (76110). Phone 817/923-6941.* Mexican menu. Breakfast, lunch, dinner. Closed Sun-Mon evenings. Bar. Casual attire. **$**

★ ★ **JOE T. GARCIA'S.** *2201 N Commerce, Fort Worth (76106). Phone 817/626-4356; fax 817/626-0581. www.joets.com.* Mexican menu. Lunch, dinner. Closed Thanksgiving, Dec 25. Bar. Outdoor seating. **$$**

★ **MANCUSO'S.** *9500 White Settlement Rd, Fort Worth (76108). Phone 817/246-7041.* The building is more than 100 years old. Italian menu. Lunch, dinner. Closed Sun; holidays. Children's menu. Outdoor seating. **$$**

★ ★ ★ **MICHAELS RESTAURANT & ANCHO CHILE BAR.** *3413 W 7th St, Fort Worth (76107). Phone 817/877-3413; fax 817/877-3430. www.michaelscuisine.com.* Southwestern menu. Lunch, dinner. Closed Sun; holidays. Bar. Business casual attire. Outdoor seating. **$$**

★ ★ **RANDALL'S GOURMET CHEESECAKE CO.** *907 Houston St, Fort Worth (76102). Phone 817/336-2253; fax 817/336-5476.* This trendy American bistro is located in the lower downtown area. A clubby, romantic atmosphere and a well-executed menu make a winning combination. American bistro menu. Lunch, dinner. Closed Sun-Mon. **$$**

★ **TOKYO STEAKHOUSE.** *8742 Hwy 80 W, Fort Worth (76116). Phone 817/560-3664; fax 817/560-2093.* Japanese, Thai menu. Lunch, dinner. Closed holidays. Bar. Children's menu. **$$$**

Fredericksburg (C-7)

See also Johnson City, Kerrville, Mason

Founded 1846
Population 8,911
Elevation 1,742 ft
Area Code 830
Zip 78624
Information Chamber of Commerce/Convention & Visitors Bureau, 106 N Adams; phone 830/997-6523
Web Site www.fredericksburg-texas.com

Nearly 600 Germans came here to settle under the auspices of the Society for the Protection of German Immigrants in Texas. Surrounded by Comanches, isolated, plagued with epidemics, unfamiliar with the country, they fought a bitter battle for survival. Upright and industrious, they prospered until the Civil War when, disapproving of slavery, men hid out in the hills and fled to Mexico to avoid joining the Confederate Army. Their troubles continued during Reconstruction, but these folks persevered by being self-reliant. In 1912, they built their own railroad to connect with the nearest line; this was discontinued in 1941. In 1937, Highway 87 was built through the town; now Highway 290 and Highway 16 also run through here. Today, Fredericksburg, the center of diversified farming and ranching activity, is a picturesque community with many stone houses.

What to See and Do

Admiral Nimitz Museum State Historical Park. *340 E Main St, Fredericksburg. Phone 830/997-4379.* Dedicated to the more than 2 million men and women of all services who served under Fleet Admiral Chester W. Nimitz, a Fredericksburg native. The restored steamboat-shaped Nimitz Hotel (1852) contains three floors of exhibits in the Museum of the Pacific War. History Walk is lined with rare guns, planes, and tanks from the Pacific theater. Captured Japanese minisub. The Garden of Peace was built by the Japanese. (Daily; closed Dec 25) **$$**

Enchanted Rock State Natural Area. *16710 Ranch Rd 965, Fredericksburg (78624). 18 miles N off Rural Rte 965. Phone 915/247-3903; toll-free 800/792-1112. www.tpwd.state.tx.us/park/enchantd.* One of the nation's largest batholiths, Enchanted Rock is a climber's dream, attracting hikers and rock climbers in droves—so many, in fact, that parking sometimes reaches capacity as early as 10 or 11 am on weekends. Legend has it that the sight of "ghost fires" and the sound of unearthly creaking and groaning, first observed by the Tonkawa Indians, led to this huge rock formation's name. Geologists are less romantic, explaining that the noises result from the rock's heating by day and contracting during the cool of the night. Conquer the rock via a short, steep trail. There's also a 4-mile backpacking/day-hiking trail in the park, as well as an interpretive center. Wildlife is plentiful—you may even spot the odd armadillo—and plant communities are many and varied, ranging from Texas persimmon to live oak to bushybeard bluestem. Camping and picnicking are allowed, and the park's a good place for bird-watching and stargazing. **$**

Pioneer Museum. *309 W Main St, Fredericksburg. Phone 830/990-8431.* Complex of several buildings, including Weber Sunday House, log cabin. Relics of German colonists. (Daily; closed holidays) **$$**

Vereins Kirche Museum. *Market Sq, Fredericksburg. Off 100 block W Main St; opposite courthouse. Phone 830/997-7832.* (Pioneer Memorial Building) Reproduction of the original (1847) octagonal community building; archives and local history collection. (Daily) **FREE**

Special Events

Candlelight Tour of Homes. *312 W San Antonio St, Fredericksburg (78624). Phone 830/997-2835.* Second week in Dec. **$$$$**

Easter Fires Pageant. *2000 S Hwy 16, Fredericksburg (78624). Phone 830/997-2359.* Dates back more than 100 years. Sat evening before Easter.

Educational Festival. *312 W San Antonio St, Fredericksburg (78624). Phone 830 997-2835.* Pioneer period crafts, dancing, entertainment. Second Sat in May.

Food and Wine Fest. *100 W Main St, Fredericksburg (78624). Phone 830/997-8515.* Texas wine, food, music. Late Oct.

Gillespie County Fair. *2000 S State Hwy 16, Fredericksburg (78624). Phone 830/997-2359.* Oldest county fair in Texas. Fourth weekend in Aug.

Night in Old Fredericksburg. *106 N Adams, Fredericksburg. Phone 830/997-8515.* German food, entertainment. Third weekend in July.

Limited-Service Hotels

★ **FREDERICKSBURG INN AND SUITES.** *201 S Washington St, Fredericksburg (78624). Phone 830/997-0202; toll-free 800/446-0202; fax 830/997-5740. www.fredericksburg-inn.com.* 103 rooms, 2 story. Complimentary continental breakfast. Check-in 3 pm, check-out 11 am. High-speed Internet access, wireless Internet access. Two outdoor pools, whirlpool. **$**
🏊

★ **SUNDAY HOUSE INN & SUITES.** *501 E Main St, Fredericksburg (78624). Phone 830/997-4484; toll-free 800/274-3762; fax 830/997-5607. www.sunday houseinnandsuites.com.* 124 rooms, 3 story. Pets accepted, some restrictions; fee. Check-in 3 pm, check-out noon. Outdoor pool. **$**
🐾 🏊

Specialty Lodging

The following lodging establishment is approved by Mobil Travel Guide, but due to its unique and individualized nature has not been given a traditional Mobil Star rating. Included in this listing you may find bed-and-breakfasts, limited-service inns, guest ranches, and other unique hotel properties.

MAGNOLIA HOUSE. *101 E Hackberry St, Fredericksburg (78624). Phone 830/997-0306; toll-free 800/880-4374; fax 830/997-0766. www.magnolia-house.com.* Built in 1923. 5 rooms, 2 story. Children over 12 years only. Complimentary full breakfast. Check-in 2 pm, check-out 11 am. Airport transportation available. **$**
🏷

Restaurants

★ **FRIEDHELM'S BAVARIAN.** *905 W Main St, Fredericksburg (78624). Phone 830/997-6300; fax 830/997-6302.* German menu. Lunch, dinner. Closed Mon; Thanksgiving, Dec 25. Bar. Children's menu. Casual attire. **$$**

★ **MAMACITA'S.** *506 E Main St, Fredericksburg (78624). Phone 830/997-9546; fax 830/997-6818.* Mexican menu. Lunch, dinner. Closed Thanksgiving, Dec 25. Bar. Children's menu. Casual attire. Reservations recommended. **$**

Fritch (E-3)

See also Amarillo, Pampa

Population 2,235
Area Code 806
Zip 79036
Information Chamber of Commerce, 104 N Robey, PO Box 396; phone 806/857-2458

What to See and Do

Hutchinson County Historical Museum. *618 N Main St, Borger. 12 miles E. Phone 806/273-0130.* Professionally designed museum emphasizes oil boom of the 1920s and the story of Hutchinson County. Photos of Boomtown Borger; models of early houses and Fort Adobe Walls. Painting of Chief Quanah Parker, the Battle of Adobe Walls, and early Native American fighter Billy Dixon. Tools and oil field equipment, Panhandle Pueblo artifacts; dancehall, pioneer house, changing exhibits. (Mon-Sat; closed holidays) **FREE**

Lake Meredith Aquatic & Wildlife Museum. *104 N Robey, Fritch. Phone 806/857-2458.* Life-size dioramas of small game found around lake area. Five aquariums holding 11,000 gallons of water display the variety of fish found in Lake Meredith. (Daily; closed Jan 1, Thanksgiving, Dec 25) **FREE**

Lake Meredith National Recreation Area. *419 E Broadway, Fritch. Phone 806/857-3151.* Created by the Sanford Dam on the Canadian River and stocked with walleye, bass, channel and blue catfish, crappie, and perch. Swimming, water-skiing, fishing, boating (ramps); picnicking, primitive camping (some sites restrooms, dump stations). (Daily) **FREE** On south edge of lake is

Alibates Flint Quarries National Monument. *419 E Broadway, Fritch. Phone 806/857-3151.* Includes area of flint quarries used by Native Americans of several periods from 10,000 BC to AD 1700. Contact Lake Meredith Recreation Area, PO Box 1460. **FREE**

Special Event

World's Largest Fish Fry. *Phone 806/274-2211.* June. **$$**

Gainesville (A-8)

See also Denison, Denton, Sherman

Founded 1849
Population 15,538
Elevation 738 ft
Area Code 940
Zip 76240
Information Chamber of Commerce, 101 S Culberson, 76240; phone toll-free 888/585-4468.
Web Site www.gainesville.tx.us

Once a stop on the Butterfield Stage Line, Gainesville today is an industrial center producing airplane interiors, cutting tools, and foodstuffs.

What to See and Do

Leonard Park. *1000 W California, Gainesville. Phone toll-free 888/585-4468.* Swimming pool, bathhouse (mid-May-Labor Day; fee); picnicking, playground, ballfields. Frank Buck Zoo is also here. Park (daily).

Morton Museum of Cooke County. *210 S Dixon St, Gainesville. Phone 940/668-8900.* Former city fire station (1884) now houses items of county history dating to 1850. Tours of historic downtown area (by appointment). (Tues-Sat; closed holidays) **FREE**

Moss Lake. *E Hwy 70, Gainesville. 12 miles NW. Phone toll-free 888/585-4468.* A 1,125-acre lake with 15 miles of shoreline. Fishing, camping; picnicking.

Limited-Service Hotels

★ **BEST WESTERN SOUTHWINDS.** *2103 N I-35, Gainesville (76240). Phone 940/665-7737; toll-free 800/731-1501; fax 940/668-2651. www.bestwestern.com.* 35 rooms. Pets accepted; fee. Complimentary continental breakfast. Check-out 11 am. Outdoor pool. **$**

★ **RAMADA INN.** *600 Fair Park Blvd, Gainesville (76241). Phone 940/665-8800; fax 940/665-8709.* 118 rooms, 2 story. Check-out noon. Outdoor pool. **$**

Restaurant

★ **CLARK'S OUTPOST BBQ.** *101 N Hwy 377, Tioga (76271). Phone 940/437-2414; fax 940/437-5529.* Barbecue menu. Lunch, dinner. Closed Jan 1, Thanksgiving, Dec 24-25. Bar. Children's menu. **$$**

Galveston (D-9)

See also Angleton, Baytown, Houston, Texas City

Founded 1816
Population 57,247
Elevation 20 ft
Area Code 409
Information Galveston Island Convention & Visitors Bureau, 2428 Seawall Blvd, 77550; phone toll-free 888/425-4753
Web Site www.galvestontourism.com

Few American cities have histories as romantic and adventurous as Galveston's. It is generally agreed that the Spanish explorer Cabeza de Vaca, the first European to see Texas, was shipwrecked on Galveston Island in 1528. From here he began his wanderings through Texas, New Mexico, and finally to Mexico, where his tales inspired later expeditions.

The pirate Jean Lafitte was lord of Galveston from 1817 until 1821. He built a house and fortress called Maison Rouge (Red House). Under Lafitte, the town was a nest of slave traders, saloon keepers, gamblers, smugglers, and pirates. One hundred Spanish ships were seized and looted during Lafitte's time, but Spain was powerless against him. Many slaves were on the pirated vessels; Lafitte's standard price for slaves was a dollar a pound.

Lafitte's occupation ended in May 1821, after the United States Navy ordered him to leave. He set fire to the town, fleeing southward and into oblivion with his remaining followers.

During the Texas Revolution, the four ships of the Texas Navy were based in Galveston and managed to prevent a blockade of the Texas coast. When David Burnet, interim President of the Republic of Texas, and his cabinet came here in 1836, fleeing from Santa Ana, the town became the capital of Texas.

After the Civil War, Congress appropriated money to make Galveston a deep-water port. The town had a population of 38,000 in 1900. On September 8 of that year, a hurricane with 110-mph winds struck, flooding the city, killing 6,000 and leaving 8,000 homeless. The storm drove a 4,000-ton vessel to a point 22 miles from deep water. Galveston rebuilt itself with inspired fortitude. The level of land was raised from 5 to 17 feet and a 17-foot-high, 16-foot-wide reinforced concrete seawall was built. The wall has withstood subsequent hurricane tides.

Galveston's wharves can berth 38 oceangoing vessels. It is the state's leading cotton port and is a sulphur and grain shipping center. It is an island city colored with blooming tropical flora. Forty blocks of the East End Historical District, protected from future development, may be seen on walking or driving tours.

With 32 miles of sandy beaches, fishing piers, deep-sea fishing, cool breezes off the Gulf and plenty of places to stay, eat, and enjoy oneself, Galveston is an ideal spot for a seaside vacation. Such vacations are its specialty, although the city is also an important medical center and international seaport.

What to See and Do

1839 Williams Home. *3601 Ave P, Galveston. Phone 409/762-3933. www.galvestonhistory.org/plc-williamshouse.htm.* Home of Texas pioneer, patriot, and entrepreneur Samuel May Williams, the house was saved from the wrecker's ball and meticulously restored. (Sat-Sun noon-4 pm; closed holidays) **$$**

Ashton Villa. *2328 Broadway, Galveston (77550). At 23rd St. Phone 409/762-3933. www.galvestonhistory.org/plc-ashtonvilla.htm.* (1859) This three-story brick Italianate mansion has been restored to reflect life in Galveston during the late 1800s; period furniture, many interesting details include ornate cast-iron verandas in Gothic Revival-style. Tours begin in carriage house, located on grounds, and include the ornate Gold Room and second-floor family quarters. (Memorial Day-Labor Day: Mon-Sat 10 am-4 pm, Sun from noon; winter: daily noon-4 pm; closed Thanksgiving, Dec 24-25) **$$$**

The Bishop's Palace. *1402 Broadway, Galveston (77550). Phone 409/762-2475.* (1886) Four-story stone Victorian mansion, former residence of Bishop Byrne (1923-1950), is an outstanding example of this style and period; marble, mosaics, stained- and jeweled-glass windows, hand-carved stairwell and woodwork,

art objects from many lands. Tours. (June-early Sept: noon-4 pm; mid-Sept-May: daily 10 am-4:45 pm) **$$**

Factory Stores of America. *11001 Delany Rd, LaMarque (77568). Approximately 15 minutes on I-45, exit 13, in LaMarque. Phone 409/938-3333. www.factorystores.com.* More than 30 outlet stores can be found in this outdoor shopping area. (Mon-Thurs 10 am-5 pm, Fri-Sat to 7 pm, Sun noon-7 pm; closed holidays) **FREE**

Galveston Island State Park. *14901 Farm Market Rd, Galveston (77554). 11 miles SW on FM 3005. Phone 409/737-1222. www.tpwd.state.tx.us/park/galvesto.* A 2,000-acre recreational area. Swimming, fishing, boating in bay and Gulf; nature trails, picnicking (shelters), improved campsites (hook-ups, showers, dump station). (Daily) **$**

Galveston-Port Bolivar Ferry. *State Hwy 87 and Ferry Rd, Galveston. Phone 409/763-2386.* Taking this 2.7-mile trip is the only way that motorists can cross the waterway between Bolivar Peninsula and Galveston Island. Operated by the Texas Department of Transportation. (Daily) **FREE**

Grand 1894 Opera House. *2020 Postoffice St, Galveston (77550). Phone 409/765-1894. wwww.thegrand.com.* Extraordinary theater with magnificent restoration hosts national touring shows and other performing arts year-round. (Call for schedule)

"The Great Storm." *Pier 21 Theater, 21st St and Harbor Side Dr (formerly Port Industrial Blvd), Galveston (77550). Phone 409/763-8808.* A 27-minute documentary tells the story of the devastating hurricane that killed more than 6,000 people and destroyed one third of the city in September 1900. (Hourly presentations Sun-Thurs: 11 am-6 pm; Fri-Sat 11 am-8 pm) **$**

Gulf Greyhound Park. *1000 FM 2004 Rd, La Marque (77568). One block W of I-45 S at exit 15; 30 miles S of Houston and 15 miles N of Galveston. Phone 409/986-9500. www.gulfgreyhound.com.* The world's largest greyhound racing operation, Gulf Greyhound Park, has attracted close to 9 million visitors since it opened in November 1992. Dog races are held in the evenings Tuesday through Saturday, with additional matinees on Friday, Saturday, and Sunday. The air-conditioned complex features four levels, each with a variety of dining and viewing options, including Texas's largest full-service dining room, which has the capacity to seat 1,900 with a view of the track. There are 318 teller windows and more than 1,100 close-circuit televisions. The park's 18 kennels house 60 greyhounds each. Dogs race on a sand-composition track on 5/16-,

3/8-, and 7/16-mile courses. Call ahead for information about special events, ranging from wife-carrying contests to dachshund races. (Tues-Sun) **$**

Moody Gardens Aquarium & Rainforest. *1 Hope Blvd, Galveston (77554). Phone toll-free 800/582-4673. www.moodygardens.com.* Rising from the edge of Galveston Island like three polished gems, the massive pyramid structures that house Moody Gardens Aquarium & Rainforest are architectural wonders. Inside, guests have a plethora of entertainment options to choose from. The ten-story glass Rainforest Pyramid includes thousands of tropical plants, exotic fish, birds, and butterflies native to the rain forests of Africa, Asia, and the Americas. It also houses "Toadally Frogs," the largest frog and toad collection in the country. With 1.5 million gallons of water, the Aquarium at Moody houses exhibits representing the North Pacific, South Pacific, Antarctic, and Caribbean regions with 8,000-plus specimens of marine life. The Discovery Pyramid focuses on science, with interactive demonstrations of science experiments and traveling exhibits. IMAX 3D and Ridefilm theaters offer visual thrills, and the Garden's Palm Beach water park is a relaxing outdoor oasis. (Winter: Sun-Fri 10 am-6 pm, Sat 10 am-8 pm; June-Aug: daily 10 am-9 pm) **$$$**

Ocean Star. *Pier 19, Harborside St, Galveston (77550). Phone 409/766-7027. www.oceanstaroec.com.* Step aboard an offshore rig and experience the oil and gas production work at sea through videos, interactive displays, and models from around the world. (Daily 10 am-5 pm; to 6 pm in summer) **$$**

Railroad Museum at the Center for Transportation and Commerce. *123 Rosenberg, Galveston (77550). Phone 409/765-5700.* At the foot of the historic Strand in the restored Santa Fe Union Station, this 5-acre museum contains the largest collection of restored railroad equipment in the Southwest. Sound and light shows portray the history and development of Galveston Island; the miniature layout of the Port of Galveston features an HO-scale railroad. Building includes a 1930s waiting room. (Daily, hours vary; call for schedule; closed holidays, Mardi Gras week) **$**

Recreational facilities. *Phone 409/763-5668. www.galveston.com/beachparks.* Galveston offers 32 miles of beaches with fishing piers, boats for rent, and amusements. Stewart Beach (6th and Seawall Blvd; closed Nov-Feb), a municipal development, is at the east end of the island. Fishing is allowed from five free county piers, by boat rental, or by charter boat for deep-sea sport. There are riding stables at Jamaica Beach on Stewart Rd and two golf courses and several tennis courts in the area. Anchorage for 300 pleasure boats and yachts at the Galveston Yacht Club (715 Holiday Dr); also for 556 (400 covered) at the marina, 11th St at Pier 7.

Seawolf Park. *Pelican Island via Seawolf Pkwy (51st St), Galveston (77550). Phone 409/744-5738. www.galveston.com/beachparks/seawolfpark.shtml.* World War II submarine USS *Cavalla* and destroyer escort USS *Stewart* are located here; also an Army tank and Navy fighter plane. Playground, picnicking, fishing pier (fee), pavilion. Parking (fee). Park (daily). **$**

⭐ **The Strand National Historic Landmark District.** *502 20th St, Galveston (77550). Extends between 20th and 25th sts. Phone 409/766-7068.* This historic area is restored to late 1800s appearance. The Strand, once known as the "Wall Street of the Southwest," contains one of the finest concentrations of 19th-century commercial structures in the United States. Many are now restored and used as apartments, restaurants, shops, and galleries. Various events take place here throughout the year (see SPECIAL EVENTS). Contact the Galveston Historical Foundation, 2016 Strand (77550).

Texas Seaport Museum. *Pier 21, #8, Galveston (77550). Phone 409/763-1877. www.tsm-elissa.org.* Features the tallship *Elissa*, built in Scotland in 1877. The ship, crafted by Alexander Hall & Company, shipbuilders famous for their beautiful iron sailing ships, traded under five different flags and visited ports throughout the world. Rescued from the scrapyard in 1974 and restored by Galveston Historical Foundation. Audiovisual presentation on *Elissa*; galleries with maritime exhibits. (Daily 10 am-5 pm; closed Thanksgiving, Dec 25) **$$**

Treasure Island Tour Train. *2106 Seawall Blvd, Galveston (77550). Departs from Beach Central. Phone 409/765-9564.* Ninety-minute, 17-mile trip around Galveston. (June-Aug: 9 am, 11 am, 1:30 pm, 3:30 pm, and 5:30 pm; Sept-Dec, Mar-May: daily 11 am and 1:30 pm, weather permitting; May: daily 9 am, 11 am, 1:30 pm, and 3:30 pm; closed holidays) **$$**

Special Events

Dickens on the Strand. *2016 Strand, Galveston (77550). Phone 409/766-7068. www.dickensonthe strand.org.* Located in the Strand National Historic

Landmark District. Yuletide celebration recreates 19th-century London street scene including live representations of Charles Dickens' characters, carolers, dancers, puppeteers, and outdoor handbell festival. First weekend in Dec. **$$**

Galveston Island Outdoor Musicals. *Moody Gardens Convention Center, One Hope Blvd, Galveston (77554). I-45 S, exit 61st St, make a right then right on Seawall Blvd. Right on 81st St to Jones Rd. Left on Hope Blvd to Moody Gardens. Phone 409/737-1744. www.galveston musicals.com.* Broadway, other productions. Mid-June-early Sept.

Historic Homes Tour. *502 20th St, Galveston (77550). Phone 409/765-7834. www.galvestonhistory.org.* Tour of 19th-century private houses not normally open to the public. Contact Galveston Historical Foundation. May. **$$$**

Mardi Gras. *502 20th St, Galveston (77550). Phone 409/766-7068. www.mardigrasgalveston.com.* The largest Mardi Gras celebration in Texas, this event lasts for 12 days and 11 nights and features parades, live music, masquerade balls, and many ornate costumes. Mid-late Feb. **$$$$**

Limited-Service Hotels

★ **HARBOR HOUSE.** *Pier 21, Galveston (77550). Phone 409/763-3321; toll-free 800/874-3721; fax 409/765-7721.* 42 rooms, 3 story. Complimentary continental breakfast. Check-in 4 pm, check-out noon. **$**

★ ★ **HOLIDAY INN.** *5002 Seawall Blvd, Galveston (77551). Phone 409/740-3581; toll-free 800/465-4329; fax 409/740-6677. www.holiday-inn.com.* 179 rooms, 8 story. Check-in 3 pm, check-out noon. Restaurant, bar. Fitness room. Beach. Outdoor pool, children's pool. Airport transportation available. **$**
🛉 🛏

★ **LA QUINTA INN & SUITES GALVESTON.** *8710 Seawall Blvd, Galveston (77554). Phone 409/740-9100; fax 409/744-0782. www.lq.com.* 70 rooms. Check-in 3 pm, check-out noon. Outdoor pool, whirlpool. **$**
🛏

Full-Service Hotel

★ ★ ★ **WYNDHAM TREMONT HOUSE HOTEL.** *2300 Ship Mechanic Row, Galveston (77550). Phone 409/763-0300; toll-free 800/996-3426; fax 409/763-1539. www.wyndham.com.* This 1879 building features 11-foot-high windows. 119 rooms, 4 story. Check-in 4 pm, check-out noon. High-speed Internet access. Restaurant, bar. Fitness room. **$$**
🛉

Full-Service Resorts

★ ★ ★ **HILTON GALVESTON ISLAND RESORT.** *5400 Seawall Blvd, Galveston (77551). Phone 409/744-5000; toll-free 800/475-3386; fax 409/740-2209. www.galvestonhilton.com.* With no better place to meet and relax, this hotel ensures comfort with attentive service and all the comforts of home. 150 rooms, 6 story. Check-in 4 pm, check-out 11 am. Restaurant, two bars. Fitness room. Outdoor pool, whirlpool. **$**
🛉 🛏

★ ★ ★ **SAN LUIS RESORT AND CONFERENCE CENTER.** *5222 Seawall Blvd, Galveston (77551). Phone 409/744-1500; toll-free 800/445-0090; fax 409/744-8452. www.sanluisresort.com.* This hotel offers its guests a relaxing stay whether they are traveling for business or leisure. The property is on a 22-acre island and has a heated pool with swim-up bar and whirlpool, full spa, and much more. 241 rooms, 16 story. Check-in 4 pm, check-out 11 am. High-speed Internet access. Two restaurants, two bars. Children's activity center. Fitness room (fee), fitness classes available, spa. Outdoor pool, children's pool, whirlpool. Tennis. Airport transportation available. Business center. **$$**
🛉 🛏 🛝 🛉

★ ★ ★ **WYNDHAM HOTEL GALVEZ.** *2024 Seawall Blvd, Galveston (77550). Phone 409/765-7721; toll-free 800/996-3426; fax 409/765-5623. www.wyndham.com.* 226 rooms, 7 story. Check-in 3 pm, check-out noon. High-speed Internet access, wireless Internet access. Restaurant, two bars. Fitness room. Beach. Outdoor pool, whirlpool. Business center. **$**
🛉 🛏 🛉

Restaurants

★ ★ **CLARY'S.** *8509 Teichman Rd, Galveston (77554). Phone 409/740-0771; fax 409/740-1872.* Seafood menu. Lunch, dinner. Closed Mon. Bar. **$$**

★ ★ **GAIDO'S.** *3800 Seawall Blvd, Galveston (77550). Phone 409/762-9625; fax 409/762-4825. www.galveston.com/gaidos.* Established in 1911.

Seafood menu. Lunch, dinner. Closed Dec 25. Bar. Children's menu. Casual attire. **$$**

★ ★ **LUIGI'S RISTORANTE ITALIANO.** *2328 Strand, Galveston (77550). Phone 409/763-6500; fax 409/763-0270.* Roman décor in historic Victorian building (1895). Italian menu. Lunch, dinner. Closed Sun. Bar. Children's menu. Business casual attire. Reservations recommended. **$$**

★ ★ **MERCHANT PRINCE.** *2300 Ship's Mechanic Row, Galveston (77550). Phone 409/763-0300; fax 409/763-1539.* Atrium dining. American menu. Breakfast, lunch, dinner. Bar. Children's menu. Casual attire. Reservations recommended. Valet parking. **$$$**

Georgetown (C-8)

See also Austin, Burnet, Salado

Founded 1848
Population 28,339
Elevation 758 ft
Area Code 512
Information Convention and Visitor's Bureau, PO Box 409, 78627-0346; phone 512/930-3545 or toll-free 800/436-8696
Web Site www.georgetown.org

Established as a trade center for this agricultural region, Georgetown is the seat of Williamson County, one of Texas's most productive farming areas and home of Southwestern University. The town's Main Street has some of the best Victorian architecture in the state.

What to See and Do

Inner Space Cavern. *Directly underneath I-35, Georgetown (78627). Take exit 259 off I-35. Phone 512/931-2283. www.innerspace.com.* Go underground with the kids at the most accessible cavern in central Texas, located just 24 miles north of Austin, literally underneath Interstate 35. The stalactites, helectites, and soda straws will wow the little ones, and probably even you. Be sure to pan for gems and minerals in the mine, and don't miss the fossil displays in the visitor's center. (Daily; closed Thanksgiving, Dec 11-25) **$$$**

Lake Georgetown. *500 Cedar Breaks Rd, Georgetown (78628). 4 miles W of I-35 via FM 2338. Phone 512/930-5253.* This 1,300-acre lake is surrounded by four developed park areas. Hiking trail (16 1/2 miles), camping (fee). (Daily) **FREE**

San Gabriel Park. *1003 N Austin Ave, Georgetown (78626). N edge of town, on the San Gabriel River. Phone 512/930-3595.* Eighty acres with fishing, swimming; picnicking (shelters, barbecue facilities), ballfield, hiking; livestock show barns, rodeo arena. **FREE**

Southwestern University. *1001 E University Ave, Georgetown. Phone 512/863-6511.* (1840) (1,200 students.) Oldest university in Texas. Several historic buildings; chapel. Self-guided tours. (Mon-Sat)

Special Event

Mayfair. *Phone 512/930-3545.* Air show, art walk. May.

Limited-Service Hotels

★ **COMFORT INN.** *1005 Leander Rd, Georgetown (78628). Phone 512/863-7504; fax 512/819-9016. www.comfortinn.com* 54 rooms. Pets accepted; fee. Complimentary continental breakfast. Check-in 2 pm, check-out noon. High-speed Internet access, wireless Internet access. Outdoor pool. **$**

★ **LA QUINTA INN.** *333 N I-35, Georgetown (78628). Phone 512/869-2541; toll-free 800/531-5900; fax 512/863-7073. www.lq.com.* 99 rooms, 3 story. Pets accepted. Complimentary continental breakfast. Check-in 3 pm, check-out noon. Outdoor pool, whirlpool. **$**

Glen Rose (B-7)

Web Site www.glenrosetexas.net

What to See and Do

Fossil Rim Wildlife Center. *2155 County Rd 2008, Glen Rose (76043). S on Hwy 144, then 3 miles SW of Glen Rose off Hwy 67. Phone 254/897-2960.* A 3,000-acre wildlife conservation center with more than 1,000 endangered, threatened, and exotic animals. Breeding programs for endangered species include white rhinoceros, Mexican wolf, red wolf, Grevy's zebra, Arabian oryx, scimitar-horned oryx, addax, and cheetah. Ten-mile drive-through with nature trail; fossil area; petting pasture. Restaurant; gift shop. Some fees.

(Daily 8:30 am-5:30 pm; closed Thanksgiving, Dec 24-25) **$$$$**

Full-Service Resort

★ ★ ★ **ROUGH CREEK LODGE.** *Country Rd 2013, Glen Rose (76043). Phone 254/965-3700; toll-free 800/864-4705; fax 254/965-3170. www.roughcreek.com.* 39 rooms, 2 story. Pets accepted, some restrictions; fee. Check-in 3 pm, check-out 11 am. Restaurant, bar. Children's activity center. Fitness room, spa. Outdoor pool, whirlpool. Tennis. **$$$**

Specialty Lodging

The following lodging establishment is approved by Mobil Travel Guide, but due to its unique and individualized nature has not been given a traditional Mobil Star rating. Included in this listing you may find bed-and-breakfasts, limited-service inns, guest ranches, and other unique hotel properties.

INN ON THE RIVER. *205 SW Barnard, Glen Rose (76043). Phone 254/897-2929; toll-free 800/575-2101; fax 254/897-7729. www.innontheriver.com.* 22 rooms, 2 story. Children over 16 years only. Complimentary full breakfast. Check-in 4 pm. Check-out noon. Outdoor pool. **$$**

Goliad (D-8)

See also Victoria

Founded 1749
Population 1,975
Elevation 171 ft
Area Code 361
Zip 77963
Information Chamber of Commerce, Market and Franklin sts, PO Box 606; phone 361/645-3563
Web Site www.goliad.org/goliad.html

A Mexican garrison stationed in Goliad was conquered in 1835 by American settlers in Texas; in December of that year, the first Declaration of Texas Independence was issued from the city of Goliad. Three weeks after the fall of the Alamo, in March 1836, Colonel James W. Fannin and 350 men holding the town were overwhelmed by Mexican forces, and surrendered. They were promised they would be treated as prisoners of war; instead, they were massa-

cred. Spurred on by the resultant wrath and the battle cry "Remember the Alamo, remember Goliad," Texas Republic forces devastated Santa Ana at San Jacinto.

Now a farm and ranching market town, Goliad remains a monument to the Texas Revolution.

What to See and Do

Goliad State Park. *108 Park Rd 6, Goliad (77963). 1 mile S on Hwy 183 to Park Rd 6. Phone 361/645-3405. www.tpwd.state.tx.us/park/goliad.* Goliad is saturated in history, figuring prominently in everything from the origin of the Cinco de Mayo holiday to the beginning of Texas cattle ranching to the signing of the first Declaration of Texas Independence. But the thing that makes this state park an outstanding attraction is that there's something to please everyone else in the family: a gorgeous setting, quaint special events that coincide with holidays (twinkling lights leading up to Christmas, the Messiah at Easter), plus a petting zoo and some of the best camping around. There's also access to the San Antonio River for fishing and canoeing and a junior Olympic-size swimming pool. Built in 1749, Mission Espiritu Santo was the first great cattle ranch in Texas. Reconstructed in the 1930s, the mission now serves as historical focal point of the park. Across the river is Presidio La Bahia, the fort built to protect the mission. It was here that 92 citizens hoisted the first flag of Texas independence. (Daily 7 am-10 pm; closed Dec 25) **$** Includes

Mission Espiritu Santo de Zuñiga. A reconstruction of the original mission established in 1749. The interpretive center in the mission contains artifacts and displays illustrating the Spanish colonial era. (Daily 8 am-noon, 1-5 pm)

Market House Museum. *131 S Courthouse Sq, Goliad. Corner of Franklin and Market sts. Phone 361/645-3563.* The Market House, restored in 1967 as a museum, was built in 1870 with stalls that were rented to sellers of meat and produce. In 1886 the building became a firehouse, home to the volunteer fire department. Chamber of commerce offices are here as well. (Wed-Sat 11 am-5 pm; closed holidays) **FREE**

Presidio La Bahia. *1 mile S on Hwy 183. Phone 361/645-3752.* (1721) The only completely restored Spanish Colonial Presidio in the Western Hemisphere and the only one in North America to have participated in six wars for independence. Spanish, Mexican, and Texan soldiers once garrisoned its fortified walls. The first Declaration of Texas Independence was signed here; the first flag of Texas independence flew here. Site of the longest siege in American military history (1812-1813) and the Goliad Massacre (1836), the largest loss of life for Texas independence. Living history programs, battle reenactments, seasonal fiestas throughout the year. (Daily; closed holidays) **$$**

Special Events

Goliad County Fair & Rodeo. *Fairgrounds. Phone 361/645-2492.* Third weekend in Mar.

Stock car racing. *Shady Oaks Speedway, 6878 County Rd 283, Edna (77957). 6 miles N off Hwy 77A on FM 622. Phone 361/645-1963.* Mar-Oct.

Tour de Goliad Bike Ride. *Phone 361/645-3563.* Third week in Oct. **$$$$**

Gonzales (D-8)

See also San Marcos, Seguin

Settled 1825
Population 7,202
Area Code 830
Zip 78629
Information Chamber of Commerce, 414 St. Lawrence St, PO Box 134; phone 830/672-6532

In 1835, the city of Gonzales had a small brass cannon that the Mexican government had left for defense in case of Native American attack. When the American settlers grew dissatisfied with Mexican rule, they refused to return the cannon. Mexico then sent a detachment to take it by force. The first Texas battle flag, with a single star and the words "Come and Take It," was unfurled. When the Mexicans came, the first shots of the Texas Revolution were fired (October 2, 1835), and the Mexicans withdrew. Later, Gonzales's men went to the Alamo to aid Colonel William Travis, although they knew the cause was hopeless.

What to See and Do

Gonzales County Jail Museum. *414 St. Lawrence, Gonzales (78629). Phone 830/672-6532.* Restored cells, gallows, dungeon, and jailer's room. (Daily; closed holidays) **FREE**

Gonzales Memorial Museum. *414 Smith St, Gonzales. Phone 830/672-6350.* Collection of toys, guns, clothing, pictures, and letters that depict Gonzales and its

history. Includes the legendary cannon. (Tues-Sun) **FREE**

Gonzales Pioneer Village. *N Hwy 183, Gonzales. 1 mile N on Hwy 183. Phone 830/672-2157.* Village consists of more than ten reconstructed buildings from before 1900. Includes log house, blacksmith shop, printing press, grainery, working broom factory, 1890s house, and 1870s church. Special tours, programs (fees). Adjacent is Fort Waul, an earthen-walled Confederate fort (1864). (Sept-May: Sat-Sun; Jun-Aug: Fri-Sun) **$$**

Palmetto State Park. *Park Rd 11 and FM 291, Gonzales (78649). 12 miles NW on Hwy 183, 2 miles W on Park Rd 11. Phone 830/672-3266.* Approximately 270 acres. Swimming, fishing (pier); picnicking (shelter; fee), playground, nature and hiking trails, improved camping (hook-ups, dump station). (Daily) **$**

Special Events

Come and Take It Celebration. *414 St. Lawrence, Gonzales (78629). Phone 830/672-6532.* Honors first shot fired for Texas independence. Parade, street dance, vintage house tours, battle reenactments. First weekend in Oct.

Springfest. *Phone 830/672-6532.* Tour of historic homes. Last weekend in Apr.

Graham (A-7)

See also Mineral Wells

Founded 1872
Population 8,716
Elevation 1,045 ft
Area Code 940
Zip 76450
Information Chamber of Commerce, 608 Elm St, PO Box 299; phone 940/549-3355 or toll-free 800/256-4844
Web Site www.visitgraham.com

The Cattle Raisers Association of Texas was organized here in 1877. Today, Graham is a farming, ranching, and oil commercial center.

What to See and Do

Fort Richardson State Historical Park. *Park Rd 61 and Hwy 281 S, Jacksboro. 30 miles E via Hwy 380. Phone 940/567-3506.* Approximately 400 acres. Most northerly of frontier army posts in Texas, active 1867-1878. Seven restored buildings and two replicas. Interpretive center and period displays. Fishing; hiking, nature study, picnicking, improved campsites (hook-ups, dump station). (Daily) **$**

Possum Kingdom State Park. *15 miles E of Breckenridge on Hwy 180 to Caddo, then 17 miles N on Park Rd 33. Phone 940/549-1803.* This park, on the shores of Possum Kingdom Reservoir, is located in the Brazos River Valley. The reservoir covers 19,800 acres behind the Morris Sheppard Dam and has a 310-mile shoreline. Water sports are popular; catfish, striped bass, white bass, and crappie abound. Fishing pier. Hiking trail. Canoe, boat, pontoon, bass boat rentals available at park store. The park covers more than 1,500 acres and offers swimming, water-skiing, boating (ramps); picnicking, playground, concessions, improved campsites, cabins.

Limited-Service Hotel

★ ★ **GATEWAY INN.** *1401 Hwy 16 S, Graham (76450). Phone 940/549-0222.* 77 rooms, 2 story. Pets accepted, some restrictions; fee. Check-out noon. Restaurant. Outdoor pool, whirlpool. Airport transportation available. **$**

Granbury (B-7)

See also Arlington-Grand Prairie, Cleburne, Fort Worth

Population 5,718
Elevation 722 ft
Area Code 817
Zip 76048
Information Granbury Convention and Visitors Bureau, 100 N Crockett; phone 817/573-5548 or toll-free 800/950-2212
Web Site www.granbury.org

What to See and Do

Granbury Opera House. *133 E Pearl St, Granbury. Phone 817/573-9191.* (1886) Restored opera house on historic town square. Musicals, plays, special events. (Summer: Thurs-Sun; rest of year: Fri-Sun)

Special Event

General Granbury Civil War Reenactment. *Phone 817/573-5548.* Late Sept.

Limited-Service Hotels

★ **COMFORT INN.** *1201 N Plaza Dr, Granbury (76048). Phone 817/573-2611; fax 817/573-2695. www.comfortinn.com.* 48 rooms, 2 story. Complimentary continental breakfast. Check-out noon. Outdoor pool, whirlpool. **$**

★ **PLANTATION INN ON THE LAKE.** *1451 E Pearl St, Granbury (76048). Phone 817/573-8846; toll-free 800/422-2403; fax 817/579-0917.* 53 rooms, 2 story. Pets accepted, some restrictions; fee. Complimentary continental breakfast. Check-out 11 am. Outdoor pool, children's pool. **$**

Specialty Lodging

The following lodging establishment is approved by Mobil Travel Guide, but due to its unique and individualized nature has not been given a traditional Mobil Star rating. Included in this listing you may find bed-and-breakfasts, limited-service inns, guest ranches, and other unique hotel properties.

NUTT HOUSE HISTORICAL HOTEL. *119 E Bridge St, Granbury (76048). Phone toll-free 888/678-0813. www.nutt-house-hotel.com.* 7 rooms, all suites. Complimentary full breakfast. Check-in 3-6 pm, check-out 11 am. Restaurant. **$$**

Restaurant

★ **KELLY'S ON THE SQUARE.** *115 E Pearl, Granbury (76048). Phone 817/573-9722; fax 817/579-5114. www.kellysonthesquare.com.* Historic building; antique furnishings. Steak menu. Lunch, dinner. Closed Mon; also Dec 24-Jan 1. Children's menu. **$$**

Greenville (A-8)

See also Bonham, Dallas, McKinney, Sulphur Springs

Population 23,960
Elevation 550 ft
Area Code 903
Information Chamber of Commerce, 2713 Stonewall St, PO Box 1055, 75403; phone 903/455-1510
Web Site www.greenville-chamber.org

Greenville was once known as the Cotton Capital of the World; in 1912, the Greenville Cotton Compress set the world's record for number of bales pressed and loaded into freight cars in a day. Today, Greenville is a manufacturing and processing center of aerospace, electronics, food, and other products. Fishing is available in five city reservoirs and a number of nearby lakes.

What to See and Do

American Cotton Museum. *600 E I-30, Garland. At exit 95. Phone 903/450-4502.* The story of cotton from seed to modern products. Includes history and impact of cotton in the area and special exhibits. (Tues-Sun; closed holidays) **$$**

Lake Tawakoni. *6553 State Park Rd 55, Granbury (75453). 16 miles S off Hwy 69. Phone 903/662-5134.* Fishing, boating (ramps), water-skiing; picnicking, cabins, tent and trailer sites. Some fees. (Daily)

Mary of Puddin Hill. *201 I-30 E, exit 95, Greenville. Phone 903/455-6931; toll-free 800/545-8889.* Fruitcake bakery, candy kitchen, and store. Tours (Oct-Dec, Mon-Sat; rest of year varies; group tours by appointment) **FREE**

Special Events

Cotton Jubilee. *600 E I-30, Garland (75043). Phone 903/455-1510.* Multicultural and environmental fair; dancing, carnival, arts and crafts show. Third weekend in Oct.

Hunt County Fair. *Fairgrounds, 2713 Stonewall St, Greenville. Phone 903/455 1510.* Second week in June.

Limited-Service Hotel

★ **BEST WESTERN INN AND SUITES.** *1216 I-30 W, Greenville (75402). Phone 903/454-1792; toll-free 800/795-2300; fax 903/454-6804. www.bestwestern .com.* 99 rooms, 2 story. Complimentary continental breakfast. Check-out noon. Bar. Outdoor pool. **$**
🏊

Groesbeck (B-8)

See also Waco

Founded 1869
Population 4,291
Elevation 478 ft
Area Code 254
Zip 76642

Information Chamber of Commerce, 110 N Ellis, PO Box 326; phone 254/729-3894

Groesbeck is a trade center for area farms and ranches. Site of several small manufacturing industries and large deposits of lignite coal, it has some oil and gas production.

What to See and Do

Confederate Reunion Grounds State Historical Park. *S Hwy 14, Mexia. 7 miles N via Hwy 14, then 2 1/2 miles W on FM 2705. Phone 254/562-5751.* Approximately 80 acres. Encampment formed in 1889 to perpetuate memories of fallen Confederate soldiers and to aid disabled survivors and indigent widows and orphans of the deceased. Canoeing to Fort Parker State Park on Navasota River. Swimming, fishing; hiking, bird-watching, picnicking, playground. Contact Park Superintendent, c/o Fort Parker State Park, 194 Pork Rd 28, Mexia 76667. (Daily) **$**

Fort Parker State Park. *S Hwy 14, Mexia. 6 miles N via Hwy 14, to entrance on Park Rd 28. Phone 254/562-5751.* On Lake Fort Parker, approximately 1,500 acres. Swimming, fishing, boating (ramp), canoeing; hiking, picnicking, concession, improved campsites (hookups, shelters, dump station). (Daily) **$**

Lake Limestone. *18 miles SE via FM 937.* This 14,200-acre dammed lake offers two marinas with public access areas at various locations. (Daily)

Limestone County Historical Museum. *210 W Navasota St, Groesbeck. Phone 254/729-5064.* Artifacts and information relating to Limestone County; Old Fort Parker memorabilia. (Mon-Fri; closed holidays) **$**

Old Fort Parker State Historical Park. *Reunion Grand Rd, Groesbeck. 4 miles N via Hwy 14 and Park Rd 35. Phone 254/729-5253.* (1834) Built by the Parker family to protect a small settlement of families. In 1836, Comanches overran the fort, killing five people and capturing five more, including Cynthia Ann Parker, 9 years old. She grew up, married a Comanche chief, and lived with the tribe until captured 24 years later. She was the mother of the last great Comanche chief, Quanah Parker. Log blockhouse and stockade. (Daily) **$**

Special Event

Christmas at the Fort. *Old Fort Parker, Groesbeck. Phone 254/562-5751.* Live demonstration of life in 1840s. Second weekend in Dec.

Guadalupe Mountains National Park (B-3)

See also Carlsbad, El Paso, Van Horn

Web Site www.nps.gov/gumo

Approximately 50 miles N of Van Horn via Hwy 54.

Standing like an island in the desert, this spectacular expanse of the Capitan Reef is part of the world's most extensive fossil reef complex (Permian reef complex). The 86,416-acre park encompasses the most scenic and rugged portion of these mountains. Elevations range from 3,650 feet to 8,749 feet at Guadalupe Peak, the highest point in Texas. Besides the lofty peaks and coniferous forests, there are deep canyons, a tremendous earth fault, desert lowlands, historic sites, unusual flora and fauna, outstanding scenery, and more than 80 miles of hiking trails, with possible trips ranging from five minutes to five days. Several precautions are necessary. Check with a ranger before leaving the main road; do not climb the cliffs; many desert plants have sharp spines; watch for and respect rattlesnakes; be prepared in the backcountry (stout shoes, sun protection, appropriate clothing, and water). Pets must be leashed or restrained and are not permitted on the trails or in the backcountry; firearms are not permitted in the park; wood or charcoal fires are not permitted in the park. Plan to cook on a stove using containerized fuel. Sightseeing by car is limited to the highway, but scenic. Camping, backpacking, hiking, and horseback trails (no rentals). Two drive-in campgrounds (no showers or hook-ups; fee): one on the southeast side at Pine Springs, and one on the north at Dog Canyon. All individual campsites are on a first-come, first-served basis. Permits (free) required for backpacking; check with the visitor center first. For information contact Superintendent, HC 60, Box 400, Salt Flat, TX 79847-9400; 915/828-3251.

Harlingen (F-8)

See also Brownsville, Edinburg, McAllen, Port Isabel, South Padre Island

Population 57,564
Elevation 36 ft
Area Code 956
Information Chamber of Commerce, 311 E Tyler St, 78550; phone 956/423-5440 or toll-free 800/531-7346
Web Site www.harlingen.com

Formerly known as "Six-Shooter Junction" because in the 1800s there were more six-shooters than city residents, Harlingen has become the transportation and medical center of a rich farming territory. It is also a central area of distribution, processing, and marketing. The Harlingen Channel (Arroyo Colorado Canal) links the Port of Harlingen with the Intracoastal Waterway and 30,000 miles of inland waterways. The Harlingen area is a popular location for bird-watching and other outdoor recreation.

What to See and Do

Iwo Jima Memorial & Museum. *320 Iwo Jima Blvd, Harlingen. Phone 956/412-2207.* Features the original sculpture used to cast the bronze Marine Corp Memorial in Arlington, VA, depicting the raising of the United States flag over Iwo Jima during World War II. (Daily) **FREE**

Laguna Atascosa National Wildlife Refuge. *Buena Vista Rd, Rio Hondo. 18 miles E on FM 106, then follow signs. Phone 956/748-3607.* Approximately 45,000 acres with walking trails. Fishing along the Harlingen Ship Channel only. Visitor center (Oct-May, sunrise to sunset; closed June-Sept) Administrative office (all year, Mon-Fri; closed holidays). **$$**

Special Events

RioFest. *1204 Fair Park Blvd, Harlingen (78550). Phone 956/425-2705; toll-free 800/531-7346.* Late Apr.

Rio Grande Valley Birding Festival. *Harlingen Municipal Auditorium Complex and Plaza de Amistad, 1204 Fair Park Blvd, Harlingen (78550). Phone toll-free 800/531-7346.* Early-mid-Nov.

Limited-Service Hotel

★ ★ **COURTYARD BY MARRIOTT.** *1725 W Filmore Ave, Harlingen (78550). Phone 956/412-7800; toll-free 888/267-8927; fax 956/412-7889. www.courtyard.com.* 114 rooms, 3 story. Check-in 3 pm, check-out noon. Fitness room. Outdoor pool, whirlpool. **$**

Henderson (B-9)

See also Longview, Tyler

Founded 1844
Population 11,273
Elevation 506 ft
Area Code 903
Zip 75652
Information Tourist Development Department, Chamber of Commerce, 201 N Main St; phone 903/657-5528
Web Site www.hendersontx.com

What to See and Do

Depot Museum and Children's Discovery Center. *514 N High St, Henderson. Phone 903/657-4303.* Covers Rusk County history; many activities for children ages 3-11 in renovated cotton warehouse. Several other buildings include T. J. Walling Cabin (1841) and Arnold Outhouse (1908), the first such structure to receive a state historical marker. (Mon-Sat; closed holidays) **$**

Howard-Dickinson House. *501 S Main St, Henderson. Phone 903/657-5256.* (1805) One of the first brick houses in the county. Frame wing added in 1905. Period furnishings; books, paintings, photographs, original documents. (By appointment; closed holidays) **$$**

Special Events

Rural Heritage Weekend. *Downtown Historic District, Henderson. Phone 903/657-5528.* Arts and crafts, antique tractor shows. Third weekend in Apr.

Syrup Festival. *514 N High St, Henderson (75652). Phone 903/657-5528.* Syrup making, arts and crafts, entertainment. Second Sat in Nov.

Hereford (E-3)

See also Amarillo, Canyon

Population 14,597
Elevation 3,806 ft
Area Code 806
Zip 79045
Information Chamber of Commerce, 701 N Main, PO Box 192; phone 806/364-3333

Seat of Deaf Smith County and named for the many herds of Hereford cattle, this area's economy is largely dependent on agriculture. Huge quantities of wheat, grain sorghum, and corn are produced; more than 3 million cattle are raised in feed-lots.

What to See and Do

Deaf Smith County Historical Museum. *400 Sampson St, Hereford. Phone 806/363-7070.* Furniture, clothes, farming tools, artifacts used by pioneers of the area; also E. B. Black Home (1909). (Mon-Sat; closed holidays) **FREE**

Limited-Service Hotel

★ **BEST WESTERN RED CARPET INN.** *830 W 1st St, Hereford (79045). Phone 806/364-0540; toll-free 877/512-6777; fax 806/364-0818. www.bestwestern.com.* 90 rooms, 2 story. Pets accepted, some restrictions. Check-out noon. Outdoor pool. **$**

Hillsboro (B-8)

See also Arlington-Grand Prairie, Cleburne, Corsicana, Dallas, Lake Whitney, Waco

Founded 1853
Population 8,232
Elevation 634 ft
Area Code 254
Zip 76645
Information Chamber of Commerce, 115 N Covington St, PO Box 358; phone 254/582-2481 or toll-free 800/445-5726
Web Site www.hillsborochamber.org

Center of a rich agricultural region and gateway to lakes Aquilla and Whitney, Hillsboro is also noted for its many antiques and crafts shops. The imposing Hill

County Courthouse (1890) at the center of the town square is surrounded by many restored turn-of-the-century buildings.

What to See and Do

Confederate Research Center. *112 Lamar Dr, Hillsboro. Hill College, in Library Building. Phone 254/582-2555.* Archives and displays with emphasis on Confederate military history. Also here is the Audie L. Murphy Gun Museum. (Mon-Fri; closed school holidays) **FREE**

Hillsboro Outlet Center. *104 NE I-35, Hillsboro (76645). Phone 254/582-2047.* More than 100 outlet stores can be found here. Café. (Mon-Sat 10 am-8 pm, Sun 11 am-6 pm; closed holidays)

Special Event

Hill County Fair. *Phone 254/582-2481.* Livestock, food, arts and crafts exhibits. First week in Feb.

Houston (D-9)

See also Angleton, Baytown, Brazosport, Eagle Lake, Galveston, Texas City

Founded 1836
Population 1,953,631
Elevation 55 ft
Area Code 713 and 281
Information Greater Houston Convention & Visitors Bureau, 901 Bagby, 77002; phone 713/437-5200
Web Site www.houston-guide.com

Houston and Texas, it has been said, grew up together. The city was founded in the same year as the Republic of Texas by brothers Augustus and John Allen, speculators from New York. The town became the new nation's first capital, named after Sam Houston, hero of the Battle of San Jacinto and the first elected president of the Republic. When the first steamboat chugged up the Buffalo Bayou, its captain found stakes marking the streets of what is today the largest city in both Texas and the South.

Buffalo Bayou is now part of the Houston Ship Channel, a 400-foot-wide, 40-foot-deep, 52-mile-long man-made waterway flowing into the Gulf of Mexico. More than 200 industries, including petrochemical and steel plants, line its shore. Houston is a leader in both total tonnage and foreign tonnage handled by a United States port.

The space industry has thrived here for years, following the establishment in 1962 of NASA's Mission Control Center (now known as the NASA Lyndon B. Johnson Space Center), 16 miles southeast, near Clear Lake City. A number of research and development and other space-related concerns are located in the greater Houston area.

Several construction and redevelopment projects have been undertaken in Houston. The city already boasts one of the tallest buildings in the United States west of the Mississippi in the JP Morgan Chase Tower. Projects have included a convention center, theater center, and Space Center Houston. The face of Houston promises to change continuously through the 21st century.

Conventions and tourism play an important role in the local economy. Relying on its cosmopolitan image, temperate climate, Gulf Coast location, and myriad shops, accommodations, and recreational and cultural activities, Houston attracts millions of visitors each year.

Public Transportation

Buses (Metro Transit), phone 713/635-4000

Airport William P. Hobby Airport; weather phone toll-free 877/792-3225; cash machines, near Southwest Airlines.

Information Phone 713/643-4597

Lost and Found Phone 713/643-4597

Airport George Bush Intercontinental; weather phone toll-free 877/792-3225; cash machines, Terminals A, B, C.

Information Phone 281/230-3000

Lost and Found Phone 281/230-3299

Airlines Aero Mexico, Air Canada, Air France, Air Jamaica, American Trans Air, America West, American Airlines, American Connection, Atlantic Southeast Airlines, Aviasca, British Airways, Cayman Airways, Comair, Continental, Continental Express, Delta Air Lines, Frontier Airlines, KLM Royal Dutch, Lufthansa, Northwest Airlines, SkyWest, Southwest Airlines, TACA, United Airlines, US Airways

What to See and Do

Allen's Landing Park. *100 Main St, Houston (77002). Downtown, at Main St and Buffalo Bayou.* Site where Houston was founded (1836) by the Allen brothers. Served as first port for steamers and sailing vessels from 1837. (Daily) **FREE**

Armand Bayou Nature Center. *8500 Bay Area Blvd, Pasadena (77507). From Houston, take I-45 S, exit 26 at Bay Area Blvd, and go E 7 miles just past Bay Area Park. Phone 281/474-2551. www.abnc.org.* With canoe and pontoon boat trips and stargazing and birding classes, Armand Bayou Nature Center gives families visiting the Houston area multiple opportunities to learn about nature on the bayou, night and day. "Breakfast on the Bayou" is a Saturday morning feature in which guests enjoy a continental breakfast as they drift down the bayou on a pontoon boat nature tour. There are also family star parties, night hikes, and sunset cruises. Along the Central Flyway, the largest migratory bird route in North America, the bayou is home to more than 220 species of birds. The preserve also shelters everything from armadillos to swamp rabbits, bobcats, and coyotes. Weekend demonstrations and talks teach about wildlife and also demonstrate turn-of-the-century farm tasks (rope-making, cheese-making, etc.) at the Center's Martyn farm site. Guided trail hikes are also offered on weekends. Call the center for current schedules. (Tues-Sun 9 am-5 pm, Sun noon-6 pm; closed Dec 25) **$**

Bayou Bend Collection and Gardens. *1 Westcott St, Houston (77007). Phone 713/639-7758. www.mfah.org/bayoubend.* Garden enthusiasts and American decorative arts buffs alike will appreciate Bayou Bend, the former home of Houston philanthropist Ima Hogg, daughter of Texas's first native-born governor. The mansion now houses the Museum of Fine Arts, Houston's 5,000-object American decorative arts collection. The collection includes furniture by John Townsend and John Henry Belter, paintings by John Singleton Copley and Charles Willson Peale, and silver by Paul Revere. The 14 acres surrounding the main building include eight formal gardens of azaleas, gardenias, antique roses, and the rare Duchess De Caze pink camellias. Tours ($$) hosted by the River Oaks Garden Club lead visitors through the 28 rooms of the Hogg mansion, which chronicles the evolution of style in America from 1620 to 1870. (Sorry, no kids under 10 are allowed in the house.) Outside, garden tours take visitors past regional plants such as magnolias and crepe myrtles. Unusual highlights include topiar-

ies shaped to resemble native Texas animals, a goddess statuary, and a planting in the shape of a butterfly. Self-guided garden tours ($). (Guided tour: Tues-Fri 10-11 am and 1-2:45 pm, Sat 10-11:15 am. Reservations are required. Audio tours of the home Sat-Sun 1-5 pm) **$$**

Byzantine Fresco Chapel Museum. *4011 Yupon at Branard, Houston (77006). Phone 713/521-3990. www.menil.org/byzantine.html.* The story of how the only intact Byzantine frescoes in the entire Western Hemisphere came to be housed in Houston is a dramatic one. Back in the 1980s, thieves ripped the frescoes (a dome showing Christ surrounded by angels and an apse with a painting of the Virgin Mary and two archangels) from a chapel near Lysi in the Turkish-occupied section of Cyprus. Hoping to sell the works piece by piece, the thieves cut them up and smuggled them off the island. A curator from the Menil Foundation (of Houston's Menil Art Collection) got wind of the frescoes and rescued them. The foundation then spent two years carefully restoring the paintings. In gratitude, the Church of Cyprus made a "long-term loan" of the frescoes, which are displayed in a much-acclaimed building custom designed for the frescoes by Francois de Menil. (Fri-Sun) **FREE**

Children's Museum of Houston. *1500 Binz, Houston (77004). Phone 713/522-1138. www.cmhouston.org.* Kids can explore an Oaxacan village, get up to their elbows in bubbles, play cashier in a "real-life" grocery store, and participate in dozens of hands-on activities that promote creative thinking and learning. One of the most visited youth museums in the country, the Children's Museum of Houston is constantly expanding and improving on its permanent exhibits and brings in many more that are showcased temporarily. For the active ones in the bunch, there are loads of things to climb on, from a 25-ton caboose to a Victorian playhouse. Weekend visitors are treated to storytellers, musicians, magicians, and dancers who perform in the museum's 164-seat auditorium as part of its Spotlight Performance series. If you have toddlers in tow, visit the Tot Spot for stimulating toddler activities. (Memorial Day-Labor Day and most federal holidays: Mon-Sat 9 am-5 pm, Sun from noon; rest of year: Tues-Sat 9 am-5 pm, Sun from noon) **$**

Contemporary Arts Museum. *5216 Montrose Blvd, Houston (77006). Phone 713/284-8250. www.camh.org.* Changing exhibits by international and regional artists of contemporary painting, sculpture, photography, video. (Tues-Wed, Fri-Sat 10 am-5 pm, Thurs to 9 pm, Sun noon-5 pm; closed Jan 1, Thanksgiving, Dec 25) **FREE**

George Ranch Historical Park. *10215 FM 762, Richmond (77406). Phone 281/343-0218. www.georgeranch.org.* The George Foundation set aside 480 of its 23,000 acres of ranch and farmlands to create this time capsule illustrating 100 years of Texas's past. Costumed interpreters help visitors understand what it was like to be a colonial pioneer struggling to make it on a stock farm. There's also a taste of Old West cattle drives, chuck wagons and cattle camps, plus a glimpse of Victorian-era Texas at the ranch's 1890s Victorian manse—Davis House. The property's working ranch from the 1930s includes original barns and cattle-working pens where visitors can see demonstrations of cattle sorting and roping. Hands-on opportunities abound from harvesting crops at the Jones Stock Farm to weaving cloth and grinding corn. Special events throughout the year range from a Victorian Easter egg hunt at Davis House to a working cowboy competition at the ranch every May. (Daily 9 am-5 pm; closed holidays) **$$**

Heritage Society Tours. *Sam Houston Park, 1100 Bagby St, Houston (77002). Phone 713/655-1912. www.heritagesociety.org.* Museum complex of eight historic structures dating from 1820 to 1905; structures include frontier cabin, Texas plantation house, Greek Revival and Victorian houses, church (circa 1890), and museum gallery. Period furnishings. One-hour tours through four structures. (Tues-Sat 10 am, 11:30 am, 1 pm, 2:30 pm, Sun 1 pm and 3 pm; no tours holidays) **$$**

⭐ **Hermann Park.** *6001 Fannin, Houston (77030). Bounded by Fannin and Main sts on the W, Hermann Dr on the N, Almeda Rd on the E, and N MacGregor Dr on the S. Phone 713/845-1000. www.hermannpark.org.* Approximately 400 acres donated by businessman and philanthropist George Hermann. A bronze statue and fountain honoring him are located at the intersection of Fannin and N MacGregor Dr. Also in the park are the Garden Center; an ancient Korean pavilion; a Japanese garden; the Miller Outdoor Theatre, which stages free summer music, ballet, and theater productions; and

Burke Baker Planetarium. *1 Hermann Circle Dr, Houston (77030). Phone 713/639-4600. www.hmns.org.* Offers planetarium programs as well as laser light shows on Fridays and Saturdays.

(Daily; call or visit Web site for current schedule; closed Jan 1, Dec 25) **$**

Houston Museum of Natural Science. *1 Hermann Circle Dr, Houston (77030). Phone 713/639-4600. www.hmns.org.* This museum is home to the Burke Baker Planetarium, the Wortham IMAX Theatre, the Cockrell Butterfly Center, and three floors of natural science halls and exhibits. Most popular is the Hall of Paleontology, featuring dinosaur and Egyptian artifacts. Other exhibits include vast displays of gems and minerals, a 100,000-specimen dried insect collection, and Native American artifacts. The Welch Chemistry Hall includes hands-on interactive displays and a live demonstration theater. The Fondren Discovery Place provides more fun, hands-on learning. (Daily) **$**

Houston Zoo. *1513 N MacGregor Dr, Houston (77030). N of Texas Medical Center. Phone 713/533-6500. www.houstonzoo.org.* Small mammals, including a vampire bat colony; reptile and primate houses, hippopotamus building, alligator display, gorilla habitat, birdhouse with tropical rain forest; aquarium with marine life; large cat facility; education center. Three-acre discovery zoo with separate contact areas. (Mar-Sept: daily 9 am-6 pm; rest of year: to 5 pm) **$$**

Mecom Rockwell Fountain. *Between Fannin and San Jacinto sts. www.hmns.org.* Considered one of the most beautiful structures in the city. Colonnade around the fountain resembles a Roman temple; the water jet in the pool rises 12 feet.

Wortham IMAX Theatre. *1 Herman Circle Dr, Houston (77030). Phone 713/639-4600. www.hmns .org.* Multimedia auditorium (seats 394) featuring films on natural science topics shown on a 60-by-80-foot screen. (Daily; closed Jan 1, Dec 25)

Houston Arboretum and Nature Center. *Memorial Park, 4501 Woodway, Houston (77024). Phone 713/681-8433. www.houstonarboretum.org.* A 155-acre non-profit nature sanctuary for the protection of native trees, shrubs, and wildlife. Five miles of nature trails (daily). Guided tours (Sat-Sun afternoons). Special events and educational programs. (Daily 8:30 am-6 pm; closed holidays) **FREE**

Houston Astros (MLB). *Minute Maid Park, 501 Crawford St, Houston (77002). At Texas St. Phone toll-free 800/278-7672. houston.astros.mlb.com.* **$$$$**

Houston Ballet. *501 Texas Ave, Houston (77019). Texas and Smith sts. Phone 713/227-2787; toll-free 800/828-2787. www.houstonballet.org.* Hailed as "one of the nation's best ballet companies" by *The New York Times* and "one of America's most vibrant ballet companies" by *The London Times,* the Houston Ballet is something special to see. An extensive repertoire of works includes 19th-century classics such as *The Nutcracker, Swan Lake,* and *Don Quixote,* as well as new works by contemporary choreographers including Trey McIntyre, Stanton Welch, and Natalie Weir. You can see the ballet's ensemble of 54 dancers perform at the Wortham Theater Center in downtown Houston. Fees vary per performance ($$$-$$$$). (Sept-June; call or visit Web site for specific dates and times)

Houston Comets (WNBA). *Toyota Center, 1510 Polk St, Houston (77002). Phone 713/627-9622. www.wnba.com/comets.* Professional basketball team. **$$**

Houston Grand Opera. *Wortham Theater Center, 501 Texas Ave, Houston (77002). Phone 713/546-0200 (information); toll-free 800/828-2787 (tickets). www.houstongrandopera.org.* Multiple performances of several major productions featuring international stars (Oct-May); also special events. Wheelchair seating, infrared and live narration, headphones. **$$$$**

Houston Rockets (NBA). *Toyota Center, 1510 Polk St, Houston (77002). Phone 713/627-3865. www.nba.com/rockets.* **$$$$**

Houston Texans (NFL). *2 Reliant Park, Houston (77054). Phone 832/667-2000. www.houstontexans.com.* In 2002, Houstonians were overjoyed to have a pro football team of their own to cheer for again, having been abandoned by the Oilers several years earlier. Visitors can see the NFL's newest team in action at Houston's 69,500-seat Reliant stadium, the first NFL stadium with a retractable roof. The Texans play in the AFC South Division along with the Indianapolis Colts, Jacksonville Jaguars, and Tennessee Titans. Individual game tickets are available by calling Ticketmaster (713/629-3700).

Houston Walks. *Phone 713/222-9255. www.discoverhoustontours.com.* Professional tour guide Sandra Lord has made a career out of creating interesting city tours. Take, for example, her Tunnel Loop tour, a unique jaunt through downtown Houston's tunnel system, a network of concourses linking 75 buildings—many with historic significance—20 feet below the streets. Anyone interested in Houston's hottest nightspots can join in on one of Discover Houston Tours's NiteCrawls, an adults-only tour of clubs, restaurants, and hotels, replete with colorful stories of oil magnates and shady ladies, ghosts, and suicides. There are also walking tours of Houston's six historic wards, as well as Spiritual Journeys—walks to eight of Houston's downtown religious institutions. Holiday-inspired Ghost Walks in October include urban legends and tales of deceased Houstonians (wear a costume and get a discount) and the December Holiday Lights Walks, which tour downtown's holiday decorations. Reservations are a must. Call or visit the Web site for tour locations. **$$**

John P. McGovern Museum of Health and Medical Science. *1515 Hermann Dr, Houston (77004). Phone 713/942-7054. www.mhms.org.* A 22-foot-long backbone with ribs descending from the ceiling, a 10-foot-tall walk-through brain, and a 27-foot intestine—the sheer novelty and gross-out value of the exhibits at the McGovern Museum of Health and Medical Science make it a must-see for all ages. Designed as a voyage through a Texas-sized body, the museum's Jim Hickox Amazing Body Pavilion includes dozens of hands-on exhibits and science stations, interspersed with the giant organs. Sixty-one interactive video and audio kiosks ask and answer interesting questions about human health and anatomy. Skin-morphing demos show kids the effects of sunlight on the skin. There's a huge walk-in eyeball that shows how the eye receives and perceives images. There are also exhibits that let you look down the throat at vocal chords in action or see what a clogged artery really looks like. Two theaters, a science lab, and learning center add "edutainment" options. Traveling exhibits are also on display. (Daily; closed Thanksgiving, Dec 25, also Mon in spring and fall) **$**

Menil Collection. *1500 W Alabama St, Houston (77006). Phone 713/525-9400. www.menil.org.* Considered one of the most outstanding private art collections in the world, endowed by Mr. and Mrs. John de Menil. Includes contemporary, surrealistic, and prehistoric art and antiquities. Housed in a museum designed by renowned Italian architect Renzo Piano. (Wed-Sun 11 am-7 pm) **FREE**

Museum of Fine Arts. *5601 Main St, Houston (77005). Phone 713/639-7300. www.mfah.org.* You could spend days viewing the MFAH's vast collections, housed in six locations (four within walking distance of one another, two a few miles away). More than 45,000 artworks represent the major civilizations of Europe,

Asia, North and South America, and Africa. The strongest holdings include Italian Renaissance paintings, French Impressionist works, photographs, American and European decorative arts, African and Pre-Columbian gold, American art, and European and American paintings and sculpture from 1945 and later. Traveling exhibits rotate in and out, sharing focus with special exhibits drawn from the museum's permanent collection. The MFAH's two house museums, Bayou Bend Collection and Gardens (American works) and Rienzi (European works), are well worth the trip off-campus. Families with children should stop by the Lillie and Hugh Roy Cullen Sculpture Garden and the gardens at Bayou Bend and call ahead to check times for Family Flicks and arts-and-crafts projects on Sundays. (Tues-Wed 10 am-5 pm, Thurs to 9 pm, Fri-Sat to 7 pm, Sun 12:15 pm-7 pm; closed Thanksgiving, Dec 25) **$$**

Old Market Square. *301 Milam St, Houston (77002). One block park on Congress. Phone 713/845-1000.* Site of city's first commercial center (early 1800s). An extensive redevelopment project features a central plaza and sidewalks paved with collages of paving material taken from old Houston buildings. Photos commemorating city history are reproduced on porcelain-enameled panels decorating benches in the square. (Daily dawn-dusk) **FREE**

Port of Houston. *7300 Clinton Dr, Houston (77020). At Gate 8. Phone 713/670-2416. www.portofhouston.com.* Boat tours of the port. Reservations required. Call for schedule. **FREE**

Reliant Park. *8400 Kirby Dr, Houston (77054). Phone 832/667-1400. www.reliantpark.com.* Complex of entertainment and meeting/display facilities include Reliant Center, Reliant Arena, and

> **Reliant Stadium.** *1 Reliant Park, Houston (77054). South Loop 610 and Kirby Dr. Phone 713/629-3700.* Site of sporting events, conventions, exhibitions, and concerts. Parking (fee). **$$**

> **Six Flags AstroWorld.** *9001 Kirby Dr, Houston (77054). Phone 713/799-8404. www.sixflags.com.* This 75-acre theme park with more than 100 rides, shows, and attractions includes the Texas Cyclone roller coaster; Dungeon Drop, a 20-story freefall; suspended coaster; children's section. Concerts at the Southern Star Amphitheatre (adjacent). (Summer: daily; spring and fall: weekends) **$$$$**

> **Six Flags WaterWorld.** *9001 Kirby Dr, Houston (77054). Phone 713/799-8404. www.sixflags.com.*

This 15-acre family water recreation park features water slides, river rapids ride, wave pool, speed slides, diving platforms, and a children's play area. (Apr: weekends; June-Aug: daily) Free admission with Six Flags AstroWorld ticket. **$$$$**

Rothko Chapel. *1409 Sul Ross St, Houston (77006). Phone 713/524-9839. www.rothkochapel.org.* Octagonal chapel houses canvases of the late Mark Rothko, Russian-born painter. On the grounds are a reflecting pool and the Broken Obelisk, a sculpture by Barnett Newman, dedicated to Dr. Martin Luther King Jr. (Daily 10 am-6 pm) **FREE**

Sam Houston Park. *1100 Bagby, Houston (77002). Phone 713/655-1912. www.heritagesociety.org.* A haven of quiet and green in the midst of downtown Houston's bustle, Sam Houston Park is also a parcel of the city's past. Nestled in the park's 19 acres, eight historic structures dating from 1823 to 1905 have been carefully restored. Buildings range from a cedar log cabin believed to be the oldest surviving structure in the county to St. John Church, a country parish relocated here. Heritage Society guided tours of the buildings ($$) give guests a glimpse into the life and times of the Houstonians who used to live, work, and worship here. (You choose four of the eight structures for each tour.) Soak up more history at the park's free-admission Heritage Society Museum, where exhibits range from 19th-century paintings to priceless pieces of early Texas furniture to an exact replica of a general store from Egypt, Texas. (Museum daily 10 am-4 pm)

Sam Houston Race Park. *7575 N Sam Houston Pkwy W, Houston (77064). Phone toll-free 800/807-7223. www.shrp.com.* Thoroughbreds, American quarter horses, and Arabians are the draw here. The park offers ten races nightly throughout its season, which runs from fall through spring. Simulcast races are broadcast 364 days a year on 1,200 TV monitors. Track amenities include the Winners' Circle restaurant, featuring fine dining for 750 in a multi-tiered seating arrangement. (No need to worry about table turns—once booked, your seat is yours for the entire evening.) Call ahead to reserve a luxury suite on the track's third level, and check out the schedule for a wide assortment of special events. Kids' days, for example, include pony rides, moonwalks, and more, and during the summer there are concerts almost every weekend. (Fri-Sat 7 pm, Sun 1:30 pm; closed Dec 25) **$**

San Jacinto Battleground. *3523 Hwy 134, Houston (77571). 6 miles SE on Gulf Frwy (I-45) to I-610*

(South Loop), then 1 1/2 miles E to Hwy 225 (La Porte Frwy), then 10 1/2 miles E to Hwy 134 and 3 miles W to Battleground; highway signs identify the battlefield exits beginning on the Gulf Frwy. Phone 281/479-2421. www.tpwd.state.tx.us/park/sanjac. A 570-foot reinforced concrete shaft, faced with Texas fossilized buff limestone and a lone star on top, marks the site of the Battle of San Jacinto. On April 21, 1836, General Sam Houston suddenly attacked the superior forces of Dictator-General Santa Ana of Mexico, routed them and took Santa Ana himself prisoner. This victory ended Texas's War of Independence with Mexico, avenged the massacre at the Alamo six weeks earlier, and led to the founding of the Republic of Texas. Elevator in monument (fee). Museum with exhibits on the cultural development of Texas from Native American civilization to statehood. Multimedia presentation (fee). Monument (daily 8 am-6 pm; closed Thanksgiving, Dec 24-25). Museum (daily 9 am-6 pm; closed Thanksgiving, Dec 24-25). Battleground (May-Sept: daily 8 am-9 pm; rest of year to 7 pm) **FREE** Moored nearby is the

> **Battleship USS *Texas*.** 3523 Hwy 134, LaPorte (77571). Phone 281/479-2411. www.tpwd.state.tx.us/parks/battlesh. Presented to the state by the US Navy. The ship, a dreadnought built in 1914, saw action in World War I and World War II. (Daily 10 am-5 pm; closed Thanksgiving, Dec 24-25) **$$**

⭐ **Space Center Houston.** 1601 Nasa Rd 1, Houston (77058). 25 miles S of downtown Houston in the NASA/Clear Lake area. Phone 281/244-2100. www.spacecenter.org. Designed by Disney, Space Center Houston puts space travel at kids' fingertips. Interactive exhibits help them understand what it's like for astronauts to eat and shower in space, as well as perform complicated tasks such as landing the space shuttle, retrieving satellites, and using the Manned Maneuvering Unit. At Mission Status Center, guests hear the latest info about NASA space flights and training activities. At Kids Space Place, kids can ride across the moon in a Lunar Rover, perform experiments, and command a space shuttle. Exhibits at the center include Robotics, which lets kids build and program their own robots, and ISS Odyssey, which features a 30-foot model of the space station and six virtual reality stations that "transport" visitors to the station for a tour—including a space walk. Also fun is the Martian Matrix, a five-story play structure that provides plenty of crawl space composed of mazes, tunnels, and passageways. Tram tours to Johnson Space Center depart every half hour. (June: Mon-Fri 10 am-7 pm; July: Mon-Fri 9 am-7 pm; Aug: Mon-Fri 10 am-5 pm, Sat-Sun 10 am-7 pm; winter: Mon-Fri 10 am-5 pm, Sat-Sun 10 am-7 pm) **$$$$**

Sur La Table. 1996 W Gray, Houston (77019). Phone 713/533-0400. www.surlatable.com. In the 1970s, Seattle spawned this clearinghouse for hard-to-find kitchen gear, and it soon became known as a source for cookware, small appliances, cutlery, kitchen tools, linens, tableware, gadgets, and specialty foods. Sur La Table has since expanded to include cooking classes ($$$$), chef demonstrations, and cookbook author signings, as well as a catalog and online presence. Cooking connoisseurs discover such finds as cool oven mitts, zest graters, copper whisks, onion soup bowls, and inspired TV dinner trays. (Mon-Sat 10 am-6 pm, Sun 11 am-6 pm)

Trader's Village. 7979 N Eldridge Rd, Houston (77041). Phone 281/890-5500. www.tradersvillage.com. Billed as a "Texas-sized marketplace with a little bit of everything," Trader's Village is a bargain-hunter's boon. Browse, shop, and trade your way through thousands of booths featuring wares from 600 dealers—everything from belt buckles to bulldozers. Covering more than 70 acres, Trader's Village opened in 1989 and has become the largest flea market on the Texas Gulf coast. In addition to shopping options, there are camping, an RV park, kiddie rides and games, snack stands, mobile beverage carts, and covered rest areas. Food vendors serve festival foods such as hot links, roasted corn-on-the-cob, made-to-order burgers, pizzas, turkey legs, and baked potatoes. Special events range from BBQ and chili cook-offs to square dancing and bluegrass festivals (call for events and dates). (Sat-Sun 9 am-6 pm; closed Dec 25) **FREE**

University of Houston. 4800 Calhoun Road, Houston (77204). Phone 713/743-2255. www.uh.edu. (1927) (33,000 students) Located on 392 acres. University Center has an arboretum; the Hofheinz Pavilion is the site of many sports events and concerts. The Lyndall Finley Wortham Theater complex offers mime and drama productions.

Special Events

Bayou City Art Festival. Memorial Park, Houston. Phone 713/521-0133. www.bayoucityartfestival.com. As Houston's premier outdoor fine arts event, the Bayou City Art Festival celebrates both visual and performing arts. Performing arts groups became a part of the festivities for the first time in 2003, joining more than 300 accomplished visual artists. Dancers, musicians, and singers are spotlighted on the Theater District Stage, while visual artists present paintings, drawings, photographs, sculpture, furniture, jewelry, and works in clay, glass, wood, fiber, textiles, and metal throughout Memorial Park. The kid-focused Creative Zone gives young artists the chance to try their hand at spin art, hat-painting, sand-casting, jewelry-making, drawing, and more. (Kids take home whatever they create.) A wide variety of ethnic restaurants, wine cafés, and beer gardens offer refreshment. Late Mar. **$$**

Greek Festival. *3511 Yoakum Blvd, Houston (77006). Phone 713/526-5377. greekfestival.org.* Annunciation Greek Orthodox Cathedral. Cultural festival with Greek food, music, and dancing. Early Oct. **$**

Houston International Festival. *1221 Lamar St, Houston (77010). Phone 713/654-8808. www.ifest.org.* Houston's huge international festival spotlights a different culture each year and celebrates dozens more. Festival-goers delve into a wide variety of cultural traditions, participating in performances by more than 1,500 regional, national, and international artists on eight main stages and four cultural stages. The fest is divided into seven entertainment zones featuring music, art, and food. Pick a zone and zero in on one culture, or mix and match. Past zones have included a Mexico zone, with Mexican cuisine, traditional arts and crafts, and music from different Mexican states (Tamaulipas, Veracruz, Mexico, and Puebla); an African Caribbean zone, with world beats keeping toes tapping; and a Latin zone, which pulsed with Tejano and mariachi music. There's also an arts market and, to keep the little ones happy, an entire kids' zone with arts and crafts, kid food, and a petting zoo. Two weekends in late Apr. (11 am-8 pm)**$**

Houston Livestock Show & Rodeo. *Reliant Stadium, 8334 Fannin St, Houston (77054). Phone 713/629-3700. www.hlsr.com.* Mar. **$$**

Houston Symphony. *Jesse H. Jones Hall for the Performing Arts, 615 Louisiana St, Houston (77002). Phone 713/224-4240. www.houstonsymphony.org.* Classical and Exxon Pops series (Sept-May). Sounds Like Fun children's festival (various locations; June, free). Free summer concerts at Miller Outdoor Theatre in Hermann Park. Summer concerts at Cynthia Woods Mitchell Pavilion, Jones Hall, and other locations.

Juneteenth Festival. *Miller Outdoor Theatre, 100 Concert Dr, Houston (77030). Phone 713/284-8352.* Gospel, blues, and other music celebrates the abolition of slavery in Texas in June 1865. June.

River Oaks Garden Club's Azalea Trail. *2503 Westheimer Rd, Houston (77098). Phone 713/523-2483. www.riveroaksgardenclub.org.* Tour of seven historical homes and their gardens. First two weekends in Mar. **$$$$**

Summer concerts. Musical performances take place at various venues around Houston, including Traders Village and the Miller Outdoor Theatre May-Aug.

Limited-Service Hotels

★ ★ **COURTYARD BY MARRIOTT.** *3131 W Loop S, Houston (77027). Phone 713/961-1690; toll-free 800/321-2211; fax 713/627-8434. www.courtyard.com.* 209 rooms, 6 story. Check-in 3 pm, check-out noon. High-speed Internet access, wireless Internet access. Restaurant, bar. Fitness room. Outdoor pool, children's pool, whirlpool. Business center. **$**
🧍 ⛱ 🏃

★ ★ **COURTYARD BY MARRIOTT HOUSTON/WESTCHASE.** *9975 Westheimer Rd, Houston (77042). Phone 713/784-3003; toll-free 800/321-2211; fax 713/784-9009. www.courtyard.com.* 153 rooms. Check-in 3 pm, check-out noon. High-speed Internet access. Fitness room. Outdoor pool, whirlpool. **$**
🧍 ⛱

★ ★ **DOUBLETREE GUEST SUITES.** *5353 Westheimer Rd, Houston (77056). Phone 713/961-9000; toll-free 800/222-8733; fax 713/877-8835. www.houstonsuites.doubletree.com.* This luxurious hotel is found in the Uptown/Galleria area. Its location puts it near premier shopping, restaurants and entertainment, as well as near many area attractions. 335 rooms, 26 story, all suites. Pets accepted; fee. Check-in 3 pm, check-out noon. High-speed Internet access, wireless Internet access. Restaurant, bar. Fitness room. Outdoor pool, whirlpool. Business center. **$**
🐾 🧍 ⛱ 🏃

★ ★ **EMBASSY SUITES.** *2911 Sage Rd, Houston (77056). Phone 713/626-5444; toll-free 800/362-2779; fax 713/626-3883. www.embassysuites.com.* This hotel is near shopping; lots of restaurants; and many attractions like the Astrodome, the Galleria Mall and Six Flags amusement park. 150 rooms, 6 story, all suites. Complimentary full breakfast. Check-in 3 pm, check-out noon. High-speed Internet access. Restaurant, bar. Fitness room. Indoor pool, whirlpool. **$$**
🧍 ⛱

★ ★ **HILTON HOUSTON NASA CLEAR LAKE.**
*3000 Nasa Rd One, Houston (77058). Phone 281/
333-9300; toll-free 800/634-7230; fax 281/333-3750.
www.hilton.com.* Located on Clear Lake, directly across
from the Johnson Space Center, this property has an
83-slip marina and many water activities, including jet
skiing and boat charters. 243 rooms, 13 story. Check-
in 2 pm, check-out noon. High-speed Internet access.
Restaurant, bar. Fitness room. Outdoor pool. Business
center. **$**

★ **HOMEWOOD SUITES.** *2424 Rodgerdale Rd,
Houston (77042). Phone 713/334-2424; toll-free 800/
225-5466; fax 713/787-6749. www.homewoodsuites.com.*
96 rooms, 3 story, all suites. Pets accepted, some restrictions; fee. Complimentary full breakfast. Check-in
3 pm, check-out noon. High-speed Internet access,
wireless Internet access. Fitness room. Indoor pool,
whirlpool. Tennis. Business center. **$**

★ ★ **LEXINGTON HOTEL SUITES HOUSTON.**
*16410 N Frwy 45, Houston (77090). Phone 281/821-
1000; fax 281/821-1420.* 247 rooms, 3 story.
Complimentary continental breakfast. Check-in 3 pm,
check-out noon. Outdoor pool. Airport transportation available. **$**

Full-Service Hotels

★ ★ ★ **CROWNE PLAZA.** *12801 Northwest Frwy,
Houston (77040). Phone 713/462-9977; toll-free 800/
826-1606; fax 713/690-8098. www.crowneplaza.com/
brookhollowtx.* This property is a short drive from
Galleria shopping and Sam Houston Race Park. 291
rooms, 10 story. Pets accepted, some restrictions; fee.
Check-in 3 pm, check-out noon. Restaurant, bar.
Fitness room. Outdoor pool. **$**

★ ★ ★ **DOUBLETREE HOTEL.** *400 Dallas St,
Houston (77002). Phone 713/759-0202; toll-free 800/772-
7666; fax 713/752-2734. www.doubletreehotels
.com.* Located in Houston's business district, this hotel
offers both business and leisure travelers a relaxing stay.
Guests can enjoy spacious rooms offering a sensational
skyline view and warm and friendly service. 350 rooms,
20 story. Pets accepted, some restrictions; fee. Check-in 3
pm, check-out noon. High-speed Internet access. Restau-
rant, bar. Fitness room. Business center. **$$**

★ ★ **DOUBLETREE HOTEL.** *2001 Post Oak Blvd,
Houston (77056). Phone 713/961-9300; fax 713/923-
6685. www.doubletreehotels.com.* Ideally situated within
the heart of uptown Houston's business district, this
hotel offers spacious guest rooms and warm service.
Nearby attractions include the Galleria Mall, the Pavil-
ion, Astrodome, and the George R. Brown Convention
Center. 486 rooms, 14 story. Pets accepted, some restric-
tions; fee. Check-in 3 pm, check-out noon. Restaurant,
bar. Fitness room. Outdoor pool. Business center. **$**

★ ★ ★ ★ **FOUR SEASONS HOTEL
HOUSTON.** *1300 Lamar St, Houston (77010). Phone
713/650-1300; toll-free 800/545-4000; fax 713/652-6220.
www.fourseasons.com.* The Four Seasons is a perfect
complement to the urbane spirit of Houston. Close to
the Convention Center and Enron Field Stadium, it is
conveniently located near the downtown business and
financial districts. Thoughtful car service makes doing
business or visiting the sites carefree. Shoppers adore
this hotel for its proximity to Park Shops, a three-level
mall connected to the hotel via a climate-controlled
skywalk. The guest rooms are a sophisticated blend
of European furniture, Asian decorative objects, and
Southwestern splash. The sparkling outdoor pool,
fitness center, and spa give the hotel a resort-in-the-
city ambience. Guests sample tequila, taste wine, and
savor tapas from around the world in the relaxing
atmosphere of the Lobby Lounge. Quattro (see) is a
feast for the eyes and the senses with its vivacious décor
and simply delicious Italian cuisine. 404 rooms, 30
story. Pets accepted, some restrictions. Check-in 3 pm,
check-out 1 pm. High-speed Internet access, wireless
Internet access. Restaurant, two bars. Fitness room, spa.
Outdoor pool, whirlpool. Airport transportation avail-
able. Business center. **$$$**

★ ★ ★ **HILTON AMERICAS HOUSTON.** *1600
Lamar, Houston (77010). Phone 713/739-8000; fax
713/739-8007. www.americashouston.hilton.com.* 1,203
rooms. Pets accepted, some restrictions; fee. Check-in
3 pm, check-out noon. High-speed Internet access,
wireless Internet access. Three restaurants, three bars.
Fitness room, spa. Indoor pool, whirlpool. **$$**

★ ★ ★ **HILTON HOUSTON PLAZA.** *6633 Travis
St, Houston (77030). Phone 713/313-4000; toll-free 800/
445-8667; fax 713/313-4660. www.hilton.com.* Adjacent

to museums, parks, Rice University. 183 rooms, 19 story. Check-in 3 pm, check-out noon. High-speed Internet access. Restaurant, bar. Fitness room. Outdoor pool, whirlpool. Business center. **$$**

★ ★ ★ HILTON HOUSTON WESTCHASE.

9999 Westheimer Rd, Houston (77042). Phone 713/974-1000; toll-free 800/445-8667; fax 713/974-2108. www.hilton.com. 297 rooms, 13 story. Check-in 3 pm, check-out noon. High-speed Internet access. Restaurant, two bars. Fitness room. Outdoor pool, whirlpool. Business center. **$**

★ ★ ★ HOTEL DEREK. *2525 W Loop S, Houston (77027). Phone 713/961-3000; fax 713/297-4392.* Modernists adore the Hotel Derek for its fresh, hip look and feel. Houston's chic alternative appeals to contemporary travelers with a penchant for minimalist design and maximum attention. Guests are ferried about town in the hotel's stretch SUV, nicknamed the "Derek Mobile." While its Houston Galleria location makes it a favorite choice of fashionistas, this hotspot lures executives with its plentiful business amenities. Designed to feel like a rock star's pad, the loftlike rooms and suites are the very definition of cool, contemporary luxury and are fitted with every possible detail. The people-watching is first-rate here, especially at the Southwestern-influenced Maverick's restaurant and amid the Las Vegas-meets-Houston ambience at Derek's Bar. 314 rooms, 14 story. Pets accepted, some restrictions; fee. Check-in 3 pm, check-out noon. High-speed Internet access. Restaurant, bar. Fitness room. Outdoor pool. Business center. **$$**

★ ★ ★ HOTEL ICON. *220 Main St, Houston (77002). Phone 713/224-4266; toll-free 800/877-4266; fax 713/223-3223. www.hotelicon.com.* 135 rooms. Check-in 2 pm, check-out noon. High-speed Internet access. Restaurant, two bars. Fitness room. Airport transportation available. Business center. **$$**

★ ★ ★ THE HOUSTONIAN HOTEL. *111 N Post Oak Ln, Houston (77024). Phone 713/680-2626; fax 713/680-2992.* Shaded by trees and surrounded by greenery, The Houstonian Hotel gives guests the impression of being in the country while remaining in the city center. Guests are greeted with a warm Texas-size welcome at this gracious hotel. Rustic elegance meets European panache here, where

a magnificent 30-foot hand-carved stone fireplace dominates the lobby. The guest rooms have an inviting atmosphere enhanced by floor-to-ceiling windows that showcase the wooded grounds. Guests enter a privileged world in this superb location, where they have access to the private Houstonian Golf Club and the Houstonian Club, considered one of the finest private fitness facilities in the country. From the rock-climbing wall to boxing, yoga, and martial arts classes, exercise takes on an exciting edge here. The spa is the picture of serenity, offering standby favorites and signature treatments. Several cafés delight diners with light fare, while Olivette offers tastes of the French, Italian, and Spanish Mediterranean. 287 rooms, 4 story. Check-in 4 pm, check-out noon. High-speed Internet access, wireless Internet access. Three restaurants, bar. Children's activity center. Fitness room, fitness classes available, spa. Outdoor pool, children's pool, whirlpool. Golf, 90 holes. Tennis. Airport transportation available. Business center. **$$**

★ ★ ★ HYATT REGENCY HOUSTON. *1200 Louisiana St, Houston (77002). Phone 713/654-1234; toll-free 800/233-1234; fax 713/951-0934. www.hyatt.com.* Built around 30-story atrium; glass-enclosed elevators. Covered passage to downtown buildings. 977 rooms, 30 story. Check-in 3 pm, check-out noon. High-speed Internet access, wireless Internet access. Three restaurants, two bars. Fitness room. Outdoor pool. Business center. **$$**

★ ★ ★ HYATT REGENCY HOUSTON AIRPORT. *15747 John F Kennedy Blvd, Houston (77032). Phone 281/987-1234; toll-free 800/633-7313; fax 281/590-8461. www.hyatt.com.* This hotel is situated a block from Houston Intercontinental Airport and set on 5 acres of wooded grounds. Nearby golf courses include the World Houston, the Woodlands, and the Tour 18. 314 rooms, 7 story. Check-in 3 pm, check-out noon. Restaurant, bar. Fitness room. Outdoor pool, whirlpool. Airport transportation available. Business center. **$**

★ ★ ★ INN AT THE BALLPARK. *1520 Texas Ave, Houston (77002). Phone 713/228-1520; fax 713/228-1555. www.innattheballpark.com.* 201 rooms. Check-in 3 pm, check-out noon. High-speed Internet access, wireless Internet access. Two restaurants, bar. Fitness room. Business center. **$$**

★ ★ ★ **INTERCONTINENTAL HOTEL HOUSTON.** *2222 West Loop S, Houston (77459). Phone 713/627-7600; toll-free 866/342-0831; fax 713/961-3327. www.intercontinental.com.* 485 rooms, 23 story. Check-in 3 pm, check-out noon. High-speed Internet access. Restaurant, bar. Fitness room. Outdoor pool, whirlpool. Business center. **$$**

★ ★ ★ **JW MARRIOTT HOTEL BY THE GALLERIA.** *5150 Westheimer, Houston (77056). Phone 713/961-1500; toll-free 800/228-9290; fax 713/961-5045. www.marriott.com/houjw.* The JW Marriott Hotel wins high marks from demanding travelers for its attention to detail, business-friendly services, and convenient location. Situated in the heart of Houston's Uptown business and shopping neighborhood, this hotel is a perfect base for those visiting for business or pleasure. Nearly 350 shops and restaurants await just outside the door of this hotel, although all-day dining is available at the hotel's own Brasserie. 514 rooms, 23 story. Check-in 3 pm, check-out noon. High-speed Internet access, wireless Internet access. Restaurant, bar. Fitness room. Indoor pool, outdoor pool, whirlpool. Business center. **$$**

★ ★ ★ **LANCASTER HOTEL.** *701 Texas Ave, Houston (77002). Phone 713/228-9500; toll-free 800/231-0336; fax 713/223-4528. www.lancaster.com.* The Lancaster Hotel is a Houston landmark. Located in the heart of Houston's theater district, this historic hotel's convenient setting places it within walking distance of area businesses and cultural attractions. Opened in 1926, the Lancaster feels like an exclusive private club with its intimate scale, jewel-toned walls, and European furnishings. Floral fabrics and distinctive furnishings give the traditional-style rooms and suites a welcoming ambience, while luxurious details enhance the experience. The flavors of the Gulf Coast are celebrated at Bistro Lancaster, where guests dine to the sounds of the piano on weekends. Both the restaurant and the bar are popular spots for theatergoers, who book tables before and after the show. 93 rooms, 12 story. Check-in 3 pm, check-out 1 pm. High-speed Internet access, wireless Internet access. Restaurant, bar. Fitness room. Business center. **$$$**

★ ★ **MAGNOLIA HOTEL HOUSTON.** *1100 Texas Ave, Houston (77002). Phone 713/221-0011; toll-free 888/915-1110; fax 713/221-0022. www.magnoliahotels.com.* 314 rooms. Pets accepted, some restrictions. Check-in 3 pm, check-out noon. High-speed Internet access, wireless Internet access. Restaurant, bar. Fitness room. Outdoor pool, whirlpool. **$$**

★ ★ ★ **MARRIOTT HOUSTON MEDICAL CENTER.** *6580 Fannin St, Houston (77030). Phone 713/796-0080; toll-free 800/228-9290; fax 713/770-8100. www.marriott.com.* This hotel is perfectly located near many attractions. It is found in the heart of the Texas Medical Center, adjacent to Rice University and only minutes from downtown Houston. 386 rooms, 26 story. Pets accepted, some restrictions; fee. Check-in 4 pm, check-out noon. High-speed Internet access. Three restaurants, bar. Fitness room. Indoor pool, whirlpool. Business center. **$**

★ ★ ★ **MARRIOTT SUGAR LAND TOWN SQUARE.** *16090 City Walk, Sugar Land (77479). Phone 281/275-8400; fax 281/275-8401. www.marriott.com.* 300 rooms. Check-in 4 pm, check-out noon. High-speed Internet access, wireless Internet access. Restaurant, bar. Fitness room. Outdoor pool, whirlpool. Airport transportation available. Business center. **$$**

★ ★ ★ **OMNI HOUSTON HOTEL.** *4 Riverway, Houston (77056). Phone 713/871-8181; toll-free 800/843-6664; fax 713/871-0719. www.omnihotels.com.* Only 30 minutes from downtown, the Omni Houston Hotel occupies an enviable location in the Post Oak/Galleria section. Nestled on lush grounds overlooking a 3-acre lake, this hotel enables visitors to leave the world behind. The gracious lobby dazzles with its water garden of cascading waterfalls and brightly colored fish. Rich reds, golds, and persimmons are used in the public spaces, creating an exotic sophistication. Lush foliage dominates the lobby, and abundant floral displays add touches of beauty throughout the hotel. The guest rooms have a relaxed, contemporary style, while modern amenities allow visitors to keep in touch. A well-equipped fitness center, tennis and basketball courts, and the nearby jogging trails of Hershey Park provide athletic diversions. An American bistro and English-style pub offer pleasantly casual surroundings, while the refined French cuisine of La Reserve is an award-winning local sensation. 378 rooms, 11 story. Pets accepted, some restrictions; fee. Check-in 3 pm, check-out noon. High-speed Internet access, wireless Internet access. Two restaurants, two bars. Fitness room. Outdoor pool, whirlpool. Tennis. Business center. **$$**

★ ★ ★ RENAISSANCE HOUSTON HOTEL.
6 Greenway Plz E, Houston (77046). Phone 713/629-1200; toll-free 800/468-3571; fax 713/629-4702. www.renaissancehotels.com. This hotel is situated in the same complex as numerous corporate headquarters and adjacent to the Compaq Center Complex. 388 rooms, 20 story. Pets accepted, some restrictions. Check-in 3 pm, check-out 1 pm. High-speed Internet access. Two restaurants, two bars. Fitness room. Outdoor pool. Business center. **$$**

★ ★ ★ THE SAM HOUSTON HOTEL.
1117 Prairie St, Houston (77002). Phone 832/200-8800; toll-free 877/348-8800; fax 832/200-8811. www.samhoustonhotel.com. In the heart of downtown near the theater district and the Houston Astros ballpark, this hip hotel is a National Historic Landmark. Still, it's a modern facility, with ultracontemporary décor and flat-screen TVs in the rather small guest rooms. Business travelers appreciate the Aeron chairs, laptop safes, and complimentary high-speed Internet access, while all guests enjoy granite baths with separate glassed-in showers. The hotel's restaurant, 17, serves regional American cuisine. 100 rooms. Pets accepted; fee. Check-in 3 pm, check-out noon. High-speed Internet access. Restaurant, bar. Fitness room. **$$**

★ ★ ★ SHERATON SUITES HOUSTON NEAR THE GALLERIA.
2400 W Loop S, Houston (77027). Phone 713/586-2444; toll-free 800/325-2525; fax 713/586-2445. www.sheratonsuiteshouston.com. 281 rooms, 14 story, all suites. Pets accepted, some restrictions. Check-in 3 pm, check-out noon. High-speed Internet access, wireless Internet access. Restaurant, bar. Fitness room. Outdoor pool, whirlpool. Business center. **$$**

★ ★ ★ SOFITEL.
425 N Sam Houston Pkwy E, Houston (77060). Phone 281/445-9000; toll-free 800/763-4835; fax 281/445-9826. www.sofitel.com. This hotel is conveniently located 7 miles from the airport and situated in the heart of the North Houston business district. Nearby attractions include the Sam Houston Race Park and Old Towne Spring. 334 rooms, 8 story. Pets accepted. Check-in 3 pm, check-out 1 pm. High-speed Internet access, wireless Internet access. Restaurant, bar. Fitness room. Outdoor pool, whirlpool. Airport transportation available. Business center. **$$**

★ ★ ★ ★ THE ST. REGIS, HOUSTON.
1919 Briar Oaks Ln, Houston (77027). Phone 713/840-7600; toll-free 888/625-5144; fax 713/840-8036. www.stregis.com. The St. Regis echoes the grace and elegance of its pedigreed neighbors in the River Oaks section of Houston. The world-class shopping of the Galleria is just a short distance, as are the businesses and attractions of downtown. While staying here, guests are assured of a singular experience. The guest rooms are lovely homes away from home, with rich mahogany furnishings juxtaposed with subtle cream, white, and taupe color schemes. Large windows are swathed in luxurious fabrics, and appealing art adorns the walls. The climate-controlled outdoor pool offers a perfect place for reflection. Bathed in sunshine, the Tea Lounge offers one of the most elegant ways to spend an afternoon, and the quality seafood and steaks at Remington Grill make for a memorable dining experience. 232 rooms, 12 story. Pets accepted. Check-in 3 pm, check-out noon. High-speed Internet access. Two restaurants, bar. Fitness room, spa. Outdoor pool. Business center. **$$$**

★ ★ ★ THE WARWICK HOTEL HOUSTON.
5701 Main St, Houston (77005). Phone 713/526-1991; toll-free 866/460-1532; fax 713/639-4545. www.thewarwick.dolce.com. 308 rooms, 10 story. Pets accepted, some restrictions; fee. Check-in 3 pm, check-out noon. High-speed Internet access, wireless Internet access. Restaurant, bar. Fitness room. Outdoor pool, whirlpool. Business center. **$$**

★ ★ ★ THE WESTIN GALLERIA HOUSTON.
5060 W Alabama, Houston (77056). Phone 713/960-8100; toll-free 800/937-8461; fax 713/960-6553. 487 rooms, 17 story. Pets accepted, some restrictions. Check-in 3 pm, check-out noon. High-speed Internet access, wireless Internet access. Restaurant, bar. Outdoor pool. Business center. **$$**

★ ★ ★ THE WESTIN OAKS.
5011 Westheimer at Post Oak, Houston (77056). Phone 713/960-8100; toll-free 800/937-8461; fax 713/960-6554. 406 rooms,

15 story. Pets accepted, some restrictions. Check-in 3 pm, check-out noon. High-speed Internet access, wireless Internet access. Two restaurants, bar. Outdoor pool. **$$**

★ ★ ★ THE WOODLANDS RESORT & CONFERENCE CENTER. *2301 N Millbend Dr, The Woodlands (77380). Phone 281/367-1100; toll-free 800/433-2624; fax 281/364-6345. www.woodlandsresort.com.* 490 rooms, 3 story. Check-in 3 pm, check-out noon. High-speed Internet access, wireless Internet access. Four restaurants, three bars. Children's activity center. Fitness room, fitness classes available, spa. Outdoor pool, children's pool, whirlpool. Golf, 36 holes. Tennis. Airport transportation available. Business center. **$$**

★ ★ ★ WOODLANDS WATERWAY MARRIOTT HOTEL. *1601 Lake Robbins Dr, The Woodlands (77380). Phone 281/367-9797; toll-free 800/228-9290; fax 281/681-5656. www.marriott.com/houmw.* 345 rooms. Check-in 4 pm, check-out 11 am. High-speed Internet access. Restaurant, bar. Fitness room. Outdoor pool, whirlpool. Business center. **$$**

Full-Service Inn

★ ★ ★ LA COLOMBE D'OR HOTEL. *3410 Montrose Blvd, Houston (77006). Phone 713/524-7999; fax 713/524-8923. www.lacolombedor.com.* Prairie-style mansion built in 1923 by Walter Fondren, founder of Humble Oil (now Exxon). 13 rooms, 3 story, all suites. Check-in flexible, check-out noon. Restaurant, bar. **$$**

Specialty Lodgings

The following lodging establishments are approved by Mobil Travel Guide, but due to their unique and individualized nature have not been given a traditional Mobil Star rating. Included in this listing you may find bed-and-breakfasts, limited-service inns, guest ranches, and other unique hotel properties.

BOGART'S ON THE BOULEVARD. *1536 Heights Blvd, Houston (77008). Phone 713/864-2500; fax 713/426-1016. www.bogarts.org.* 7 rooms. Children over 12 years only. Complimentary full breakfast. Check-in 3 pm, check-out noon. High-speed Internet access. Outdoor pool, whirlpool. **$**

LOVETT INN. *501 Lovett Blvd, Houston (77006). Phone 713/522-5224; toll-free 800/779-5224; fax 713/528-6708. www.lovettinn.com.* 10 rooms. Pets accepted, some restrictions. Complimentary continental breakfast. Check-in 2 pm, check-out noon. Wireless Internet access. Outdoor pool, whirlpool. **$**

SARA'S BED AND BREAKFAST INN. *941 Heights Blvd, Houston (77008). Phone 713/868-1130; toll-free 800/593-1130; fax 713/868-3284. www.saras.com.* This bed-and-breakfast in Houston Heights has the area's small-town charm as well as a convenient location to downtown Houston. The rooms are individual mixtures of vintage, antiques, and modern convenience. 12 rooms, 2 story. Children over 8 years only. Complimentary full breakfast. Check-in 3 pm, check-out noon. Wireless Internet access. **$**

Spa

★ ★ ★ ★ TRELLIS, THE SPA AT THE HOUSTONIAN. *111 N Post Oak Ln, Houston (77024). Phone 713/685-6790; toll-free 800/378-4010. www.trellisspa.com.* In addition to a fabulous 125,000-square-foot fitness center complete with an indoor track, a rock climbing wall, a variety of courts, and three pools, The Houstonian boasts one of the best spas in Texas. Popular with hotel guests and local denizens in the know, this Mediterranean-style spa focuses on beauty and well-being with a variety of European-inspired treatments. This facility simply sparkles and is the perfect place to celebrate a special occasion or to unwind after a pressure-filled day. An indoor float pool encourages total relaxation, while the lovely lounge—complete with a fireplace—is an ideal spot to sip Texas sweet tea before or after a treatment. The spa even offers programs tailored to teenagers and mothers-to-be, allowing them to enjoy days created specifically for them. Unlike many spas, where men often are considered only as afterthoughts, Trellis features a treatment menu that caters to male guests. Leave the rat race behind as you relax with a Swedish, stone, or aromatic massage. Active contouring helps reduce unwanted cellulite, while the body bronzing treatment adds a healthy glow to your skin. Increase your circulation and improve your skin tone with a hydrotherapy treatment or let the seven heads of the Vichy shower rain down on you. Designed around two lauded European products, Carita and Decléor, the facials offer intense hydrating, lifting, and firming to help renew and revive your skin; specialized facials are available

for sensitive and oily complexions. Whether you choose a body wrap that invigorates and detoxifies or a unique treatment that banishes stretch marks or relieves leg discomfort, treat yourself to much deserved pampering.

Restaurants

★★★**AMERICAS.** *1800 Post Oak Blvd, Houston (77056). Phone 713/961-1492; fax 713/626-2701. www.cordua.com.* Influences from North, South, and Central America converge here into the eclectic "New World Cuisine" menu. The dramatic dark-wooded, high-ceilinged bar is a mere prelude for the impressive dining room above. This restaurant is a must when wanting to impress or indulge someone special. Suspension bridge to second level. Latin American menu. Lunch, dinner. Closed Sun. Bar. Children's menu. Business casual attire. Reservations recommended. Valet parking. **$$**

★★**ARCODORO.** *5000 Westheimer, Houston (77056). Phone 713/621-6888; fax 713/621-6859. www.arcodoro.com.* This gorgeous Galleria-area favorite pairs the comfort of owner Efisio Farris's Sardinian homeland with the joys of sophisticated yet rustic Sardinian cuisine. The Grill is the place for seeing and being seen, with a lovely al fresco dining option and a wood-burning pizza oven, while the Dining Room feels dressier. Favorites include the grilled, marinated portobello with lightly fried polenta over a pecorino fondue and squid-ink risotto with cuttlefish and grilled prawns. Don't miss the special drink—a grappa-rita. Italian menu. Lunch, dinner, late-night, brunch. Closed Jan 1, Thanksgiving, Dec 25. Bar. Business casual attire. Reservations recommended. Valet parking. Outdoor seating. **$$$**

★★**BACKSTREET CAFE.** *1103 S Shepherd, Houston (77019). Phone 713/521-2239; fax 713/521-2219. www.backstreetcafe.net.* American menu. Lunch, dinner, brunch. Closed Thanksgiving, Dec 24-25. Bar. Children's menu. Business casual attire. Reservations recommended. Valet parking. Outdoor seating. **$$$**

★★**BAROQUE.** *1700 Sunset Blvd, Houston (77005). Phone 713/523-8881.* Eighteenth-century Baroque décor; ornate chandeliers, murals, antiques. Eclectic menu. Lunch, dinner. Closed Sun-Mon; also during the summer. Bar. **$$**

★★**BENJY'S.** *2424 Dunstan, Houston (77005). Phone 713/522-7602; fax 713/522-7655. www.benjys.com.* American menu. Lunch, dinner, late-night, brunch. Closed holidays. Bar. Children's menu. Casual attire. Reservations recommended. **$$**

★**BIRRAPORETTI'S.** *500 Louisiana St, Houston (77002). Phone 713/224-9494; fax 713/224-2608. www.birrafun.com.* In the Theater District. Italian menu. Lunch, dinner, late-night, Sun brunch. Closed Thanksgiving, Dec 25. Bar. Business casual attire. Reservations recommended. **$$**

★★**BISTRO LANCASTER.** *701 Texas Ave, Houston (77002). Phone 713/228-9502; toll-free 800/231-0336; fax 713/223-4528. www.lancaster.com.* Smart and sleek, this bistro attracts all types, from the downtown worker to the restaurant savvy jetsetter. American menu. Breakfast, lunch, dinner. Bar. Business casual attire. Reservations recommended. Valet parking. **$$$**

★★★**BRENNAN'S.** *3300 Smith St, Houston (77006). Phone 713/522-9711; fax 713/522-9142. www.brennanshouston.com.* From the famed New Orleans restaurant family, Brennan's is considered *the* place in Houston for fine dining and gracious Southern hospitality. The unique "Texas Creole" menu at Brennan's is a brilliant blend of Southwestern ingredients and Creole dishes and is complemented by an incredible wine list (and a team of sommeliers to steer you through it). If romance is the order of the day, request a table on the charming patio, set under the cool shade of tall oak trees. If you plan ahead, you and your companions can dine at the coveted chef's table, a petite, glass-enclosed dining room in the center of the high-octane kitchen. As if you needed another bite (the portions here are quite filling), on your way out you'll receive a complimentary homemade praline for the ride home. If you can wait until morning to finish it off, you've got a will of steel. Creole, French menu. Lunch, dinner. Closed holidays. Bar. Children's menu. Business casual attire. Reservations recommended. Valet parking. Outdoor seating. **$$$**

★★★**BROWNSTONE.** *2736 Virginia St, Houston (77098). Phone 713/520-5666; fax 713/520-7001. www.brownstone-houston.com.* While the wine list is notable and the food is good, people go to Brownstone for the ambiance. The luxurious and relaxed atmosphere is created by the ceiling to floor windows facing out to a lush courtyard with a small pool. American, French menu. Lunch, dinner. Closed Sun. Bar. Business casual attire. Reservations recommended. Valet parking. Outdoor seating. **$$$**

★ ★ ★ **CAFE ANNIE.** *1728 Post Oak Blvd, Houston (77056). Phone 713/840-1111; fax 713/840-1558. www.cafe-annie.com.* Cafe Annie is one of Houston's most beloved restaurants. Under the watchful care of chef/owner Robert Del Grande, Cafe Annie's bold regional American menu has a strong Southwestern flair. Although the house is best known for two haute Southwestern plates—cocoa-roasted chicken with barbecued sweet potatoes and cinnamon-roasted pheasant with applewood smoked bacon, red chile pecan sauce, apricot jam, and creamy mashed spuds—simpler fare from the Mixed Grill section also shines. Cafe Annie's features sleek mahogany walls, checkered limestone floors, vaulted ceilings, artistic floral arrangements, and leather banquettes. the room has a chic, stylish vibe. It is constantly abuzz with a passionate following of visiting celebrities, moneyed locals, salivating foodies, and knowledgeable wine connoisseurs. Southwestern menu. Lunch, dinner. Closed Sun; holidays. Bar. Business casual attire. Reservations recommended. Valet parking. **$$$**

★ **CAFE JAPON.** *3915 Kirby Dr, Houston (77098). Phone 713/529-1668; fax 713/529-1682.* Japanese menu. Lunch, dinner, late-night. Bar. Casual attire. Outdoor seating. **$$**

★ ★ **CANYON CAFE.** *5000 Westheimer, Suite 250, Houston (77056). Phone 713/629-5565; fax 713/629-5570. www.canyoncafe.com.* A mainstay on the Southwestern dining scene and a fixture in the Galleria area, this shopping center jewel delights with its outdoor seating option on a balcony. Solid starters include the poblano chicken chowder and the corn-crusted calamari with a chipotle remoulade sauce. Chile-rubbed sirloin with sautéed spinach is a nice entrée pick. Southwestern, Spanish menu. Lunch, dinner, late-night. Closed Thanksgiving, Dec 25. Bar. Children's menu. Casual attire. Reservations recommended. Outdoor seating. **$$**

★ ★ ★ **THE CAPITAL GRILLE.** *5365 Westheimer Rd, Houston (77056). Phone 713/623-4600; fax 713/623-4606. www.thecapitalgrille.com.* Steak menu. Dinner. Closed Super Bowl Sun, Thanksgiving, Dec 25. Bar. Children's menu. Business casual attire. Reservations recommended. Valet parking. **$$$**

★ ★ **CARRABBA'S.** *3115 Kirby Dr, Houston (77098). Phone 713/522-3131; fax 713/522-1526. www.carrabbas.com.* Italian menu. Lunch, dinner. Closed Thanksgiving, Dec 25. Bar. Valet parking. Outdoor seating. **$$$**

★ ★ **CHARLEYS 517.** *517 Louisiana St, Houston (77002). Phone 713/224-4438; fax 713/229-8112. www.charleys517.com.* Chef/owner Clive Berkman's restaurant is sophisticated and urban yet casually comfortable. American menu. Lunch, dinner. Closed Sun; holidays. Bar. Business casual attire. Reservations recommended. Valet parking. **$$$**

★ ★ ★ **CHEZ NOUS.** *217 S Ave G, Humble (77338). Phone 281/446-6717.* This well-known French spot, located near Bush International Airport in a small, renovated church, has garnered many kudos for its authentic cuisine. French menu. Dinner. Closed Sun. Bar. Business casual attire. Reservations recommended. **$$$**

⊙ ★ **CHUY'S COMIDA DELUXE.** *2706 Westheimer Rd, Houston (77098). Phone 713/524-1700; fax 713/524-2766. www.chuys.com.* Tex-Mex menu. Lunch, dinner, late-night. Closed Thanksgiving, Dec 25. Bar. Children's menu. Casual attire. Outdoor seating. **$$**

★ ★ **DAILY REVIEW CAFE.** *3412 W Lamar, Houston (77019). Phone 713/520-9217; fax 713/520-1916. www.dailyreviewcafe.com.* American menu. Lunch, dinner, Sun brunch. Bar. Casual attire. Reservations recommended. Valet parking. Outdoor seating. **$$**

★ ★ **DAMIAN'S CUCINA ITALIA.** *3011 Smith St, Houston (77006). Phone 713/522-0439; fax 713/522-4408. www.damians.com.* For a large array of food, visit this warm and comfortable downtown restaurant. If patrons are indecisive, the sheer mountain of attractive entrées will not make selecting dinner an easy task. Italian menu. Lunch, dinner. Closed Sun; holidays. Bar. Business casual attire. Reservations recommended. Valet parking. **$$$**

★ **DONERAKI.** *7705 Westheimer Rd, Houston (77063). Phone 713/975-9815; fax 713/975-9111. www.doneraki.com.* Mexican menu. Breakfast, lunch, dinner, late-night. Bar. Children's menu. Casual attire. Reservations recommended. **$$**

★ ★ **ESCALANTE'S MEXICAN GRILLE.** *6582 Woodway, Houston (77057). Phone 713/461-5400; fax 713/461-5490. www.escalantesmexicangrille.com.* Large mural; indoor colonnade. Mexican menu. Lunch, dinner. Bar. Children's menu. Casual attire. Outdoor seating. **$$**

★ ★ **THE FLYING DUTCHMAN.** *9 Kemah Broadwalk, Kemah (77565). Phone 281/334-7575.*

Seafood menu. Lunch, dinner. Closed Thanksgiving, Dec 25. Bar. Children's menu. Outdoor seating. **$$**

★ **GARSON RESTAURANT.** *2926 Hillcroft, Houston (77057). Phone 713/781-0400; fax 713/781-0870.* Mediterranean, Persian menu. Lunch, dinner. Bar. Casual attire. Reservations recommended. **$$**

★ ★ **GLASS MENAGERIE.** *2301 N Millbend Dr, Houston (77380). Phone 281/364-6326; fax 281/364-6272. www.woodlandsresort.com.* Both elegant and relaxing, this restaurant features one of the loveliest views in town. American menu. Dinner, Sun brunch. Closed Mon; Jan 1. Bar. Business casual attire. Valet parking. **$$$**

★ **GOLDEN ROOM.** *1209 Montrose Blvd, Houston (77019). Phone 713/524-9614; fax 713/524-9621. www.thegoldenroom.com.* Chinese, Thai menu. Lunch, dinner. Closed Sun; Dec 25-Jan 1. Casual attire. **$$**

★ **GOODE COMPANY SEAFOOD.** *2621 Westpark, Houston (77098). Phone 713/523-7154; fax 713/523-0774. www.goodecompany.com.* Seafood menu. Lunch, dinner. Bar. Children's menu. Casual attire. Valet parking. **$$**

★ **GOODE COMPANY TEXAS BAR-B-Q.** *5109 Kirby Dr, Houston (77098). Phone 713/522-2530; fax 713/522-3873. www.goodecompany.com.* Barbecue menu. Lunch, dinner. Closed Jan 1, Thanksgiving, Dec 25. Casual attire. Outdoor seating. **$**

★ ★ **GREAT CARUSO.** *10001 Westheimer Rd, Houston (77042). Phone 713/780-4900. www.houstondinnertheater.com.* Broadway and light operetta performances nightly; singing waiters and dancers. American menu. Dinner. Closed Mon-Tues; Jan 1, Dec 25. Bar. Casual attire. Valet parking. **$$**

★ ★ **GROTTO.** *4715 Westheimer Rd, Houston (77027). Phone 713/622-3663; fax 713/622-6284. www.grottohouston.com.* Long one of the most popular restaurants in Houston, this trattoria aims to transport diners to the Amalfi Coast. Murals befitting the mood of Fellini and the warmth of comfy pastas and the old-fashioned wood-burning pizza oven make you want to sit back and savor the experience. Almond-crusted trout with artichoke hearts is one of the restaurant's good seafood efforts. Italian menu. Lunch, dinner. Closed Dec 25. Bar. Children's menu. Casual attire. Reservations recommended. Valet parking. **$$**

★ **GUADALAJARA HACIENDA.** *9799 Katy Frwy, Houston (77024). Phone 713/461-5300; fax 713/461-8401.* Mexican menu. Lunch, dinner, brunch. Bar. Children's menu. Casual attire. Outdoor seating. **$$**

★ ★ **HUNAN.** *1800 Post Oak Blvd, #184, Houston (77056). Phone 713/965-0808; fax 713/965-0701.* Chinese menu. Lunch, dinner. Closed Thanksgiving. Bar. Casual attire. Reservations recommended. Valet parking. **$$**

★ **KIM SON.** *2001 Jefferson St, Houston (77003). Phone 713/222-2461; fax 713/227-8612. www.kimson.com.* Chinese, Vietnamese menu. Lunch, dinner, late-night. Bar. Children's menu. Casual attire. Valet parking (Sat). **$**

★ **KING FISH MARKET.** *11335 Katy Frwy, Houston (77057). Phone 713/467-4400; fax 713/974-2082. www.kingfishmarket.com.* Seafood menu. Lunch, dinner. Closed Thanksgiving, Dec 25. Bar. Children's menu. Casual attire. Outdoor seating. **$$**

★ ★ ★ **LA COLOMBE D'OR.** *3410 Montrose Blvd, Houston (77006). Phone 713/524-7999; fax 713/524-8923. www.lacolombedorhouston.com.* American, French menu. Lunch, dinner. Bar. Business casual attire. Reservations recommended. Valet parking. Outdoor seating. **$$$**

★ ★ ★ **LA GRIGLIA.** *2002 W Gray St, Houston (77019). Phone 713/526-4700; fax 713/526-9249. www.lagrigliarestaurant.com.* True to its name (which means "the grill"), most of the food at this brightly decorated restaurant is prepared on one of two huge grills. Italian menu. Lunch, dinner. Closed Dec 25. Bar. Children's menu. Casual attire. Reservations recommended. Valet parking. Outdoor seating. **$$$**

★ ★ **LA MORA.** *912 Lovett, Houston (77006). Phone 713/522-7412; fax 713/522-0761.* Italian menu. Dinner. Closed Sun; holidays. Bar. Business casual attire. Reservations recommended. Valet parking. Outdoor seating. **$$**

★ ★ ★ **LA RESERVE.** *4 Riverway, Houston (77056). Phone 713/871-8177; toll-free 800/843-6664; fax 713/871-0719. www.omnihotels.com.* Set in the Omni Houston Hotel and surrounded by 32 acres of pastoral parkland in the heart of the city, La Reserve is a plush, upscale hotel dining spot that has gained a dedicated following. Houstonians flock to La Reserve for its innovative, contemporary continental cuisine that playfully borders on the exotic. The menu relies on local flavors, global ingredients, and impeccable

French technique, and the formula is winning. You'll find farm-raised fowl, game, and beef, as well as an eclectic selection of outstanding freshwater and saltwater fish. The lengthy wine list is a thrill as well, with a terrific variety of bottles from the Pacific Coast and around the world. French menu. Dinner, Sun brunch. Closed Mon. Bar. Children's menu. Jacket required. Reservations recommended. Valet parking. **$$$**

★ ★ **LA STRADA.** *322 Westheimer, Houston (77006). Phone 713/523-1014; fax 713/522-7999. www.lastrada.org.* Italian menu. Lunch, dinner, Sun brunch. Closed Mon; Memorial Day, Labor Day, Dec 25. Bar. Children's menu. Casual attire. Reservations recommended. Valet parking. Outdoor seating. **$$**

★ ★ **LAS ALAMEDAS.** *8615 Katy Frwy, Houston (77024). Phone 713/461-1503; fax 713/461-8635. www.lasalamedas.com.* Replica of 19th-century Mexican hacienda; entrance arch, stained glass. Valet parking. Mexican menu. Lunch, dinner, Sun brunch. Closed holidays. Bar. Children's menu. **$$**

★ ★ ★ **MARK'S AMERICAN CUISINE.** *1658 Westheimer Rd, Houston (77006). Phone 713/523-3800; toll-free 800/523-3800; fax 713/523-9292. www.marks1658.com.* From the spare décor to the eclectic dishes, chef/owner Mark Cox (formerly of Tony's) has displayed a penchant for catching everyone off guard. Cox's creations include five-pepper-crusted Atlantic salmon, maple leaf duck, and grilled veal medallions. Built in 1926; former Gothic-style church. American menu. Lunch, dinner. Bar. Casual attire. Reservations recommended. Valet parking. **$$$**

★ ★ ★ **MASRAFF'S.** *1025 S Post Oak Ln, Houston (77056). Phone 713/355-1975; fax 713/355-1965. www.masraffs.com.* American menu. Lunch, dinner, late-night, Sun brunch. Closed Thanksgiving, Dec 25. Bar. Business casual attire. Reservations recommended. Valet parking. **$$$**

★ ★ **MINGALONE ITALIAN BAR AND GRILL.** *540 Texas Ave, Houston (77002). Phone 713/223-0088; fax 713/223-5255. www.mingalone.com.* Italian menu. Lunch, dinner, late-night. Closed Thanksgiving, Dec 25. Bar. Business casual attire. Reservations recommended. Valet parking. Outdoor seating. **$$**

★ **MO MONG.** *1201 Westheimer Rd, Houston (77006). Phone 713/524-5664; fax 713/524-3631.* Vietnamese menu. Lunch, dinner, late-night. Closed Easter, Thanksgiving, Dec 25. Bar. Casual attire. Outdoor seating. **$$**

★ ★ ★ **MORTON'S, THE STEAKHOUSE.** *5000 Westheimer Rd, Houston (77056). Phone 713/629-1946; fax 713/629-4548. www.mortons.com.* Steak, seafood menu. Dinner. Closed holidays. Bar. Valet parking. **$$$**

★ ★ **NIT NOI.** *2426 Bolsover, Houston (77005). Phone 713/524-8114; fax 713/524-2838. www.nitnoithai.com.* Thai menu. Lunch, dinner. Bar. Casual attire. **$$**

★ ★ ★ **OLIVETTE.** *111 N Post Oak Ln, Houston (77024). Phone 713/685-6713; fax 713/680-2992. www.houstonian.com.* Addresses don't get more elegant than the Houstonian Hotel, and Olivette lives up to its setting. Mediterranean accents, bench seating, and the Hearth Room, with its oversized fireplace, make this a compelling place. The changing menu is likely to feature dishes along the lines of paella and rice pudding with mission figs and black currants. French, Mediterranean menu. Breakfast, lunch, dinner, brunch. Bar. Children's menu. Business casual attire. Valet parking. **$$$**

★ **OTTO'S BARBECUE.** *5502 Memorial Dr, Houston (77007). Phone 713/864-2573; fax 713/864-1881. www.ottosbarbecue.com.* Barbecue menu. Lunch, dinner. Closed Sun. Casual attire. Outdoor seating. **$**

★ ★ **OUISIE'S TABLE.** *3939 San Felipe, Houston (77027). Phone 713/528-2264; fax 713/961-4560. www.ouisiestable.com.* The country chic interior with all its antique treasures is the perfect showcase for the stylish comfort food found on Ouisie's menu. Try to get a table in the lovely herb garden, which is a treat. Southern menu. Lunch, dinner, brunch. Closed holidays. Bar. Children's menu. Business casual attire. Reservations recommended. Valet parking. Outdoor seating. **$$$**

★ ★ **PAPPADEAUX.** *6015 Westheimer Rd, Houston (77057). Phone 713/782-6310; fax 713/782-5614. www.pappadeaux.com.* Cajun, seafood menu. Lunch, dinner. Closed Thanksgiving, Dec 25. Bar. Children's menu. Casual attire. Outdoor seating. **$$**

★ ★ ★ **PAPPAS BROTHERS STEAKHOUSE.** *5839 Westheimer Rd, Houston (77057). Phone 713/780-7352. www.pappas.com.* The local minds behind the wildly successful BBQ and seafood chains have another hit with their latest venture, a by-the-book steak joint. Steak menu. Dinner. Closed Sun; holidays. Bar. **$$$**

★ **PAPPASITO'S CANTINA.** *6445 Richmond Ave, Houston (77082). Phone 713/784-5253; fax 713/789-2118. www.pappasrestaurants.com.* Mexican menu. Lunch, dinner. Closed Thanksgiving, Dec 25. Bar. Children's menu. Casual attire. Outdoor seating. **$$**

★ ★ ★ **POST OAK GRILL.** *1415 S Post Oak Ln, Houston (77056). Phone 713/993-9966; fax 713/993-0180. www.postoakgrill.com.* American, seafood menu. Lunch, dinner. Closed Sun; week of Dec 25. Bar. Children's menu. Reservations recommended. Valet parking. **$$**

★ ★ **PREGO.** *2520 Amherst St, Houston (77019). Phone 713/529-2420; fax 713/526-3181. www.prego-houston.com.* Bistro-style dining. Italian menu. Lunch, dinner. Closed Thanksgiving, Dec 25. Bar. Children's menu. Casual attire. Reservations recommended. Valet parking. **$$**

★ ★ ★ **QUATTRO.** *1300 Lamar St, Houston (77010). Phone 713/652-6250; fax 713/276-4720. www.fourseasons.com.* Contemporary Italian-American cuisine is the order of the day at Quattro, the brightly colored ultramodern restaurant in the Four Seasons Hotel Houston (see). After a $3 million makeover, the space has been reborn as a dynamic restaurant, replete with lipstick-red, leather-upholstered walls; stainless steel beaded curtains; pillared candles; and vibrant, jewel-toned, stained-glass paneled walls. With its new look, Quattro's bar is drawing twenty-somethings and after-work revelers in numbers. Despite the buzz at the bar, the dining room maintains a sense of calm, and the food remains a top priority. The kitchen focuses on local, seasonal ingredients and presents plates that are as visually alluring as the space. American, Italian menu. Breakfast, lunch, dinner, late-night, Sun brunch. Bar. Children's menu. Business casual attire. Reservations recommended. Valet parking. **$$$**

★ ★ ★ **RAINBOW LODGE.** *1 Birdsall St, Houston (77007). Phone 713/861-8666; toll-free 866/861-8666; fax 713/861-8405. www.rainbow-lodge.com.* On Buffalo Bayou; garden, gazebo. American menu. Lunch, dinner, Sun brunch. Closed Mon; Jan 1, July 4, Dec 25. Bar. Business casual attire. Reservations recommended. Valet parking. Outdoor seating. **$$$**

★ ★ **RIVER OAKS GRILL.** *2630 Westheimer Rd, Houston (77098). Phone 713/520-1738; fax 713/520-5748.* American menu. Dinner, late-night. Closed Sun. Bar. Business casual attire. Reservations recommended. Valet parking. **$$$**

★ ★ **RUGGLES GRILL.** *903 Westheimer Rd, Houston (77006). Phone 713/524-3839; fax 713/526-6548. www.rugglesgrill.com.* American menu. Lunch, dinner, late-night, Sun brunch. Closed Mon; holidays. Bar. Business casual attire. Valet parking. **$$$**

★ ★ **RUGGLES GRILL 5115.** *5115 Westheimer, Houston (77056). Phone 713/963-8067; fax 713/843-5815. www.rugglesgrill.com.* American menu. Lunch, dinner. Closed Sun; Jan 1, Thanksgiving, Dec 25. Business casual attire. Reservations recommended. Valet parking. **$$**

★ ★ ★ **RUTH'S CHRIS STEAK HOUSE.** *6213 Richmond Ave, Houston (77057). Phone 713/789-2333; fax 713/789-4136. www.ruthschris.com.* Steak menu. Dinner. Closed Thanksgiving, Dec 25. Bar. Valet parking. **$$**

★ ★ **SHANGHAI RIVER.** *2407 Westheimer Rd, Houston (77098). Phone 713/528-5528; fax 713/528-4057.* Chinese menu. Lunch, dinner. Closed Thanksgiving. Bar. Business casual attire. Reservations recommended. **$$**

★ ★ **SIMPOSIO.** *5591 Richmond Ave, Houston (77056). Phone 713/532-0550; fax 713/532-7712. www.simposiorestaurant.com.* Italian menu. Lunch, dinner. Closed Sun; holidays. Bar. Reservations recommended. **$$**

★ ★ ★ **THE STATE GRILLE.** *2925 Weslayan St, Houston (77027). Phone 713/622-1936; fax 713/622-7190. www.thestategrill.com.* Formerly known as the Confederate House, this elegant dining room features foods of the American South. Regulars rave about the cheese grits, fried oysters, and chicken stuffed with andouille sausage and goat cheese. Look for locals from the River Oaks-Memorial Park area nearby. Seafood, steak menu. Lunch, dinner. Closed Sun; holidays. Bar. Business casual attire. Reservations recommended. Valet parking. **$$**

★ ★ **TASTE OF TEXAS.** *10505 Katy Frwy, Houston (77024). Phone 713/932-6901; fax 713/461-6177. www.tasteoftexas.com.* Historical Texan décor; many local antiques, memorabilia. Steak menu. Lunch, dinner. Closed Thanksgiving, Dec 25. Bar. Children's menu. **$$$**

★ **TEXADELPHIA.** *5535 Memorial Dr, Suite O, Houston (77007). Phone 713/868-3100; fax 713/868-6330.* American menu. Lunch, dinner. Bar. Children's menu. Casual attire. **$$**

★ ★ **TONY MANDOLA'S GULF COAST KITCHEN.** *1962 W Gray St, Houston (77019). Phone 713/528-3474; fax 713/528-4438. www.tonymandolas.com.* Seafood menu. Lunch, dinner. Bar. Children's menu. Business casual attire. Reservations recommended. Outdoor seating. **$$**

★ ★ ★ **TONY'S.** *3755 Richmond Ave, Houston (77056). Phone 713/622-6778; fax 713/626-1232. www.tonyshouston.com.* Tony's is one of the best places to see and be seen in Houston. It has become the de facto dining room of the famous (or almost famous) and fabulous, crowded with marquee names and the stylish set. This is a jewel box of a restaurant, decked out in ruby red and coral fabrics, fine art, and glossy Italian wood and lit with ornate antique chandeliers. The appealing setting is stunning and is matched by the heavenly, Italian-inspired menu, featuring premium seasonal ingredients and imported "boutique" seafood. The house signature—a wood oven-roasted, truffle-scented baby hen with wild mushroom risotto—leaves no question that dining at Tony's is a decadent eating exercise. Indeed, this is the best kind of exercise. Continental menu. Lunch, dinner, late-night. Closed Sun; Jan 1, Thanksgiving, Dec 25. Bar. Business casual attire. Valet parking. **$$**

★ ★ **VARGO'S INTERNATIONAL CUISINE.** *2401 Fondren Rd, Houston (77063). Phone 713/782-3888. www.vargos.net.* Seafood, steak menu. Dinner, Sun brunch. Closed Dec 25. Bar. Valet parking. **$$$**

Huntsville (C-9)

See also Bryan/College Station, Crockett

Population 35,078
Elevation 400 ft
Area Code 936
Zip 77340
Information Chamber of Commerce, 1327 11th St; phone 936/295-8113 or toll-free 800/289-0389
Web Site www.chamber.huntsville.tx.us

Huntsville was the home of Sam Houston, winner of Texas independence at San Jacinto, first elected president of the Texas Republic, and twice governor of Texas. It is also the headquarters of the Texas Department of Criminal Justice, and home of Sam Houston State University, whose Criminal Justice Center is one of the largest criminal justice education and research facilities in the nation. Lumber and woodworking are important to its economy.

What to See and Do

Huntsville State Park. *6 miles S on I-45, exit 109 at Park Rd 40. Phone 936/295-5644.* On Lake Raven, 2,083 acres. Swimming, fishing, boating (ramp, rentals); nature and hiking trails, picnicking, concession, improved campsites (hook-ups, dump station). (Daily) **$$**

Sam Houston's Grave. About three blocks north of courthouse in Oakwood Cemetery, follow signs. Inscription is the tribute of Andrew Jackson, once his military commander: "The world will take care of Houston's fame."

Sam Houston Memorial Museum Complex. *1836 Sam Houston Ave, Huntsville. Phone 936/294-1832.* Eight-structure complex surrounding a 15-acre park. Exhibits with artifacts pertaining to the Republic of Texas and relating to Houston and his family. Tours. (Tues-Sun; closed holidays) **FREE** Includes

Steamboat House. *1836 Sam Houston Ave, Huntsville. Phone 936/295-7824.* (1858) Where Sam Houston died. Built by Dr. Rufus W. Bailey, this house is modeled after a Mississippi steamboat, with decklike galleries running its full length.

Woodland Home, Sam Houston's Residence. *1836 Sam Houston Ave, Huntsville.* (1848) Residence with original law office and detached replica log kitchen. Tours.

Sam Houston National Forest. *394 FM 1375 W, New Waverly (77358). 50 miles N of Houston; 3 miles W of New Waverly on FM 1375. ; toll-free 888/361-6908. www.southernregion.fs.fed.us/texas.* Located where the pine forests of the southeastern United States meet the prairies of central Texas, Sam Houston National Forest boasts a wide variety of both eastern and western species of birds and other wildlife. Look for animals and enjoy the outdoors through a variety of activities here. Primitive camping is permitted throughout the general forest area, except during deer-hunting season or when posted otherwise; there are three developed campgrounds as well. The 128-mile Lone Star Hiking Trail—a portion of which has gained National Recreation Trail status—winds through the forest. Cagle Recreation Area, on the shore of Lake Conroe, offers shoreline wading and swimming, boating, water sports, and fishing. There are additional hiking and biking trails, plus 56 miles of equestrian and mountain bike trails. This is also a good spot to view the thousands of wildflowers that Texas is known for—look for flowering redbud trees in February followed by dogwoods in March. (Daily)

Texas Prison Museum. *1113 12th St, Huntsville. Opposite courthouse. Phone 936/295-2155.* Items on display include a Texas electric chair ("Old Sparky"), rifles, contraband items, and examples of inmate art. (Daily; closed holidays) **$$**

Limited-Service Hotel

★ **LA QUINTA INN.** *124 I-45 N, Huntsville (77320). Phone 936/295-6454; toll-free 800/531-5900; fax 936/295-9245. www.lq.com.* 120 rooms, 2 story. Pets accepted. Complimentary continental breakfast. Check-in 2 pm, check-out noon. High-speed Internet access. Fitness room. Outdoor pool. **$**
🔦 🧍 🏊

Restaurant

★ **JUNCTION STEAK AND SEAFOOD.** *2641 11th St, Huntsville (77340). Phone 936/291-2183.* Seafood, steak menu. Lunch, dinner. Closed Jan 1, Thanksgiving, Dec 24-25. Children's menu. Casual attire. **$$**

Jacksonville (B-9)

See also Palestine, Rusk, Tyler

Population 13,868
Elevation 531 ft
Area Code 903
Zip 75766
Information Chamber of Commerce, 526 E Commerce, PO Box 1231; phone 903/586-2217 or toll-free 800/376-2217
Web Site www.jacksonvilletexas.com

What to See and Do

Lake Jacksonville. *Peoples St, Jacksonville. 3 miles SW via Hwy 79, College Ave exit. Phone 903/586-5977.* A 1,760-acre recreation area with swimming, water-skiing, bass fishing, boating; camping and cabins (fee). (Daily)

Love's Lookout State Park. *3 1/2 miles N via Hwy 69, Lookout exit.* A large roadside park with a beautiful overlook of the countryside. Woodlands, play areas, picnicking, rest rooms. (Year-round) **FREE**

Special Events

Tomato Fest. *Downtown Jacksonville. Phone 903/586-2217.* Children's activities. Second Sat in June.

Tops in Texas Rodeo. *Phone 903/586-3285.* Three days. Second week in July.

Jasper (C-10)

Founded 1837
Population 8,247
Elevation 228 ft
Area Code 409
Zip 75951
Information Chamber of Commerce, 246 E Milam; phone 409/384-2762
Web Site www.jaspercoc.org

Jasper is the county seat of Jasper County, where much of the land is covered with timber. The economy is based on lumbering, wood products, and by-products, but there are also many small industries.

The reservoirs resulting from the construction of dams on the Angelina, Sabine, and Neches rivers provide recreational facilities.

What to See and Do

Angelina National Forest. *701 N First St, Jasper. NW on Hwy 63. Phone 936/639-8620.*

B. A. Steinhagen Lake. *890 FM 92, Woodville (75979). Headquarters located 15 miles SW on Hwy 190, then 5 miles S on FM 92. Phone 409/429-3491.* Water-skiing, fishing, boating (ramps); picnicking, concession, camping (tent and trailer sites, fee). (Daily) **FREE**

Beaty-Orton House. *200 S Main, Jasper. Phone 409/384-2765.* Restored Victorian gingerbread house. Museum; tours. (Mon-Fri, weekends by appointment) **$**

Lake Sam Rayburn. *Rte 3, Box 486, Jasper (75951). Headquarters located 9 miles N on Hwy 96, then 8 miles W on TX 255. Phone 409/384-5716.* Swimming, water-skiing, fishing, boating (ramps); picnicking, camping (tent and trailer sites, fee).

Martin Dies Jr. State Park. *13 miles SW on Hwy 190 to Park Rd 48, on the eastern shore of B. A. Steinhagen Lake. Phone toll-free 800/792-1112.* Approximately 700 acres. Swimming, water-skiing, fishing piers, canoeing, boating (ramps); picnicking, camping (tent and trailer sites, hook-ups, dump station). (Daily)

Sabine National Forests. *201 S Palm, Jasper (75948). N and E via Hwy 96.* Phone 936/639-8620. Approximately 160,600 acres of rolling clay, sand hills covered with pine, hardwood forests. Toledo Bend Reservoir is on the eastern boundary of forest. Five recreation areas. Swimming, boating (launch); hiking, birding, camping (fee). (Daily) Fees vary. Contact District Ranger office.

Toledo Bend Dam and Reservoir. *Spur Rd 135, Burkeville. Project headquarters, 9 miles N on Hwy 96, then 26 miles E on Hwy 255.* Phone 409/565-2273. *www.sra.dst.tx.us.* Maintained by the Sabine River Authorities of Texas and Louisiana. Swimming, water-skiing, fishing, boating; picnicking, camping. Approximately 1,200 miles of shoreline. Some fees. (Daily, hours vary; closed holidays) **$$**

Special Events

Fall Fest. *Liars Club rodeo grounds., 246 E Milam, Jasper (75951).* Phone 409/384-2762. Early Oct.

PRCA Lion's Club Championship Rodeo. *633 S Wheeler St, Jasper (75951).* Phone 409/384-4322. Early May. **$$$$**

Limited-Service Hotels

★ **HOLIDAY INN EXPRESS.** *2100 N Wheeler St, Jasper (75951).* Phone 409/384-8600; toll-free 800/465-4329; fax 409/384-9551. *www.holiday-inn.com.* 57 rooms, 2 story. Complimentary continental breakfast. Check-out noon. Outdoor pool. **$**
🛏️

★ ★ **RAMADA INN.** *239 E Gibson St, Jasper (75951).* Phone 409/384-9021; fax 409/384-9021. *www.ramada.com.* 100 rooms. Check-out noon. Restaurant, bar. Outdoor pool. **$**
🛏️

Jefferson (A-10)

See also Marshall

Founded 1836
Population 2,024
Elevation 200 ft
Area Code 903
Zip 75657
Information Marion County Chamber of Commerce,

118 N Vale; phone 903/665-2672 or toll-free 888/467-3529
Web Site www.jefferson-texas.com

On Big Cypress Bayou, this was once Texas's largest inland river steamboat port. The town had gaslights in 1867, which used gas made from pine knots. Trees were harvested for lumber until the area was nearly stripped of its natural resource. Iron ore was found nearby, and Jefferson was the home of an early foundry. In 1872, this community had a population of more than 35,000.

What to See and Do

Atalanta. *211 W Austin, Jefferson (75657).* Phone 903/665-2513. Personal rail car of railroad magnate and financier Jay Gould. (Mon-Sat 10 am-4 pm, Sun noon-4 pm; closed holidays) **$**

Caddo Lake State Park. *2198 FM Rd, Jefferson. E on Hwy 134.* Phone 903/679-3351. (See MARSHALL.)

Excelsior House. *211 W Austin St, Jefferson.* Phone 903/665-2513. Built in the 1850s. President Ulysses S. Grant, President Rutherford B. Hayes, Jay Gould, and Oscar Wilde stayed here. Period furnishings. Tours (Daily; closed Dec 25). **$$** Opposite is

> **Freeman Plantation.** *Hwy 49 W, Jefferson (75657). 1 mile W on Hwy 49.* Phone 903/665-2320. Antebellum home built in 1850; restored and furnished with Victorian antiques. Tours (Mon-Tues, Thurs-Sun; closed Easter, Thanksgiving, Dec 25). **$$**

House of the Seasons. *409 S Alley, Jefferson.* Phone 903/665-1218. (1872) Example of the transition period between the Greek Revival and Victorian styles of architecture. The unique feature of the house is the cupola, from which the house gets its name. Each wall contains a different color stained-glass window that creates the illusion of a season of the year. Many original furnishings and art pieces. Tours (daily; closed Thanksgiving, Dec 25). **$$$**

Jefferson Historical Museum. *223 W Austin St, Jefferson.* Phone 903/665-2775. Former post office and federal court building (1888) houses Native American exhibits, gun collection, early American items, art display. (Daily; closed holidays) **$$**

Jefferson Riverboat Landing & Depot. *Bayou St, Jefferson (75657). At Bayou St and Cypress River Bridge.* Phone 903/665-2222. *www.historicjefferson.com/*

bayoutours. Narrated tour of Big Cypress Bayou. Historical sites are detailed. (Mar-Dec, daily 10 am-noon, 2-4 pm) **$$$**

Lake o' the Pines. *FM Rd 729 and Johnson Creek, Jefferson. 4 miles W on Hwy 49, then 4 miles W on FM 729, and 2 miles W on FM 726. Phone 903/755-2530; toll-free 800/284-2267 (reservations).* Swimming, fishing, boating; picnicking, camping (tent and trailer sites, dump station; fee). (Daily)

Special Events

Christmas Candlelight Tour. *Phone 903/665-2672. www.holidaytrailoflights.com/calendar-jefferson.html.* Tour of four Victorian houses decorated for the season. First two weeks in Dec, 3-9 pm. **FREE**

Historical Pilgrimage. *211 W Austin St, Jefferson. Phone 903/665-2513.* Tours of four old houses. Surrey rides. "Diamond Bessie Murder Trial," Jefferson Playhouse; Henderson and Market streets. Late Apr-early May.

Specialty Lodgings

The following lodging establishments are approved by Mobil Travel Guide, but due to their unique and individualized nature have not been given a traditional Mobil Star rating. Included in this listing you may find bed-and-breakfasts, limited-service inns, guest ranches, and other unique hotel properties.

1ST BED AND BREAKFAST IN TEXAS - PRIDE HOUSE. *409 E Broadway St, Jefferson (75657). Phone 903/665-2675; toll-free 800/894-3526; fax 903/665-3901. www.jeffersontexas.com.* Victorian residence (1889) restored with original materials. Ornate woodwork, period furnishings. 6 rooms, 2 story. Complimentary full breakfast. Check-in noon-3 pm, check-out 11 am. Airport transportation available. **$**
🅳

EXCELSIOR HOUSE. *211 W Austin St, Jefferson (75657). Phone 903/665-2513; fax 903/665-9389. www.theexcelsiorhouse.com.* Restored hotel (1856); elegant antique Victorian furnishings. 15 rooms, 2 story. Closed Dec 24-25. Check-in 2:30 pm, check-out 11:30 am. **$**
🅳

MCKAY HOUSE. *306 E Delta St, Jefferson (75657). Phone 903/665-7322; fax 903/665-8551. www.mckay house.com.* Victorian house restored with authentic an-

tiques. 8 rooms, 2 story. Complimentary full breakfast. Check-in 3 pm, check-out 11 am. **$**
🅳

Restaurants

★**THE BAKERY.** *201 W Austin St, Jefferson (75657). Phone 903/665-2253.* In historic district. Breakfast, lunch, dinner. Closed Thanksgiving, Dec 25.**$**

★★**GALLEY.** *121 W Austin St, Jefferson (75657). Phone 903/665-3641; fax 903/665-6135.* Victorian décor, antiques. Lunch, dinner. Closed Sun, Mon; Dec 24-25. Bar. **$$**

★★★**STILLWATER INN.** *203 E Broadway, Jefferson (75657). Phone 903/665-8415; fax 903/665-8416. www.stillwaterinn.com.* French, American menu. Dinner. Closed Sun; Dec 25. Reservations recommended. **$$$**
🅳

Johnson City (C-7)

See also Austin, Burnet, Fredericksburg

Population 1,191
Elevation 1,193 ft
Area Code 830
Zip 78636
Information Tourism & Visitors Bureau, PO Box 485; phone 830/868-7684
Web Site www.johnsoncity-texas.com

President Lyndon B. Johnson's Hereford ranch is 13 miles west at Stonewall, just off Highway 290. During his term of office, it was referred to as the Texas White House; it is now a National Historical Park.

What to See and Do

⭐**Lyndon B. Johnson National Historical Park.** *100 Lady Bird Lane, Johnson City (78636). 1 block off Main St. Phone 830/868-7128.* Composed of two units: the Johnson City Unit consists of the boyhood home with visitor center and the 1860s Johnson Settlement; the LBJ Ranch Unit consists of the LBJ birthplace, family cemetery, Texas White House, and the ranch. Access to Ranch Unit by bus tour only (1 1/4 hours; fee). (Daily; closed Jan 1, Dec 25) Contact Superintendent, PO Box 329. **FREE**

   Birthplace. *13 miles W of visitors center via Hwy 290, Park Rd 49.* Reconstructed two-bedroom farmhouse, typical of late 1800s structures of this region, with "dog-trot," an open hallway for ventilation. The Johnson family occupied the house from 1907 to 1913 and 1920 to 1922. Adjacent to Birthplace is the family cemetery where Johnson is buried. LBJ State Park is nearby. **FREE**

Boyhood Home. (1901) Folk Victorian-style frame house, period furnishings, family heirlooms; Johnson lived here from 1913 to 1934. (Daily; closed Jan 1, Dec 25) **FREE**

Johnson Settlement. Restoration of cabin and surrounding pastures owned by the President's grandfather, a longhorn cattle driver in the mid-1800s. (Daily; closed Jan 1, Dec 25) **FREE**

LBJ Ranch House ("Texas White House"). *401 E Pecan, Johnson City.* Built of limestone and wood; ranch has registered Hereford cattle. Bus tour drives by (not open to public).

Lyndon B. Johnson State Historical Park. *Park Rd 52 and Hwy 290, Johnson City (78671). 14 miles W on Hwy 290, enter on Park Rd 52. Phone 830/644-2252.* On Pedernales River, 733 acres. Swimming and wading pools (fee), fishing; nature and hiking trails, picnicking, playground, tennis courts. Visitor center (daily; closed Dec 25) has Johnson family memorabilia and relics of previous settlers of the area. Adjacent is Behrens Cabin (1840), a "dog-trot" building with period furnishings. Sauer-Beckmann homestead of early 1900s is site of living history program; tours. (Daily) **FREE**

Pedernales Falls State Park. *117 Pedernales Falls, Johnson City. 9 miles E on Ranch Rd 2766. Phone 830/868-7304.* Approximately 5,000 acres. Swimming, fishing; nature, hiking, and bicycle trails; picnicking, primitive and improved camping (hook-ups, dump station). (Daily)

Selah Bamberger Ranch Preserve. *2341 Blue Ridge Dr, Johnson City (78636). Phone 830/868-2630. www.bambergerranch.org.* Dinosaur tracks, fossil hunts, and the largest herd of endangered scimitar-horned oryx in the world are just a few of the many reasons to visit this 5,500-acre ranch, the largest habitat restoration project on private land in Texas. You'll also find a chiroptorium, a manmade bat cave built to house 1 million bats, and a nice selection of hikes, tours, seminars, and art classes. Madrone Art Workshops range from an informal class introducing the basic principles of landscape drawing to a day spent learning about the artistic anatomy of trees. The pub-

lic ranch tour, which includes visits to the fossil beds, dino tracks, and bat cave, is 3 1/2 hours long, with transportation provided by an open trailer. Weekend nature journaling workshops hone observation skills through the use of simple sketching exercises and informal writing techniques. Reservations for all Bamberger Ranch events are a must—call for information about class times and prices. Fees for events vary.

Kerrville (C-7)

See also Bandera, Fredericksburg, Mason, San Antonio

Population 20,425
Elevation 1,645 ft
Area Code 830
Zip 78028
Information Convention and Visitors Bureau, 1700 Sidney Baker, Suite 200; phone 830/792-3535 or toll-free 800/221-7958
Web Site www.kerrville.org

A resort area in the hill country, this community is also a popular conference center and winter destination for Texans. Among the many activities available are fishing, swimming, boating, hunting, horseback riding, tennis, and golf. River and ranch cabins are open year-round.

What to See and Do

Hill Country Museum (Captain Charles Schreiner Mansion). *226 Earl Garrett, Kerrville. Phone 830/896-8633.* Residence restored to house the memorabilia of more than a century of area history. (Mon, Wed-Sat noon-4 pm; closed holidays)

Kerrville-Schreiner State Park. *2385 Bandera Hwy (Hwy 173), Kerrville (78028). 3 miles S via Hwy 173. Phone 830/257-5392.* Approximately 500 acres. Swimming, fishing, boating (ramps); hiking trail, picnicking, playground, camping (hook-ups, dump station). (Daily) **$$**

National Center for American Western Art. *1550 Bandera Hwy (Hwy 173), Kerrville. Phone 830/896-2553. www.americanwesternart.org.* Rotating and permanent collections of works and memorabilia devoted to the art of the West; Western art library. (Memorial Day-Labor Day: Mon-Sat, Sun afternoons; rest of year: Tues-Sat, Sun afternoons) **$$**

Y. O. Ranch. *2033 Sidney Baker St, Kerrville (78028). I-10 W, 18 miles W to Hwy 41, then 16 miles SW.* Phone 830/640-3222. Acquired in 1880 by Captain Charles Schreiner, this 60-square-mile ranch, one of the largest in Texas, has a herd of more than 1,500 longhorn cattle. The terrain resembles that of Africa. Approximately 55 different species of exotic game animals, including antelope, zebras, giraffes, ostriches, and emus roam free. Game animals are also abundant (limited hunting); photo safaris. Tours (by reservation). Ranch includes general store, cabins, pool, lodge. (Daily, by reservations only; closed Easter, Dec 25) (See SPECIAL EVENTS) Some fees.

Special Events

Kerr County Fair. *2108 Sidney Baker St, Kerrville.* Phone 830/792-3535. Music, food, crafts, livestock. Oct.

Kerrville Folk Festival. *Quiet Valley Ranch, 5600 Medina Hwy, Kerrville. 9 miles S on Hwy 16.* Phone 830/257-3600. Outdoor music festival. Children's concerts, crafts, camping. Late May-early June.

Kerrville Wine & Music Festival. *Quiet Valley Ranch, 5600 Medina Hwy, Kerrville. 9 miles S on Hwy 16.* Phone 830/257-3600. Outdoor festival; concerts, wine tastings, arts and crafts, camping. Labor Day weekend.

Longhorn Trail Drive. *Y. O. Ranch, 2033 Sidney Baker St, Kerrville (78028).* Phone 830/640-3222. Heritage celebration, camping under the stars, covered wagons, and "trailblazers." Memorial Day weekend. **$$$$**

Smith/Ritch Point Theatre. *507 W Hwy 39, Ingram, (78025). 6 miles W via Hwy 39.* Phone 830/367-5122. Four productions in outdoor amphitheater on the banks of the Guadalupe River. Thurs-Sat, nightly. May-Aug.

Texas State Arts & Crafts Fair. *Schreiner College campus, 2100 Memorial Blvd, Kerrville (78028).* Phone 830/896-5711. Concessions, entertainment, demonstrations. Memorial Day weekend.

Limited-Service Hotels

★ ★ **BEST WESTERN SUNDAY HOUSE INN.** *2124 Sidney Baker St, Kerrville (78028).* Phone 830/896-1313; toll-free 800/677-9477; fax 830/896-1336. www.bestwestern.com. 97 rooms, 2 story. Pets accepted, some restrictions; fee. Complimentary full breakfast. Check-in 3 pm, check-out noon. Restaurant, bar. Outdoor pool. **$**

★ ★ **INN OF THE HILLS CONFERENCE RESORT.** *1001 Junction Hwy, Kerrville (78028).* Phone 830/895-5000; toll-free 800/292-5690; fax 830/895-6820. www.innofthehills.com. 167 rooms, 6 story. Complimentary continental breakfast. Check-in 4 pm, check-out noon. Wireless Internet access. Restaurant, bar. Outdoor pool, children's pool, whirlpool. Tennis. **$**

★ ★ **Y.O. RANCH RESORT HOTEL.** *2033 Sidney Baker St, Kerrville (78028).* Phone 830/257-4440; toll-free 877/967-3767; fax 830/896-8189. www.yoresort.com. Visitors who are looking to experience the Old West will love this Texas hotel. Stepping into the lobby, which is filled with antiques and more than 40 game trophies, is like stepping back in time. Guest rooms are spacious with Western décor. 185 rooms, 2 story. Pets accepted, some restrictions. Check-in 4 pm, check-out noon. Restaurant, bar. Outdoor pool, children's pool, whirlpool. Tennis. **$**

Specialty Lodging

The following lodging establishment is approved by Mobil Travel Guide, but due to its unique and individualized nature has not been given a traditional Mobil Star rating. Included in this listing you may find bed-and-breakfasts, limited-service inns, guest ranches, and other unique hotel properties.

LAZY HILLS GUEST RANCH. *Henderson Branch Rd, Ingram (78025).* Phone 830/367-5600; toll-free 800/880-0632; fax 830/367-5667. www.lazyhills.com. 25 rooms. Check-in 4 pm, check-out noon. Restaurant. Children's activity center. Outdoor pool, children's pool, whirlpool. Tennis. **$$**

Restaurant

★ ★ **ANNEMARIE'S ALPINE LODGE.** *1001 Jct Hwy, Kerrville (78028).* Phone 830/257-8282; fax 830/895-6091. www.innofthehills.com. Swiss menu. Breakfast, lunch, dinner, Sun brunch. Bar. Casual attire. Reservations recommended. Outdoor seating. **$$**

Kilgore (B-9)

See also Longview, Marshall, Tyler

Population 11,301

Elevation 370 ft
Area Code 903
Zip 75662
Information Chamber of Commerce, 813 N Kilgore St, PO Box 1582, 75663; phone 903/984-5022
Web Site www.kilgorechamber.com

The discovery of the largest oil field in the continental United States transformed Kilgore into a thriving boomtown in the 1930s. More than 1,200 producing wells were drilled within the city limits during the boom, including 24 in a half-block area of downtown.

What to See and Do

East Texas Oil Museum at Kilgore College. *Kilgore College campus, Hwy 259 and Ross St, Kilgore (75662). Phone 903/983-8295.* Re-creation of oil discovery and production in 1930s in largest oil field in the United States. Full-scale town depicting oil boom days. (Tues-Sun; special Dec holiday schedule; closed Easter, Thanksgiving) **$$** Also on campus is

> **Rangerette Showcase.** *1100 Broadway, Kilgore. Phone 903/983-8265.* Museum depicts history of the famous Kilgore Rangerettes, college football's first precision drill and dance team, with photographs, scrapbooks, memorabilia, and film footage. (Mon-Sat; closed holidays) **FREE**

Killeen (C-7)

See also Burnet, Temple

Population 86,911
Elevation 833 ft
Area Code 254
Information Greater Kileen Chamber of Commerce, One Santa Fe Plaza, 76541; phone 254/526-9551 or toll-free 800/869-8265
Web Site www.gkcc.com

What to See and Do

Belton Lake. *99 FM 2271, Killeen. 8 miles E and N via Hwy 190 then Hwy 317. Phone 254/939-1829.* (see TEMPLE)

Fort Hood. *Fort Hood Rd and Hwy 190 (visitor center), Killeen (76544). W of town. Phone 254/287-8506.* This 339-square-mile army installation has the nation's largest concentration of armored power. Houses the US Army III Corps, the first Cavalry Division and the fourth Infantry. The fourth Infantry and first Cavalry museums feature military equipment and campaign exhibits.(Daily, limited hours) **FREE**

Stillhouse Hollow Lake. *6 miles SE via FM 2410 and Hwy 190.* (see SALADO)

Special Event

Killeen Festival of Flags. Memorial Day weekend.

Limited-Service Hotel

★ **LA QUINTA INN.** *1112 S Fort Hood St, Killeen (76541). Phone 254/526-8331; toll-free 800/531-5900; fax 254/526-0394. www.lq.com.* 106 rooms, 3 story. Pets accepted, some restrictions. Complimentary continental breakfast. Check-in 1 pm, check-out noon. Outdoor pool. Airport transportation available. **$**
🐾 🏊

Kingsville (E-7)

See also Alice, Corpus Christi

Founded 1904
Population 25,575
Elevation 66 ft
Area Code 361
Zip 78363
Information Visitors Center, 1501 S Hwy 77, PO Box 1562; phone 361/592-8516 or toll-free 800/333-5032
Web Site www.kingsville.org

This is the home of the King Ranch, an 825,000-acre property in four main sections stretching down the coastal bend between Corpus Christi and Harlingen. It is one of the world's largest privately owned ranches and one of the most scientifically run. Richard King, a steamboat captain, came into this unpromising area in 1853 and built an empire. His son-in-law, Robert Kleberg Sr., and grandson Robert J. Kleberg Jr. developed the first beef breed in the Western Hemisphere—the hardy, cherry-red Santa Gertrudis. Planning and genetic engineering went into the ranch's pursuit of the perfect cow horse, the Old Sorrel family of quarter horses. King's descendants still own and run the vast territory. Many varieties of wildlife live on the ranch. Driving south along Highway 77, traffic passes right through the ranch, though there are no signs to indicate this.

Also near Kingsville are a large petrochemical plant and the Kingsville Naval Air Station, a jet pilot training facility.

What to See and Do

King Ranch. *Hwy 141 W, Kingsville (78354). W of town via Santa Gertrudis Ave or Hwy 141. Phone 361/592-8055; toll-free 800/333-5032. www.king-ranch.com.* Texas visitors who want to have real-life encounters with cowboys, cattle, and horses can do no better than a visit to King Ranch, one of the oldest and largest working ranches in the United States today. Bigger than Rhode Island, the ranch sprawls over 825,000 acres of south Texas. A wide variety of tours let you dictate what you want to view—and how intensely. On one end of the spectrum, there are guided bus tours that hit the agricultural and historical highlights. (For example, you'll see various breeds of cattle, plus the ranch's famous quarter horses.) Nature enthusiasts can choose from eight different tours of the vast acreage, ranging from half-day wildlife and bird-watching excursions to full-day birding tours and customized excursions. (There's even a "Little Winged Wonder Foray" devoted to finding the ranch's many butterfly and dragonfly species.) Get oriented for your visit with a stop at the visitor center, and don't leave without checking out the saddle shop for everything from hunting gear to luggage. (Daily; closed holidays) **$$**

Texas A&M University-Kingsville. *Armstrong St between Santa Gertrudis and Corral aves. Phone 361/593-2111.* (1925) (6,400 students) A 1,600-acre campus. Changing exhibits in Gallery of Art Building featuring famous Southwestern artists. Observatory in Lon C. Hill Science Hall. Also on campus is

John E. Conner Museum. *905 W Santa Gertrudis Ave, Kingsville. Phone 361/593-2819.* Historical exhibits and collections of southern Texas; Kleberg Hall of Natural History; Peeler Hall of Horns. Regional and photo archives. Changing exhibits. (Mon-Sat; closed holidays) **DONATION**

Special Events

Cactus Festival. *2231 Brahma Blvd, Kingsville (78363). Phone 361/592-8516.* Apr.

Fiesta de Colores. *Northway Exposition Center.* First weekend in Oct.

Texas A&M National Intercollegiate Rodeo. *Northway Exposition Center, Kingsville. Phone 361/595-8595.*

Contestants from across Texas and Louisiana. Late Mar.

Specialty Lodging

The following lodging establishment is approved by Mobil Travel Guide, but due to its unique and individualized nature has not been given a traditional Mobil Star rating. Included in this listing you may find bed-and-breakfasts, limited-service inns, guest ranches, and other unique hotel properties.

B BAR B RANCH. *325 E CR 2215, Kingsville (78363). Phone 361/296-3331; fax 261/296-3337. www.b-bar-b.com.* This lodge is located in a mesquite grove and is surrounded by a working ranch. Nilgai game, quail and turkey hunting, and bird-watching are all outdoor acitivities available. A great location for workshops or weddings, guests can also put their dogs in kennels for training in everything from basic obedience to hunting. Part of the King Ranch. 16 rooms. Closed Dec 24-25. Children over 16 years only. Complimentary full breakfast. Check-in 3 pm, check-out 11 am. Restaurant. Outdoor pool. **$**
🏊

La Grange (D-8)

See also Austin, Bastrop

Population 4,478
Elevation 277 ft
Area Code 979
Zip 78945
Information Chamber of Commerce, 171 S Main, "In the Old Jail"; phone 979/968-5756 or toll-free 800/524-7264.
Web Site www.lagrangetx.org

What to See and Do

Fayette Heritage Museum. *855 S Jefferson, La Grange. Phone 979/968-6418.* Historical museum; changing displays; archives. (Tues-Sun; closed holidays) **FREE**

Fayette Power Project Lake & Parks. *10 miles E via Hwy 159, junction Hwy 71. Phone 979/249-3504.* On 2,400-acre cooling pond for generating station. Swimming, water-skiing, fishing, boating (launch, ramps); picnicking, tent camping (showers). (Daily) **$$$**

Jersey Barnyard. *3117 Hwy 159, La Grange. Phone 979/249-3406.* Home of Belle, the "singing and talking" cow. Tours of dairy farm; barnyard, country store. (Mon-Sat, also Sun afternoons; closed holidays) **$$$**

Monument Hill & Kreische Brewery State Historical Park. *414 State Loop 92, La Grange (78945). 2 miles S off Hwy 77 on Spur 92, on bluff overlooking Colorado River. Phone 979/968-5658.* Memorial monument, tomb of Texans massacred during the Mexican uprisings (1842) and Black Bean Episode (1843). Ruins of a German brewery; guided tours (weekends). Picnic area, nature trails. (Daily) **$**

Old Fayette County Jail. *171 S Main St, La Grange (78945). Phone 979/968-5756.* A 114-year-old jail; memorabilia. Information center; maps, brochures. (Mon-Sat)

Winedale Historical Center. *3841 Farm Market #2714, Round Top (78954). 17 miles NE on Hwy 237 to Round Top, then 4 1/2 miles E via FM 1457, 2714. Phone 979/278-3530. www.rtis.com/reg/roundtop/winedale.htm.* Outdoor museum maintained by the University of Texas. Six restored farm buildings; antique furniture, tools; guided tours. (Sat 9 am-5 pm, Sun noon-5 pm; Mon-Fri by appointment; closed holidays) **$$**

Special Events

Chilispiel. *20 miles SW on I-10 and Hwy 609 In Flatonia.* Three-day festival is one of the largest chili cook-offs in Texas. Fourth weekend in Oct.

Fayette County Country Fair. *Hwy 77, N 2 miles, 1800 block of N Jefferson, La Grange (78945). Phone 979/968-3911. www.fayettecountychamberoh.com.* Labor Day weekend. **$**

Lake Whitney (B-8)

See also Hillsboro, Waco.

Web Site www.lakewhitney.com
17 miles SW of Hillsboro on Hwy 22.

This is one of the largest lakes in Texas: 49,710 acres on the Brazos River near Whitney. This area, offering many resorts and fishing camps, has been increasing in popularity among vacationers since 1953, when the Whitney Dam was completed.

What to See and Do

Whitney Lake. *285 Corps Rd, #3602, Laguna Park. Headquarters is 7 miles SW of Whitney on Hwy 22.*

Phone 254/694-3189. Swimming, water-skiing, fishing, boating (ramps); picnicking, concession, camping (tent and trailer sites, some fees). An Army Corps of Engineers Project office is located below the dam.

Lake Whitney State Park. *FM 1244, Whitney. 4 miles SW of Whitney. Phone 254/694-3793.* More than 900 acres offering swimming, water-skiing, fishing, boating (ramp); hiking, picnicking, playground, improved campsites (tent and trailer sites). (Daily) **$**

Laredo (E-6)

Founded 1755
Population 176,576
Elevation 420 ft
Area Code 956
Information Laredo Convention & Visitor's Bureau, 501 San Agustin, 78040; phone 956/795-2200 or toll-free 800/361-3360
Web Site www.visitlaredo.com

Laredo is the most important US gateway to Mexico for rail, highway, and tourist traffic, with a fine highway to Monterey and Mexico City. Many white brick and stone buildings grace the streets of the business district; areas of the city date from the Spanish colonial period and reflect that heritage.

Thomas Sanchez founded the town in 1755 and established a ferry across the Rio Grande, for which he received 15 square leagues (about 110 square miles) of rangeland from the Spanish authorities. After the Texas Revolution, because of a dispute over the boundaries of Texas, Laredo was in a no-man's land. For a time in the 1840s, a government of "The Republic of the Rio Grande" was set up; the capitol building still stands opposite San Agustin Plaza, on Zaragoza Street.

Large-scale cattle ranching is done in the mesquite, chaparral, and cactus country north and east of town. In the 1990s, the NAFTA accord made international trade the leading industry for this inland port. Today, the port of Laredo processes more than 35 percent of all imports and exports between the United States and Mexico.

What to See and Do

Lake Casa Blanca International State Park. *5201 Bob Bullock Loop, Laredo. 5 miles E off Hwy 59 on Loop 20.*

Phone 956/725-3826. Water-skiing, fishing, boating (ramp); 18-hole golf, picnicking, playground, primitive camping. (Daily) **$$**

Laredo Children's Museum. *Washington St, Laredo (78040). At Laredo Community College, West End Washington St. Phone 956/725-2299.* Two fort buildings dating from the mid-1800s house the museum. Changing hands-on exhibits and demonstrations. (Daily; closed holidays) **$**

LIFE Downs. *Hwy 59 E and Arkansas Ave, Laredo. Near Casa Blanca Lake. Phone 956/722-9948.* Site of youth rodeos, livestock shows, other events. **$$$**

Nuevo Laredo, Tamaulipas, Mexico. (Population 575,000) Across the bridge at the end of Convent Avenue. For a limited visit, it is easier to park in Laredo and walk across. (For Border Crossing Regulations, see MAKING THE MOST OF YOUR TRIP.) Nuevo Laredo is a typical border town, with stores and stands featuring Mexican goods lining the street south of the bridge. There are also many parks, fine restaurants, and popular entertainment spots.

Villa de San Agustin. *Downtown area.* Laredo's historical district contains many of the city's older buildings. They include

> **Republic of the Rio Grande Museum.** *1003 Zaragoza St, Laredo. Opposite San Agustin Plaza. Phone 956/727-3480.* (Circa 1830) An example of "Laredo" architecture, this was the former capitol of the short-lived Republic; period rooms, furniture. (Tues-Sun; closed holidays) **$**

> **San Agustin Church.** *214 San Agustin Ave, Laredo. E of Plaza.* (1872) The original church was built in 1767 on the site where the city was founded. Genealogical records date to 1789. (Daily) **FREE**

Special Events

Diez Y Seis Celebration. *Laredo and Nuevo Laredo.* Mexican National Independence Day celebration. Mid-Sept.

Expomex. *Nuevo Laredo (Mexico), at Carranza Park.* Fiesta, stock show, bullfight. Early Sept.

George Washington's Birthday Celebration. *1819 E Hillside Rd, Laredo (78041). Phone 956/722-0589.* International fiesta with parades; jalapeño-eating festival, colonial pageant, dances, bullfights. Ten days in mid-Feb.

Laredo International Fair & Exposition. *LIFE Downs, Hwy 59 E and Arkansas Ave, Laredo (78043). Phone 956/722-9948.* Stock, arts and crafts shows; horse racing, barbecue, dance. Early Mar.

Limited-Service Hotels

★ **HAMPTON INN.** *7903 San Dario Ave, Laredo (78041). Phone 956/717-8888; toll-free 800/426-7866; fax 956/717-8391. www.hamptoninn.com.* 119 rooms, 5 story. Pets accepted. Complimentary continental breakfast. Check-in 3 pm, check-out noon. Wireless Internet access. Outdoor pool, whirlpool. **$**

★ ★ **HOLIDAY INN.** *800 Garden St, Laredo (78040). Phone 956/727-5800; toll-free 800/379-8741; fax 956/727-0278. www.holiday-inn/laredotx.com.* 203 rooms, 14 story. Check-in 3 pm, check-out noon. Restaurant, bar. Fitness room. Outdoor pool, whirlpool. Airport transportation available. Business center. **$**

★ **LA QUINTA INN.** *3610 Santa Ursula Ave, Laredo (78041). Phone 956/722-0511; toll-free 800/531-5900; fax 956/723-6642. www.lq.com.* 153 rooms, 2 story. Pets accepted. Check-in 2 pm, check-out noon. Outdoor pool. **$**

Full-Service Hotel

★ ★ ★ **LA POSADA HOTEL.** *1000 Zaragoza St, Laredo (78040). Phone 956/722-1701; toll-free 800/444-2099; fax 956/722-4758. www.laposadahotel.com.* 208 rooms. Check-in 4 pm, check-out noon. Wireless Internet access. Two restaurants, two bars. Fitness room. Outdoor pool. Airport transportation available. Business center. **$**

League City (D-9)

Full-Service Resort

★ ★ ★ **SOUTH SHORE HARBOUR RESORT.** *2500 S Shore Blvd, League City (77573). Phone 281/334-1000; fax 281/334-1157. www.sshr.com.* 242 rooms. Check-in 3 pm, check-out noon. Two restaurants, two bars. Fitness room. Outdoor pool, whirlpool. Business center. **$$**

Longview (B-9)

See also Henderson, Kilgore, Marshall, Tyler

Founded 1870
Population 73,344
Elevation 289 ft
Area Code 903
Web Site www.longviewtx.com/lcvb.html

Longview, in the Sabine River Valley, is a center for beef cattle production. This is also a manufacturing center with petroleum and earthmoving equipment plants, a brewery, and other diversified industry.

What to See and Do

Gregg County Historical Museum. *214 N Fredonia St, Longview. In Everett Building, downtown. Phone 903/753-5840.* Artifacts, photographs; displays on timber, cotton, corn, farming, railroads, printing, early business, and commerce; extensive military collection. Period room settings include bank president's and dentist's offices, early 1900s parlor and bedroom, log cabin, general store. Audiovisual presentation. Tours. (Tues-Sat; closed holidays) **$**

LeTourneau University. *2100 S Mobberly Ave, Longview. Memorial Student Center, 3rd floor. Phone 903/753-0231.* (1946) (1,700 students) Engineering, business, technology, education, aviation, arts, and sciences. Displays on campus contain early scale models of earthmoving equipment invented by R. G. Le-Tourneau, founder of the university; also personal mementos.

Longview Museum of Fine Arts. *215 E Tyler St, Longview. Phone 903/753-8103.* Collection of Southwestern and contemporary artists; changing exhibits; lectures, workshops and classes. (Tues-Fri, Sat afternoons; closed holidays) **FREE**

Limited-Service Hotels

★ ★ **BEST WESTERN INN OF LONGVIEW.** *3119 Estes Pkwy, Longview (75602). Phone 903/758-0700; fax 903/758-8705. www.bestwestern.com.* 193 rooms, 4 story. Check-out 1 pm. Restaurant. Indoor pool, outdoor pool, whirlpool. Airport transportation available. **$**

★ **LA QUINTA INN.** *502 S Access Rd, Longview (75602). Phone 903/757-3663; fax 903/753-3780. www.lq.com.* 105 rooms, 2 story. Pets accepted, some restrictions. Complimentary continental breakfast. Check-out noon. Outdoor pool. **$**

Restaurants

★ ★ **JOHNNY CACE'S SEAFOOD & STEAK.** *1501 E Marshall Ave, Longview (75601). Phone 903/753-7691; fax 903/758-9064. www.johnnycaces.com.* Creole, Cajun menu. Lunch, dinner. Closed holidays. Bar. Children's menu. **$$$**

★ **PAPACITA'S MEXICAN RESTAURANT.** *305 W Loop 281, Longview (75605). Phone 903/663-1700; fax 903/663-4936. www.papacitas.com.* Mexican menu. Lunch, dinner. Closed Thanksgiving, Dec 25. Bar. Children's menu. Outdoor seating. **$$**

Lubbock (A-5)

See also Plainview

Founded 1891
Population 199,564
Elevation 3,241 ft
Area Code 806
Information Convention & Tourism Bureau, 1301 Broadway, Suite 200, 79401; phone 806/747-5232 or toll-free 800/692-4035
Web Site www.lubbockhospitality.com

Named after Colonel Thomas S. Lubbock, Confederate officer and brother of Texas's Civil War governor, this was originally a headquarters for buffalo hunters, trail drivers, and early ranchers. Lubbock is now an important commercial and shipping center for a large and rich ranching, oil, and agricultural territory.

Lubbock is one of the largest inland cotton markets in the nation, the center of a farm area also producing grain sorghums, wheat, and corn. Wineries, the historic Depot District, and Texas Tech University are also important to the area.

What to See and Do

Buddy Holly Statue and Walk of Fame. *Sixth St and*

Ave Q, Lubbock. Larger-than-life bronze statue of the rock-and-roll pioneer and Lubbock native. Bronze plaques honor famous country and western musicians from the area. **FREE**

Buffalo Springs Lake Recreational Area. *5 miles SE on FM 835. Phone 806/747-3353.* A 1,223-acre area with 225 acres of water. Water-skiing, fishing, boating, beach, water slides (Fri-Sun); picnicking, concession, hiking, volleyball, primitive and improved camping (tent and trailer sites; fee; two-week maximum). Store. (Daily) **$**

Cap-Rock Winery. *Woodrow Rd and Hwy 87, Lubbock. 5 miles S on Hwy 87, 1/2 mile E on Woodrow Rd. Phone 806/863-2704.* Modern facilities with the look of a Southwest mission utilize classic European wine grape varieties grown in the winery's own vineyard. Tasting room, gift shop. Tours on the hour and half hour. (Daily) **FREE**

Llano Estacado Winery. *5 miles S on Hwy 87, 3 miles E on FM 1585. Phone 806/745-2258.* Founded in 1976, this was the first modern Texas winery. Grows award-winning grapes. Tours, tastings (daily). **FREE**

Mackenzie Park. *301 I-27, Lubbock (79401). Off I-27, 4 miles E on Broadway to Park Rd 18. Phone 806/763-2719.* Approximately 500 acres. Includes 36-hole golf course (fee). Picnicking, grills. Amusement area (fee); prairie dog town. (Daily) **FREE**

Science Spectrum-Omnimax. *2579 S Loop 289, Lubbock. Between University and Indiana aves. Phone 806/745-2525. www.sciencespectrum.com.* Hands-on science and technology museum with more than 100 exhibits, films, and demonstrations. Kidspace; Hall of Flight. Traveling exhibits. Seventy-millimeter projection system with domed theater screen, 58 feet in diameter. (Mon-Fri 10 am-5 pm, Sat 10 am-6 pm, Sun 1-5 pm; closed Thanksgiving, Dec 25) **$$**

Texas Tech University. *University and Broadway aves, Lubbock. Phone 806/742-1299.* (1923) (25,573 students) One of Texas's four major state universities; 1,800-acre campus. It offers major sports and arts attractions, including a noted Peter Hurd mural. Also here is Texas Tech University Health Sciences Center (1969). On campus are

Lubbock Lake Landmark State Historic Park. *2202 Landmark Ln, Lubbock (79415). 2 miles N of campus at Loop 289 and Landmark Dr. Phone 806/741-0306.* This major archaeological excavation has yielded evidence of ancient peoples and extinct animals. (Tues-Sun) **$**

Museum of Texas Tech University. *4th St and Indiana Ave, Lubbock. Phone 806/742-2490.* Exhibits on art, natural sciences, and history of semi-arid and arid lands. Moody Planetarium. (Tues-Sun; closed holidays) **FREE**

Ranching Heritage Center. *3121 4th St, Lubbock (79409). Phone 806/742-2482.* This 14-acre restoration of 36 structures represents the development of ranching in the West. (Daily; closed holidays) **FREE**

Special Events

Buddy Holly Music Festival. *Historic Depot District, 1801 Avenue G, Lubbock. Phone 806/767-2686.* Early Sept.

Lubbock Arts Festival. *South Plains Fairgrounds, 2109 Broadway St, Lubbock. Phone 806/744-2787.* Three days in Apr.

Limited-Service Hotels

★ ★ **ASHMORE INN AND SUITES.** *4019 S Loop 289, Lubbock (79423). Phone 806/785-0060; toll-free 800/785-0061; fax 806/785-6001.* 100 rooms, 2 story. Complimentary continental breakfast. Check-out noon. Fitness room. Outdoor pool, whirlpool. Airport transportation available. **$**

★ ★ **FOUR POINTS BY SHERATON.** *505 Ave Q, Lubbock (79401). Phone 806/747-0171; toll-free 800/368-7764; fax 806/747-9243. www.fourpoints.com/lubbock.* 141 rooms, 6 story. Check-out noon. Restaurant, bar. Fitness room. Indoor pool. Airport transportation available. **$**

★ ★ **HOLIDAY INN.** *801 Ave Q, Lubbock (79401). Phone 806/763-1200; toll-free 800/765-0330; fax 806/763-2656. www.holiday-inn.com.* 295 rooms, 6 story. Check-out noon. Restaurant, bar. Fitness room. Indoor pool, whirlpool. Airport transportation available. **$**

★ **LA QUINTA INN.** *601 Ave Q, Lubbock (79401). Phone 806/763-9441; fax 806/747-9325. www.lq.com.* 137 rooms, 2 story. Pets accepted, some restrictions.

Complimentary continental breakfast. Check-out noon. Outdoor pool. **$**

★ ★ **LUBBOCK INN.** *3901 19th St, Lubbock (79410). Phone 806/792-5181; toll-free 800/545-8226; fax 806/792-1319. www.lubbockinn.com.* 119 rooms, 3 story. Check-out noon. Restaurant, bar. Outdoor pool, children's pool. Airport transportation available. **$**

Restaurants

★ ★ **CHEZ SUZETTE.** *4423 50th St, Lubbock (79414). Phone 806/795-6796; fax 806/796-1295. www.chezsuzette.com.* French, Italian menu. Lunch, dinner. Closed Sun; Jan 1, Thanksgiving, Dec 25. Bar. Children's menu. **$$**

★ **GARDSKI'S.** *2009 Broadway, Lubbock (79401). Phone 806/744-2391; fax 806/744-0181. www.gardskis.com.* Steak menu. Lunch, dinner. Closed Thanksgiving, Dec 25. **$$**

★ ★ **HARRIGAN'S.** *3801 50th St, Lubbock (79413). Phone 806/792-4648; fax 806/792-6185.* American menu. Lunch, dinner. Bar. **$$**

★ **ORLANDO'S.** *2402 Ave Q, Lubbock (79411). Phone 806/747-5998; fax 806/747-3501. www.orlandos.com.* Italian menu. Lunch, dinner. Closed holidays. Bar. Children's menu. **$$**

Lufkin (B-9)

See also Crockett, Nacogdoches

Settled 1881
Population 32,709
Area Code 409
Zip 75901
Information Visitor & Convention Bureau, PO Box 1606; phone 409/634-6644
Web Site www.ci.lufkin.tx.us

Lumber and a newsprint mill combine with iron foundries, farming, and ranching to give Lufkin a well-diversified income base. The headquarters for the Sam Houston (see HUNTSVILLE), Sabine (see JASPER), Angelina, and Davy Crockett national forests are here.

What to See and Do

Angelina National Forest. *3121 4th St, Lubbock (79409). 21 miles E on Hwy 103 or 16 miles SE on Hwy 69. Phone 409/639-8620.* Approximately 153,000 acres of rolling, forested sandhills; Sam Rayburn Reservoir (see JASPER) bisects the forest. Swimming, fishing, boating (ramps); hunting, hiking, picnicking, camping (fee). Audio tape tour (free) available at ranger station. Fees are charged at recreation sites.

Davy Crockett National Forest. *17 miles W on Hwy 94 or Hwy 103. District Ranger office. Phone 409/544-2046.* Ratcliff Lake is in the forest, which comprises approximately 163,000 acres. The area includes the Big Slough Wilderness Area. Swimming, fishing (bass, bream, catfish), boating; hunting (deer), hiking, picnicking, concession, camping (fee) in shortleaf-loblolly pinewoods. Fees are charged at recreation sites. A free audio tour of Ratcliff Lake and the surrounding forest area is available from the camp concessionaire.

Forest Information. *701 N First St, Lufkin (75901). Phone 409/639-8501.* A visitor guide to the forests may be obtained from Forest Supervisor, 701 N First St, Lufkin.

Ellen Trout Park Zoo. *402 Zoo Cir, Lufkin (75901). Loop 287 N at Martin Luther King Dr, 2 miles N. Phone 409/633-0399.* More than 500 species of birds, reptiles, mammals; miniature train rides (summer, daily; rest of year, weekends; fee); lake, fishing; picnicking, playground. (Daily) **$**

Museum of East Texas. *503 N Second St, Lufkin. Phone 409/639-4434.* Explores visual arts and history through changing exhibits, lectures, performances, multidisciplinary programs, and films. (Tues-Fri 10 am-5 pm, Sat-Sun 1-5 pm; closed Thanksgiving, Dec 25) **FREE**

Texas Forestry Museum. *1905 Atkinson Dr, Lufkin. Phone 409/632-9535. www.treetexas.com.* Artifacts from early days of Texas logging and timber industry include logging train, working sawmill steam engine, 100-foot fire tower, photographs, and memorabilia. (Mon-Sat 10 am-5 pm, Sun 1-5 pm; closed holidays) **FREE**

Limited-Service Hotels

★ ★ **DAYS INN.** *2130 S 1st St, Lufkin (75904). Phone 936/639-3301; fax 936/634-4266. www.daysinn.com.* 126 rooms, 2 story. Pets accepted; fee. Complimentary continental breakfast. Check-out noon. Restaurant, bar. Outdoor pool, children's pool, whirlpool. **$**

★ ★ **HOLIDAY INN.** *4306 S First St, Lufkin (75901). Phone 936/639-3333; toll-free 888/639-3382; fax 936/639-3382. www.holiday-inn.com.* 102 rooms, 2 story. Pets accepted, some restrictions; fee. Check-out noon. Restaurant, bar. Outdoor pool. Airport transportation available. **$**

Marfa (C-3)

See also Alpine

Founded 1883
Population 2,121
Elevation 4,688 ft
Area Code 915
Zip 79843
Information Chamber of Commerce, 200 S Abbot, PO Box 635; phone 915/729-4942 or toll-free 800/650-9696
Web Site www.marfacc.com

Texas's highest incorporated city, Marfa, is surrounded by unspoiled mountain country, rising to more than 8,000 feet in some areas. Marfa is the best starting point to travel the highway to Mexico and Chihuahua City; the Camino del Rio (River Road) to Big Bend National Park (see); and the Scenic Loop through the Davis Mountains. It offers various outdoor recreation activities and the puzzling "Marfa mystery lights," which have remained a mystery for more than 100 years. The Presidio County Courthouse (1886) and El Paisano Hotel (1930) are also notable landmarks.

With mild winters and cool summers, the area offers abundant opportunities for camping, hunting, hiking, picnicking, and golfing.

What to See and Do

Chinati Foundation. *1 Calvary Row, Marfa. Phone 915/729-4362.* The museum is spread over 15 buildings of the former army post Fort D. A. Russell. It houses permanent collections of Donald Judd, John Chamberlain, and others; temporary exhibits. (Thurs-Sat or by appointment) **$$$**

Special Event

Marfa Lights Festival. *Presidio County Courthouse, Marfa (79843). Phone toll-free 800/650-9696.* Labor Day weekend.

Marshall (B-10)

See also Jefferson, Kilgore, Longview

Founded 1841
Population 23,935
Elevation 412 ft
Area Code 903
Zip 75670
Information Chamber of Commerce, 213 W Austin, PO Box 520; phone 903/935-7868
Web Site www.marshall-chamber.com

For a time, this was the Confederate state capital of Missouri. Orders were issued, vouchers drawn, and official business transacted in exile; Missouri itself was in Northern hands, but the governor held himself to be legitimately in office nonetheless. Marshall was also important in the administration of Confederate affairs. The Confederate Trans-Mississippi Agency of the Post Office Department, Quartermaster, and Commissary Departments were all in Marshall. The basements of the First Methodist Church and Odd Fellows Hall were used for storage of military supplies. Marshall is now an educational and manufacturing center that includes 13 potteries.

What to See and Do

Caddo Lake State Park. *2198 FM Rd, Karnack. 14 miles NE on Hwy 43, then 1/2 mile E on FM 2198. Phone 903/679-3351.* Approximately 32,000 acres include bayous and cypress swamp. Swimming, water-skiing, fishing, boating (ramp, rentals); nature and hiking trails, picnicking, playground, screened shelters, improved campsites, RV facilities, cabins (dump station). (Daily) **$$**

Harrison County Historical Museum. *707 N Washington, Marshall (75670). In the old Ginocchio Hotel, a few blocks N of Hwy 80 on Washington. Phone 903/938-2680.* Business, transportation, and communication displays; medical items; Victorian needlecraft; pressed glass, toys, Caddo Indian artifacts, pioneer relics. Memorabilia collections of Lady Bird Johnson, journalist Bill Moyers, Olympic gold medalist George Foreman, and others. Military Room, Ethnic Group

Heritage Room, Caddo Lake Room. Art gallery. (Tues-Sat 10 am-5 pm; closed holidays) **$**

Marshall Pottery. *4901 Elysian Fields Rd, Marshall. Hwy 59 to FM 31.* Phone 903/938-9201. Twenty shops, restaurants, RV park. Tours (by appointment). (Daily) **FREE**

Michelson Museum of Art. *Southwestern Bell Bldg, 216 N Bolivar, Marshall.* Phone 903/935-9480. *www.michelsonmuseum.org.* Features paintings of Russian-born, post-impressionist Leo Michelson; special exhibits. (Tues-Fri noon-5 pm, Sat-Sun 1-4 pm; closed Thanksgiving, Dec 24-Jan 1) **$**

T. C. Lindsey & Company. *2293 FM 134, Jonesville. 2 miles W of Louisiana state line via I-20, 2 miles N on FM 134.* Phone 903/687-3382. General store, in continuous operation since 1847; antiques, rural relics on display. Setting for two Walt Disney productions. (Mon-Sat; closed holidays) **FREE**

Special Events

Fireant Festival. *2501 East End Blvd, Marshall (75672).* Phone 903/935-7868. Second weekend in Oct.

Stagecoach Days Celebration. *213 W Austin St, Marshall.* Phone 903/935-7868. *www.marshall-chamber.com.* Stagecoach rides, gunfighters, arts and crafts. May. **FREE**

Wonderland of Lights. *213 W Austin St (Chamber of Commerce), Marshall.* Phone 903/935-7868. Christmas festival. Courthouse, entire neighborhoods decorated by 7 1/2 million lights. Thanksgiving-Dec.

Mason (C-7)

See also Fredericksburg, Kerrville

Population 2,134
Elevation 1,550 ft
Area Code 915
Zip 76856
Information Mason County Chamber of Commerce, PO Box 156; phone 915/347-5758
Web Site www.masontxcoc.com

This town grew under the protection of Fort Mason in the rolling, scenic hill country. Hunting for white-tailed deer and wild turkey and fishing in the Llano River are popular. Citizens and cattle rustlers once participated in a bloody feud known as the Mason County War.

What to See and Do

Eckert James River Bat Cave Preserve. *SW of Mason, near Hwy 290, Mason.* Phone 915/347-5970. One of America's largest known Mexican free-tailed bat colonies and the only bat maternity cave owned by a conservation agency. Visitors are instructed on how best to view the colony without disturbing the bats (May-Oct, Thurs-Sun eves). Preserve (year-round). **FREE**

Fort Mason. *612 San Antonio, Mason. Post Hill St.* Reconstructed four-room officers' quarters on crest of Post Hill. Original foundations and stone used in reconstruction. Robert E. Lee's last command before the Civil War. Picnicking. (Daily) **FREE**

Mason County Museum. *300 Moody St, Mason.* Historical items housed in old schoolhouse (1870) built with stone from Fort Mason. (Mon-Fri or by appointment) **FREE**

Rocks & Minerals. Collectors from all over the nation come to this area of ancient geologic outcroppings for variety of rocks and minerals, especially topaz, the state gemstone.

McAllen (F-7)

See also Edinburg, Harlingen, Mission

Population 106,414
Elevation 124 ft
Area Code 956
Information Chamber of Commerce, 10 N Broadway, PO Box 790, 78505; phone 956/682-2871 or toll-free 800/250-2591
Web Site www.mcallen.org

This is a winter resort area surrounded by orange and grapefruit groves and irrigated vegetable and cotton fields. McAllen packs and markets this produce. Food manufacturing and processing machinery, petroleum products, dehydrated foods, and carotene are also local industries. McAllen is a favorite crossing place for excursions into Mexico. The area is also rated as one of the top birding spots in the country.

What to See and Do

McAllen International Museum. *1900 Nolana Loop, McAllen. Phone 956/682-1564. www.artcom.com/ Museums/nv/mr/78504-4R.htm.* Art and natural science exhibits and programs. (Tues-Sat 9 am-5 pm, Sun 1-5 pm; closed holidays) Free admission Thurs evenings. **$**

McAllen Nature Center. *4104 W Business Hwy 83, McAllen (78501). Phone 956/682-1517.* Cactus gardens, nature trails, bird-watching. (Mon-Fri 7:30 am-5:30 pm; closed Thanksgiving, Dec 25) **FREE**

Reynosa, Mexico. *8 miles S on Hwy 336.* (Population 400,000) Parking area on United States side of bridge. (For Border Crossing Regulations, see MAKING THE MOST OF YOUR TRIP.) Reynosa is a picturesque border town, well worth a leisurely visit. The plaza has a beautiful renovated church with high belfries and a soaring arched façade. There are nightclubs; several restaurants serve game dinners—venison and wild turkey. Dancing to Mexican music outdoors or indoors; occasional bullfights. *The Mercado* (market) tests visitors' bargaining skills.

Santa Ana National Wildlife Refuge. *Hwy 281, Pharr. 8 miles E on Hwy 83, then 7 miles S on FM 907 and 1/4 mile E on Hwy 281. Phone 956/784-7500.* More than 2,000 acres of forest and lakes include 450 plant species, 380 species of North American and Mexican birds, 12 miles of hiking trails, and 7 miles of wildlife auto tour road (available when tram tour is not in operation). Interpretive tram tour; photo blinds; visitor center. Nature trail accessible to wheelchairs and the visually impaired. Contact Refuge Manager, Rte 2, Box 202-A, Alamo 78516. (Daily; closed Jan 1, Thanksgiving, Dec 25) **$**

Virgin de San Juan del Valle Shrine. *E on Hwy 83, between McAllen and San Juan. Phone 956/787-0033.* Original statue of the Virgin, rescued from flames, now stands in a new shrine.

Special Event

Candlelight Posada. *Archer Park, 10 N Broadway, McAllen (78501). Phone 956/682-2871.* Citywide Christmas celebration. Blends traditions of Mexico with those of America. Dec.

Limited-Service Hotels

★ ★ **EMBASSY SUITES.** *1800 S 2nd St, McAllen (78503). Phone 956/686-3000; toll-free 800/362-2779;* *fax 956/631-8362. www.embassy-suites.com.* 252 rooms, 9 story, all suites. Complimentary full breakfast. Check-in 3 pm, check-out noon. High-speed Internet access, wireless Internet access. Restaurant, bar. Fitness room. Indoor pool, children's pool, whirlpool. Airport transportation available. **$**

★ ★ **FOUR POINTS BY SHERATON.** *2721 S 10th St, McAllen (78503). Phone 956/984-7900; toll-free 800/325-3535; fax 956/984-7997. www.fourpoints.com.* 148 rooms, 5 story. Complimentary full breakfast (weekends). Check-in 3 pm, check-out noon. Restaurant, bar. Fitness room. Outdoor pool, children's pool, whirlpool. Tennis. Airport transportation available. Business center. **$**

★ **HAMPTON INN.** *300 W Expy 83, McAllen (78501). Phone 956/682-4900; toll-free 800/426-7866; fax 956/682-6823. www.hamptoninn.com.* 91 rooms, 4 story. Pets accepted. Complimentary continental breakfast. Check-in noon, check-out noon. Outdoor pool. **$**

Full-Service Hotel

★ ★ ★ **RENAISSANCE CASA DE PALMAS HOTEL.** *101 N Main St, McAllen (78501). Phone 956/631-1101; fax 956/631-7934.* This property is a destination for both leisure and business guests. 165 rooms, 3 story. Pets accepted, some restrictions; fee. Check-in 3 pm, check-out noon. High-speed Internet access, wireless Internet access. Restaurant, bar. Fitness room. Outdoor pool. Airport transportation available. Business center. **$**

Restaurant

★ ★ **SANTA FE STEAK.** *1918 S 10th St, McAllen (78501). Phone 956/630-2331.* Southwestern menu. Dinner. Closed Sun; holidays. Outdoor seating. **$$**

McKinney (A-8)

See also Dallas, Denton, Greenville, Sherman

Founded 1848
Population 54,369
Elevation 632 ft
Area Code 972

Information Chamber of Commerce, 1801 W Louisiana St, 75069; phone 972/542-0163
Web Site www.mckinneytexas.org

The north Texas artificial lake area has eight lakes of more than 10,000 acres each within 60 miles of this town. McKinney is known as one of the state's largest historic districts; Chestnut Square is a block of restored 1800s houses.

What to See and Do

Heard Natural Science Museum and Wildlife Sanctuary. *1 Nature Pl, McKinney. Exit 38 E off Hwy 75 to Hwy 5 S, follow signs (FM 1378). Phone 972/562-5566. www.heardmuseum.org.* Natural history exhibits of north central Texas; marine life, rock, and mineral displays; historical exhibit of museum founder Bessie Heard (1886-1988); live animals; changing art shows; bird of prey rehabilitation facility; a 274-acre sanctuary along Wilson Creek including bottomland, upland, woodland, and prairie; guided and self-guided tours of nature trails. Free museum and sanctuary admission Mon. (Mon-Sat 9 am-5 pm, Sun 1-5 pm; closed holidays) **$$**

Lavon Lake. *3375 Sky View Dr, McKinney (75098). 15 miles E on Hwy 380, then 10 miles S on Hwy 78. Phone 972/442-5711 (recording).* Swimming, water-skiing, fishing, boating; hiking, horseback trail, picnicking, camping (tent and trailer sites). Some fees. (Daily) **FREE**

Special Events

Heritage Guild's Christmas Tour of Homes. *Phone toll-free 888/649-8499.* First weekend in Dec.

Wild West Fest. *Downtown Square, 105 1/2 E Virginia, McKinney. Phone 972/562-6880.* Antiques, crafts, entertainment. First Sat in Oct.

Mesquite (A-8)

Web Site www.cityofmesquite.com

Special Event

Mesquite Championship Rodeo. *1818 Rodeo Dr, Mesquite (75149). Phone 972/285-8777; toll-free 800/833-9339. www.mesquiterodeo.com.* When in Texas, do as many Texans do: hoot and holler at an action-packed rodeo. In an air-conditioned arena with 5,500 seats, real-live cowpokes compete in barrel-racing, bull riding, calf-roping, chuck-wagon racing, steer wrestling, and other events that fire up the crowd. In the calf scramble, kids scurry out onto the arena floor trying to remove ribbons from two calves, with prizes for the winners. A barbecue dinner and pony rides precede all the buckin' and ridin'. Fri-Sat in early Apr-early Oct **$$$$**

Midland (B-5)

See also Big Spring, Odessa

Population 94,996
Elevation 2,779 ft
Area Code 915
Information Chamber of Commerce/Convention & Visitors Bureau, 109 N Main, PO Box 1890, 79702; phone 915/683-3381 or toll-free 800/624-6435
Web Site www.visitmidlandtx.com

Midland (midway between Fort Worth and El Paso) is at the south edge of the high plains. The administrative center for the Permian oil basin, many oil companies have their offices in Midland, as do manufacturers and distributors.

What to See and Do

Commemorative Air Force and American Airpower Heritage Museum. *Midland International Airport, 9600 Wright Dr, Midland. Phone 915/563-1000.* Dedicated to the preservation of World War II combat aircraft. Planes on display change every three months. (Daily; closed Thanksgiving, Dec 25) (See SPECIAL EVENTS). **$$$**

Haley Library and History Center. *1805 W Indiana, Midland. Phone 915/682-5785.* Rare books, archives, and Western art. Emphasis on range country and cattle industry history in Texas and the Southwest. Includes original mission bell from the Alamo, cast in 1722. Research room. (Mon-Fri; closed holidays) **FREE**

Midland Community Theatre. *2000 W Wadley Ave, Midland. Phone 915/682-2544.* Eight dramas, comedies, or musicals annually, includes special summer features. (Thurs-Sun) **$$$$**

Museum of the Southwest. *1705 W Missouri Ave, Midland. Phone 915/683-2882. www.museumsw.org.* Former residence (1934) of Texas oil man Fred Turner houses permanent collection of Southwestern art and anthropology; traveling exhibits on display; children's museum with hands-on exhibits. Marian Blakemore Planetarium sky programs (Fri evenings; fee). (Tues-Sat 10 am-5 pm, Sun 2-5 pm; closed holidays) **FREE**

Permian Basin Petroleum Museum. *1500 W I-20, Midland (79707). Exit 136. Phone 915/683-4403.* Animated exhibits explain the history and development of the oil industry and the Permian Basin; walk-through diorama of ocean floor as it was 230 million years ago; oil well blowout action display; collection of paintings of west Texas and southeastern New Mexico. World's largest collection of antique drilling and production equipment. (Daily; closed holidays) **$$**

Special Events

Commemorative Airforce Airshow. *Midland International Airport, 9600 Wright Dr, Midland. Phone 915/563 1000.* First weekend in Oct.

Mex-Tex Menudo. *Centennial Plaza, 1410 N Lamesa Rd, Midland. Phone 915/682-2960.* Chili and fajita cook-off. June.

Summer Mummers. *Yucca Theatre (1927), 208 N Colorado St, Midland. Phone 915/682-4111.* Topical satire staged in the manner of 1890s melodrama. Fri-Sat in June-Labor Day.

Limited-Service Hotels

★ ★ **HOLIDAY INN.** *4300 W Wall St, Midland (79703). Phone 432/697-3181; toll-free 800/465-4329; fax 432/694-7754. www.holiday-inn.com.* 252 rooms, 2 story. Pets accepted, some restrictions; fee. Check-out noon. Restaurant, bar. Fitness room. Indoor pool, whirlpool. Airport transportation available. Business center. **$**

★ **LA QUINTA INN.** *4130 W Wall Ave, Midland (79703). Phone 432/697-9900; fax 432/689-0617. www.lq.com.* 146 rooms, 2 story. Pets accepted, some restrictions. Complimentary continental breakfast. Check-out noon. Outdoor pool. **$**

Full-Service Hotel

★ ★ ★ **HILTON MIDLAND AND TOWERS.** *117 W Wall St, Midland (79701). Phone 915/683-6131; toll-free 800/725-6131; fax 915/683-0958.*

www.hilton.com. Access to all major business and government offices is guaranteed from this central downtown location. Even more convenient, the Midland Convention Center is located just across the street, and the travel time to the airport is only 15 minutes. 249 rooms, 11 story. Check-out noon. Restaurant, bar. Fitness room. Outdoor pool, whirlpool. Airport transportation available. **$**

Restaurants

★ **BLUE STAR INN.** *2501 W Wall, Midland (79701). Phone 915/682-4231.* Chinese, American menu. Lunch, dinner. **$$**

★ **LUIGI'S ITALIAN.** *111 N Big Spring St, Midland (79701). Phone 915/683-6363.* Lunch, dinner. Closed Sun; holidays. Bar. Children's menu. **$$**

★ **SHOGUN.** *4610 N Garfield, Midland (79705). Phone 915/687-0734; fax 915/570-8888.* Japanese menu. Lunch, dinner. Bar. Children's menu. **$$**

★ **TAMPICO SPANISH INN.** *2411 W Wall, Midland (79701). Phone 915/682-5074.* Mexican, American menu. Lunch, dinner. Closed Mon; July 4. Children's menu. **$$**

★ ★ **VENEZIA.** *2101 W Wadley Ave #20, Midland (79705). Phone 915/687-0900.* Italian menu. Lunch, dinner. Closed Sun; holidays. Outdoor seating. **$$**

Mineral Wells (A-7)

See also Fort Worth, Graham, Weatherford

Population 16,946
Elevation 911 ft
Area Code 940
Zip 76067
Information Chamber of Commerce, PO Box 1408; phone 940/325-2557 or toll-free 800/252-6989
Web Site www.mineralwellstx.com

What to See and Do

Swimming, water sports, fishing, boating. On several nearby lakes and the Brazos River. Lake Mineral Wells State Park, 4 miles E; Lake Palo Pinto, 20 miles SW; Possum Kingdom Lake, 25 miles NW.

Special Event

Palo Pinto County Livestock Association Rodeo. *1200 FM Rd 18212, Mineral Wells (76067). Phone 940/325-2557.* Early May.

Mission (F-7)

See also Edinburg, McAllen

Population 45,408
Elevation 134 ft
Area Code 956
Zip 78572
Information Chamber of Commerce, 220 E 9th St; phone 956/585-2727 or toll-free 800/580-2700
Web Site www.missionchamber.com

This center of the Texas citrus industry started when the Oblate Fathers planted a citrus grove on the north bank of the Rio Grande near here. La Lomita Mission, located south of town, has been restored using many of the original bricks and foundations.

What to See and Do

Bentsen-Rio Grande Valley State Park. *3 miles W on Hwy 83, then 3 miles S on FM 2062 to Park Rd 43. Phone 956/585-1107.* Approximately 600 acres. Fishing, boat ramp; nature and hiking trails, picnicking, playground, camping, tent and trailer sites (dump station). (Daily) **$$**

La Lomita Farms State Historic Site. *3 3/4 miles S on FM 1016. Phone 956/581-2725.* Spanish-style structure once used as novitiate for oblate priests now houses exhibits. (Mon-Fri) **FREE** Nearby is

La Lomita Mission. *3 miles S on FM 1016. Phone 956/580-8760.* One of several missions established. Tiny (12 by 25 feet) chapel, still used as place of worship by locals. Built by oblate priests in 1845; the town of Mission is named for chapel.

Los Ebanos International Ferry. *17 miles W via Hwy 83.* The only hand-drawn ferry across the US border. (Daily, weather permitting) **$**

Special Events

Texas Border Botanical & Butterfly Festival. *Phone 956/585-2727.* Nature expo, seminars, butterflying field trips, park and garden tours, children's activities. Three days in late Mar.

Texas Citrus Fiesta. *1420 E Kika de la Garza St, Mission. Phone 956/585-9724.* Late Mar.

Restaurant

★ **FERRELL'S PIT.** *2224 E Business Hwy 83, Mission (78572). Phone 956/585-2381.* American menu. Lunch, dinner. Closed Tues; Thanksgiving, Dec 25. **$$**

Monahans (B-4)

See also Fort Stockton, Odessa, Pecos

Population 6,821
Elevation 2,613 ft
Area Code 915
Zip 79756
Information Chamber of Commerce, 401 S Dwight; phone 915/943-2187
Web Site www.monahans.org

What to See and Do

Million Barrel Museum. *400 Museum Blvd, Monahans (79756). 2 miles E on Business Loop 20. Phone 915/943-8401.* Texas oil boom prompted construction of an oil tank 522 feet by 426 feet to hold more than 1 million gallons; it was filled only once. Includes the Holman House with period furnishings; antique farming and railroad memorabilia, caboose; eclipse windmill; first Ward County jail; amphitheater; gift shop. (Tues-Sun; closed Thanksgiving, Dec 25) **DONATION**

Monahans Sandhills State Park. *I-20, exit 86, Monahans. 6 miles E on I-20, exit mile marker 86 to Park Rd 41. Phone 915/943-2092.* Sand dunes, some 70 feet high, believed to be from the Trinity sandstone formation and collected by the Permian Sea. On 3,840 acres. Nature trail, picnicking, improved campsites (dump station). (Daily) **$** Also here is the

Sandhills Interpretive Center. *I-20, exit 86, Monahans.* Natural history, historical, archaeological, botanical, and geological displays on the area. (Daily) Included with entrance to park.

Mount Pleasant (A-9)

Population 13,935
Elevation 416 ft
Area Code 903
Zip 75456

Information Mount Pleasant/Titus County Chamber of Commerce, 1604 N Jefferson, PO Box 1237; phone 903/572-8567
Web Site www.mtpleasant-tx.com

This town is a commercial center for shopping, manufacturing, and medicine. State records for largemouth bass have been set in two nearby lakes; many catches have weighed in at seven pounds or more.

Special Events

Deck the Halls. *Civic Center, 1800 N Jefferson Ave, Mount Pleasant (75455). Phone 903/575-4190.* Arts and crafts. Sat after Thanksgiving.

Mount Pleasant Championship Rodeo. *Phone 903/572-3381.* First weekend in June.

Titus County Fair. *Fairgrounds, 1620 N Washington Ave, Mount Pleasant (75455).* Carnival, cattle show, entertainment. Last full week in Sept.

Limited-Service Hotel

★ **SUPER 8.** *401 W I-30, Mount Vernon (75457). Phone 903/588-2882; fax 903/588-2844. www.super8.com.* 43 rooms, 2 story. Pets accepted, some restrictions; fee. Complimentary continental breakfast. Check-out 11 am. Bar. **$**

Nacogdoches (B-9)

See also Lufkin, Rusk

Founded 1691
Population 29,914
Elevation 277 ft
Area Code 936
Zip 75961
Information Convention & Visitors Bureau, 513 North St, PO Drawer 631918; phone 936/564-7351 or toll-free 888/564-7351
Web Site www.nacogdoches.org

Nacogdoches was founded as one of the five original Spanish missions in Texas. The initial mission was abandoned until 1779, when Captain Antonio Gil Y'Barbo returned with a group of settlers who had been evicted from their land by Spanish authorities. Here in 1826, Haden Edwards brashly declared Texas independent of Mexico and named it the Republic of Fredonia. He got no support from other colonists and soon fled to the United States.

Surrounded by 460,000 acres of pine timber, Nacogdoches is in the east Texas pine belt. Chicken, egg, and milk production along with industry, business, and education are the mainstays of the town's economy.

What to See and Do

Millard's Crossing. *6020 North St, Nacogdoches. 4 miles N via Hwy 59. Phone 936/564-6631.* Historic village of restored 19th-century east Texas homes furnished with period antiques. Log cabin, corn crib, chapel, Victorian parsonage, and farmhouse reflect life of east Texas pioneers. Guided tours. (Daily; closed holidays) **$$**

Sterne-Hoya Home. *211 S Lanana St, Nacogdoches. Phone 936/560-5426.* (1830) Pioneer home of Adolphus Sterne. (Mon-Sat; closed holidays) **FREE**

Stone Fort Museum. *Vista and Griffith blvds, Nacogdoches. Stephen F. Austin State University campus. Phone 936/468-2408.* Rebuilt by the state in 1936 from the original structure probably erected by Gil Y'Barbo in 1779. Focus on east Texas history and Spanish Nacogdoches. Guided tours. (Tues-Sun; closed school holidays) **FREE**

Limited-Service Hotels

★ **COMFORT INN.** *3400 South St, Nacogdoches (75964). Phone 936/569-8100; toll-free 800/465-4329; fax 936/569-0332. www.comfortinn.com.* 126 rooms, 2 story. Check-out noon. Restaurant. Fitness room. Indoor pool, outdoor pool, whirlpools. **$**

★ ★ **FREDONIA HOTEL & CONVENTION CENTER.** *200 N Fredonia St, Nacogdoches (75961). Phone 936/564-1234; toll-free 800/594-5323; fax 936/564-1234. www.fredoniahotel.com.* 113 rooms, 6 story. Pets accepted; fee. Check-out 1 pm. Restaurant. Outdoor pool. **$**

Natural Bridge Caverns

Web Site www.naturalbridgecaverns.com

8 miles NE of I-35 exit 175, on FM 3009 (Natural Bridge Caverns Rd).

With names like "Castle of the White Giants," "Sherwood Forest," and "The Hall of the Mountain King," the vast underground rooms that form Natural Bridge Caverns are as fittingly fantastic as the delicate crystalline formations and massive stone monuments that fill them. Guided tours of the caverns are accessible to walking guests as well as more adventurous types. Discovered in 1960 and opened to the public in 1964, the North Cavern is the most spectacular part, with room after room of both delicate and rugged rock formations. Seventy-five-minute tours of the cavern leave every 30 minutes. Encompassing 3/4 mile, this walking tour takes visitors to a depth of 180 feet. Also discovered in 1964, the South Cavern extends 1/2 mile beyond the North. Here, delicate, hollow formations called soda straws are among the longest in North America, and limestone crystals are so pure that light shines through them. Accessed by rappelling down a 160-foot-long shaft, the tour through this cave takes three to four hours and is available by reservation only. (Attraction ownership provides caving gear.) Visitors can also try their luck at panning for gems and minerals at the Natural Bridge Mining Company. (Early Sept-May: daily 9 am-4 pm; June-Labor Day: daily 9 am-6 pm) **$$$$**

New Braunfels (D-7)

See also San Antonio, San Marcos, Seguin

Founded 1844
Population 36,494
Elevation 639 ft
Area Code 830
Information Chamber of Commerce, 390 S Seguin Ave, PO Box 311417, 78131; phone 830/625-2385 or toll-free 800/572-2626
Web Site www.nbcham.org

Prince Carl of Solms-Braunfels, Commissioner-General for the Society for the Protection of German Immigrants in Texas, founded New Braunfels in 1844.

He built his headquarters on a hilltop, lived there for a short while, and then returned to Germany to marry. Within a few months of his return to Texas, nearly 6,000 German immigrants followed him, landing at Indianola, 125 miles away from New Braunfels. There was little shelter, food and supplies were scarce, and no transportation to New Braunfels was available. In desperation, many began to walk. Disease, hunger, and exposure wiped out as many as 2,000 of these pioneers. Unfamiliarity with the land and conditions in their new homeland caused much privation and suffering, but they persevered. Today, New Braunfels still has a strong German influence.

What to See and Do

Canyon Lake. *601 COE Rd, New Braunfels (78133). Headquarters, 15 miles NW via FM 306. Phone 830/964-3341; toll-free 800/528-2104.* A 224-foot-high earthen dam. Swimming, water-skiing, fishing, boating (ramps), canoeing, tubing; picnicking, concession, camping (tent and trailer sites, some hook-ups; fee). **$**

Fishing. For bass, catfish, perch in Lake Dunlap and Canyon Lake; for rainbow trout in Guadalupe River.

Landa Park. *110 Golf Course Rd, New Braunfels (78130). Landa St, 5 blocks NW on Hwy 46. Phone 830/608-2160.* A 190-acre park with spring-fed pool, swimming pool, tubing on river, glass-bottom boat rides; 18-hole golf, miniature golf, miniature train, picnicking, playground, concession. Historical markers, arboretum. Park (daily, schedule varies with season). Some fees. **FREE**

Lindheimer Home. *491 Comal Ave, New Braunfels. Phone 830/629-2943.* (Circa 1852) Restored house of Ferdinand Lindheimer (1801-1879), educator, guide, botanist, and editor. (May-Aug: Mon-Tues, Thurs-Sun; rest of year: Sat-Sun, or by appointment; closed Jan 1, Dec 25) **$**

Natural Bridge Caverns. *26495 Natural Bridge. 15 miles W via Hwy 46, FM 1863. Phone 210/651-6101.* **$$$$**

New Braunfels Museum of Art and Music. *1259 Gruene Rd, New Braunfels. Phone 830/625-5636; toll-free 800/456-4866. www.nbmuseum.org.* Affiliate of Smithsonian Institute. Ongoing and changing exhibits featuring Texas visual and folk artist and music history. World's largest collection of original paintings and drawings by Sister Maria Innocentia Hummel; the popular German porcelain figurines are modeled on her work. Gift shop. (Wed-Sat 10 am-6 pm, Sun noon-6 pm; closed holidays) **$**

Schlitterbahn Water Park. *3150 I-35 S, New Braunfels (78130). Phone 830/625-2351. www.schlitterbahn.com.* Water parks typically include lots of canvas and concrete, but Schlitterbahn (German for "slippery road"), with its location on the tree-lined banks of the spring-fed Comal River, is a pleasant exception. Also unique is that parking is free, and families are allowed to bring their own picnics with them. Attracting more visitors than any other seasonal water park in the United States, the park offers more than a dozen kinds of family water fun: the Master Blaster (which blasts riders up six stories of hills and valleys), tub chutes, body-boarding, a wave pool, swimming pools, hot tubs, and children's water playgrounds. Seventeen water slides rate from tame to scary. Likewise, tubing adventures include fast and slow options. You'll also find water and sand volleyball courts and more than 20 refreshment centers. The park has two separate riverfront sections, with free trams and buses to shuttle you back and forth. (Daily) **$$$$**

Sophienburg Museum & Archives. *401 W Coll St, New Braunfels. Phone 830/629-1900.* Memorabilia, archives of pioneer days. Changing exhibits. Museum (daily; closed holidays). Archives (Mon-Fri; closed holidays). **$**

Special Events

Comal County Fair. *801 E Common St, New Braunfels. Phone 830/608-2100.* Carnival and rodeo. Late Sept.

Wurstfest. *178 Landa Park Dr, New Braunfels (78130). Phone 830/625-9167. www.wurstfest.com/general/ info.htm.* German music and food, displays, dancing. Late Oct-early Nov.**$$**

Limited-Service Hotel

★ **BEST WESTERN INN & SUITES.** *1493 N I-35, New Braunfels (78130). Phone 830/625-7337; toll-free 800/937-8376; fax 830/625-7133. www.bestwestern.com.* 60 rooms, 2 story. Pets accepted; fee. Complimentary continental breakfast. Check-in 3 pm, check-out noon. High-speed Internet access. Outdoor pool, whirlpool. **$**

Restaurants

★ ★ **GRISTMILL.** *1287 Gruene Rd, New Braunfels*

(78130). Phone 830/625-0684; fax 830/629-6729. www.gristmillrestaurant.com. American menu. Lunch, dinner. Bar. Casual attire. Outdoor seating. **$$**

★ **NEW BRAUNFELS SMOKEHOUSE.** *146 Hwy 46 E, New Braunfels (78130). Phone 830/625-2416; fax 830/626-3785. www.nbsmokehouse.com.* American, German menu. Breakfast, lunch, dinner, brunch. Children's menu. Casual attire. Outdoor seating. **$**

Odessa (B-4)

See also Midland, Monahans

Founded 1881
Population 90,943
Elevation 2,890 ft
Area Code 915
Information Chamber of Commerce, 700 N Grant, Suite 200, 79760; phone 915/332-9111 or toll-free 800/780-4678
Web Site www.odessachamber.com

An oil field supply and equipment center for the Permian Basin, Odessa also has liquefied petroleum, synthetic rubber, cement, and petrochemical plants.

Odessa is the home of the "Chuck Wagon Gang," a group of businessmen who travel worldwide each year preparing Texas-style barbecue "feeds" to promote good will for their city.

What to See and Do

Globe Theatre. *2308 Shakespeare Rd, Odessa. Phone 915/332-1586.* Authentic re-creation of Shakespeare's original playhouse showcases drama ranging from Shakespeare to Broadway. Guided tours (Mon-Fri; weekends by appointment). **$$** Also here is

    Ann Hathaway Cottage Archival & Shakespearean Library. *2308 Shakespeare Rd, Odessa.* Contains many old books, documents pertaining to Shakespeare; costumes, furnishings, and other items of the Elizabethan era.

Hero's Water World. *12300 W Hwy 80 E, Odessa. Phone 915/563-1933.* The 18-acre park includes giant wave pools, swimming pools, water slides, inner-tube rides, bumper boats, go-karts, Kiddieland. (Late Apr-Memorial Day: weekends; Memorial Day-Labor Day: Tues-Sat) **$$$$**

Meteor Crater. *8 miles W via I-20 or Hwy 80 to Meteor Crater Rd exit.* Large crater formed more than 20,000 years ago. Paths through crater have interpretive signs. Picnic facilities. **FREE**

Presidential Museum. *622 N Lee, Odessa. Phone 915/332-7123.* Changing exhibits and educational programs devoted to the people who have held or run for the office of President of the United States. Collections include images of the presidents, campaign memorabilia, signatures, political cartoons, miniature replicas of First Lady inaugural dresses. (Tues-Sat; closed holidays) **$**

Special Events

Jazz Festival. *3181 E University Blvd, Odessa. Phone 915/362-1191.* Week-long jazz entertainment. May.

Sandhill Hereford and Quarter Horse Show and Rodeo. *4201 Andrews Hwy, Odessa. Phone 915/366-3951.* First week in Jan.

Limited-Service Hotels

★ ★ **BEST WESTERN GARDEN OASIS.** *110 W I-20, Odessa (79761). Phone 432/337-3006; toll-free 877/574-9231; fax 432/332-1956. www.bestwestern.com.* 118 rooms, 2 story. Pets accepted, some restrictions. Check-out noon. Restaurant. Indoor pool, whirlpool. Airport transportation available. **$**
🐾 🛏

★ **LA QUINTA INN.** *5001 E Business 20, Odessa (79761). Phone 432/333-2820; fax 432/333-4208. www.lq.com.* 122 rooms. Pets accepted, some restrictions. Check-out noon. Outdoor pool. **$**
🄳 🐾 🛏

★ ★ **MCM HOTEL GRANDE.** *6201 E Business Loop 20, Odessa (79762). Phone 432/362-2311; fax 432/362-9810.* 244 rooms, 3 story. Pets accepted, some restrictions. Restaurant, bar. Fitness room. Indoor pool, outdoor pool, whirlpool. Airport transportation available. **$**
🐾 🏃 🛏

Restaurants

★ ★ **BARN DOOR.** *2140 N Andrew Hwy, Odessa (79761). Phone 915/337-4142.* Victorian country décor. American menu. Lunch, dinner. Closed Sun; Labor Day, Dec 24 evening, Dec 25. Bar. **$$**

★ **MANUEL'S CRISPY TACOS.** *1404 E 2nd St, Odessa (79761). Phone 915/333-2751; fax 915/333-2753.* Mexican menu. Lunch, dinner. Closed holidays. Bar. Children's menu. **$**

Orange (C-10)

See also Beaumont, Port Arthur

Founded 1836
Population 18,643
Elevation 14 ft
Area Code 409
Zip 77630
Information Convention & Visitors Bureau, 1012 Green Ave; phone 409/883-3536 or toll-free 800/528-4906
Web Site www.org-tx.com/chamber

Orange is on the Sabine River, at its junction with the Intracoastal Waterway. The deepwater port is connected with the Gulf by the Sabine-Neches Waterway. Bayous nearby are shaded with cypress and pine trees. Cattle, timber, shipbuilding, oil, and chemical processing provide a diverse economy. There are several historic structures and a branch of Lamar University of Beaumont in town. The imposing First Presbyterian Church with art glass windows and a marble staircase was among the first public buildings in the country to be air-conditioned.

What to See and Do

Boating and fishing. On Sabine River and Lake and in surrounding bayous. Launching, dock facilities, marinas in area.

Heritage House Museum. *905 W Division St, Orange. Phone 409/886-5385.* (1902) Historic house; changing exhibits. (Tues-Fri; closed holidays) **$**

Lutcher Theater for the Performing Arts. *Orange Civic Plaza. Phone 409/886-5535 (box office); toll-free 800/828-5535.* Professional performances of top stars in concert, Broadway musicals, and plays. **$$$$**

Stark Museum of Art. *712 Green Ave, Orange. Phone 409/883-6661.* Built to house the collections of the Stark family. Fine collections of Western art, including originals by Russell, Remington, Audubon, and the Taos Society of Artists of New Mexico. The American Indian collection includes many art forms of the tribes of the Great Plains and the Southwest. Displays of Doughty and Boehm porcelain bird sculpture and Steuben crystal. (Tues-Sat; closed holidays) **FREE**

W. H. Stark House. *610 Main St, Orange (77630). 6th and Green sts. Phone 409/883-0871.* (1894) Restored Victorian house typical of wealthy southeast Texas family; 15 rooms, three stories built of longleaf yellow pine with gables, galleries, and windowed turret. Original furniture, silver, woodwork, lighting, and decorative accessories; collection of cut glass in carriage house. Stairs are a major part of the tour. Reservations required. (Tues-Sat; closed holidays) Over 14 years only. **$**

Limited-Service Hotels

★ **BEST WESTERN ORANGE INN.** *2630 I-10 W, Orange (77632). Phone 409/883-6616; fax 409/883-3427. www.bestwestern.com.* Near Orange County Airport. 60 rooms, 2 story. Check-out noon. Outdoor pool. **$**

★ ★ **RAMADA INN–ORANGE.** *2610 I-10, Orange (77632). Phone 409/883-0231; toll-free 800/272-6232; fax 409/883-8839. www.ramada.com.* 125 rooms, 2 story. Pets accepted, some restrictions. Check-out noon. Restaurant, bar. Outdoor pool, children's pool. **$**

Ozona (C-5)

See also Sonora

Population 3,436
Elevation 2,348 ft
Area Code 915
Zip 76943
Information Chamber of Commerce, 1110 Avenue E, PO Box 1135; phone 915/392-3737

The only town in the 3,215-square-mile area of Crockett County, Ozona is a ranching community that calls itself the "biggest little town in the world."

What to See and Do

Crockett County Museum. *404 11th St, Ozona. Courthouse Annex. Phone 915/392-2837.* Local historical exhibits, including objects from early Spanish explorers; minerals, mammoth bones. Murals depicting big-game animals hunted by Paleo-Indians; simulated rock overhang shelter, artifacts dating to

10,000 BC. (Mon-Fri 9 am-5 pm, Sat 10 am-4 pm; closed holidays) **$**

Davy Crockett Monument. *S end of town square.* Unveiled in 1939, this statue of the famous frontiersman bears the inscription "Be sure you are right, then go ahead."

Fort Lancaster State Historical Park. *33 miles W on I-10, exit 343 then 11 miles W on Hwy 290, near Sheffield. Phone 915/836-4391.* Ruins of Army outpost (1855-1861); 82 acres. Museum containing exhibits relating to 18th-century military life. (Daily; closed Dec 25) **$**

Limited-Service Hotel

★ **BEST WESTERN OZONA INN.** *1307 Avenue A, Ozona (76943). Phone 325/392-3791; toll-free 800/780-7234; fax 325/392-5277. www.bestwestern.com.* 50 rooms. Complimentary continental breakfast. Check-in 3 pm, check-out 11 am. High-speed Internet access, wireless Internet access. Outdoor pool. **$**

Padre Island National Seashore (F-8)

See also Port Isabel

Web Site www.nps.gov/pais

From I-37, turn onto Hwy 358. The highway changes its name from 358 to South Padre Island Dr and then crosses over the Laguna Madre on the JFK causeway and becomes Park Rd 22. At the end of Park Rd 22 is the National Seashore.

A visit to Texas's Gulf Coast would be incomplete without surf, sun, sand, and shells. Padre Island National Seashore scores big in all categories. There are 65 miles of Gulf beach, 55 miles of which comprise the Big Shell and Little Shell Beaches, with excellent areas for shell seeking. You can also camp throughout. In addition to swimming, sunbathing, and hiking, all but 4 miles of the seashore (Malaquite Beach) are open to four-wheel-drive vehicles. Rent or drive one to travel down the island to Bird Island Basin on the Laguna Madre, where the warm, shallow waters and persistent winds make this one of the top spots in the world for windsurfing. Windsurfing gear is available here for rental, and there's also a boat-launching ramp. For budding naturalists, the park participates in a sea turtle rescue project, hatching eggs at the park's incubation facility and then releasing the hatchlings when they're mature enough to survive. The park welcomes audiences for the hatchling releases—just phone the Hatchling Hotline (phone 361/949-7163). (Daily; closed Jan 1, Dec 25) **$$**

Palestine (B-9)

See also Athens, Crockett, Fairfield, Jacksonville, Rusk

Founded 1846
Population 17,598
Elevation 510 ft
Area Code 903
Information Convention and Visitors Bureau, PO Box 1177, 75802; phone 903/723-3014 or toll-free 800/659-3484
Web Site www.palestine-online.org

Surrounded by wooded areas and lakes, Palestine (pronounced PAL-es-teen) offers a wide array of outdoor recreation. It is the home of an atmospheric research station as well as petroleum, retail, and agricultural operations.

What to See and Do

Community Forest. *2 miles NW on Hwy 287.* Fishing, piers, boat ramp; nature trails, picnicking. Fishing also on Lake Palestine, 20 miles N. **FREE**

National Scientific Balloon Facility. *3224 Farm Market Rd, Palestine (75801). 5 miles N via Hwy 287 to FM 3224.* Phone 903/729-0271. Research facility employs high-altitude balloons in various experiments. Interpretive video (30 minutes). Guided tour of facility (weather permitting; one week advance notice requested) includes launch vehicle "Tiny Tim" and weather station. (Mon-Fri 8 am-4:30 pm; closed holidays) **FREE**

Rusk-Palestine State Park. *Park Rd 76, Palestine. 6 miles E on Hwy 84.* Phone 903/683-5126. (See RUSK)

Special Events

Hot Pepper Festival. Phone 903/723-3014. *www.palestinechamber.org/events.asp.* Early Oct. **FREE**

Texas Dogwood Trail Festival. *3121 W Oak St, Palestine.* Phone 903/729-7275. Last two weekends in Mar and first weekend in Apr.

Limited-Service Hotel

★ ★ **BEST WESTERN PALESTINE INN.** *1601 W Palestine Ave, Palestine (75801).* Phone 903/723-4655; toll-free 800/523-0121; fax 903/723-2519. *www.bestwestern.com.* 66 rooms, 2 story. Pets accepted. Check-out 1 pm. Restaurant. Outdoor pool. **$** 🐾 🏊

Pampa (E-4)

See also Amarillo, Fritch

Population 17,887
Elevation 3,234 ft
Area Code 806
Information Chamber of Commerce, 200 N Ballard, PO Box 1942, 79066; phone 806/669-3241
Web Site www.pampa.com

From a little cattle town of perhaps 1,000 people, Pampa (so named because the country around it resembles the Argentine *pampas*) has grown, since the discovery of oil in 1926, into a thriving industrial city. Carbon black, petrochemical, and manufacturing plants now stand alongside grain elevators and livestock businesses.

What to See and Do

White Deer Land Museum. *116 S Cuyler St, Pampa.* Phone 806/669-8041. Arrowhead and Native American photo collection, pioneer artifacts, historical records; room displays with antique furnishings, machines and utensils. (Tues-Sun 1-4 pm; closed holidays) **FREE**

Special Events

Top O'Texas Junior Livestock Show & Sale. *Clyde Carruth Bull Barn, Hwy 60 E, Pampa (79065).* Phone 806/665-5946. Mid-Jan.

Top O'Texas Rodeo, PRCA. *200 N Ballard, Pampa.* Phone 806/669-0434. Second weekend in July.

Limited-Service Hotel

★ ★ **BEST WESTERN NORTHGATE INN.** *2831 Perryton Pkwy, Pampa (79065).* Phone 806/

665-0926; toll-free 888/665-0926; fax 806/665-8027. www.bestwestern.com. 100 rooms, 2 story. Complimentary continental breakfast. Check-out noon. Restaurant. Outdoor pool. **$**

Restaurants

★ **DYER'S BAR-B-QUE.** Hwy 60 W, Pampa (79065). Phone 806/665-4401. Lunch, dinner. Closed Sun; holidays. Children's menu. **$**

★ **TEXAS ROSE STEAKHOUSE.** 2537 Perryton Pkwy, Pampa (79065). Phone 806/669-1009. Kitchen visible behind glass partition. Lunch, dinner. Closed Sun; holidays. Children's menu. **$$**

Paris (A-9)

See also Bonham

Settled 1836
Population 25,898
Elevation 602 ft
Area Code 903
Zip 75460
Information Visitor & Convention Office, 1651 Clarksville St; phone 903/784-2501 or toll-free 800/727-4789
Web Site www.paristexas.com

Farm produce and cattle are raised outside the city limits; Paris proper relies on manufacturing. Rebuilt by plan after a great fire in 1916, the downtown area is a time capsule of the 1920s. Paris has nearly 1,400 acres of parks and flower beds.

What to See and Do

Fishing. Lake Crook, 3 miles N. Lake Pat Mayse, 12 miles N.

Sam Bell Maxey House State Historical Park. 812 S Church, Paris. Phone 903/785-5716. Two-story house (1867), in high Victorian Italianate style, was built by Sam Bell Maxey, Confederate major general and US Senator. Occupied by his family until 1966. Family heirlooms and furniture, some dating to 1795. (Wed-Sun; closed Jan 1, Thanksgiving, Dec 25) **$**

Senator A. M. and Welma Aikin Jr. Regional Archives. 2400 Clarksville, Paris. On campus of Paris Junior College. Phone 903/782-0415. Includes a gallery of memorabilia from the noted senator's career as an

educational reformer; replica of his office in Austin. Local and regional archives. (Mon-Fri; closed campus holidays) **FREE**

Special Events

CRCA Annual Rodeo. 570 E Center St, Fairgrounds, Paris. (75460) Aug.

Municipal Band Concerts. Paris Visitors and Convention Office, 1651 Clarksville St, Paris (75460). In Bywaters Park. Phone 903/784-2501. Fri nights. Second weekend in June-second weekend in July.

Red River Valley Exposition. Fairgrounds, 570 E Center St, Paris (75460). Phone 903/785-7971. Eight days in early Sept.

Limited-Service Hotel

★ ★ **COMFORT INN.** 3505 NE Loop 286, Paris (75460). Phone 903/784-7481; fax 903/784-0231. www.comfortinn.com. 62 rooms, 2 story. Complimentary continental breakfast. Check-out noon. Restaurant. Outdoor pool. **$**

Restaurants

★ **FISH FRY.** 3500 NE Loop 286, Paris (75460). Phone 903/785-6144. Nine dining areas. Seafood menu. Dinner. Closed Sun-Mon; Jan 1, Thanksgiving, Dec 25. Children's menu. **$**

★ **TA MOLLY'S.** 2835 NE Loop 286, Paris (75460). Phone 903/784-4706. Water fountain in the center of the room. Mexican menu. Lunch, dinner. Closed holidays. Children's menu. **$$**

Pasadena (E-9)

What to See and Do

Armand Bayou Nature Center. 8500 Bay Area Blvd (77507). From Houston, take I-45 S, take exit 26 at Bay Area Blvd, and go E 7 miles just past Bay Area Park. Phone 281/474-2551. www.abnc.org. With canoe and pontoon boat trips and stargazing and birding classes, Armand Bayou Nature Center gives families visiting the Houston area multiple opportunities to learn about nature on the bayou, night and day. "Breakfast on the Bayou" is a Saturday morning feature in which guests enjoy continental breakfast as they drift down the bayou on a pontoon boat nature tour. There are also family star parties, night hikes, and sunset cruises. Along the Central Flyway, the largest migratory bird route in North America, the bayou is home to more than 220 species of birds. The preserve also shelters everything from armadillos to swamp rabbits, bobcats, and coyotes. Weekend demonstrations and talks teach about wildlife and also demonstrate turn-of-the-century farm tasks (rope-making, cheese-making, etc.) at the Center's Martyn farm site. Guided trail hikes are also offered on weekends. Call the center for current schedules. (Tues-Sun 9 am-5 pm, Sun noon-6 pm; closed Dec 25.) **$**

Pecos (B-4)

See also Fort Stockton, Monahans

Population 9,501
Elevation 2,580 ft
Area Code 915
Zip 79772
Information Chamber of Commerce, 111 S Cedar, PO Box 27; phone 915/445-2406
Web Site www.pecostx.com

This one-time rough cattle town is now a modern producing and shipping point for cotton, cantaloupes, and vegetables produced in the large area irrigated by water pumped from underground. It is also an oil, gas, and sulphur center. The town has not forgotten its colorful past. The annual rodeo commemorates the fact that Pecos invented this sporting event in 1883, with a contest among cowpokes from local ranches.

What to See and Do

Balmorhea State Park. *9207 Hwy 17 S, Toyahvale. 32 miles S on Hwy 17, near the Davis Mountains. Phone 915/375-2370.* Spring-fed swimming pool (daily; fee); picnicking, playground, lodging, camping, tent and trailer sites (dump station). (Daily) **$$**

West of the Pecos Museum. *120 E 1st St, Pecos. 1st St and Hwy 285. Phone 915/445-5076.* Renovated 1904 hotel; more than 50 rooms cover history of western Texas from the 1880s; includes restored Old #11 Saloon (1896), where two gunslingers were killed. (Memorial Day-Labor Day: daily; rest of year: Tues-Sat; closed Thanksgiving, also one week in mid-Dec) **$$**

Special Event

West of the Pecos Rodeo. *Buck Jackson Memorial Rodeo Arena, 111 S Cedar St, Pecos. Phone 915/445-2406.* Includes Golden Girl of the Old West contest, Old-Timer Reunion at museum, Fiesta Night in Old Pecos. Parade of floats, riding groups, and antique vehicles; barbecue. Four days in early July.

Limited-Service Hotel

★ ★ **BEST WESTERN SWISS CLOCK INN.** *133 S Frontage Rd, Pecos (79772). Phone 432/447-2215; toll-free 800/780-7234; fax 432/447-4463.* www.bestwestern.com. 105 rooms. Pets accepted, some restrictions; fee. Complimentary full breakfast. Check-in 3 pm, check-out 11 am. Restaurant, bar. Outdoor pool. **$**

Plainview (A-5)

See also Lubbock

Founded circa 1880
Population 22,336
Elevation 3,300 ft
Area Code 806
Zip 79072
Information Chamber of Commerce, 710 W 5th; phone 806/296-7431 or toll-free 800/658-2685
Web Site www.plainviewtex.com

This is one of the four chief commercial centers of the High Plains, where cotton, corn, sunflowers, and soybeans are nurtured by the vast, shallow, underground water belt.

What to See and Do

Abraham Family Art Gallery. *1900 W 7th St, Plainview. Phone 806/296-5521.* Dr. Malouf Abraham's donation of select artwork to the Wayland Baptist University. (Mon-Sat) Lower level of J. E. & L. E. Mabee Learning Resources Center on Wayland campus. **FREE**

Llano Estacado Museum. *1900 W 8th St, Plainview. On Wayland Baptist University campus. Phone 806/291-3660.* Regional history and archaeology; art and science collections. Major events held year-round. (Mar-Nov: Mon-Fri 9 am-5 pm, Sat-Sun 1-5 pm; closed holidays and Easter weekend) **FREE**

Special Events

Bar None Rodeo. *So Bate St, Plainview (79072). Phone 806/293-2661.* Third weekend in July.

High Plains Gem & Mineral Show. Early Apr.

Limited-Service Hotel

★ **BEST WESTERN CONESTOGA.** *600 N I-27, Plainview (79072). Phone 806/293-9454; toll-free 800/780-7234; fax 806/291-9985. www.bestwestern.com.* 83 rooms, 2 story. Pets accepted; fee. Complimentary continental breakfast. Check-out noon. Outdoor pool. **$**

Plano (A-8)

Restaurant

★ ★ **NAKAMOTO JAPANESE CUISINE.** *3309 N Central Expy, Plano (75023). Phone 972/881-0328.* Japanese menu. Lunch, dinner. Bar. Casual attire. **$$$**

Port Aransas (E-8)

See also Aransas Pass, Corpus Christi, Rockport

Population 3,370
Elevation 7 ft
Area Code 361
Zip 78373
Information Chamber of Commerce, 421 W Cotter, PO Box 356; phone 361/749-5919 or toll-free 800/452-6278
Web Site www.portaransas.org

This resort town on Mustang Island is accessible from Aransas Pass by causeway and ferryboat or from Corpus Christi via causeway. Padre Island (see) is also nearby. Eighteen miles of coastline provides good surf fishing as well as chartered-boat, deep-sea fishing for sailfish and kingfish. Swimming and surfing on the beach are popular activites. **Mustang Island State Park,** 14 miles south on Highway 361, while relatively unspoiled, does have swimming with a bathhouse and showers; picnicking and camping. Beach driving is permitted. A hardtop road goes to Corpus Christi.

What to See and Do

***Texas Treasure* Casino Cruise.** *229 Hwy 361 S, Port Aransas (78373). Phone 361/758-4444; toll-free 800/472-5215. www.txtreasure.com.* Sailing twice daily, the adults-only *Texas Treasure* gives guests good value, combining casino games, fine dining, live entertainment, and a trip over Gulf of Mexico waters into one tempting package. Rules require that gaming can't begin until the cruise reaches international waters 9.3 miles from port, which is why most guests choose to start their cruise with the International Buffet, a smorgasbord of meats, poultry, seafood, veggies, salads, and desserts. Gambling options include more than 400 slot machines and 20 table games, including blackjack, Caribbean stud, craps, and three-card poker. Patrons who opt for the evening cruise have the added option of a late-night snack/early breakfast on the cruise back to port. (Sun noon-6 pm; Tues-Wed 11 am-5 pm, 6:30 pm-12:30 am; Thurs 11 am-5 pm; Fri-Sat 11 am-4:30 pm, 6:30 pm-1 am) **$$$$**

Special Event

Deep-Sea Roundup. *Phone 361/749-6339.* Fishing contest. Early July.

Port Arthur (C-10)

See also Beaumont, Orange

Founded 1895
Population 57,755
Elevation 18 ft
Area Code 409
Information Convention & Visitor Bureau, 3401 Cultural Center Dr, 77642; phone 409/985-7822 or toll-free 800/235-7822
Web Site www.portarthur.com

Hernando De Soto was shipwrecked nearby in 1543. Later a secret anchorage for the pirate Jean Lafitte, the area became known as the "Cajun Capital of Texas" when settled by thousands of French Acadians.

In 1895, Arthur Edward Stilwell, builder of the Kansas City, Pittsburg, and Gulf Railroad (now the Kansas City Southern), chose Port Arthur as his Gulf terminus. He said the "brownies" had suggested the site, and that the plan of the city had been suggested to him in dreams inspired by the spirit world. He named the town after himself.

The Lucas well in the Spindletop field, 15 miles north, gushed forth in 1901, flooding 100 acres with oil before it was capped. John W. "Bet-a-million" Gates came to town, lent Stilwell some needed money and soon took over the industrial development of the booming new city.

This city on the shores of Lake Sabine is now called the "energy city" because it has the largest petroleum refining center in the country. It is also a thriving commercial, shipping, and chemical center. Since the Sabine-Neches Ship Channel is built within the city, ships passing through appear to be moving through the city streets. An interesting mix of industry and tourism fuels the local economy.

What to See and Do

J. D. Murphree Wildlife Management Area. *10 Parks and Wildlife Dr, Port Arthur (77640). W on Hwy 73. Phone 409/736-2551. www.tpwd.state.tx.us.* A 24,000-acre marsh. Fishing (spring, summer); waterfowl and alligator hunting (fall, winter).

Museum of the Gulf Coast. *700 Procter, Port Arthur. Phone 409/982-7000. www.co.jefferson.tx.us/museums .htm.* Exhibits cover history and culture of area; also history of oil refining; southeast Texas musical heritage exhibit includes Janis Joplin, Tex Ritter; sports legends exhibit features Jimmy Johnson, Babe Zaharias, and others. (Mon-Sat 9 am-5 pm, Sun 1-5 pm; closed holidays) **$$**

Nederland Windmill Museum. *1500 Boston Ave, Nederland. 5 miles N via Hwy 347. Phone 409/722-0279.* Located in Tex Ritter Park is a replica of a Dutch windmill built to honor 1898 immigrants from Holland; artifacts from Holland; memorabilia of country-western star Tex Ritter. (Mar-Sept: Tues-Sun 1-5 pm; rest of year: Thurs-Sun; closed holidays) **FREE** Adjacent is

> **La Maison Acadienne Museum.** *1500 Boston Ave, Nederland. Phone 409/723-1545.* Replica of French Acadian home preserves heritage of French and Cajun immigrants who settled in Nederland in early 1900s; period furniture. (Days same as Windmill Museum) **FREE**

Pleasure Island. *Sabine Lake, across the channel on Hwy 82.* Fishing (four fishing piers, free; also charter boat fishing), crabbing (from 16 1/2 miles of shoreline), boating (launch, marina, supplies, repair; also regattas); horseback riding (stables), picnicking,

camping. Music park. Lake connects to the Intracoastal Waterway at its north end and the Port Arthur Ship Channel at its south end, 16 miles from the Gulf of Mexico. **FREE**

Pompeiian Villa. *1953 Lakeshore Dr, Port Arthur. Phone 409/983-5977.* Built as a winter house for Isaac Ellwood of DeKalb, Illinois, in 1900, the villa, with its three-sided courtyard and decorative trim, is a copy of a Pompeiian house of AD 79; furnishings include a Louis XVI parlor set; diamond-dust mirror; art nouveau Baccarat chandelier, French Savannerie rug. (Mon-Fri; closed holidays) **$**

Port of Port Arthur. *100 W Lakeshore, Port Arthur. Phone 409/983-2011.* Port where vessels are loaded and unloaded; 75-ton gantry crane, "Big Arthur." Tours (Mon-Fri; closed holidays). **FREE**

Rose Hill Manor. *100 Woodworth Blvd, Port Arthur. Phone 409/985-7292.* Palatial colonial residence of Rome H. Woodworth, early Port Arthur mayor. Greek Revival style; borders the Intracoastal Waterway. Tours. (Tues-Sat, by appointment; closed holidays) **$**

Sabine Woods. *15 miles E on Hwy 87. Phone 409/985-7822; toll-free 800/235-7822. www.portarthurtexas.com.* The Audubon Society maintains two wooded bird sanctuaries near Pleasure Island. (Daily) **FREE**

Sea Rim State Park. *Hwy 87, Sabine Pass. 24 miles SW on Hwy 87. Phone 409/971-2559.* Approximately 15,000 acres with a 5 1/2-mile-long beach and some marsh areas. Swimming, fishing; nature trail, picnicking, camping (hook-ups, dump station); primitive beach camping. (Daily) **$**

Special Events

CavOILcade. *1 Plaza Sq, Port Arthur (77642). Phone 409/983-1009.* Festival honoring the oil industry; coronation of queen; carnival, parades, fireworks. Mid-Oct.

Mardi Gras of SE Texas. *Downtown, Port Arthur.* Family event. Parades, carnival, entertainers, food fair. Late Feb.

Mexican Independence Day Festival. *3401 Cultural Center Dr, Port Arthur. Phone 409/724-6134.* Music, children's costume parade, folk dances, food. Sept.

Limited-Service Hotel

★ ★ **HOLIDAY INN.** *2929 Jimmy Johnson Blvd, Port Arthur (77642). Phone 409/724-5000; toll-free 800/*

465-4329; fax 409/724-7644. www.holiday-inn.com.
163 rooms, 4 story. Check-out noon. Restaurant, bar.
Outdoor pool. Airport transportation available. **$**

Port Isabel (F-8)

*See also Brownsville, Harlingen, South Padre Island,
Padre Island National Seashore*

Founded 1790
Population 4,865
Elevation 15 ft
Area Code 956
Zip 78578
Information Chamber of Commerce, 421 E Queen
Isabella Blvd; phone 956/943-2262 or toll-free 800/
527-6102
Web Site www.portisabel.org

This is a fishing, shrimping, and resort town near
the southernmost tip of Texas. The Queen Isabella
Causeway stretches to the town of South Padre Island
(see) via the state's longest bridge (2.6 miles). Port
Isabel has a yacht harbor, marinas, and fishing
charters for the Bay and Gulf.

Special Events

Shrimp Cook-off. *Phone 956/943-2262.* Mid-Oct.

Texas International Fishing Tournament. *Marlin
Marina, 110 W Jefferson St, Port Isabel. Phone 956/943-
8438.* Marlin, tarpon, sailfish, and offshore categories;
bay, tag and release, and junior divisions. Late July-
early Aug.

Restaurant

★ ★ **MARCELLO'S ITALIAN RESTAURANT.**
*110 N Tarnava, Port Isabel (78578). Phone 956/943-
7611; fax 956/943-7200. www.marcellositalian.com.*
Marble fountain at entrance. Italian, seafood menu.
Lunch, dinner. Closed Thanksgiving, Dec 25. Bar.
Children's menu. Casual attire. Reservations recom-
mended. **$$**

Port Lavaca (D-8)

See also Victoria

Founded 1815

Population 12,035
Elevation 22 ft
Area Code 361
Zip 77979
Information Port Lavaca-Calhoun County Chamber
of Commerce, 2300 TX 35 Bypass, PO Box 528; phone
361/552-2959 or toll-free 800/552-7678

Founded by the Spanish in 1815 and established as a
community in 1840, Port Lavaca became an impor-
tant shipping port. In 1856, camels were landed in
nearby Indianola, bound for Camp Verde, Texas. They
had been purchased for the US Army to transport
supplies between forts along the western frontier. The
camel experiment was abandoned following the Civil
War, and the herd was sold to a San Antonio entrepre-
neur.

The great hurricane of 1886 destroyed Indianola, then
the county seat. Port Lavaca became the county seat
but did not regain its importance as a shipping point
until much later. A deepwater port serves the city's
major industries.

What to See and Do

Fishing. In Lavaca Bay (3,200-foot-long pier, lighted
for night fishing) and the Gulf. Charter boats; also a
number of fishing camps in area.

Special Events

Calhoun County Fair. *County Rd 101, Port Lavaca
(77979). Phone 512/552-2959.* Second week in Oct.

Summerfest. Centers on the town's man-made beach.
Beauty pageant, music, evening dances, sports tourna-
ments, and recreational games. Third weekend in
June.

Limited-Service Hotel

★ **BEST WESTERN PORT LAVACA INN.**
*2202 N Hwy 35, Port Lavaca (77979). Phone 361/
553-6800; toll-free 877/686-7900; fax 361/553-6900.
www.bestwestern.com.* 50 rooms, 2 story. Pets accepted.
Complimentary continental breakfast. Check-in 2 pm,
check-out noon. Outdoor pool. **$**

Quanah (F-5)

See also Childress, Vernon

Population 3,022
Elevation 1,568 ft
Area Code 940
Zip 79252
Information Chamber of Commerce, 220 S Main, PO Box 158; phone 940/663-2222
Web Site www.quanahtx.com

Named for Quanah Parker, last great war chief of the Comanche, who was the son of a Comanche chief and Cynthia Ann Parker, a captive girl raised by the Comanche. Today, the town of Quanah is a marketing and shipping point.

What to See and Do

Copper Breaks State Park. *131 Park Rd 62, Quanah. 12 miles S on Hwy 6.* Phone 940/839-4331. Approximately 1,900 acres. Swimming, fishing; hiking, picnicking, playground, primitive and improved camping. Museum of local history with dioramas, artifacts; Texas Longhorn herd. Contact 777 Park Rd 62. (Daily) **$**

Rockport (E-8)

See also Aransas Pass, Corpus Christi, Port Aransas

Founded 1870
Population 7,385
Elevation 6 ft
Area Code 361
Zip 78382
Information Chamber of Commerce, 404 Broadway; phone 361/729-6445 or toll-free 800/242-0071
Web Site www.rockport-fulton.org

With its weathered buildings and wind-twisted trees, this resort town calls to mind a Maine fishing village. Year-round fishing in Aransas Bay and the Gulf, a mile-long sand beach, and water sports add to its attractions. The town is also a haven for artists and bird-watchers.

What to See and Do

Aransas National Wildlife Refuge. *2040 Farm Market Rd, Rockport (77950). 22 miles N on Hwy 35, then 9 miles E on FM 774, then 7 miles SE on FM 2040.* Phone 361/286-3559. southwest.fws.gov/refuges.texas/aransas.html. More than 110,000 acres, includes Matagorda Island overlooking Gulf of Mexico. This is the principal wintering ground for the endangered whooping crane; it also houses deer, alligators, and a variety of birds. Early mornings and late afternoons are best for viewing wildlife. Observation tower; interpretive center; 15-mile auto tour loop; nature trails. Wheelchair access to observation tower (ramps). Contact Refuge Manager, PO Box 100, Austwell 77950. (Daily 8:30 am-4:30 pm; closed Thanksgiving, Dec 25) Nearest gas 14 miles. **$$**

Beaches. *N end of downtown on Hwy 35 Business.* **Rockport.** Sand beach, park, ski and yacht basins, boat launch, bird sanctuary. **Fulton.** *3 miles N on Hwy 35.* Yacht basin, boat launch, 1,000-foot fishing pier, sand beach.

Boat trips. *Rockport Harbor, Rockport (77950).* Phone 361/729-4855. Into Aransas National Wildlife Refuge. Bird-watching, sightseeing, and photography tours. *Wharf Cat* leaves Rockport Harbor (Nov-Mar). **$$$$**

Center for the Arts. *902 Navigation Cir, Rockport.* Phone 361/729-5519. www.rockportartcenter.org. Restored Victorian home hosts shows from sporting art to modern expression. (Tues-Sat 10 am-4 pm, Sun 1-4 pm) **FREE**

Copano Bay Causeway. *5 miles N on Hwy 35.* Phone 361/729-8633. Fishing piers, boating (ramp); picnicking. Some fees.

Fulton Mansion State Historic Site. *317 Fulton Beach Rd, Fulton (78358). Between Fulton and Rockport via Hwy 35; turn E on Henderson St.* Phone 361/729-0386. www.tpwd.state.tx.us/park/fulton. This Second Empire/Victorian mansion overlooking Aransas Bay was built in the mid-1870s. The first and second floors are authentically furnished, and the spacious lawns slope toward the beach. (Wed-Sun; closed Dec 25) **$**

Goose Island. *202 Palmetto Ave, Rockport. 10 miles NE on Hwy 35, then E on Park Rd 13, partly on mainland and partly on nearby islands.* Phone 361/729-2858. Swimming permitted, lighted fishing pier, boating (ramp); picnicking, bird-watching, improved campsites. (Daily) **$$**

Texas Maritime Museum. *1202 Navigation Cir, Rockport. At Rockport Harbor.* Phone 361/729-1271. www.texasmaritimemuseum.org. Explores Texas's seafaring history, from early Spanish discovery, through Texas independence, emergence of river trade, Civil

War blockade-running, and growth of fishing and offshore drilling industries. (Tues-Sat 10 am-4 pm, Sun 1-4 pm; closed holidays) **FREE**

Special Events

Hummer/Bird Celebration. *404 Broadway St, Rockport (78382). Phone 361/729-6445.* Sept.

OysterFest. *402 Fulton Beach Rd, Rockport. Phone 361/729-2388.* Food and music. First weekend in Mar.

SeaFair Rockport. *404 Broadway St, Rockport. Phone 361/729-6445.* Columbus Day weekend.

Texas State Kite Festival. *404 Broadway, Rockport (78382). Phone 361/729-6445; toll-free 800/826-6441. www.rockport-fulton.org.* Texas's most colorful aerial display happens each year at the Texas State Kite Festival. Scheduled in conjunction with the state kite-flying championships, the event gives spectators amazing displays of showmanship and athletic skill. Kite flyers ranging in age from 8 to 80 show their prowess at single, dual, and quad line kite-flying in individual, team, and pair competitions—precision and ballet. Chinese fighter kites battle for dominance of the air and on the ground, and kite buggy races are held. Creative kite craftspeople display homemade kites competing to win titles in the Largest Kite, Highest Flying Kite, and Most Unusual Kite categories. Kite workshops are included for kids. Call the Rockport Chamber of Commerce for the current schedule of events. Mid-May.

Limited-Service Hotel

★ **BEST WESTERN INN BY THE BAY.** *3902 Hwy 35 N, Fulton (78358). Phone 361/729-8351; toll-free 800/235-6076; fax 361/729-0950. www.bestwestern.com.* 72 rooms, 2 story. Pets accepted; fee. Complimentary full breakfast. Check-out 11 am. Outdoor pool. **$**

🐾 🏞

Restaurant

★ **DUCK INN.** *701 Hwy 35 N, Rockport (78382). Phone 361/729-6663; fax 361/729-3824.* American, seafood menu. Breakfast, lunch, dinner, brunch. Closed Mon; also one week in Sept and week of Dec 25. Bar. Casual attire. **$$**

🅳

Rusk (B-9)

See also Jacksonville, Nacogdoches, Palestine

Population 5,085
Elevation 489 ft
Area Code 903
Zip 75785
Information Chamber of Commerce, 415 N Main St, PO Box 67; phone 903/683-4242
Web Site www.rusktx.com

Rusk was a supply center for salt, iron ore, and lumber during the Civil War. Oil production began in 1914; fruit, vegetables, and dairy products are handled here. Many old houses have been restored. A 546-foot wooden footbridge (1861) is thought to be the longest in the nation.

What to See and Do

Jim Hogg State Historical Park. *Reklaw Hwy, Rusk. 2 miles NE off Hwy 84. Phone 903/683-4850.* Approximately 170 acres. "Mountain Home" plantation; replica of the pioneer home of Governor Hogg and his family. Family cemetery, trails. Picnicking, playground. Flowering trees. (Fri-Sun; closed Dec 25) **$**

Rusk-Palestine State Park. *Park Rd 76, Rusk. 3 miles W on Hwy 84. Phone 903/683-5126.* Includes a 15-acre lake, tennis courts, picnic area, and campsites. (Daily) **$** Also here is

Texas State Railroad Historical Park. *2503 W 6th St, Rusk. Phone 903/683-2561.* Four-hour round-trip excursions aboard turn-of-the-century steam-powered train to Palestine (see). Tour through locomotive cab before departure; slide show. Also runs from Palestine. (Summer: Mon, Thurs-Sun; spring and fall: Sat-Sun only) Advance reservations recommended. Camping adjacent (full hook-ups). **$$$$**

Salado (C-8)

See also Georgetown, Temple

Population 3,475
Elevation 520 ft
Area Code 254
Zip 76571

Information Chamber of Commerce, PO Box 849; phone 254/947-5040
Web Site www.salado.com

What to See and Do

Stillhouse Hollow Lake. *3740 FM 1670, Salado (76513). Approximately 5 miles NW on FM 1670. Phone 254/939-2461.* Swimming, fishing, boating (ramps, storage); picnicking, concession, primitive and improved camping (fee). Fee for some recreation areas. (Daily) **FREE**

Special Event

Art Fair. *Pace Park, 601 N Main St, Salado. Phone 254/947-5040.* First full weekend in Aug.

Full-Service Hotel

★ ★ **STAGECOACH INN.** *1 Main St, Salado (76571). Phone 254/947-5111; toll-free 800/732-8994; fax 254/947-0671. www.stagecoach-inn.com.* On Salado Creek. 82 rooms, 2 story. Check-in 3 pm, check-out noon. Two restaurants, bar. Outdoor pool, whirlpool. Tennis. **$**

Restaurants

★ ★ **SALADO MANSION.** *128 S Main St, Salado (76571). Phone 254/947-5157; fax 254/947-5019. www.saladomansion.com.* Built in 1857 for a judge; antiques displayed. Southwestern menu. Lunch, dinner. Closed Thanksgiving, Dec 25. Bar. Children's menu. Casual attire. Reservations recommended. Outdoor seating. **$$**

★ **STAGECOACH INN DINING ROOM.** *1 Main St, Salado (76571). Phone 254/947-9400; fax 254/947-0671. www.stagecoach-inn.com.* Former stagecoach stop; Early-American décor. American menu. Lunch, dinner. Bar. Casual attire. Reservations recommended. **$$**

San Angelo (B-6)

Founded 1867
Population 88,439
Elevation 1,847 ft
Area Code 915
Information Chamber of Commerce, 500 Rio Concho

Dr, 76903; phone 915/655-4136
Web Site www.sanangelo-tx.com

From its beginnings as a lawless frontier village and the site of one of the last Indian Wars forts, San Angelo has become a regional trade center complemented by a diversified economy. While ranching and farming predominate, the city's economy is also based on education, health care, tourism, and recreation. San Angelo is where the North and South Concho rivers combine to form the Concho River; visitors enjoy strolling along the River Walk or in the numerous nearby parks.

What to See and Do

Fishing and boating. *Lake Nasworthy, 6 miles SW on Knickerbocker Rd. Twin Buttes Lake, 5 miles W of city, off Hwy 67. San Angelo State Park, 4 miles N on Arden Rd, off Mercedes St. North, Middle, and South Concho rivers.*

Fort Concho National Historic Landmark. *630 S Oakes, San Angelo. Downtown near Concho River. Phone 915/481-2646. www.fortconcho.com.* Indian Wars fort comprising of 21 restored stone buildings on 40 acres. Museum covers infantry, cavalry, artillery, and civilian life during fort's active period (1867-1889). Visitor center on corner of Avenue C and South Oakes. (Tues-Sat 10 am-5 pm, Sun 1-5 pm; closed holidays) **$**

San Angelo State Park. *FM 2288, San Angelo (76901). Just W of town off of FM 2288. Phone 915/949-4757.* Swimming, water-skiing, fishing, boating (ramps); nature, bicycle, and jogging trails; picnicking, camping (tent and trailer sites) at Dry Creek and Red Arroyo. Two off-road vehicle areas. Fees for some activities. (Daily) **$**

Special Event

Texas Wine & Food Festival. *El Paseo de Santa Angela, San Angelo. Phone 915/653-6793.* Apr.

Limited-Service Hotels

★ ★ **HOLIDAY INN.** *441 Rio Concho Dr, San Angelo (76903). Phone 325/658-2828; toll-free 800/465-4329; fax 325/658-8741. www.holiday-inn.com.* This high rise features not only convention and meeting spaces, but also recreational facilities. 148 rooms, 6 story. Pets accepted; fee. Check-out noon. Restaurant, bar. Indoor pool, whirlpool. **$**

★ **INN OF THE CONCHOS.** *2021 N Bryant Hwy 87 N, San Angelo (76903). Phone 915/658-2811; toll-free 800/621-6091; fax 915/653-7560. www.inn-of-the-conchos.com.* 125 rooms, 2 story. Pets accepted. Check-out noon. Bar. Outdoor pool. **$**

★ **LA QUINTA INN.** *2307 Loop 306, San Angelo (76904). Phone 325/949-0515; toll-free 800/687-6667; fax 325/944-1187. www.lq.com.* 170 rooms, 2 story. Pets accepted, some restrictions. Complimentary continental breakfast. Check-out noon. Outdoor pool. **$**

Restaurant

★ ★ **ZENTNER'S DAUGHTER STEAK HOUSE.** *1901 Knickerbocker Rd, San Angelo (76904). Phone 915/949-2821; fax 915/949-4705.* Steak menu. Lunch, dinner. Closed Thanksgiving, Dec 25. Bar. **$$**

San Antonio (D-7)

See also Austin, Bandera, Kerrville, New Braunfels, Natural Bridge Caverns, Seguin

Founded 1718
Population 1,144,646
Elevation 701 ft
Area Code 210
Information Convention & Visitors Bureau, 203 S St. Mary's St, PO Box 2277, 78298; phone 210/207-6700 or toll-free 800/447-3372
Web Site www.sanantoniocvb.com

In the course of its colorful history, this beautiful old city has been under six flags: France, Spain, Mexico, the Republic of Texas, Confederate States of America, and United States of America. Each has definitely left its mark.

The Mission San Antonio de Valero (the Alamo) was founded by Friar Antonio de San Buenaventura Olivares in May, 1718, near the tree-lined San Antonio River. Four more missions were built along the river during the next 13 years. All continued to operate until about 1794. In 1718, Don Martin de Alarcon, Captain General and Governor of the Province of Texas, established a military post here. San Antonio has been a military center ever since.

The Alamo is in the center of town. Here, from February 23 to March 6, 1836, Davy Crockett, Colonel James Bowie, Colonel William B. Travis, and 186 other Texans stood off General Antonio López de Santa Anna, dictator-president of Mexico, and his 5,000 men. Nearly every defender died in the battle. Their heroic stand was the inspiration for the famous Texas battle cry "Remember the Alamo!" Three months after the Alamo tragedy, San Antonio was almost deserted. Within a few years, however, it became a great Western outpost. In the 1840s, there was a heavy influx of Germans whose descendants still add to the city's cosmopolitan air. In the 1870s, new settlers, adventurers, and cowboys on long cattle drives made this a tough, hard-drinking, hard-fighting, gambling town. San Antonio has evolved into a modern, prosperous city, but it retains much of the flavor of its past.

Additional Visitor Information

The Visitor Information Center has many helpful leaflets; contact 317 Alamo Plaza, 78205; 210/270-8748. For further information contact the Convention & Visitors Bureau, PO Box 2277, 78298; phone toll-free 210/207-6700 or 800/447-3372. San Antonio Conservation Society, 107 King William St, 78204, 210/224-6163, provides brochures for a walking tour of the King William Historic District.

Public Transportation

Buses, trolleys (Metropolitan Transit Authority), phone 210/362-2020

Airport **San Antonio International Airport**; cash machines, Terminals 1 and 2

Information Phone 210/207-3411

Lost and Found Phone 210/207-3451

What to See and Do

Alamodome. *100 Montana St, San Antonio (78203). Just E of HemisFair Park, across I-37. Phone 210/207-3663; toll-free 800/884-3663. www.sanantonio.gov/dome.* This multipurpose dome boasts a cable-suspended roof, which is anchored from four concrete towers. The sports, concert, and convention center employs 160,000 gross square feet of exhibit space and 30,000 square feet of conference space, with configurations for basketball, hockey, football, and major concerts (maximum seating 73,200). Guided tours include executive suites, locker rooms, mechanical features, and the playing field (phone for schedule). **$$**

Brackenridge Park. *3910 N Saint Mary's St, San Antonio (78212). N Broadway (Hwy 81), 2 miles N of the Alamo. Phone 210/207-8000.* This 340-acre park has picnicking, playground, athletic fields, golf, carousel, miniature train, pedal boats. Some fees. (Daily 5 am-11 pm) **FREE** Also here are

Japanese Tea Gardens. *3800 N Saint Mary's St, San Antonio (78212). Phone 210/821-3120.* Floral displays on walls and floor of abandoned quarry. Outdoor Grecian theater is also here. (Daily dawn-dusk) **FREE**

Pioneer Memorial Hall. *3805 Broadway, San Antonio (78209). Phone 210/822-9011.* Houses collections of Texas trail drivers, pioneers, and the Texas Rangers. Saddles, guns, tools, furniture, and other memorabilia illustrate the lifestyle of early Texans. (Mon-Sat 11 am-4 pm, Sun from noon) **$$**

San Antonio Zoo. *3903 N Saint Mary's St, San Antonio (78212). Phone 210/734-7184. www.sazoo.org.* Get up close and personal with more than 40 lories—colorful medium-sized parrots from Australia—at the zoo's Lory Landing. The friendly birds range in color from scarlet and green to royal blue and fiery orange—so social that they flock close, landing on visitors' shoulders and even their heads. (Encourage them with a little lory nectar (fee), available from the zoo concession stand.) Beyond birds, you can visit more than 3,500 animals of 750 species here, making this one of the largest zoos in the United States. At the African Hill—a microcosm of life as it might be encountered on the African plains—look for ostriches, zebras, giraffes, cranes, ducks, gazelles, and antelope. Farther on, visit the lushly planted Amazonia exhibit, including more than 30 species of tropical animals. There are large and small cats, venomous reptiles, tamarins, and marmosets, as well as bats, fish, and birds. The Pad is another popular zoo location, with 17 habitats for amphibians including salamanders, horned frogs, poison dart frogs, and toads. (Memorial Day-Labor Day: daily 9 am-6 pm; Labor Day-Memorial Day: daily 9 am-5 pm) **$$**

Witte Museum. *3801 Broadway, San Antonio (78209). At Tuleta St. Phone 210/357-1900. www.wittemuseum.org.* History, science, and the humanities collections and exhibits. Special at-

tractions include "Ancient Texans: Rock Art and Lifeways Along the Lower Pecos" and "Texas Wild: Ecology Illustrated." On the museum grounds are four reconstructed early Texas houses. Changing exhibits. Free admission Tues 3-9 pm. (Mon, Wed-Sat 10 am-5 pm; Tues to 9 pm; Sun noon-5 pm; closed Thanksgiving, Dec 24-25; also the third Mon in Oct) **$$**

Buckhorn Saloon and Museum. *318 E Houston St, San Antonio (78205). Phone 210/247-4000. buckhornmuseum.com.* Buckhorn Hall of Horns houses a vast collection of horns, animal trophies, and memorabilia dating to 1881. Also Hall of Fins and Feathers, a collection of birds, fish, and marine life. Buckhorn Saloon and O. Henry House. Hall of Texas History depicts memorable periods from 1534 to 1898. (Memorial Day-Labor Day: daily 10 am-6 pm; Labor Day-Memorial Day: 10 am-5 pm; closed Thanksgiving, Dec 25) **$$**

Cascade Caverns Park. *226 Cascade Caverns Rd, Boerne (78015). 14 miles NW on I-10, exit 543 Cascade Caverns Rd, then W and follow signs. Phone 830/755-8080. www.cascadecaverns.com.* Located on a 105-acre park is a water-formed underground cavern with spectacular rock formations. A special feature of this natural attraction is a 100-foot underground waterfall, viewed as the grand finale of a 45-minute guided tour. The park has picnic facilities. (Memorial Day-Labor Day: daily 9 am-6 pm; Labor Day-Mar: Sat-Sun 10 am-4 pm; Mar-Memorial Day: Mon-Fri 10 am-4 pm, Sat-Sun 9 am-5 pm) **$$$**

Coach USA bus tours. *217 Alamo Plz, Suite B, San Antonio (78205). Phone toll-free 800/472-9546. www.coachusa.com.* Tours include the Alamo & Mission Trail (3 1/2 hours), Texas Hill Country Escape (9 hours), Shopping in Nuevo Laredo, Mexico (10 hours), and San Antonio Sampler (3 1/2 hours). (Call or check Web site for days and departure times) **$$$$**

Fort Sam Houston Museum and National Historic Landmark. *3600 Fort Sam, San Antonio (78201). Off I-35, Walters St exit. Phone 210/221-1211.* Fort Sam Houston is headquarters for both the US Fifth Army and Brooke Army Medical Center. Museum depicts history of fort and US Army in this region from 1845 to the present. Exhibits of uniforms, equipment, and photographs detail growth of the post and events that occurred here. Audiovisual exhibits. More than 900 historic structures on base represent the era 1876-1935; the historic quadrangle once detained Geronimo and his renegade Apaches; self-guided tours. (Wed-Sun 10 am-4 pm; closed holidays) **FREE**

Institute of Texan Cultures. *801 S Bowie St, San Antonio (78205). In HemisFair Park. Phone 210/458-2300. www. texancultures.utsa.edu/public/index.htm.* Exhibits depicting lives and contributions of the people of Texas. Multimedia presentation (four shows daily); part of the University of Texas at San Antonio. (Tues-Wed 10 am-6 pm, Thurs-Sat to 8 pm, Sun noon-5 pm; closed holidays, Thanksgiving, Dec 24-25) Parking (fee). **$$**

McNay Art Museum. *6000 N New Braunfels, San Antonio (78209). At Austin Hwy. Phone 210/824-5368. www.mcnayart.org.* Includes Gothic, medieval, late 19th- and 20th-century American and European paintings; sculpture, graphic arts; rare books on theater arts, architecture, and fine arts; changing exhibits (some fees). Patio with fountains; gardens. (Tues-Sat 10 am-5 pm, Sun from noon; closed holidays) **FREE**

Plaza Wax Museum/Ripley's Believe It or Not! *301 Alamo Plz, San Antonio (78205). Phone 210/224-9299. www.plazawaxmuseum.com/flash/default.asp.* Wax museum with more than 225 historical and entertainment figures; horror chamber. In the same building, Ripley's museum with more than 500 exhibits of the strange and bizarre. (Mon-Thurs 9:30 am-6 pm, Fri-Sun 9 am-7 pm) **$$$**

Rivercenter Mall. *849 Commerce St, San Antonio (78205). Phone 210/225-0000. www.shoprivercenter.com.* Located steps away from the Alamo on San Antonio's famed Riverwalk, Rivercenter Mall welcomes visitors with several unique attractions. Enjoy daily free entertainment from strolling musicians at indoor/outdoor dining venues (both casual and upscale) encircling Rivercenter's Lagoon. There are more than 125 shops and restaurants—everything from Dillard's and Foleys to Heavenly Hands and Godiva Chocolatier. Open and airy with glass walls, marble floors, and fiesta color (purple, orange, turquoise) accents, the mall keeps the river as its focal point. Parking is free for two hours with a validated ticket. (Mon-Sat 10 am-9 pm, Sun noon-6 pm; closed Easter) **FREE**

San Antonio Botanical Gardens. *555 Funston Pl, San Antonio (78029). At N New Braunfels Ave. Phone 210/207-3255. www.sabot.org.* Thirty-three acres include formal gardens, Japanese garden, rose garden, herb gardens, xeriscape gardens, garden for the visually impaired. Native Texas area features lake, native flora, and 1800s dwellings. Lucile Halsell Conservatory is a complex of five glass exhibition greenhouses. Self-guided tours. (Daily 9 am-5 pm; closed Jan 1, Dec 25) **$**

San Antonio Missions National Historical Park. *2202 Roosevelt Ave, San Antonio (78210). Phone 210/534-8833 (headquarters). www.nps.gov/saan.* Four Spanish colonial missions in San Antonio are administered by the National Park Service, with exhibits, talks, and cultural demonstrations. Parishes within the missions are still active. (Daily 9 am-5 pm; closed Jan 1, Thanksgiving, Dec 25) **FREE**

Espada Aqueduct. (1735) This 120-foot-long Spanish colonial aqueduct carried water over Piedras Creek continuously for more than 200 years. Nearby farms still use water from this system. Return to Espada Road South, turn right to Ashley, and turn right again on Roosevelt Avenue to return to San Antonio.

Espada Dam. (1740) Constructed to divert river water into irrigation ditches. Waters flow into Espada Aqueduct (see), which carries water to Mission Espada. Continue on Padre Drive (through low-water crossing) through Villamain to

Mission Concepcion. *807 Mission Rd, San Antonio (78210). Phone 210/534-1540.* Established in 1731, this is one of the best preserved missions in Texas and the oldest unrestored stone mission church in the country. It is built of porous limestone found nearby. There are some fine 18th-century frescoes; the acoustics of the building are remarkable. (Daily; closed Jan 1, Thanksgiving, Dec 25)

Mission Espada. *10040 Espada Rd, San Antonio (78214). Phone 210/627-2021.* (1731) Southernmost of the San Antonio chain of missions. Unusual arched doorway. Friary and chapel (except for façade) are restored. (Daily 9 am-5 pm)

Mission San Jose. *6539 San Jose Dr, San Antonio (78214). Phone 210/932-1001.* (1720) One of the largest and most successful missions in the Southwest; the church, Native American quarters, granary, and old mill have been restored. Built of tufaceous limestone, the church is famous for its carvings and masonry. The sacristy window is sometimes referred to as "Rosa's Window." Follow Napier Ave, right on Padre Dr and through underpass to Espada park. (Daily 9 am-5 pm; closed Jan 1, Thanksgiving, Dec 25)

Mission San Juan. *9101 Graf Rd, San Antonio (78214). Phone 210/534-0749.* (1731) A self-sufficient community was centered around this mission. Indian artisans and farmers established a trade network with their surplus. (Daily 9 am-5 pm)

San Antonio Museum of Art. *200 W Jones Ave, San Antonio (78215). Phone 210/978-8158. www.sa-museum.org.* An art museum in a former brewery? It works—especially given the beauty of the 1884 brick structure. Opened in 1981, this art museum is known for its Greek and Roman collection, Asian Art, Latin American and folk art, and American paintings. The latter collection includes landscapes and portraits dating from the Colonial Period to the early 20th century. Collections include more than 3,000 objects including Egyptian antiquities, ancient glass, classical sculptures, and more. The Nelson A. Rockefeller Center for Latin American Art includes pre-Columbian, Spanish Colonial, and Latin American Folk art. The museum has its own café, open from 9:30 am to 3:30 pm (Wed-Sat 10 am-5 pm, Third Thurs 10 am-8 pm, Sun noon-6 pm; closed holidays) **FREE**

San Antonio Spurs (NBA). *SBC Center, 1 SBC Center, San Antonio (78219). Phone 210/554-7700.* Established in 1967 as the Dallas Chaparrals, the team was rechristened the San Antonio Spurs in 1973. They are 1999 and 2003 NBA champions. **$$$$**

San Antonio Symphony. *228 E Houston St, San Antonio (78205). Phone 210/554-1010. www.sasymphony.org.* Making music accessible to many tastes, the San Antonio Symphony's 39-week season (Sept-May) includes more than 100 concerts—26 POPS concerts, 32 classical concerts, and special interactive Sunday events for families with young children. There are also nine seasonal events, including holiday performances of *The Nutcracker*, and, on New Year's Eve, *Night in Old Vienna*. Concerts are performed at the Majestic, a stunning vintage theater in downtown San Antonio. After three years without a resident conductor, the symphony welcomed new music director Larry Rachleff for its 2003-04 season. Featured headliners at the symphony include pianist Andre Watts and violinist Pinchas Zukerman. **$$$$**

SeaWorld San Antonio. *10500 SeaWorld Dr, San Antonio (78251). At the intersection of Ellison Dr and Westover Hills Blvd, just off Hwy 151 between Loop 410 and Loop 1604, 16 miles NW of downtown San Antonio. Numerous directional signs are visible. Phone 210/523-3000. www.buschgardens.com/seaworld/tx.* The world's largest marine life adventure park and family entertainment venue, SeaWorld San Antonio includes four parks within its 250 acres. There are animal attractions, rides, slides, and shows ranging from "The Steel Eel" (billed as the Southwest's first hypercoaster) to "Fools with Tools," a comic sea lion adventure poking fun at do-it-yourselfers. Visitors can also touch and feed Atlantic bottle-nose dolphins, feed sea lions and seals, encounter penguins, and observe killer whale behaviors. SeaWorld's "Viva!" show combines the fluid movements of synchronized swimmers, professional high divers, and aerialists with the antics of Pacific white-sided dolphins and beluga whales. For an additional fee, you can add behind-the-scenes visits with sharks and stingrays or learn all about belugas in the educational beluga interaction program. The Sea Star Theater is where patrons don 3-D glasses to maximize visual effects, and speakers are synchronized to shoot air and water during the show. (Mar-Nov: park opens at 10 am; closing times vary) **$$$$**

Six Flags Fiesta Texas. *17000 I-10 W, San Antonio (78257). At jct Loop 410. Phone 210/697-5050. www.sixflags.com.* A 200-acre amusement park dramatically set in a former limestone quarry. Four themed areas—Spassburg (German), Los Festivales (Hispanic), Crackaxle Canyon (Western), and Rockville (1950s)—arranged around central Texas Square, highlight live entertainment productions on seven theater stages. Features include the aeroflight thrill ride, *Dornrschen;* an early 1900s-style carousel; and *Kinderspielplatz,* a major area devoted to children's rides and amusements. Many restaurants and shops. (Mid-late Mar and Memorial Day weekend-Labor Day weekend: daily; late Mar-late May and early Sept-early Nov: Fri-Sun; hours vary) **$$$$**

Southwest School of Art & Craft. *300 Augusta, San Antonio (78205). On grounds of Old Ursuline Academy and Convent (1848). Phone 210/224-1848. www.swschool.org.* Offers adult studio programs in such fields as ceramics, painting, drawing, and photography; young artists programs; exhibitions highlighting the works of local and national artists as well as students (Mon-Sat 9 am-5 pm, Sun 11 am-4 pm); public programs that include lectures, conferences, and musical performances; and the visitors center museum, a Texas Historic Landmark on the National Register of Historic Places, which presents the history of the school (Mon-Sat 9 am-5 pm, Sun 11 am-4 pm; closed holidays). **FREE**

Splashtown. *3600 N I-35, San Antonio (78219). I-35 at exit 160. Phone 210/227-1400. www.splashtownsa.com.* An 18-acre water recreation theme park with 17 rides and attractions, including wave pool, slide complexes, and large children's play area. Changing rooms, showers, lockers, rafts available. (Apr-mid-Sept; days and hours vary) **$$$**

Steves Homestead. *509 King William St, San Antonio (78204). Phone 210/225-5924.* (1876) Victorian-era mansion on banks of the San Antonio River in the King William Historic District. Period furnishings; landscaped grounds have carriage house, stable, wash house. Tours available. (Daily 10 am-4:15 pm) **$**

Sunset Station. *1174 E Commerce, San Antonio (78205). Phone 210/222-9481. www.sunset-station.com.* This restored 1902 train depot serves as a downtown entertainment destination with live music clubs, restaurants, and shopping. Call for an event schedule.

Texas Adventure. *307 Alamo Plz, San Antonio (78205). Phone 210/227-0388. www.texasadventure.com.* Multimedia show portraying the story of Texas independence with the Alamo drama as its centerpiece. Computerized technology with digital 3-D images and the 4,800-watt stereo sound system make the 1836 battle come alive with fire, blasting cannons, and other sounds of battle. (Winter: daily 10 am-8 pm; summer: daily 10 am-10 pm) **$$$**

Tower of the Americas. *HemisFair Park, 600 HemisFair Park, San Antonio (78205). Phone 210/207-8615.* Stands 750 feet high; observation level at 579 feet; glass-walled elevators. Revolving restaurant at 550-foot level. (Sun-Thurs 9 am-10 pm, Fri-Sat to 11 pm) **$**

VIA Streetcar. *1021 San Pedro Ave, San Antonio (78212). Phone 210/362-2020. www.riverwalkguide.com.* A reproduction of a rail streetcar that traveled the streets of San Antonio during the 1920s. The downtown route includes St. Paul's Square, the King William District, Market Square, and Alamo Plaza. (Mon-Fri 7 am-6 pm, Sat 9 am-2 pm) **$**

Vietnam War Memorial. *In front of Municipal Auditorium, at the corner of E Martin and Jefferson sts.* This memorial depicts a scene from the Battle for Hill 881 South—a radioman calling for help for a wounded comrade.

⭐ **Walking tour.** Start at east side of Alamo Plaza (south of E Houston St, north of Crockett St, and east of N Alamo). Visit

The Alamo. *300 Alamo Plz, San Antonio (78299). Phone 210/225-1391. www.thealamo.org.* No place in America has come to symbolize courage for the cause of liberty more strongly than the Alamo. This old mission, San Antonio de Valero (established in San Antonio in 1718), was the spot at which a small band of Texans—including legendary figures such as James Bowie, Davy Crockett, and William B. Travis—held out for 13 days against the centrist army of General Antonio Lopez de Santa Anna. Although the Alamo fell on the morning of March 6, 1836, the legacy of the courageous Alamo Defenders lives on. More than 2.5 million visitors come to the Alamo each year. Located on Alamo Plaza in downtown San Antonio, its three buildings span 300 years of history. Managed by the Daughters of the Republic of Texas since 1905, the 4.2-acre complex includes the Shrine, Long Barrack Museum, Gift Museum, and gardens. (Mon-Sat 9 am-5:30 pm, Sun from 10 am; closed Dec 24-25) **FREE**

Arneson River Theatre. *418 Villita St, San Antonio (78205). Phone 210/207-8610.* The audience sits on one side of the river; the stage is on the other. Climb the steps through the theater and go through the arch. Performances include plays and musical performances.

Casa Navarro State Historical Park. *228 S Laredo St, San Antonio. Phone 210/226-4801. www.tpwol.state.tx.us/park/jose/feecasa.htm.* Complex of three limestone and adobe houses built circa 1850; home of a Texas patriot. Period furnishings; exhibits and documents. Tours. (Wed-Sun 10 am-4 pm) **$**

Cos House. *418 Villita St, San Antonio. Phone 210 207 8610.* Here, on Dec 10, 1835, General Perfecto de Cos signed the Articles of Capitulation after Texans had taken the town.

HemisFair Park. *222 HemisFair Park, San Antonio (78205). Bounded by Alamo, Bowie, Market, and Durango sts. Phone 210/207-8572. www.sanantoniocvb.com.* Among the 68 buildings that remain are the Tower of the Americas and the Institute of Texan Cultures. Also here are the Henry B. Gonzalez Convention Center and Theater for the Performing Arts, an urban water park, shops, and restaurants. Turn left (west) on Market Street to the river. (Daily 8 am-11 pm) **FREE**

La Villita. *418 Villita St, San Antonio (78205). South of Paseo de La Villita, west of S Alamo St, north of Nueva St, and east of S Presa St. Phone 210/207-8610. www.lavillita.com.* This 250-year-old Spanish settlement was reconstructed during 1939 to preserve its unique buildings. A haven in the midst of the city where the old arts and crafts continue to flourish, the area has three patios where various functions and festivals are held. (Daily 10 am-6 pm; closed Jan 1, Thanksgiving, Dec 25)

Market Square. *514 W Commerce St, San Antonio (78207). Phone 210/207-8600. tavernini.com/mercado.* Dating to the late 1890s, San Antonio's Market Square is a colorful, bustling, two-block district of shops, restaurants, and art galleries. Best known are El Mercado—the largest Mexican goods emporium outside of Mexico—and, next door, the Farmer's Market Plaza Building. Here, shoppers can browse more than 80 stores that offer such items as Southwestern arts and crafts and worldwide imports. In addition to shopping, the Square hosts 14 different festivals throughout the year, ranging from Dia de los Muertos (Day of the Dead) to Freedom Fest, a Mexican-flavored Independence Day celebration. The Square's two best-known restaurants are Mi Tierra, famous since the 1940s for authentic Mexican cuisine, and La Marguerita, specializing in many varieties of fajitas. Soon to come: Museo Americano, a museum the city is launching with the Smithsonian to celebrate and promote Latino arts and culture. (Daily; closed holidays)

Menger Hotel. *204 Alamo Plz, San Antonio (78205). Phone toll-free 210/223-4361. www.historicmenger.com.* A famous hostelry in which Robert E. Lee, Theodore Roosevelt, and William Jennings Bryan stayed. The bar where Roosevelt recruited his "Rough Riders" is still in use. (Daily 24 hours)

Military Plaza. City Hall stands in the center; on the northwest corner is a statue of Moses Austin, often called the Father of Texas.

Paseo del Rio. *213 Broadway St, San Antonio (78205). Phone 210/227-4262.* This 2 1/2-mile "River Walk" along the meandering San Antonio River is lined with colorful shops, galleries, hotels, popular nightspots, and many sidewalk cafés. Water taxis provide transportation. To the west, a short distance from the Tower Life Building exit, is Main Plaza.

San Fernando Cathedral. *115 W Main Plz, San Antonio (78205). Phone 210/227-1297.* The original parish church of Canary Islands settlers.

Spanish Governor's Palace. *105 Plaza de Armas, San Antonio. Phone 210/224-0601.* (1749) Note date and Hapsburg crest in the keystone. This was the office and residence of Spanish administrators. (Daily; closed Jan 1, Thanksgiving, Dec 25; also Fiesta Fri and two weeks following) **$**

Special Events

Boerne Berges Fest. *30 miles NW on I-10, in Boerne, 1 Main Plz, San Antonio. Phone 830/249-4773.* German Festival of the Hills; continuous German and country and western entertainment, arts and crafts, horse races, pig races, parade, 10K walk, special events. Father's Day weekend.

Dawn at The Alamo. *300 Alamo Plz, San Antonio (78299). Phone 210/225-1391.* Early Mar.

Diez y Seis. *1327 Guadalupe St, San Antonio. Phone 210/223-3151.* Citywide. Three days of celebration mark the Sept 16 Mexican independence from Spain. Includes a gala, Market Square celebrations, parade, festivals, dance presentations, and charreadas (rodeos). Mid-Sept.

Fiesta San Antonio. *Phone 210/227-5191; toll-free 877/723-4378. www.fiesta-sa.org.* Floats that really float, a battle of flowers, and an illuminated night parade—they're all part of Fiesta, a nine-day party in the streets of San Antonio held to honor the heroes from the battles of the Alamo and San Jacinto and to celebrate the city's diversity. Buoyant floats are the feature in the Texas Cavalier's parade down the San Antonio River that kicks off the Fiesta, which has been going on for more than 110 years. A second parade, The Battle of Flowers, is a colorful, modern-day adaptation of an 1891 event, and the illuminated Fiesta Flambeau is the largest parade of its kind in the United States. But Fiesta's much more than that—there's an arts and crafts fair; a week's worth of nightly entertainment; international cuisine in La Villita, San Antonio's restored 17th-century village; a street fair in the Victorian charm of downtown's King William historic district; and almost constant musical performances, sporting competitions, and other events. Fiesta del Mercado is another focal point, featuring live entertainment on six stages. Fees vary with event. Mid-late Apr.

Fiestas Navidenas. *Market Sq, 514 W Commerce St, San Antonio. Phone 210/207-8600.* Christmas festival;

bands; Mexican folk dances; Christmas foods. Late Nov-mid-Dec.

Las Posadas. *River Walk, 107 King William, San Antonio. Phone 210/224-6163.* Procession assembles at La Mansion del Rio Hotel (see FULL-SERVICE HOTELS). Song and candlelight procession has been a tradition for more than 250 years. Held in conjunction with Fiesta de las Luminarias, the fiesta of lights, when the River Walk is lined with candles. Reenactment of the Holy Family's search for an inn. Evening ends with piñata party in Plaza Juárez in La Villita. Mid-Dec.

San Antonio New World Wine and Food Festival. *Phone 210/930-3232. www.newworldwinefood.org.* Sailing into San Antonio in time for Columbus Day, the city's celebrated New World Wine and Food Festival celebrates the wines and cuisines of the Americas, with the accent on Nuevo Latino fare. Sample culinary creations from talented chefs—both seasoned professionals and rising stars. Taste the best of both old-world and new-world wines at luncheons, dinners, tastings, and seminars. The festival's events take place at an assortment of high-profile restaurants downtown. Fees for events vary. Mid-Oct.

San Antonio Stock Show & Rodeo. *3201 E Houston St, San Antonio (78219). Phone 210/225-5851. www.sarodeo.com.* You've heard of steer wrestling and bull riding, but what about mutton busting? The event—where kids ages 4 to 7 hang on to a hank of wool and try to stay on the back of a sheep for six seconds with a little panache and style—is one highlight of many at the San Antonio Stock Show & Rodeo. The event, which has been going on for more than 50 years, is now held at SBC Center, giving the rodeo 6,500 seats more than were offered at its previous venue. That's more room for you and your family to enjoy events, including the traditional seven: bareback bronc riding, steer wrestling, calf roping, team roping, saddle bronc riding, barrel racing, and bull riding—plus lots more. San Antonio has the largest junior livestock show in the world, highlighting today's livestock industry through multimedia exhibits, demonstrations, and displays of animals. Equine shows display strength, style, and precision. There's a midway with rides and games, plus a petting zoo, pony rides, and lots of food. Early-mid-Feb. **$**

Summer Festival. *505 Villita St, San Antonio. Phone 210/207-8610.* Performances of Latin-flavored *Fiesta Noche del Rio, Fiesta Flamenca,* and *Fandango* at Arneson River Theatre. May-Aug.

Texas Folklife Festival. *Institute of Texan Cultures, HemisFair Park, 801 S Bowie St, San Antonio. Phone 210/458-2300.* Crafts, folk music and dancing, entertainment, food representing more than 30 ethnic groups in Texas. Early June.

Limited-Service Hotels

★ **BEST WESTERN HILL COUNTRY SUITES.** *18555 US Hwy 281 N, San Antonio (78258). Phone 210/490-9191; toll-free 866/784-8346; fax 210/490-3465. www.bestwestern.com.* 76 rooms, 2 story, all suites. Complimentary full breakfast. Check-in 3 pm, check-out noon. High-speed Internet access. Fitness room. Outdoor pool, whirlpool. Business center. **$**

★ ★ **COURTYARD BY MARRIOTT.** *8585 Marriott Dr, San Antonio (78229). Phone 210/614-7100; toll-free 800/321-2211; fax 210/614-7110. www.courtyard.com.* 146 rooms, 3 story. Pets accepted; fee. Check-in 3 pm, check-out noon. High-speed Internet access, wireless Internet access. Restaurant. Fitness room. Outdoor pool, whirlpool. Business center. **$**

★ ★ **DOUBLETREE HOTEL.** *37 NE Loop 410, San Antonio (78216). Phone 210/366-2424; toll-free 800/535-1980; fax 210/341-0410. www.sanantonioairport.doubletree.com.* 290 rooms, 5 story. Pets accepted, some restrictions. Check-in 3 pm, check-out noon. High-speed Internet access, wireless Internet access. Restaurant, bar. Fitness room, spa. Outdoor pool, whirlpool. Airport transportation available. Business center. **$**

★ ★ **EMBASSY SUITES.** *10110 US Hwy 281 N, San Antonio (78216). Phone 210/525-9999; fax 210/525-0626. www.embassysuites.com.* This hotel is only 1/2 mile north of the airport and 2 miles from the area's largest shopping complex. 261 rooms, 9 story, all suites. Complimentary full breakfast. Check-in 3 pm, check-out 1 pm. Restaurant, bar. Fitness room. Indoor pool, whirlpool. Airport transportation available. Business center. **$**

★ **HAMPTON INN.** *414 Bowie St, San Antonio (78205). Phone 210/225-8500; toll-free 800/426-7866; fax 210/225-8526. www.hamptoninn.com.* 169 rooms, 6 story. Complimentary continental breakfast. Check-in 4 pm, check-out 11 am. High-speed Internet access, wireless Internet access. Outdoor pool. **$**

★ **HAMPTON INN.** *11010 I-10 W, San Antonio (78230). Phone 210/561-9058; toll-free 877/731-4331; fax 210/690-5566. www.hamptoninn.com.* 120 rooms, 6 story. Pets accepted, some restrictions; fee. Complimentary full breakfast. Check-in 3 pm, check-out noon. High-speed Internet access. Fitness room. Outdoor pool. Business center. **$**

★ **HAWTHORN INN & SUITES ON THE RIVERWALK.** *830 N St. Mary's St, San Antonio (78205). Phone 210/527-1900; toll-free 800/527-1133; fax 510/527-9969. www.hawthorn.com.* 149 rooms, all suites. Complimentary full breakfast. Check-in 3 pm, check-out 11 am. High-speed Internet access, wireless Internet access. Fitness room. Outdoor pool. Business center. **$$**

★ ★ **HOLIDAY INN.** *217 N Saint Mary's St, San Antonio (78205). Phone 210/224-2500; toll-free 800/445-8475; fax 210/223-1302. www.holiday-inn.com.* 313 rooms, 23 story. Pets accepted. Check-in 3 pm. Check-out noon. Restaurant, bar. Fitness room. Outdoor pool, whirlpool. **$$**

★ **HOMEWOOD SUITES.** *432 W Market St, San Antonio (78205). Phone 210/222-1515; toll-free 800/225-5466; fax 210/222-1575. www.homewoodsuites.com.* 146 rooms, 10 story, all suites. Complimentary continental breakfast. Check-in 3 pm, check-out noon. High-speed Internet access. Fitness room. Outdoor pool, whirlpool. Business center. **$$**

★ ★ **HOWARD JOHNSON.** *9735 I-35 N, San Antonio (78233). Phone 210/655-3510; toll-free 800/406-1411; fax 210/655-0778. www.hojo.com.* 161 rooms, 2 story. Complimentary full breakfast. Check-in 3 pm, check-out noon. Restaurant, bar. Outdoor pool, children's pool, four whirlpools. **$**

★ **LA QUINTA INN.** *900 Dolorosa St, San Antonio (78207). Phone 210/271-0001; fax 210/228-0663. www.lq.com.* 184 rooms, 2 story. Pets accepted, some restrictions. Complimentary continental breakfast. Check-in 3 pm. Check-out noon. Outdoor pool. **$**

★ ★ **RADISSON HILL COUNTRY INN.** *502 W Durango, San Antonio (78207). Phone 210/224-7155; toll-free 800/333-3333; fax 210/224-9130. www.radisson.com.* 250 rooms. Check-in 3 pm, check-out noon. Restaurant, bar. Fitness room. Outdoor pool, whirlpool. Business center. **$**

★ **WOODFIELD SAN ANTONIO.** *100 W Durango, San Antonio (78204). Phone 210/212-5400; toll-free 800/338-0008; fax 210/212-5407. www.woodfieldsuites.com.* 151 rooms, 6 story, all suites. Pets accepted, some restrictions. Complimentary continental breakfast. Check-in 3 pm, check-out noon. High-speed Internet access. Bar. Fitness room. Outdoor pool, whirlpool. **$**

Full-Service Hotels

★ ★ ★ **THE FAIRMOUNT HOTEL.** *401 S Alamo, San Antonio (78205). Phone 210/224-8800; fax 210/475-0082.* 37 rooms, 4 story. Pets accepted; fee. Check-in 3 pm, check-out noon. High-speed Internet access. Restaurant, bar. Fitness room. **$**

★ ★ ★ **HILTON PALACIO DEL RIO.** *200 S Alamo St, San Antonio (78205). Phone 210/222-1400; toll-free 800/774-1500; fax 210/270-0761. www.palaciodelrio.hilton.com.* 483 rooms, 22 story. Pets accepted, some restrictions; fee. Check-in 3 pm, check-out noon. High-speed Internet access, wireless Internet access. Restaurant, three bars. Fitness room. Outdoor pool, whirlpool. Business center. **$$**

★ ★ ★ **HOTEL VALENCIA RIVERWALK.** *150 E Houston St, San Antonio (78205). Phone 210/227-9700; fax 210/227-9701. www.hotelvalencia.com.* 213 rooms. Check-in 3 pm, check-out noon. High-speed Internet access. Restaurant, bar. Fitness room. **$$**

★ ★ ★ **HYATT REGENCY SAN ANTONIO.** *123 Losoya St, San Antonio (78205). Phone 210/222-1234; toll-free 800/633-7313; fax 210/227-4925. www.hyatt.com.* 632 rooms, 11 story. Check-in 3 pm, check-out noon. High-speed Internet access, wireless Internet access. Restaurant, bar. Fitness room. Outdoor pool, whirlpool. Business center. **$$**

★ ★ ★ **LA MANSION DEL RIO.** *112 College St, San Antonio (78205). Phone 210/518-1000; toll-free 800/292-7300; fax 210/226-0389. www.lamansion.com.* La Mansion del Rio is the pride of San Antonio. This Spanish Colonial treasure built in 1852 pays tribute to the area's heritage in its architecture and interior design, and its location overlooking the city's cherished River Walk makes it a tourist's dream. Romantic views are the hallmark of this hotel; the flowing river and tropical courtyard vistas are enjoyed from the balconies of guest accommodations or at the sensational Las Canarias Restaurant (see). The restaurant is a cherished spot, both for its intimate setting and for its creative contemporary menu with Texas inflections. The rooms and suites have a unique character, and Spanish and Mexican antiques provide a sense of place. In-room spa services are available, and guests are invited to experience the sister property's (see Watermark Hotel & Spa) full-service spa nearby. La Mansion del Rio guests have full charging privileges at the Watermark, including at their spa. 337 rooms, 7 story. Pets accepted, some restrictions; fee. Check-in 3 pm, check-out 1 pm. High-speed Internet access, wireless Internet access. Restaurant, two bars. Fitness room, fitness classes available. Outdoor pool. Business center. **$$**

★ ★ ★ **MARRIOTT PLAZA SAN ANTONIO.** *555 S Alamo St, San Antonio (78205). Phone 210/229-1000; toll-free 800/421-1172; fax 210/229-1418. www.plazasa.com.* The fountains, courtyards and gardens of this hotel are a pleasant surprise in this downtown San Antonio location. The more adventuresome can explore the historic district by foot or complimentary bicycle. 258 rooms, 7 story. Pets accepted, some restrictions. Check-in 3 pm, check-out noon. High-speed Internet access. Restaurant, bar. Fitness room. Outdoor pool, whirlpool. Business center. **$$**

★ ★ ★ **MARRIOTT SAN ANTONIO RIVERWALK.** *711 E Riverwalk St, San Antonio (78205). Phone 210/224-4555; toll-free 800/648-4462; fax 210/224-2754. www.marriott.com.* Many rooms overlook the San Antonio River. 512 rooms, 28 story. Pets accepted; fee. Check-in 4 pm, check-out noon. High-speed Internet access. Two restaurants, bar. Fitness room. Indoor pool, outdoor pool, whirlpool. Airport transportation available. Business center. **$$**

★ ★ ★ **MENGER HOTEL.** *204 Alamo Plz, San Antonio (78205). Phone 210/223-4361; toll-free 800/345-9285; fax 210/228-0022. www.historicmenger.com.* This hotel was built in 1859 and is a historic landmark situated next door to the Alamo. There is a 19th-century wing with Victorian-style guest rooms. Visitors can enjoy a drink in the bar where "Teddy Roosevelt recruited his Rough Riders" for the Spanish-American War. 316 rooms, 5 story. Check-in 3 pm, check-out noon. Restaurant, bar. Fitness room, spa. Outdoor pool, whirlpool. **$**

★ ★ ★ **OMNI SAN ANTONIO HOTEL.** *9821 Colonnade Blvd, San Antonio (78230). Phone 210/691-8888; toll-free 800/843-6664; fax 210/691-1128. www.omnihotels.com.* 326 rooms, 20 story. Pets accepted, some restrictions; fee. Check-in 3 pm, check-out noon. High-speed Internet access, wireless Internet access. Restaurant, bar. Fitness room. Indoor pool, outdoor pool, whirlpool. Airport transportation available. Business center. **$**

★ ★ ★ **RADISSON HILL COUNTRY RESORT & SPA.** *9800 Westover Hills Blvd, San Antonio (78251). Phone 210/509-9800; toll-free 800/333-3333; fax 210/509-9814. www.radisson.com.* 227 rooms. Check-in 3 pm, check-out noon. Restaurant, bar. Children's activity center. Fitness room, spa. Outdoor pool, children's pool, whirlpool. Business center. **$**

★ ★ ★ **SHERATON GUNTER HOTEL SAN ANTONIO.** *205 E Houston St, San Antonio (78205). Phone 210/227-3241; toll-free 888/999-2089; fax 210/227-3299. www.gunterhotel.com.* This hotel, built in 1909, is a small jewel decorated in Texan elegance. It radiates personal charm and comfort. It is only a short stroll away from the River Walk. 322 rooms, 12 story. Pets accepted, some restrictions. Check-in 3 pm, check-out noon. High-speed Internet access. Restaurant, bar. Fitness room. Outdoor pool, whirlpool. Business center. **$**

★ ★ ★ **THE ST. ANTHONY HOTEL.** *300 E Travis St, San Antonio (78205). Phone 210/227-4392; fax 210/227-0915. www.wyndham.com.* This landmark property, built in 1909, is famous for its elegant lobby. 352 rooms, 10 story. Check-in 3 pm, check-out noon. Wireless Internet access. Restaurant, bar. Fitness room. Indoor pool. Business center. **$**

★ ★ ★ ★ **THE WATERMARK HOTEL & SPA.**
212 W Crockett St, San Antonio (78205). Phone 210/223-8500; toll-free 866/605-1212; fax 121/022-6389. www.watermarkhotel.com. Overlooking the historic River Walk, the Watermark Hotel & Spa is one of San Antonio's finest destinations. This luxurious property provides a respite from the hectic everyday with its plush accommodations and world-class spa. The rooms and suites are handsomely appointed with iron four-poster beds, British Colonial furnishings, and distinctive local artwork. The rooftop pool is a relaxing spot with lovely views, and the adjacent café serves breakfast and lunch. The buzzworthy Pesca on the River spotlights international seafood in a dazzling contemporary space. The Watermark spa is an urban oasis complete with a state-of-the-art fitness facility, mind/body awareness classes, and a comprehensive, nature-based treatment menu. Guests of the Watermark are granted privileges at its sister property, La Mansion del Rio (see). This historic gem directly across the river enjoys a storied past, and its Las Canarias restaurant (see) is a highlight of any visit to San Antonio. 99 rooms. Pets accepted, some restrictions; fee. Check-in 3 pm, check-out 1 pm. High-speed Internet access. Two restaurants, bar. Fitness room, fitness classes available, spa. Outdoor pool, whirlpool. Airport transportation available. **$$$**

★ ★ ★ **THE WESTIN RIVERWALK HOTEL.**
420 W Market St, San Antonio (78205). Phone 210/224-6500; toll-free 800/937-8461; fax 210/444-6000. www.westin.com/riverwalk. 473 rooms, 15 story. Pets accepted, some restrictions. Check-in 3 pm, check-out noon. High-speed Internet access. Restaurant, bar. Fitness room. Outdoor pool. Business center. **$$**

Full-Service Resorts

★ ★ ★ **HYATT REGENCY HILL COUNTRY.**
9800 Hyatt Resort Dr, San Antonio (78251). Phone 210/647-1234; toll-free 800/647-1234; fax 210/681-9681. www.hillcountry.hyatt.com. Two hundred acres of woods are the setting for this hotel just across from the Texas SeaWorld. Located just 15 minutes from Six Flags Fiesta Texas theme park and 20 minutes from downtown, this a great place to stay for a family vacation. 500 rooms, 4 story. Check-in 3 pm, check-out noon. Five restaurants, bar. Children's activity center. Fitness room, fitness classes available, spa. Beach. Outdoor pool, whirlpool. Golf. Tennis. **$$$**

★ ★ ★ **THE WESTIN LA CANTERA RESORT.** *16641 La Cantera Pkwy, San Antonio (78256). Phone 210/558-6500; fax 210/558-2400. www.westinlacantera.com.* The Westin La Cantera Resort is a slice of paradise in Texas Hill Country. Located on one of the highest points above San Antonio, this 300-acre resort treats its guests to breathtaking views of the city and the rolling hills of the countryside. Red tiles and stucco walls pay tribute to the region's Spanish-Mediterranean heritage, while inside, the wrought-iron details, fabrics, and decorative objects are pure Southwest. This resort is a premier destination with the renowned Castle Rock Health Club and Spa, 36 holes of championship golf, and a well-regarded golf academy. The Lost Quarry Pools area beckons visitors of all ages. Fun-filled yet luxurious, the resort offers something for the entire family. Taste buds are tickled pink by gourmet offerings, from Texas-style barbecue and fine Southwestern fare to grilled steaks and comfort food favorites. 508 rooms, 7 story. Check-in 3 pm, check-out noon. Restaurant, bar. Children's activity center. Fitness room, spa. Outdoor pool, children's pool, whirlpool. Golf. Tennis. Business center. **$$**

Full-Service Inn

★ ★ ★ **HAVANA RIVERWALK HOTEL.** *1015 Navarro St, San Antonio (78205). Phone 210/222-2008; fax 210/227-2717.* This boutique hotel was built in 1914. 27 rooms, 3 story. Children over 14 years only. Complimentary continental breakfast. Check-in 3 pm, check-out noon. Restaurant, bar. **$$**

Specialty Lodgings

The following lodging establishments are approved by Mobil Travel Guide, but due to their unique and individualized nature have not been given a traditional Mobil Star rating. Included in this listing you may find bed-and-breakfasts, limited-service inns, guest ranches, and other unique hotel properties.

A BECKMANN INN & CARRIAGE HOUSE BED AND BREAKFAST. *222 E Guenther St, San Antonio (78204). Phone 210/229-1449; toll-free 800/945-1449; fax 210/229-1061. www.beckmanninn.com.* Victorian house (1886) with wraparound porch. 5 rooms, 2 story. Children over 12 years only. Complimentary full breakfast. Check-in 4-6 pm. Check-out 11 am. Restaurant. **$**

A YELLOW ROSE BED & BREAKFAST. *229 Madison, San Antonio (78204). Phone 210/229-9903; toll-free 800/950-9903; fax 210/229-1691. www.ayellowrose.com.* Built in 1878; antiques. 5 rooms, 2 story. Children over 12 years only. Complimentary full breakfast. Check-in 3 pm, check-out 11 am. **$$**

BEAUREGARD HOUSE. *215 Beauregard, San Antonio (78204). Phone 210/222-1198; toll-free 888/667-0555; fax 210/222-9338. www.beauregardhouse.com.* Restored Victorian house (1908) in the King William District; Riverwalk is one block away. 6 rooms, 3 story. Complimentary full breakfast. Check-in 3 pm, check-out 11 am. **$**

BONNER GARDEN B&B. *145 E Agarita Ave, San Antonio (78212). Phone 210/733-4222; toll-free 800/396-4222; fax 210/733-6129. www.bonnergarden.com.* 5 rooms. Complimentary full breakfast. Check-in 1 pm, check-out 11 am. High-speed Internet access, wireless Internet access. Outdoor pool. Airport transportation available. **$**

BRACKENRIDGE HOUSE. *230 Madison, San Antonio (78204). Phone 210/271-3442; toll-free 800/221-1412; fax 210/226-3139. www.brackenridgehouse .com.* 5 rooms, 2 story. Children over 12 years only. Complimentary full breakfast. Check-in 3 pm, check-out 11:30 am. Wireless Internet access. Whirlpool. **$**

BULLIS HOUSE INN. *621 Pierce Ave, San Antonio (78208). Phone 210/223-9426; toll-free 877/477-4100; fax 210/299-1479. www.sanantoniobb.org.* 8 rooms, 3 story. Complimentary continental breakfast. Check-in 2 pm, check-out noon. Pool.

THE INN AT CRAIG PLACE. *117 W Craig Pl, San Antonio (78212). Phone 210/736-1017; toll-free 877/427-2447; fax 210/737-1562. www.craigplace.com.* 4 rooms. Children over 12 years only. Complimentary full breakfast. Check-in 4 pm, check-out 11 am. Wireless Internet access. **$$**

NOBLE INNS. *107 Madison St, San Antonio (78204). Phone 210/225-4045; toll-free 800/221-4045; fax 210/227-0877. www.nobleinns.com.* This bed-and-breakfast was built as a house in 1894 for Moses Jackson. The Victorian-style building provides a parlor for guests to enjoy inside or a landscaped garden outside. The conservatory is surrounded by Victorian stained-glass windows. Turndown service, robes, and fresh flowers are provided. 7 rooms, 2 story. Children over 12 years only. Complimentary full breakfast. Check-in 3 pm, check-out 11 am. Indoor pool. **$**

OGE HOUSE. *209 Washington St, San Antonio (78204). Phone 210/223-2353; toll-free 800/242-2770; fax 210/226-5812. www.ogeinn.com.* Built in 1857, this inn is full of history and decorated with antiques. Each floor has its own private veranda for relaxing, or guests can sit in the grand foyer. 10 rooms, 3 story. No children allowed. Complimentary full breakfast. Check-out 11 am. **$$**

RIVERWALK VISTA. *262 Losoya St, San Antonio (78205). Phone 210/223-3200; toll-free 866/898-4782; fax 210/223-4278. www.riverwalkvista.com.* 17 rooms. Complimentary continental breakfast. Check-in 3 pm, check-out 11 am. High-speed Internet access, wireless Internet access. Business center. **$$**

Spa

★ ★ ★ ★ WATERMARK SPA @ WATERMARK HOTEL & SPA. *212 W Crockett St, San Antonio (78205).* The Watermark Spa is a true urban oasis. Despite its location in the city center, this spa transports guests to a serene location far away from the hectic pace of city life. Feminine without being frilly, it is marked by a cool, fresh décor complete with soft colors and contemporary furnishings.

Purity is a guiding force behind this spa, where natural essential oil-based products are the inspiration behind most of the treatments. This spa's menu features many signature therapies exclusive to the Watermark. Signature body treatments include gentle citrus scrubs, mesquite scrubs, and purple sage salt glows, along with mesquite clay body wraps, aloe skin quenchers, and avocado lime blossom scalp and body treatments. Be sure to try one of the signature massages. The Watermark Restoration massage begins with a Spanish rosemary massage and is followed by the application of yucca, a plant beloved by Native Americans for its healing properties. Other signature massages include the summer rain therapy, a refreshing and stimulating warm water massage, and the blue mint foot repair, which cools and soothes tired soles. The nature-based facials are wonderfully relaxing and rejuvenating, with therapies such as aloe skin renewal, restorative organics, ultimate hydration, and vitamin C aromatherapy among the many offerings. Male clients are especially pampered at the Watermark, with a special menu designed specifically for their needs. From clarifying back treatments to rescue facials, men are treated with special care here.

Restaurants

★ ★ **ALDINO CUCINA ITALIANA.** *1203 NW Loop 1604, San Antonio (78258). Phone 210/340-0000; fax 210/366-1066. www.aldinos.com.* Italian menu. Lunch, dinner, brunch. Bar. Business casual attire. Outdoor seating. **$$**

★ ★ ★ **ANAQUA GRILL.** *555 S Alamo St, San Antonio (78205). Phone 210/229-1000; toll-free 800/ 421-1172; fax 210/229-1418. www.anaquagrill.com.* Immediately south of downtown in the Plaza San Antonio Hotel, this elegant space allows diners to gaze upon exotic birds in an old-world-style courtyard while dining on some of the city's most special dishes. Typical starters include pan-seared calamari with a roasted chile-tomato sauce and lamb chop lollipops with porcini sauce, while the tempting list of entrées is likely to offer grilled salmon in a mango-barbecue sauce and prime tenderloin stuffed with roasted garlic. Look for a vast wine list, too. American menu. Breakfast, lunch, dinner, late-night, brunch. Bar. Children's menu. Business casual attire. Valet parking. Outdoor seating. **$$**

★ ★ ★ **ANTLERS LODGE.** *9800 Hyatt Resort Dr, San Antonio (78251). Phone 210/520-4001; fax 210/ 681-9681.* The gourmet dining room of the Hyatt Regency Country Resort features modern Texas cooking using fresh ingredients from the local Hill Country. The restaurant gets its name from the impressive antler chandelier. A cozy fireplace and sweeping view of the golf course complete the lodge ambience. Southwestern menu. Dinner. Closed Mon. Bar. Business casual attire. Reservations recommended. Valet parking. **$$$**

★ ★ ★ **BIGA ON THE BANKS.** *203 S St. Mary's St, Suite 100, San Antonio (78205). Phone 210/225-0722; fax 210/225-1052. www.biga.com.* Contemporary yet very warm, this downtown showplace overlooking the Riverwalk from within the International Building offers what's easily the most sought-after meal in San Antonio. That's because superstar chef/owner Bruce Auden works marvels with such dishes as seared Hudson Valley foie gras on a maple waffle with black trumpet mushrooms and grapefruit-duck glaze and axis venison with a goat cheese strudel. Ask about

Table 31, which provides a kitchen view and Auden's special tasting menu. American menu. Dinner, Sun brunch. Closed Jan 1, Dec 25; also week of July 4. Bar. Children's menu. Business casual attire. Reservations recommended. Valet parking. Outdoor seating. **$$$**

★ ★ **BISTRO TIME.** *5137 Fredericksburg, San Antonio (78229). Phone 210/344-6626; fax 210/344-5654. www.bistro-time.com.* Open for lunch and dinner, this casual yet elegant bistro caters to a fashion-conscious crowd. American menu. Lunch, dinner. Closed Sun; holidays. Business casual attire. Reservations recommended. **$$$**

★ ★ **BOUDRO'S A TEXAS BISTRO.** *421 E Commerce St, San Antonio (78205). Phone 210/224-8484; fax 210/225-2839. www.boudros.com.* Historic building; pictographs on walls, original artwork. Seafood, steak menu. Lunch, dinner, late-night. Bar. Children's menu. Casual attire. Reservations recommended. Outdoor seating. **$$**

★ ★ **CAPPY'S.** *5011 Broadway St, San Antonio (78209). Phone 210/828-9669; fax 210/828-3041. www.cappysrestaurant.com.* A fashionable favorite in the upscale Alamo Heights neighborhood, this inviting spot makes for a special lunch or dinner that's decidedly unfussy. Choice menu selections include comforting roasted chicken given an Italian treatment with tomatoes, olives, and mushrooms, as well as potstickers with a Texas twang, thanks to a stuffing of pork, corn, and peppers. American menu. Lunch, dinner. Closed holidays. Bar. Children's menu. Casual attire. Outdoor seating. **$$**

★ **CASA RIO.** *430 E Commerce St, San Antonio (78205). Phone 210/225-6718; fax 210/225-2216. www.casa-rio.com.* Riverboat dining by reservations. On the San Antonio River. Mexican menu. Lunch, dinner. Closed holidays. Bar. Children's menu. Casual attire. Reservations recommended. Outdoor seating. **$$**

★ ★ **CRUMPET'S.** *3920 Harry Wurzbach, San Antonio (78209). Phone 210/821-5454; fax 210/821-5624.* American menu. Lunch, dinner. Closed Jan 1, Dec 25. Bar. Casual attire. Outdoor seating. **$$**

★ ★ **EL JARRO DE ARTURO.** *13421 San Pedro Ave, San Antonio (78216). Phone 210/494-5084; fax 210/496-6885. www.eljarro.com.* A local favorite since 1975, El Jarro prides itself on offering healthful preparations of true Mexican cuisine by cooking with canola and olive oils. Among prime menu picks are the carne asada, a grilled tenderloin steak with sautéed poblano chiles and a side of green chicken enchilada; and the salmon with garlic mashed potatoes over a chipotle mushroom sauce. Don't forget to try the margaritas or to stop by for live jazz on weekends. Mexican menu. Lunch, dinner, brunch. Closed holidays. Bar. Casual attire. Outdoor seating. **$$**

★ ★ **EL MIRADOR.** *722 S St. Mary's St, San Antonio (78205). Phone 210/225-9444; fax 210/271-3236.* Locals crowd this little hangout on a daily basis, in part for the sensational soups and otherwise for the welcoming spirit of the dining room and the outdoor patio. Puffy tacos are special, with the addition of shredded cabbage, and the chorizo quesadillas are unforgettable. Evening meals get extra oomph from seafood enchiladas and a veal chop with chilies. Mexican menu. Breakfast, lunch, dinner. Closed holidays. Casual attire. Outdoor seating. **$**

★ ★ **ERNESTO'S.** *2559 Jackson Keller, San Antonio (78230). Phone 210/344-1248.* A romantic spirit pervades this secluded find deep within a shopping center. Owner Ernesto Torres has created a special menu known for seafood with rich, butter-enhanced sauces and inventive salsas. Combination options include a steak with enchilada, both of which receive the same creative treatments given to the seafood. At this refined and popular spot, you may need a reservation. Mexican menu. Lunch, dinner. Closed Sun; Jan 1, Dec 25. Bar. Children's menu. Casual attire. Reservations recommended. **$$**

★ ★ ★ **FIG TREE.** *515 Villita St, San Antonio (78205). Phone 210/224-1976; fax 210/271-9180. www.figtreerestaurant.com.* American menu. Dinner. Closed Jan 1, Thanksgiving, Dec 25. Business casual attire. Reservations recommended. Valet parking. Outdoor seating. **$$$**

★ ★ ★ **FRANCESCA'S AT SUNSET.** *16641 La Cantera Pkwy, San Antonio (78256). Phone 210/558-6500; fax 210/641-0721. www.westinlacantera.com.* Located in the beautiful Westin La Cantera Resort (see), this romantic restaurant is decorated in the Spanish-colonial style. Outdoor seating with views of the Texas hill country is available. Southwestern menu. Dinner. Closed Sun-Mon. Bar. Children's menu. Business casual attire. Reservations recommended. Valet parking. Outdoor seating. **$$$**

⊙ ★ **GAZEBO AT LOS PATIOS.** *2015 NE Loop 410, San Antonio (78217). Phone 210/655-6171; fax 210/655-6317. www.lospatios.com.* Although it's within five minutes of the San Antonio International Airport,

Los Patios feels like a country retreat. A tree-shaded patio and the light-filled Gazebo combine to offer a delightful lunch spot, with a menu that's been popular since 1968. Classic dishes include green chicken enchiladas; chicken-mushroom crepes; quiche; shrimp with angel hair pasta; the combo of shrimp salad, chicken salad, and fruit salad with poppy seed dressing; and fresh strawberry pie for dessert. Southwestern menu. Lunch, Sun brunch. Closed Jan 1, Thanksgiving, Dec 25. Bar. Children's menu. Casual attire. Outdoor seating. **$**

★ ★ **GREY MOSS INN.** *19010 Scenic Loop Rd, Helotes (78023). Phone 210/695-8301; fax 210/695-3237. www.grey-moss-inn.com.* American menu. Dinner. Closed Thanksgiving, Dec 25. Casual attire. Reservations recommended. Outdoor seating. **$$$**
⃟

★ **GUENTHER HOUSE.** *205 E Guenther St, San Antonio (78204). Phone 210/227-1061; toll-free 800/235-8186; fax 210/351-3672. www.guentherhouse.com.* House built by founder of Pioneer Flour Mills (1860). American menu. Breakfast, lunch. Closed Jan 1, Thanksgiving, Dec 24-25. Casual attire. Outdoor seating. **$**

★ **INDIA OVEN.** *1031 Patricia Dr, San Antonio (78213). Phone 210/366-1030; fax 210/366-1033. www.indiaoven.com.* Indian menu. Lunch, dinner. Bar. Children's menu. **$$**

★ ★ **LA FOGATA.** *2427 Vance Jackson Rd, San Antonio (78213). Phone 210/340-1337; fax 210/349-6467. www.lafogata.com.* Mariachis Fri-Sat. Mexican menu. Lunch, dinner, late-night. Closed Jan 1, Thanksgiving, Dec 24-25. Bar. Children's menu. Casual attire. Reservations recommended. Valet parking. Outdoor seating. **$$**

★ ★ **LA FONDA.** *2415 N Main Ave, San Antonio (78212). Phone 210/733-0621; fax 210/733-8957. www.lafondaonmain.com.* Mexican menu. Lunch, dinner. Closed holidays. Bar. Children's menu. Casual attire. Reservations recommended. Outdoor seating. **$$**

★ **LA MARGARITA.** *120 Produce Row, San Antonio (78207). Phone 210/227-7140; fax 210/271-3097.* Restored farmers' market building (1910). Mexican menu. Lunch, dinner. Bar. Children's menu. Casual attire. Outdoor seating. **$**

★ ★ ★ **LAS CANARIAS.** *112 College St, San Antonio (78205). Phone 210/518-1000; toll-free 800/292-7300; fax 210/225-8601. www.lamansion.com.* This romantic, elegant restaurant is full of Spanish colonial charm. For a special treat, experience a specially designed three-course meal while drifting along the San Antonio Riverwalk on board the Las Canarias riverboat. Reservations are recommended. American, French menu. Breakfast, lunch, dinner, Sun brunch. Bar. Children's menu. Business casual attire. Reservations recommended. Valet parking. Outdoor seating. **$$$**

★ ★ ★ **LE REVE.** *152 E Pecan St, San Antonio (78205). Phone 210/212-2221; fax 210/212-6221. www.restaurantlereve.com.* Filled nightly with glamorous foodies, Riverwalk's Le Reve is a charming, cubbyhole of a restaurant that is fast becoming one of San Antonio's best bets for innovative French cuisine. Le Reve may be tiny, with minimal décor and only 12 tables, but it has an intimate, cozy feel that does not stray into claustrophobic territory. The kitchen focuses on lavish French fare with a modern edge and deftly contrasting textures, flavors, and spices, always keeping the complete dish in graceful balance. Fresh ingredients make beautiful visuals, and plates resemble edible culinary art. Dining here is French in style and in substance, which means that dinner is served at a leisurely pace (pencil in about three memorable hours), allowing you to relax and have a lovely experience. French menu. Dinner. Closed Sun-Mon; holidays; also two weeks in Jan and Aug. Jacket required. Reservations recommended. Valet parking. **$$$$**

★ **LIBERTY BAR.** *328 E Josephine, San Antonio (78215). Phone 210/227-1187; fax 210/227-9248.* Oldest bar in Texas in continuous operation. American menu. Lunch, dinner, late-night. Closed Jan 1, Thanksgiving, Dec 25. Bar. Casual attire. Valet parking. **$$**

★ ★ **LITTLE RHEIN STEAK HOUSE.** *231 S Alamo St, San Antonio (78205). Phone 210/225-2111; fax 210/271-9180. www.littlerheinsteakhouse.com.* Within the 1847 stone building, thought to be the city's first two-story structure, is a former German saloon that became a steakhouse in 1967. Hand-cut, aged steaks include a prime porterhouse, sirloin, and ribeye; other top picks include lobster tail, lamb chops, Roquefort mashed potatoes, and exceptional stuffed mushrooms. The great Riverwalk setting is high among appeal factors, as is the quiet, romantic mood. Steak menu. Dinner. Children's menu. Casual attire. Reservations recommended. Valet parking. Outdoor seating. **$$$**

★ **LONE STAR CAFE SAN ANTONIO RIVER.** *237 Losoya, San Antonio (78205). Phone 210/223-9374; fax 210/223-4634.* Seafood, steak menu. Lunch, dinner. Closed Dec 25. Bar. Children's menu. Casual attire. Outdoor seating. **$$**

★ **LOS BARRIOS.** *4223 Blanco Rd, San Antonio (78212). Phone 210/732-6017; fax 210/732-9720.* Mexican menu. Breakfast, lunch, dinner. Closed Easter, Thanksgiving, Dec 25. Bar. Children's menu. Casual attire. **$**

★ ★ **MI TIERRA.** *218 Produce Row, San Antonio (78207). Phone 210/225-1262; fax 210/225-7101. www.mitierracafe.com.* Deep within El Mercado is one of the city's favorite spots for authentic Mexican and Tex-Mex food. It is located in an old farmers' market building, which was built in 1910. Loud, bright, and bustling, Mi Tierra is part bakery and part dining room, and mariachi music is likely to fill your ears as you try to choose among dishes of cabrito, green enchiladas, or fajitas. Best of all, it's open 24 hours. Be sure to try one of the egg dishes if a late-night craving takes over. Tex-Mex menu. Breakfast, lunch, dinner, late-night, brunch. Bar. Children's menu. Casual attire. Valet parking. Outdoor seating. **$**

★ **MICHELINO'S.** *521 Riverwalk, San Antonio (78205). Phone 210/223-2939; fax 210/224-8209.* Italian menu. Lunch, dinner. Bar. Children's menu. Outdoor seating. **$$**

★ ★ ★ **MORTON'S, THE STEAKHOUSE.** *849 E Commerce St, Suite 283, San Antonio (78205). Phone 210/228-0778; fax 210/228-0770. www.mortons.com.* Although sometimes it may seem like Texas has more than its fair share of steakhouses, this national chain can compete with the best of them. Along with steak, steak and more steak, there are also several seafood selections and a nice variety of side dishes. Steak menu. Dinner. Closed holidays. Bar. Business casual attire. Reservations recommended. Valet parking. **$$$**

★ ★ **OLD SAN FRANCISCO STEAK HOUSE.** *10223 Sahara St, San Antonio (78216). Phone 210/342-2321; fax 210/366-1623. www.osfsteakhouse.com.* Victorian décor, dueling pianos, and a woman in a red velvet swing take you back to the gold rush days, and an old-fashioned menu of prime rib, aged steaks, and cherries jubilee brings back memories of classic 20th-century dining. Dinners begin with a giant block of Swiss cheese and warm, fresh loaves of authentic San Francisco sourdough rye bread, followed by salads and grilled, charbroiled, or sautéed meat, chicken, or fish.

Steak menu. Dinner. Bar. Children's menu. Business casual attire. Valet parking. **$$$**

★ **PICO DE GALLO.** *111 S Leona St, San Antonio (78207). Phone 210/225-6060; fax 210/225-7344. www.picodegallo.com.* Mexican menu. Breakfast, lunch, dinner. Closed Thanksgiving. Bar. Children's menu. Casual attire. Outdoor seating. **$**

★ ★ **PIECA D'ITALIA.** *Crockett and N Presa sts, San Antonio (78205). Phone 210/227-5511; fax 210/ 227-5905. www.italiariverwalk.com.* This restaurant features patio dining overlooking the river, with many tables under the Crockett Street Bridge. Italian menu. Lunch, dinner, late-night. Bar. Children's menu. Reservations recommended. Outdoor seating. **$$**

★ **RIO RIO CANTINA.** *421 E Commerce St, San Antonio (78205). Phone 210/226-8462; fax 210/226-8443. www.rioriocantina.com.* One of many Tex-Mex restaurants on the famed Riverwalk, Rio Rio serves up gargantuan portions of south-of-the-border favorites like fajitas, enchiladas, and pitchers of tangy margaritas. Request a table on the upper level to distance yourself from the crowds strolling past. Tex-Mex menu. Lunch, dinner. Closed Thanksgiving. Bar. Children's menu. Casual attire. Outdoor seating. **$$**

★ **ROSARIO'S.** *910 S Alamo, San Antonio (78205). Phone 210/223-1806; fax 210/223-3924.* Mexican menu. Lunch, dinner. Closed Sun; Thanksgiving, Dec 25. Bar. Casual attire. Outdoor seating. **$$**

★ ★ ★ **RUTH'S CHRIS STEAK HOUSE.** *7720 Jones Maltsberger Rd, San Antonio (78216). Phone 210/ 821-5051; toll-free 800/544-0808; fax 210/821-5095. www.ruthschris-sanantonio.com.* This outlet of the New Orleans-based chain is located near the convention center. Seafood, steak menu. Dinner, late-night. Closed Thanksgiving, Dec 25. Bar. Business casual attire. Reservations recommended. Valet parking. **$$$**

★ **SCHILO'S DELICATESSEN.** *424 E Commerce, San Antonio (78205). Phone 210/223-6692; fax 210/ 329-9525.* Deli menu. Breakfast, lunch, dinner. Closed Sun; holidays. Children's menu. Casual attire. **$**

★ ★ **SILO RESTAURANT AND BAR.** *1133 Austin Hwy, San Antonio (78209). Phone 210/824-8686; fax 210/805-8452. www.siloelevatedcuisine.com.* A mixed bag of international treats within an old market, Silo's offerings include superb chicken-fried oysters and Greek-style braised lamb shank. The menu changes with the seasons and always takes advantage of fresh, seasonable produce, meats, and

fish. An on-site bakery provides the freshest breads imaginable, and live music by Texas artists is served up on weekends. American menu. Lunch, dinner. Closed Jan 1, Thanksgiving, Dec 25; also Super Bowl Sun. Bar. Children's menu. Business casual attire. Reservations recommended. Valet parking (Fri-Sat). **$$**

★ ★ **ZUNI GRILL.** *511 Riverwalk St, San Antonio (78205). Phone 210/227-0864; fax 210/227-0868. www.zunigrill.com.* Southwestern menu. Breakfast, lunch, dinner, brunch. Closed Thanksgiving, Dec 25. Bar. Children's menu. Casual attire. Reservations recommended. Outdoor seating. **$$**

San Marcos (D-7)

See also Austin, Bastrop, Gonzales, New Braunfels, Seguin

Founded 1851
Population 34,733
Elevation 578 ft
Area Code 512
Zip 78666
Information Convention & Visitors Bureau, PO Box 2310; phone 512/393-5900 or toll-free 800/200-5620
Web Site www.sanmarcostexas.com/tourism/ default.htm

Fissures in the rocks of the Balcones escarpment pour out clear spring water to form the San Marcos River. A group of Franciscan monks is said to have discovered these springs on St. Mark's Day in 1709, giving the river, and hence the town, its name. This is the center of farming and ranching for this part of the black lands. To the west above the Balcones escarpment lies scenic hill country with fine deer hunting and bird-watching.

What to See and Do

Aquarena Springs. *1 Aquarena Springs Dr, San Marcos. Phone 512/245-7575; toll-free 800/999-9767.* Glass-bottom boats, from which aquatic plants, fish, and spring formations can be seen; ferry boat to Hillside Gardens; Texana Village. Restaurants. Gift shop. (Daily; closed Dec 25) **$$**

Blair House Inn Cooking School. *100 Spoke Hill Rd, Wimberly (78676). Phone toll-free 877/549-5450. www.blairhouseinn.com.* Blair House Inn is a magnet for home chefs with culinary aspirations. Located in the heart of Texas's Hill Country, 50 miles from both San Antonio and Austin, Blair House offers dozens of cooking classes taught by classically trained chef Christopher Stonesifer. Three-day theme classes (offered once a month, year-round) train students in techniques necessary for proper preparation of everything from French Provincial fare to the cuisine of the Pacific Rim. (Two nights' lodging plus meals and complimentary wine are included in the price.) Two-day seminars are also offered: one is an abbreviated, weekend version of the three-day theme class, and the other features one-on-one training with the chef on the preparation of a five-course meal. In summer, look for combination cooking/adventure packages, which follow kitchen training with two days of kayaking and fly fishing on the San Marcos River. If you're not staying at the inn, you can still reserve a place on Saturday night for five-course fixed-price dinners.

Fishing. From banks of the San Marcos River (license required); also scuba diving.

Lockhart State Park. *Park Rd, Lockhart. Approximately 20 miles NE via Hwy 80/142. Phone 512/398-3479.* Approximately 260 acres. Pool (Memorial Day-Labor Day); 9-hole golf (fee), picnicking, improved camping. (Daily) **$**

San Marcos Factory Shops. *3939 I-35 S 300, San Marcos (78666). At exit 200. Phone 512/396-2200. www.outletsonline.com.* More than 100 outlet stores can be found in this outdoor shopping mall. Food court. (Mon-Sat 10 am-9 pm, Sun 11 am-6 pm; closed holidays)

Wonder World. *1000 Prospect St, San Marcos. W side of town. Phone 512/392-3760.* Tours of a cave formed by an earthquake. Cave temperature is approximately 70° F. Antigravity House, observation tower, train ride through wildlife park and waterfall. Picnic areas, snack bar. (Daily) **$$$$**

Special Events

Republic of Texas Chilympiad. *Hays County Civic Center, 1253 Civic Center Loop, San Marcos (78666). Phone 512/396-5400.* Men's state chili championship cook-off (more than 500 entries); parade; 5K race; nightly concerts. Third weekend in Sept.

Texas Water Safari. *9515 FM 1979, Martindale (78655). Phone 512/357-6113.* Five-day, 262-mile "world's toughest boat race." Canoe race starts in San Marcos at Aquarena Center and ends in Seadrift. Second Sat in June.

Tours of Distinction. *400 E Hopkins, San Marcos. Phone 512/353-1258.* Spring tour of historic houses and restored buildings. Departs from Charles S. Cock House Museum; docents and map/brochure. First weekend in May.

Full-Service Inn

★ ★ ★ **INN ABOVE ONION CREEK.** *4444 Hwy 150 W, Kyle (78640). Phone 512/268-1617; toll-free 800/579-7686; fax 512/268-1090. www.innaboveonioncreek.com.* Located on a 500-acre bluff that overlooks Onion Creek, this bed-and-breakfast has rooms with entertainment centers and feather mattresses on either queen- or king-size beds. A hearty breakfast and a three-course evening dinner are included. 10 rooms, 2 story. Closed Dec 24-25. Children over 12 years only. Complimentary full breakfast. Check-in 3-6 pm, check-out 11 am. Outdoor pool. **$$**

Specialty Lodgings

The following lodging establishments are approved by Mobil Travel Guide, but due to their unique and individualized nature have not been given a traditional Mobil Star rating. Included in this listing you may find bed-and-breakfasts, limited-service inns, guest ranches, and other unique hotel properties.

BLAIR HOUSE. *100 Spoke Hill Rd, Wimberley (78676). Phone 512/847-1111; toll-free 877/549-5450; fax 512/847-8820. www.blairhouseinn.com.* Art gallery. 10 rooms. Children over 12 years only. Complimentary full breakfast. Check-in 3 pm, check-out noon. **$$**

CRYSTAL RIVER INN. *326 W Hopkins St, San Marcos (78666). Phone 512/396-3739; toll-free 888/396-3739; fax 512/396-6311. www.crystalriverinn.com.* Indulge in the romantic spirit of this hill country getaway with its rooms surrounding the fountain, roses, and old pecan trees in the garden. Or come for one of the theme weekends such as original murder mystery, river-trips or ladies' shopping. 11 rooms, 2 story. Pets accepted, some restrictions; fee. Complimentary full breakfast. Check-in 3 pm, check-out noon. **$**

Seguin (D-7)

See also Gonzales, New Braunfels, San Antonio, San Marcos

Founded 1838
Population 22,011
Elevation 520 ft
Area Code 830
Zip 78155
Information Chamber of Commerce, 427 N Austin St, PO Box 710; phone 830/379-6382 or toll-free 800/580-7322
Web Site www.seguintx.org

Seguin (pronounced se-GEEN), on the Guadalupe River, was first settled by Southern planters. The town later became a haven for German immigrants. Widely diversified crops and light manufacturing contribute to its prosperity. Within the county, six power dams on the Guadalupe form lakes providing generous recreational facilities for water sports and fishing.

Special Events

Biggest Small Town Parade. *205 N River, Seguin (78155). Phone 830/401-2448.* July 4.

Guadalupe County Fair and PRCA Rodeo. *728 Midway, Seguin. Phone 830/379-1333.* Four days in early Oct.

Texas Ladies' State Chili Cook-off. *600 River Dr W, Seguin (78155). Phone 830/401-2480.* Mid-Apr.

Texas Youth Rodeo Association State Finals. *728 Midway, Seguin. Phone 830/379-9997.* Late July or early Aug.

Limited-Service Hotel

★ ★ **HOLIDAY INN.** *5100 Marshall St, Seguin (78155). Phone 830/372-0860; toll-free 800/465-4329; fax 830/372-3020. www.holiday-inn.com/seguintx.* 139 rooms, 2 story. Check-out noon. Restaurant, bar. Fitness room. Outdoor pool. **$**
🏋 🏊

Shamrock (E-4)

See also Amarillo

Population 2,029
Elevation 2,310 ft

Area Code 806
Zip 79079
Information Chamber of Commerce, 207 N Main; phone 806/256-2501
Web Site www.shamrocktx.net

Located in the eastern part of the Panhandle natural gas field, Shamrock has a gas pumping station and is also a farming center. The town's water tower on Main Street is said to be the tallest in the state.

What to See and Do

Pioneer West Museum. *204 N Madden St, Shamrock. Phone 806/256-3941. www.shamrocktx.net/museum .html.* Renovated hotel furnished with items depicting pioneer days; kitchen, parlor and bedroom, doctor and dentist offices, Native American room, country store, school room, chapel, early barbershop, war room, Fort Elliot room and "Prairie-to-the-Moon" room honoring astronaut Alan Bean. Located on the grounds is Justice of the Peace office and lawyer's office building. (Mon-Sat 10 am-noon, 1-3 pm; closed holidays) **DONATION**

Special Event

St. Patrick's Day Celebration. Parade, Miss Irish Rose Pageant, TRA team roping, entertainment, dances, carnival, banquet. Weekend nearest Mar 17.

Limited-Service Hotel

★ ★ **IRISH INN MOTEL.** *301 I-40 E, Shamrock (79079). Phone 806/256-2106; toll-free 800/538-6747; fax 806/256-2106.* 157 rooms, 2 story. Pets accepted, some restrictions; fee. Check-out 1 pm. Restaurant. Indoor pool, whirlpool. **$**
🐾 🏊

Restaurant

★ **IRISH INN.** *303 I-40 E, Shamrock (79079). Phone 806/256-2332.* Breakfast, lunch, dinner, late-night, Sun brunch. Bar. Children's menu. **$$**

Sherman (A-8)

See also Bonham, Denison, Gainesville, McKinney

Population 35,082
Elevation 745 ft
Area Code 903

Zip 75090
Information Convention & Visitors Bureau, 307 W Washington, Suite 100, PO Box 1029, 75091; phone 903/893-1184 or toll-free 888/893-1188
Web Site www.shermantexas.com

Sherman is a major manufacturing and processing center, supplying a list of items ranging from wheat and pharmaceuticals to cotton gin machinery and truck bodies. This, along with Lake Texoma's tourism, contributes to a broad economic base.

What to See and Do

Hagerman National Wildlife Refuge. *6465 Refuge Rd, Sherman (75092). NW via Hwy 82, exit at FM 1417, go N to Refuge Rd, follow signs to headquarters. Phone 903/786-2826.* An 11,320-acre area on Lake Texoma provides food and rest for migratory waterfowl of the central flyway. Fishing, boating (Apr-Sept); trail, self-guided auto tour route, picnicking. Visitor center. (Daily; closed holidays) **FREE**

Lake Texoma. *13 miles N.*

Red River Historical Museum. *301 S Walnut, Sherman. In the historic Carnegie Library bldg (1914). Phone 903/893-7623.* Quarterly exhibits; permanent exhibits include "Black Land, Red River," artifacts and furniture from Glen Eden, early plantation house whose site is now under Lake Texoma; country store, local history, and farm and ranch room. (Tues-Fri, also Sat afternoons; closed holidays) **$**

Special Event

Sherman Preservation League Tour of Homes. *Phone 903/893-4067.* Third weekend in Apr.

Limited-Service Hotels

★★**EXECUTIVE INN.** *2105 Texoma Pkwy, Sherman (75090). Phone 903/892-2161; fax 903/893-3045. www.4executiveinn.com.* 150 rooms, 2 story. Check-out noon. Restaurant. Outdoor pool, whirlpool. Airport transportation available. **$**
🏊

★★**HOLIDAY INN.** *3605 S Hwy 75, Sherman (75090). Phone 903/868-0555; toll-free 800/325-3535; fax 903/892-9396. www.holiday-inn.com.* 142 rooms, 2 story. Pets accepted; fee. Check-out noon. Restaurant. Fitness room. Outdoor pool, children's pool, whirlpool. **$**
🐾 🎿 🏊

Snyder (B-5)

See also Big Spring

Founded 1876
Population 10,783
Elevation 2,316 ft
Area Code 915
Zip 79549
Information Chamber of Commerce, 2302 Avenue R, PO Box 840; phone 915/573-3558
Web Site www.snydertex.com/chamber

Snyder is the county seat for Scurry County, one of the nation's top oil-producing counties. Its modern sports complex and public parks make it a center for recreational activities.

What to See and Do

Lake J. B. Thomas. *17 miles SW on Hwy 350.* Swimming, fishing, boating; picnicking.

Scurry County Museum. *6200 College Ave, Snyder (79549). 1/4 mile E off Hwy 350 on Western Texas College campus. Phone 915/573-6107. www.snydertex.com/semuseum.* Local and county historical exhibits from prehistory to oil boom. Changing exhibits. (Mon-Fri 10 am-4 pm, Sun 1-4 pm; closed holidays) **FREE**

Special Events

Legends of Western Swing Music Festival. *900 E Coliseum Dr, Snyder (79549). Phone 903/573-3558.* Mid-June.

Scurry County Fair. *900 E Coliseum Dr, Snyder. Phone 915/573-3558.* Mid-Sept.

Western Texas College Rodeos. *900 E Coliseum Dr, Snyder (79549). Phone 915/573-9811.* First three weekends in Apr.

White Buffalo Festival. *900 E Coliseum Dr, Snyder (79549). Phone 915/573-3558.* Early Oct.

Limited-Service Hotel

★ **PURPLE SAGE MOTEL.** *1501 E Coliseum Dr, Snyder (79549). Phone 915/573-5491; toll-free 800/545-5792; fax 915/573-9027.* 45 rooms. Pets accepted, some restrictions. Complimentary continental breakfast. Check-out noon. Outdoor pool. **$**
🐾 🏊

Restaurant

★ ★ **SHACK.** *1005 25th St, Snyder (79549). Phone 915/573-4921.* Seafood, steak menu. Lunch, dinner. Closed holidays. **$$**

Sonora (C-6)

See also Ozona

Settled 1890
Population 2,924
Elevation 2,120 ft
Area Code 915
Zip 76950
Information Chamber of Commerce, 707 N Crockett Ave, PO Box 1172; phone 915/387-2880
Web Site www.sonoratx-chamber.com

The longest fenced cattle trail in the world once stretched from Sonora to the town of Brady; it was 100 miles long, 250 feet wide, and had holding pastures along the route. Today, the seat of Sutton County is a livestock and wool processing center.

What to See and Do

Caverns of Sonora. *8 miles W on I-10, then 7 miles S on FM 1989. Phone 915/387-3105.* Unusually beautiful caverns with many rare and fine formations; guided tours within 30 minutes. Picnicking, camping and RV park available (fee). (Daily) **$$$$**

Special Event

Sutton County Days and Outlaw Pro Rodeo. *Phone 915/387-5645.* Rodeo, dance, parade, children's activities. Arts and crafts, barbecue. Aug.

Limited-Service Hotel

★ **DAYS INN.** *1312 N Service Rd, Sonora (76950). Phone 325/387-3516; toll-free 800/329-7466; fax 325/387-2854. www.daysinn.com.* 99 rooms, 2 story. Pets accepted; fee. Complimentary continental breakfast. Check-in 3 pm, check-out noon. Wireless Internet access. Outdoor pool. **$**

South Padre Island (F-8)

See also Brownsville, Harlingen, Port Isabel

Population 2,422
Elevation 0 ft
Area Code 956
Zip 78597
Information Convention & Visitors Bureau, 600 Padre Blvd; phone 956/761-6433 or toll-free 800/343-2368
Web Site www.sopadre.com

South Padre Island, located 2 1/2 miles off Port Isabel, at the southern tip of Padre Island (see), has long been a favored vacationing spot; the Karankawa were known to have spent the winter months in this area as long as 400 years ago. The town, which averages only a 1/2 mile wide, relies on tourism as its economic basis; activities from beachcombing to parasailing are popular, and numerous charter boat operators offer bay and deep-sea fishing excursions and dolphin-watching cruises.

Special Events

Independence Day Celebration & Fireworks Extravaganza. *Ling and Laguna Blvd, South Padre Island (78597). Phone 956/761-3000.* July 4.

Island of Lights Festival. *Phone 956/761-5419.* Late Nov-early Dec.

South Padre Island Windsurfing Blowout. *Phone toll-free 800/767-2373.* May.

Full-Service Hotel

★ ★ ★ **SHERATON SOUTH PADRE ISLAND BEACH HOTEL.** *310 Padre Blvd, South Padre Island (78597). Phone 956/761-6551; toll-free 800/222-4010; fax 956/761-6570. www.sheraton.com/sopadre.* Conveniently located near the S.P.I. Convention Center, and situated directly on the beach, this hotel features more than meeting space. The pool's swim-up bar, the two lounges with entertainment, seasonal water sports and beachfront horseback riding are some of the fun recreational activities offered. 251 rooms, 12 story. Check-in 3 pm, check-out 11 am. Restaurant, two bars. Fitness room. Outdoor pool, children's pool. Business center. **$$$**

Full-Service Resort

★ ★ **RADISSON RESORT SOUTH PADRE ISLAND.** *500 Padre Blvd, South Padre Island (78597). Phone 956/761-6511; fax 956/761-1602. www.radisson.com.* This property is a beachfront resort with a cascading waterfall into the heated swimming pool. Tennis and volleyball courts are on the beachfront and lit for night play. Condos with views of the Gulf of Mexico are available. 128 rooms, 12 story. Check-in 3 pm, check-out 11 am. Restaurant, two bars. Children's activity center. Outdoor pool, whirlpool. **$$**

Specialty Lodging

The following lodging establishment is approved by Mobil Travel Guide, but due to its unique and individualized nature has not been given a traditional Mobil Star rating. Included in this listing you may find bed-and-breakfasts, limited-service inns, guest ranches, and other unique hotel properties.

BROWN PELICAN INN. *207 W Aires Dr, South Padre Island (78597). Phone 956/761-2722; fax 956/761-8683. www.brownpelican.com.* View of bay. 7 rooms. Children over 12 years only. Complimentary full breakfast. Check-in 3 pm, check-out 11 am. High-speed Internet access. **$**

Restaurants

★ ★ **AMBERJACKS.** *209 W Amberjack St, South Padre Island (78597). Phone 956/761-6500; fax 956/761-4470. www.spadre.com.* American menu. Lunch, dinner. Closed one week in Nov. Bar. Children's menu. Casual attire. Reservations recommended. Outdoor seating. **$$**

★ **LA JAIBA SEAFOOD.** *2001 Padre Blvd, South Padre Island (78597). Phone 956/761-9878.* Seafood menu. Lunch, dinner. Closed Mon; Jan 1, Easter, Dec 25. Bar. Children's menu. Casual attire. Reservations recommended. **$$**

★ ★ **SCAMPI'S.** *206 W Aires Dr, South Padre Island (78597). Phone 956/761-1755; fax 956/761-2534. www.scampisspi.com.* American menu. Dinner. Closed ten days in mid-late Dec. Bar. Casual attire. Outdoor seating. **$$$**

★ ★ **SEA RANCH.** *1 Padre Blvd, South Padre Island (78597). Phone 956/761-1314; fax 956/761-1616.* American menu. Dinner. Closed mid-late Dec. Bar. Children's menu. Casual attire. **$$$**

Stephenville (B-7)

See also Cleburne, Comanche

Settled 1850
Population 14,921
Elevation 1,277 ft
Area Code 254
Zip 76401
Information Chamber of Commerce, 187 W Washington; phone 254/965-5313 or toll-free 800/658-6490
Web Site www.stephenvilletexas.org

What to See and Do

Cross Timbers Country Opry. *Lower Dublin Rd, Stephenville. 1 mile E of Hwy 281 via Hwy 377 Bypass. Phone 254/965-4132.* Family entertainment by country and western variety performers. (Sat evenings) **$$$**

Dinosaur Valley State Park. (See CLEBURNE) *29 miles E on Hwy 67.*

Historical House Museum Complex. *525 E Washington, Stephenville. Phone 254/965-5880. www.rootsweb.com/~txerath/museum.htm.* Rock English cottage (1869), two-story with bargeboards and vents with Pennsylvania hex signs. Church with fish-scaled steeple (1899); three log cabins; log corn crib (1861); late 1800s ranch house where John Tarleton (of Tarleton State University) lived; 1890s two-room schoolhouse; replica of carriage house containing museum of local history items. (Fri-Sun 2-5 pm; closed holidays) **FREE**

Hoka Hey Fine Arts Gallery & Foundry. *Hwy 377, Dublin. 10 miles SW via Hwy 377. Phone 254/445-2017.* One of the foremost bronze foundries in the United States. Here stands Robert Summers' original 9-foot sculpture of John Wayne, among various other bronzes, paintings, and prints. (Daily; closed holidays. Foundry tours by appointment). **FREE**

Tarleton State University. *1333 W Washington St, Stephenville. Phone 254/968-9000.* (1899) (6,500 students) An affiliate of Texas A&M University. Clyde Wells Fine Arts Center. Horse breeding program is one of the finest in the nation; tours of campus farm.

Special Event

Dairy Fest. Family fun, games, picnic. Concert. Mid-June.

Limited-Service Hotels

★ **DAYS INN.** *701 S Loop, Stephenville (76401). Phone 254/968-3392; fax 254/968-3527. www.daysinn.com.* 65 rooms, 2 story. Check-out 11 am. Outdoor pool. **$**

★ ★ **HOLIDAY INN.** *2865 W Washington St, Stephenville (76401). Phone 254/968-5256; toll-free 800/465-4329; fax 254/968-4255. www.holiday-inn .com.* 100 rooms, 2 story. Pets accepted, some restrictions; fee. Check-out noon. Restaurant. Outdoor pool. **$**

Restaurant

★ **JOSE'S.** *1044 W Washington, Stephenville (76401). Phone 254/965-7400; fax 254/965-6447.* Mexican, American menu. Lunch, dinner. Closed Jan 1, Thanksgiving, Dec 25. **$$**

Sulphur Springs (A-9)

See also Greenville

Population 14,551
Elevation 530 ft
Area Code 903
Zip 75482
Information Tourism & Visitors Bureau, 1200 Houston St, PO Box 347; phone 903/885-6516 or toll-free 888/300-6623
Web Site www.tourtexas.com/sulphursprings

Seat of Hopkins County with a Richardsonian Romanesque courthouse (1894), Sulphur Springs is the center of Texas's leading dairy region. The Leo St. Clair music box collection, the Regional Livestock Exposition and Civic Center, Heritage Park, and the Southwest Dairy Center make this an interesting area to visit.

What to See and Do

City Park. *Connally and League sts, Sulphur Springs.* Kids kingdom playground; lake, fishing, swimming pool (summer; fee). (Daily) **FREE**

Southwest Dairy Center. *1210 Houston St, Sulphur Springs. Phone 903/439-6455.* Exhibits demonstrate practical application of antique processing equipment and life on an early dairy farm to modern production and transportation. Guided tours (groups by appointment). (Mon-Sat 9 am-4 pm, Sun 1-4 pm; closed holidays) **FREE**

Special Events

CRA Finals Rodeo. *Civic Center, 1200 Houston St, Sulphur Springs (75482). Phone 903/885-8071.* Second weekend in Nov.

Fall Festival. *1200 Houston St, Sulphur Springs (75482). Phone 903/885-6515.* Carnival, arts and crafts exhibits, special events. Second Sat-third Sat in Sept.

Hopkins County Dairy Festival. *Civic Center, 1200 Houston St, Sulphur Springs (75482). Phone 903/885-8071.* Third week in June.

Limited-Service Hotels

★ **BEST WESTERN TRAIL DUST INN.** *1521 Shannon Rd E; I-30 E, exit 127, Sulphur Springs (75483). Phone 903/885-7515; toll-free 800/980-2378; fax 903/885-7515. www.bestwestern.com.* 102 rooms, 2 story. Complimentary continental breakfast. Check-out noon. Outdoor pool. **$**

★ ★ **HOLIDAY INN.** *1495 Industrial Dr E, Sulphur Springs (75482). Phone 903/885-0562; toll-free 800/566-4431; fax 903/885-0562. www.holiday-inn.com.* 96 rooms, 2 story. Pets accepted; fee. Check-out noon. Restaurant, bar. Outdoor pool. **$**

Sweetwater (B-6)

See also Abilene

Founded 1881
Population 11,415
Elevation 2,164 ft
Area Code 915
Zip 79556
Information Chamber of Commerce, 810 E Broadway, PO Box 1148; phone 915/235-5488 or toll-free 800/658-6757

Sweetwater is a manufacturing center for electronics, wearing apparel, and gypsum products. Hereford cattle, quarter horses, and sheep are raised in large numbers in the area.

Hunting is good for deer, quail, and turkey in the south and central portions of the county.

What to See and Do

City-County Pioneer Museum. *610 E 3rd St, Sweetwater. Phone 915/235-8547. www.sweetwatertexas.org/ museum.html.* Historic house displays antique furniture, pioneer tools, early photographs of area; Indian artifacts; Women Air Force Service Pilots memorabilia. (Tues-Sat 1-5 pm; closed holidays) **FREE**

Special Events

American Junior Rodeo National Finals. *Nolan County Coliseum, 1699 Cypress St, Sweetwater (79556). Phone 915/235-9259.* Late July-early Aug.

Rattlesnake Roundup. *Nolan County Coliseum, 1699 Cypress St, Sweetwater (79556). Phone 915/235-9259.* Also Gun & Coin Show. Second weekend in Mar.

Limited-Service Hotel

★ ★ **HOLIDAY INN.** *500 NW Georgia St, Sweetwater (79556). Phone 915/236-6887; toll-free 800/465-4329; fax 915/236-6887. www.holiday-inn.com.* 107 rooms, 2 story. Pets accepted; fee. Check-out noon. Restaurant. Outdoor pool. **$**

Temple (C-8)

See also Killeen, Salado, Waco

Population 54,514
Elevation 736 ft
Area Code 254
Information Convention & Visitors Bureau, Municipal Building, 2 N Main, 76501; phone 254/298-5720
Web Site www.temple-tx.org

Temple is the principal commercial center for a large area of central Texas. Items manufactured here encompass industries as diverse as agriculture, plastics, machinery, and electronics. Also in Temple are the Scott and White Clinic and Hospital, founded in 1904, and Texas A&M University School of Medicine.

What to See and Do

Belton Lake. *3110 FM 2271, Temple (76513). I-35 S, exit W on FM 2305. Phone 254/939-1829.* Swimming, water-skiing, fishing, boating (ramps); picnicking, concession, camping (tent and trailer sites, fee; hookups, dump station). (Daily) **$$**

Railroad & Heritage Museum. *315 W Ave B, Temple (75601). Phone 254/298-5172. www.rrhm.org.* Exhibits in restored Santa Fe Railroad depot (1907). Baldwin locomotive 3423, Santa Fe caboose. World War II troop sleeper and other pieces of rolling stock on grounds. Picnicking, playground. (Tues-Sat 10 am-4 pm, Sun noon-4 pm; closed holidays) **$**

Recreation areas. The Recreation Department maintains 26 parks, five with swimming, seven with tennis courts, three with 9-hole golf. Also 222-acre area on Belton Lake.

Special Event

Independence Day Celebration & Belton PRCA Rodeo. *412 E Central Ave, Temple. 8 miles SW on I-35, in Belton. Phone 254/939-3551.* Carnival, fiddlers' contest, parade, rodeo. Four days in early July.

Limited-Service Hotel

★ **LA QUINTA INN.** *1604 W Barton Ave, Temple (76501). Phone 254/771-2980; toll-free 800/531-5900; fax 254/778-7565. www.lq.com.* 106 rooms, 3 story. Pets accepted, some restrictions. Complimentary continental breakfast. Check-out noon. Outdoor pool. **$**

Texarkana (A-10)

Founded 1873
Population 34,782
Elevation 336 ft
Area Code 903 (TX); 870 (AR)
Information Chamber of Commerce, 819 State Line Ave, PO Box 1468, 75504; phone 903/792-7191
Web Site www.texarkanachamber.com

State Line Avenue divides this area into two separate cities: Texarkana, Arkansas, and Texarkana, Texas. The post office, which houses the Federal offices for both states, is centered on this line. The two civil governments cooperate closely. Texarkana is an agricultural, transportation, wholesale, and manufacturing center serving four states and produces paper, tires, tank cars, furniture, food, metal, and wood items. The Army's Red River Depot and Lone Star Army Ammunition Plant are located just to the west of the city.

Fishing is good on many nearby lakes, and on the Sulphur, Red, Cossatot, and Little rivers.

At the southeast corner of Third and Main streets is a mural honoring one of Texarkana's most noted native sons, ragtime pioneer Scott Joplin.

What to See and Do

Perot Theatre. *219 Main St, Texarkana. Phone 903/792-4992.* (1924) Designed by Emil Weil to accommodate both live theater and films. This historic, 1,606-seat performing arts facility features professional and local amateur entertainment.

Texarkana Historical Museum. *219 State Line Ave, Texarkana. Phone 903/793-4831. www.texarkanamuseums.org/texarkana_historical-museum.htm.* Local history displays include Caddo artifacts, Victorian parlor, doctor's office, 1885 kitchen; changing exhibits. (Tues-Fri 10 am-4 pm, Sat-Sun noon-3 pm; closed holidays) **$**

Wright Patman Dam and Lake. *12 miles SW on US 59. Phone 903/796-2419 (Rocky Point).* Water sports (marina, ramps); hunting, picnicking, playgrounds, camping (Rocky Point, Clear Springs, Piney Point; hook-ups). Fee for some activities. (Daily)

Special Event

Four States Fair & Rodeo. *Fairgrounds, Loop 245 and E 50th St, Texarkana (71854). Phone 870/773-2941; toll-free 800/776-1836. www.fourstatesfair.com.* Partake of the live entertainment, stroll through the livestock exhibits, and take in the Demolition Derby (fee). Sept. **$**

Limited-Service Hotel

★ **HOLIDAY INN EXPRESS.** *5401 N State Line Ave, Texarkana (75503). Phone 903/792-3366; toll-free 800/342-4942; fax 903/792-5649. www.holiday-inn.com.* 116 rooms, 3 story. Complimentary continental breakfast. Check-out noon. Outdoor pool, whirlpool. Airport transportation available. **$**

Specialty Lodging

The following lodging establishment is approved by Mobil Travel Guide, but due to its unique and individualized nature has not been given a traditional Mobil Star rating. Included in this listing you may find bed-and-breakfasts, limited-service inns, guest ranches, and other unique hotel properties.

MANSION ON MAIN BED & BREAKFAST INN. *802 Main St, Texarkana (75501). Phone 903/792-1835; fax 903/793-0878. www.mansiononmain.com.* Built in 1895; veranda columns from St. Louis World's Fair. 5 rooms, 2 story. Complimentary full breakfast. Check-in 2 pm, check-out 11 am. **$**

Texas City (D-9)

See also Galveston, Houston

Population 41,521
Elevation 12 ft
Area Code 409
Information Chamber of Commerce, 8419 Emmett F. Lowry Expy, Suite 105, PO Box 1717, 77592; phone 409/935-1408 or 281/280-3917 (Houston)
Web Site www.texas-city-tx.org

Texas City is located on the mainland, opposite Galveston. A 40-foot ship channel connects to the gulf. Several large oil refineries and chemical plants are located here.

What to See and Do

Fishing. From three municipal fishing piers on dike extending 5 miles into Galveston Bay. Also at Memorial and Bay Street parks. Swimming, water-skiing, boating (ramps free); picnicking.

Texas City Museum. *409 6th St N, Texas City. Phone 409/643-5799. www.texas-city.tx.org/docs/events/tx_museum.htm.* Two-story facility houses exhibits on history, science, technology, education, and culture. Replicas of filling station, railway depot. Discovery Center. (Tues-Sat 10 am-4 pm, Sun afternoons; closed holidays) **$$**

Special Events

Funfest. *Phone 409/935-1408.* Competition tennis, golf, soccer; rides, dances, children's activities, fun run; barbecue cook-off. June.

Shrimp Boil. *Rotary Pavilion, Nessler Park, 8419 Emmet F Lowry Expwy, Texas City. Phone toll-free 888/860-1408.* Food, dancing. Aug.

Limited-Service Hotel

★ **LA QUINTA INN.** *1121 Hwy 146 N, Texas City (77590). Phone 409/948-3101; toll-free 800/687-6667; fax 409/945-4412. www.lq.com.* 120 rooms, 2 story. Pets accepted, some restrictions. Complimentary continental breakfast. Check-out noon. Outdoor pool. **$**

The Colony

What to See and Do

The Tribute Golf Club. *1000 Boyd Rd (75056). Phone 972/370-5465.* You may be deep down south in Texas on the shores of Lake Lewisville, but you'd swear you were in the British Isles when shooting a round at this par-72, links-style golf course. In designing Tribute, Tripp Davis was influenced by some of the great holes at St. Andrews, Troon, Prestwick, and other famous Scottish links where the game was born so many years (and swings) ago. Eat and drink like the Scottish as well, in a pub and restaurant in the clubhouse. (Daily dawn-dusk; closed holidays) **$$$$**

Tow

What to See and Do

Fall Creek Vineyards. *1820 County Rd 222 (78672). Phone 915/379-5361. www.fcv.com.* You might not expect to find a winery that creates much of a buzz in the Texas Hill Country, but Fall Creek has won more than 500 awards since Ed and Susan Auler, a businessman-rancher and his wife, planted their first grapes in 1975. On 65 acres bordering Lake Buchanan, the Aulers produce primarily white wines, although some of their reds have also been toasted. For those who make the scenic drive out to the 15,000-square-foot winery, the Aulers offer daily tours and tastings. (Daily; closed holidays)

Tyler (B-9)

See also Athens, Henderson, Jacksonville, Kilgore, Longview

Founded 1846
Population 83,650
Elevation 545 ft
Area Code 903
Information Convention & Visitors Bureau, 315 N Broadway, 75702; phone 903/592-1661 or toll-free 800/235-5712
Web Site www.tylertexas.com

More than 1/3 of the commercially grown rose bushes in the United States come from the Tyler area. An area of diversified resources such as livestock, crops, forest products, and iron ore, Tyler is also a headquarters for the East Texas oilfield.

What to See and Do

Brookshire's World of Wildlife Museum & Country Store. *1600 W SW Loop 323, Tyler. Phone 903/534-2169. www.texas-on-line.com/graphic/tyler.htm.* More than 200 specimens of animals from all over the world, some in natural habitat exhibits. Replica of 1920s country store stocked with authentic items. Reservations advised. (Tues-Fri 9 am-noon, 1-4 pm, Sat 10 am-4 pm; closed holidays) **FREE**

Caldwell Zoo. *2203 W Martin Luther King Jr. Blvd, Tyler. Gentry Pkwy and Martin Luther King Jr. Blvd, NW part of town. Phone 903/593-0121.* More than 120 acres; domestic and wild animals. (Daily 9:30 am-5:30 pm; closed holidays) **FREE**

Goodman Museum. *624 N Broadway, Tyler. Phone 903/531-1286.* Antebellum artifacts, antiques, 19th-century medical instruments in a house built circa 1860. (Tues-Fri 10 am-4 pm, Sat noon-5 pm; closed holidays) **FREE**

Hudnall Planetarium. *On Tyler Junior College campus, two blocks from Hwy 64. Phone 903/510-2312. www.tyler.cc.tx.us/planet/planet.htm.* Astronomy exhibits (Sept-mid-May, Mon-Thurs; closed college vacations). Shows (Sept-mid-May, Sun and Wed; closed college vacations). **$**

Smith County Historical Society. *201 S College, Tyler. In former Carnegie Public Library. Phone 903/392-5993.* Exhibits cover history of Tyler and Smith County. (Tues-Sun afternoons; closed holidays) Tours by appointment. **FREE**

✪ **Tyler Rose Garden and Museum.** *420 Rose Park Dr, Tyler. Phone 903/531-1212.* The formal garden has 500 varieties on 15 acres; museum, community center. Museum and visitor center displays photos, memorabilia, past Rose Festival gowns. (Mon-Sat 9 am-4:30 pm, Sun 1-4 pm; closed holidays) **$$**

Tyler State Park. *789 Park Rd 16, Tyler (75706). 2 miles N of I-20, exit 562. Phone 903/597-5338.* Swimming, fishing, boating (ramp, rentals); picnicking, concession, improved campsites (hook-ups, dump station). Six lakes are within a few miles. Reservations advised. (Daily)

Special Events

Azalea Trail. Early Apr.

East Texas State Fair. *East Texas State Fairgrounds, 2112 W Front St, Tyler (75702). Phone 903/597-2501.* Late Sept.

Texas Rose Festival. *420 South Rose Park, Tyler (75702). Phone 903/597-3130.* Parade, pageantry; tours of rose fields. Rose show. Late-Oct.

Limited-Service Hotels

★ **HAMPTON INN.** *3130 Troup Hwy, Tyler (75701). Phone 903/596-7752; fax 903/596-7765. www.hamptoninn.com.* 78 rooms, 3 story. Complimentary continental breakfast. Check-out noon. Indoor pool, whirlpool. **$**
🛏

★★ **HOLIDAY INN.** *5701 S Broadway Ave, Tyler (75703). Phone 903/561-5800; fax 903/561-9916. www.holiday-inn.com.* 185 rooms, 8 story. Check-out noon. Restaurant. Outdoor pool, children's pool, whirlpool. Airport transportation available. **$**
🛏

Restaurants

★★ **LIANG'S CHINESE RESTAURANT.** *1828 E Southeast Loop 323, Tyler (75701). Phone 903/593-7883; fax 903/593-7308.* Large wood dragon sculpture. Chinese menu. Lunch, dinner. Closed Mon; Thanksgiving. Bar. Children's menu. **$$**

★★ **POTPOURRI HOUSE.** *3320 Troup Hwy, Tyler (75701). Phone 903/592-4171; fax 903/593-7484. www.potpourrihouse.com.* Victorian garden décor. Seafood, steak menu. Lunch, dinner. Closed Sun; holidays. **$$**

Uvalde (D-6)

See also Brackettville, Del Rio, Eagle Pass

Founded 1855
Population 14,929
Elevation 913 ft
Area Code 830
Zip 78801
Information Chamber of Commerce/Convention & Visitors Bureau, 300 E Main; phone 830/278-3361 or toll-free 800/588-2533
Web Site www.uvalde.org

The Balcones escarpment divides Uvalde County into rugged upland hills and valleys to the north and low, flat mesquite country to the south. Livestock, cotton, vegetables, pecans, and large quantities of honey from desert blossoms, called "Uvalde honey," come from the area.

What to See and Do

First State Bank. *200 E Nopal St, Uvalde. Phone 830/278-6231.* Former governor's art and antique collections on display. (Mon-Fri) **FREE**

Garner Memorial Museum. *333 N Park St, Uvalde. Phone 830/278-5018. www.museumsusa.org/data/museums/TX/187782.htm.* Home of Vice President John Nance Garner; houses displays on the life and career of Garner, and Uvalde County history. (Tues-Sat 9 am-5 pm; closed holidays) **$**

Garner State Park. *30 miles N on Hwy 83, off Hwy 1050 onto Park Rd 29. Phone 830/232-6132.* Swimming, fishing; hiking trail, bird-watching, miniature golf (seasonal), picnicking, concessions, improved campsites, screened shelters, cabins (dump station). (Daily) **$$**

Uvalde Grand Opera House. *104 W North St, Uvalde. Phone 830/278-4184.* (1891) Used for plays, ballets, orchestra performances; also includes historical room. Tours (Mon-Fri; closed holidays).

Special Events

Air Fiesta. *Garner Field Rd, Uvalde.* Soaring competitions. Aug.

Sahawe Indian Dance Ceremonials. *117 Studer St, Uvalde (78801).* Phone 830/278-2016. Two weekends in Feb, one week in July.

Limited-Service Hotel

★ ★ **HOLIDAY INN.** *920 E Main St, Uvalde (78801). Phone 830/278-4511; toll-free 800/465-4329; fax 830/591-0413. www.holiday-inn.com.* 150 rooms, 2 story. Pets accepted. Check-out noon. Restaurant, bar. Outdoor pool. **$**

Van Horn (C-3)

See also Guadalupe Mountains National Park

Population 2,435
Elevation 4,010 ft
Area Code 915
Zip 79855
Information Convention Center and Visitors Bureau, 1801 W Broadway, PO Box 488; phone 915/283-2682

The mountains surrounding Van Horn provide an exceptional setting for the town. Once a cattle and sheep market, the town now bases its economy on tourism. It is also a center for cotton, vegetables, and grain, first grown here in 1950 after discovery of a great underground water deposit. Milling talc and marble are equally important industries.

Just west of town in the Diablo Mountains roams the last remaining flock of bighorn sheep in Texas. These sheep are the subject of a successful breeding program. Deer, antelope, quail, and dove are abundant in the rugged mountains of the area.

Special Events

Culberson County Fair. *Rodeo Arena, 1801 W Broadway, Van Horn.* Phone 915/283-2682. Late Sept.

Frontier Days & Rodeo Celebration. *1801 W Broadway, Van Horn.* Phone 915/283-2682. Held since 1899. Parade, AJRA rodeo, Rodeo Queen contest, golf tournament, dance. Late June.

Vernon (A-6)

See also Childress, Quanah, Wichita Falls

Founded 1889
Population 11,660
Elevation 1,216 ft
Area Code 940
Zip 76384
Information Chamber of Commerce, 1725 Pease St, PO Box 1538, 76385; phone 940/552-2564 or toll-free 800/687-3137

Vernon is headquarters of the 500,000-acre W. T. Waggoner Ranch, one of the largest in the United States. In its early days it was a supply point for trail riders driving herds of cattle north. Doan's Crossing, 16 miles northeast, was a famous cattle trail crossing for the Red River.

What to See and Do

Lake Kemp. *25 miles S via Hwy 183, 283.* Swimming, water-skiing, fishing, boating.

Red River Valley Museum. *4600 College Dr (Hwy 70), Vernon (76384). On Hwy 70, just off Hwy 287.* Phone 940/553-1848. www.rrvm.org. Archaeological exhibits and Native American artifacts. Big-game collection includes more than 130 trophies, including black rhino and polar bear; History of Texas Ranching Room includes a 10-by-20-foot Waggoner mural. Sculpture exhibit includes busts of famous people; traveling exhibits room. (Tues-Sun 1-5 pm; closed holidays) **FREE**

Special Event

Santa Rosa Roundup. Phone 940/552-2321. Rodeo, parade, specialty acts, Santa Rosa Palomino Club. Third weekend in May.

Limited-Service Hotels

★ ★ **BEST WESTERN VILLAGE INN.** *1615 Expressway, Vernon (76384). Phone 940/552-5417; toll-free 800/780-7234; fax 940/552-5417. www.bestwestern.com.* 46 rooms. Check-in noon, check-out 11 am. Restaurant, bar. Outdoor pool. **$**

★ **GREEN TREE INN.** *3029 Morton St, Vernon (76384). Phone 940/552-5421; toll-free 800/600-5421;*

fax 940/552-5421. 30 rooms. Pets accepted, some restrictions. Complimentary continental breakfast. Check-out 11 am. Outdoor pool. **$**

Victoria (D-8)

See also Goliad, Port Lavaca

Founded 1824
Population 60,603
Elevation 220 ft
Area Code 361
Information Convention & Visitors Bureau, 700 Main Center, Suite 101, PO Box 2465, 77902; phone 361/573-5277 or toll-free 800/926-5774
Web Site www.victoriachamber.org

In 1685, Robert Cavelier, Sieur de La Salle, established a fort at the head of Lavaca Bay and claimed the area for France. The Spanish set up a fort and a mission in 1722. Victoria itself was settled by the Spanish, founded in 1824 by Martin DeLeon and named after a Mexican President, Guadalupe Victoria. Anglo-Americans soon moved in and were active in the Texas Revolution.

Victoria County is one of the leading cattle areas in Texas. Brahmans and crossbreeds are a big part of the economy. Victoria, with its oil and chemicals, is a part of the booming Texas Gulf Coast. Shipping is aided by the 35-mile-long Victoria Canal, connecting link to the Intracoastal Waterway.

What to See and Do

Coleto Creek Reservoir. *365 Coleto Rd, Fannin. 14 miles SW via Hwy 59 S. Phone 361/575-6366.* Approximately 3,100 acres of fresh water. Extensive lakefront, water-skiing, fishing (lighted pier), boating; nature trail, pavilions, picnicking, playground, improved camping (fee). (Daily) **$$$**

Memorial Square. *700 Main Center S, Victoria.* Oldest public burial ground in the city. Three monuments outline history of the area. A steam locomotive and Dutch windmill are also here.

Riverside Park. *700 Main Center, Victoria. Red River and Memorial sts. Phone 361/572-2767.* A 562-acre site on the Guadalupe River. Picnic areas, barbecue pits, playgrounds, duck pond, rose garden, hiking/biking

trail; boat ramp; 27-hole golf, baseball fields, RV campsites (fee). (Daily) **FREE** Within the park is

Texas Zoo. *110 Memorial Dr, Victoria.* Indoor and outdoor exhibits of animals native to Texas include margays, ocelots, jaguarundis, and a pair of rare red wolves. (Daily; closed Jan 1, Thanksgiving, Dec 25) **$**

Special Events

Bach Festival. *Phone 361/570-5788.* June.

PRCA Rodeo. *Victoria Community Center, 2905 E North St, Victoria (77901). Phone 361/573-2651.* Last weekend in Feb.

Victoria Jaycees Stockshow. *2905 E North St, Victoria (77901). Phone 361/576-4300.* Second weekend in Mar.

Limited-Service Hotel

★ **FAIRFIELD INN.** *7502 N Navarro St, Victoria (77904). Phone 361/582-0660; fax 361/582-0660. www.fairfieldinn.com.* 64 rooms, 3 story. Complimentary continental breakfast. Check-in 3 pm, check-out noon. Indoor pool, whirlpool. **$**

Waco (B-8)

See also Groesbeck, Hillsboro, Lake Whitney, Temple

Founded 1849
Population 113,726
Elevation 427 ft
Area Code 254
Information Tourist Information Center, PO Box 2570, 76702; phone 254/750-8696 or toll-free 800/922-6386 (outside Waco)
Web Site www.wacocvb.com

Named for the Huaco (WAY-co) Indians, this area has been a trade, distribution, and travel center since the first permanent white settler, Captain Shapley P. Ross, ran a ferry across the Brazos River. The ferry put Waco on the main thoroughfare to the West.

From 1857 to 1865, the city was at the center of the Texas secessionist movement. Consequently it suffered considerable disruption of civic and business affairs, making a slow recovery after the Civil War. Waco is now alive with industries and modern businesses.

What to See and Do

Art Center Waco. *1300 College Dr, Waco (76706). Phone 254/752-4371. www.artcenterwaco.org.* Permanent and changing exhibits in renovated Mediterranean-style house. (Tues-Sat 10 am-5 pm, Sun 1-5 pm; closed holidays) **$**

Baylor University. *1311 S 5th St, Waco. Phone 254/710-1011.* (1845) (14,122 students) Chartered by the Republic of Texas in 1845, Baylor University is the oldest university in continuous existence in the state. On the 425-acre campus are

> **Armstrong Browning Library.** *700 Speight St, Waco. Phone 254/710-3566. www.browninglibrary.org/visitor.htm.* World's largest collection of books, letters, manuscripts, and memorabilia of Robert Browning and Elizabeth Barrett Browning. (Mon-Fri 9 am-5 pm, Sat 9 am-noon; closed holidays) **FREE**

> **Governor Bill & Vara Daniel Historic Village.** *1218 S University Parks Dr, Waco (76706). Behind Alumni Center. Phone 254/710-1160.* A reconstructed 1890s Texas river town. (Mon-Sat) **$$**

> **Strecker Museum.** *Speight and 4th sts, Waco (76706). Basement of Sid Richardson Science Bldg. Phone 254/710-1110. www.baylor.edu/museum_studies/strecker.htm.* Biology, geology, archaeology, and anthropology exhibits; "Man's Cultural Heritage in Central Texas;" 1835 log cabin. World's largest fossil sea turtle; exhibit of local reptiles. (Mon-Sat 10 am-4 pm; closed holidays) **FREE**

Dr. Pepper Museum. *300 S 5th St, Waco. Phone 254/757-1024. www.drpeppermuseum.com/visit.html.* This 1906 "Home of Dr. Pepper" features exhibits, memorabilia, and a working turn-of-the-century soda fountain. (Mon-Sat 10 am-4 pm, Sun noon-4 pm; closed holidays) **$$**

Fort Fisher Park. *106 Texas Rangers Trail, Waco (76706). I-35 and University Dr, exit 335B. Phone 254/750-8630.* Headquarters for Company F, Texas Rangers, Waco Tourist Information Center, and the Texas Rangers Hall of Fame and Museum. Approximately 30 acres. (Park closed to public) (Tourist information and museum only) (Daily) Within the park is

> **Texas Ranger Hall of Fame & Museum.** *100 Texas Ranger Trail, Waco. Phone 254/750-8631. www.texasranger.org/visitor/location/tours.htm.* Texas Ranger memorabilia, firearms exhibits and dioramas with wax figures depict more than 170-year history of Texas Rangers; 20-minute film, "*Story of Texas Rangers;*" Western art; library. (Daily 9 am-6 pm; closed holidays) **$$**

Lake Waco. *FM 1637, Waco (76706). Headquarters is 2 miles NW on FM 1637 (N 19th St), then approximately 1 1/2 miles W, follow signs. Phone 254/756-5359.* Swimming, water-skiing, fishing, boating (ramps); nature trail, picnicking, camping (tent and trailer sites, dump station). Some fees. (Daily)

Restored houses. Earle-Napier-Kinnard House. *814 S 4th St, Waco (76706). Phone 254/753-5166.* (1867) Two-story Greek Revival home; furnished in 1860s style (summer tours Thurs-Mon). **East Terrace** (circa 1872) *100 Mill St.* Two-story Italianate villa-style house built with bricks made from Brazos River clay; period furnishings. **Fort House** (1868) *503 S 4th St.* Antiques and local historical exhibits in Greek Revival home. **Champe Carter McCulloch House** (1866) *407 Columbus Ave.* Two-story Greek Revival home, period furnishings. (All houses: Sat-Sun; closed Easter and Thanksgiving weeks, Dec-Jan 2) Combination ticket available. **$**

Special Events

Brazos River Festival. *Cameron Park E. Phone 254/753-5166.* Art show, karaoke, the Great Texas Raft Race, food, fun, games, music. Last full weekend in Apr.

Christmas on the Brazos. *810 S 4th St, Waco.* First full weekend in Dec.

Heart o' Texas Fair & Rodeo. *Coliseum and Fairgrounds, 46th and Bosque Blvd, Waco (76710).* Early Oct.

Heart o' Texas Speedway. *203 Trailwood, Waco (76712). Phone 254/829-2294.* Stock car racing. Mar-Sept.

Limited-Service Hotels

★ **BEST WESTERN OLD MAIN LODGE.** *I-35 and 4th St, Waco (76706). Phone 254/753-0316; toll-free 800/299-9226; fax 254/753-3811. www.bestwestern.com.* Near Baylor University. 84 rooms. Pets accepted, some restrictions. Complimentary full breakfast. Check-in 3 pm, check-out 1 pm. High-speed Internet access, wireless Internet access. Outdoor pool. **$**

★ **CLARION INN WACO.** *801 S 4th St, Waco (76706). Phone 254/757-2000; toll-free 800/275-9226;*

fax 254/757-1110. www.choicehotels.com. Baylor University one block. 148 rooms, 2 story. Complimentary full breakfast. Check-in 3 pm, check-out noon. Wireless Internet access. Indoor pool. Airport transportation available. Business center. **$**

★ **COMFORT INN.** 1430 I-35 S, Waco (76706). Phone 254/752-1991; toll-free 800/228-5150; fax 254/752-2084. www.choicehotels.com. 53 rooms, 2 story. Complimentary continental breakfast. Check-in 3 pm, check-out 11 am. High-speed Internet access. Outdoor pool. **$**

Full-Service Hotel

★ ★ ★ **HILTON WACO.** 113 S University Parks Dr, Waco (76701). Phone 817/754-8484; toll-free 800/234-5244; fax 817/752-2214. www.hiltonwaco.com. This hotel is conveniently located downtown and close to the convention center. 196 rooms, 11 story. Pets accepted, some restrictions; fee. Check-in 3 pm, check-out noon. High-speed Internet access, wireless Internet access. Restaurant, bar. Fitness room. Indoor pool, whirlpool. Tennis. Airport transportation available. Business center. **$**

Restaurant

★ **ELITE CAFE.** 2132 S Valley Mills Dr, Waco (76706). Phone 254/754-4941; fax 254/754-7145. American menu. Lunch, dinner, late-night. Closed Thanksgiving, Dec 25. Bar. Children's menu. Casual attire. **$$**

Weatherford (B-7)

See also Eastland, Fort Worth, Mineral Wells

Population 19,000
Elevation 1,052 ft
Area Code 817
Zip 76086
Information Chamber of Commerce, 401 Fort Worth St, PO Box 310; phone 817/594-3801
Web Site www.weatherford-chamber.com

What to See and Do

Holland Lake Park. *Off Clear Lake Rd, exit 409 from I-20.* Ten-acre municipal park; living museum of nature. An original dog-run log cabin, the first built in the county. Playground, picnicking. (Daily)

Lake Weatherford. *8 miles NE on FM 1707.* Water sports, fishing, boating; picnicking. (Daily)

Special Event

Peach Festival. *Courthouse Sq, 401 Fort Worth St, Weatherford (76086). Phone 817/596-3801.* Second Sat in July.

Wichita Falls (A-7)

See also Vernon

Founded 1882
Population 104,197
Elevation 946 ft
Area Code 940
Information Convention and Visitors Bureau, 1000 Fifth St, 76301; phone 940/716-5500 or toll-free 800/799-6732
Web Site www.wichitafalls.org

Wichita Falls was named for the Wichita who lived on the Big Wichita River, near a waterfall that disappeared around the turn of the century. A re-creation of the falls was completed in 1987 and has become the symbol of a prosperous community. Wichita Falls is an industrial center for many manufacturing plants that produce a variety of products, such as fiberglass reinforcements, plate glass, gas turbine components, oil field equipment, and electronic components. Livestock, wheat, oil, and cotton also contribute to the economy. Sheppard AFB, one of the largest air force technical training centers in the nation, is 5 miles north on Highway 277/281.

The rebuilt falls can be seen from Interstate 44 heading into town from the north. They are 54 feet high and recirculate the river's waters at a rate of 3,500 gallons per minute.

What to See and Do

Diversion Reservoir. *25 miles W via Hwy 82, Hwy 258.* Swimming, water-skiing, fishing, boating.

Kell House. *900 Bluff St, Wichita Falls. Phone 940/723-0623.* (1909) Landmark with original family furnishings. High ceilings, oak floors, ornate woodwork, period pieces. Guided tour relates history of the early settlement of the area. Tours (Tues-Wed, Sun afternoons). **$$**

Lake Arrowhead State Park. *229 Park Rd 63, Wichita Falls (76310). 15 miles SE of town via Hwy 281 and FM 1954.* Phone 940/528-2211. Swimming, water-skiing, fishing, boating (ramp, rentals); nature and bridle trails, picnicking, playground, improved camping (hook-ups, dump station). **$**

Lake Kickapoo. *25 miles SW via Hwy 82 to Mankins, then S off Hwy 25.* Swimming, water-skiing, fishing, boating.

Trails & Tales of Boomtown, USA. *104 W 3rd St, Burkburnett. 15 miles N on I-44 E to TX 240 W, Burkburnett exit.* Phone 940/569-0460. www.trailsand tales.org. Displays, photographs, and audiovisual presentations illustrate the famous 1918 Burkburnett oil boom and surrounding events. Guided bus tour (two hours) of various sites relevant to the boom. (June-Oct, Fri-Sat 8 am-5 pm; tour, Sat only; closed Thanksgiving, Dec 25.) **$$$**

Wichita Falls Museum & Art Center. *2 Eureka Cir, Wichita Falls.* Phone 940/692-0923. www.wfmuseum.org. Permanent and changing art and hands-on science exhibits; children's activities. Planetarium shows (Sat afternoons, fee). Museum (Tues-Sat 10 am-5 pm, Sun 1-5 pm; closed holidays). **$$**

Special Events

Fantasy of Lights. *Midwestern State University, 3400 Taft Blvd, Wichita Falls.* Phone 940/397-4352. More than 30 magnificent Christmas displays and 18,000 lights outlining campus buildings. Begun in 1920s. Dec.

Home and Garden Festival. *1000 5th St, Wichita Falls.* Phone 940/696-5262. Yard and garden plants, demonstrations, seminars. Late Feb.

Hotter 'n Hell Bicycle Ride. *1000 5th St, Wichita Falls (76301).* Phone 940/322-3223. Trails varying in length from 6-100 miles; race. Music; homemade ice cream contest; food and beverages. Late Aug.

Texas-Oklahoma Fair. *1000 5th St, Wichita Falls.* Phone 940/720-2999. Carnival, arts and crafts, entertainment. Mid-Sept.

Texas Ranch Roundup. *1005 Midwestern Pkwy, Wichita Falls.* Phone 940/322-0771. Team competition among 11 of the largest ranches in Texas. Mid-Aug.

Texas Weapon Collectors Association Gun & Knife Shows. *MPEC Exhibit Hall, 1000 5th St, Wichita Falls.* Phone 940/692-3766. 350 exhibitors from an eight-state area; antique and modern firearms. Weekends in Jan, Mar, Aug, Nov.

Zephyr Days Train Show. *Ohio and 9th St, Wichita Falls.* Phone 940/723-0623. Old-time demonstrations and dress, carriage rides, food. Early Oct.

Limited-Service Hotels

★ ★ **HOLIDAY INN.** *401 Broad St, Wichita Falls (76301).* Phone 940/766-6000; toll-free 800/465-4329; fax 940/766-5942. www.holiday-inn.com. 241 rooms, 4 story. Check-out noon. Restaurant, bar. Fitness room. Indoor pool, outdoor pool, children's pool, whirlpool. **$**
🏃 ⛱

★ **LA QUINTA INN.** *1128 Central Frwy N, Wichita Falls (76305).* Phone 940/322-6971; fax 940/723-2573. www.lq.com. 139 rooms, 2 story. Pets accepted, some restrictions. Complimentary continental breakfast. Check-out noon. Outdoor pool. Airport transportation available. **$**
🐾 ⛱

Restaurant

★ **EL CHICO.** *1028 Central Frwy, Wichita Falls (16306).* Phone 940/322-1455; fax 940/766-5636. www.elchico.com. Tex-Mex menu. Lunch, dinner. Closed Thanksgiving, Dec 25. Bar. Children's menu. **$$**

Set aside a few days to venture out of the Lone Star state and discover what its neighbors have to offer. From Dallas, Hot Springs and Little Rock, Arkansas, and Oklahoma City are within a few hours drive. If you've been touring the Houston area, consider the six-hour drive to New Orleans. Carlsbad Caverns and White Sands National Monument in New Mexico are within a day's drive from El Paso. Santa Fe, Georgia O'Keeffe's inspiration, is a five-hour drive from Amarillo. Expand your horizons; you never know what interesting attractions you might come across.

Hot Springs & Hot Springs National Park, AR

5 hours, 286 miles from Dallas

Settled Town of Hot Springs: 1807
Population 35,750
Elevation 632 ft
Area Code 501
Information Convention & Visitors Bureau, 134 Convention Blvd, PO Box K, 71902; phone 501/321-2277 or toll-free 800/772-2489
Web Site www.nps.gov/hosp and www.hotsprings.org

One of the most popular spas and resorts in the United States, the colorful city of Hot Springs surrounds portions of the nearly 4,700-acre Hot Springs National Park. Approximately 1 million gallons of thermal water flow daily from the 47 springs within the park. The springs have been administered by the federal government since 1832.

At an average temperature of 143° F, the water flows to a reservoir under the headquarters building; here it is distributed to bathhouses through insulated pipes. Some of it is cooled to 90° F without being exposed to air or mixed with other water. Bathhouses mix cooled and hot thermal water to regulate bath temperatures. The only differences among bathhouses are in the appointments and service.

The Libbey Memorial Physical Medicine Center specializes in hydrotherapy treatments given under the supervision of a registered physical therapist. Patients may be referred to this center by registered physicians or may get a standard bath without a referral.

Hot Springs, however, is more than a spa. It is a cosmopolitan city visited by travelers from all over the world; it is also a delightful vacation spot in the midst of beautiful wooded hills, valleys, and lakes of the Ouachita region. Swimming, boating, and water sports are available at nearby Catherine, Hamilton, and Ouachita lakes. All three offer good year-round fishing for bream, crappie, bass, and rainbow trout. The 42nd President of the United States, William Jefferson Clinton, grew up here. A Ranger District office of the Ouachita National Forests is located in Hot Springs.

What to See and Do

Arkansas Alligator Farm & Petting Zoo. *847 Whittington Ave. Phone 501/623-6172. www.hotsprings usa.com/gatorfarm.* Houses alligators, rhesus monkeys, mountain lions, llamas, pygmy goats, ducks, and other animals. (Daily) **$$**

Auto tours. *Fountain St and Hot Springs Mountain Dr. Phone 501/321-2277.* Just north of Bathhouse Row, drive from the end of Fountain Street up Hot Springs Mountain Drive to scenic overlooks at Hot Springs Mountain Tower and a picnic area on the mountaintop. West Mountain Drive, starting from either Prospect Avenue (on the south) or from Whittington Avenue (on the north) also provides excellent vistas of the city and surrounding countryside.

Bath House Show. *701 Central Ave. Phone 501/623-1415. www.thebathhouseshow.com.* Two-hour show of music and comedy acts derivative of 1930s-present; musical anthologies, reenactments of radio shows. (Feb-Dec, schedule varies; closed Jan) **$$$$**

Belle of Hot Springs. *5200 Central Ave (Hwy 7 S), Hot Springs (71913). Phone 501/525-4438. www.belle*

riverboat.com. Sightseeing, lunch, and dinner cruises along Lake Hamilton on the 400-passenger vessel (Feb-Nov, daily). Charter cruises available.

Coleman's Crystal Mine. *5386 N Hwy 7. 16 miles N on Hwy 7 N. Phone 501/984-5328.* Visitors may dig for quartz crystals; tools supplied. Shop. (Daily; closed Dec 25) **$$$**

Dryden Potteries. *341 Whittington Ave. Phone 501/623-4201. www.drydenpottery.com.* Pottery-making demonstrations. (Mon-Fri 9 am-3:30 pm, Sat from 9:30 am; closed Jan 1, Thanksgiving, Dec 25) **FREE**

Hot Springs Mountain Tower. *401 Hot Springs Mountain Dr, atop Hot Springs Mountain. Phone 501/623-6035.* Tower rises 216 feet above Hot Springs National Park; glass-enclosed elevator rides 1,256 feet above sea level for spectacular view of Ouachita Mountains; fully enclosed viewing area and, higher up, open-air deck. (Daily; closed Jan 1, Thanksgiving, Dec 24-25) **$$$**

Josephine Tussaud Wax Museum. *250 Central Ave. Phone 501/623-5836. www.rideaduck.com.* Set in the former Southern Club, which was the city's largest casino and supper club until the late 1960s, this museum displays more than 100 wax figures. (Summer: Sun-Thurs 9 am-8 pm, Fri-Sat 9 am-9 pm; winter: Sun-Thurs 9:30 am-5 pm, Fri-Sat 9:30 am-8 pm; closed Jan 1, Thanksgiving, Dec 25) **$$**

Lake Catherine State Park. *5386 N Hwy 7, Hot Springs Village (71909). S and E via Hwy 128, 171. Phone 501/984-5396. www.arkansasstateparks.com.*

Mid-America Science Museum. *500 Mid-America Blvd. Phone 501/767-3461. www.midamerica museum.com.* Exhibits focus on life, energy, matter, perception, state of Arkansas. Museum features 35,000-gallon freshwater aquarium; erosion table; laser theater. Snack bar (seasonal), gift shop. (Memorial Day-Labor Day: daily 9:30 am-6 pm; rest of year: Tues-Sun 10 am-5 pm; closed Jan 1, Thanksgiving, Dec 24-25) **$$$**

National Park & Hot Springs Duck Tours. *406 Central Ave. Phone 501/321-2911; toll-free 800/682-7044. www.rideaduck.com.* The "Amphibious Duck" travels on both land and water. Board in the heart of Hot Springs and proceed onto Lake Hamilton around St. John's Island. (Mar-Oct, daily; Nov-Feb, as weather permits) **$$$**

Ouachita National Forest. *100 Reserve St, Hot Springs (71902). 12 miles W on Hwy 270 or 20 miles N on Hwy 7. Phone 501/321-5202. www.fs.fed.us.oonf/*

ouachita.htm. The Ouachita (WASH-i-taw), located in 15 counties in west-central Arkansas and southeast Oklahoma, covers approximately 1.7 million acres and includes 7 wilderness areas, 35 developed recreation areas, 7 equestrian trails, 9 navigable rivers, and 8 lakes suitable for boating. Some recreation areas charge fees. For more information, contact the Forest Supervisor, PO Box 1270, 71902. (Daily) On Lake Ouachita is

Lake Ouachita State Park. *5451 Mountain Pine Rd, Mountain Pine (71956). 3 miles W on Hwy 270, 12 miles N on Hwy 227. Phone 501/767-9366. www.lakeouachita.com.* Approximately 400 acres. Swimming, fishing, boating (rentals, marina); hiking trails, picnicking, camping (hook-ups, dump station), cabins. Interpretive programs, exhibits. (Daily)

Tiny Town. *374 Whittington Ave (71901). Phone 501/624-4742.* Indoor train town with trains across America; mechanical display; handmade miniatures. (Apr-Nov, Mon-Sat) **$$**

⭐ **Walking tour.** Start at

Park Headquarters and Visitor Center. *101 Reserve St, Hot Springs (71901). Phone 501/624-3383.* Exhibit on workings and origin of the hot springs. A self-guided nature trail starts here and follows the Grand Promenade. Visitor center is located in the Hill Wheatley Plaza at the park entrance (daily; closed Jan 1, Dec 25). Gulpha Gorge Campground is available for stays limited to 14 days April-October, and to 30 days in a calendar year (fee). Inquire at National Park Fordyce Visitor Center on Bathhouse Row.

Grand Promenade. *Grand Promenade and Fountain sts. Phone 501/624-3383.* Leads through a landscaped park above and behind Bathhouse Row, offering pleasant vistas of the city.

Bathhouse Row. *Central Ave. Phone 501/624-3383.* Self-guided tours of the Fordyce Bathhouse are offered. (Daily; closed July 4, Thanksgiving, Dec 25)

Two Open Hot Springs. *At the S end of Bathouse Row. Phone 501/623-6172.*

Special Event

Thoroughbred racing. Oaklawn Jockey Club. *2705 Central Ave, Hot Springs (71902). Phone 501/623-4411; toll-free 800/625-5296. www.oaklawn.com.* While watching and wagering on live races at Oaklawn, fans can also follow simulcast races or dine on a variety of tasty treats. Jan-Apr, daily.

Limited-Service Hotels

★ **DAYS INN.** *106 Lookout Pt, Hot Springs (71913). Phone 501/525-5666; toll-free 800/995-9559; fax 501/525-5666. www.daysinn.com.* 58 rooms, 2 story. Check-out 11 am. Outdoor pool, whirlpool. **$**

★ **HAMPTON INN.** *151 Temperance Hill Rd, Hot Springs (71913). Phone 501/525-7000; toll-free 800/426-7866; fax 501/525-7626. www.hamptoninn.com.* 82 rooms, 4 story. Complimentary continental breakfast. Check-out 11 am. Outdoor pool. **$**

Full-Service Hotels

★ ★ ★ **ARLINGTON RESORT HOTEL AND SPA.** *239 Central Ave, Hot Springs (71901). Phone 501/623-7771; toll-free 800/643-1502; fax 501/623-2243. www.arlingtonhotel.com.* Guests will find total relaxation and enjoyment at this resort in the beautiful Ouachita Mountains of the Hot Springs National Park. Guests can unwind in twin cascading pools or in the refreshing outdoor mountainside hot tub. Grand old hotel (circa 1925); overlooks park. 484 rooms, 11 story. Check-out 11 am. Restaurant, bar. Fitness room. Two outdoor pools, whirlpool. Tennis. **$**

★ ★ ★ **THE AUSTIN HOTEL & CONVENTION CENTER.** *305 Malvern Ave, Hot Springs (71901). Phone 501/623-6600; toll-free 877/623-6697; fax 501/624-7160. www.theaustinhotel.com.* This wonderful getaway is located in the Hot Springs Park with a spectacular view of the Ouachita Mountains. It is a unique setting for guests to rejuvenate themselves with a visit to the famous spa in the park. Art galleries and music shows are just a few miles away. 200 rooms, 14 story. Check-out 11 am. Restaurant, bar. Spa. Indoor, outdoor pool; whirlpool. **$$**

Restaurants

★ ★ **BOHEMIA.** *517 Park Ave, Hot Springs (71901). Phone 501/623-9661; fax 501/623-9661.* Czech, German menu. Lunch, dinner. Closed Sun; holidays; also part of Dec, Jan. Children's menu. **$**

★ **CAJUN BOILERS.** *2806 Albert Pike Hwy, Hot Springs (71913). Phone 501/767-5695; fax 501/767-0952.* Dock for boat dining. Cajun menu. Dinner. Closed Sun-Mon; Thanksgiving, Dec 25. Children's menu. **$$**

★ ★ **COY'S STEAK HOUSE.** *300 Coy St, Hot Springs (71901). Phone 501/321-1414; fax 501/321-1497.* Seafood, steak menu. Dinner. Closed Thanksgiving, Dec 24-25, 31. Bar. Children's menu. Valet parking. **$$$**

★ **FADED ROSE.** *210 Central Ave, Hot Springs (71901). Phone 501/624-3200; fax 501/624-5380.* Seafood, steak menu. Lunch, dinner. Closed Thanksgiving, Dec 25. In former hotel (1889). **$$**

★ ★ ★ **HAMILTON HOUSE.** *130 Van Lyell Trail, Hot Springs (71913). Phone 501/525-2727; fax 501/525-1717.* This is the most appropriate choice in town for a dress-up, fine-dining occasion. The restaurant occupies four stories of an old estate home with seating in several cozy dining rooms. The quiet, peninsula setting is on beautiful Lake Hamilton. American menu. Dinner. Closed holidays. Bar. Children's menu. Valet parking. Outdoor seating. **$$$**

★ ★ **HOT SPRINGS BRAU-HOUSE.** *801 Central Ave, Hot Springs (71901). Phone 501/624-7866.* This restaurant is located in the cellar of 110-year-old building. German menu. Dinner. Closed Mon; holidays. Bar. Children's menu. Outdoor seating. **$**

★ **MCCLARD'S BAR-B-Q.** *505 Albert Pike, Hot Springs (71913). Phone 501/624-9586.* Barbecue menu. Lunch, dinner. Closed Sun-Mon; Thanksgiving, Dec 25. Children's menu. Casual attire. **$**

★ **MILLER'S CHICKEN AND STEAK HOUSE.** *4723 Central Ave, Hot Springs (71913). Phone 501/525-8861.* American, steak menu. Dinner. Closed Mon; also Dec-mid-Jan. Bar. Children's menu. **$$**

★ **MOLLIE'S.** *538 W Grand Ave, Hot Springs (71901). Phone 501/623-6582.* Kosher menu. Lunch, dinner. Closed Sun; Jan 1, Thanksgiving, Dec 25. Bar. Children's menu. Outdoor seating. **$$**

Little Rock, AR

5 hours 12 minutes, 319 miles from Dallas

Settled 1812
Population 183,133
Elevation 286 ft

Area Code 501
Information Little Rock Convention & Visitors Bureau, Robinson Center, Markham & Broadway, PO Box 3232, Little Rock 72203; phone 501/376-4781 or toll-free 800/844-4781
Web Site www.littlerock.com

Little Rock apparently got its name from French explorers who called this site on the Arkansas River "La Petite Roche" to distinguish it from larger rock outcroppings up the river. The first shack probably was built on the site in 1812, and by 1819, a town site had been staked. The community became the territorial capital in 1821 when the seat of government was moved here from Arkansas Post. The first steamboat, the *Eagle*, came up the Arkansas River in 1822.

Additional Visitor Information

Travelers may stop at the visitor information centers (daily) at the Statehouse Convention Center, and Little Rock National Airport to get more information. Telefun, 501/372-3399, is a 24-hour prerecorded entertainment hotline with a bi-weekly update on events in the Little Rock area. For any additional information, contact the Little Rock Convention & Visitors Bureau, Statehouse Plaza, PO Box 3232, Little Rock 72203; phone 501/376-4781 or toll-free 800/844-4781.

What to See and Do

Arkansas Arts Center. *MacArthur Park, 501 E 9th St, Little Rock (72202). Phone 501/372-4000. www.arkarts.com.* Exhibits include paintings, drawings, prints, sculpture, and ceramics; public classes in visual and performing arts; library, restaurant, theater. Performances by the Arkansas Arts Center Children's Theater; community events. (Tues-Sat 10 am-5 pm, Sun from 11 am; closed Dec 25) **FREE**

Arkansas Repertory Theatre. *601 Main St, Little Rock (72203). Phone toll-free 866/684-3737. www.therep.org.* Professional theatrical productions.

Arkansas Symphony Orchestra. *Robinson Center Music Hall, 2417 N Tyler St, Little Rock (72207). Phone 501/666-1761. www.arkansassymphony.org.* For schedule, contact Arkansas Symphony Orchestra Society, PO Box 7328, Little Rock 72217. (Sept-May)

Burns Park. *1 Eldor Johnson Dr, North Little Rock (72119). Off I-40 at exit 150. Phone 501/791-8537.* More than 1,500 acres with fishing, boating; wildlife trail; 27-hole golf, miniature golf, tennis. Camping (10-day maximum). Amusement rides; 9-hole Frisbee golf course. Fee for some activities. (Daily) **FREE**

Decorative Arts Museum. *501 E 9th St, Little Rock (72202). Phone 501/372-4000.* Restored Greek Revival mansion (1839) houses decorative art objects ranging from Greek and Roman period to contemporary American; ceramics, glass, textiles, crafts, Asian works of art. (Tues-Sat) **FREE**

Museum of Discovery. *500 President Clinton Ave, Little Rock (72201). In River Market Entertainment District. Phone 501/396-7050; toll-free 800/880-6475. www.amod.org.* Exhibits on the sciences, social sciences, and technology. (Mon-Sat; closed holidays) **$$$**

Old Mill. *Lakeshore and Fairway Ave, North Little Rock (72116). Phone 501/791-8537.* (1828) Old waterwheel gristmill. Two stones on the road to the mill are original milestones laid out by Jefferson Davis. This scenic city park is famous for its appearance in the opening scene of *Gone with the Wind*. (Daily) **FREE**

Pinnacle Mountain State Park. *11901 Pinnacle Valley Rd, Roland (72135). 7 miles W via Hwy 10, 2 miles N via Hwy 300. Phone 501/868-5806. www.arkansasstateparks.com.* A cone-shaped mountain juts 1,000 feet above this heavily forested, 1,800-acre park; bordered on the west by 9,000-acre Lake Maumelle. Fishing; boating (ramps); hiking, backpacking, picnicking, playground. Gift shop. Visitor center with natural history exhibits; interpretive programs. (Daily; closed Thanksgiving, Dec 25)

⭐ **Quapaw Quarter Historic Neighborhoods.** *1315 Scott St, Little Rock and North Little Rock. Phone 501/371-0075.* Encompassing the original town of Little Rock and its early additions through the turn of the century, this area contains three National Register historic districts and well over 150 buildings listed on the National Register of Historic Places. Named for Arkansas's native Quapaw, the area includes sites and structures associated with the history of Arkansas's capital city from the 1820s to the present. A tour of historic houses in the area is held the first weekend of May. Contact the Quapaw Quarter Association, PO Box 165023, 72216. Restored sites in the area include

Historic Arkansas Museum. *200 E 3rd St, Little Rock (72201). Phone 501/324-9351. www.arkansashistory.com.* Built in the 1820s-1850s, the restoration includes four houses, outbuildings, and a log house arranged to give a realistic picture of pre-Civil War Arkansas. The museum houses

Arkansas-made exhibits and a crafts shop. Guided tours. (Mon-Sat 9 am-5 pm, Sun 1-5 pm; closed holidays) **$**

The Old State House. *300 W Markham St, Little Rock (72201). Phone 501/324-9685. www.oldstatehouse.com.* Originally designed by Kentucky architect Gideon Shryock, this beautiful Greek Revival building was the capitol from 1836 to 1911; it now houses a museum of Arkansas history. Features include: restored governor's office and legislative chambers; Granny's Attic, a hands-on exhibit; President William J. Clinton exhibit; interpretive display of Arkansas's First Ladies' gowns. Self-guided tours. (Mon-Sat 9 am-5 pm, Sun 1-5 pm) **FREE**

Villa Marre. *1321 Scott St, Little Rock (72202). Phone 501/371-0075. www.quapaw.com/villa_marre.html.* (1881) Restored Italianate mansion reflects the exuberance of the period with ornate parquet floors, walnut woodwork, and highly decorated stenciled ceilings; antique furnishings are mainly Victorian with some American empire and Edwardian pieces. The house is featured in the opening credits of TV series *Designing Women.* Tours (Mon-Fri mornings, also Sun afternoons). **$$**

State Capitol. *1 State Capitol, Little Rock (72201). W end of Capitol Ave. Phone 501/682-5080.* A reduced-scale replica of the nation's capitol, the building is constructed of Batesville (AR) limestone. On the south lawn is a 1,600-bush rose garden comprising 150 varieties. The legislature meets the second Monday in January of odd-numbered years for 60 days. Self-guided and guided tours (Mon-Fri). **FREE**

Toltec Mounds Archeological State Park. *490 Toltec Mounds Rd, Scott (72142). 15 miles SE of North Little Rock, off Hwy 165 on Hwy 386. Phone 501/961-9442. www.arkansasstateparks.com.* This 182-acre park is the site of one of the largest and most complex prehistoric Native American settlements in the Lower Mississippi Valley; several mounds and a remnant of the embankment are visible. Guided on-site tours (by appointment; fee); a paved trail is accessible to the disabled. Tours depart from the visitor center, which has exhibits explaining how archaeologists work and the history of the site, as well as audiovisual programs and an archaeological laboratory. (Tues-Sat, also Sun afternoons; closed holidays) **$$**

War Memorial Park. *1 Jonesboro Dr, Little Rock (72205). Phone 501/664-6976.* On approximately 202 acres are rides and amusements. Golf, tennis, fitness center. Picnicking. (Daily) Also here is

Little Rock Zoo. *Phone 501/666-2406. www.littlerockzoo.com.* More than 500 animals on 40 acres. (Nov-Mar daily, 9:30 am-4:30 pm, rest of year to 5 pm; closed Jan 1, Thanksgiving, Dec 25) **$$$**

Wild River Country. *6820 Crystal Hill Rd, North Little Rock (72118). Jct I-40 and I-430, Crystal Hill Rd. Phone 501/753-8600. www.wildrivercountry.com.* A 23-acre themed water park with nine different water attractions. (June-Labor Day: daily; May: weekends) **$$$$**

Special Events

Arkansas All-Arabian Horse Show. *Barton Coliseum, 2600 Howard St, Little Rock (72206). Phone 501/372-8341.* Second full weekend in Apr.

Arkansas State Fair and Livestock Show. *2300 W Roosevelt Rd, Little Rock (72206). Phone 501/372-8341. www.arkfairgrounds.com.* Enjoy some down-home fun at this popular fair, which attracts more than 400,000 people over its ten-day run. Live music, motor sports, rodeos, and children's shows, as well as a 10-acre Midway with carnival rides, food, and games will surely please every member of the family. Early-mid-Oct. **$$**

Riverfest. *Riverfront Park, Little Rock. Phone 501/255-3378. www.riverfestarkansas.com.* Visual and performing arts festival includes exhibits by 60 artists; ballet, symphony, opera, theater, jazz, bluegrass, and rock groups; children's area; bike race, 5-mile run; concessions. Memorial Day weekend.

Wildwood Festival. *20919 Denny Rd, Little Rock (72223). Phone 501/821-7275; toll-free 888/278-7727.* Series of musical programs, exhibits, lectures, and events centered on the performing arts. Late May-June.

Limited-Service Hotels

★ **BEST WESTERN GOVERNORS SUITES.** *1501 Merrill Dr, Little Rock (72211). Phone 501/224-8051; toll-free 800/422-8051; fax 501/224-8051. www.bestwestern.com.* 49 rooms, 3 story, all suites. Complimentary full breakfast. Check-out noon. Outdoor pool, whirlpool. **$**

★ ★ **COURTYARD BY MARRIOTT.** *10900 Financial Centre Pkwy, Little Rock (72211). Phone 501/227-6000; toll-free 800/321-2211; fax 501/227-6912. www.courtyard.com.* 149 rooms, 3 story. Check-out noon. Restaurant, bar. Fitness room. Outdoor pool, whirlpool. **$**

★ **HAMPTON INN.** *6100 Mitchell Dr, Little Rock (72209). Phone 501/562-6667; toll-free 800/426-7866; fax 501/568-6832. www.hamptoninn.com.* 122 rooms, 4 story. Complimentary continental breakfast. Check-out noon. Outdoor pool. **$**

★ ★ **LA QUINTA INN.** *11701 I-30, Little Rock (72209). Phone 501/455-2300; toll-free 800/687-6667; fax 501/455-5876. www.laquinta.com.* 145 rooms, 3 story. Pets accepted, some restrictions. Complimentary continental breakfast. Check-out noon. Restaurant, bar. Outdoor pool, whirlpool. **$**

Full-Service Hotels

★ ★ ★ **THE CAPITAL HOTEL.** *111 W Markham St, Little Rock (72201). Phone 501/374-7474; toll-free 800/766-7666; fax 501/370-7091. www.thecapitalhotel.com.* Built in 1876, this hotel is at home amidst Little Rock's historical district. Turn-of-the-century ambiance and attentive service will be found throughout the hotel. 125 rooms, 4 story. Check-out 1 pm. Restaurant, bar. **$$**

★ ★ ★ **THE PEABODY LITTLE ROCK.** *3 Statehouse Plz, Little Rock (72201). Phone 501/375-5000; fax 501/375-4721.* Travelers to historic Little Rock would be hard-pressed to find a place more heartwarming than The Peabody, located on the banks of the Arkansas River. Special memories are made here, where twice daily the hotel's five North American mallards, four hens, and one drake march to the tune of John Philip Sousa's *King Cotton March* to take a splash in the fountain. The ducks aren't the only ones treated with kid gloves here; guests can expect to be cosseted in this thoroughly modern hotel. Whether traveling for business or pleasure, visitors appreciate the plentiful guest services and sophisticated accommodations. Gourmet dining at Capriccio rounds out the unique experience at this cherished hotel. 417 rooms, 19 story. Check-out 11 am. Three restaurants, bar. Fitness room. Airport transportation available. Business center. **$$**

Full-Service Inn

★ ★ ★ **EMPRESS OF LITTLE ROCK.** *2120 S Louisiana, Little Rock (72206). Phone 501/374-7966; toll-free 877/374-7966. www.theempress.com.* Step back in time to the 19th century at this fully restored Queen Anne-style mansion built in 1888. With ornate architecture and unique antique-filled suites, guests will feel like royalty as they experience a high dose of southern hospitality here. All rooms are named after historic Arkansas figures. 5 rooms. Complimentary full breakfast. Check-in 3 pm, check-out 11 am. **$$**

Restaurants

★ ★ **1620.** *1620 Market St, Little Rock (72211). Phone 501/221-1620; fax 501/221-1921.* American menu. Dinner. Closed Sun; holidays. Bar. **$$**

★ **BROWNING'S.** *5805 Kavanaugh Blvd, Little Rock (72207). Phone 501/663-9956.* Mexican, American menu. Lunch, dinner. Closed Sun-Mon; holidays. Children's menu. **$$**

★ **BRUNO'S LITTLE ITALY.** *315 N Bowman Rd #15, Little Rock (72211). Phone 501/224-4700. www.brunoslittleitaly.com.* Italian menu. Dinner. Closed Sun; holidays. Children's menu. **$$**

★ **BUFFALO GRILL.** *1611 Rebsamen Park Rd, Little Rock (72202). Phone 501/663-2158; fax 501/663-7698.* Lunch, dinner. Closed Sun; Thanksgiving, Dec 25. Children's menu. **$**

★ **CHIP'S BARBECUE.** *9801 W Markham St, Little Rock (72205). Phone 501/225-4346; fax 501/225-1056.* Barbecue menu. Lunch, dinner. Closed Mon. Children's menu. **$**

★ **FADED ROSE.** *1615 Rebsamen Park Rd, Little Rock (72207). Phone 501/663-9734.* American, Cajun menu. Lunch, dinner. Closed Thanksgiving, Dec 25. Bar. Children's menu. Casual attire. **$$**

★ ★ **GRAFFITI'S.** *7811 Cantrell Rd, Little Rock (72207). Phone 501/224-9079; fax 501/224-9161.* Italian menu. Dinner. Closed Sun; holidays. Bar. **$$**

★ ★ **SIR LOIN'S INN.** *801 W 29th St, North Little Rock (72115). Phone 501/753-1361; fax 501/753-3379.* Dinner. Closed Sun; holidays. Bar. **$$$**

New Orleans, LA

6 1/2 hours, 390 miles from Houston

Founded 1718
Population 484,674
Elevation 5 ft
Area Code 504
Information New Orleans Metropolitan Convention & Visitors Bureau, 1520 Sugar Bowl Dr, 70112; phone 504/566-5011 or toll-free 800/672-6124
Web Site www.neworleanscvb.com
NOTE: This section of southern Louisiana coastline was the hardest hit by hurricane Katrina in 2005. Most businesses are trying to recover from hurricane damage, but it is still advisable to phone ahead.

New Orleans is a beguiling combination of old and new. Named for the Duc d'Orléans, Regent of France, it was founded by Jean Baptiste Le Moyne, Sieur de Bienville. From 1763 to 1801, the territory of Louisiana was under Spanish rule. In 1801, Napoleon regained it for France, though no one in Louisiana knew of this until 1803, only 20 days before the Louisiana Purchase made it US territory. The first institution of higher learning in Louisiana, the College of Orleans, opened in New Orleans in 1811. The following year, the first steamboat went into service between New Orleans and Natchez. Louisiana was admitted to the Union on April 30, 1812, with New Orleans as the capital. The War of 1812 was over on January 8, 1815, when General Sir Edward Pakenham attacked New Orleans with a British force and was decisively defeated by General Andrew Jackson at Chalmette Plantation (now a National Historical Park). During the Civil War, New Orleans was captured by Union forces and held under tight military rule for the duration.

The population is extremely cosmopolitan, with its Creoles (descendants of the original French and Spanish colonists), Cajuns (descendants of the Acadians who were driven from Nova Scotia by the British in 1755), and other groups whose ancestors came from Italy, Africa, and the islands of the Caribbean.

Among tourists, New Orleans is famous for the old-world charm of its French Quarter. Visitors come from all over the country to dine in superb restaurants, listen to incomparable jazz, and browse in Royal Street's fine antiques shops. In the world of trade, New Orleans is known as one of the busiest and most efficient international ports in the country. More than 100 steamship lines dock here. As many as 52 vessels can be berthed at one time.

Public Transportation

Streetcars and buses (Regional Transit Authority), phone 504/248-3900

Airport New Orleans International Airport; weather phone 504/828-4000

Information Phone 504/464-0831

Lost and Found Phone 504/464-2672

What to See and Do

735 Nightclub. *735 Bourbon St, New Orleans (70116). Phone 504/581-6740. www.club735.com.* New wave, electrosynth, and techno music are the mainstays of this dance club, which has not one, but two dance floors. The snap-o-matic dancers add to the excitement on Wednesday, Friday, and Saturday nights. A popular meat market for folks of all persuasions, 735 draws a fair number of gay and lesbian patrons. (Thurs-Sat from 2 pm-9 pm) **$$$**

Adelina Patti's House and Courtyard. *631 Royal St, New Orleans (70130).* Former residence of the famous 19th-century opera diva.

Ampersand. *1100 Tulane Ave, New Orleans (70112). Phone 504/587-3737. www.ampersandnola.com.* Sophisticatedly naughty, this converted bank building features two levels, two bars, a huge dance floor, an outdoor courtyard, and several sitting rooms—one in the former bank vault. Appealing to serious clubbers of all stripes, Ampersand offers DJs from around the world spinning music of the techno and industrial persuasion. (Fri-Sat at 11 pm) **$$$$**

Audubon Park. *6500 Magazine St, New Orleans (70118). Phone 504/861-2537. www.auduboninstitute .org.* This 400-acre park designed by the Olmstead brothers is nestled between St. Charles Avenue and the Mississippi River and is surrounded by century-old live oak trees. The park features a par-62 18-hole golf course ($$$$), bicycle and jogging paths, and tennis courts. (Daily)

Audubon Zoo. *6500 Magazine St, New Orleans (70118). Phone 504/861-2537; toll-free 866/487-2966. www.auduboninstitute.org/zoo.* More than 1,800 animals from every continent call this top-ranked zoo, part of the Audubon Nature Institute, home. Check out kangaroos from Australia, llamas from South America, white tigers from Asia, and zebras from Africa, all in naturalistic habitats. Indigenous furry, feathered, and scaly creatures are featured at the Louisiana Swamp Exhibit. You can get up close during the sea lion show and personal in the Embraceable Zoo. Discovery walks, the EarthLab, and other interactive programs make the zoo an "edutaining" experience. Combination Zoo/Aquarium and Zoo/Aquarium/IMAX tickets are available. (Daily from 9: 30 am; closed Thanksgiving, Christmas, Mardi Gras, and the first Fri in May) **$$$**

Auto or streetcar tour of universities and Audubon Park. *St. Charles Ave and Canal St, New Orleans (70130).* The St. Charles Avenue streetcar can be boarded here. **$** The first point of interest is

Audubon Aquarium of the Americas. *#1 Canal St, Riverfront Area, New Orleans (70130). Phone 504/861-2537; toll-free 800/774-7394. www.auduboninstitute.org/aoa.* True to its name, this aquarium houses more than 10,000 aquatic creatures from all areas of the Americas. For total immersion—without getting wet—walk through the aquatic tunnel in the Caribbean Reef section or catch a glimpse of a rare white alligator through the RiverView window in the Mississippi section. Boasting the largest collection of jellyfish in the world, the aquarium also houses penguins, sea otters, and sharks—and lets you actually touch one! Combination Aquarium/Zoo, Aquarium/IMAX, and Aquarium/IMAX/Zoo tickets are available. (Sun-Thurs 9:30 am-6 pm, Fri-Sat until 7 pm; closed Mardi Gras Day, Dec 25) **$$$**

The Garden District. *Magazine St and Washington Ave, New Orleans (70130). gardendistrict.neworleans.com.* It was once the social center of New Orleans American (as opposed to Creole) aristocracy. There are still beautiful Greek Revival and Victorian houses with palms, magnolias, and enormous live oaks on the spacious grounds in this area. A walking tour of the Garden District, conducted by a national park ranger, departs from the corner of 1st and St. Charles (by appointment; closed Mardi Gras, Dec 25).

Lafayette Square. *6000 St. Charles Ave, New Orleans (70118).* With statues of Franklin, Clay, and McDonough.

Lee Circle. *Howard Ave.* With a statue of Robert E. Lee by Alexander Doyle.

Loyola University. *6363 St. Charles Ave, New Orleans (70118). Phone 504/865-3240; toll-free 800/ 465-9652. www.loyno.edu.* (1912) (3,500 students) Buildings on the 21-acre campus are Tudor Gothic in style. Tours are arranged through the Office of Admissions (Mon-Fri, twice daily).

Tulane Green Wave. *Tulane University, New Orleans. tulanegreenwave.ocsn.com.* Tulane University fields 13 sports teams, all using the Green Wave nickname. The logo for Tulane evolved from a pelican riding a surfboard to the fierce Riptide pelican mascot. The Superdome is home to the football team; other Tulane teams play at a variety of venues including Fogelman Arena and Turchin Stadium.

Tulane University. *6823 St. Charles Ave, New Orleans (70118). Phone 504/865-5000 (main campus). www.tulane.edu.* (1834) (12,381 students) The 110-acre main campus, located uptown, offers art galleries and other exhibits. The Tulane University Medical Center, located downtown, includes the School of Medicine, the School of Public Health and Tropical Medicine, and a 300-bed private hospital.

Auto tour to City Park and Lake Pontchartrain. *Drive NW on Esplanade or NE on N Carrollton Ave to the Esplanade entrance.* Allow two to four hours. Proceed along Lelong Drive to the

Dueling Oaks. *1 Palm Dr, New Orleans (70124).* Where many an affair of honor was settled in the early 18th century. Located in City Park.

Lake Pontchartrain. *Lakeshore Dr, New Orleans (70122).* A favorite spot of locals for picnicking, fishing, running, cycling, skating, or simply watching sailboats pass by.

Lake Pontchartrain Causeway. *www.thecauseway .com.* This, the longest bridge in the world, is 24-miles-long (toll).

New Orleans Botanical Garden. *1 Palm Dr, New Orleans (70124). Phone 504/483-9386. www.new orleanscitypark.com/nobg.php.* This beautiful public garden features a collection of antique roses, as well as azaleas, camellias, and gardenias. In the center of the garden is the Pavilion of the Two Sisters, named for Eminia Wadsworth and Marion Wadsworth Harve, who helped fund the Education Pavilion. (Tues-Sun 10 am-4:30 pm; closed Mon) **$**

Composing History

He usually played sitting in a chair, leaning against a wall, with a derby tilted over one eye—his bad eye, which was blinded when he was a kid. It is said that when we talk about "hot jazz," we are talking about the style he perfected: the art of playing collective improvisations instead of solos. He used mutes, bottles, cups, and derbies to coax different sounds out of his horn, and he mesmerized a young boy named Louis Armstrong who used to sit in the smoky New Orleans clubs to hear him play. The guy's name was Joe Oliver. He gave Armstrong his first cornet and became his mentor. Until the day Oliver died—broke, in pain from a bad back, and working as a janitor in a pool room in Georgia—Louis referred to him as Papa Joe.

Papa Joe Oliver is one of the legends of turn-of-the-century New Orleans, a time when jazz was becoming jazz; Buddy Bolden, whose band began playing in 1895, was another. "The blowingest man ever lived since Gabriel," Jelly Roll Morton called him, himself a French Quarter luminary. While Jelly Roll is credited with being the first true jazz composer—the first to put notes to paper—Bolden established the organization of the jazz ensemble—one or two cornets, a clarinet, trombone, double bass, guitar, and drums. Like Joe Oliver, he died tragically. After suffering a breakdown while playing his cornet in a street parade, he was committed to a mental institution and never emerged. He died 25 years later.

New Orleans is filled with the echoes of musicians like Buddy Bolden and Papa Joe, people who carved out America's musical heritage. Take a walk through the French Quarter and you'll hear them all. Over there is Jelly Roll Morton, smiling at the audience with a diamond in his teeth, tickling the ivories and creating the transition between ragtime and jazz. There are the strains of Mahalia Jackson singing gospel in a Baptist church. There's Louis Prima, singing and playing his trumpet before heading to New York, where he all but created swing and composed Benny Goodman's greatest hit, "Sing Sing Sing."

The legendary musician known as Professor Longhair started here. "The first instrument I played was the bottom of my feet, working out rhythms," he once said. He danced for tips in the French Quarter before becoming one of the fathers of rhythm and blues. His style greatly influenced Fats Domino, who brought popular appeal to the "classic New Orleans R&B sound." However, Domino's first recording, 1949's "The Fat Man," is considered a contender (along with many, many others) for the first rock and roll record. That always confused Fats. Rock and roll? He was only doing what he'd been doing in New Orleans for many years.

Farther down the block, you hear the horns of Al Hirt and Pete Fountain, the bluesy voice of Marva Wright, and the R&B trumpet of Charlie Miller. And then, finally, you hear the sounds of The Man himself: Satchmo. Louis Armstrong's musical ability, knowledge, technique, and irrepressible inventiveness—all honed here—made him one of the greatest of all jazz musicians. And in this town, even more than in most, he is legendary. His rags-to-riches story includes picking up his first cornet at reform school. He made a name for himself in the French Quarter, left, came back, and left, but never forgot his roots, they say. And because he popularized the "New Orleans sound," he paved the way for musicians to head north to play in cities like Chicago and New York and create even newer sounds.

Still, the New Orleans notes keep coming. From the Marsalis boys, Wynton and Branford. From the Neville Brothers. From Harry Connick, Jr. They sing with different voices, perhaps, and with different rhythms and beats. But that is New Orleans— New Orleans as it has always been.

New Orleans Museum of Art. *City Park, 1 Collins Diboll Cir, New Orleans (70124). Phone 504/488-2631. www.noma.org.* Established in 1911, NOMA boasts more than 40,000 objects in its permanent collection. The strengths of the permanent collection lie in its photography and glassware exhibits, as well as notable collections of American, African, Japanese, and French art, including works by Edgar Degas, who visited New Orleans in the early 1870s. World-class traveling exhibits, extensive children's programs, and a sculpture garden, which opened in 2002 in the adjacent City Park, round out the attractions. (Tues-Sun 10 am-5 pm; closed Mon, holidays) **$$$**

Southern Regional Research Center. *1100 Robert E. Lee Blvd, New Orleans (70124). Phone 504/286-4200. msa.ars.usda.gov/la/srcc.* Part of the US Department of Agriculture, which finds and develops new and improved uses for Southern farm crops. Guided tours by appointment. (Mon-Fri; closed holidays) **FREE**

University of New Orleans. *2000 Lake Shore Dr, New Orleans (70122). Phone 504/280-6000. www.uno.edu.* (1958) (17,000 students) On the shores of Lake Pontchartrain, the 345-acre campus is the center of a residential area. Fine Arts Gallery (Mon-Fri; closed holidays).

Bally's Casino. *1 Stars and Stripes Blvd, New Orleans (70126). Phone toll-free 800/572-2559. www.parkplace .com/ballys/neworleans.* Floating in Lake Pontchartrain, Bally's boasts high-limit gambling with games including blackjack, mini baccarat, craps, and roulette. You can choose from traditional or video slot machines and participate in weekly tournaments. The Showroom brings in musical acts from the 1960s, '70s, and '80s. You can also find live entertainment at the Wild Card Sports Bar, along with 16 sports-filled TV screens. Food choices include an all-you-can-eat buffet, a bakery specializing in desserts, and a deli. (Daily, 24 hours)

Bayou Barriere Golf Course. *7427 Hwy 23, Belle Chasse (70037). Phone 504/394-9500.* This course is fairly flat but strives to offer variety from hole to hole. The fairways differ in width and water comes into play, but at different points in each hole. The prices are reasonable, and the course is open year-round. With 27 holes on site, the facility accommodates high levels of traffic well, and you can explore various combinations of holes to find your favorite 18. The most challenging nine is the third, as the tee boxes are mostly on the course's levee. **$$$$**

Bayou Oaks. *1040 Fillmore Ave, New Orleans (70124). Phone 504/483-9396. www.neworleanscitypark.com/ golf.html.* The four courses at Bayou Oaks vary greatly in length in order to appeal to every type of golfer at every skill level. The two best courses are the championship West and the Wisner. The West course is more than 7,000 yards long and features water on many holes, like a lot of New Orleans courses do. White cranes, alligators, and great blue herons can often been seen on the course, which uses the natural borders of the bayou for many of its boundaries. Wide fairways, large greens, and easy access from downtown make

this one of the best places for any golfer to spend time while in the Big Easy. **$$$$**

Beauregard-Keyes House and Garden. *1113 Chartres St, New Orleans (70116). Phone 504/523-7257.* (Circa 1826) Greek Revival, Louisiana-raised cottage restored by its former owner, the novelist Frances Parkinson Keyes. Confederate Army General Pierre G. T. Beauregard lived here for more than a year following the Civil War. Exhibits include the main house and servant quarters, which together form a handsome shaded courtyard. (Keyes actually lived informally in the servant quarters, which are filled with her books, antiques, and family heirlooms.) To the side of the main house is a formal garden (visible from both Chartres and Ursulines streets) that is part of the guided tour conducted by costumed docents. (Mon-Sat 10 am-3 pm; closed holidays) **$**

Bourbon Street. *Bourbon Street, New Orleans.* No place in the world can match Bourbon Street for 24-hours-a-day, gaudy, bawdy fun. With elegant hotels next door to garish strip clubs, Bourbon Street encapsulates the ever-beating heart of the French Quarter. Visit its shops and restaurants in the daytime if you're not up for the always-rowdy nighttime crowds. But if you're visiting the Big Easy to let the good times roll, there's no better place to start a night of rambunctious partying.

Brechtel Park Golf Course. *4401 Lennox Blvd, New Orleans (70131). Phone 504/364-4014.* Built in 1965, Brechtel Park has been a favorite recreational course in New Orleans for some time. Not as challenging as some of the more exclusive clubs in the area, the course still requires a moderate level of skill to hit shots accurate enough to keep scores down. Brechtel Park is a good bargain if you're looking for a quick, fun, and inexpensive round of golf. **$$$$**

Brulatour Courtyard. *520 Royal St, New Orleans (70130).* The Courtyard is lined with interesting shops.

The Cabildo. *701 Chartres St, New Orleans (70118). Phone 504/568-6968. lsm.crt.state.la.us.* Part of the Louisiana State Museum, the Cabildo offers exhibits on life in early New Orleans, including plantation and slave life. Construction was completed in 1799, and the building housed the city council and the Louisiana Supreme Court at various times. In 1803, the transfer of the Louisiana Purchase took place here. Though a 1988 fire did significant damage, many artifacts were saved, the structure was authentically restored, and the building re-opened in 1994. (Tues-Sun 9 am-5 pm) **$$**

Cathedral Garden. *615 Pére Antoine Alley, New Orleans (70116).* The monument in the center of the garden was erected in honor of French marines who died while nursing New Orleans' citizens during a yellow fever outbreak. Picturesque, narrow Pirate's Alley, bordering the garden, is a favorite spot for painters. On the Alley is the house in which William Faulkner lived when he wrote his first novel. The garden is also called St. Anthony's Square in memory of a beloved priest known as Pére Antoine.

Cemetery & Voodoo History Tour. *Café Beignet, 334-B Royal St, New Orleans (70130). In the courtyard of Café Beignet. Phone 504/947-2120.* Tour (approximately two hours) features St. Louis Cemetery #1, the oldest and most significant burial ground in New Orleans; visits to a practicing Voodoo priestess at her temple; Congo Square, the site of early slave gatherings; and a visit to the home of legendary Voodoo Queen Marie Laveau. (Mon-Sat 10 am and 1 pm; Sun 10 am) **$$$**

Center of Banking. *403 Royal, New Orleans (70130). At the corner of Royal and Bienville, turn right, away from the river, four blocks to N Rampart, turn right and walk five blocks.* The old Louisiana State Bank was designed in 1821 by Benjamin Latrobe, one of the architects of the Capitol in Washington. The 343 Royal building was completed in the early 1800s for the old Bank of the United States. The old Bank of Louisiana, 334 Royal, was built in 1826; it is now the French Quarter Police Station.

City Park. *1 Palm Dr, New Orleans (70124). Phone 504/482-4888. www.neworleanscitypark.com.* The 1,500 acres of City Park provide room for all sorts of family fun. Step into Storyland to slide down the dragon-flame slide, board Captain Hook's ship, or engage with actors portraying storybook characters. Board one of two minitrains and mount a steed on one of the oldest wooden carousels in the US. Catch some spray from Popp Fountain, get a license and catch some fish in one of the many lagoons, or bask in Marconi Meadow and catch some rays. Admire a range of architectural styles in various buildings and bridges. Appreciate the natural beauty in the Botanical Garden and see more mature oak trees than anyplace in the world. Get active and rent a boat or play tennis, golf, or softball in the park's facilities. Check for events at Tad Gormley Stadium. Also in City Park are

Bandstand and Peristyle. The latter is an attractive classical structure.

Recreation areas. Four 18-hole golf courses, a driving range, lighted tennis courts, and lagoons for boating (fee).

Contemporary Arts Center. *900 Camp St, New Orleans (70130). Phone 504/528-3800. www.cacno.org.* Established in 1976, the Contemporary Arts Center (CAC) is housed in an award-winning building renovated in 1990. Each year, CAC hosts as many as two dozen exhibitions in its 10,000 square feet of gallery space. Taking a multidisciplinary approach, the center promotes art forms as traditional as painting, photography, and sculpture, and as diverse as performance art, dance, music, and video. Artists' Studio Days offer children and their elders a glimpse into the creative process. The Dog & Pony Theater company-in-residence presents workshops, rehearsals, and dance and theater productions. CAC also hosts the annual Black Theater Festival during the first two weekends in October. (Tues-Sun 11 am-5 pm; closed Mon) **$$**

Crescent City Farmers' Market. *700 Magazine St, New Orleans (70116). Phone 504/861-5898. www.crescent cityfarmersmarket.org.* Choose the day and location to suit your needs. At this market, regional vendors offer fresh produce, seafood, baked goods, and other edibles, as well as cut flowers and bedding plants. Each location offers frequent cooking demonstrations with area chefs and a variety of food-related events. Market founders promote sound ecological and economic development in the greater New Orleans area. The Tuesday Market is situated between Levee and Broadway in the parking lot of Uptown Square, at 200 Broadway from 10 am to 1 pm. The Wednesday Market is located between French Market Place and Governor Nicholls Street from 10 am to 2 pm. The Thursday Market sits on the American Can Company residential development at 3700 Orleans Avenue from 3-7 pm. The Saturday Market is in the downtown neighborhood known as the Warehouse District (originally known as the American Sector), on the corner of Magazine and Girod streets, at 700 Magazine Street from 8 am-12 pm.

Destrehan Plantation. *13034 River Rd, Destrehan (70047). Approximately 30 miles W via Hwy 48. Phone 985/764-9315. www.destrehanplantation.org.* Built in 1787, this is the oldest plantation house left intact in the lower Mississippi Valley, with ancient live oaks adorning the grounds. Guided tours are available. (Daily; closed holidays) **$$$**

Dragon's Den. *435 Esplanade Ave, New Orleans (70116). Phone 504/949-1750.* Located above a Thai restaurant, the Den echoes the Eastern atmosphere with a dark, red-lit ambience and tasseled pillows strewn on the floor. Live music styles range from jazz to bluegrass to hip-hop to the latest local sounds. The club also hosts spoken-word performances, which feature local poets. (After 2 am)

Eastover Country Club. *5690 Eastover Dr, New Orleans (70128). Phone 504/245-7347. www.eastovercc.com.* A semi-private club, Eastover features two courses, named Rabbit's Foot and Teeth of the Gator. The courses were designed by the team of Joe Lee and Rocky Rocquemore, who also helped design courses such as Cog Hill and Doral. Teeth of the Gator is the longer of the two at more than 7,000 yards, and 12 holes feature water hazards. Rabbit's Foot is more for everyone, at 300 yards shorter than its more difficult sister course. Membership to the club brings benefits, but anyone can play these two great courses on most days of the year. (Mon-Fri 7:50 am-5:30 pm, Sat-Sun 6:50 am-5:30 pm) **$$$$**

Entergy IMAX Theatre. *#1 Canal St, New Orleans (70130). Phone 504/581-IMAX; toll-free 800/774-7394. www.auduboninstitute.org/imax.* Adjacent to the Audubon Aquarium of the Americas (see) and part of the Audubon Nature Institute, this theater showcases several films at a time in larger-than-life format and hosts a summer film festival. Combination IMAX/Aquarium and IMAX/Aquarium/Zoo tickets are available. (Daily from 10 am; closed Mardi Gras Day, Dec 25) **$$**

F & F Botanica. *801 N Broad St, New Orleans (70119). Phone 504/482-9142.* The oldest and largest spiritual supply store in the French Quarter, F & F Botanica offers herbs, oils, potions, candles, incense—whatever you need to enhance your spiritual practice, whether it be Santeria, Voodoo, or what have you. The store offers free spiritual consultations to help you figure out how to find what your spirit is searching for. At least one staffer is sure to speak Spanish to help customers who share owner Felix Figueroa's heritage. (Mon-Sat 8 am-6 pm)

French Market. *813 Decatur St, New Orleans (70116).* Which has been a farmers' market for nearly two centuries. The market's "Café du Monde" (see RESTAURANTS) is a popular and famous coffee stand specializing in café au lait (half coffee with chicory, half hot milk) and beignets (square-shaped doughnuts sprinkled with powdered sugar). The café never closes (except Dec 25), and café au lait and beignets are inexpensive. The downriver end of the French Market houses booths in which produce is sold.

French Quarter. *Bourbon St, New Orleans (70130). From Canal St to Esplanade Ave, and from Decatur St on the Mississippi River to Rampart St. www.frenchquarter.com.* Whether you're in New Orleans to party hearty, shop 'til you drop, soak up Creole (or voodoo) charms, sample Southern hospitality, delve into history, or admire architecture, you can find what you want in the Vieux Carré. The oldest—and only remaining—French and Spanish settlement in the country, the Quarter offers sights, sounds, tastes, and treasures to suit every interest.

★ **French Quarter Walking Tours.** *Phone 504/523-3939.* Both the Friends of Cabildo (1850 House Museum Store, 523 St. Ann St on Jackson Square; phone 504/523-3939) and the French Quarter Visitor Center (419 Decatur St; phone 504/589-2636) offer walking tours that cover the Quarter's history and architecture. The pace isn't strenuous, but factor in the heat and humidity, and dress accordingly. Licensed guides conduct the two-hour Friends of Cibaldo tours, while interpreters from the National Park Service lead a 90-minute free tour, which is restricted to the first 25 people who show up each day. A Cibaldo tour ticket entitles you to a discount on items at the 1850 House Museum Store. (Daily; no tours holidays, Mardi Gras) **$$$**

Gallier House. *1126 Royal St, New Orleans (70116). Phone 504/525-5661. www.gnofn.org/~hggh.* For a slice of pre-Civil War life in New Orleans, check out the home of architect James Gallier Jr. which he designed for himself in 1857. Thoroughly modern for its time, the house boasts hot-and-cold running water and an indoor bathroom. Painstakingly restored, the house is one of New Orleans's more beautiful historic landmarks. (Mon-Fri 10 am-4 pm; closed holidays) **$$$**

Gray Line bus tours. *#1 Toulouse St, New Orleans (70130). Phone 504/569-1401; toll-free 800/535-7786. www.graylineneworleans.com.* See all of New Orleans's must-see sites from the comfort of an air-conditioned coach. Besides its comprehensive city tour, Gray Line offers numerous other sightseeing options, including tours of plantations, swamps and bayous, the Garden District, and cemeteries. An off-the-beaten path trek takes you to such places as the childhood neighborhood of jazz great Louis Armstrong and Faubourg Marigny, one of the earliest Creole suburbs, where the striking architecture will surely grab your attention.

NEW ORLEANS, LA/SIDE TRIPS

The French Quarter

Since the founding of New Orleans, Royal Street has been the most prestigious address in the city. Today it remains the most refined street in the Quarter, lined with historic buildings, famous restaurants, galleries, and of course, banks. A good starting point for exploring this part of New Orleans is behind St. Louis Cathedral, a block up from Jackson Square, where a lush collection of tropical plants fills the compact St. Anthony's Garden. Follow the alleyway upriver to 324 Pirate's Alley, where author William Faulkner lived in 1925. His fans still flock to that corner, now the home of a popular bookstore featuring the works of this bard of Southern letters. Continue down Pirate's Alley and away from the river along St. Peter to return to Royal Street.

Near the corner of St. Peter and Royal streets, the brick Labranche buildings, with their dramatic cast-iron galleries, were built starting in 1835. Proceed upriver along Royal Street. Beyond Toulouse Street, the 1798 Court of Two Lions at 541 Royal Street features marble lions atop the entry posts. The same architect built the neighboring house (527-533 Royal Street) in 1792. Now home to the Historic New Orleans Collection (phone 504/523-4662), the house museum displays exhibits on New Orleans history. At 613 Royal, the Court of Two Sisters is among the city's most venerable restaurants for French-Creole cuisine.

Between St. Louis and Conti streets, the huge, white marble State Supreme Court Building dominates the block; between Conti and Bienville streets, it's the block-long Monteleone Hotel. You might turn around before you hit the harsher realities of contemporary life outside the Quarter at Canal Street. Loop around Bourbon Street for a change of scene, pass restaurants, nightclubs, and saloons, and drop down St. Ann Street back to Royal Street, where the Café des Exiles marks the historical gathering spot of French refugees from the Revolution. Further downriver, a detour down Dumaine toward the river lands you in front of Madame John's Legacy (632 Dumaine; phone 504/568-6968). This French cottage was one of the few structures to survive the fire that destroyed most of the city in 1794. Returning to Royal and proceeding downriver, the cornstalk fence at 915 Royal draws onlookers and carriage tours, who stop to admire the intricate tasseled design of the ironwork.

The Gallier House museum at 1118-32 Royal Street (phone 504/525-5661) was built in the 1860s by acclaimed local architect James Gallier Jr. Drop down Ursulines Avenue here to the old Ursulines Convent at the corner of Chartres Street. The 1745 convent is among the oldest structures in the city. Continue down Ursulines towards the River to visit the French Market, or return upriver along Chartres Street to return to Jackson Square.

If you want to ply the Mississippi, the company also offers a riverboat cruise. (Closed Mardi Gras) **$$$$**

Griffin Fishing Charters. *2629 Privateer Blvd, Lafitte (70036). Phone toll-free 800/741-1340. www.neworleans fshintours.com.* Specializing in shallow-sea fishing for speckled trout and redfish in saltwater marshes from Lafitte down to the Gulf of Mexico, owners Raymond and Belinda Griffin can also set you up for a day of deep-sea fishing. Or combine two pursuits—play golf in the morning and then head out to the water for some fishing. Prices include an out-of-state fishing license, rods, reels, bait, tackle, ice, Po-boy sandwiches, soda, water, and cleaning and packaging of caught fish. Package plans that include lodging, meals, and transportation are also available. **$$$$**

Harrah's New Orleans. *8 Canal St, New Orleans (70130). Phone 504/533-6000; toll-free 800/847-5299.*

www.harrahs.com. The oldest of New Orleans's land-based casinos, Harrah's is 115,000 square feet of non-stop gambling fun. More than 100 tables offer 10 different games, including poker, craps, Baccarat, and roulette. You can play the slots for a penny, a dollar, or up to $500 at any of 2,500 slot machines. Live jazz, Creole cuisine, Mardi Gras décor, and an attached hotel means that you can immerse yourself in a total Harrah's New Orleans experience. (Daily, 24 hours)

Hermann-Grima House. *820 St. Louis St, New Orleans (70112). Phone 504/525-5661. www.gnofn.org/~hggh.* (1831) The Georgian design reflects the post-Louisiana Purchase American influence on traditional French and Spanish styles in the Quarter; the furnishings typify a well-to-do lifestyle during the period of 1831-1860. The restored house has elegant interiors, two landscaped courtyards, slave quarters, a stable, and a working period kitchen; Creole cooking demonstrations on open hearth (Oct-May, Thurs). Tours. (Mon-Fri; closed holidays) **$$$**

Historic New Orleans Collection. *533 Royal St, New Orleans (70130). Phone 504/523-4662. www.hnoc.org.* Established in 1966 by local collectors, General and Mrs. Kemper Williams, the Collection is composed of several historic buildings housing a museum and comprehensive research center for state and local history. The main exhibition gallery presents changing displays on Louisiana's history and culture. The 1792 Merieult House features a pictorial history of New Orleans and Louisiana; the Williams Residence shows the elegant lifestyle of the collection's founders. Changing exhibits grace several galleries. There is also a touch tour for the visually impaired. (Tues-Sat 9:30 am-4:30 pm)

House of Blues. *225 Decatur St, New Orleans (70130). Phone 504/529-2624. www.hob.com.* Even in the eye-catching French Quarter, it's hard to miss the gaudy, neon-lit entrance to the House of Blues. Past the wildly decorated porch and inside, you're liable to hear musical styles ranging from Cajun to country and reggae to rock and roll, not to mention pure, soulful blues. And the music is live, of course. The Sunday Gospel Brunch is justly famous and surprisingly inexpensive.

The Howlin' Wolf. *828 S Peters, New Orleans (70130). Phone 504/522-9653. www.howlin-wolf.com.* The live music here tends more toward local and national rock and roll and alternative sounds than traditional New Orleans jazz and blues. After opening in 1988 in nearby Metairie, the Wolf successfully transplanted its relaxed ambience to the Warehouse District in 1991, where it remains popular with college students and those looking for original music and up-and-coming acts. Check out the acoustic open-mike nights on Mondays. **$$$$**

Jackson Brewery. *600 Decatur St, New Orleans (70130). Phone 504/566-7245. www.jacksonbrewery.com.* This historic brewery was converted into a large retail, food, and entertainment complex with 75 shops and restaurants, outdoor seating, and a riverfront promenade. (Mon-Sat 10 am-8 pm; Sun 10 am-7 pm; closed Dec 25)

Jackson Square. *615 Pére Antoine Alley, New Orleans (70116). www.jackson-square.com.* Bordered by Chartres, St. Peter, Decatur, and St. Ann streets, this area was established as a drill field in 1721 and was called the *Place d'Armes* until 1848, when it was renamed for Andrew Jackson, hero of the Battle of New Orleans. The statue of Jackson, the focal point of the square, was the world's first equestrian statue with more than one hoof unsupported; the American sculptor, Clark Mills, had never seen an equestrian statue and therefore did not know that the pose was thought impossible. Today, the square and surrounding plaza is one of the best places in the Quarter to catch your breath, watch people, and listen to jazz. It attracts local artists, food vendors, and street performers such as mimes, magicians, and musicians.

Jean Bragg Antiques & Gallery. *600 Julia St, New Orleans (70115). Phone 504/895-7375. www.jeanbragg antiques.com.* The focus of this shop and gallery is on Louisianian and Southern art, especially paintings, watercolors, and etchings of Louisiana and the French Quarter. Specializing in George Ohr pottery and Newcomb College pottery and craft work, the shop also offers museum-quality pieces from the late 19th and early 20th centuries. Discover vintage linens, jewelry, and glassware along with Victorian furniture. (Mon-Sat 10 am-5 pm)

Lafitte's Blacksmith Shop. *941 Bourbon St, New Orleans (70116). www.atneworleans.com/body/ blacksmith.htm.* This popular bar is arguably the oldest French-style building left in the French Quarter after the Spanish style dominated rebuilding efforts following two fires in the 1700s that destroyed much of the city. Local lore has it that the original smithy, built sometime before 1772, served as a front for pirate Jean Lafitte's more notorious activities. The bar retains a dark, historical feel, although the local and exotic patrons lighten the atmosphere. (Daily from 11 am)

Le Chat Noir. *715 St Charles Ave, New Orleans (70130). Phone 504/581-6333. www.cabaretlechatnoir.com.* Get decked out (no jeans or shorts) to check out the Cat (*chat noir* means black cat) for an ever-changing schedule of cabaret, live theater, and musical performances. The Bar Noir is a cozier room, perfect for a pre-show cocktail (try the house specialty Black Cat) or for quiet conversation with friends.

Levee and docks. *Canal St and Mississippi River, New Orleans.* From the foot of Canal Street, turn right and walk along the busy docks to the coffee and general cargo wharves, which are most interesting. Smoking is forbidden in the dock area. Rides on the Canal Street Ferry are free. Along the docks are paddlewheel and other excursion boats.

Longue Vue House & Gardens. *7 Bamboo Rd, New Orleans (70124). I-10, Metairie Rd exit. Phone 504/488-5488. www.longuevue.com/.* A grand city estate furnished with original English and American antiques is located on 8 acres of formal and picturesque gardens; changing exhibits in galleries and seasonal horticultural displays in gardens. Tours on the hour. (Mon-Sat 10 am-5 pm; Sun 1-5 pm; closed holidays) **$$**

Louis Armstrong Park. *N Rampart St, New Orleans (70130).* To the left of the entrance—built to resemble a Mardi Gras float—is a stand of very old live oak trees. This area was originally known as Congo Square, where slaves were permitted to congregate on Sunday afternoons; it was also the scene of voodoo rites. After the Civil War, the square was named for General P. G. T. Beauregard. Louis Armstrong Park, which includes an extensive water garden that focuses upon a larger-than-life-size statue of Armstrong, was expanded from the original square and contains the municipal auditorium and the Theatre of the Performing Arts. Located in the 800 block of North Rampart Street.

Louisiana's Children's Museum. *420 Julia St, New Orleans (70130). Phone 504/523-1357. www.lcm.org.* Catering to toddlers and the young at heart of any age, this museum encourages hands-on exploration. Take a ride in a simulated police cruiser in the Safety First area, anchor a newscast in the Kidswatch Studio, or experience bayou life in the Cajun Cottage. Other areas include Waterworks, Big City Port, Art Trek, and the Challenge area, where you can try your hand at reading Braille, a print language for the blind. Children under 16 must be accompanied by an adult. (Tues-Sat 9:30 am-4:30 pm, Sun noon-4:30 pm; open Mon during the summer; closed holidays) **$$**

Louisiana Nature Center. *5601 Read Blvd, New Orleans (70127). Phone 504/246-5672; toll-free 800/774-7394. www.auduboninstitute.org/lnc.* You can lead yourself on an audio tour of local plant and animal life through the nature center's trails and boardwalks, or set off to explore some of the 86 acres on your own. On Turtle Pond offers, yes, turtles and tortoises, along with other amphibian life. The public is invited to a schedule of shows in the planetarium on Saturdays and Sundays. (Tues-Fri 9 am-5 pm, Sat 10 am-5 pm, Sun noon-5 pm) **$**

Louisiana State Museum. *751 Chartres, New Orleans (70116). Phone 504/568-6968; toll-free 800/568-6968. lsm.crt.state.la.us.* The Museum comprises five proper-ties in the French Quarter city and three sites outside of the city. Though only the residence is open to the public (a kitchen and servants' quarters complete the complex), Madame John's Legacy is a fine example of Creole architecture. Built in 1789 after the great fire of 1788, it's notable for also surviving the 1795 fire. The 1850 House, named for the year it was built, holds an authentic collection of period furnishings. Built in 1791 on the site of a monastery, one of the Presbytere's functions was as a courthouse. It currently holds not-to-be-missed Mardi Gras exhibits. The Old US Mint was the only mint in the country that printed currency for both the Confederacy and the US government. The Mint now holds state and local research materials and exhibits. (Tues-Sun 9 am-5 pm; closed holidays) **$**

Louisiana Superdome. *Sugar Bowl Dr, New Orleans (70112). Phone 504/587-3663. www.superdome.com.* The Dome is home field for the New Orleans Saints (NFL football), Tulane University Green Wave (NCAA Division I football), and host to a variety of other sports events, including college baseball and the 1996 NCAA men's basketball Final Four and 2003 games. The annual Endymion Extravaganza Mardi Gras Parade and Party happens here, as well as the New Orleans Home & Garden Show, the Boat & Sport Fishing Show, the Kid's Fair & Expo, and numerous concerts and other special events.

M. S. Rau Antiques. *630 Royal St, New Orleans (70130). Phone 504/523-5660; toll-free 800/544-9440. www.rauantiques.com.* Founded in 1912, this family-owned and family-run business is so confident of its merchandise that it offers a 125 percent guarantee on all in-store purchases (online purchases include a slightly modified guarantee). Internationally known names such as Paul Revere, Meissen, Fabergé, Wedgwood, Tiffany, and Chippendale are represented in the 25,000-square-foot showroom and extensive catalogue. You can also pick up fabulous diamonds, jewelry, silver, and objets d'art among the vast array of American and European antiques. (Mon-Sat 9 am-5:15 pm; closed Sun)

Madame John's Legacy. *632 Dumaine St, New Orleans (70116). Phone 504/568-6968. lsm.crt.state.la.us/madam.htm.* This home is one of the oldest domestic buildings in the Mississippi Valley, built about 1727, rebuilt in 1788, and restored in 1981. It is part of the Louisiana State Museum. (Tues-Sun 9 am-5 pm) **$**

Magazine Street. *Magazine St, New Orleans (70115). Phone 504/455-1224. www.magazinestreet.com.* Fun and funky, Magazine Street offers 6 miles of clothing retailers, antique establishments, gift shops, eateries, and more. Most of the businesses are housed in 19th-century buildings or brick-faced cottages, which helps the area maintain its other-worldly charm. You can stroll from the French Quarter through Magazine Street to the Audubon Zoo, picking up a piece of jewelry, a piece of furniture, a book, or some food along the way. Make a point to stop off at the Magazine Arcade, a mini-mall that houses eclectic shops offering antique music boxes and musical instruments, period medical equipment, dolls and their furnishings, as well as antique household items for real people. Most shops open daily 10 am-5 pm.

Maison Le Monnier. *640 Royal St (private), New Orleans (70130).* Built in 1811 and sometimes called the "skyscraper," this was the first building in the Vieux Carré more than two stories high. This house was used as the setting of George W. Cable's novel *Sieur George.* Notice the YLR, for Yves LeMonnier, worked into the grillwork.

Mardi Gras World. *233 Newton St, New Orleans (70114). Phone 504/361-7821; toll-free 800/362-8213. www.mardigrasworld.com.* For a fascinating look at where about 75 percent of Mardi Gras props and floats are made, visit this unique establishment—the world's largest. You can try on costumes; watch painters, sculptors, and carpenters at work; and tour rooms filled with props and Mardi Gras paraphernalia. The Kern family's business also provides floats and props for parades across the country. (Daily 9:30 am-4:30 pm) **$$$**

Memorial Hall–Confederate Museum. *929 Camp St, New Orleans (70130). Phone 504/523-4522. www.con federatemuseum.com.* Louisiana veterans of the War Between the States founded the Hall as a repository for artifacts and memorabilia of the Confederate side of the Civil War. Opened in 1891, it is the nation's longest continuously operating museum. The museum houses flags, swords, and uniforms from both officers and foot solders as well as an extensive collection of photographs. The widow of Confederate president Jefferson Davis donated many family items. (Mon-Sat 10 am-4 pm; closed holidays, Mardi Gras) **$**

Metairie Cemetery. *5100 Pontchartrain Blvd, New Orleans (70112). Phone 504/486-6331.* On the former grounds of the Metairie Race Course, the largest (150 acres) and loveliest of New Orleans' cemeteries is home to a variety of eye-catching memorials and mausoleums. Styles range from Egyptian pyramids

to Celtic crosses to European castles. At least one of the numerous bronze statues is said to wander the grounds, a lovely setting for a quiet stroll. You can rent a taped audio tour or choose to drive around the grounds. (Daily 8:30 am-5 pm)

Mid-19th-century townhouse. *826 St. Ann St, New Orleans (70116). Phone 504/581-1367.* Headquarters of the New Orleans Spring Fiesta Association (see SPECIAL EVENTS). Early 19th-century antiques, Victorian pieces; objets d'art. Guided tours (Mon-Fri afternoons). **$$**

Moonwalk. *615 Pére Antoine Alley, New Orleans (70116). www.neworleansonline.com.* Running the length of the French Quarter along the river levee, the Moonwalk is a pedestrian thoroughfare that connects many attractions along the river, including the Aquarium of the Americas and paddleboat cruises, as well as shops and restaurants. Or, you can park yourself on a bench and watch the crowds and the river flow by. Locals and tourists make this a popular venue for an evening stroll, especially on a clear, moonlit night.

Musee Conti Historical Wax Museum. *917 rue Conti, New Orleans (70112). Phone 504/581-1993; toll-free 800/233-5405. www.get-waxed.com.* In addition to the obligatory dungeon of horrors featuring Dracula and the Wolfman, more than 150 wax figures illustrate the history of the city. Catch Napolean Bonaparte in his bath, Voodoo Queen Marie Laveau and her dancers, and Duke Ellington playing some jazz. The figures are painstakingly constructed (even clean-shaven men have stubble) using a process that makes them seem nearly life-like, and are set in historically accurate tableaux. (Mon-Sat 10 am-5:30 pm; closed Mardi Gras, Thanksgiving, Dec 20-26) **$$**

National D-Day Museum. *945 Magazine St, New Orleans (70130). Phone 504/527-6012. www.ddaymuseum.org.* Opened on June 6, 2000, the 16,000 square feet of gallery space houses exhibits, many interactive, that trace the political and economic events leading up to the D-Day invasion in 1944. Founded by the late historian and author Stephen Ambrose, the museum offers oral histories of the men and women who participated and rare film footage that help bring World War II to life. Free lunchbox lectures on Wednesdays give insight into specific topics or personalities. (Daily 9 am-5 pm; closed Thanksgiving, December 24, December 25, Mardi Gras) **$$$**

New Orleans Centre. *1400 Poydras, New Orleans (70112). Phone 504/568-0000.* This three-story mall is located in the heart of the business district adjacent to the Louisiana Superdome, the New Orleans Sports Arena, and the Hyatt Regency New Orleans. Anchored by Macy's and Lord & Taylor, the mall houses more than 60 shops including national chains and local specialty shops. Food offerings run the gamut from fast-food outlets to well-reviewed restaurants. (Mon-Sat 10 am-8 pm, Sun noon-6 pm)

New Orleans Custom House. *423 Canal St, New Orleans (70130). Decatur and Canal sts.* Begun in 1848, interrupted by the Civil War, and completed in 1881, the Greek Revival building with neo-Egyptian details was used in part as an office by Major General Benjamin "Spoons" Butler during Union occupation, and in part as a prison for Confederate soldiers. A great dome was planned but the great weight of the existing building caused the foundation to settle and the dome was never completed. (In 1940, the building had sunk 30 inches, while the street level had been raised three feet.) Of particular interest is the famed Marble Hall, an architectural wonder. Self-guided tour. (Mon-Fri) **FREE**

New Orleans Fairgrounds. *1751 Gentilly Blvd, New Orleans (70119). Phone 504/944-5515. www.fgno.com.* The horses have been darting out of the starting gates at this Mid-City racetrack since 1852, making it the oldest one still operating in the United States. When you're not placing bets and watching the fast-paced action on the track, wander through the Racing Hall of Fame, which honors 110 of the sport's most revered, such as legendary jockey Bill Shoemaker and Duncan Kenner, the founding father of racing in this country. The 145-acre facility also hosts the city's annual Jazz and Heritage Festival. (Thanksgiving Day-Mar: races start at 12:30 pm) **$**

New Orleans Ghost Tour. *625 St. Phillip, New Orleans (70129). Phone 504/628-1722. www.neworleansghosttour.com.* This walking tour carries on rain or shine (though not gloom of night) and covers creepy happenings in the French Quarter ranging from the mad butcher, who may have butchered more than beef, to the sultan reportedly buried alive. Tour host Thomas Duran has extensive ghost-hunting credentials from England and is a licensed New Orleans tour guide. **$$$$**

⭐ **New Orleans Historic Voodoo Museum.** *724 rue Dumaine, New Orleans (70116). www.voodoomuseum.com.* Marie Laveau reigned as Voodoo Queen of New Orleans throughout much of the 19th century. The Voodoo Museum displays her portrait and memorabilia. Although it sells the stereotypical voodoo supplies, the museum also offers serious exhibits on voodoo history and its artifacts. You can also purchase your own *gris-gris* bag filled with herbs, bones, and charms to bring luck or love into your life (a local addition to the trappings of the practice).(Daily 10 am-dusk) **$$$$**

New Orleans Hornets (NBA). *New Orleans Arena, 1501 Girod St, New Orleans (70113). Phone 504/301-4000. www.nba.com/hornets.* The Hornets moved from Charlotte for the 2002-2003 NBA season to give New Orleans a National Basketball Association team for the first time since the Jazz moved to Utah in 1979. They play home games at the New Orleans Arena, where the Honeybees cheer them on and mascot Hugo the Hornet is a three-time NBA Mascot Slam Dunk Champion. **$$$$**

New Orleans Opera. *801 N Rampart St, New Orleans (70116). Phone 504/529-2278; toll-free 800/881-4459. www.neworleansopera.org.* Operating from the Mahalia Jackson Theatre of the Performing Arts, the New Orleans Opera Association presents four operas each season, which runs from October through March. The association was founded in 1943 and stages high-quality performances of renowned operas as well as world premieres. English translations appear in subtitles above the stage. **$$$$**

New Orleans Pharmacy Museum (*La Pharmacie Francaise*). *514 Chartres St, New Orleans (70130). www.pharmacymuseum.org.* Louis Dufilho, the first licensed pharmacist in the US, operated an apothecary shop here from 1823 to 1855. The ground floor contains pharmaceutical memorabilia of the 1800s, such as apothecary jars filled with medicinal herbs and voodoo powders, surgical instruments, pharmacy fixtures, and a black-and-rose Italian marble soda fountain (circa 1855). (Tues-Sun 10 am-5 pm; closed Mon, holidays) **$**

New Orleans Saints (NFL). *Louisiana Superdome, Sugar Bowl Dr, New Orleans (70112). Phone 504/731-1700. www.neworleanssaints.com.* One of the few NFL teams that remains in its original city, the Saints joined the National Football League in 1967. They play their home games in the Superdome, which also regularly hosts the Super Bowl. **$$$$**

New Orleans School of Cooking & Louisiana General Store. *524 St. Louis St, New Orleans (70130). Phone 504/525-2665; toll-free 800/237-4841. www.nosoc.com.* After a session at the School of Cooking, you'll be a convert to Louisiana cuisine—"ga-ron-teed." Make a reservation for a three-hour or a two-hour lunch class to learn the basics of Louisiana cooking, and, even better, to sample the four dishes cooked up. An early 1800s-era converted molasses warehouse is home to the school and to the Louisiana General Store, where you can pick up ingredients, a cookbook, and cooking utensils. **$$$$**

New Orleans Steamboat Company. *#2 Canal St, Suite 2500, New Orleans (70130). Phone 504/586-8777; toll-free 800/233-2628. www.neworleanssteamboat.com.* Cruise from the heart of the French Quarter on the steamboat *Natchez*. She's the ninth steamer to have the name. Her predecessor, *Natchez VI*, won the race against the *Robert E. Lee* in the most famous steamboat race of all time. The *Natchez* has never lost a race. She was launched in 1975, and is one of only six true steam-powered sternwheelers sailing on the Mississippi today. Cruises last two hours, and there is an optional creole lunch available for an additional fee. Each cruise features live narration of historical facts and highlights, jazz music in the main dining room, and a calliope concert during boarding times. The Harbor/Jazz Cruises at 11:30 am and 2:30 pm offer jazz by "Duke Heitger and the Steamboat Stompers." The 7 pm Dinner/Jazz Cruise features the world-renowned "Dukes of Dixieland" performing nightly. The Dinner/Jazz Cruise offers buffet-style dining and indoor/outdoor seating. Cruises depart from the Toulouse Street Wharf. **$$$$**

New Orleans Walking and Driving Tour. *2020 St. Charles Ave, New Orleans (70115). Phone 504/566-5011. www.neworleanscvb.com.* For a more thorough tour of the many interesting points in the Vieux Carré and surrounding area, see the visitor information center.

No Problem Raceway Park. *6470 Hwy 996, Bella Rose (70341). Phone 985/369-3692. www.noproblemraceway.com.* This drag racing park hosts, you guessed it—drag races—on its 4,000-foot dragstrip. Part of the Grand Bayou Circuit, the park also has a 1.8-mile, 15-turn asphalt road course and sponsors kart races as well. (Wed, Fri-Sat, some Sun; race times vary with event) Also here is

Grand Bayou Circuit. You can race your own car on the 1.8-mile asphalt track.

Oak Alley Plantation. *3645 Hwy 18 (Great River Rd), Vacherie (70090). W on I-10, Gramercy exit 194, S on Hwy 641, W on Hwy 18. Phone 225/265-2151; toll-free 800/442-5539. www.oakalleyplantation.com.* (1839) This quintessential antebellum, Greek Revival plantation house has been featured in many films: an *allee* of 300-year-old live oaks leads to the mansion surrounded by first- and second-floor galleries supported by massive columns. The interior was remodeled in the 1930s with antiques and modern furnishings of the day. Extensive grounds with many old trees. Picnicking, restaurant. Cottages. (Daily tours 9 am-5 pm; closed Thanksgiving, Dec 25) **$$**

The Old US Mint. *400 Esplanade Ave, New Orleans (70116). Esplanade and Decatur sts. Phone 504/568-6968. lsm.crt.state.la.us.* Designed by William Strickland in 1835, the mint produced coins for both the US and for the Confederate States. Today, the Mint houses permanent exhibitions of jazz and the Louisiana State Museum's Historical Center, a research facility. (Tues-Sun 9 am-5 pm; historical center also Mon, by appointment; closed holidays) **$**

Pitot House. *1440 Moss St, New Orleans (70119). Phone 504/482-0312. www.pitothouse.org/.* (1799) One of the last remaining French colonial/West Indies-style plantation houses along Bayou St. John. It was the residence of James Pitot, the first elected mayor of incorporated New Orleans. Restored; furnished with antiques. (Wed-Sat 10 am-3 pm; closed Sun-Tues, holidays) **$**

Pontalba Building. *523 St. Anne St, New Orleans (70116). Phone 504/524-9118.* Completed in 1850 and 1851 by the Baroness Pontalba to beautify the square. Still occupied and used as intended (with duplex apartments above ground-floor offices and shops), the buildings are now owned by the city and the Louisiana State Museum. The 1850 House is furnished in the manner of the period (Tues-Sun 9 am-5 pm; closed holidays). **$**

The Presbytere. *751 Chartres St, New Orleans (70116). Phone 504/568-6968. lsm.crt.state.la.us.* Architecturally similar to the Cabildo, this 1791 building was intended to house clergy serving the parish church. A series of fires kept the Presbytère incomplete until 1813, when it was finished by the US government. It is now a museum with a permanent exhibit on the history of Mardi Gras. The Presbytère, like the Cabildo, is part of the Louisiana State Museum complex. (Tues-Sun; closed holidays) **$$**

Preservation Hall. *726 St. Peter St, New Orleans (70116). Phone 504/522-2841. www.preservationhall .com.* Since 1961, people have been warming the benches at this rustic music hall in the French Quarter for one reason—to hear traditional New Orleans Jazz, which dates back to the early 1900s. If you know your music, you know this type of jazz is slower than other forms and features simple arrangements usually led by the sweet sounds of the trumpet. But even if you're no jazzman, you'll still want to jive to the beat at this swingin' joint. Bring the kids, too; the hall welcomes all ages. (Daily 8 pm-midnight) **$**

River cruises. *2 Canal St, New Orleans (70130).* Daily excursions depart from the riverfront.

Delta Queen and **Mississippi Queen Sternwheelers.** *Phone 504/586-0631; toll-free 800/543-1949. www.deltaqueen.com.* The sternwheelers *Delta Queen* and *Mississippi Queen* offer 3- to 12-night cruises on the Mississippi, Ohio, Cumberland, and Tennessee rivers year-round. Contact the Delta Queen Steamboat Co, 30 Robin St Wharf, 70130-1890.

John James Audubon Riverboat. *1 Canal St, New Orleans (70130). Phone 504/586-8777; toll-free 800/ 233-2628.* The riverboat *John James Audubon* provides river transportation between the Aquarium of the Americas and the Audubon Zoo 7 miles up-river, round-trip or one-way; return may be made via the St. Charles Avenue Streetcar (additional fee). Round-trip ticket price includes admission to both the Audubon Zoo and the Aquarium of the Americas.

Paddlewheeler Creole Queen and **Riverboat Cajun Queen.** *610 S Peters, New Orleans (70130). Phone 504/524-0814. www.neworleanspaddlewheels.com.* The paddlewheeler *Creole Queen* offers 2 1/2-hour sightseeing cruises to Chalmette National Historical Park, the site of the Battle of New Orleans, as well as three-hour dinner jazz cruises. The riverboat *Cajun Queen* offers harbor cruises from the Aquarium of the Americas (one-hour tour with narration).

Steamboat Natchez. *2 Canal St, New Orleans (70130). Toulouse St Wharf in the French Quarter behind Jackson Brewery. Phone 504/586-8777; toll-free 800/233-2628. www.steamboatnatchez.com.* This sternwheeler steamboat, the only one in New Orleans, takes passengers on two- and three-hour harbor cruises and evening dinner cruises. Live jazz is featured on all cruises. Tours depart from the Toulouse Street Wharf. **$$$$**

Riverfront Streetcar Line. *www.norta.com.* Vintage streetcars follow a 1 1/2-mile route along the Mississippi riverfront from Esplanade past the French Quarter to the World Trade Center, Riverwalk, Convention Center, and back. **$**

Riverwalk. *1 Poydras St, New Orleans (70130). Phone 504/522-1555. www.riverwalkmarketplace.com.* This 1/2-mile-long festival marketplace has more than 140 national and local shops, restaurants, and cafés. The Riverwalk structure was converted from World's Fair pavilions. (Mon-Sat 10 am-9 pm; Sun 11 am-7 pm; closed Thanksgiving, Dec 25)

Saenger Theatre. *143 N Rampart St, New Orleans (70112). Phone 504/525-1052. www.saengertheatre.com.* Opened in 1927 as a movie house, the Saenger now hosts national theatrical tours, musical acts, and other performing arts organizations. Entered in the National Register of Historic Places in 1977, the building's Italian Baroque interior includes Greek and Roman statuary and a ceiling embedded with lights to evoke a starry night sky. The 778-pipe organ is the largest the Robert Morton Wonder Organ Company ever built.

San Francisco Plantation. *2646 Hwy 44 (River Rd), Garyville (70051). Approximately 35 miles W via Hwy 61 or I-10 and Hwy 44. Phone 985/535-2341; toll-free 888/322-1756. www.sanfranciscoplantation.org.* (1853-1856) While a remarkable example of the "Steamboat Gothic" style in detail, the structure is typical of a Creole building: galleried with the main living quarters on the second floor, dining room and various service rooms on the ground floor. Authentically restored, the interior features five decorated ceilings (two are original). The house was used as the setting of Frances Parkinson Keyes's novel *Steamboat Gothic.* (Daily tours 9:30 am-4:40 pm, 4 pm in winter; closed holidays, Mardi Gras) **$$**

Shim-Sham Club and Juke Joint. *615 Toulouse St, New Orleans (70130). www.shimshamclub.com.* Nothing if not distinctive, the Shim-Sham Club offers everything from punk/heavy metal karaoke nights to alternative live theater. Boogie to the tunes at the weekly '80s dance party, or spin your own discs at the Juke Joint's jukebox. The Shim-Sham Revue offers burlesque complete with striptease and comedy acts. (Daily 2 pm-6 am)

The Shops at Canal Place. *333 Canal St, New Orleans (70130). Phone 504/522-9200. www.theshopsatcanal*

place.com. Three levels of name and designer shops give this shopping center at the edge of the French Quarter lots of cachet. Saks Fifth Avenue anchors the mall, which also offers Gucci, Kenneth Cole, and Betsey Johnson stores, along with Williams-Sonoma, Pottery Barn, and other clothing, jewelry, and shoe shops—about 30 in all. Additional amenities include a fitness club, a post office, and, of course, an ATM. The Southern Repertory Theater stage is located here also. (Mon-Sat 10 am-7 pm, Sun noon-6 pm)

Six Flags New Orleans. *12301 Six Flags Pkwy, New Orleans (70129). Phone 504/253-8100. www.sixflags.com.* Formerly known as Jazzland, this 140-acre amusement park is divided into six theme areas, including Looney Tunes Adventures, which offers rides and amusements for smaller children. Get wet on the flume ride in Ponchartrain Beach or watch the Batman Water Stunt Show there. Visit New Orleans-themed Cajun Country, Mardi Gras, and Kid's Carnival areas as well. Batman: The Ride roller coaster is one of six coasters in the park. **$$$$**

Southern Repertory Theater. *365 Canal St, New Orleans (70118). Phone 504/522-6545. www.southernrep.com.* Permanently housed in The Shops at Canal Place mall since 1991, the Southern Repertory Theater (SRT) was founded in 1986 to promote Southern plays and playwrights. Plays by Southern luminaries such as Tennessee Williams, Pearl Cleage, Beth Henley, and SRT founding member Rosary H. O'Neill form the basis of the theater's September-to-May season. (Thurs-Sat 8 pm, Sun 3 pm) **$$$$**

St. Bernard State Park. *501 St. Bernard Pkwy, Braithwaite (70040). 18 miles SE on Hwy 39. Phone 504/682-2101; toll-free 888/677-7823. www.lastateparks.com/stbernar.* Approximately 358 acres near the Mississippi River, with many viewing points of the river and a network of artificial lagoons. Swimming; picnicking, playground, trails, camping. (Daily) **FREE**

⭐ **St. Charles Avenue Streetcar.** *6700 Plaza Dr, New Orleans (70127). Phone 504/827-7802. www.regionaltransit.org.* The streetcars (never call them trolleys!) entered the National Registry of Historic Places in 1973. A ride is a quaint and relaxing way to view the varied architecture and exotic greenery of the aptly named Garden District. The 13.2-mile route can take you to tour Tulane University, drop you off at Audubon Park (where the zoo is located), and provide you with safe transport after imbibing in the French Quarter. **$**

St. Louis Cathedral. *615 Pére Antoine Alley, New Orleans (70116). Phone 504/525-9585. www.saint louiscathedral.org.* Consecrated in 1794 and named for French king and Saint Louis IX, this is the oldest cathedral in the United States and is the third church to stand on the site. (The two earlier churches were destroyed by hurricane and fire, respectively.) A mural inside depicts Louis announcing the seventh crusade. The triple steeple makes this French Quarter landmark easy to spot. (Daily; closed during Mardi Gras) **DONATION**

St. Louis Cemetery #1. *425 Basin St, New Orleans (70112). Phone 504/483-2064.* It's not a place to be after dark if you care about your physical health (it's in a high-crime area), but the oldest cemetery in the city is still worth a visit with a tour guide. Because New Orleans itself is below sea level, all the tombs are above ground and range in size and opulence from small, simple crypts to towering, ornate mausoleums. Don't be surprised to see flowers at Voodoo Queen Marie Laveau's tomb. (Mon-Sat 9 am-3 pm, Sun 9 am-noon)

Tipitina's. *501 Napolean Ave, New Orleans (70125). Phone 504/895-8477. www.tipitinas.com.* Live music is what you find at Tip's, as it's known to the locals. The emphasis is on rock, but funk, Cajun, and jazz all make the calendar. Tuesdays feature various local artists at the no-cover 8th Floor "Homegrown Nights," and Sundays often offer a $5 cover for the Cajun Fais Do Do. Shows featuring nationally and locally known talent start at 10 pm. (Thurs-Sun)

Toulouse Street Wharf. *At the foot of Toulouse St and the river.* Sales office and departure point for riverboat cruises and bus tours of the city and countryside.

Washington Artillery Park. *Frenchman and Royal sts, New Orleans (70152).* Between the muddy Mississippi and elegant Jackson Square lies this park named for the 141st Field Artillery, which has fought in every major conflict since the 1845 Mexican War. Broad steps serve as an amphitheater from which you can catch the escapades of the kids in the playground, the antics of the street performers, the lazy flow of the river, or a great view of the French Quarter.

Whiskey Blue. *333 Poydras St, New Orleans (70130). Phone 504/252-9444. www.whotels.com.* Located in the nouveau-chic W Hotel, Whiskey Blue upholds the hotel's chic, edgy tone with low-slung chairs, clear blue lighting, and pricey, (and expertly made) martinis. Smallish (it holds just 91 patrons) and intimate (there's a queen-sized bed in the middle of the place), the Blue caters to a stylish crowd taking a break from the French Quarter's free-for-all atmosphere. (Mon-Sat 4 pm-4 am, Sun to 2 am)

Woldenberg Riverfront Park. *1 Canal St, New Orleans (70130). Between Toulouse and Canal sts. Phone 504/565-3033.* Covering 17 acres on the riverfront, Woldenberg Park offers the city its first direct access to the river in 150 years; ships and paddlewheelers dock along the park. Visitors can choose from a variety of riverboat tours. (Sun-Thurs 6 am-10 pm, Fri-Sat 6 am-midnight)

World Trade Center of New Orleans. *2 Canal St, New Orleans (70130). Phone 504/529-1601. wtc-no.org.* This center houses the offices of many maritime companies and foreign consulates involved in international trade. Top of the Mart, a revolving restaurant and cocktail lounge on the 33rd floor, offers fine views of the city and the Mississippi River. (Daily; closed holidays) **$**

Special Events

Bridge City Gumbo Festival. *Gumbo Festival Park on Angel Square, 1701 Bridge City Ave, New Orleans (70130). On the other side of Huey P. Long Bridge from New Orleans. Phone 504/436-4712. www.hgaparish.org/gumbofestival.htm.* In the Gumbo Capital of the World, festival organizers cook up more than 2,000 gallons of chicken, sausage, and seafood gumbos. Jambalaya, another local specialty, is also available, along with a variety of accompaniments. You can enter a cooking contest, listen to live music, enjoy carnival rides, and participate in many other activities. Early Nov.

French Quarter Festival. *French Quarter, 100 Conti St, New Orleans (70130). Phone 504/522-5730; toll-free 800/673-5725. www.frenchquarterfestival.com.* Fabulous and free, the French Quarter Festival showcases local musicians on 15 stages throughout the Vieux Carré. Marching bands, brass bands, and jazz and Dixieland bands play early to late three days running, usually the second weekend in April. You can also hear Cajun, country, zydeco, and everything in between. Music stages are located at Jackson Square, Woldenberg Riverfront Park, Bourbon Street, Royal Street, the French Market, Le Petit Theatre at St. Peter and Chartres, and Louisiana State Museum's Old US Mint at Esplanade and Decatur. Don't miss the "World's Largest Jazz Brunch" —booths can be found in Jackson Square, Woldenberg Riverfront Park, and Louisiana State Museum's Old US Mint. Art exhibits,

dance troupes, and workshops for young and young at heart guarantee something for everyone.

Horse racing. Fair Grounds Racetrack. *1751 Gentilly Blvd, New Orleans (70119). Phone 504/944-5515. www.fgno.com.* (1872) America's third-oldest race-track. Pari-mutuel betting. Jacket required in clubhouse. Wed-Sun, late Nov-Mar.

Louisiana Crawfish Festival. *8200 W Judge Perez Dr, Chalmette (70043). Phone 504/271-3836.* Rides, games, live entertainment, and an array of dishes featuring crawfish. Early Apr.

Louisiana Swampfest. *6500 Magazine St, New Orleans (70118). Phone 504/581-4629; toll-free 866/487-2966. www.auduboninstitute.org/swampfest/.* Ever wondered how alligator tastes? Head to the Swampfest to try fried gator tidbits while listening to local bands play Cajun and Zydeco tunes. You may want to participate in the 5K run before indulging in the food and music treats, checking out the craft village, or getting some hands-on experience with live creatures in the swamp exhibit. Early-mid-Nov.

Mardi Gras Festival. *The main parade route travels down St. Charles Ave and the heart of Bourbon St. Phone 504/566-5011. www.mardigras.com or www.mardigrasday.com.* The biggest party of the year offers something for everyone—especially if you're into raucous, bawdy partying. The party starts weeks before the actual date of Mardi Gras, which, because it's 46 days before Easter, varies each year. Parades and parties are scheduled throughout the weeks leading up to Ash Wednesday and Lent (the French term *mardi gras* means "fat Tuesday"). Though most of the balls are invitation-only, you pay nothing to watch the numerous parades sponsored by the secret societies (krewes) that organize the festivities. The parades range in theme and name from Barkus (animals of all kinds), to the Phunny Phorty Phellows, to Comus, New Orleans' oldest krewe. If you're looking to enjoy the festivities without offending too many sensibilities, head to the family-friendly Garden District and avoid the French Quarter, where it's nearly impossible to avoid seeing lots of flesh and usually concealed body parts. Early Jan-late Feb.

New Orleans Jazz & Heritage Festival. *Fairgrounds Racetrack, 1751 Gentilly Blvd, New Orleans (70119). Phone 504/522-4786. www.nojazzfest.com.* Each year, Jazz Fest draws 500,000 visitors from around the world for an experience that embraces music, food, art exhibits, and craft workshops. You know that the music is eclectic when the acts for one day range from Lil' Romeo to Crosby, Stills & Nash to Buckwheat Zydeco. The main action is at the Fair Grounds, but the fun spreads to venues throughout the city. New Orleans's own Neville Brothers are always a big draw. Late Apr-early May. **$$$$**

Nokia Sugar Bowl College Football Classic. *Louisiana Superdome, Sugar Bowl Dr, New Orleans (70112). Phone 504/525-8573. www.nokiasugarbowl.com.* Each year, two top-ranked college football teams compete in this prestigious bowl game, part of the Bowl Championship Series. From 4 pm to kickoff, all football lovers can party at Fan Jam, on the Gate C Bridge located on the Superdome's east side. The spirited event features live music, contests, hot food, and ice-cold beverages. Sugar Bowl week also includes a basketball classic and a regatta on Lake Pontchartrain. Jan.

Spring Fiesta. *826 St. Ann St, New Orleans (70116). Phone 504/581-1367.* For two weekends every year, New Orleans celebrates its unique heritage with this springtime festival. The fun-packed festivities include a parade of horse-drawn carriages through the French Quarter, the coronation of the festival's queen at Jackson Square, and tours of private homes and courtyards and the historic Metairie Cemetery. Mid-late Apr.

Tennessee Williams New Orleans Literary Festival. *French Quarter, Le Petit Theatre du Vieux Carré, 616 St. Peter St, New Orleans (70116). Phone 504/581-1144; toll-free 800/965-4827. www.tennesseewilliams.net.* Born in Mississippi, playwright Tennessee Williams adopted New Orleans as his spiritual home. The city honors him with an annual festival held around his March 26 birthday. The five days of the festival are filled with workshops on writing and publishing, a one-act play competition, and a book fair, as well as performances of some of Williams' plays. You can join a literary walking tour or compete in a Stanley and Stella contest. Le Petit Theatre du Vieux Carré is the festival headquarters, but other venues also house activities. Late Mar.

White Linen Night. *900 Camp St, New Orleans (70130). Phone 504/528-3805. www.cacno.org.* Catch some culture during this annual art walk and street party. August in the bayou is always hot and humid, so patrons and partiers don their coolest clothes—white linen is a popular choice—and stroll through the Arts District, popping into galleries that stay open late, catching live dance and theater performances,

and ending up at the Contemporary Arts Center for a party that goes on until the wee hours. First Sat in Aug. **FREE**

Limited-Service Hotels

★ ★ **BEST WESTERN FRENCH QUARTER LANDMARK.** *920 N Rampart St, New Orleans (70116). Phone 504/524-3333; toll-free 800/780-7234; fax 504/523-5431. www.bestwestern.com.* 100 rooms, 3 story. Check-in 4 pm, check-out noon. Restaurant, bar. Outdoor pool. **$**
🅳 🏊

★ ★ **BIENVILLE HOUSE HOTEL.** *320 Decatur St, New Orleans (70130). Phone 504/529-2345; toll-free 800/535-9603; fax 504/525-6079. www.bienvillehouse .com.* One of the first things to strike you about the Bienville House Hotel is how much the lobby feels like your living room—assuming that your living room has a chandelier and looks somewhat like a French Quarter manor home from the late-18th-century. Elegantly cushy chairs and coffee tables aside, a recent multimillion-dollar renovation that included the creation of hand-painted wall murals has steeped this French Quarter treat with a stately, old-world charm. The allure continues outside in a lush courtyard surrounding a pool with four sundecks and wonderful city views. 83 rooms, 4 story. Complimentary continental breakfast. Check-out noon. Restaurant. Outdoor pool. **$**
🏊

★ ★ **DOUBLETREE HOTEL.** *300 Canal St, New Orleans (70130). Phone 504/581-1300; fax 504/522-4100. www.doubletree.com.* Location is what distinguishes this fairly standard hotel. It's conveniently located in the business district, just three blocks from the convention center and overlooking the river. Harrah's Casino is next door, and the French Quarter is just across the street. 363 rooms, 17 story. Check-in 3 pm, check-out noon. Restaurant, bar. Fitness room. Outdoor pool. Business center. **$$**
🏋 🏊 🚶

★ ★ **EMBASSY SUITES.** *315 Julia St, New Orleans (70130). Phone 504/525-1993; toll-free 800/362-2779; fax 504/525-3437. www.embassyneworleans. com.* This hotel is located in the convention center and is convenient to the French Quarter, the St. Charles Streetcar, and the waterfront. 282 rooms, 16 story, all suites. Pets accepted; fee. Complimentary full breakfast. Check-in 3 pm, check-out noon. Restaurant, bar. Fitness room. Outdoor pool, whirlpool. **$$**

★ ★ **HOTEL PROVINCIAL.** *1024 rue Chartres, New Orleans (70116). Phone 504/581-4995; toll-free 800/535-7922; fax 504/581-1018. www.hotelprovincial.com.* Haunted? Rumor has that it soldiers who were treated here when it was a Civil War hospital still come around every once in a while. If you see one, ask him to bring you a beignet; if he's anything like any other employee at the hotel, you'll have it before the request leaves your lips. The service at Hotel Provincial is nearly as wonderful as its award-winning architecture, which is nearly as wonderful as the warm, relaxing atmosphere that can be soaked up within its restored old buildings. 105 rooms, 4 story. Check-out noon. Restaurant, bar. Outdoor pool. **$**

★ ★ **IBERVILLE SUITES.** *910 Iberville St, New Orleans (70112). Phone 504/523-2400; fax 504/524-1320. www.ibervillesuites.com.* Its location in the historic Maison Blanche building in the French Quarter gives you a clue as to what you'll find inside this hotel: warm Southern hospitality from check-in to check-out. The antique-filled lobby, with classic wood touches, comfortable chairs and sofas, and plenty of sitting room for relaxing and people-watching, is the sort of place you want to sit for a while, or perhaps take tea. If you'd prefer to have tea in your room or suite, take comfort in the fact that your tea (or coffee) will be served in a silver pot and poured into china cups. Guests also enjoy signing privileges at the Ritz-Carlton's food and beverage outlets and spa and fitness facilities. Elegantly decorated guest rooms boast warm, rich colors and more antiques. 230 rooms, 7 story, all suites. Pets accepted, some restrictions; fee. Complimentary continental breakfast. Check-in 3 pm, check-out noon. Restaurant, bar. Fitness room, spa. Indoor pool, whirlpool. Airport transportation available. Business center. **$$**

★ ★ **MAISON DE VILLE AND AUDUBON COTTAGES.** *727 rue Toulouse, New Orleans (70130). Phone 504/561-5858; fax 504/528-9939.* In the heart of the French Quarter, this charming hotel offers antique-filled main-house rooms and historic Audubon Cottages (believed to be former slave quarters). All accommodations include continental breakfast and evening port and sherry served in the courtyard or salon. 23 rooms, 3 story. Children over 12 years only.

Complimentary continental breakfast. Check-in 3 pm, check-out noon. Restaurant. **$$**

★ ★ **MAISON DUPUY.** *1001 rue Toulouse, New Orleans (70112). Phone 504/586-8000; toll-free 800/535-9177; fax 504/566-7450. www.maisondupuy.com.* A low-key, semitropical courtyard complete with gas lamps and potted palms may be just the thing after a long day of hustle-bustling your way through the nearby French Quarter. The courtyard emerged as part of the renovation and preservation project that took seven French Quarter townhouses and created Maison Dupuy. It is the heart of this quiet hotel, the place where guests can be found starting their day, relaxing before dinner, and enjoying a dip in the whirlpool before retiring for the night. 200 rooms, 5 story. Check-out 11 am. Restaurant, bar. Fitness room. Outdoor pool. **$$**

★ ★ **PRYTANIA PARK HOTEL.** *1525 Prytania St, New Orleans (70130). Phone 504/524-0427; toll-free 888/498-7591; fax 504/522-2977. www.prytaniapark hotel.com.* Huey Long's girlfriend slept here. No doubt she wanted to be a tad removed from the center of things; but the Pyrtania Park has a shuttle to take you to the French Quarter, the Convention Center, and the Central Business District. A group of 1980 buildings wrapped around an 1834 townhouse, the Prytania Park is a tourist-class hotel with peaceful courtyards and outside stairwells, provoking a sense of old New Orleans. Several wooden picnic tables and chairs line shady, narrow walkways, providing a lovely place for breakfast. 62 rooms, 2 story. Complimentary continental breakfast. Check-out noon. **$**

★ ★ ★ **W NEW ORLEANS - FRENCH QUARTER.** *316 Chartres St, New Orleans (70130). Phone 504/581-1200; fax 504/523-2910. www.whotels.com.* 98 rooms, 5 story. Pets accepted, some restrictions. Check-out noon. Restaurant, bar. Outdoor pool. **$$**

★ ★ **WYNDHAM BOURBON ORLEANS HOTEL.** *717 Orleans St, New Orleans (70116). Phone 504/523-2222; fax 504/525-8166. www.bourbonorleans.com.* After a wild beginning as the famous Orleans Ballroom, the site of the city's earliest masquerade balls, things took a 180 degree turn and this property was purchased by an order of African-American nuns devoted to teaching, who turned it into a school. Today, the hotel has recaptured its lavish roots: a huge spiral staircase, columns, chandeliers, marble floors, and Queen Anne and Chippendale furnishings in the lobby and foyer create an air of restrained opulence. And Mardi Gras balls again take place here, now in the sumptuous banquet room. 216 rooms, 6 story. Check-out noon. Restaurant, bar. Outdoor pool. **$**

★ ★ **WYNDHAM RIVERFRONT HOTEL.** *701 Convention Center Blvd, New Orleans (70130). Phone 504/524-8200; fax 504/524-0600. www.wyndham.com.* The Wyndham Riverfront is a pleasant hotel in the heart of New Orleans's business district, across the street from the Ernest N. Memorial Convention Center. This is a business traveler's delight—great amenities and a staff that understands the importance (and occasional urgency) of getting a job done. Its location adjacent to downtown New Orleans and the French Quarter, near Cafe du Monde, Pat O'Brien's, Jackson Square, Canal Place, and the Audubon Aquarium of the Americas means that the staff is also well versed in the art of having fun and can give you guidance on things to do. 202 rooms, 6 story. Check-out noon. Restaurant, bar. Fitness room. Business center. **$$**

Full-Service Hotels

★ ★ ★ **CHATEAU SONESTA HOTEL.** *800 Iberville St, New Orleans (70112). Phone 504/586-0800; fax 504/586-1987.* Not only are the guest rooms at this elegant Sonesta extra-large (with 12-foot ceilings), but most come with good views of well-landscaped courtyards or Bourbon Street, which sits just steps away. As an added bonus for business travelers, all the rooms come with T-1 high-speed Internet access. If you wake up hungry, La Chatelaine serves breakfast. For lunch or dinner, savor scrumptious seafood dishes at Ralph Brennan's Red Fish Grill. The unique-looking hotel dates all the way back to 1849, when Daniel Henry Holmes opened his D. H. Holmes Department Store, which did a booming business on this very site until 1989. 251 rooms, 4 story. Pets accepted, some restrictions; fee. Check-in 3 pm, check-out noon. High-speed Internet access. Restaurant, bar. Fitness room. Outdoor pool. **$$$**

★ ★ ★ **DAUPHINE ORLEANS HOTEL.** *415 Dauphine St, New Orleans (70112). Phone 504/586-1800; toll-free 800/521-7111; fax 504/586-1409. www.dauphineorleans.com.* Head to the French Quarter and step back into the New Orleans of yesteryear when you check into this jewel with quite a past. May Baily's Place, the hotel's bar, was one of the more popular bordellos in the city's red-light district in 1857. In the Audubon Cottage, now the main meeting room, John James Audubon painted his well-known "Birds of America" series from 1821 to 1822. And a townhome built for a wealthy merchant in 1834 now houses 14 patio rooms. Besides all this history, the charming boutique hotel also serves guests a welcome cocktail, continental breakfast, and afternoon tea (with cookies)—all complimentary. 111 rooms, 4 story. Complimentary continental breakfast. Check-in 3 pm, check-out noon. Bar. Fitness room. Outdoor pool, whirlpool. **$$**

★ ★ ★ **THE FAIRMONT NEW ORLEANS.** *123 Baronne St, New Orleans (70112). Phone 504/529-7111; toll-free 800/441-1414; fax 504/522-2303. www.fairmont.com.* The genteel Fairmont offers the perfect introduction to the sultry city of New Orleans. Situated at the edge of the French Quarter in the center of the business district, this posh hotel has been the preferred choice of gentlemen and ladies since 1893. Eight presidents have slept here. When it was called The Roosevelt (in honor of Teddy), rumor has it that Governor Huey Long built a 90-mile road from the state capital in Baton Rouge to the hotel so that he could get there more easily; a right turn upon leaving The Fairmont does indeed put you on Highway 61 to Baton Rouge. Its location makes it ideal for exploring the city's renowned streets by foot, although it is the Victorian-era elegance and sparkling interiors that really make this hotel a standout. Its atmosphere is distinctly historic, yet the hotel remains relevant with the latest technology and amenities. The elegance of the glorious lobby, with huge bouquets of fresh flowers and a snap-to-it bellstaff, parallels that of the guest rooms, most with huge bathrooms, and many with claw-foot bathtubs and marble showers. Foodies flock to New Orleans for its top-notch restaurants, and The Fairmont's Sazerac Bar & Grill rarely disappoints with its fantastic Creole cuisine. 700 rooms, 14 story. Pets accepted, some restrictions; fee. Check-in 4 pm, check-out 1 pm. Restaurant, bar. Fitness room. Outdoor pool. Tennis. Business center. **$$**

★ ★ ★ **HILTON NEW ORLEANS RIVERSIDE.** *2 Poydras St, New Orleans (70140). Phone 504/561-0500; fax 504/568-1721. www.neworleans.hilton.com.* With its multiple levels, intimate sitting areas, soaring ceilings, a long crosswalk, and entrances in several different lobbies, the Hilton New Orleans Riverside lives up to its own moniker: "a city within a city." This is not a quaint, cozy hotel. A feeling of excitement and high energy prevails from check-in, past the "main street" of shops and dining venues and up to the guest rooms. Although this sophisticated hotel can't be summed up by any one particular style, the rooms can be termed either "traditional" or French Provinçial, the latter perhaps fitting with the hotel's location on the banks of the Mississippi. Privileges to a nearby racquet and health club are available to guests for a small fee. 1,616 rooms, 29 story. Check-in 3 pm, check-out noon. Restaurant. Fitness room. Two outdoor pools, whirlpool. Tennis. Business center. **$**

★ ★ ★ **HOTEL LE CIRQUE.** *2 Lee Cir, New Orleans (70130). Phone 504/962-0900. www.hotellecirque.com.* A stylish and hip crowd checks into this chic hotel, thanks to its location in the oh-so-funky Arts and Warehouse District, home to many cutting-edge galleries, restaurants, and shops. You'll feel positively cosmopolitan in one of its smart-looking guest rooms, and you'll feel like a local when you dine in its Lee Circle Restaurant, which dishes up tasty French Creole cuisine. The hotel has one of the best locations for enjoying Mardi Gras festivities because more than 23 krewes parade right by its front doors. 137 rooms, 10 story. Check-out noon. Restaurant, bar. Fitness room. Airport transportation available. Business center. **$**

★ ★ ★ **HOTEL MONTELEONE.** *214 rue Royal, New Orleans (70130). Phone 504/523-3341; fax 504/561-5803.* Truman Capote. Tennessee Williams. Paul Newman and Joanne Woodward. Since 1886, the French Quarter's oldest and largest hotel has been rolling out the red carpet for its guests, many of them celebrated authors, movie stars, royalty, and other notables. The guest rooms in this family-owned and operated property are spacious and well appointed, as one would expect after seeing the elegant lobby, with its unique art and antiques. For decades, locals have favored the Monteleone's Carousel Bar, where some seats revolve around the room (hence the watering hole's name). After cocktails, take a seat inside the Hunt Room Grill for fine dining. For recreation, head up to the rooftop for a dip in the pool or a workout in the well-equipped fitness center, which offers splendid views of the French Quarter and the Mississippi River. 600 rooms, 17 story. Check-in 3 pm, check-out noon.

Restaurant, bar. Fitness room. Outdoor pool. Business center. **$$**

★ ★ ★ **INTERCONTINENTAL HOTEL NEW ORLEANS.** *444 St. Charles Ave, New Orleans (70130). Phone 504/525-5566; toll-free 800/445-6563; fax 504/523-7310. www.new-orleans.interconti.com.* With translation services available, a foreign currency exchange on the premises, a global newspaper service, and a staff that speaks 14 languages, the InterContinental Hotel New Orleans can't help but have a European flair. This large, modern hotel is a mecca for business travelers. Yet while the furnishings are modern and the business accoutrements are top-notch, so are the elements that bring pleasure to even "have to" travel—a terrific health club and a restaurant that serves lavish breakfast and lunch buffets, fine traditional New Orleans cuisine, and a traditional jazz Sunday brunch. 482 rooms, 15 story. Check-in 3 pm, check-out noon. Restaurant, bar. Fitness room. Outdoor pool. Airport transportation available. Business center. **$$$**

★ ★ ★ **INTERNATIONAL HOUSE.** *221 Camp St, New Orleans (70130). Phone 504/553-9550; toll-free 800/633-5770; fax 504/553-9560. www.ihhotel.com.* At this top-rated boutique hotel, the décor is a winning mix of New Orleans style and contemporary chic. The charming folk art and handmade furniture created by Louisiana artisans serve as a pleasant reminder you're in Cajun country, but the stainless steel and marble accents give the ritzy, intimate hotel a cosmopolitan feel. Get in touch with the spirits at Loa (the Voodoo word for deities), a dark bar lighted only by candles. And dine at Lemon Grass (see) for Vietnamese cuisine with some French touches. After drinks and dinner, could romance come next? At the International House, definitely. 119 rooms, 12 story. Check-in 4 pm, check-out noon. Restaurant, bar. Golf. **$$**

★ ★ ★ **LAFAYETTE HOTEL.** *600 St. Charles Ave, New Orleans (70130). Phone 504/524-4441; toll-free 888/524-4441; fax 504/523-7327. www.thelafayettehotel.com.* In 1916, this small and luxurious hotel originally opened in the same Beaux Arts building in which it still pampers guests. Located on Lafayette Square in the Central Business District, it often hosts executives in town on business. Its old-world-style rooms and suites are individually decorated and come well appointed—many have French doors and wrought-iron balconies, and all have English botanical prints, overstuffed easy chairs, and marble bathrooms with French-milled soaps and thick terry bathrobes. Off its small but elegant lobby, guests can dine at Mike Ditka's, a gourmet steakhouse that also serves Creole and Cajun favorites. 44 rooms, 5 story. Check-in 4 pm, check-out 11 am. Restaurant, bar. **$**

★ ★ ★ **LE PAVILLON HOTEL.** *833 Poydras St, New Orleans (70112). Phone 504/581-3111; fax 504/620-4130.* This hotel, listed on the National Register of Historic Places, has seen it all: wars, prohibition, and the birth of the horseless carriage. Through it all, it has kept its reputation as a Great Lady of New Orleans. In 1970, the Hotel Denechaud, as it was called, passed into new hands and was renamed Le Pavillon, receiving a facelift and some spectacular accoutrements: crystal chandeliers from Czechoslovakia, railings from the lobby of Paris's Grand Hotel, and fine art and antiques from around the world. The Crystal Suite contains a hand-carved marble bathtub, a gift from Napoleon to a wealthy Louisiana plantation owner—just like the one in the Louvre. 226 rooms, 10 story. Check-in 3 pm, check-out noon. Restaurant, bar. Fitness room. Outdoor pool, whirlpool. Airport transportation available. **$**

★ ★ ★ **LE RICHELIEU IN THE FRENCH QUARTER.** *1234 Chartres St, New Orleans (70116). Phone 504/529-2492; toll-free 800/535-9653; fax 504/524-8179. www.lerichelieuhotel.com.* This family-owned hotel offers an amenity you won't find at any other hotel in the French Quarter: free self-parking. As good as that sounds, many guests keep coming back to this people-pleaser for other reasons as well—including affordable rates; comfortable, homey rooms decorated in Creole style with mirrored walls and ceiling fans; a cozy bar and café; and an attractive courtyard with a pool. All these pluses got the attention of ex-Beatle Paul McCartney, who checked in here for two months in the late 1970s while in town doing some recording work. A suite is now named after him. 86 rooms, 4 story. Check-in 3 pm, check-out 1 pm. Restaurant, bar. Outdoor pool. **$**

★ ★ ★ **OMNI ROYAL CRESCENT HOTEL.** *535 Gravier St, New Orleans (70130). Phone 504/527-0006; toll-free 800/578-3200; fax 504/571-7575. www.omniroyalcrescent.com.* A first impression of the Omni Royal Crescent makes you want to straighten your posture: this is a place where the staff will allow

no slouching, and you just don't want to. The lobby is an impeccable blend of modern and traditional, with shiny brass elevators, a concierge stand, and colorful fresh flowers, plus refined artwork and potted palms. Unusual in New Orleans, the Omni has a restaurant serving Thai food (with American food for breakfast). The comfortable guest rooms feature touches of wood and brass. 98 rooms, 8 story. Pets accepted; fee. Check-in 3 pm, check-out noon. Restaurant. Fitness room. Outdoor pool, whirlpool. **$**

★ ★ ★ **OMNI ROYAL ORLEANS.** *621 St. Louis St, New Orleans (70140). Phone 504/529-5333; fax 504/529-7089. www.omniroyalorleans.com.* For royal treatment in the French Quarter, settle into one of the many plush rooms at this luxury hotel, which has been pampering visitors to the city since 1960. In the comfort of your room, this chain property will spoil you with Irish linen sheets, marble baths, and windows overlooking all the action in the Quarter. Dine on steak and seafood in the award-winning Rib Room, a local favorite for decades; or refresh yourself with a mint julep or two at the Touche Bar or the Esplanade Lounge (in the lobby). Up on the rooftop, go for a relaxing swim in the pool, work up a sweat in the fitness center, or take in the sensational views. 346 rooms, 7 story. Pets accepted, some restrictions; fee. Check-in 4 pm, check-out noon. Restaurant, bar. Fitness room. Outdoor pool. Business center. **$$$**

★ ★ ★ **THE PONTCHARTRAIN HOTEL.** *2031 St. Charles Ave, New Orleans (70140). Phone 504/524-0581; fax 504/529-1165.* For more than 75 years, this *grande dame* has been mixing European elegance with Southern hospitality in the city's charming Garden District. In years gone by, dignitaries and celebrities frequently registered here, explaining why some of the suites bear the names of famous folks—Richard Burton, Joan Fontaine, and Mary Martin, among them. But these days, business travelers like to settle into its comfortable rooms, all of which are individually decorated with antiques and original art. At breakfast, lunch, or dinner, savor classic Creole and Cajun specialties at Lafitte's Restaurant. If you start your morning there, you'll likely spot local politicos and civic leaders drinking café au lait and biting into beignets. After the workday, local professionals often wind down in the Bayou Bar. 104 rooms, 12 story. Pets accepted; fee. Check-in 3 pm, check-out noon. Restaurant, bar. Airport transportation available. **$**

★ ★ ★ **RENAISSANCE PERE MARQUETTE HOTEL.** *817 Common St, New Orleans (70112). Phone 504/525-1111; fax 504/525-0688. www.renaissance hotels.com.* Although it's housed in a historic building, this hotel has a contemporary look that appeals to those who like modern, chic décor. Given its location in the Central Business District, the Renaissance attracts plenty of business travelers, especially since every room comes with high-speed Internet access, two-line phones with data ports, and work desks with lamps. But leisure travelers book its rooms, as well, because of its close proximity to some of the city's best shopping, restaurants, and attractions, including the French Quarter. Rene Bistrot serves award-winning French cuisine at affordable prices, so you'll be vying for a table with the locals who work downtown and know where to find the best deals. 275 rooms, 7 story. Check-in 3 pm, check-out noon. High-speed Internet access. Restaurant, bar. Fitness room. Outdoor pool, whirlpool. Business center. **$$**

[icons]

★ ★ ★ **THE RITZ-CARLTON, NEW ORLEANS.** *921 Canal St, New Orleans (70112). Phone 504/524-1331; toll-free 800/241-3333; fax 504/524-7675. www.ritzcarlton.com.* The Ritz-Carlton transports visitors to 19th-century New Orleans with its French *savoir-faire* and gracious styling. On the edge of the French Quarter, this refined hotel is a delightful refuge in the vibrant Crescent City. The guest rooms have a timeless elegance. Feather beds and deep-soaking tubs add to the luxurious atmosphere. The bistro-style FQB is a casually elegant spot, while Victor's dazzles with its formal setting and refined cuisine. The exquisite lounge offers an unrivaled afternoon tea set to the gentle strains of a harp. Reviving many treatments favored by royals like Marie Antoinette and Princess Eugenie and incorporating the citrus scent created for Napoleon, the sensational spa is a celebration of all things French. 527 rooms, 14 story. Pets accepted, some restrictions; fee. Check-in 3 pm, check-out noon. Restaurant, bar. Fitness room, spa. Indoor pool, whirlpool. Airport transportation available. Business center. **$$**

[icons]

★ ★ ★ **ROYAL SONESTA HOTEL NEW ORLEANS.** *300 Bourbon St, New Orleans (70130). Phone 504/586-0300; fax 504/586-0335.* Gabled windows. French doors. Wrought-iron lace balconies. Gilded mirrors. Furniture reminiscent of 18th-century France. Tranquil, beautifully landscaped courtyards. This cozy but elegant property occupies a full block right on Bourbon Street, and it looks like it belongs in this historic district. If you crave a gourmet meal, sample the contemporary French and Creole cuisine served at Begue's Restaurant (see). For something more casual, opt for the Desire Oyster Bar (see), where the chefs cook up both Creole and seafood dishes. Party at the Mystick Den cocktail lounge or the Can-Can Café and Jazz Club. If you just want to rest and relax, lounge out by the pool on an appealing third-floor terrace. 484 rooms, 7 story. Pets accepted, some restrictions; fee. Check-in 3 pm, check-out noon. Restaurant, bar. Fitness room. Outdoor pool. Business center. **$$$**

[icons]

★ ★ ★ **ST. JAMES HOTEL.** *330 Magazine St, New Orleans (70130). Phone 504/304-4000; toll-free 888/856-4485; fax 504/569-0640. www.saintjameshotel.com.* Even though the St. James opened just a few years ago, it has the look of a distinguished older property because it occupies a renovated building that dates back to the 1850s. The hotel looks vintage New Orleans, as well, with wrought-iron balconies and some rooms with exposed-brick walls. Business travelers like its downtown location and the two-line phones in every room. Rooftop terraces overlook a small pool in a charming courtyard. Cuvee restaurant (see) offers contemporary Creole cuisine and more than 500 wine choices. 90 rooms, 3 story. Check-out noon. Restaurant, bar. Fitness room. Indoor pool. Airport transportation available. Business center. **$$**

[icons]

★ ★ ★ **ST. LOUIS HOTEL.** *730 rue Bienville, New Orleans (70130). Phone 504/581-7300; toll-free 888/535-9111; fax 504/524-8925. www.stlouishotel.com.* All guest rooms in this French Quarter boutique hotel overlook a lovely Mediterranean courtyard lush with tropical greenery, banana trees, flowering plants, and a Baroque fountain. Inside, they are decked out in French period reproductions, and fabulous French cuisine is featured in the Louis XVI Restaurant, a New Orleans tradition. At breakfast, however, the hotel serves Eggs Sardou and other local favorites in its courtyard. 85 rooms, 5 story. Check-in 3 pm, check-out noon. Restaurant; **$**

★ ★ ★ **W NEW ORLEANS.** *333 Poydras St, New Orleans (70130). Phone 504/525-9444; toll-free 800/522-6963; fax 504/581-7179. www.whotels.com.* This style-soaked chain is designed for savvy business travelers, but even leisure guests won't mind the down comforters, Aveda products, and great fitness center.

Zoe Bistro offers creative French food, and the lobby's Whiskey Blue (see) bar delivers a dose of Randy Gerber-style nightlife. 423 rooms, 23 story. Pets accepted, some restrictions; fee. Check-in 3 pm, check-out noon. Restaurant, bar. Fitness room. Outdoor pool. **$$$**

★ ★ ★ ★ **WINDSOR COURT HOTEL.** *300 Gravier St, New Orleans (70130). Phone 504/523-6000; fax 504/596-4513.* Not far from the French Quarter, in the city's Business District, the Windsor Court Hotel welcomes guests with open arms. Set around a courtyard, this elegant hotel brings a bit of the English countryside to New Orleans. Traditional English furnishings and unique artwork define the rooms, while bay windows focus attention on lovely views of the city or the Mississippi River. This full-service hotel also includes a pool, sundeck, and comprehensive business and fitness centers under its roof. In a city hailed for its works of culinary genius, the Windsor Court is no exception. The Grill Room (see) is one of the hottest tables in town; the Polo Club Lounge is ideal for enjoying brandy and cigars; and Le Salon is the "in" spot for afternoon tea. 324 rooms, 23 story. Pets accepted, some restrictions; fee. Check-in 3 pm, check-out noon. Restaurant, bar. Fitness room. Outdoor pool, whirlpool. Airport transportation available. Business center. **$$$**

★ ★ ★ **WYNDHAM NEW ORLEANS AT CANAL PLACE.** *100 rue Iberville, New Orleans (70130). Phone 504/566-7006; fax 504/553-5120. www.wyndham.com.* Its downtown location isn't the only reason business travelers give this upscale hotel a thumbs up. They also like the oversized guest rooms and the worker-friendly amenities in them, including direct high-speed Internet access, ergonomic work chairs, and cordless telephones. But the Wyndham also appeals to leisure travelers since it's convenient to most of the city's main attractions. In fact, it's in the Canal Place Tower, home to the Shops at Canal Place, where visitors (and locals) like to go on buying sprees in the many top-name stores, such as Saks Fifth Avenue. Everyone who beds down here appreciates the stellar views of the city from both the marble-adorned lobby (on the tower's 11th floor) and the rooms that rise above it. For the hungry, the Wyndham dishes up American cuisine with a Louisiana twist in the Riverbend Grill. 438 rooms, 18 story. Check-in 3 pm, check-out noon. Restaurant, bar. Fitness room. Outdoor pool. Business center. **$$$**

★ ★ ★ **WYNDHAM WHITNEY HOTEL.** *610 Poydras St, New Orleans (70130). Phone 504/581-4222; fax 504/207-0100. www.wyndham.com.* The fact that this building used to be a branch of the Whitney National Bank is what puts the "fun" in "functional." Take some time to check out the private dining room, once the bank's vault; the grand public dining room, once the actual bank space; the impossibly thick doors, which once kept out bank robbers; and the intricate old plasterwork in the public spaces. The atmosphere makes it easy to understand what it all must have been like, although your imagination is helped by the hotel's location—right next to the US federal buildings. 293 rooms, 7 story. Check-in 3 pm, check-out noon. Restaurant, bar. Fitness room. Business center. **$**

Full-Service Inns

★ ★ ★ **HOUSE ON BAYOU ROAD.** *2275 Bayou Rd, New Orleans (70119). Phone 504/945-0992; toll-free 800/882-2968; fax 504/945-0993. www.houseon bayouroad.com.* Experience old New Orleans at this converted Indigo plantation home (1798), offering 2 acres of gardens, ponds, and patios, as well as a plantation-style breakfast. 9 rooms, 2 story. Children over 12 years only. Complimentary full breakfast. Check-in 3 pm, check-out noon. Restaurant. Outdoor pool, whirlpool. **$**

★ ★ ★ **LAFITTE GUEST HOUSE.** *1003 Bourbon St, New Orleans (70116). Phone 504/581-2678; toll-free 800/331-7971; fax 504/581-2677. www.lafitteguest house.com.* If you want to feel like you're staying with friends in the mid-19th century, this three-story bed-and-breakfast will do the trick. At this guest house-cum-small inn—there is a concierge to attend to your needs—you'll receive the type of warm welcome that only a guest house can truly provide. One can just imagine a proper cup of tea while sitting in the 1849 Victorian ground-floor sitting room, a fire crackling, couches and chairs adorning an Oriental rug. Most of the guest rooms have private balconies with views of what makes New Orleans New Orleans—Bourbon Street or the French Quarter. 14 rooms, 4 story. Complimentary continental breakfast. Check-in 2 pm, check-out noon. **$**

★ ★ ★ **MELROSE MANSION.** *937 Esplanade Ave, New Orleans (70116). Phone 504/944-2255;*

toll-free 800/650-3323; fax 504/945-1794. www. melrosemansion.com. The Melrose Mansion, overlooking the French Quarter, was built in 1884 and purchased a few years later by a New Orleans nightclub owner as a home for the girls in his conga line. Conga girls don't live there anymore, but those who love the atmosphere in which they did can, at least for a night or two. Approaching the front door of a brick "welcome" path, you'll walk past a wrought-iron gate and ascend the grand staircase to your suite (the suites have names like Prince Edward and Miss Kitty). You'll descend the next morning for fresh-baked pastries and hazelnut coffee—taken in the parlor, of course. 8 rooms, 2 story. Complimentary continental breakfast. Check-in 3 pm, check-out noon. Fitness room. Outdoor pool. **$$**

★ ★ ★ **SONIAT HOUSE HOTEL.** *1133 Chartres St, New Orleans (70116). Phone 504/522-0570; toll-free 800/544-8808; fax 504/522-7208. www.soniathouse.com.* Don't let its location in the bustling French Quarter fool you. The quiet and intimate Soniat House offers an elegant respite from all the revelry out on the streets of this boisterous entertainment district. Its cozy rooms are housed in three Creole-style town houses dating back to the early 1800s, and they're tastefully decorated with English, French, and Louisiana antiques. What the property lacks in amenities—no pool, restaurant, or fitness center—it more than makes up for with all its charm and the superior service of its friendly, attentive staff. 33 rooms, 3 story. Children over 12 years only. Check-in 3 pm, check-out noon. **$$**

Specialty Lodgings

The following lodging establishments are approved by Mobil Travel Guide, but due to their unique and individualized nature have not been given a traditional Mobil Star rating. Included in this listing you may find bed-and-breakfasts, limited-service inns, guest ranches, and other unique hotel properties.

CHIMES BED & BREAKFAST. *1146 Constantinople St, New Orleans (70115). Phone 504/488-4640; toll-free 800/729-4640; fax 504/488-4639. www.historiclodging.com/chimes.* Jill and Charles Abbyad were pioneers in 1987 when they opened a bed and breakfast in the servants' quarters behind their charming Victorian home near the French Quarter. The bed-and-breakfast craze had not yet caught on in this city of historic hotels. They are

warm, inviting hosts, offering both comfort and good cheer to their guests. Breakfast is served in the main house along with knowledgeable advice on where to go and what to do in the city the owners know so well. 5 rooms. Pets accepted, some restrictions; fee. Complimentary full breakfast. **$**

GIROD HOUSE. *835 Esplanade Ave, New Orleans (70116). Phone 504/944-7993; toll-free 866/877-1024; fax 504/945-1794. www.girodhouse.com.* Girod House was constructed in 1833 by New Orleans first mayor (1812-1815), Nicholas Girod, as a gift to his son François. Now a historic Creole townhouse with six sunny suites, this charming three-story bed-and-breakfast is filled with antique furnishings, has balconies overlooking peaceful Esplanade Avenue, and beckons you to enjoy its tropical patio filled with exotic flowers. Its quiet location between Bourbon and Dauphine streets provides easy access to the French Quarter. 6 rooms, 2 story. Children over 12 years only. Complimentary continental breakfast. Check-out 1 pm. **$**

HISTORIC FRENCH MARKET INN. *501 rue Decatur, New Orleans (70130). Phone 504/561-5621; toll-free 888/256-9970; fax 504/566-0160. www.new orleansfinehotels.com.* Built in the 1800s for the fabulously wealthy Baron Joseph Xavier de Pontalba, the Historic French Market Inn was the official government house when Louisiana was still a French colony. The atmosphere has changed since the baron shot his daughter-in-law and then turned the gun on himself: today, the original 19th-century brick walls, elegant brass beds, and lush courtyard speak of romance. The wrought-iron gates guarding the entrance whisper of a different pace; a grand staircase sweeps from the ground floor rotunda to the second-floor lobby, and antique period pieces convey two centuries of New Orleans history. 108 rooms, 4 story. Complimentary continental breakfast. Check-out 11 am. Bar. Outdoor pool. **$**

Spa

★ ★ ★ **THE SPA AT THE RITZ-CARLTON, NEW ORLEANS.** *921 Canal St, New Orleans (70112). Phone 504/670-2929; toll-free 800/241-3333. www.ritzcarlton.com.* Soft lighting, gleaming marble, brass chandeliers, and gentle colors set a regal tone for The Spa at The Ritz-Carlton, New Orleans. This tranquil spa lets you relax and indulge like the royals once did with a treatment menu inspired in part by favorite practices of French aristocrats. From the four-hands massage that Marie Antoinette adored to the citrus scent that Napoleon once wore, this spa takes you on a fascinating journey, enabling you to unwind in splendor.

Your body is primped and pampered in style here, whether you opt for a massage, a hydrotherapy soak, or a body treatment. The Napoleon royal massage is a spa signature that includes a heavenly citrus-scented bath prior to a lemon verbena-scented Swedish massage. Hydrotherapy soaks include therapeutic, couples, and even color therapy-themed baths. The body treatments are superb, and the spa's signature magnolia sugar scrub gently exfoliates and polishes your skin while the heady scent of Louisiana's luscious magnolias blended with botanical extracts envelops you. The magie violete therapy uses marine clay with lemon, lavender, pine, cinnamon, cypress, sweet marjoram, and ylang ylang essential oils and offers an innovative approach to the body wrap without the actual wrapping. In the magie noire treatment, moor mud draws out the skin's impurities and is followed by an exfoliating massage and a refreshing Vichy shower. Whether you want to add a glow to your skin with a body bronzing treatment or to banish unwanted cellulite with a body contour treatment, this spa satisfies all requests, while manicures, pedicures, and hair care services ensure that you leave looking your best.

A delightful café invites you to linger before or after a treatment and is a lovely spot to enjoy salads, sandwiches, and light dishes that please your palate without adding to your waistline. The spa's well-stocked gift shop warrants some retail therapy; the magnolia-scented signature products are wonderful reminders of this sweet Southern getaway.

Restaurants

★ ★ ★ ALEX PATOUT'S LOUISIANA RESTAURANT. 720 St. Louis St, New Orleans (70130). Phone 504/525-7788; fax 504/525-7809. www.patout.com. Those who want to experience New Orleans' Best Creole (as voted by the readers of both *Where* and *New Orleans* magazines) and other dishes created by Alex Patout ("One of America's 25 Hot Chefs," says *Food and Wine* magazine) have a choice of a first-floor bistro with dark wood, mirrors, and ceiling fans or a second-floor dining room with an old New Orleans feel. The dining room's floor-to-ceiling windows open onto St. Louis Street. Cajun menu. Dinner. Closed Easter, Thanksgiving, Dec 25. Casual

attire. Outdoor seating. **$$$**

★ ★ ALLEGRO BISTRO. 1100 Poydras, New Orleans (70163). Phone 504/582-2350; fax 504/582-2351. American menu. Lunch, dinner. Closed Sat-Sun; holidays. Bar. Outdoor seating. **$**

★ ★ ANDREW JAEGER'S HOUSE OF SEAFOOD. 300 Decatur St, New Orleans (70130). Phone 504/581-2534; fax 504/581-9314. www.andrewjaegers.com. There are three distinct levels of dining in this 1832 Creole cottage. Seafood menu. Dinner. Closed Thanksgiving, Dec 25. Bar. Outdoor seating. **$$**

★ ★ ★ ANTOINE'S. 713 rue St. Louis, New Orleans (70130). Phone 504/581-4422; fax 504/581-3003. www.antoines.com. A fixture since 1840, this Creole/classic French dining spot still exudes quality fare. It is in the French Quarter, just a short distance from Bourbon Street. The locals know which entrées are the best— the filet and any oyster dish— Rockefeller, Bienville, and Foch included. Creole menu. Lunch, dinner. Closed Sun; holidays. Jacket required. **$$$**

★ ★ ★ ARNAUD'S. 813 rue Bienville, New Orleans (70112). Phone 504/523-5433; toll-free 866/230-8891; fax 504/581-7908. www.arnauds.com. In the French Quarter near Bourbon Street, this exquisite restaurant heaps refined service on diners. Partake of the trout meuiere and shrimp remoulade. A wonderful romantic atmosphere prevails. Built in 1790 and opened in 1918, it has been restored to its original design. French, Creole menu. Lunch, dinner, Sun brunch. Closed Dec 25. Bar. Jacket required. **$$$**

★ ★ ★ BACCO. 310 Chartres St, New Orleans (70130). Phone 504/522-2426; fax 504/521-8323. www.bacco.com. A member of the Brennan family, located at the W Hotel in the French Quarter (see), this romantic Creole/Italian restaurant fuses local products with traditional Italian recipes. Guests can even pick up some Italian; they play tapes in the rest rooms. Italian menu. Lunch, dinner. Closed Mardi Gras, Dec 24-25. Bar. **$$$**

★ BANGKOK CUISINE. 4137 S Carroltown Ave, New Orleans (70119). Phone 504/482-3606; fax 504/486-0090. Thai menu. Lunch, dinner. Closed July 4, Thanksgiving, Dec 25. **$$**

★ ★ ★ ★ BAYONA. 430 Dauphine St, New Orleans (70112). Phone 504/525-4455; fax 504/522-0589. www.bayona.com. A little slice of the romantic Mediterranean awaits you at Bayona, a jewel of a

restaurant tucked into a 200-year-old Creole cottage, in the heart of the French Quarter. The warm, cozy room is often set with fresh flowers and is warmed by sunny lighting and bright colors. Settle in and get ready for chef Susan Spicer's terrific interpretation of New Orleans cuisine, blending the ingredients of the Mediterranean with the flavors of Alsace, Asia, India, and the Southwest. Spicer is indeed a talented chef, capable of surprising her loyal fans by successfully combining textures and spices that have never before met on a plate. To match the exquisite fare, you'll find an outstanding waitstaff eager to guide you and answer questions about the menu. A great selection of beers, including several local brews, plus an extensive wine list, make it difficult to choose a beverage to accompany dinner, so you may just have to come back a few times. Eclectic menu. Lunch, dinner. Closed Sun; Jan 1, Mardi Gras, Dec 25. Bar. Casual attire. Reservations recommended. Outdoor seating. **$$$**
🅓

★ ★ ★ **BEGUE'S.** *300 Bourbon St, New Orleans (70140). Phone 504/553-2220. www.sonesta.com/ begues.* This French Quarter restaurant is located in the Royal Sonesta Hotel. (see) Meals are served in a relaxed atmosphere overlooking a tropical courtyard filled with orange trees. The specialty here is Creole-French cuisine, prepared beautifully, and an all-you-can-eat Sunday brunch that makes you wonder if there are any crawfish or snapper left in any other part of the world. A children's menu keeps the little ones happy. French, Creole menu. Breakfast, lunch, dinner, Sun brunch. Children's menu. Casual attire. Outdoor seating. **$$$**

★ ★ ★ **BELLA LUNA.** *914 N Peters St, New Orleans (70116). Phone 504/529-1583; fax 504/522-4858. www.bellalunarestaurant.com.* Guests get a choice of two views, the French Quarter on one side and a great romantic view of the Mississippi River on the other side. The cuisine is mostly American, with a spicy Creole flavor. Local favorites are the pecan-crusted pork chops, battered soft shell crabs, and the giant stuffed gulf shrimp. Cajun/Creole menu, Mediterranean menu. Dinner. Closed Dec 25, Mardi Gras. Bar. Valet parking. **$$$**

★ ★ **BISTRO AT MAISON DE VILLE.** *733 Toulouse St, New Orleans (70130). Phone 504/528-9206; toll-free 800/634-1600; fax 504/528-9939. www.maisondeville.com.* This intimate restaurant in an 18th-century house is steps from Bourbon Street. The lustrous mahogany and soft lighting relax guests prior to a fine dining experience. There are stylish, flavorful Creole and American creations like grilled salmon with pecan-flavored wild rice, and saffron-sage broth with quail ravioli. Patio dining is also available, weather permitting. French Bistro menu. Lunch, dinner. Outdoor seating. **$$**

★ ★ **BON TON CAFE.** *401 Magazine St, New Orleans (70130). Phone 504/524-3386.* This restaurant features a wrought-iron chandelier, shuttered windows, and wildlife prints on exposed brick walls. Cajun menu. Lunch, dinner. Closed Sat-Sun; holidays. Children's menu. **$$**

★ ★ ★ **BRENNAN'S.** *417 Royal St, New Orleans (70130). Phone 504/525-9711; fax 504/525-2302. www.brennansneworleans.com.* Breakfast is king at this sister restaurant to Commander's Palace (see) in the heart of the French Quarter, but guests will enjoy the classic upscale Creole cuisine at any meal of the day. Dine in the courtyard on the decadent egg dishes. French, Creole menu. Breakfast, lunch, dinner. Closed Dec 24-25. Bar. Children's menu. Casual attire. Reservations recommended. Outdoor seating. **$$$**

★ ★ ★ **BRIGTSEN'S.** *723 Dante St, New Orleans (70118). Phone 504/861-7610; fax 504/866-7397. www.brigtsens.com.* Frank Brigsten is the chef/owner of this delightful Uptown spot with excellent food and even better service. This local favorite offers Cajun/Creole dishes, with specialties of the house including blackened tuna and roast duck. It is located in a restored 1900s house built from river barge timbers. Reservations recommended. Creole menu. Dinner. Closed Sun-Mon; holidays. **$$**

★ ★ ★ **BROUSSARD'S.** *819 Conti St, New Orleans (70112). Phone 504/581-3866; fax 504/581-3873. www.broussards.com.* This award-winning restaurant has been family-owned for 75 years, albeit by different families. The current owners run things with as much loving care and attention to detail as the Broussards did in the early 1800s, with wife Evelyn tending to personal touches—impeccable table settings, romantic candles, courtyard greenery, and blooming flowers. Her husband, classically French-trained chef Gunter, prepares unmatched Creole fantasies; try the lump crab in ravigote sauce with shrimp rémoulade and house-cured salmon; or grilled pompano on puff pastry accompanied by shrimp, scallops, and mustard-caper sauce. Wine aficionados: prepare for the 20-page wine list. French menu. Dinner. Closed Dec 25. Bar. Reservations recommended. Outdoor seating. **$$$**

★ **CAFE DU MONDE.** *1039 Decatur St, New Orleans (70116). Phone 504/525-4544; toll-free 800/ 772-2927; fax 504/587-0847. www.cafedumonde.com.* The appeal of fried dough blanketed in powdered sugar cannot be understood or underestimated. The Café du Monde is world famous for its beignets, as well as for its roasted chicory-and-coffee combinations. The original café is located on the edge of the French Quarter and provides a perfect place to stop in for a sweet treat between bouts of shopping at the adjacent French Market or before or after whooping it up in the Quarter. French menu. Breakfast, lunch, dinner, late-night. Closed Dec 25. Casual attire. Outdoor seating. No credit cards accepted. **$**

★ ★ **CAFE GIOVANNI.** *117 rue Decatur, New Orleans (70130). Phone 504/529-2154; fax 504/529-3352. www.cafegiovanni.com.* New world Italian menu. Lunch, dinner. Closed Sun (July-Aug); holidays; Mardi Gras. Valet parking. **$$**

★ **CAFE PONTALBA.** *546 St. Peter St, New Orleans (70116). Phone 504/522-1180; fax 504/522-1186.* Cajun, Creole menu. Lunch, dinner. Closed Dec 25. Bar. **$$**
🄳

★ ★ **CAFE VOLAGE.** *720 Dublin St, New Orleans (70118). Phone 504/861-4227; fax 504/861-4207.* This restaurant comprises two intimate dining areas in an 1800s Victorian cottage. French, Mediterranean menu. Lunch, dinner, Sun brunch. Closed holidays; Mardi Gras. Children's menu. Outdoor seating. **$$**

★ **CAMELLIA GRILL.** *626 S Carrollton Ave, New Orleans (70118). Phone 504/866-9573; fax 504/861-9311.* Popular night spot. American menu. Breakfast, lunch, dinner. Closed Thanksgiving, Dec 25. **$**
🄳

★ **CENTRAL GROCERY.** *923 Decatur St, New Orleans (70116). Phone 504/523-1620; fax 504/523-1670.* Italian menu. Lunch. Closed holidays. Casual attire. No credit cards accepted. **$**
🄳

★ **CHEZ NOUS CHARCUTERIE.** *5701 Magazine St, New Orleans (70115). Phone 504/899-7303; fax 504/891-8583.* Gourmet delicatessen within a grocery store. Creole menu. Lunch, dinner. Closed Sun; holidays. Outdoor seating. **$**
🄳

★ ★ **CHRISTIAN'S.** *3835 Iberville St, New Orleans (70119). Phone 504/482-4924; fax 504/482-6852.* www.christiansrestaurantneworleans.com. The well-lit steeple is a beacon for those looking for elegant dining in an unusual setting. From a masterful remodeling of a church dating to 1914 that created an atmosphere awash with dark wood and soaring ceilings, Christian's provides a heavenly dining experience. New Orleans Creole and classic French combine to offer creative cuisine that is not for those watching calories or fat grams, but is worth every Gulf shrimp sautéed with pearl onions, mushrooms, sun-dried tomatoes, and garlic, flambéed in brandy and finished with a Dijon butter sauce. Creole, French menu. Lunch, dinner. Closed Sun-Mon; Dec 25. Bar. Jacket required. Reservations recommended. **$$**
🄳

★ ★ ★ **COMMANDER'S PALACE.** *1403 Washington Ave, New Orleans (70130). Phone 504/899-8221; fax 504/891-3242. www.commanderspalace.com.* In the center of the Garden District stands this turquoise and white Victorian monument to Creole cuisine. The famed Brennan family has presided over the dining room since 1974, but Emile Commander originally founded it in 1880 as a fine restaurant for distinguished neighborhood families. The lush garden setting hosts live Dixieland music for the lively Saturday and Sunday jazz brunches. Creole menu. Lunch, dinner, brunch. Closed Mardi Gras, Dec 24-25. Bar. Jacket required. Reservations recommended. Valet parking. Outdoor seating. **$$$**

★ ★ **COURT OF TWO SISTERS.** *613 Royal St, New Orleans (70130). Phone 504/522-7261; fax 504/581-5804. www.courtoftwosisters.com.* Creole, French menu. Dinner, brunch (daily). Closed Dec 25. Bar. Children's menu. Built in 1832 with a spacious patio and courtyard. Outdoor seating. **$$$**

★ ★ **CRESCENT CITY BREWHOUSE.** *527 Decatur St, New Orleans (70130). Phone 504/522-0571; toll-free 888/819-9330; fax 504/522-0577. www.crescent citybrewhouse.com.* American menu. Lunch, dinner. Closed Thanksgiving, Dec 25. Bar. Children's menu. Casual attire. Outdoor seating. **$$**

★ ★ ★ **CUVEE.** *322 Magazine St, New Orleans (70130). Phone 504/587-9001; fax 504/587-9006. www.restaurantcuvee.com.* Excellent advice on wine and food pairings is just one of the highlights of this New Orleans bright star. Opened in 1999 and considered an upstart in this city of decades-old dining establishments, Cuvee nevertheless has gained a reputation as one of New Orleans's finest gourmet restaurants. Intimate, with just 85 seats, the restaurant

is housed in a landmark 1833 building whose age strangely complements its "nouveau New Orleans cuisine"—dishes like sugar cane-smoked duck breast and crispy confit leg served with Hudson Valley foie gras and Roquefort-pecan risotto. Eclectic menu. Lunch, dinner. Closed Sun. **$$**
🔲

★ ★ **DESIRE OYSTER BAR.** *300 Bourbon St, New Orleans (70140). Phone 504/586-0300; fax 504/586-0335.* American, Creole, seafood menu. Lunch, dinner. Bar. Children's menu. Casual attire. **$$**

★ ★ ★ **DOMINQUE'S.** *1001 rue Toulouse St, New Orleans (70112). Phone 504/586-8000; fax 504/525-5334. www.dominiquesrestaurant.com.* This French Quarter location in the beautiful Maison Dupuy Hotel (see) features the innovative cuisine of chef Dominique Macquet. Ingredients are always the freshest available, and the breads and pastries are baked on the premises. French menu. Dinner, Sun brunch. Bar. Valet parking. Outdoor seating. **$$$**

★ ★ **DOOKY CHASE.** *2301 Orleans Ave, New Orleans (70119). Phone 504/821-0600; fax 504/821-0600.* Creole menu. Lunch, dinner. Closed Dec 25. Bar. **$$**

★ ★ ★ ★ **EMERIL'S DELMONICO.** *1300 St. Charles Ave, New Orleans (70130). Phone 504/525-4937; fax 504/595-2206. www.emerils.com.* As if Emeril Lagasse—the celebrity chef and man behind the "Bam!"—wasn't busy enough, in 1998 he decided to reopen and revive Delmonico, an icon of the New Orleans dining scene since 1895. Apparently, this man thrives on juggling many projects at once, because Delmonico is a smashing success. Lagasse pays homage to the restaurant's classic menu (steaks, chops, creamed spinach, and the like) but adds his distinct signature "kick" as well, treating plates to bold flavor twists. Seasonal ingredients, farm-raised poultry, dry-aged beef, and an impressive selection of seafood make this a restaurant for all appetites and cravings. Though formal—gentlemen wear jackets—a warm, soft glow and a casual atmosphere pervade the well-appointed room. This is a wonderful and easy space in which to relax and unwind. Flaming desserts like baked Alaska are the perfect end to a meal at Delmonico; the dessert is the ultimate mix of old-world charm and blazing Emeril style. Creole menu. Lunch, dinner, Sun brunch. Bar. **$$$**

★ ★ ★ ★ **EMERIL'S RESTAURANT.** *800 Tchoupitoulas St, New Orleans (70130). Phone 504/*528-9393; fax 504/558-3925. www.emerils.com.* Still glimmering from its 2000 renovation by famed restaurant designer David Rockwell, Emeril's is a chic and stylish hotspot. With lofty ceilings, an open kitchen, custom-made cast metal door handles, and a towering wooden wine wall, the restaurant is a dynamic space that suits its urban, Warehouse District neighborhood. The slick food bar is a fun spot to take in the buzzing, see-and-be-seen crowd. If you are looking for intimacy and romance, this is not the place. The room can get loud, but like a ride on a roller coaster, it's a great rush. The menu—French Creole-meets-the-Southwest-meets-Emeril—liberally employs a world of herbs, spices, and chiles that awaken the palate with a wonderful jolt. Emeril's trademarks include barbecued shrimp served over flaky, rosemary-scented buttermilk biscuits and a tamarind-glazed double-cut Niman ranch pork chop with green chili mole and roasted sweet potatoes. American, Creole menu. Lunch Mon-Fri, dinner daily. Closed Mardi Gras, holidays. Bar. Jacket required. Reservations recommended. Free valet parking. **$$$**

★ ★ **FEELINGS CAFE.** *2600 Chartres St, New Orleans (70117). Phone 504/945-2222; fax 504/945-7019. www.feelingscafe.com.* Located in an outbuilding of an 18th-century plantation, this restaurant features antiques and original artwork. Creole menu. Lunch, dinner, Sun brunch. Closed Thanksgiving, Dec 25; Mardi Gras. Outdoor seating. **$$**

★ ★ **FIVE HAPPINESS.** *3605 S Carrollton Ave, New Orleans (70118). Phone 504/482-3935; fax 504/486-0743. www.fivehappiness.com.* Chinese menu. Lunch, dinner. Closed Thanksgiving. Bar. **$$**

★ **FRENCH MARKET.** *1001 Decatur St, New Orleans (70116). Phone 504/525-7879; fax 504/568-1522.* Seafood menu. Lunch, dinner. Closed Good Friday, Thanksgiving, Dec 25. Bar. Casual attire. Outdoor seating. **$$**

★ ★ ★ **GABRIELLE.** *3201 Esplanade Ave, New Orleans (70119). Phone 504/948-6233; fax 504/949-7459. www.gabriellerestaurant.com.* This is a place where locals go—or used to, when they could get in. Tourists have discovered it, and Gabrielle's popularity has overtaken its 62 seats (which, divided between two dining rooms, make this a wonderfully cozy dining experience). The menu is "contemporary Creole," lighter than what many think of as traditional New Orleans cooking. Entrées include Creole cream cheese-crusted lamb chops and a very un-Creole dish of chicken served with tomatoes, provolone, and mixed greens with balsamic vinaigrette. Creole menu. Lunch, dinner. Closed Sun-Mon; holidays; Mardi Gras. Bar. Outdoor seating. **$$$**

★ ★ ★ **GALATOIRE'S.** *209 Bourbon St, New Orleans (70130). Phone 504/525-2021; fax 504/525-5900. www.galatoires.com.* Jean Galatoire, a Frenchman from the foothills of the Pyrenees, founded this landmark French Quarter restaurant in 1905. To this day, it continues on in the hands of his descendants. Cajun/Creole menu. Lunch, dinner. Closed Mon; holidays; Mardi Gras. Bar. Jacket required. **$$$**

★ ★ ★ **GAUTREAU'S.** *1728 Soniat St, New Orleans (70115). Phone 504/899-7397; fax 504/899-0154. www.gautreaus.net.* This quintessential neighborhood bistro in Uptown is in an old pharmacy, with an antique apothecary serving as a liquor cabinet and embossed tin ceilings. Chef John Harris lends his classical French-trained style to a Creole-influenced menu. American, seafood menu. Dinner. Closed Sun; holidays. Valet parking. **$$$**
🅳

★ ★ ★ ★ **THE GRILL ROOM.** *300 Gravier St, New Orleans (70130). Phone 504/522-1992; fax 504/596-4649. www.windsorcourthotel.com.* Dining at The Grill Room may be one of the most luxurious ways to spend an evening in New Orleans. With a menu that changes monthly and features locally grown and organic foods whenever possible, The Grill Room is known for its fabulous contemporary New Orleans cuisine. The kitchen's robust and inventive brand of cuisine—international dishes jazzed up with a bold mixture of Creole and Southern style—is complemented by one of the finest wine cellars in the city. The room is lavishly appointed with cushy, napworthy armchairs and banquettes, brocade drapes, and suntan-glow lighting. Add to the serene surroundings the extreme pampering the warm and attentive staff will treat you to, and you'll come to realize that The Grill Room experience is nothing short of marvelous. American menu, Lunch, dinner, Sun jazz brunch. Bar. Jacket required. Free valet parking. **$$$**

★ ★ **GUMBO SHOP.** *630 St. Peter St, New Orleans (70116). Phone 504/525-1486; fax 504/524-0747. www.gumboshop.com.* Creole, seafood menu. Lunch, dinner. **$$**
🅳

★ ★ **K-PAUL'S LOUISIANA KITCHEN.** *416 Chartres St, New Orleans (70130). Phone 504/524-7394; fax 504/571-1214. www.chefpaul.com.* Seafood,

steak menu. Lunch, dinner. Closed Sun; Jan 1, Mardi Gras, Dec 24-25. Bar. Reservations recommended. **$$$**

★ ★ **LA MADELEINE.** *547 St. Ann St, New Orleans (70116). Phone 504/568-0073; fax 504/525-1680. www.lamadeleine.com.* French menu. Breakfast, lunch, dinner. Closed Dec 25. **$**
🅳

★ ★ ★ **LEMON GRASS.** *217 Camp St, New Orleans (70130). Phone 504/523-1200; toll-free 800/633-5770; fax 504/523-1208. www.lemongrassrest.com.* A shrimp dumpling in the land of jambalaya? Mostly Vietnamese with a touch of French, even the American dishes have an Asian flair—grilled double pork chop with lemon grass rice, baby bok choy, and tamarind sauce, for instance. You'll find a tip of the hat to New Orleans among the wok dishes, with entrées like crawfish with Oriental veggies over Shanghai noodles. But the Saigon-born and -educated chef knows what he does best, and he does it beautifully. Also beautiful is the cozy feng shui atmosphere, perfect for those looking for a break from Cajun and Creole in every way. Vietnamese, French menu. Lunch, dinner. Children's menu. **$$$**

★ **LUCY'S RETIRED SURFERS BAR & RESTAURANT.** *701 Tchoupitoulas St, New Orleans (70130). Phone 504/523-8995; fax 504/523-9198. www.lucysretiredsurfers.com.* Mexican, California menu. Lunch, dinner. Closed holidays. Bar. Children's menu. Casual attire. Outdoor seating. **$$**

★ ★ ★ **MARTINIQUE.** *5908 Magazine St, New Orleans (70115). Phone 504/891-8495; fax 504/862-8549.* French menu. Dinner. Closed Jan 1, Dec 25. Outdoor seating. **$$**

★ ★ ★ **MAXIMO'S ITALIAN GRILL.** *1117 Decatur St, New Orleans (70116). Phone 504/586-8883; fax 504/586-8891. www.maximositaliangrill.com.* The old rules are out: it's no longer just white wine with pasta. For proof, go to this northern Italian restaurant, replete with a wine list of 100 bottles. Maximo's menu has a variety of pastas, seafood, and veal specialties served in a casual but elegant setting. Jazz emanates from a well-integrated sound system in this renovated 1829 building, which has won a Vieux Carré award for architectural excellence. Italian menu. Dinner. Closed Thanksgiving. Bar. Casual attire. Outdoor seating. **$$$**
🅳

★ ★ **MICHAUL'S.** *840 St. Charles Ave, New Orleans (70130). Phone 504/522-5517; toll-free 800/563-4055; fax 504/529-2541. www.michauls.com.* Cajun menu. Dinner. Closed Sun; Easter, Thanksgiving, Dec 25; also the last two weeks in Aug. Bar. Children's menu. **$$**

★ ★ **MIKE ANDERSON'S SEAFOOD.** *215 Bourbon St, New Orleans (70130). Phone 504/524-3884. www.mikeandersons.com.* Seafood menu. Lunch, dinner. Closed Easter, Thanksgiving, Dec 25. Bar. Children's menu. Casual attire. **$$**

★ **MOTHER'S.** *401 Poydras St, New Orleans (70130). Phone 504/523-9656; fax 504/525-7671. www.mothersrestaurant.net.* Former residence (1830); extensive collection of US Marine memorabilia. Creole menu. Breakfast, lunch, dinner. Casual attire. Cafeteria-style service. **$**

★ ★ **MR B'S BISTRO.** *201 Royal St, New Orleans (70130). Phone 504/523-2078; fax 504/521-8304. www.mrbsbistro.com.* This famous Brennan family institution in the French Quarter offers Creole cuisine specializing in local and organically grown products. It is the power lunch spot in the French Quarter and is very popular among locals and tourists alike for dinner. Creole menu. Lunch, dinner, Sun brunch. Closed Mardi Gras, Dec 24-25. Bar. Casual attire. **$$$**

★ ★ ★ **NOLA.** *534 St. Louis St, New Orleans (70130). Phone 504/522-6652; fax 504/524-6178. www.emerils.com.* As the most accessible of Emeril's restaurants, the innovative cuisine at this French Quarter location complements the unique Art Deco ambience. Efficient service and elegant presentations bring life to the "Bam!" Creole menu. Lunch, dinner. Closed Mardi Gras, Thanksgiving, Dec 24-25. Bar. **$$$**

★ ★ ★ **PALACE CAFE.** *605 Canal St, New Orleans (70130). Phone 504/523-1661. www.palacecafe.com.* Crabmeat cheesecake, anyone? Both contemporary and classic Creole seafood dishes are available at this upscale, lively café on historic Canal Street. Owned by Dickie Brennan of the famous restaurant family, Palace Café's signature dishes include a creamy oyster pan roast and white chocolate bread pudding. If you can't bear to leave said bread pudding, fear not: that, plus 169 other Palace Café recipes, are available in *The Flavor of New Orleans Palace Café* cookbook, available for purchase. What must be experienced in person, however, is the popular Sunday brunch with live blues music. Cajun/Creole menu. Lunch, dinner, brunch.

Closed Mardi Gras, Dec 24-25. Bar. Children's menu. Casual attire. **$$**

★ ★ ★ **PELICAN CLUB.** *312 Exchange Alley, New Orleans (70130). Phone 504/523-1504; fax 504/522-2331. www.pelicanclub.com.* For fine dining in the French Quarter, look no further than this restaurant tucked away in a converted townhouse in charming Exchange Alley. Excellent cuisine and professional service make for an enjoyable dining experience. International menu. Dinner. Closed holidays; Mardi Gras. Bar. **$$$**

★ ★ ★ **PERISTYLE.** *1041 Dumaine St, New Orleans (70116). Phone 504/593-9535; fax 504/529-6942.* A fire in 1999 was the catalyst for the present look of this two-story 19th-century French Quarter building, once a family-owned oyster house near the red light district. A basement office was converted into a wine cellar with something to complement every dish on the decidedly French menu, with items like l'assiette du charcutier and rosemary lamb loin chop with red onion marmalade and pine nut-sultana red wine reduction. Also on the menu: a touch of romance, with antique-framed mirrors on the walls, a polished copper-topped bar, fresh flowers, and a row of hopper-transom windows above the bar's banquette. French menu. Dinner. Closed Sun-Mon; holidays. Bar. Reservations recommended. Free valet parking. **$$$**

★ **PRALINE CONNECTION.** *542 Frenchmen St, New Orleans (70116). Phone 504/943-3934; fax 504/943-7903. www.pralineconnection.com.* Creole menu. Lunch, dinner. Closed Dec 25. Bar. Children's menu. **$$**

★ ★ **RED FISH GRILL.** *115 Bourbon St, New Orleans (70130). Phone 504/598-1200; fax 504/581-9795. www.redfishgrill.com.* This restaurant is located in a converted deparment store. Seafood menu. Lunch, dinner. Closed Mardi Gras, Dec 24-25. Bar. Children's menu. Casual attire. **$$**

★ ★ ★ **RESTAURANT AUGUST.** *301 Tchoupitoulas St, New Orleans (70130). Phone 504/299-9777; fax 504/299-1199. www.rest-august.com.* The instant you walk into Restaurant August—a beautiful place set in an 18th-century townhouse in New Orleans's historic warehouse district—you feel at ease. The host who greets you at the door smiles, welcomes you heartily, and escorts you to your table in a warm, exposed-brick room with vaulted ceilings, old-world antiques, and floral arrangements. Your waiter is there in an instant to offer you an aperitif. If you are cold, you will receive a pashmina shawl. And so it goes. Dining at August is all about being pampered, and chef Jon Besh, a *Food & Wine* Best New Chef (1999), does a wonderful job of continuing the love from the kitchen with an innovative and delicious menu of dishes that marry robust ingredients from Spain and France with regional flavors. His menu changes seasonally, but two flawless signatures are the Moroccan-spiced duck with polenta and tempura dates and the "BLT," made from fat, meaty fried Buster crabs (the owner's uncle farms them), lettuce, and heirloom tomatoes on a slab of brioche. You'll leave warm, full, and very happy indeed. French menu. Lunch, dinner. Closed Sun. Business casual attire. Reservations recommended. Valet parking. **$$$$**

★ **SNUG HARBOR JAZZ BISTRO.** *626 Frenchmen St, New Orleans (70116). Phone 504/ 949-0696. www.snugjazz.com.* Seafood, steak menu. Dinner. Closed Dec 25. Bar. **$$**

★★ **TONY MORAN'S.** *240 Bourbon St, New Orleans (70130). Phone 504/523-3181; fax 504/410-0750. www.oldabsinthehouse.com.* Italian menu. Dinner. Closed Mardi Gras. Bar. Casual attire. Reservations recommended. Outdoor seating. **$$$**

★★ **TUJAGUE'S.** *823 Decatur St, New Orleans (70116). Phone 504/525-8676; fax 504/525-8785. www.tujaguesrestaurant.com.* This restaurant opened its doors before New Orleans had a name. Back then, it was a Spanish armory. Today, it's the second-oldest restaurant in New Orleans, boasts the city's first stand-up bar, and has a mirror over the bar that's been there for 150 years. The restaurant has a decidedly 19th-century atmosphere. Located in the middle of the French Quarter, facing the historic French Market, Tujague's (pronounced "two Jacks") plays to repeat customers—no menu, six courses (five plus coffee), and you take whatever entrée they give you. French, Creole menu. Lunch, dinner. Bar. Children's menu. **$$$**

★★ **UPPERLINE.** *1413 Upperline St, New Orleans (70115). Phone 504/891-9822. www.upperline.com.* The gracious service and excellent Creole food make this neighborhood restaurant in Uptown a local favorite. Cajun/Creole menu. Dinner. Closed Mon-Tues; Mardi Gras, July 4, Thanksgiving, Dec 25. Bar. Children's menu. **$$**

★★★ **VERANDA.** *444 St. Charles Ave, New Orleans (70130). Phone 504/525-5566; fax 504/523-1710.* Situated on the second floor of the InterContinental Hotel New Orleans (see), opening onto the hotel's enormous faux-streetlamp-lined atrium, Veranda is an open, airy, delightful arena for a calming meal. Regional fare is the ticket here; Cajun, gumbo, crawfish, and other New Orleans cuisine is done up in imaginative ways, but Veranda is known primarily for its lavish breakfast and lunch buffets. And the Sunday champagne jazz brunch draws both locals and visitors from throughout the city. American, Creole menu. Breakfast, lunch, dinner, Sun brunch. Free valet parking. **$$**

Carlsbad Caverns National Park, NM

4 hours, 152 miles from El Paso, TX

Web Site www.nps.gov/cave

27 miles SW of Carlsbad on Hwy 62/180.

One of the largest and most remarkable in the world, this cavern extends approximately 30 miles and is as deep as 1,037 feet below the surface.

It was once known as Bat Cave because of the spectacular bat flights, still a daily occurrence at sunset during the warmer months. Cowboy and guano miner Jim White first explored and guided people through the caverns in the early 1900s, later working for the National Park Service as the Chief Park Ranger. Carlsbad Cave National Monument was established in 1923, and in 1930 the area was enlarged and designated a national park. The park contains 46,755 acres and more than 80 caves. Carlsbad Cavern was formed by the dissolving action of acidic water in the Tansill and Capitan limestones of the Permian age. When an uplift drained the cavern, mineral-laden water dripping from the ceiling formed the stalactites and stalagmites.

The main cavern has two self-guided routes, a Ranger-guided Kings Palace tour, and several "off-trail" trips. The "Cavern Guide," an audio tour rented at the visitor center, enhances self-guided tours with interpretations of the caverns, interviews, and historic re-creations. Also available are tours in two backcountry caves: Slaughter Canyon Cave and Spider Cave. All guided tours require reservations.

Since the temperature in the cavern is always 56° F, be sure to carry a sweater even if it is hot outside; comfortable rubber-soled shoes are also recommended for safety. No pets; there is a kennel available. Photography, including flash and time exposures, is permitted on self-guided trips and some guided tours. Wheelchairs can be accommodated in the elevator for a partial tour. Rangers patrol the cave. Holders of Golden Access and Golden Age passports receive a 50 percent discount. Picnic area at Rattlesnake Springs. Scenic 9 1/2-mile loop drive, hiking trails, observation tower, exhibits on surface, restaurant. No camping in park, but available nearby. Bat flight programs are held each evening during the summer at the cavern entrance amphitheater.

Visitor center and museum with educational exhibits and displays. For tour reservations and fees, contact the Superintendent, 3225 National Parks Hwy, Carlsbad 88220. Phone 505/785-2232 (ext 429 for reservations).

Santa Fe, NM

5 hours, 290 miles from Amarillo

Founded 1607
Population 62,203
Elevation 7,000 ft
Area Code 505
Information Convention & Visitors Bureau, PO Box 909, 87504; phone 505/984-6760 or toll-free 800/777-2489
Web Site www.santafe.org

This picturesque city, the oldest capital in the United States, is set at the base of the Sangre de Cristo (Blood of Christ) Mountains. A few miles south, these mountains taper down from a height of 13,000 feet to a rolling plain, marking the end of the North American Rocky Mountains. Because of the altitude, the climate is cool and bracing. Tourists and vacationers will find much to do and see here all year.

Santa Fe was founded by Don Pedro de Peralta, who laid out the plaza and built the Palace of the Governors in 1610. In 1680, the Pueblo revolted and drove the Spanish out. In 1692, led by General Don Diego de Vargas, the Spanish made a peaceful reentry. Mexico gained its independence from Spain in 1821. This was followed by the opening of the Santa Fe Trail. In 1846, General Stephen Watts Kearny led US

troops into the town without resistance and hoisted the American flag. During the Civil War, Confederate forces occupied the town for two weeks before they were driven out.

In addition to its own attractions, Santa Fe is also the center of a colorful area, which can be reached by car. It is in the midst of the Pueblo country. The Pueblo, farmers for centuries, are also extremely gifted craftsworkers and painters. Their pottery, basketry, and jewelry are especially beautiful. At various times during the year, especially on the saint's day of their particular pueblo, they present dramatic ceremonial dances. Visitors are usually welcome. Since these are sacred rites, however, visitors should be respectful. As a rule, photographs are forbidden. A list of many of these ceremonies is given under SPECIAL EVENTS.

The high altitude may cause visitors accustomed to lower altitudes to have a little shortness of breath for a day or two. A short walking tour taken slowly will be helpful; the tour covers many centrally located sights.

What to See and Do

Atalaya Mountain Hiking Trail. *From downtown Santa Fe take Alameda Ave eastbound. Turn right onto Camino Cabra and continue to the intersection with Camino Cruz Blanca where you will turn left. Look for the signs for St. John's College and the parking area for Atalaya Mountain Trailhead. For the shorter trail, keep driving .8 miles past the college on Camino Cruz Blanca to the small parking lot on the left side of the road.* The Atalaya Mountain Trail, accessible from the parking lot at St. John's College, is one of the most popular and easily accessible hiking trails in Santa Fe. Hikers have the option of taking the longer route (Trail 174), which is approximately 7 miles round-trip, or parking farther up near the Ponderosa Ridge development and doing a 4.6-mile loop (Trail 170) instead. Both trials eventually join and take you toward the top of Atalaya Mountain, a 9,121-foot peak. The first few miles of the trail are relatively easy, but it becomes increasingly steep and strenuous as you near the summit of Atalaya Mountain. Hikers who make it to the top are afforded great views of the Rio Grande valley and the city below.

Santa Fe's Art and Architecture

Every tourist's Santa Fe exploration begins at the Plaza, plotted when the town was built in 1610. A square block planted with trees and grass, it's a place to sit on park benches to study a map or just watch the parade of visitors go by. Lining the Plaza on the east, south, and west are art galleries, Native American jewelry shops, boutiques, a vintage hotel, and restaurants. Facing the Plaza on the north is the Palace of the Governors, the first stop on your walking tour. Sheltered along the portal (porch) that spans the front of the block-long, pueblo-style building—which also dates from 1610—are dozens of craft and art vendors from the region's nearby pueblos. Only pueblo Indians can sell their jewelry, blankets, beadwork, pottery, and other goods here. Inside the palace, a museum exhibits nearly 20,000 historic objects, including pottery, books, documents, and artifacts.

One block west along Palace Avenue, the Museum of Fine Arts was built in 1917 and represents the Pueblo Revival style of architecture, also called Santa Fe style. Site of chamber music concerts, the museum exhibits work by local artists and by noted painters of the Santa Fe and Taos art colonies. Continue west on Palace another block, turning north on Grant Avenue one block, then west on Johnson Street one block. Stop inside the relatively new Georgia O'Keeffe Museum to see the world's largest collection of the artist's work.

Backtrack to the Plaza, heading to the Catron Building, which forms the east "wall" of the Plaza. Inside the 1891 office building are several art galleries and stores. At the building's southern end, anchoring the southeast corner of the Plaza, is La Fonda, the oldest hotel in Santa Fe. The lobby's art and décor are worth a look, and the rooftop bar is a favorite gathering place. From the plaza, walk south two blocks on Old Santa Fe Trail to Loretto Chapel. The beautiful chapel has an irresistible story in its Miraculous Staircase. Now walk east on Water Street one block to Cathedral Place, turning left (north) on Cathedral one block to the magnificent St. Francis Cathedral, built over several years in the latter 1800s.

Directly across the street, see the Institute of American Indian Arts Museum, housing thousands of pieces of sculpture, basketry, paintings, and pottery. Cathedral ends here at Palace Avenue, which you'll follow east one long block to explore two excellent bookstores, Nicholas Potter Bookseller and Palace Avenue Books. Backtracking on Palace again to the west, Sena Plaza is on your right (on the north side of the street). Inside the lovely, flower-filled courtyard, you'll find a 19th-century hacienda that once belonged to the Sena family and is now filled with art galleries, shops and a restaurant. Wind up back at the Plaza by following Palace another long block to the west; head to the Ore House on the Plaza's west side to review the day over refreshments.

⭐ **Canyon Road Tour.** *Go E on San Francisco St to the cathedral and bear right to the end of Cathedral Pl. Turn left on Alameda.* Many artists live on this thoroughfare. This tour totals about 2 or 3 miles, and there is no better way to savor the unique character of Santa Fe than to travel along its narrow, picturesque old streets. On the left is

> **Camino del Monte Sol.** Famous street on which many artists live and work. Turn left up the hill. Off this road are a number of interesting streets worth exploring.

> **Cristo Rey Church.** This is the largest adobe structure in the United States. It contains beautiful ancient stone reredos (altar screens). (Mon-Fri; closed holidays)

Museum of Indian Arts and Culture. *710-708 Camino Lejo, Santa Fe (87505). Phone 505/476-1250. www.miaclab.org.* When the Spanish arrived in the Southwest in the 16th century they found many sprawling towns and villages which they referred to as Pueblos, a name that is still used to identify Indian communities in New Mexico to this day. The Museum of Indian Arts and Culture houses an extensive collection of historic and contemporary Pueblo art from throughout the Southwest. One of the highlights of the museum is an excellent interpretive section where you can encounter Pueblo cultures from the viewpoint and narrative of modern-day Pueblo natives and exhibit designers. The museum itself is housed in a large, adobe-style building that blends architecturally into the surroundings, and also houses many outstanding examples of Pueblo textiles, pottery, jewelry, contemporary paintings, and other rotating exhibits. An adjacent building houses the Laboratory of Anthropology, which contains an extensive library and supports continuing research into Southwestern archeology and cultural studies. (Tues-Sun 10 am-5 pm; closed holidays) **$$**

St. John's College in Santa Fe. *1160 Camino Cruz Blanca, Santa Fe (87505). Just W of Camino del Monte Sol. Phone 505/984-6000. www.sjcsf.edu.* (1964) (400 students) The first campus of St. John's College is in Annapolis, Maryland (1696). Liberal arts.

Wheelwright Museum. *704 Camino Lejo, Santa Fe (87505). Phone 505/982-4636; toll-free 800/607-4636. www.wheelwright.org.* Founded in 1937 by Mary Cabot Wheelwright and Navajo singer/medicine man Hastiin Klah to help preserve Navajo art and traditions, the Wheelwright now devotes itself to hosting major exhibits of Native American artists from tribes throughout North America. The Case Trading Post in the basement sells pottery, jewelry, textiles, books, prints, and other gift items. (Mon-Sat 10 am-5 pm, Sun 1-5 pm; closed Jan 1, Thanksgiving, Dec 25) **DONATION**

Cathedral of St. Francis. *Santa Fe Plaza, 231 Cathedral Pl, Santa Fe (87501). Phone 505/982-5619.* (1869) French Romanesque cathedral built under the direction of Archbishop Lamy (prototype for Bishop Latour in Willa Cather's *Death Comes for the Archbishop*). La Conquistadora Chapel, said to be the country's oldest Marian shrine, is here. (Daily 8 am-5:45 pm, except during mass) Tours (summer).

College of Santa Fe. *1600 St. Michael's Dr, Santa Fe (87505). 3 miles SW at Cerrillos Rd and St. Michael's Dr. Phone 505/473-6011; toll-free 800/456-2673. www.csf.edu.* (1947) (1,400 students) On campus are the Greer Garson Theatre Center, Garson Communications Center, and Fogelson Library.

Cross of the Martyrs. *Paseo de la Loma, Santa Fe (87504). Access from the stairs on Paseo de la Loma. Phone 505/983-2567.* An ideal destination for history fans and anyone looking for a sensational city view, this large, hilltop cross weighing 76 tons and standing 25 feet tall honors the memory of more than 20 Franciscan priests and numerous Spanish colonists who were killed during the 1680 Pueblo Revolt against Spanish dominion. Dedicated in 1920, this cross shouldn't be confused with the newer one at nearby Fort Marcy Park. Vistas from the old cross include those of the Sangre de Cristos mountain range immediately northeast, the Jemez about 40 miles west, and the Sandias, 50 miles south near Albuquerque.

Dragon Room. *406 Old Santa Fe Trail, Santa Fe (87501). Phone 505/983-7712.* The rustic Dragon Room in the Pink Adobe Restaurant is one of the best places to mingle with locals, spot celebrities, and enjoy the Santa Fe ambience while sipping on house specialty drinks like the "Rosalita" or "Silver Coin Margarita." The *Santa Fe Reporter* voted this the top bar in Santa Fe, and it's always a hot social spot on Friday and Saturday nights.

El Farol. *808 Canyon Rd, Santa Fe. Phone 505/983-9912.* El Farol ("The Lantern" in Spanish) is the oldest restaurant and cantina in Santa Fe, dating to 1835. Located near the top of Canyon Road, it serves up award-winning Mediterranean food and continues to be one of the most popular late-night watering holes, offering patrons live music and a usually packed dance floor Wednesday through Saturday nights. The music tends towards Famenco, Latin, Jazz, Soul and Blues and usually gets hopping after 10 pm.

★ El Rancho de las Golondrinas. *334 Los Pinos Rd, Santa Fe (87507). 13 miles S, off I-25. Phone 505/471-2261. www.golondrinas.org.* This living history museum is set in a 200-acre rural valley, and depicts Spanish Colonial life in New Mexico from 1700 to 1900. It was once a stop on the Camino Real, and is one of the most historic ranches in the Southwest. Original colonial buildings date to the 18th century, and special festivals and theme weekends offer visitors a glimpse of the music, dance, clothing, crafts, and celebrations of Spanish colonial New Mexico. Self-guided tours. (June-Sept: Wed-Sun 10 am-4 pm) **$**

Federal Court House. *Federal Pl and Paseo De Peralta, Santa Fe.* There is a monument to Kit Carson in front.

Genoveva Chavez Recreation Center. *3221 Rodeo Rd, Santa Fe (87507). Phone 505/955-4001.* The Chavez Recreation Center is housed in a massive, architecturally imposing solar complex covering several city blocks. Inside, for a small daily fee, visitors can get access to a 50-meter lap pool, leisure pool, spa, sauna, and therapy pool, competition-sized ice-skating rink, basketball and racquetball courts, numerous fitness classes (extra charge), and a full line of state-of-the-art exercise equipment. **$$**

Georgia O'Keeffe Museum. *217 Johnson St, Santa Fe (87501). Phone 505/946-1000. www.okeeffemuseum.org.* One of the most important American artists of the 20th century, Georgia O'Keeffe lived and worked at Ghost Ranch near Abiqui for much of her career, drawing inspiration from the colors and forms of the surrounding desert environment. This museum houses the world's largest permanent collection of her artwork and is also dedicated to the study of American Modernism (1890-present), displaying special exhibits of many of her contemporaries. (Nov-June: Mon-Tues, Thurs, Sat-Sun 10 am-5 pm, Fri 10 am 8 pm; rest of year: daily; closed holidays) **$$**

Hyde Memorial State Park. *740 Hyde Park Rd, Santa Fe (87501). 8 miles NE via Hwy 475. Phone 505/983-7175.* Perched 8,500 feet up in the Sangre de Cristo Mountains near the Santa Fe Ski Basin; used as base camp for backpackers and skiers in the Santa Fe National Forests. Cross-country skiing, rentals, picnicking (shelters), playground, concession, camping (electric hook-ups, dump station). (Daily)

Hyde Park hiking/biking trails. *From the Santa Fe Plaza go N on Washington Ave, and continue several blocks to the light at Artist's Rd and turn right. Continue on Artist's Rd for about 8.6 miles to a parking lot on the left side of the road just before you reach the Hyde Park RV campground.* One of the closest hiking opportunities to Santa Fe is available in the Hyde Park area on the road to the ski basin. From the Hyde Park parking lot, you can access a loop covering three different trails offering easy hiking that's popular with runners, hikers, dog walkers, and weekenders looking for a quick getaway. The loop consists of switchbacks, moderate grades, creek crossings, and fine views of the mixed conifer forest. If you come during the fall you can view the spectacularly colorful changing of the Aspen leaves. Start with the common trailhead at the far side of the parking lot. Look for the Borrego Trail (150), Bear Wallow Trail (182), and Winsor Trail (254) markings. A loop covering all three is about 4 miles long.

Institute of American Indian Arts Museum. *108 Cathedral Pl, Santa Fe (87501). Phone 505/983-1777. www.iaiancad.org.* The Institute of American Indian Arts, established in 1962, runs a college in south Santa Fe in addition to a museum just off the Plaza. The museum is the only one in the country dedicated solely to collecting and exhibiting contemporary Native American art, much of it produced by the staff and faculty of the college. Inside you can view educational films, exhibits of contemporary artists, and outdoor sculptures in an enclosed courtyard. (June-Sept: daily 9 am-5 pm; Oct-May: daily 10 am-5 pm; closed holidays) **$$**

Kokopelli Rafting Adventures. *541 W Cordova Rd, Santa Fe (87501). Phone toll-free 800/879-9035. www.kokopelliraft.com.* Kokopelli Rafting offers a full range of whitewater rafting trips to the Rio Grande and Rio Chama rivers as well as sea kayaking trips to Cochiti lake, Abiqui lake, and Big Bend National Park in Texas. Rafting trips cover Class II through IV rapids. Excursions include half-day, full-day, overnight and 2- to 8-day wilderness expeditions. Transportation from Santa Fe included. (Apr-Sept) **$$$$**

La Fonda Hotel. *100 E San Francisco St, Santa Fe (87501). Phone 505/982-5511; toll-free 800/523-5002. www.lafondasantafe.com.* A longtime center of Santa Fe social life. Former meeting place of trappers, pioneers, merchants, soldiers, and politicians; known as the "Inn at the End of the Trail."

Las Cosas School of Cooking. *DeVargas Center, 181 Paseo de Peralta, Santa Fe (87501). Phone 505/988-3394. www.lascosascooking.com.* Found within a beautiful store stocked with gourmet kitchen tools and elegant tableware, this cooking center offers hands-on culinary education experiences that fill a morning or evening. Taught by school director John Vollertsen and by chefs from New Mexico's leading restaurants, the classes cover a wide range of topics, such as artful risotto, Atkins diet dishes, soups and stocks, Oaxacan moles, the best in fish preparations, grilling, one-dish wonders, and fresh herb recipes. All kitchen supplies are provided, as are alcoholic beverages, and private classes can be arranged, too. (Classes usually at 10 am and 6 pm; closed Thanksgiving, Dec 25, Jan 1) **$$$$**

Lensic Performing Arts Center. *211 W San Francisco St, Santa Fe (87501). Phone 505/988-7050. www.lensic.com.* The Lensic Theater is one of Santa Fe's historical and architectural gems. The structure was first built in 1931 in a Moorish/Spanish Renaissance style and has always been Santa Fe's premiere theater space, having played host to celebrities such as Roy Rogers and Judy Garland over the years. It has provided a constantly changing schedule of quality theater, symphony, and performing arts events.

Loretto Chapel. *207 Old Santa Fe Trail, Santa Fe (87501). Phone 505/982-0092. www.lorettochapel.com.* The Loretto Chapel was built in 1873 and is one of the few non adobe-style buildings in downtown Santa Fe.

Modeled after St. Chapelle cathedral in Paris, it was the first Gothic building built west of the Missisippi. The chapel itself is not particularly impressive, but what draws countless tourists is the "miraculous stairway", a two-story spiral wooden staircase built without any nails or central supports that seems to defy engineering logic. (Summer: Mon-Sat 9 am-6 pm, Sun 10:30 am-5 pm; winter: Mon-Sat 9 am-5 pm, Sun 10:30 am-5 pm)

Museum of Fine Arts. *107 W Palace Ave, Santa Fe (87501). Phone 505/476-5072. www.museumofnewmexico.org.* Designed by Isaac Hamilton Rapp in 1917, the museum is one of Santa Fe's earliest Pueblo revival structures and its oldest art museum. It contains more than 20,000 holdings, with an emphasis on Southwest regional art and the artists of Santa Fe and Taos from the early 20th century. The St. Francis Auditorium inside the museum also presents lectures, musical events, plays, and various other performances. Free admission on Friday evenings. (Tues-Sun 10 am-5 pm, Fri 5-8 pm) **$$$**

Museum of International Folk Art. *706 Camino Lejo, Santa Fe (87505). Phone 505/476-1200. www.moifa.org.* The Museum of International Folk Art, first opened in 1953, contains more than 130,000 objects, billing itself as the world's largest folk museum dedicated to the study of traditional cultural art. Much of the massive collection was acquired when the late Italian immigrant, architect/designer Alexander Girard donated his 106,000-object collection of toys, figurines, figurative ceramics, miniatures, and religious/ceremonial art that he had collected from more than 100 countries around the world. In addition to the collection in the Girard wing, you'll also find a large collection of Hispanic art in the Hispanic Heritage Wing, as well as costumes and folk art from many cultures in the Neutrogena Collection. Several smaller collections and major temporary exhibits add to a rich museum experience that can easily take several hours to explore. Two museum shops offer a wide variety of folk-oriented books, clothing, and jewelry to choose from. (Tues-Sun 10 am-5 pm; closed holidays) **$$**

Museum of Spanish Colonial Art. *Museum Hill, Santa Fe (87502). Phone 505/982-2226. www.spanishcolonial.org.* This small museum holds some 3,000 objects showcasing traditional Hispanic art in New Mexico dating from conquest to present day. The galleries are housed in a building designed in 1930 by famous local architect John Gaw Meem, gracefully restored with historically accurate appointments. The collection includes many early works in wood, tin, and other local materials as well as numerous works by contemporary New Mexican artists who continue the rich Hispanic artistic traditions to this day. (Tues-Sun 10 am-5 pm; closed Thanksgiving, Dec 25) **$$$**

Oldest House. *De Vargas St and Old Santa Fe Trail, Santa Fe.* Believed to be pre-Spanish; built by Native Americans more than 800 years ago.

Palace of the Governors. *105 Palace Ave, Santa Fe (87501). Phone 505/476-5100. www.palaceofthegovernors.org.* Built in 1610, this is the oldest public building in continuous use in the United States. It was the seat of government in New Mexico for more than 300 years. Lew Wallace, governor of the territory (1878-1881), wrote part of *Ben Hur* here in 1880. It is now a major museum of Southwestern history. The Palace, Museum of Fine Arts, Museum of Indian Arts and Culture, Museum of International Folk Art, and state monuments all make up the Museum of New Mexico. Free admission Friday evenings. Tours (Mon-Sat 10:15 am-noon). (Tues-Sun 10 am-5 pm, Fri 5-8 pm; closed holidays) **$$**

Pecos National Historical Park. *Pecos. 25 miles SE via Hwy 25. Phone 505/757-6414. www.nps.gov/peco.* The ruins of Pecos Pueblo lie on a mesa along the Santa Fe Trail that served as a strategic trade route and crossroads between Pueblo and Plains Indian cultures. At its peak, the Pueblo housed a community of as many as 2,000 people, and was occupied for nearly 500 years. When the Spanish arrived, it became an important missionary outpost that continued to be occupied until the 1800s when its last inhabitants relocated to Jemez Pueblo. Ruins of the original multistory structures survive in the form of large stone walls and several ceremonial kivas that have been restored. The largest ruins are of two Spanish missionary churches that were destroyed in the Pueblo revolt of 1680. An easy 1.25-mile hike and self-guided tour allows visitors to explore the ruins at their own pace. The visitor center includes historical exhibits and shows an introductory film covering the area's history. (Daily 8 am-5 pm; closed Dec 25) **$$**

The Santa Fe Plaza. *100 Old Santa Fe Trail, Santa Fe.* The Santa Fe Plaza, steeped in a rich history, has been a focal point for commerce and social activities in Santa Fe since the early 17th century. The area is marked by a central tree-lined park surrounded by some of Santa Fe's most important historical landmarks, many of which survive from Spanish colonial times. The most important landmark is the Palace of the Governors, which was the original seat of local government and is the oldest public building in the United States still in use. Native American artists from nearby Pueblos sell handmade artwork in front of the Palace, and various museums, shops, and dining establishments surround the Plaza, making it the top tourist destination in Santa Fe. Numerous festivals and activities are held in the Plaza throughout the year, including the Spanish Market and the Indian Market.

San Felipe's Casino Hollywood and Hollywood Hills Speedway. *25 Hagan Rd, San Felipe (87001). 30 miles S of Santa Fe via I-25. Phone 505/867-6700; toll-free 877/529-2946. www.sanfelipecasino.com.* This multiuse complex situated midway between Santa Fe and Albuquerque on the San Felipe Pueblo brings something akin to Las Vegas-style entertainment to New Mexico. Within the casino, guests find abundant gaming opportunities, as well as showroom entertainment. (Mon-Thurs 8 am-4 pm, Fri-Sat 24 hours) Also on-site is the Hollywood Hills Speedway, opened in 2002 and known as the state's premier venue of its kind. The 3/8-mile clay oval speedway for auto and motorcycle racing is viewed from a grandstand seating 10,000, as well as from sky boxes. Also look for monster truck shows, extreme sports events, and outdoor concerts, with entertainers ranging from country music acts to specialty cultural performers.

San Ildefonso Pueblo. *16 miles N on Hwy 84, 285, then 6 miles W on Hwy 502. Phone 505/455-2273.* (Population: 447) This pueblo is famous for its beautiful surroundings and its black, red, and polychrome pottery, made famous by Maria Poveka Martinez. (Daily; closed winter weekends; visitors must register at the visitor center) Photography permit may be purchased at the visitor center (fee). Various festivals take place here throughout the year (see SPECIAL EVENTS). The circular structure with the staircase leading up to its rim is a *kiva,* or ceremonial chamber. There are two shops in the pueblo plaza, and a tribal museum adjoins the governor's office. One-half mile west is a fishing lake. **$$**

San Miguel Mission. *401 Old Santa Fe Trail, Santa Fe (87501). Phone 505/983-3974.* Built in the early 1600s, this is the oldest church in the United States still in use. Construction was overseen by Fray Alonso de Benavidez, along with a group of Tlaxcala Indians from Mexico who did most of the work. The original adobe still remains beneath the stucco walls, and the interior has been restored along with Santa Fe's oldest

wooden reredos (altar screen). Church services are still held on Sundays. (Sun 1-4:30 pm; summer: Mon-Sat 9 am-4:30 pm; winter: Mon-Sat 10 am-4 pm; closed holidays) **DONATION**

Santa Fe Children's Museum. *1050 Old Pecos Trail, Santa Fe (87505). Phone 505/989-8359. www.santa fechildrensmuseum.org.* Happy activity fills a creative space that absorbs the attention of children of all ages. Hands-on exhibits invite kids to make magnetic structures, route water streams, create paintings, illustrate cartoon movies, discover plants on a greenhouse scavenger hunt, scale an 18-foot-high climbing wall, use an old-fashioned pitcher pump, and weave beads and fabric on a loom. Local artists and scientists make appearances to teach kids in playful, inventive ways. Especially interesting are regularly scheduled events like "Music Under the Big Top" and "Ice Cream Sunday." (Wed-Sat 10 am-5 pm, Sun noon-5 pm; closed holidays) **$**

Santa Fe National Forest. *1474 Rodeo Rd, Santa Fe (87504). Phone 505/438-7840.* This forest consists of over 1 1/2 million acres. Fishing is excellent in the Pecos and Jemez rivers and tributary streams. Hiking trails are close to unusual geologic formations. Hot springs in the Jemez Mountains. Four wilderness areas within the forest total more than 300,000 acres. Campgrounds are provided by the Forest Service at more than 40 locations; for reservations phone toll-free 800/280-2267. There are user fees for many areas. Forest headquarters are located here.

Santa Fe Premium Outlets. *8380 Cerrillos Rd, Santa Fe (87507). Phone 505/474-4000. www.premiumoutlets.com.* Shop for bargain-priced designer apparel, shoes, luggage, jewelry, housewares, and other accessories at New Mexico's only outlet center. Located on the south side off Cerrillos Road, the more than 40 stores include such well-known brands as Bass, Bose, Brooks Brothers, Dansk, Eddie Bauer, Liz Claiborne, Nautica, Samsonite, Van Hausen, and many more. (Daily)

Santa Fe Rafting Company. *1000 Cerrillos Rd, Santa Fe (87505). Phone 505/988-4914; toll-free 800/467-7238. www.santaferafting.com.* The Rio Grande and Rio Chama rivers north of Santa Fe provide excellent opportunities for river running and white waterrafting, offering Class II through Class IV rapids. Santa Fe Rafting Company offers several rafting trips including half-day, full-day and multiday camping excursions, some of which include a boxed lunch. The biggest rapids are found on their Taos Box full-day trip, open to anyone over age 12. All trips include roundtrip transportation from Santa Fe. (Apr-Sept) **$$$$**

Santa Fe School of Cooking. *116 W San Francisco St, Santa Fe. Phone 505/983-4511. www.santafeschoolof cooking.com.* Sign up for classes offered several times weekly in traditional and contemporary Southwestern cuisine. Culinary tours involve classes with nationally renowned chefs with trips to local farms and wineries. Call for schedule.

Santa Fe Southern Railway. *410 S Guadalupe St, Santa Fe (87501). Phone 505/989-8600; toll-free 888/989-8600. www.sfsr.com.* Made famous by the 1940s swing tune "Atchison, Topeka & Santa Fe," a small part of this historical rail line continues as the Santa Fe Southern Railway, which still carries freight and tourists between Santa Fe and nearby Lamy, an 18-mile trip. The start of the route is housed in the old Santa Fe Depot, where you can view vintage railcars and shop for gifts and memorabilia in the original mission-style train depot. Several scenic train rides in restored vintage cars are offered to the public, following the original high desert route to and from Lamy. The rides cater to tourists and range from short scenic roundtrips to longer outings that include picnics, BBQs, and various holiday-themed events, such as the Halloween Highball Train and New Year's Eve Party Train. **$$$$**

Santa Fe Trail Museum. *614 Maxwell Ave, Springer (87747). Phone 505/483-2682.* The Santa Fe Trail Museum displays artifacts and exhibits about pioneer life on and around the trail from 1880 to 1949. (Open daily 9 am-4 pm, summer only) **$**

Santuario de Guadalupe. *100 Guadalupe St, Santa Fe. Phone 505/988-2027.* Built in 1781, and the oldest shrine in America dedicated to Our Lady of Guadalupe, the Santuario has been converted into an art and history museum specializing in religious art and iconography. The holdings include a large collection of northern New Mexican santos (carved wooden saints) and paintings in the Italian Renaissance and Mexican baroque styles. A famous rendering of Our Lady of Guadalupe by renowned Mexican artist Jose de Alzibar is also on display. (Nov-Apr: Mon-Fri 9 am-4 pm; May-Oct: Mon-Sat 9 am-4 pm; closed holidays) **FREE**

Scottish Rite Temple. *463 Paseo De Peralta, Santa Fe (87501). Phone 505/982-4414.* Modeled after part of the Alhambra. (Mon-Fri 9 am-noon, 1-4 pm)

Sena Plaza and Prince Plaza. *Washington and E Palace aves, Santa Fe (87501).* Small shops, formerly old houses, built behind portals and around central patios.

Shidoni Bronze Foundry and Gallery. *1508 Bishop's Lodge Rd, Santa Fe (87501). Phone 505/988-8001. www.shidoni.com.* A fantastic resource for art collectors and sculptors, Shidoni consists of a bronze foundry, art gallery, and outdoor sculpture garden set in an 8-acre apple orchard 5 miles north of Santa Fe. Artists from around the country come to work at Shidoni's 14,000-square-foot foundry, open to the general public for self-guided tours. Explore the lovely sculpture garden during daylight hours or shop for works of bronze and metal in the adjacent gallery. Gallery (Mon-Sat 9 am-5 pm). Foundry (Mon-Fri noon-1 pm, Sat 9 am-5 pm).

Shona Sol Sculpture Garden. *Turquoise Trail, Hwy 14, Santa Fe (87506). Phone 505/473-5611.* Exhibits of some of the world's finest stone sculptors, whose work is also shown around the world. Also features the work of fine Zimbabwean artists. (Weekends 10 am-6 pm) **FREE**

Ski Santa Fe. *2209 Brothers Rd, Santa Fe (87505). Take Paseo de Peralta to Bishop Lodge Rd and turn N onto Bishop Lodge Rd. Continue one block and turn right on Artist Rd (which becomes Hyde Park Rd) and follow to the top of the mountain (approximately 16 miles). Phone 505/982-4429. www.skisantafe.com.* World-class skiing and snowboarding in the majestic Sangre de Cristo mountains is only a 20-minute drive from the downtown Santa Fe Plaza. Ski Santa Fe is a family-owned resort catering to skiers and snowboarders of all levels, from beginning to expert. In addition to breathtaking views of the city below, the 12,053-foot summit offers 6 lifts and 44 runs (20 percent easy, 40 percent more difficult, 40 percent most difficult), with a total of 660 acres of terrain. The longest run is 3 miles, and the mountain offers a vertical drop of 1,700 feet. The average yearly snowfall is 225 inches. A PSIA-certified ski school offers group and private lessons for adults and children, and there are restaurants, rental shops, and a clothing boutique on-site. The Chipmunk Corner offers activities and lessons for children ages 4-9. (Late Nov-early Apr, daily) **$$$$**

State Capitol. *Old Santa Fe Trail at Paseo de Peralta, Santa Fe (87501). Phone 505/986-4589.* (1966) This unique building, in modified Territorial-style, is round and intended to resemble a Zia sun symbol. Self-guided tours. (Mid-May-Aug: Mon-Sat 8 am-

7 pm; Sept-mid-May: Mon-Fri 8 am-7 pm; closed holidays) **FREE**

Swig. *135 W Palace Ave, Level 3, Santa Fe (87501). Phone 505/955-0400.* This is Santa Fe's swankiest bar/nightclub. Swig offers four different bar areas (mostly nonsmoking) and a very red dance floor all set in an intoxicatingly contemporary atmosphere. Sip the expensive but refreshingly creative martinis (starting at $11) or sample the excellent pan-Asian tapas. The dance floor will keep you entertained while a fresh roster of rotating DJs spin. Be sure to dress the part: Swig does enforce a dress code. (Tues-Thurs 5 pm-midnight, Fri-Sat 5 pm-1 am)

Ten Thousand Waves. *3451 Hyde Park Road, Santa Fe (87501). Take Paseo de Peralta to Bishop Lodge Rd and turn N onto Bishop Lodge Rd. Continue one block and turn right at Artist Rd (which becomes Hyde Park Rd) and follow to the sign on left side of winding road (approximately 4 miles). Phone 505/982-9304. www.ten thousandwaves.com.* When you feel like being pampered, this exquisite Japanese-themed spa and bathhouse is a genuine treat. Located in a unique Zen-like setting in the Sangre de Cristo Mountains, Ten Thousand Waves offers soothing hot tubs, massages, facials, and other spa treatments to make you forget your cares. The choices here are endless: hand, foot, scalp, and full-body massages, herbal wraps, rejuvenating facials, and a variety of open-air hot tubs, including coed public hot tubs (where clothing is optional before 8:15 pm), a women-only tub, secluded private tubs, and large private tubs that can accommodate up to 20. Whichever you choose, you'll find all tubs clean and inviting (and chlorine-free), and amenities such as kimonos, towels, sandals, lotion, and lockers provided for you. Be sure to call ahead for reservations, especially for massage services. (Daily) **$$$$**

⭐ **Turquoise Trail.** *Sandia Park (87047). Drive S from Santa Fe via I-25, exiting New Mexico Hwy 14 S toward Madrid. Phone 505/281-5233. www.turquoisetrail.org.* Undeniably the most interesting path between Albuquerque and Santa Fe, this poetically named route is the 50-mile reach of New Mexico 14 that parallels Interstate 25 north from Interstate 40 and a National Scenic Byway. Cutting a course along the backside of the Sandias just north of Albuquerque, the trail winds through a rolling countryside of sumptuous, cactus-littered hills populated by tiny burgs. Along the way, watch for the mountain sun to cast spectacular purples and roses on crumbling rock houses, ancient family cemeteries, and long-

abandoned ranch houses and barns. Stops include the town of Golden, where the first discovery of gold west of the Mississippi was made and where a silver boom once employed more than 1,200 workers; and Madrid (pronounced MAD-rid), once rich in coal mines but today the refuge of artists whose galleries and shops have become lucrative businesses. The wonderful Mine Shaft Tavern offers burgers, buffalo steaks, and cold beer, along with live entertainment on weekends.

Special Events

AID and Comfort Gala. *Eldorado Hotel, 309 W San Francisco St, Santa Fe (87504). Phone 505/989-3399. www.aidandcomfort.org.* Since 1989, the organization Aid and Comfort has raised money to benefit those suffering from HIV and AIDS. The annual gala kicks off the holiday season on the Saturday after Thanksgiving with a lavish bash at the Eldorado Hotel, featuring live music for dancing, a buffet, and a silent auction. Sat after Thanksgiving. **$$$$**

Christmas Eve Canyon Road Walk. *Santa Fe Plaza, Canyon Rd, Santa Fe. Starts at the foot of Canyon Rd near Paseo De Peralta. Phone toll-free 800/777-2489.* Adorned with thousands of *farolitos*, traditional luminaries (lights made of a single small candle inside a paper bag), the streets and homes around Canyon Road play host to a unique and colorful festival each Christmas Eve. Literally thousands of pedestrians stroll up and down the streets while singing Christmas carols, lighting bonfires, and enjoying hot apple cider. A major Santa Fe tradition not to be missed. Dec 24. **FREE**

Christmas Eve Celebrations. *Phone toll-free 800/777-2489.* In Santa Fe and nearby villages, with street fires and *farolitos* (paper bag lanterns) "to guide the Christ Child," candlelit Nacimientos (nativity scenes), and other events. Santo Domingo, Tesuque, Santa Clara, and other pueblos have Christmas dances the following three days. Late Dec.

Eight Northern Pueblos Arts & Crafts Show. *San Juan Pueblo, Santa Fe. artnewmexico.com/eightnorthern/index.shtml.* This annual festival features traditional and contemporary Native American art at more than 500 booths. Approximately 1,500 artists attend and have their work judged for prizes before being displayed for sale. Third weekend in July.

Fiesta and Green Corn Dance. *San Felipe Pueblo, Santa Fe.* Early May.

Fiesta at Santo Domingo Pueblo. *Santo Domingo Pueblo, Santa Fe. Phone 505/465-2214.* Corn dance. This fiesta is probably the largest and most famous of the Rio Grande pueblo fiestas. Early Aug.

Indian Market. *Santa Fe Plaza, Santa Fe (87504). Phone 505/983-5220. www.swaia.org/indianmrkt.html.* Each year in late August, the Santa Fe Indian Market attracts a swarm of national and international buyers and collectors to the largest and oldest Native American arts show and market in the world. More than 1,200 artists from over 100 North American tribes participate in the show, with around 600 outdoor booths set up in the middle of the ancient Santa Fe Plaza. The market is a great opportunity to meet the artists and buy directly from them instead of going through the usual galleries and other middlemen. Quality of work is stressed, as all sale items are strictly screened for quality and authenticity. Numerous outdoor booths sell food, and the event draws an estimated 100,000 visitors to Santa Fe during the weekend, so make your lodging reservations well in advance. Late Aug.

International Folk Art Market. *Milner Plaza, Camino Lejo, Santa Fe. On Museum Hill off the Old Santa Fe Trail. Phone 505/476-1203. www.folkartmarket.org.* This two-day event brings together 75 master folk artists from around the world, from Bangladesh to Zimbabwe, in a celebration of color, music, and cuisine. Mediums represented include everything from textiles to woodblock prints to ceramics and sculptures. In addition to shopping for works to take home, visitors can attend demonstrations and lectures, tour local folk art collections, bid on works at an auction, and participate in children's activities. Mid-July. **$**

Invitational Antique Indian Art Show. *Sweeney Center, 201 W Marcy, Santa Fe (87501). Phone 505/984-6760.* Largest show of its kind in the country. Pre-1935 items; attracts dealers, collectors, museums. Two days in mid-Aug.

Mountain Man Rendezvous and Festival. *105 W Palace Ave, Santa Fe (87504). Phone 505/476-5100. www.palaceofthegovernors.org.* In early August, costumed mountain men ride into town on horseback for the Museum of New Mexico's annual buffalo roast, part of a large gathering of trappers and traders from the pre-1840 wilderness. Participants sell primitive equipment, tools, and trinkets and compete in period survival skills such as knife and tomahawk throwing, muzzleloader rifle shooting, cannon firing, storytelling, and foot races. Early Aug.

Santa Fe Chamber Music Festival. *St. Francis Auditorium, Museum of Fine Arts, and the Lensic Performing Arts Center, Santa Fe (87501). Phone 505/983-2075. www.sfcmf.org.* Since the first season of the festival in 1973, when Pablo Casals was the founding, honorary president, this artistic tradition has grown into a major event consisting of more than 80 performances, open rehearsals, concert previews, and roundtable discussions with composers and musicians during the annual summer season. The celebrated "Composer-in-Residence" Program has hosted luminaries such as Aaron Copland, Ellen Taafe Zwilich, and John Harbison, and the festival has sent ensembles on national tours since 1980. Performances are frequently heard on National Public Radio, and the festival fosters a significant outreach program to Santa Fe schools. Check for performances scheduled at St. Francis Auditorium, Museum of Fine Arts, and the Lensic Performing Arts Center. July-Aug.

Santa Fe Fiesta. *Santa Fe Plaza, Santa Fe. Phone 505/988-7575.* This ancient folk festival, dating to 1712, features historical pageantry, religious observances, arts and crafts shows, and street dancing. It also celebrates the reconquest of Santa Fe by Don Diego de Vargas in 1692. Make reservations well in advance. First weekend in Sept.

Santa Fe Opera. *Hwys 84/285, Santa Fe (87505). Drive N from Santa Fe about 7 miles via Hwy 84/285; the Opera is on the W side of the highway. Phone 505/986-5900; toll-free 800/280-4654. www.santafeopera.org.* Founded in 1957, this opera company presents one of the world's most famous and respected opera festivals each summer from early July through late August. Each season, the company stages five works, including two classics, a lesser-known work by a well-known composer, a Richard Strauss offering, and a world premiere or new American staging. Possibly more dramatic and appealing, even to an opera novice, is the Santa Fe Opera's home, a breathtaking hilltop amphitheater found about 7 miles north of the city. Designed by Polshek & Partners of New York, who refurbished Carnegie Hall in Manhattan, the Opera incorporates bold, swooping lines with excellent sight lines and is known for superb acoustics. Featured stars frequently include those from New York's Metropolitan Opera, among many others, and the festival is known for offering an exemplary apprentice program to young opera hopefuls. Backstage tours (early July-late Aug: Mon-Sat at 1 pm, fee)(Performances begin between 8 pm and 9 pm) **$$$$**

Santa Fe Pro Musica. *Lensic Performing Arts Center, 211 W San Francisco St, Santa Fe (87504). Phone 505/988-4640; toll-free 800/960-6680. www.santafepromusica.com.* Chamber orchestra and chamber ensemble perform classical and contemporary music, also performance of *Messiah* during Christmas season, Mozart Festival in Feb. Sept-May. **$$$$**

Santa Fe Rodeo. *Santa Fe Rodeo Grounds, 2801 W Rodeo Rd, Santa Fe (87502). Phone 505/471-4300. www.rodeodesantafe.com.* The Santa Fe Rodeo offers the chance to see real live cowboys and bucking broncos in action at the outdoor rodeo fairgrounds. Various professional competitions and public exhibitions open to the public are put on during the brief summer season. Rodeo events generally happen during evening and weekend matinee hours. A downtown rodeo parade takes place in mid-June at the start of the season. **$$$$**

Santa Fe Stages. *Performances held at the Lensic Performing Arts Center and the Armory for the Arts. Phone 505/982-6683. www.santafestages.org.* With presentations offered primarily at the historic Lensic Performing Arts Center, Santa Fe Stages hosts a season of dance, music, and theater with national and regional appeal. The season typically begins before Memorial Day and ends in late September, and may offer Irish folk dance, classical ballet, opera, jazz, drama, comedy, or cabaret shows. Late May-late Sept.

Santa Fe Symphony and Chorus. *Lensic Performing Arts Center, 211 W San Francisco St, Santa Fe (87501). Phone 505/983-3530. www.sf-symphony.org.* Santa Fe's orchestral company presents works in classical and jazz music, as well as specialty programs that may include the music of Spain and Mexico. Look for a blend of genres for the season-ender, which could include Copland's *Fanfare for the Modern Man,* Ellington's *The River,* and Dvorak's *Symphony No. 9 (New World).* The season generally runs from early October through Memorial Day, with matinee and evening performances at the Lensic Performing Arts Center. Early Oct-late May. **$$$$**

Santa Fe Wine and Chile Fiesta. *Santa Fe Opera grounds, 551 W Cordova Rd #723, Santa Fe (87505). Phone 505/438-8060. www.santafewineandchile.org.* Begun in 1991, this wildly popular festival honoring the best in food and drink brings in some 2,000 appreciative fans from around the state and across the country for four days of noshing and sipping on the last weekend in September. Roughly 30 local restaurants and 90 wineries from around the globe team up with a half-dozen or so of America's top celebrity chefs and cookbook authors to present a culinary extravaganza in a variety of venues around town. Wine seminars, cooking demonstrations, special vintners' lunches and dinners, and the gastronomic circus called the Grand Tasting, staged in mammoth tents on the Santa Fe Opera grounds, fill a palate-thrilling schedule. Late Sept. **$$$$**

Shakespeare in Santa Fe. *St. John's College, 1516 Pacheco St, Santa Fe (87505). Phone 505/982-2910. www.shakespearesantafe.org.* Established in 1987, the Santa Fe Shakespeare Company is a professional group that presents classical and contemporary theater to the community, with an emphasis in bringing works to young people. Each season, one of the works by William Shakespeare is presented in an outdoor setting, but the majority of presentations are made at St. John's College in the Meem Library Courtyard and at the Lensic Performing Arts Center, and a few are staged at venues like the Museum of Indian Arts and Culture. Classic Fairy Tales are among the presentations arranged specifically for Santa Fe families. Look for Shakespeare works to be presented in May and June. **$$$$**

Spanish Market. *Museum of Spanish Colonial Art, 750 Camino Lejo, Santa Fe (87501). Phone 505/982-2226. www.spanishmarket.org.* The rich and colorful Hispanic art traditions of northern New Mexico are celebrated twice a year during Spanish Market, the oldest and largest exhibition and sale of traditional Hispanic art in the United States. The smaller winter market in December is held indoors in the Sweeney Convention Center (201 W Marcy St), while the larger summer market occupies the entire Santa Fe Plaza for one weekend in July. During the market as many as 300 vendors sell and display santos (carved saints), hide paintings, textiles, furniture, jewelry, tinwork, basketry, pottery, bonework, and other locally produced handicrafts reflecting the unique and deeply religious traditional art which still flourishes in this part of New Mexico. Sponsored by the Spanish Colonial Arts Society. Dec and late July.

Spring Corn Dances. *Cochiti, San Felipe, Santo Domingo, and other pueblos. Phone 505/843-7270.* Races, contests. Late May-early June.

St. Anthony's Feast-Comanche Dance. *San Clara Pueblo, Santa Fe. Phone 505/843-7270.* Mid-June.

Tesuque Pueblo Flea Market. *Hwy 84/285, Santa Fe. From Santa Fe, take St. Francis Dr N, which turns into*

Hwy 84/285 as you leave town. Continue N for approximately 5 1/2 miles. The Flea Market is located on the left side of the highway next to the Santa Fe Opera. Phone 505/995-8626. www.tesuquepuebloflemarket.com. At the Tesuque Pueblo outdoor flea market, you'll find hundreds of vendors offering antiques, gems, jewelry, pottery, rugs, and world folk art of all descriptions at very competitive prices. Plan on devoting a couple of hours to browse all the various treasures and myriad of vendor booths stretching for several acres. Even if you don't buy anything, it's a browser's paradise well worth the 15-minute drive from Santa Fe.

Zozobra Festival. *Fort Marcy Park, 490 Washington Ave, Santa Fe (87501). Phone 505/983-7700. www.zozobra.com.* Each year on the Thursday before Labor Day, the Kiwanis Club of Santa Fe hosts the burning of Zozobra, a 50-foot effigy of "Old Man Gloom", whose passing away is designed to dispel the hardships and travails of the previous year. Zozobra started in 1924 as part of the Fiestas celebration, when a local artist conceived a ritual based on a Yaqui Indian celebration from Mexico. Over the years, Zozobra caught on and the crowd sizes have grown, making Zozobra Santa Fe's largest, most colorful and most spectacular festival. Lasting for several hours, as many as 60,000 visitors crowd into a large grassy field in Fort Marcy Park to listen to live bands, watch spectacular fireworks displays, and cheer the ritual burning. Fiestas celebrations continue during the Labor Day weekend with all day booths and activities set up in the nearby plaza. Thurs before Labor Day. **$$**

Limited-Service Hotels

★ **COMFORT INN SANTA FE.** *4312 Cerrillos Rd, Santa Fe (87505). Phone 505/474-7330; toll-free 800/635-3396; fax 505/474-7330. www.travelsouthwest.com.* 83 rooms. Pets accepted. Complimentary continental breakfast. Check-in 3 pm, check-out noon. High-speed Internet access, wireless Internet access. Indoor pool, whirlpool. **$**

★ ★ **HOTEL PLAZA REAL.** *125 Washington Ave, Santa Fe (87501). Phone 505/988-4900; toll-free 877/901-7666; fax 505/983-9322. www.buynewmexico.com.* Territorial-style architecture; fireplaces, handcrafted Southwestern furniture. 56 rooms, 3 story. Pets accepted. Check-in 3 pm, check-out noon. Restaurant, bar. **$$**

★ ★ **HOTEL SANTA FE.** *1501 Paseo De Peralta, Santa Fe (87501). Phone 800/825-9876; toll-free 800/825-9876; fax 505/955-7835. www.hotelsantafe.com.* Set in a grove of trees in a residential area about a ten-minute walk from the Plaza, this hotel is owned and operated by Native Americans it's the only venture of its kind in the United States. It exists to celebrate New Mexico's native cultures, with original pottery and paintings, an authentic Plains Indian-style tepee, ceremonial dances, and storytelling by the resident historian in front of a kiva fireplace. The 3-acre property features Native American sculptures and totems, which nicely complement the Pueblo Revival architecture of the hotel. 129 rooms, 3 story. Pets accepted. Check-in 2 pm, check-out noon. Restaurant, bar. Outdoor pool, whirlpool. Airport transportation available. **$$**

★ ★ **HOTEL ST. FRANCIS.** *210 Don Gaspar Ave, Santa Fe (87501). Phone 505/983-5700; toll-free 800/529-5700; fax 505/989-7690. www.hotelstfrancis.com.* As part of the Historic Inns of America, this hotel was built in 1880 and then rebuilt in 1923 after a fire in 1922. Each guest room has a high ceiling and original windows, some with mountain views; all are done in Victorian-style. The inn is one block from the historic Plaza and close to museums, shops, and galleries, and afternoon tea service is available. 83 rooms, 3 story. Check-in 3 pm, check-out 11 am. Restaurant, two bars. **$$**

★ **LA QUINTA INN.** *4298 Cerrillos Rd, Santa Fe (87507). Phone 505/471-1142; fax 505/438-7219. www.laquinta.com.* 130 rooms, 3 story. Pets accepted; fee. Complimentary continental breakfast. Check-in 3 pm, check-out noon. Outdoor pool. **$**

Full-Service Hotels

★ ★ **ELDORADO HOTEL.** *309 W San Francisco St, Santa Fe (87501). Phone 505/988-4455; fax 505/995-4543. www.eldoradohotel.com.* The Eldorado Hotel's imposing Pueblo Revival-style building is one of Santa Fe's largest and most important landmarks. Its lobby and interiors are lavishly decorated with an extensive collection of original Southwest art. The lobby lounge is a great spot for snacking, people-watching, and enjoying live entertainment. Sunday brunch is served in the cozy Eldorado Court, voted "Best Brunch" by the city's residents. 219 rooms, 5 story. Pets accepted; fee. Check-in 4 pm, check-out

11:30 am. High-speed Internet access. Two restaurants, bar. Fitness room. Outdoor pool, whirlpool. Business center. **$$$**

★ ★ **HILTON SANTA FE.** *100 Sandoval St, Santa Fe (87501). Phone 505/986-2811; toll-free 800/336-3676; fax 505/986-6439. www.hiltonofsantafe.com.* Located just two blocks from the historic Plaza in a 380-year-old family estate, this hotel maintains a sense of history while providing modern amenities and services. It takes up an entire city block and has the city's largest pool. Guest rooms feature locally handcrafted furnishings. 157 rooms, 3 story. Check-in 4 pm, check-out noon. Three restaurants, bar. Fitness room. Outdoor pool, whirlpool. Airport transportation available. Business center. **$$**

★ ★ ★ **INN AND SPA AT LORETTO.** *211 Old Santa Fe Trail, Santa Fe (87501). Phone 505/988-5531; toll-free 800/727-5531; fax 505/984-7988. www.hotelloretto.com.* Built in 1975, this hotel offers guests a heated outdoor pool, 12 specialty shops, and galleries. Guests can also enjoy skiing, hiking, tennis and horseback riding. 135 rooms, 4 story. Check-in 3 pm, check-out noon. Restaurant, bar. Fitness room, spa. Outdoor pool. **$$**

★ ★ ★ ★ **INN OF THE ANASAZI.** *113 Washington Ave, Santa Fe (87501). Phone 505/988-3030; fax 505/988-3277.* Native American, Hispanic, and cowboy cultures collide at the Inn of the Anasazi, where a masterful blend of New Mexican legacies results in a stunning and unusual lodging. The true spirit of Santa Fe is captured here, where enormous handcrafted doors open to a world of authentic artwork, carvings, and textiles synonymous with the Southwest. The lobby sets a sense of place for arriving guests with its rough-hewn tables, leather furnishings, unique objects, and huge cactus plants in terra-cotta pots. Located just off the historic Plaza, the inn was designed to resemble the traditional dwellings of the Anasazi. The region's integrity is maintained in the guest rooms, where fireplaces and four-poster beds reside under ceilings of vigas and latillas, and guests discover toiletries made locally with native cedar extract. Artfully prepared, the meals of the Anasazi's restaurant earn praise for honoring the area's culinary heritage. 59 rooms, 3 story. Pets accepted; fee. Check-in 3 pm, check-out noon. Restaurant, bar. Fitness room. **$$$**

★ ★ ★ **LA POSADA DE SANTA FE.** *330 E Palace Ave, Santa Fe (87501). Phone 505/986-0000; toll-free 800/727-5276; fax 505/982-5474. www.rockresorts.com.* Nestled on 6 lushly landscaped acres, La Posada de Santa Fe Resort & Spa effortlessly blends past and present. The original Staab House, dating to 1870, is the focal point of the resort, and the lovely rooms and suites are scattered throughout the gardens in a village setting. Warm colors mix with Spanish colonial and old-world style, and every amenity has been added. Relaxation is the order of the day here, especially at the fantastic Avanyu Spa with its Native American-themed treatments using local ingredients. The resort's Fuego Restaurant is a standout for its innovative food with Spanish and Mexican inflections, while the historic Staab House is an inviting setting for American classics. 157 rooms, 2 story. Check-in 4 pm, check-out noon. Restaurant, bar. Fitness room, spa. Outdoor pool, whirlpool. **$$$**

Full-Service Resorts

★ ★ ★ **BISHOP'S LODGE.** *1297 Bishop's Lodge Rd, Santa Fe (87504). Phone 505/983-6377; toll-free 800/732-2240; fax 505/983-0832. www.bishopslodge.com.* The Bishop's Lodge is a Santa Fe treasure. This historic resort has been welcoming guests since 1918, and its beloved chapel, listed on the National Register of Historic Places, remains a popular site for weddings. This resort is vintage chic, with rooms decorated with a 1930s Santa Fe flair. Lush colors, Navajo rugs, and kiva fireplaces reflect local pride. While modern American cuisine is the focus at the restaurant, the ShaNah spa is influenced by Native American traditions. Each treatment begins with a soothing drumming and blessing, adding to the uniqueness of this resort. Skiing in Santa Fe and nearby Taos attract winter visitors, while summer lures horseback enthusiasts. 88 rooms, 3 story. Pets accepted. Check-in 4 pm, check-out noon. Restaurant, bar. Children's activity center. Fitness room, spa. Outdoor pool, whirlpool. Tennis. **$$$**

★ ★ ★ **HYATT REGENCY TAMAYA RESORT & SPA.** *1300 Tamaya Trail, Santa Ana Pueblo (87004). Phone 505/867-1234; toll-free 800/554-9288; fax 505/771-6180. tamaya.hyatt.com.* Calling 500 acres of unspoiled desert beauty home, the Hyatt Regency Tamaya Resort & Spa shares the magic of New Mexico with its visitors. Pueblo-style buildings, open-air courtyards, and striking views of the Sandia Mountains and the Bosque capture the spirit of the area. Mood-elevating turquoises and bright oranges are used throughout the public and private spaces, and distinctive artwork leaves a lasting impression. Golf, tennis, and hot air ballooning are among the recreational opportunities available at this family-friendly resort, where kids can participate in special programs geared for their interests. Like the Hyatt itself, the restaurants are a showcase of Southwestern flavors, offering sophisticated takes on local favorites. 350 rooms, 4 story. Pets accepted, some restrictions. Check-in 4 pm, check-out noon. High-speed Internet access. Five restaurants, two bars. Children's activity center. Fitness room, fitness classes available, spa. Outdoor pool, children's pool, whirlpool. Golf, 18 holes. Tennis. Airport transportation available. Business center. **$$**

★ ★ ★ **RANCHO ENCANTADO RESORT.**
198 State Rd 592, Santa Fe (87501). Phone 505/982-3537; toll-free 800/722-9339; fax 505/983-8269. www.nmhotels.com. If only the walls could talk at Rancho Encantado. This legendary hideaway has played host to many of the world's most influential people, including Prince Rainier, Princess Grace, and the Dalai Lama. Once visitors catch a glimpse of this ranch nestled in the foothills of the Sangre de Cristo Mountains, it is no surprise that it has beckoned so many since the 1950s. Casitas with kiva fireplaces and outdoor whirlpools are scattered throughout the 200-acre property, offering guests the highest levels of privacy. This luxurious guest ranch-style resort is renowned for its horseback riding and equestrian center, and the Acacia spa is a relaxing addition. Western cuisine is spotlighted at The Restaurant, while the Green Room serves breakfast and sushi using ingredients from its working greenhouse. 55 rooms. Check-in 3 pm, check-out 11 am. Restaurant, bar. Outdoor pool, whirlpool. Tennis. **$$**

Full-Service Inns

★ ★ ★ **GALISTEO INN.** *9 La Vega, Galisteo (87540). Phone 505/466-8200; toll-free 866/404-8200; fax 505/466-4008. www.galisteoinn.com.* Guests can tour the area on mountain bikes, horseback, or by hiking. Located just a half hour from Pecos National Monument and nearby Santa Fe, guests can enjoy a true Southwestern vacation. This hacienda is on

8 acres built in the 1750s. 11 rooms. Children over 10 years only. Complimentary continental breakfast. Check-in 3 pm, check-out 11 am. Restaurant, bar. Outdoor pool, whirlpool. **$$**

★ ★ ★ **INN OF THE GOVERNORS.** *101 W Alameda, Santa Fe (87501). Phone 505/982-4333; toll-free 800/234-4534; fax 505/989-9149. www.innofthegovernors.com.* 100 rooms, 3 story. Complimentary full breakfast. Check-in 4 pm, check-out noon. Restaurant, bar. Outdoor pool. **$$**

Specialty Lodgings

The following lodging establishments are approved by Mobil Travel Guide, but due to their unique and individualized nature have not been given a traditional Mobil Star rating. Included in this listing you may find bed-and-breakfasts, limited-service inns, guest ranches, and other unique hotel properties.

ADOBE ABODE. *202 Chapelle St, Santa Fe (87501). Phone 505/983-3133; fax 505/424-3027. www.adobeabode.com.* Built in 1905 as officer quarters for Fort Marcy, this property offers guests a unique stay in one of the finely decorated rooms. Visitors will enjoy the complimentary sherry and Santa Fe cookies in the afternoon. 6 rooms. Complimentary full breakfast. Check-in 2 pm, check-out 11 am. **$**

CASAPUEBLO INN. *138 Park Ave, Santa Fe (87501). Phone 505/988-4455; toll-free 800/955-4455; fax 505/995-4543. www.casapueblo.com.* 32 rooms. Pets accepted; fee. Complimentary continental breakfast. Check-in 4 pm, check-out 11:30 am. **$$**

DANCING GROUND OF THE SUN. *711 Paseo De Peralta, Santa Fe (87501). Phone 505/986-9797; toll-free 800/745-9910; fax 505/982-5457. www.dancingground.com.* 21 rooms, 2 story. Pets accepted. Complimentary continental breakfast. Check-in 4 pm, check-out 11 am. **$$**

DOS CASAS VIEJAS. *610 Agua Fria St, Santa Fe (87501). Phone 505/983-1636; fax 505/983-1749. www.doscasasviejas.com.* Set in the heart of Sante Fe's Guadeloupe District, about 15 minutes from downtown, these two 1860s adobe buildings in a 1/2-acre walled/gated compound have been fully restored.

Guests looking for a quiet getaway find it here, either in the cozy rooms or by the small garden and pool area. Nearby activities include hiking, skiing, horseback riding, golf, opera, museums, art galleries, and shopping. 8 rooms. Complimentary continental breakfast. Check-in 3-6 pm, check-out noon. Outdoor pool. **$$**

EL FAROLITO BED & BREAKFAST. *514 Galisteo St, Santa Fe (87501). Phone 505/988-1631; toll-free 888/634-8782; fax 505/988-4589. www.farolito.com.* 8 rooms. Check-in 3 pm, check-out 11 am. **$$**

EL REY INN. *1862 Cerrillos Rd, Santa Fe (87505). Phone 505/982-1931; toll-free 800/521-1349; fax 505/989-9249. www.elreyinnsantafe.com.* About 2 miles from downtown, this adobe-style inn (1936) is well kept, with a cozy atmosphere and friendly staff. 86 rooms, 2 story. Complimentary continental breakfast. Check-in 3 pm, check-out noon. Outdoor pool, two whirlpools. **$**

GRANT CORNER INN. *122 Grant Ave, Santa Fe (87501). Phone 505/983-6678; toll-free 800/964-9003; fax 505/983-1526. www.grantcornerinn.com.* Located two blocks from Santa Fe's historic Plaza and next to the Georgia O'Keeffe Museum, this Colonial Manor house (1905) is a picture of tranquility, with many gardens and large trees. The air-conditioned guest rooms feature hand-painted armoires, antique photographs, and four-poster beds. The full breakfast offers such dishes as Swedish pancakes. 10 rooms, 3 story. Children over 8 years only. Complimentary full breakfast. Check-in 3-6 pm, check-out noon. **$$**

GUADALUPE INN. *604 Agua Fria St, Santa Fe (87501). Phone 505/989-7422; fax 505/989-7422. www.guadalupeinn.com.* A quiet inn offering rooms with unique style and décor. Local artists display their work in the rooms and many pieces are for sale. 12 rooms, 2 story. Complimentary full breakfast. Check-in 3-6 pm, check-out 11 am. **$**

INN OF THE TURQUOISE BEAR. *342 E Buena Vista, Santa Fe (87501). Phone 505/983-0798; toll-free 800/396-4104; fax 505/988-4225. www.turquoisebear.com.* 10 rooms. Pets accepted, some restrictions; fee. Complimentary continental breakfast. Check-in 3 pm, check-out noon. **$$$**

INN ON THE ALAMEDA. *303 E Alameda, Santa Fe (87501). Phone 505/984-2121; toll-free 888/984-2121; fax 505/982-8756. www.inn-alameda.com.* Tucked unassumingly behind adobe walls near the start of Canyon Road, this inn offers all the comforts of a luxury hotel, but has the quiet elegance of a smaller bed-and-breakfast. With lovely gardens and sheltered courtyards, the adobe-style inn offers a quiet, romantic respite. Guest rooms feature fireplaces, triple-sheeted beds with Egyptian cotton linens, and plush robes. 69 rooms, 3 story. Pets accepted, some restrictions; fee. Complimentary continental breakfast. Check-in 4 pm, check-out noon. Bar. Fitness room. Two whirlpools. **$$**

INN ON THE PASEO. *630 Paseo De Peralta, Santa Fe (87501). Phone 505/984-8200; toll-free 800/457-9045; fax 505/989-3979. www.innonthepaseo.com.* Located on the Paseo de Peralta in the heart of downtown Santa Fe, this 19-room inn offers a relaxing Southwest experience. Air-conditioned guest rooms feature down comforters, patchwork quilts, and private baths. The breakfast buffet is served on the sundeck and features a collection of healthy favorites like muffins, granola, and fresh fruit. 19 rooms, 3 story. Complimentary full breakfast. Check-in 3 pm, check-out 11 am. **$**

LAS PALOMAS. *460 W San Francisco St, Santa Fe (87501). Phone 505/988-4455; fax 505/995-4543.* 39 rooms. Pets accepted; fee. Complimentary continental breakfast. Check-in 4 pm, check-out noon. High-speed Internet access. Fitness room. Whirlpool. **$$**

TERRITORIAL INN. *215 Washington St, Santa Fe (87501). Phone 505/988-2800; toll-free 866/230-7737; fax 505/982-5457. www.territorialinn.com.* This charming 25-room Victorian home (circa 1895) is located one block from the historic Santa Fe Plaza. Rooms offer queen-size beds, alarm clocks, voice mail, cable televisions, and telephones. Relax in the rose garden or in the whirlpool. 25 rooms, 2 story. Children over 10 years only. Complimentary continental breakfast. Check-in 3 pm, check-out 11 am. **$$**

WATER STREET INN. *427 W Water St, Santa Fe (87501). Phone 505/984-1193; toll-free 800/646-6752; fax 505/984-6235. www.waterstreetinn.com.* Located just two blocks from Santa Fe's historic Plaza, this inn features Southwestern décor with art and photography lining its walls. Spacious brick-floored guest rooms have private baths, cable TV with VCRs, air conditioning, and decks/patios. The courtyard offers a sundeck with great views. 12 rooms. Pets accepted. Complimentary continental breakfast. Check-in 2 pm, check-out 11 am. Whirlpool. **$$**

Restaurants

★ ★ **AMAYA AT HOTEL SANTA FE.** *1501 Paseo de Peralta, Santa Fe (87501). Phone 505/982 1200; toll-free 800/825-9876; fax 505/984-2211. www.hotelsantafe.com.* Southwestern menu. Breakfast, lunch, dinner. Bar. Children's menu. Casual attire. Outdoor seating. **$$$**

★ ★ ★ **THE ANASAZI.** *113 Washington Ave, Santa Fe (87501). Phone 505/988-3236; toll-free 800/688-8100; fax 505/988-3277. www.innoftheanasazi.com.* The creators of memorable cuisine at this Plaza mainstay like to point out that the Navajo definition of Anasazi has come to embody an ancient wisdom that is "synonymous with the art of living harmoniously and peacefully with our environment." That philosophy is translated in the colorful Native American weavings, petroglyph-inspired art upon the walls of beautiful rock, and mesmerizing fires that crackle and warm the rooms within this dining favorite. Executive chef Tom Kerpon devotes himself to inventive uses of locally grown, organic products, from cactus and sage to chiles and corn. Plenty of satisfaction is found in his grilled basil-marinated opah with green chile risotto, buffalo osso buco, and soup of grilled corn, tortilla, and lime. Southwestern menu. Breakfast, lunch, dinner, Sun brunch. Bar. Children's menu. Casual attire. **$$$**

★ ★ **ANDIAMO.** *322 Garfield, Santa Fe (87501). Phone 505/995-9595. www.andiamoonline.com.* Italian menu. Dinner. Children's menu. Casual attire. Outdoor seating. Three dining areas. **$$**

★ **BLUE CORN CAFE.** *133 Water St, Santa Fe (87501). Phone 505/984-1800.* New Mexican menu. Lunch, dinner. Closed Thanksgiving, Dec 25. Bar. Children's menu. Casual attire. **$**

★ ★ **CAFE PARIS.** *31 Burro Alley, Santa Fe (87501). Phone 505/986-9162; fax 505/995-0008.* French menu. Lunch, dinner. Closed Mon; also Jan 1, Dec 25. Casual attire. Café-style dining. **$$$**

★ ★ **CAFE PASQUAL'S.** *121 Don Gaspar, Santa Fe (87501). Phone 505/983-9340; fax 505/988-4645.* New

Mexican, American menu. Breakfast, lunch, dinner, Sun brunch. Closed Thanksgiving, Dec 25. Casual attire. **$$$**

★ ★ **CELEBRATIONS.** *613 Canyon Rd, Santa Fe (87501). Phone 505/989-8904. www.celebrationscanyon road.com.* American menu. Breakfast, lunch, dinner. Closed Jan 1, Thanksgiving, Dec 25. Bar. Casual attire. Outdoor seating. **$$**

★ **CHOW'S CUISINE BISTRO.** *720 St. Michaels Dr, Santa Fe (87505). Phone 505/471-7120; fax 505/ 471-7120. www.mychows.com.* This cozy little restaurant tucked away in a shopping mall in south Santa Fe offers some of the best Chinese food in the city. Serving mostly Szechwan dishes in a contemporary Asian atmosphere, Chow's consistently wins the *Santa Fe Reporter*'s "Best of Santa Fe" award. Enjoy numerous unique and tasty dishes, all prepared without MSG, under large hanging Chinese lanterns. Chinese menu. Lunch, dinner. Closed Sun. Casual attire. **$$**

★ ★ ★ **COYOTE CAFE.** *132 W Water St, Santa Fe (87501). Phone 505/983-1615; fax 505/989-9026. www.coyotecafe.com.* Famed cookbook author and pioneer of Southwestern cuisine Mark Miller has enjoyed nothing but success at this bastion of trendy dining found just a block off the Plaza. Although the menu changes seasonally, patrons are assured of finding a whimsical mingling of the cuisines of New Mexico, Mexico, Cuba, and Spain in all manner of meats, fish, and vegetables. Look for chile-glazed beef short ribs with corn dumplings, pecan wood-roasted quail, and halibut in a mango-habañero blend, among many inventions, and don't miss the house drink special, a margarita del Maguey. Whether seated in the main dining room (try for a window-side table overlooking the street) or on the festive rooftop Cantina, be sure to relax and soak up the setting, decorated by magnificent folk art and artistic lighting fixtures. Southwestern menu. Dinner. Bar. Children's menu. Casual attire. Reservations recommended. Outdoor seating. **$$$**

★ **EL COMEDOR.** *727 Cerrillos Rd, Santa Fe (87501). Phone 505/989-7575; fax 505/984-8879.* Southwestern menu. Breakfast, lunch, dinner. Closed Thanksgiving, Dec 25. Children's menu. Casual attire. Outdoor seating. **$**

★ **EL FAROL.** *808 Canyon Rd, Santa Fe (87501). Phone 505/983-9912. www.elfarolsf.com.* Mexican menu. Lunch, dinner. Closed holidays. Bar. Casual attire. Outdoor seating. **$**

★ ★ **EL MESON - LA COCINA DE ESPAÑA.**
213 Washington Ave, Santa Fe (87501). Phone 505/983-6756; fax 505/983-1262. www.elmeson-santafe.com.
Spanish, tapas menu. Dinner. Closed Sun-Mon; also Jan 1, Thanksgiving, Dec 25. Bar. Children's menu. Casual attire. **$$**

★ ★ **EL NIDO.** *591 Bishops Lodge Rd, Tesuque (87574). Phone 505/988-4340; fax 505/988-2011.* Steak, seafood menu. Dinner. Closed Mon; Jan 1, Thanksgiving, Dec 25; also Super Bowl Sun. Bar. **$$**
🅳

★ ★ **GABRIEL'S.** *4 Banana Ln, Santa Fe (87506). Phone 505/455-7000; fax 505/455-3866.* Southwestern menu. Lunch, dinner. Closed Late Nov-late Dec. Bar. Casual attire. Reservations recommended. Outdoor seating. **$$**

★ ★ ★ **GERONIMO.** *724 Canyon Rd, Santa Fe (87501). Phone 505/982-1500; fax 505/820-2083. www.geronimorestaurant.com.* Housed in a restored 250-year-old landmark adobe, Geronimo (the name of the restaurant is an ode to the hacienda's original owner, Geronimo Lopez) offers robust Southwestern-spiked "Global Fusion Fare" in a stunning and cozy space. Owners Cliff Skoglund and Chris Harvey treat each guest like family, and this is a nice family to be a part of. Geronimo is inviting and warm, with a wood-burning cove-style fireplace; eggshell walls; sheer curtains; tall, rich chocolate- and garnet-leather seating; and local Native American-style sculpture and artwork decorating the walls. It feels like a Georgia O'Keeffe painting come to life. It's not just the serene and stylish space that earns Geronimo points with its regulars. The food is remarkable, fusing the distinct culinary influences of Asia, the Southwest, and the Mediterranean. Vibrant flavors, bright colors, and top-notch seasonal regional ingredients come together in perfect harmony. While Geronimo is a great place for dinner, it is also a perfect spot to take a break from gallery hopping around lunchtime. When it's warm outside, sit on the patio for prime Canyon Road people watching. Southwestern, American menu. Lunch, dinner. Bar. Casual attire. Reservations recommended. Outdoor seating. **$$$**

★ ★ **IL PIATTO.** *95 W Marcy St, Santa Fe (87501). Phone 505/984-1091; fax 505/983-6939.* Italian menu. Lunch, dinner. Closed Jan 1, Thanksgiving, Dec 25. Bar. Children's menu. Casual attire. Outdoor seating. **$$**

★ ★ **INDIA PALACE.** *227 Don Gaspar, Santa Fe (87501). Phone 505/986-5859; fax 505/986-5856. www.indiapalace.com.* The multi-award-winning India Palace, conveniently located only a block from the Santa Fe Plaza, offers some of the best authentic Indian cuisine available in New Mexico. On the menu, you'll find an excellent selection of familiar Indian dishes, including a wide variety of meat and vegetarian offerings. The real deal, though, is the popular all-you-can eat lunch buffet. East Indian menu. Lunch, dinner. Closed Super Bowl Sun. Outdoor seating. **$$**

★ ★ ★ **JULIAN'S.** *221 Shelby St, Santa Fe (87501). Phone 505/988-2355; fax 505/988-5071. www.juliansofsantafe.com.* Officially called Julian's Cucina d'Italia, this bistro has long been a favorite for romantic dining in a neighborhood cluster of high-end shops and galleries. Diners are warmed by two fireplaces within the old adobe walls, where owner-executive chef Wayne Gustafson treats them to authentic dinners designed with style. Typical of his winning ways are the antipasto of oysters baked with Parmesan and his alternative to traditional escargot, a dish of pasta shells stuffed with snails, prosciutto, garlic butter, and pesto. Signature entrées include his classic osso buco Milanese with saffron risotto and shrimp sautéed with tomatoes and graced with fresh basil and marscapone. Italian menu. Dinner. Closed Thanksgiving. Bar. Casual attire. Outdoor seating. **$$$**

★ ★ ★ **LAS FUENTES AT BISHOP'S LODGE.**
Bishop's Lodge Rd, Santa Fe (87504). Phone 505/983-6377; toll-free 800/732-2240; fax 505/989-8739. www.bishopslodge.com. Rich in history, architecture, and art, the Bishop's Lodge resort introduced Las Fuentes in the spring of 2002. Executive chef Alfonso Ramirez brings a new edition of Nuevo Latino cuisine in a vibrant blend of foods that includes tostones, mariquitas, fufu de platino, and ropa vieja from Cuba, chimmichurri from Argentina, pupusas from Salvador, aropas from Colombia, and much more from Puerto Rico, Mexico, and other Caribbean and Central and South American countries. Seared plantain-crusted salmon with fennel and chipotle juice and swordfish marinated with chile guajillo have quickly become favorites. Spa cuisine choices include gazpacho with roasted cumin seeds and Cuban black bean soup. American, Southwestern menu. Breakfast, lunch, dinner, Sun brunch. Bar. Children's menu. Outdoor seating. **$$$**

★ ★ **MARIA'S NEW MEXICAN KITCHEN.** *555 W Cordova Rd, Santa Fe (87501). Phone 505/983-7929;*

fax 505/983-4700. *www.marias-santafe.com.* If you love margaritas, this popular restaurant offers more than 100 different varieties of REAL margaritas, made with some of the best and most exotic tequilas imported from Mexico. The margarita menu is bigger than most restaurants' food menus. Maria's also offers a great selection of Mexican beers and specializes in homemade, freshly cooked New Mexican cuisine. Try the barbecued ribs or any of the fajita dishes, along with the excellent homemade salsa. New Mexican, Southwestern menu. Lunch, dinner. Closed Thanksgiving, Dec 25. Bar. Children's menu. Casual attire. Outdoor seating. **$$**

★ ★ ★ **THE OLD HOUSE RESTAURANT.** *309 W San Francisco St, Santa Fe (87501). Phone 505/988-4455; toll-free 800/855-4455; fax 505/995-4555. www.eldoradohotel.com.* Supping on the culinary genius of chef Martin Rios produces a sensation much like that of falling in love—sweet, seductive, and intensely pleasurable. Taking time to prepare every element in the most fastidious fashion, Rios is known for making all sauces from stock reductions and finishing with butter and cream, and for introducing unexpected flavors in otherwise everyday items. Witness his roasted pork tenderloin, accompanied by sweet potatoes pureed with oranges that he's preserved for nine days, and his duck confit and foie gras in puff pastry with pistachios and cherry-celery compote. Take just a moment from swooning over chilled sweet corn soup and lobster soup with lobster tempura and osetra caviar to enjoy the candlelit stucco room, which is adorned with Mexican folk art and bold, oversized paintings, and is part of one of the city's oldest buildings. Southwestern menu. Dinner. Closed Thanksgiving, Dec 25. Bar. Casual attire. Valet parking. **$$$**

★ ★ **ORE HOUSE ON THE PLAZA.** *50 Lincoln Ave, Santa Fe (87505). Phone 505/983-8687; fax 505/920-6892. www.orehouseontheplaza.com.* A perennial favorite on every list of great taverns in the City Different, this comfortable hangout is in its third decade of pleasing visitors with a menu of more than 40 custom-made margaritas and dozens of sipping tequila choices. The balcony, with its unbeatable setting above the historic Plaza, is open year-round, thanks to special heating during cooler weather. A regular custom of frequent pilgrims is to wind up the day over a cocktail, noshing on complimentary snacks, listening to the evening's guitarist, and watching the stars light the sky. Happy hour is from 4-6 pm daily. Seafood, steak menu. Lunch, dinner. Closed Thanksgiving, Dec 25. Bar. Children's menu. Casual attire. Outdoor seating. **$$**

★ ★ **OSTERIA D'ASSISI.** *58 S Federal Pl, Santa Fe (87501). Phone 505/986-5858; fax 505/986-3938. www.osteriadassisi.com.* Italian menu. Lunch, dinner. Closed Jan 1, Thanksgiving, Dec 25. Casual attire. Outdoor seating. **$$**

★ ★ ★ **PALACE RESTAURANT AND SALOON.** *142 W Palace Ave, Santa Fe (87501). Phone 505/982-9891. www.palacerestaurant.com.* Recalling images of happy decadence from the Wild West, the Palace is a place where diners might expect to see a high-rolling gambler eating and drinking with the town's prettiest painted lady. Opened as a saloon by the renowned Doña Tules in 1837, the gathering spot boasts an old-fashioned red décor with ornate lighting fixtures and portrait frames reminiscent of the period. Devotees come for the fresh fish offerings, free-range veal and poultry, black Angus steaks, and locally raised lamb. Tableside Caesar salad preparations make meals special, as do house-made pastries from the cart rolled through after dinner. Expect live music, and in the summer, ask for a table on the shady old patio. American menu. Lunch, dinner. Closed Thanksgiving, Dec 25. Bar. Children's menu. Casual attire. Outdoor seating. **$$$**

★ ★ **PAUL'S.** *72 W Marcy St, Santa Fe (87501). Phone 505/982-8738. www.paulsofsantafe.com.* Chef/owner Paul Huntsicker, consistently a winner of the annual Taste of Santa Fe competition, woos patrons with a contemporary cuisine selection that includes fish, lamb, beef, and fowl, all given specialized treatments with an international assortment of herbs and exotic touches. Among the favorites are red chile wontons stuffed with duck and bathed in a ginger soy, saffron-scented fish stew, and blue crab cakes crowned with a tomato-orange-chipotle sauce. A twilight menu offers less expensive, fixed-price fare. Don't miss the chance to see folk art from New Mexico, Mexico, and Central and South America. American, Southwestern menu. Lunch, dinner. Closed July 4, Dec 25. Casual attire. **$$$**

★ ★ **THE PINK ADOBE.** *406 Old Santa Fe Trail, Santa Fe (87501). Phone 505/983-7712; fax 505/984-0691. www.thepinkadobe.com.* Historic pink adobe building circa 1700. Southwestern, Lunch, dinner. Closed holidays. Bar. Children's menu. Casual attire. Outdoor seating. **$$**

★ **PLAZA.** *54 Lincoln Ave, Santa Fe (87501). Phone 505/982-1664.* Century-old building with many original fixtures; stamped-tin ceiling; photos of early Santa Fe. American menu. Breakfast, lunch, dinner. Closed Thanksgiving, Dec 25. Children's menu. Casual attire. **$$**
🄳

★ ★ **PRANZO ITALIAN GRILL.** *540 Montezuma, Santa Fe (87501). Phone 505/984-2645; fax 505/986-1123.* Pranzo, which translates from Italian as "main" or "favorite" meal of the day, consistently ranks as one of the best Italian restaurants in Santa Fe. Situated in the Sanbusco Center in an old 19th-century lumberyard, its hardwood floors and casual ambience serve to transport diners back to Old World Italy. The experience is further enhanced by a superb menu of pastas, wood-oven pizzas, and succulent appetizers made with fresh ingredients such as goat cheese, sun-dried tomatoes, portobello mushrooms, roasted bell peppers, and plenty of garlic. You'll also find an excellent selection of wines. Late-nighters can enjoy pizza, salad, and appetizers, served in the lounge until midnight. During warm weather, patrons can dine on the rooftop patio, which offers great views of the surrounding mountains. Italian menu. Lunch, dinner. Closed July 4, Thanksgiving, Dec 25. Bar. Children's menu. Casual attire. Outdoor seating. **$$**

★ ★ **RISTRA.** *548 Agua Fria, Santa Fe (87501). Phone 505/982-8608. www.ristrarestaurant.com.* Barely off the beaten path, in a quiet neighborhood a short drive from the Plaza, this graceful Victorian adobe home provides a departure from typical Santa Fe in both setting and cuisine (although there are Southwestern elements in both). Diners gaze out of enormous windows at stands of evergreens while tucking into appetizers such as grilled foie gras and black Mediterranean mussels swept with mint and chipotle. Fresh seasonal ingredients are the key to the kitchen's successes, and a wine list of 100 French and California vintages keep local and visiting diners happy. American menu, Dinner. Casual attire. Outdoor seating. **$$$**

★ ★ **ROCIADA.** *304 Johnson St, Santa Fe (87501). Phone 505/983-3800; fax 505/983-8306. www.rociada.net.* A New York transplant, chef/owner Eric Stapelman brings country French cuisine to the near-Plaza environs with requisite panache. The interior's clean but mellow design is burnished in the golden light of small candles, allowing diners to be carried away by the food's rapture. Typical favorites have included octopus Provençal with roasted plum tomatoes, green olives, capers, and Yukon gold potatoes and California squab with applewood-smoked bacon, potato pavé, and red wine reduction. As icing to this gastronomic cake, there's a lovely, extensive selection of dessert wines (the '96 Chapoutier banyuls rouge is a huge hit) and vintage ports. French, Mediterranean menu. Dinner. Closed Sun. Bar. Casual attire. Outdoor seating. **$$$**

★ ★ **SAN MARCOS CAFE.** *3877 NM 14, Santa Fe (87505). Phone 505/471-9298.* Known for it's great Southwestern breakfasts and vegetarian cuisine. Southwestern menu. Breakfast, lunch. **$**
🄳

★ ★ ★ **SANTACAFE.** *231 Washington Ave, Santa Fe (87501). Phone 505/984-1788; fax 505/986-0110. www.santacafe.com.* Situated a block from the Plaza in the restored Padre Gallegos House, which was built by a colorful priest and politician from 1857 to 1862, Santacafe has been lauded by the *New York Times* for memorable works in globally influenced fish and meats. Simple but exquisite dishes include a salad of blood oranges and grapefruit with fennel and celeriac remoullade, shrimp-spinach dumplings in a tahini sauce, filet mignon with persillade and green chile mashed potatoes, and roasted free-range chicken with quinoa and a cranberry-chipotle chuntey. Patio dining in warmer weather is divine. American menu. Lunch, dinner. Bar. Casual attire. Outdoor seating. **$$$**

★ **SHED AND LA CHOZA.** *113 1/2 E Palace Ave, Santa Fe (87501). Phone 505/982-9030; fax 505/982-0902. www.sfshed.com.* New Mexican menu. Lunch, dinner. Closed Sun; holidays, children's menu. Casual attire. Outdoor seating. **$**

★ ★ **SHOHKO-CAFE.** *321 Johnson St, Santa Fe (87501). Phone 505/983-7288; fax 505/984-1853.* Japanese menu. Lunch, dinner. Closed holidays. Bar. Casual attire. **$$**

★ **STEAKSMITH AT EL GANCHO.** *104 B Old Las Vegas Hwy, Santa Fe (87505). Phone 505/988-3333; fax 505/988-3334. www.santafesteaksmith.com.* Steak menu. Dinner. Closed holidays. Bar. Children's menu. Casual attire. **$$$**

★ ★ **TOMASITA'S.** *500 S Guadalupe, Santa Fe (87501). Phone 505/983-5721; fax 505/983-0780.* An excellent choice for northern New Mexico cuisine, Tomasita's is housed in an old brick train station built in 1904. It's a great place to sample traditional *sopapillas,* puffy fried bread served with butter and

OKLAHOMA CITY, OK/SIDE TRIPS **227**

honey (it comes with all entrées). Be warned about the chili, though; Tomasita's makes it HOT, whether you order it red, green, or Christmas. Other specialties include quesadillas, enchiladas, burritos, and various Mexican-inspired dishes prepared with a local twist. New Mexican menu. Dinner. Closed Sun; Jan 1, Dec 25. Bar. Children's menu. Casual attire. Outdoor seating. **$**

★ ★ **VANESSIE OF SANTA FE.** *434 W San Francisco St, Santa Fe (87501). Phone 505/982-9966; fax 505/982-1507.* American menu. Dinner. Closed Easter, Thanksgiving, Dec 25. Bar. Children's menu. Casual attire. **$$$**

Oklahoma City, OK

3 1/2 hours, 205 miles from Dallas

Founded 1889
Population 444,719
Elevation 1,207 ft
Area Code 405
Information Convention & Visitors Bureau, 189 W Sheridan, 73102; phone 405/297-8912 or toll-free 800/225-5652
Web Site www.okccvb.org

What is now the site of Oklahoma's capital was barren prairie on the morning of April 22, 1889. Unassigned land was opened to settlement that day, and by nightfall the population numbered 10,000. No city was ever settled faster than during this famous run.

The city sits atop one of the nation's largest oil fields, with wells even on the lawn of the Capitol. First discovered in 1928, the field was rapidly developed throughout the city. It still produces large quantities of high-gravity oil. Oil well equipment manufacture became one of the city's major industries.

Oklahoma City's stockyards and meatpacking plants are the largest in the state. The city is also a grain milling and cotton processing center. Iron and steel, furniture, tire manufacturing, electrical equipment, electronics, and aircraft and automobile assembly are other industries. Tinker Air Force Base is southeast of the city.

Additional Visitor Information

The following organizations can provide travelers with assistance and additional information:

Oklahoma City Convention and Visitors Bureau, 189 W Sheridan, 73102, phone 405/297-8912 or toll-free 800/225-5652; Oklahoma City Chamber of Commerce, 123 Park Ave, 73102, phone 405/297-8900; Oklahoma Tourism and Recreation Department, 15 N Robinson, 73102, phone 405/521-2406. *Oklahoma Today,* the state's official magazine, has up-to-date information and articles of interest to the tourist.

Public Transportation

Buses (Central Oklahoma Transportation and Parking Authority), phone 405/235-7433

Airport Will Rogers World Airport; weather phone 405/478-3377; cash machines, located at upper level Main Terminal.

Information Phone 405/680-3200

Lost and Found Phone 405/680-3233

Airlines American, American Eagle, Champion Air, Continental, Delta, Delta Connection/Comair/ASA, Frontier, Great Plains, Northwest, Southwest, United

What to See and Do

45th Infantry Division Museum. *2145 NE 36th St, Oklahoma City (73111). Phone 405/424-5313.* Exhibits include state military history from its beginnings in the early Oklahoma Territory through World War II and Korea to the present National Guard; Desert Storm exhibit; uniforms, vehicles, aircraft, artillery, and an extensive military firearms collection with pieces dating to the American Revolution; memorabilia and original cartoons by Bill Mauldin. (Tues-Sun; closed Jan 1 and Dec 25) **FREE**

Civic Center Music Hall. *201 N Walker, Oklahoma City (73102). Phone 405/297-2584.* Home of the Oklahoma City Philharmonic, Canterbury Choral Society, Ballet Oklahoma, BLAC, and Lyric Theatre of Oklahoma. A variety of entertainment is provided, including Broadway shows and popular concerts.

Frontier City. *11501 NE Expy, Oklahoma City (73131). Phone 405/478-2412.* A 65-acre Western theme park; including more than 75 rides, shows, and attractions; entertainment; shops, restaurants. (Memorial Day-late Aug: daily; Easter-Memorial Day and late Aug-Oct: weekends only) **$$$$**

Garden Exhibition Building and Horticulture Gardens. *3400 NW 36th St, Oklahoma City (73112). Phone 405/943-0827.* Azalea trails; butterfly garden; rose, peony, and iris gardens; arboretum; the conservatory has one of the country's largest cactus and succulent collections (daily). Exhibition Building (Mon-Fri; closed holidays; open Sat-Sun during flower shows). **FREE**

Harn Homestead and 1889er Museum. *313 NE 16th St, Oklahoma City (73104). Phone 405/235-4058. www.harnhomestead.com.* Historic homestead claimed in Land Run of 1889; 1904 farmhouse furnished with pre-statehood objects dating to period of the run. Three-story stone and cedar barn; one-room schoolhouse; working farm. Ten acres of picnic area, shade trees. (Mon-Fri; closed holidays) **$$**

Metro Concourse. A downtown "city beneath the city," the underground tunnel system connects nearly all the downtown buildings in a 20-square-block area. It is one of the most extensive all-enclosed pedestrian systems in the country. Offices, shops, and restaurants line the concourse system. (Mon-Fri)

Myriad Botanical Gardens. *301 West Reno, Oklahoma City (73102). Phone 405/297-3995.* A 17-acre botanical garden in the heart of the city's redeveloping central business district. Features lake, amphitheater, botanical gardens, and seven-story Crystal Bridge Tropical Conservatory. **$$**

⭐ **National Cowboy Hall of Fame & Western Heritage Center.** *1700 NE 63rd St, Oklahoma City (73111). Off I-44 W near I-35, between Martin Luther King Jr. and Kelley aves. Phone 405/478-2250. www.nationalcowboy museum.org.* Major art collections depict America's Western heritage; Rodeo Hall of Fame; sculpture, including *End of the Trail, Buffalo Bill,* and *Coming Through the Rye*; portrait gallery of Western film stars; landscaped gardens. (Daily 9 am-5 pm; closed Jan 1, Thanksgiving, Dec 25) **$$**

National Softball Hall of Fame and Museum. *2801 NE 50th St, Oklahoma City (73111). Just W of I-35. Phone 405/424-5266.* Displays of equipment and memorabilia trace the history of the sport; Hall of Fame; stadium complex. (May-Oct: Mon-Sun; rest of year: Mon-Fri) **$$**

Oklahoma City Museum of Art. *415 Coach Dr, Oklahoma City (73102). Phone 405/236-3100.* Permanent collection of 16th-20th-century European and American paintings, prints, drawings, photographs, sculpture, and decorative arts. Changing exhibitions of regional, national, and international artists. (Tues-Sun) **$$$**

Oklahoma City National Memorial. *NW 5th St and N Robinson Ave, Oklahoma City (73102). Phone 405/235-3313. www.oklahomacitynationalmemorial.org.* A series of monuments in honor of the men, women, and children killed by a bomb at the Murrah Federal Building on April 19, 1995. The Gates of Time memorial represents the moment of the blast, forever frozen in time. The Field of Empty Chairs pays tribute to the 168 lives lost in the bombing. The Survivor Tree is an American elm tree that withstood the blast. Museum (Mon-Sat; Sun afternoon, fee). Also a reflecting pool, orchard, and children's area. (Daily) **FREE**

Oklahoma City Zoo. *2101 NE 50th, Oklahoma City (73111). Exit 50th St off I-35, 1 mile W to zoo entrance. Phone 405/424-3344.* Covers 110 acres with more than 2,000 animals representing 500 species; expansive hoofstock collection; naturalistic island life exhibit; walk-through aviaries; herpetarium; pachyderm building; big cat exhibit; primate and gorilla exhibit; children's zoo with discovery area; Safari Tram. (Daily; closed Jan 1, Dec 25) **$$$** On the zoo grounds is

> **Aquaticus.** *2101 NE 50th, Oklahoma City (73111). Phone 405/424-3344.* A unique marine-life science facility contains a comprehensive collection of aquatic life; shark tank; adaptations and habitat exhibits; underwater viewing. (Daily; closed Jan 1, Dec 25) **$**

Oklahoma Firefighters Museum. *2716 NE 50th St, Oklahoma City (73111). Phone 405/424-3440.* Antique fire equipment dating to 1736; also first fire station (1869) in Oklahoma reassembled here. (Daily; closed holidays) **$$**

Oklahoma Heritage Center. *201 NW 14th St, Oklahoma City (73103). Phone 405/235-4458.* Restored Hefner family mansion (1917) maintained as a museum; antique furnishings; collection of bells, art; Oklahoma Hall of Fame galleries (third floor) feature work by Oklahoma artists; memorial chapel and gardens. (Mon-Fri; closed holidays) **$$**

Oklahoma National Stockyards. *2501 Exchange Ave, Oklahoma City (73108). Phone 405/235-8675.* One of world's largest cattle markets; auction of cattle, hogs, and sheep; Livestock Exchange Building. (Mon-Tues; closed holidays) **FREE**

⭐ **Omniplex.** *2100 NE 52nd St, Oklahoma City (73111). Phone 405/602-6664.* Houses several museums and attractions within a 10-acre facility. (Daily; closed holidays). **$$$** Includes

International Photography Hall of Fame and Museum. *2100 NE 52nd St, Oklahoma City (73111). Phone 405/424-4055.* Permanent and traveling exhibits; one of world's largest photographic murals. (Daily; closed Thanksgiving, Dec 25)

Kirkpatrick Science and Air Space Museum. *2100 NE 52nd St, Oklahoma City (73111). Phone 405/602-6664.* Includes a hands-on science museum, Air Space Museum, Kirkpatrick Galleries, gardens/greenhouse; Kirkpatrick Planetarium (shows change quarterly). (Daily; closed Thanksgiving, Dec 25)

Red Earth Indian Center. *2100 NE 52nd St, Oklahoma City (73111). Phone 405/427-5228.* Exhibits and educational programs encourage appreciation of Native American cultures. (Daily; closed Thanksgiving, Dec 25)

Remington Park. *One Remington Pl, Oklahoma City (73111). At junction I-35 and I-44. Phone 405/424-1000.* Thoroughbred racing with a four-level grandstand and more than 300 video monitors. Restaurants. (Apr-June and Aug-Dec, Fri-Sun) **$$**

State Capitol. *2300 N Lincoln Blvd, Oklahoma City (73105). Phone 405/521-3356.* Greco-Roman, neoclassical building designed by S. A. Layton and Wemyss Smith. Oil well beneath Capitol building reaches 1 1/4 miles underground. After pumping oil from 1941 to 1986, it is now preserved as a monument. Legislature meets annually for 78 days beginning on the first Mon in Feb. Tours (daily; closed Dec 25). **FREE** Opposite is

State Museum of History. *2100 N Lincoln, Oklahoma City (73105). Phone 405/521-2491.* Exhibits on the history of Oklahoma; extensive collection of Native American artifacts. (Mon-Sat; closed holidays) **FREE**

White Water Bay. *3908 W Reno, Oklahoma City. Via I-40, Meridian exit. Phone 405/478-2412.* Outdoor water park with body surfing, water chutes, slides, rapids, and swimming pool; special playland for tots. (June-Aug: daily; late May and early Sept: weekends) **$$$$**

Special Events

Ballet Oklahoma. *7421 N Classen, Oklahoma City (73106). Phone 405/843-9898.* Oct-Apr.

Festival of the Arts. *Downtown, Hudson Ave, Oklahoma City. Phone 405/270-4848.* International foods, entertainment, children's learning and play area; craft market; artists from many states display their work. Six days in late Apr.

International Finals Rodeo. *333 Gordon Cooper Blvd, Oklahoma City (73107). Phone 405/948-6700.* International Pro Rodeo Association's top 15 cowboys and cowgirls compete in seven events to determine world championships.

Lyric Theatre. *201 N Walker, Oklahoma City (73106). Phone 405/524-9312. In Kirkpatrick Fine Arts Auditorium of Oklahoma City University.* Professional musical theater. Mid-June-early Aug.

Oklahoma City Philharmonic Orchestra. *Civic Center Music Hall, 201 N Walker, Oklahoma City (73102). Phone 405/297-2584.* Mid-Sept-May.

State Fair of Oklahoma. *333 Gorden Cooper Blvd, Oklahoma City (73107). Phone 405/948-6700.* Livestock, crafts, art exhibits; ice show, circus, rodeo; truck pull contests; auto races; concerts; international show, flower and garden show; Native American ceremonial dances; carriage collection; monorail, space tower, carnival, parades. Arena and grandstand attractions. Sept.

World Championship Quarter Horse Show. *State fairgrounds, 3313 Pershing Blvd, Oklahoma City (73107). Phone 405/948-6700.* More than 1,800 horses compete. Early-mid-Nov.

Limited-Service Hotels

★★ **BEST WESTERN SADDLEBACK INN.** *4300 SW 3rd St, Oklahoma City (73108). Phone 405/947-7000; toll-free 800/228-3903; fax 405/948-7636. www.bestwestern.com.* 220 rooms, 3 story. Pets accepted, some restrictions; fee. Check-out noon. Restaurant, bar. Fitness room. Outdoor pool, whirlpool. Airport transportation available. **$**

★★ **COURTYARD BY MARRIOTT.** *4301 Highline Blvd, Oklahoma City (73108). Phone 405/946-6500; toll-free 800/321-2211; fax 405/946-7368. www.courtyard.com.* 149 rooms, 3 story. Check-out noon. Restaurant, bar. Fitness room. Outdoor pool, whirlpool. Airport transportation available. **$**

The Oklahoma City Experience

Single-day events have shaped both the past and present of this settlement in the American heartland. Oklahoma City was born on April 22, 1889, when the area known as the Unassigned Lands in Oklahoma Territory was opened for settlement; a cannon was fired at noon that day, signaling a rush of thousands of settlers who raced into the two million acres of land to make their claims on the plains.

Just over a century later, the city's spirited energy was put to a horrific challenge with the April 19, 1995 bombing of the Alfred P. Murrah Federal Building. Today, the strength, unity, and hope generated between the city and its nation can be experienced at the new Oklahoma City National Memorial. You'll want to allow ample time to explore and appreciate this breathtaking site.

Begin at the Gates of Time, twin monuments that frame the moment of destruction: 9:02 am. The east gate represents 9:01 a.m. and the west gate 9:03 a.m. The Field of Empty Chairs consists of 168 bronze-and-stone chairs arranged in nine rows, representing the lives lost and the floor each victim was on at the time of the blast. The smaller chairs memorialize the 19 children killed. The glass seats of the chairs are etched with the names of the victims and are lit up at night. Also at the site are an American elm called the Survivors Tree; fruit and flower trees in the Rescuers Orchard; the peaceful Reflection Pool; and the Children's Area, with a wall of hand-painted tiles sent to Oklahoma City in 1995 by children across the nation.

After this sobering start, you'll walk four blocks south of Robinson to a cheerful place called the International Gymnastics Hall of Fame. Located in the First National Center, the Hall of Fame honors such Oklahoma and Olympic gymnastic greats as Shannon Miller, Bart Connor, and Nadia Comenici. Hundreds of photos, medals, uniforms, videos, and memorabilia are on display here.

Walk just another block south of Robinson to its intersection with Reno to find the beautiful Myriad Botanical Gardens, a 17-acre sanctuary in the center of downtown with lovely hills surrounding a sunken lake. At the center is the seven-story Crystal Bridge Tropical Conservatory, featuring an intriguing collection of palm trees, flowers, and exotic plants from across the globe. Along the Adventure Walk, you'll wind beneath a 35-foot-high waterfall, and you can gaze at the tropics from a skywalk. Check out the Crystal Bridge Gift Shop, featuring an outstanding collection of botanical and garden-related items.

Backtrack on Robinson just two blocks to Sheridan, turning right (east) on Sheridan. Continue walking two blocks and you'll reach Bricktown, a hot new entertainment and dining district. The old warehouse district just east of the Santa Fe railroad tracks saw its birth just before World War I, but the latest boom came in the last 15 years. Roam around the old brick streets, poke around in the shops, then take a load off at one of the restaurants, such as Crabtown, the Varsity Sports Grill, Windy City Pizza, or Bricktown Brewery (Oklahoma's first brew pub and microbrewery). Be sure to get tickets for a game at the new Bricktown Ballpark, home of the popular AAA baseball club called the Oklahoma RedHawks. Feet worn out from walking? In Bricktown, you can hop on the new rubber-wheeled trolleys, the Oklahoma Spirit, to tour downtown, or catch a ride on the *Water Taxi*, a narrated tour boat that cruises the Bricktown Canal.

★ **DAYS INN.** *12013 N I-35 Service Rd, Oklahoma City (73131). Phone 405/478-2554; toll-free 800/329-7466; fax 405/478-5033. www.daysinn.com.* 47 rooms, 2 story. Pets accepted; fee. Complimentary continental breakfast. Check-out 11 am. Indoor pool. **$**

★ ★ **EMBASSY SUITES.** *1815 S Meridian Ave, Oklahoma City (73108). Phone 405/682-6000; toll-free 800/362-2779; fax 405/682-9835. www.embassy suites.com.* This is an airport, all-suite hotel that is near the Meridian strips and more than 30 restaurants and clubs. It offers live entertainment and a dance club of its own along with exercise facilities, a pool and a whirlpool. 236 rooms, 6 story, all suites. Pets accepted, some restrictions; fee. Complimentary full breakfast. Check-out noon. Restaurant, bar. Fitness room. Indoor pool, whirlpool. Airport transportation available. Business center. **$**

★ **GOVERNORS SUITES INN.** *2308 S Meridian Ave, Oklahoma City (73108). Phone 405/682-5299; toll-free 888/819-7575; fax 405/682-3047.* 50 rooms, 3 story. Complimentary full breakfast. Check-out 11 am. Fitness room. Outdoor pool, whirlpool. Airport transportation available. **$**

★ ★ **HOLIDAY INN.** *6200 N Robinson Ave, Oklahoma City (73118). Phone 405/843-5558; toll-free 800/682-0049; fax 405/840-3410. www.holiday-inn.com.* 200 rooms, 3 story. Pets accepted, some restrictions; fee. Check-out noon. Restaurant, bar. Fitness room. Indoor pool, whirlpool. **$**

★ **LA QUINTA INN.** *8315 S I-35 Service Rd, Oklahoma City (73149). Phone 405/631-8661; toll-free 800/531-5900; fax 405/631-1892. www.laquinta.com.* 121 rooms, 2 story. Pets accepted. Complimentary continental breakfast. Check-out noon. Outdoor pool. **$**

Full-Service Hotels

★ ★ ★ **HILTON OKLAHOMA CITY NORTHWEST.** *2945 NW Expy, Oklahoma City (73112). Phone 405/848-4811; toll-free 800/774-1500; fax 405/843-4829. www.hilton.com.* Found in the business district and only 20 minutes from downtown and the Will Rogers Airport, this hotel offers guest rooms, four suites and nine poolside cabanas. The Honeymoon suite features a private swimming pool and whirlpool. 218 rooms, 9 story. Check-out noon. Restaurant, bar. Fitness room. Outdoor pool, whirlpool. Airport transportation available. **$**

★ ★ ★ **MARRIOTT WATERFORD.** *6300 Waterford Blvd, Oklahoma City (73118). Phone 405/848-4782; toll-free 800/992-2009; fax 405/843-9161. www.marriott.com.* Located in the city's premier suburb, this hotel is only 15 minutes from downtown and the airport. Guests can enjoy a drink in the waterfront lounge or take a swim in the outdoor pool. Volleyball and squash facilities are also available. 197 rooms, 9 story. Pets accepted, some restrictions; fee. Check-out noon. Restaurant, bar. Fitness room. Outdoor pool, whirlpool. Tennis. Business center. **$$**

★ ★ ★ **RENAISSANCE OKLAHOMA CITY CONVENTION CENTER HOTEL.** *10 N Broadway, Oklahoma City (73102). Phone 405/228-8000; toll-free 800/468-3571; fax 405/228-8080. www.renaissancehotels.com.* 311 rooms, 15 story. Check-out 11 am. Restaurant. Fitness room. Indoor pool, whirlpool. Business center. **$$**

★ ★ ★ **THE WESTIN OKLAHOMA CITY.** *1 N Broadway Ave, Oklahoma City (73102). Phone 405/235-2780; toll-free 800/285-2780; fax 405/232-8752. www.westin.com.* This hotel is connected to the Myriad Convention Center and many shops and businesses in the area by an underground concourse. It offers oversized guest rooms, outdoor pool, a sundeck, and fitness center. 395 rooms, 15 story. Check-out noon. Restaurant, bar. Fitness room. Outdoor pool. Business center. **$$**

Restaurants

★ ★ **ARIA GRILL.** *1 N Broadway, Oklahoma City (73102). Phone 405/815-6063; fax 408/815-6052. www.westinokc.com.* American menu. Breakfast, lunch, dinner, late-night, brunch. Closed holidays. Bar. Children's menu. Valet parking. **$$**

★ ★ ★ **BELLINI'S.** *6305 Waterford Blvd #1, Oklahoma City (73118). Phone 405/848-1065; fax 405/848-5946. www.bellinis.net.* Overlooking a charming duck pond, this casual restaurant has the ambience of an Italian piazza. It also features an open brick pizza oven. Be sure to catch the lakeside sunset. American, Italian menu. Lunch, dinner, Sun brunch. Bar. Outdoor seating. **$$**

★ ★ **BRICKTOWN BREWERY.** *1 N Oklahoma Ave, Oklahoma City (73104). Phone 405/232-2739; fax 405/232-0531. www.bricktownbrewery.com.* Renovated building in the warehouse district. American menu. Lunch, dinner, late-night. Closed holidays. Bar. Children's menu. **$$**

★ ★ **CAFE 501.** *501 S Boulevard St, Edmond (73034). Phone 405/359-1501; fax 405/341-3896. www.cafe501.com.* Eclectic menu. Lunch, dinner. Closed holidays. Children's menu. **$$**

★ ★ **CATTLEMAN'S STEAKHOUSE.** *1309 S Agnew St, Oklahoma City (73108). Phone 405/236-0416; fax 405/235-1969. www.cattlemensrestaurant.com.* In historic Stockyards City district, opened in 1910. Steak menu. Breakfast, lunch, dinner, late-night, brunch. Closed Thanksgiving, Dec 25. **$$**

★ **CLASSEN GRILL.** *5124 N Classen Blvd, Oklahoma City (73118). Phone 405/842-0428.* Seafood, steak menu. Breakfast, lunch. Closed Jan 1, Thanksgiving, Dec 25. Bar. Children's menu. **$**

★ ★ **COACH HOUSE.** *6437 Avondale Dr, Oklahoma City (73116). Phone 405/842-1000; fax 405/843-9777. www.coach-house-restaurant.com.* This intimate French restaurant highlights contemporary interpretations of classic dishes. The 50-seat restaurant also features a bar with an extensive wine list. American, French menu. Lunch, dinner. Closed Sun. Children's menu. **$$$**

★ **COUNTY LINE.** *1226 NE 63rd St, Oklahoma City (73111). Phone 405/478-4955; fax 405/478-5238. www.countyline.com.* Barbecue menu. Lunch, dinner. Closed Thanksgiving, Dec 25. Bar. Children's menu. **$$**

★ ★ **DEEP FORK GRILL.** *5418 N Western Ave, Oklahoma City (73118). Phone 405/848-7678; fax 405/840-0624. www.deepforkgrill.com.* Breakfast, lunch, lunch, dinner, late-night, brunch. Closed Thanksgiving, Dec 25. Bar. Valet parking. **$$**

★ ★ **EDDY'S OF OKLAHOMA CITY.** *4227 N Meridian Ave, Oklahoma City (73112). Phone 405/787-2944. www.eddys-steakhouse.com.* Display of crystal, collectibles. Dinner. Closed Sun. Children's menu. **$$**

★ **GOPURAM TASTE OF INDIA.** *4559 NW 23rd St, Oklahoma City (73127). Phone 405/948-7373; fax 405/948-7388.* Indian menu. Breakfast, lunch, dinner, brunch. Bar. Children's menu. **$**

★ ★ ★ **JW'S STEAKHOUSE.** *3233 NW Expressway St, Oklahoma City (73112). Phone 405/842-6633; fax 405/842-3152.* The warm, earth-toned dining room has an intimate feel. Seafood menu. Breakfast, lunch, dinner, late-night, brunch. Children's menu. Valet parking. **$$$**

♦ ★ ★ ★ **KELLER IN THE KASTLE GERMAN RESTAURANT.** *820 N MacArthur, Oklahoma City (73127). Phone 405/942-6133; fax 405/962-6202. www.kellerinthekastle.com.* Causal hometown service in a fun and interesting atmosphere. The building design is based on a castle in Normandy (France). German menu. Dinner. Closed Sun-Mon. Bar. Outdoor seating. **$$$**

★ ★ **KONA RANCH STEAKHOUSE.** *2037 S Meridian, Oklahoma City (73108). Phone 405/681-1000; fax 405/681-0265.* Hawaiian menu. Lunch, dinner. Closed Thanksgiving, Dec 25. Bar. Children's menu. **$$**

★ **LA BAGUETTE BISTRO.** *7408 N May Ave, Oklahoma City (73116). Phone 405/840-3047; fax 405/840-5104. www.labaguettebistro.com.* French menu. Breakfast, lunch, dinner, Sun brunch. Bar. Valet parking. **$$$**

★ ★ **LAS PALOMAS.** *2329 N Meridian, Oklahoma City (73107). Phone 405/949-9988; fax 405/949-9988.* Mexican menu. Lunch, dinner. Children's menu. **$$$**

★ ★ **SLEEPY HOLLOW.** *1101 NE 50th St, Oklahoma City (73111). Phone 405/424-1614; fax 405/427-1936.* Steak menu. Lunch, dinner. Bar. **$$**

★ ★ **SUSHI NEKO.** *4318 N Western Ave, Oklahoma City (73118). Phone 405/528-8862; fax 405/521-9877. www.sushineko.com.* Japanese menu. Lunch, dinner, late-night. Closed Sun. Bar. Children's menu. Valet parking. **$$**

White Sands National Monument, NM

1 1/2 hours, 70 miles from El Paso

Web Site www.nps.gov/whsa

15 miles SW of Alamogordo on Hwy 70/82.

These shifting, dazzling white dunes are a challenge to plants and animals. Here, lizards and mice are white like the sand, helping them blend in with the background. (Similarly, mice are black in the black lava area only a few miles north.)

Plants elongate their stems up to 30 feet so that they can keep their leaves and flowers above the sand. When the sands recede, the plants are sometimes left on elevated pillars of hardened gypsum bound together by their roots. Even an ancient two-wheeled Spanish cart was laid bare when the sands shifted.

Beach sand is usually silica, but White Sands National Monument sand is gypsum, from which plaster of paris is made. Dunes often rise to 60 feet; White Sands is the largest gypsum dune field in the world.

White Sands National Monument encloses 143,732 acres of this remarkable area. The visitor center has an orientation video, exhibits concerning the dunes and how they were formed, and other related material (daily; closed Dec 25). Evening programs and guided nature walks in the dunes area are conducted (Memorial Day-mid-Aug). There is a 16-mile round-trip drive from the center; free printed guide leaflet. Picnic area with shaded tables and grills (no water); primitive backpackers' campsite (by permit only). Dunes Drive (daily except Dec 25).

For further information, contact the Superintendent, PO Box 1086, Holloman AFB, NM 88330-1086; phone 505/672-2599.

Index

Notes

Notes

Notes